APOSTLES LUTHERAN CHURCH
5828 SANTA TERESA BLVD.
SAN JOSE, CA 95123

CHRISTIAN DOGMATICS

CHRISTIAN DOGMATICS

by

FRANCIS PIEPER, D. D.

Volume III

1953

CONCORDIA PUBLISHING HOUSE
SAINT LOUIS, MISSOURI

10 11 12 13 14 15 16 17 18 19   TP   91 90 89 88 87 86 85 84 83 82

Foreword

THIS third and last volume of Dr. Pieper's *Christliche Dogmatik* is issued with heartfelt thanks to God for His gracious guidance and help in the task of translation. All who had a hand in the work confess that it proved to be a larger undertaking than they had anticipated.

My thanks are offered to all, too, who supported the project and furthered it in one way or another. I shall keep in grateful remembrance particularly the sainted Dr. Theodore Engelder, who devoted the last years of his earthly life to the planning and execution of the entire work.

The first translation of this jewel of Lutheranism in America rose out of circumstances in the 1930's. My students, who no longer had an extensive knowledge of German, induced me to translate the *Dogmatik* for use as our textbook. With the permission of Dr. E. Seuel, then manager of Concordia Publishing House, the students mimeographed the manuscript. Requests made in earlier years, together with the appearance of this edition, led the General Convention of The Lutheran Church — Missouri Synod in 1944 to approve the proposal of the Synodical Centennial Committee for the printing of Dr. Pieper's work in English. The services of Dr. Engelder as chief editor were secured, and the major parts of Volumes I and II, as well as the first two sections of this volume, were the fruit of his labors. After the Lord called him to our eternal home, Dr. J. T. Mueller undertook supervision of the publication of the second volume, and the undersigned was requested to serve as editor of Volume III.

Some reviews of Volumes I and II that have come to my attention assert that Dr. Pieper's doctrinal position is an anachronism, not suited to our day, because he does not propound "the problem of knowledge," the endless, fruitless search of "scientific theology" for certainty of truth. Our answer to such criticism is: "The Word they still shall let remain." The *Sola Scriptura, Sola Gratia, Sola Fide* shall remain our shibboleth also in the future. This is the saving faith, worked in our hearts by the Holy Spirit through the Gospel of salvation. May God's Holy Spirit preserve us in this faith unto our end!

I cannot refrain from pointing out two pearls in this dogmatic compend which may escape the casual reader, but hold supreme significance for the Church. They are: "Only dogmatics is edifying" (I, 101) and "The sins of the world are forgiven" (I, 35). The first expresses the divine origin and character and the clarity of Holy Writ, the *fundamentum organicum;* the second emphasizes the objective reconciliation, the *sola gratia* and *sola fide,* or the *fundamentum substantiale,* Christ. Give Scripture its due as the verbally inspired, infallible Word of God, give Christ

His due as the sole and entire source of our salvation, and you have a truly sound theology and saving religion.

The Centennial Committee plans to publish an exhaustive index volume which will offer a topical index to facilitate reference to any particular point of doctrine, an index of the Bible passages cited and discussed, and an index of authors referred to and quoted.

May our Lord and Savior bless this translation as a means of preserving for our children the faith we inherited from our fathers, a faith that stands not on human opinion, but on the Word of God alone.

Ascension, 1952   WALTER W. F. ALBRECHT
Springfield, Illinois

Preface

IN this third volume the doctrines of the Christian life, the means of grace, the Church, eternal election, and the last things are presented. Also in the preparation of this volume I have striven to offer a dogmatics which is "up to date" in the proper sense of the term. In the preface of Volume Two, I explained what I regard as "up to date" or "abreast of the times." To deserve this distinction, a dogmatics must have particularly two characteristics. First, it must reject all human speculation and must take the Christian doctrine solely from Holy Scripture, because Holy Writ as the inspired and infallible Word of Christ is the sole source and norm of Christian doctrine till Judgment Day. Secondly, such a dogmatics must judge the doctrinal trends in Christendom, both past and present, by the doctrine of Christ as it is delivered in Scripture and must vindicate the divine truth against all contradictions.

Considerable space has been given to the doctrine of the Christian life, or the doctrine of sanctification and good works, and this for two reasons. First, Scripture describes the Christian life not only in general, but also in its many and varied phases. Secondly, and chiefly, the Scriptural order which obtains between Christian faith and Christian life is in our day, too, disarranged and in most instances completely inverted. All who, like the Roman Catholics, the Calvinists, the Arminians, and modern rationalizing Lutherans, either detract from, or deny outright, the *satisfactio Christi vicaria*, have no choice but to let sanctification precede justification in some fashion, because they regard Christ's work of reconciliation as inadequate. But this inversion of the proper order leads to the loss of both justification and sanctification.

The means of grace have been allotted more space than any other doctrine. Several reasons prompted me to offer rather too much than too little in presenting this doctrine. For one thing, here in the United States we are surrounded by Reformed church bodies, and all of them follow the same principles and use the same arguments today to separate the "Spirit" and "grace" from the means of grace which moved Zwingli and his associates to shun the "Church of the Reformation" and induce Calvin and his successors to perpetuate the separation. Ample proof for this assertion has been adduced. Secondly, there is no denying that the modern "theology of experience," pursued also by the "positive" Lutheran theologians of our day, which has abandoned the Biblical teaching of the inspiration of Scripture and of the *satisfactio Christi vicaria*, is everywhere following the paths of Reformed theology. Even some Reformed theologians have pointed this out, for instance, Schneckenburger (*Vergleichende Darstel-*

lung des luth. und ref. Lehrbegriffs, I, 264–287), though not all his observations are correct. According to the "experience theology" saving faith is not produced solely by the Word of the Gospel and does not have the Word of the Gospel as its object (that in which it believes), but is created and preserved also by the so-called "historical" work of Christ, which is to be added to the Word of Christ. Ihmels, too, expressly rejects as "intellectualistic" the "understanding of the revelation" held by the theologians of the Reformation, and states as his view: "Today also, only that is real faith in Christ which is thrust upon man through the appearance of Christ Himself" (*Zentralfragen*, 2d ed., 1912, p. 89). Thirdly, a Christian, and particularly a Christian theologian who has had practical experience in the care of souls, knows how difficult it is for a conscience crushed by the Law of God to cling to the grace offered in the means of grace, even with the correct teaching regarding the means of grace. Recall the complaints of Luther, how difficult it was for him, when attacked by Satan, to disregard all that occurred in him and about him and to trust steadfastly and solely in the gracious promise in the Word of the Gospel. And yet there is no other way to deliver us sinners in our trials and in the throes of death from doubt and despair.

In presenting the doctrine of the Church it was necessary, first, to set forth and to maintain over against Roman and Pseudo-Protestant "institutionalism" that the Church consists of Christians and hence that they are the possessors of all spiritual gifts and privileges which Christ has given His Church on earth. Secondly, it had to be shown that there is absolutely no room in the Christian Church for any word and authority of man because Christ through His Word is the sole Teacher and Ruler of His Church. The public ministry, it is true, is not a human but a divine institution, but it has no authority to teach and to prescribe anything not taught and commanded in Christ's Word.

The presentation of the doctrine of eternal election takes cognizance, of course, of the controversy which disturbed the Lutheran Church in America for decades. I have assured myself again and again that what Article XI of the Formula of Concord teaches when it maintains the *universalis gratia* over against Calvinism and the *sola gratia* over against synergism is not "untenable ground," as both of these parties have claimed, but faithfully reproduces the doctrine of Scripture.

In the doctrine of the last things, millennialism and the general conversion of the Jews have been treated in greater detail because these errors have again come to the fore in our times.

The World War and its effect on the economy of our country accounts in part for the fact that this third volume appears later than had been intended.

Soli Deo Gloria!   F. PIEPER

St. Louis, Mo., March, 1920

Contents

The Christian Life, or Sanctification and Good Works

Final Perseverance

The Means of Grace

The Lord's Supper

The Christian Church

The Public Ministry

Eternal Election

Eschatology, or the Last Things

The Christian Life, or Sanctification and Good Works

(DE SANCTIFICATIONE ET BONIS OPERIBUS)

THE Christian life in all its internal and external activities is produced, inevitably and solely, by faith in the reconciliation achieved by Christ. (This doctrine has been set forth in the "Preliminary Survey" of The Application of Salvation in Vol. II, p. 397 ff.) But the many inaccuracies and gross aberrations which have arisen in connection with the relation of justification to sanctification, also regarding sanctification itself, necessitate a detailed exposition of the doctrine of the Christian life or, in other words, the doctrine of sanctification and good works. In order to clarify this doctrine, questions such as the following will be discussed: What is the meaning of sanctification? How do justification and sanctification differ? Does sanctification play a part in the obtaining of salvation and in the perseverance in faith? By whom and by what means is sanctification effected? Is sanctification in this life perfect or imperfect? What must be taught concerning the "necessity" and the "freedom" of sanctification and good works?

1

Sanctification Defined

The term "sanctification" is used in Scripture and in theology in a wide and in a narrow sense.

In its wide sense, sanctification comprises all that the Holy Ghost does in separating man from sin and making him again God's own, so that he may live for God and serve Him. It includes the bestowal of faith, justification, sanctification as the inner transformation of man, perseverance in faith, and the complete renewal on Judgment Day. The "sanctification of the Spirit" (2 Thess. 2:13; 1 Pet. 1:2) certainly includes justification, as is evident from the phrases: "belief in the truth" (2 Thess. 2:13) and "the sprinkling of the blood of Jesus Christ" (1 Pet. 1:2). Christians are the "called saints" (Rom. 1:7; 1 Cor. 1:2), *primo loco* because of their justification by faith. The phrase "But ye are sanctified" (1 Cor. 6:11) is best taken as a synonym of justification, because it is placed between "Ye are washed" and "ye are justified in the name of the Lord Jesus." The inward renewal of man, which follows faith in the forgiveness of sins, by which he turns his back on sin and serves God in doing good works, is also designated in Scripture as "sanctification." 1 Thess. 4:3-7: "This is the will of God, even your sanctification, that ye should abstain from fornication . . . that no man go beyond and defraud his brother in any matter . . . for God hath not called us unto uncleanness, but unto holiness." Similarly holiness of life is meant in 1 Thess. 5:23 and 3:13: "unblamable in holiness"; in 2 Cor. 7:1: "perfecting holiness"; in Eph. 4:24: "Put on the new man, which after God is created in righteousness and true holiness." Finally, in Matt. 19:28 the complete and final deliverance of the Christians from all sin is called a "regeneration."

In its wide sense also Luther uses the term "sanctification" in his exposition of the Third Article of the Creed, Large Catechism: "I believe that the Holy Ghost makes us holy, as His name implies. But whereby does He accomplish this, or what are His method and means to this end? Answer: By the Christian Church, the forgiveness of sins, the resurrection of the body, and the life everlasting." (*Trigl.* 689, 40 f.) Quenstedt: " 'Sanctification' is at times used in a wide sense, including justification, as in Eph. 5:26; Heb. 10:10; at other times, however, it is used in a narrow sense and, so understood, is identical with renewal in the strict sense, as in Rom. 6:19, 22; 1 Thess. 4:3-4, 7." (II, p. 914.)

In its narrow sense, sanctification designates the internal spiritual transformation of the believer or the holiness of life which follows upon justification. It is so used in Rom. 6:22: "Now being made free from sin and become servants to God [namely, by justification],[1] ye have your fruit unto holiness." Vv. 18-19: "Being then made free from sin [namely, by faith in the Gospel, v. 17, or by justification], ye became the servants of righteousness . . . even so now yield your members servants to righteousness unto holiness." In the narrower sense of sanctification the Formula of Concord states: "In the same manner the order also between faith and good works must abide and be maintained, and likewise between justification and renewal, or sanctification. For good works do not precede faith, neither does sanctification precede justification. But first faith is kindled in us in conversion by the Holy Ghost from the hearing of the Gospel. This lays hold of God's grace in Christ, by which the person is justified. Then, when the person is justified, he is also renewed and sanctified by the Holy Ghost, from which renewal and sanctification the fruits of good works must then follow." (*Trigl.* 929, Sol. Decl., III, 40 f.)

Note that the Formula of Concord uses the terms "renewal" and

---

[1] On the entire section Rom. 6:15-23 compare Meyer, Philippi, Stoeckhardt.

"sanctification" as synonyms: "renewal or sanctification." Sanctification is called "renewal" in order to describe the activity of the new nature in contrast to the old carnal nature; and renewal is called "sanctification" in order to show that according to his new nature man is delivered from the service of sin and dedicated to the service of God. The Formula of Concord also distinguishes between sanctification and good works as *antecedens* and *consequens*. Sanctification is here taken as the new spiritual nature (καινὸς ἄνθρωπος, πνεῦμα), created through justification, while the good works are the acts flowing from this new nature. Thus Gal. 5:25-26: "If we live in the Spirit, let us also walk in the Spirit. Let us not be desirous of vainglory." Gal. 6:1: "Ye which are spiritual, restore such an one in the spirit of meekness." Gal. 5:22 represents love, joy, peace, etc., as "the fruit of the Spirit."

In another respect good works are identical with sanctification, since sanctification *in concreto* takes place through the performance of good acts, the believer avoiding, internally and externally, the evil and accomplishing, internally and externally, the good. Sanctification *in concreto* is, just as little as faith,[2] an infused substance or a dormant condition *(habitus otiosus, status otiosus)*, but it is an unceasing activity, constantly called forth and sustained by the Holy Ghost.[3] That sanctification is a matter of good works, Scripture shows by representing sanctification as the fruit of faith and then, again, by representing good works as the fruit of faith. Rom. 6:22 reads: "Ye have your fruit unto holiness," and Titus 3:8, 14 states that the believers should be "careful to maintain good works."[4] And Titus 2:11 the "grace of God that bringeth salvation" is characterized as "teaching us that, denying ungodliness and worldly lusts, we should live soberly, righteously, and godly in this present world."[5]

---

[2] See the section "Saving Faith Is *Fides Actualis*" (Vol. II, 432 ff.) and the statement by Walther: "Faith is continuous action, a continuous apprehending, though we are unable to tell how this takes place, for example, during sleep" (*ibid.*, p. 436, footnote 70).

[3] Faith is not a physical or substantial condition; see Quenstedt, II, 917.

[4] προΐστασθαι with the genitive — to devote oneself to, e. g., τέχνης, art.

[5] How sanctification (or renewal) and good works are distinguished as *antecedens* and *consequens*, and how they are actually identical, has been discussed already by the old Lutheran theologians. Baier, for instance, says: "Good works are, on the one hand, related to renewal as its *finis* [end] and *effectus* [result], and, on the other hand, they constitute the renewal. For renewal essentially consists in the good and holy actions or works which are performed through the powers of grace." (III, 315.) Chemnitz, calling attention to the fact that, e. g., in Rom. 4:5, faith and works are set in opposition, says that therefore the term "good works" designates the whole territory of the new life in which faith is active.

2

The Essential Difference Between Sanctification (in the Narrow Sense) and Justification

Justification takes place outside man. God declares a man righteous who in himself is not righteous, but unrighteous, "ungodly." True, faith through which the subjective justification takes place is in man; it is not the Holy Ghost who believes, but man himself believes through the operation of the Holy Ghost. But the sole function of faith in justification consists in apprehending a righteousness which lies outside man, namely, the righteousness which is provided by Christ's vicarious satisfaction and proclaimed and offered in the Gospel. Faith, although it is in man, is nevertheless placed in opposition to all righteousness which is in man, which inheres in man *(iustitia inhaerens)* (Rom. 4:5; Phil. 3:9). Describing this phase of the righteousness of faith, the Formula of Concord correctly says: "*Tota nostra iustitia extra nos*" (*Trigl.* 935, Sol. Decl., III, 55); describing the divine act of justification, the dogmaticians correctly say: "*Actio est non* IN *homine, sed* CIRCA *hominem.*"

But sanctification in the narrow sense, the sanctification which follows upon justification, is a divine action within man *(in homine)*. In sanctification God changes the unrighteous into a righteous man; He works in man, to use the dogmatical terms, a *iustitia inhaerens, habitualis, vitae, operum,* distinct from the *iustitia imputata* given in justification. That the sanctification which flows from faith consists in an inward moral transformation, in a *iustitia vitae, inhaerens,* is evident particularly from those Scripture passages which describe sanctification as taking place in the essential parts of the converted man. Thus 1 Thess. 5:23: "The very God of peace sanctify you wholly; and I pray God your whole spirit and soul and body [καί — καί = both soul and body] be preserved blameless unto the coming of our Lord Jesus Christ." 2 Cor. 7:1: "Having therefore these promises, [6:18] let us cleanse ourselves from all filthiness of the flesh and spirit,

---

Then he adds the admonition: "If there is agreement in the matter itself, let us not engage in controversies about the terms." (*Loci,* "*De bonis operibus,*" p. 9 *sqq.*) — By "good works" we understand "moral actions, not merely the external ones that take place through the hand and the tongue, but also the internal ones, the affections of the soul with the movements of the will. For only that is a good work which is done in obedience to God's command and performed with that affection and manner which is commanded by God." (Quenstedt, II, 1371.)

perfecting holiness in the fear of God." [6] Admonishing Christians to avoid the defilement of fornication, the Apostle urges them (1 Cor. 6:20) to glorify God in the body and in the spirit, which are God's. Rom. 12:1-2: "I beseech you, therefore, brethren, by the mercies of God, that ye present your bodies a living sacrifice, holy, acceptable unto God. . . . And be not conformed to this world, but be ye transformed by the renewing of your *mind.*" [7]

3

The Relation of Justification to Sanctification

The teaching of Scripture and of Scriptural theology on the relation between justification or faith and sanctification and good works may be epitomized in these two statements: 1. There is an inseparable connection *(nexus indivulsus)* between justification and sanctification; where there is justification, there is in every case also sanctification. 2. But in this *nexus indivulsus* the cart must not be placed before the horse, that is, sanctification must not be placed before justification, but must be left in its proper place as the consequence and effect of justification. Thus the Formula of Concord: "This should not be understood as though justification and renewal were sundered from one another in such a manner that a genuine faith sometimes could exist and continue for a time together with a wicked intention, but hereby only the order (of cause and effects, of antecedents and consequents) is indicated, how one precedes or succeeds the other. For what Luther has correctly said remains true nevertheless: Faith and good works well agree and fit together (are inseparably connected); but it is faith alone, without works, which lays hold of the blessing; and yet it is never and at no time alone." (*Trigl.* 929, Sol. Decl., II, 41.)

In view of the great importance of these two points and the strong

---

[6] Since σάρξ and πνεῦμα here designate the essential part of man, σάρξ designates the σῶμα of man.

[7] The "renewing of your mind" indicates the internal change of the disposition. — The *subiectum quod* of sanctification or renewal is the *homo iustificatus.* The *subiectum quo* is the soul as to its faculties: intellect, will, and desires; in a secondary sense also the members of the body in so far as they are the necessary instruments of the renewed or sanctified soul toward performing holy acts.

opposition which is raised against them today, the matter will have to be presented in greater detail. The two points were at issue, too, in the controversies of the Lutheran Church of the sixteenth century against Antinomianism and Majorism. On the one hand, the *nexus indivulsus* between faith and good works had to be maintained, and, on the other hand, the inversion of the proper order of faith and good works had to be rejected.

I. As to the *nexus indivulsus,* Scripture teaches that wherever the Holy Ghost works faith in the Gospel in a man, He immediately works also sanctification and good works in that same man through that faith.[8] Though justification precedes sanctification *ordine causarum et effectuum,* they both take place at the same time.[9] It is therefore correct to say that where there is no sanctification, there is also no faith.

There are all sorts of men who have no use for this *nexus indivulsus.* There are the theologians of the "critical school" who shake their heads when they see how the Apostle Paul intimately connects the inner moral transformation, the *iustitia inhaerens,* with the *actus forensis* of justification, the *iustitia imputata.* They say that such a connection is inconceivable. They insist that the Apostle inadvertently mixed up "two streams of thought," the Jewish and the Hellenistic, which are really incompatible. (See Vol. II, p. 410 ff.) There are also modern "positive" theologians who declare that the *iustitia fidei imputata* could never produce sanctification; in order to produce sanctification, justifying faith itself must be taken not merely as instrumental, but as an "ethical act" or as the "germ" of sanctification. Furthermore, it must be admitted that even the Christians who in theory maintain the inseparable connection between justification and sanctification are ever in danger, because of their flesh, of forgetting this connection in practice.

---

[8] That was done, too, in the case of the malefactor on the cross (Luke 23:40-41).

[9] Formula of Concord: Faith which lays hold of the blessing without works "is never and at no time alone" (931, Sol. Decl., III, 41). Carpzov, quoted in Baier-Walther, III, 301: "In the same instant and moment in which faith is kindled in us and in which faith, grasping the offered justification, justifies us, we are also renewed in mind and body." Quenstedt: "Regeneration" (in the sense of the generation of faith), "justification, the union with Christ and renovation all take place at the same time; their union is closer than that of a mathematical point; they cannot be separated and divorced. Nevertheless, according to our mode of conceiving (notionally), regeneration and justification precede the *unio mystica.*" (II, 896.)

But Scripture strongly emphasizes the fact that sanctification is indissolubly connected with justification. We may not be able to explain fully the "psychological connection" between these two occurrences, but the fact that they are closely connected is clearly stated in Scripture. In Rom. 3:21 to the end of chapter five the Apostle sets forth that justification is an *actus forensis*, nothing but the judicial verdict of innocence,[10] so much so that he places the faith which justifies in opposition to every moral quality in man (Rom. 4:5; 3:28; Gal. 2:16; Phil. 3:9). In Rom. 6:1 Paul at once brings up the question whether in view of such a justification a life in sin is possible; and he answers that they who are justified can self-evidently no longer live in sin, since they have died to sin. In 6:2-11 he presents this state of affairs as an established, indisputable fact and closes with this summary in v. 11: "Likewise reckon ye also yourselves to be dead indeed unto sin, but alive unto God through Jesus Christ, our Lord." The thought that justified men could still serve sin and not live unto God would be as absurd as if we assumed that men who have departed this life and are in their graves are still participating in earthly activities. The Apostle certainly teaches that there is an indissoluble connection between sanctification, or the *iustitia inhaerens*, and justification, the mere imputation of righteousness.[11]

And then there is a "psychological connection" between justification and sanctification. Why should Pfleiderer, Holtzmann, and others declare this matter to be inconceivable? They will admit that the intercourse of men is regulated by the law of psychology that love begets love. Now, God loves man with a wondrously great love. "God so (οὔτως) loved the world that He gave His only-begotten Son" (John 3:16). "Herein (ἐν τούτῳ) is love, not that we loved God, but that He loved us and sent His Son to be the propitiation for our sins" (1 John 4:10). "God commendeth [συνίστησι, proves] His love towards us in that, while we were yet sinners, Christ died for us" (Rom. 5:8). Convince a man of this wondrously great love of God for him, and he cannot help loving God in return and avoiding sin for the sake of his love to God. And God knows how to convince and assure man of His great love. He does not appeal to the natural powers of man, for the natural man will not believe in this love, but regards it as

---

[10] Holtzmann maintains correctly that Rom. 5:12-21 treats solely of justification, and not yet of sanctification (II, 153).

[11] Holtzmann: "When the believer passes from the sphere of the Law into the sphere of grace, the dominion of sin has come definitely to an end" (II, 166).

foolishness (1 Cor. 2:14; 1:23). Nor does He try to demonstrate His love by the persuasive words of man's wisdom (1 Cor. 2:4). But He simply presents this great love as a fact, and by this preaching of the Gospel the Holy Ghost creates faith in the love of God. Rom. 10:17: "Faith cometh by hearing." (John 16:14; 1 Cor. 2:5.) And when this faith in the Gospel, faith in the love of God in Christ, has been kindled in man's heart, he will, as a matter of course, love God and hate sin. Thus there is a "psychological connection" between justification and sanctification. They no longer form "two heterogeneous strata of dogmatic construction."

In Paul's own case everything was psychologically correct as to the indissoluble connection between justification and sanctification. "The life which I now live in the flesh I live by the faith of the Son of God, who loved me and gave Himself for me" (Gal. 2:20). Nor did the Christians find that they were supposed to act "unpsychologically" when they declared with John: "We love Him because He first loved us" (1 John 4:19) and with Paul: "He died for all that they which live should not henceforth live unto themselves, but unto Him which died for them and rose again" (2 Cor. 5:15). It is the experience of all Christians that the more certain they are of God's grace and of their heavenly inheritance, the more ready are they to serve God and to set their affection on things above. "I will run the way of Thy Commandments when Thou shalt enlarge my heart" (Ps. 119:32). Also love of the neighbor flows psychologically from faith in the love of God. "Beloved, if God so loved us, we ought also to love one another" (1 John 4:11), and: "Walk in love, as Christ also hath loved us and hath given Himself for us an Offering and a Sacrifice to God for a sweet-smelling savor" (Eph. 5:2). Thus the love of God and of the neighbor, in other words, the fulfillment of the Law (Matt. 22: 34-39; Rom. 13:8-10), is connected by a *nexus indivulsus* with justifying faith in a spiritual and yet most natural manner. Justification and sanctification are certainly not two heterogeneous "streams of thought" which run side by side without blending, but they clearly and certainly are "psychologically connected."

The moderns are right from their standpoint in ruling out faith as the cause of sanctification. The faith which they have in mind is wholly or in part the product of man, the result of man's self-decision or the product of scientific demonstration. Such a faith is an impotent thing. Like all the works of man's hands, it must fail. In the words of Luther: "As it [*fides acquisita*] is a human fiction and a dream, causing no real change of the heart, so it also accomplishes and is followed by no improvement" (St. L. XIV:99). But t which is kindled by the Holy Ghost without any human co-op which amidst the terrors of conscience "assents to the promise of God, in which, for Christ's sake, the remission of sins and justification are freely offered" (*Trigl.* 135, Apol., IV, 48), is virile and dynamic. This faith produces sanctification and good works. The Apology presents this psychologically: "This special faith, by which an individual believes that for Christ's sake his sins are remitted him, and that for Christ's sake God is reconciled and propitious, obtains remission of sins and justifies us. And because in repentance, i. e., in terrors, it comforts and encourages hearts, it regenerates us and brings the Holy Ghost, that then we may be able to fulfill God's Law, namely, to love God, truly to fear God, truly to be confident that God hears prayer and to obey God in all afflictions; it mortifies concupiscence, etc." (*Trigl.* 133, IV, 45.) Luther describes the power of the divinely wrought faith thus: "Faith is a divine work in us that changes us and regenerates us of God (John 1:13) and puts to death the old Adam and makes us entirely different men in heart, spirit, mind, and all powers and brings with it the Holy Ghost. Oh, it is a living, busy, active, powerful thing that we have in faith so that it is impossible for it not to do good without ceasing. Nor does it ask whether good works are to be done, but before the question is asked, it has wrought them and is always engaged in doing them. . . . Faith is a living, bold trust in God's grace, so certain that a man would die a thousand times for it. And this trust and knowledge of divine grace renders joyful, fearless, and cheerful towards God and all creatures, which [joy or cheerfulness] the Holy Ghost works through faith. And on account of this, man becomes ready and cheerful, without coercion, to do good to everyone, to serve everyone, and to suffer everything for love and praise to God, who has conferred this grace on him, so that it is impossible to separate works from faith, yea, just as impossible as it is for heat and light to be separated from fire." (St. L. XIV:99 f. *Trigl.* 941, F. C., Sol. Decl., IV, 10 ff.)

When Scripture states that faith works sanctification (Gal. 5:6: "Faith which worketh by love") and, in other passages, that the Holy Ghost works sanctification (Rom. 8:9), it presents the truth that the Holy Ghost, as the efficient cause of sanctification, works through faith as His *instrumentum.* Through faith in the grace of God, in the remission of sins for Christ's sake, He inscribes the love of God and all Christian virtues, i. e., the entire Law of God, into the heart (Gal.

2:20). Viewed also from this angle, the inseparable connection between justification and sanctification is clearly seen.

Again, Scripture states that faith is wrought by the Holy Ghost (1 Cor. 2:4-5) and, in other passages, that only by faith we can receive the Holy Ghost. Gal. 3:2, 5: "Received ye the Holy Ghost by the works of the Law or by the hearing of faith?" In the first instance the Holy Ghost is represented as approaching man from without with the Word of the Gospel and creating faith through the Word. In the latter instance He is represented as having already made His abode in man's heart. That is to say, when the Holy Ghost has created faith in the heart He does not cease working, but through faith He continues His work in the heart; from within He sustains man's faith in justification and by sustaining his faith promotes sanctification as the fruit of faith. In these various ways Scripture teaches the *nexus indivulsus* between justification and sanctification, between faith and good works.

II. Now as to the second point. Justification and sanctification cannot be separated; however, last things must not be put first. Sanctification must not be placed before justification. Sanctification is the *consequens,* never the *antecedens,* of justification.

The natural man protests against this divine order. According to his conception of religion, works must be placed before justification — the cart must be placed before the horse. That is the belief of all pagans (Acts 17:22-23; 1 Cor. 8:1; 10:20. *Trigl.* 177, Apol., III, 85) and of apostate Jewry (Rom. 10:3. *Trigl.* 177, *ibid.,* 86). That is the teaching of the Papacy; while it has put on Christian trappings, it anathematizes all who will not hitch the cart before the horse.[12] And that is the teaching of all those Protestants who in various ways and under various names let good works, "ethical" actions, correct conduct, etc., precede conversion and justification or make good works either expressly the *causa,* or at least the *conditio sine qua non* of obtaining eternal salvation (Arminians, synergists, Majorists, modern radical and positive theologians).

This general perversion of the divine order is due to the "*opinio legis,* which inheres by nature in men's mind" (*Trigl.* 197, *ibid.,* 144—145). Only when men are instructed by the Holy Ghost through the Word will they get the right view of religion and place sanctification after justification.

---

12 *Trid.,* Sess. VI, can. 24: "If anyone saith that the said works are merely the fruits and signs of justification obtained, but not a cause of the increase thereof, let him be anathema."

Because the flesh still clings to them, even Christians are always prone to assign to works a place before justification (see Luther, St. L. IV:2077 f.). And even theologians who theoretically define the relation of faith and works correctly are tempted to lose sight of this relation in practice. When they observe how the doctrine of grace is misused to neglect the doing of good works, they at times succumb to the temptation to forget the "mercies of God" (Rom. 12:1) as the sole fountainhead of good works and to approve, at least *tacito consensu,* such works as are not the fruits of justification.[13] (See further the section on "The Good Works of the Heathen.")

It is fatal folly and blindness to pervert, either openly or secretly, the proper order of justification and sanctification (Gal. 3:2). Scripture tells us that in every case where good works are placed ahead of justification two things ensue. In the first place, men do not thereby gain justification, but call down upon themselves the curse (Gal. 3:10). And, in the second place, the very opposite of sanctification and good works results, namely, sin is increased. Rom. 7:5: "The motions of sins, which were by the Law, did work in our members to bring forth fruit unto death." Either sanctification and good works follow justification, or there will be no sanctification and good works at all. Scripture sets forth this truth from several viewpoints. One who does not believe in justification by faith without the works of the Law is still under the Law; the Law, however, does not dethrone sin, but arouses it (Rom. 7:5, 7-11. Luther VIII:1455). The Law does not work sanctification, but — the flesh is at fault — hypocrisy (Jer. 31:32; Luke 18:11-12) or despair (Acts 16:27). Again: He who does not believe in the Gospel, in other words, he who trusts in his works for justification, is not ruled by the Holy Ghost, but by the devil. And such a one does not perform the holy will of God, but he thinks, wills, and does what Satan works in him (Eph. 2:2; Titus 3:3; Luke 11:21). Therefore the practical need of the individual Christian, who is concerned about his Christian faith and Christian life, and the practical need of the Church, inasmuch as it is concerned about faith and sanctification, demand that, on the one hand, the *nexus indivulsus* between justification and sanctification and, on the other hand, the *ordo antecedentium et consequentium* be clearly understood and scrupulously maintained. The following discussion also is intended to serve that purpose.

---

[13] I have in mind here, e. g., the custom of raising funds for the church by sales, socials, etc., on the plea that unless this method is followed, the necessary "good works" will not be done.

4

Who Effects Sanctification?

God, who creates faith, also produces sanctification by His infinite power. "The very God of peace sanctify you wholly. . . . Faithful is He that calleth you, who will also do it" (1 Thess. 5:23-24).[14] But in this work of sanctification the Christian also plays a part. In conversion man merely experiences the working of God *(pure passive se habet)*, but in sanctification the Christian plays an active role; he co-operates *(active se habet sive co-operatur)*.

However — and let this be clearly understood — the working of God and the working of the new man are not co-ordinate, "as when two horses draw a wagon," but the activity of the new man is always and fully subordinated to God's activity; it always takes place *dependenter a Deo*. In other words: it is the Holy Ghost who produces the activity of the new man; the new man remains the organ of the Holy Ghost.

All these points are set forth in the Formula of Concord: "From this, then, it follows that as soon as the Holy Ghost, through the Word and holy Sacraments, has begun in us His work of regeneration and renewal, it is certain that through the power of the Holy Ghost we can and should co-operate, although still in great weakness. But this (that we co-operate) does not occur from our carnal, natural powers, but from the new powers and gifts which the Holy Ghost has begun in us in conversion, as St. Paul expressly and earnestly exhorts that as workers together with Him we receive not the grace of God in vain (2 Cor. 6:1). But this is to be understood in no other way than that the converted man does good to such an extent and so long as God by His Holy Spirit rules, guides, and leads him, and that as soon as God would withdraw His gracious hand from him, he could not for a moment persevere in obedience to God. But if this were understood thus, that the converted man co-operates with the Holy Ghost in the manner as when two horses draw a wagon, this could in no way be conceded without prejudice to the divine truth." (*Trigl.* 907, Sol. Decl., II, 65 f.)

To the question as to who takes the initiative in generating the

---

[14] The Holy Ghost, dwelling in the Christians as in His temple (1 Cor. 3:16; 6:19), moves them to mortify the flesh (Rom. 8:13-14). The Christians are God's workmanship (ποίημα, creation), created unto good works (Eph. 2:10).

individual spiritual impulses or individual good works, the new man or the Holy Ghost, Scripture answers that the first suggestion and impulse to every good work proceeds from the Holy Ghost. Scripture traces even every good thought to God as its Author. 2 Cor. 3:5: "Not that we are sufficient of ourselves to think anything as of ourselves; but our sufficiency is of God." (See Calov on this passage.)

5

The Inner Motions (Motus Interni) of Sanctification

By faith in Christ a "new man" (Eph. 4:24; Col. 3:10; "the inward man," 2 Cor. 4:16) has been born, whose will agrees perfectly with the will of God. Rom. 7:22: "I delight in the Law of God after the inward man." According to the new man a Christian is therefore perfectly holy, "dead unto sin, but alive unto God" (Rom. 6:11). But in this life the Christian retains his sinful nature, the "old man" (Eph. 4:22; 2 Cor. 4:16: "our outward man"; Rom. 6:6: "the body of sin"; 7:18: "my flesh"), who is under the rule of sin (Rom. 7:18: "I know that in me, that is, in my flesh, dwelleth no good thing") and strives against the new man (Gal. 5:17: "The flesh lusteth against the Spirit"). Sanctification, therefore, is brought about only in this way that, in the struggle going on within a Christian between his new nature and his old nature, a Christian according to his new man prevails over the will and conduct of the old man. According to Scripture, sanctification, expressed negatively, consists in the putting off of the old man, and positively, in the putting on of the new man. Eph. 4:22-24: "Put off the old man . . . put on the new man."

Regarding the conflict of the spirit with the flesh we note: 1. This constant struggle does not prove that a Christian has fallen from grace, as he may perhaps think in the hour of trial, but, on the contrary, such conflict is evidence that he is living in the state of grace. Only when the struggle has ceased has the fall from grace taken place.

2. Since the old man of a Christian retains his old evil nature, just as it exists in unbelievers, Christians must not be surprised, on the one hand, when inclinations to rankest unbelief stir in their heart or temptations to commit the coarsest sins (Rom. 7:18; 1 Thess. 4:3-6); on the other hand, they must bear in mind that the spirit's struggle against the flesh does not aim at improving and reforming,

but at crucifying and mortifying the flesh.[15] Such a treatment of the flesh is demanded by Scripture. Rom. 8:13: "Mortify the deeds of the body"; Gal. 5:24: "They that are Christ's have crucified the flesh with the affections and lusts"; Col. 3:5: "Mortify your members which are upon the earth, fornication, uncleanness, etc."; 1 Cor. 9:27: "I keep under my body and bring it into subjection"; Matt. 18:8-9: "If thy hand or thy foot offend thee, cut them off. . . . If thine eye offend thee, pluck it out."

3. The struggle of the spirit against the flesh is difficult and painful: "Mortify," "crucify," "cut them off"; and the flesh which must be given that treatment is not a being separate from us, but is part and parcel of ourselves. But we find comfort in the thought that, as Luther often reminds us, "the great saints" experienced the same bitter struggle. We hear the great Apostle Paul crying out in anguish: "O wretched man that I am!" (Rom. 7:24.)[16]

4. Victory in this battle is assured to him who continues in the grace of God and God's Word and thus gives the Holy Spirit opportunity to work in him effectually with His divine power. This He does when we realize our weakness, 2 Cor. 12:10: "When I am weak, then I am strong"; Luke 18:27: "The things which are impossible with men are possible with God"; 2 Cor. 4:7 ff.: "We have this treasure in earthen vessels, that the excellency of the power may be of God and not of us." And this divine power is exerted through the Word, Eph. 6:17: "Take the sword of the Spirit, which is the Word of God"; John 15:7: "If ye abide in Me and My words abide in you, ye shall ask what ye will, and it shall be done unto you." And what will happen if we thus employ the Word of God? Rom. 8:37: "In all these things we are more than conquerors" (ὑπερνικῶμεν — we keep achieving the most brilliant victory). Paul describes the victorious outcome in detail. 2 Cor. 4:8 ff. (Paul's play upon words cannot be reproduced in the translation): "We are troubled on every side, yet not distressed; we are perplexed, but not in despair; persecuted, but not forsaken; cast down, but not destroyed; always bearing about in the body the

---

15 Meyer on 2 Cor. 7:1: "Never is the demand made that the σάρξ be or become holy."

16 Luther: "Not one of you who suffers or is tempted in soul or body, even though it be in the highest and severest degree, should imagine that he suffers something special, new, or rare, or that no one, in the past and in the present, ever experienced and endured such hard and terrible trials; no, you are not the only ones. Your brethren, both the dead and the living, have experienced the same and indeed even greater and worse trials." (St. L. IX:1292.)

dying of the Lord Jesus, that the life also of Jesus might be made manifest in our body."

Regarding the use of God's Word in the conflict of the spirit with the flesh, Luther says: "You must be sober and vigilant in order that the body may become fit" (Luther often speaks of the proper training of the body in this connection, but he does not overestimate this *paedagogia externa*). "But thereby the devil is not yet vanquished; more than the outward training of the body against sin is needed. The real sword is this, that you are strong and firm in the faith. If with your heart you take hold of the Word of God and cling to it in faith, the devil cannot win, but must flee. If you can say: 'This my God hath said; on this I take my stand,' you will see that he slinks away, and with him will depart the sluggishness, the evil desires, anger, miserliness, melancholy, and doubt. But the devil is sly; he will not have you put your trust in the Word and reaches out to wrest it out of your hand; if he can make you lazy, so that your body becomes unfit and filled with knavish desires, he will soon wrest the sword out of your hand. He thus had his way with Eve; she had God's Word, and if she had clung to it, she would not have fallen. But when the devil saw that she held the Word so loosely, he tore it out of her heart, so that she let go of it; and thus he had won. (2 Cor. 11:3; Gen. 3:4, 13.) Thus St. Peter has sufficiently instructed us how we are to fight the devil. Running to and fro will not do, nor any work that you might perform; what is needed is that you cling to the Word by faith. When he comes and would drive you into despondency because of your sin, just take hold of the Word of God which promises forgiveness of sins and take that to heart, then he will soon have to leave off." (St. L. IX:1108, on 1 Pet. 5:9.)

5. An important rule in this warfare is to do at once the very opposite of what the flesh and the devil propose. When we are tempted to murmur against God, then the best answer is to praise God for His many mercies. When we are tempted to entertain our own or other men's thoughts about matters of doctrine and life, we should simply ask: What has God revealed on this matter in Scripture? [17] It is important for the Christian not only to read God's Word

[17] Experience proves that following this rule will insure success. Do not wait with the praise of God until your heart feels that God should be praised, but in the midst of your discontent take up the strains of "Now thank we all our God," and your discontent and murmuring will melt away. When death rises up as a frightening specter before our eyes, words of Scripture such as "Today shalt thou be with Me in Paradise" will banish the frightening specter. The feeling that our affliction entails very deep and persistent sorrow will vanish in the light

daily, but to commit to his memory as many Scripture texts as possible,
so that he will be ready to repel the attacks of the flesh, the world,
and the devil with the Word of Scripture, whenever and wherever
they occur. Christ taught us by His example that in this way the
victory is obtained (Matt. 4:1-11).

6

The Means by Which Sanctification Is Effected

Strictly speaking, only that Word which mortifies the old man and
supplies strength to the new man is the means of sanctification, namely,
the Gospel (the means of grace), not the Law. It is only the Gospel
which dethrones sin; the Law can only multiply sin (Rom. 6:14; 7:5-6;
Jer. 31:31 ff.). However, the Law has its place in the work of sanctification; it serves the Gospel. Over against the inexact statements
of some Lutheran theologians Carpzov shows that only the Gospel
(*solum evangelium*) is the means (*organum*) of renewal and sanctification, but that "the work of the Law is needed to accomplish a certain
purpose." [18]

of passages such as "Rejoice in the Lord alway (πάντοτε)." The thought that
the temptation besetting us is too strong to be borne is silenced, e. g., by 1 Cor.
10:13: "God is faithful, who will not suffer you to be tempted above that ye
are able." — When he was tempted by false doctrine, Luther confessed: "Often
I have not been able to refute the devil's arguments" (St. L. IX:1339), but the
doubts disappeared like fog before the sun as soon as the Holy Spirit reminded
him of the words of Scripture dealing with the matter. "The Word they still shall
let remain." See Luther's words on the ability not merely of teachers, but of all
Christians to overcome all error by taking their stand on the clear Word of God
without "glosses" (St. L. IX:1235 ff.).

[18] *Disputatt. isagog.*, 1146 *sq.*, quoted in Baier-Walther, III, 308 *sq.* Baier
is using inaccurate language when he says: "The instrumental cause on the part
of God is the Word of the Law and the Gospel" (he thus co-ordinates Law and
Gospel), and "the Law suppresses the remaining evil desires of the flesh in the
regenerate." The *supprimere* holds good only in regard to certain external out-
bursts of the flesh (*Trigl.* 969, F. C., Sol. Decl., VI, 24), not in regard to the
evil desires of the flesh, the *concupiscentiae carnis.* Baier appeals to Gal. 5:15-16
to prove the statement that the Law suppresses the evil desires of the flesh;
but in this passage the suppression of the evil desires is ascribed to the Spirit,
not to the Law. Carpzov's statement corrects Baier; he writes: "The Law indeed
is said 'to be inscribed in the heart,' Jer. 31:33, but it does not inscribe. The
inscription takes place solely through the Gospel. Solely that which regenerates us
renews us; now, we are born again solely by the Gospel; ergo, we are also renewed
solely by the Gospel. This statement does not deny that the Law does some
service in the work of sanctification."

How does the Law assist in the work of sanctification? The Law continually prepares the way for the Gospel. Since the Christian, having the old evil flesh clinging to him, is ever inclined to make light of the sin which still adheres to him, it is necessary that the Law continually show him his sinfulness and damnableness. Where the knowledge of sin ceases, there also faith in the remission of sins, faith in the Gospel, has come to an end (cf. Luther against the Antinomians, St. L. XX:1646), and thus the Gospel, the only source of sanctification, is choked off. Again, according to his flesh the Christian is always inclined to follow his own ideas as to what constitutes a saintly, God-pleasing life, and he will look upon certain sins as virtues and upon certain virtues as sins. And in view of this fact that by nature he is but dimly conscious of the holy will of God, he is in constant need of the revealed Law as a "rule" to show him at all times the true nature of the God-pleasing life and truly good works.[19]

But we must bear in mind that the strength to do good works and to abstain from evil works is supplied solely by the Gospel. Paul admonishes the Christians "by the mercies of God" (Rom. 12:1) to present their bodies a sacrifice unto God. The only thing that will create the love of God and of the brethren in us is "because He first loved us" (1 John 4:19, 11). In every case the Gospel must write the Law of God into our hearts.[20] Luther reminds us that those preachers who use the Law instead of the Gospel to effect sanctification are to blame for the paucity of sanctification and good works.[21]

Finally, are the vicissitudes of life — poverty and wealth, sickness and health, misfortune and good fortune — conducive to holiness? These external things do not in themselves work sanctification,[22] but by the providence of God they contribute to sanctification by leading men into God's Word. So, too, when the Law is applied as a curb,

---

[19] Formula of Concord: "So, too, this doctrine of the Law is needful for believers, in order that they may not hit upon a holiness and devotion of their own, and under the pretext of the Spirit of God set up a self-chosen worship, without God's Word and command" (*Trigl.* 969, Sol. Decl., VI, 20. So also 963, *ibid.*, 3).

[20] Formula of Concord: "The Law says indeed that it is God's will and command that we should walk in a new life, but it does not give the power and ability to begin and do it; but the Holy Ghost, who is given and received, not through the Law, but through the preaching of the Gospel, Gal. 3:14, renews the heart" (*Trigl.* 965, Sol. Decl., VII, 11).

[21] Luther, on Rom. 12:1, in St. L. XII:318 f. Walther, *Pastorale,* p. 86 ff. [Fritz, *Pastoral Theology,* p. 76 ff.]

[22] In themselves they produce, because of the flesh, either murmuring and despair or pride and self-conceit.

to keep the flesh of the Christians in subjection by the threat of hell and other punishments,[23] the Law serves the Gospel in promoting holiness. A powerful illustration of this use of the Law is found in Mark 9:42-48, where Christ exhorts us to apply merciless self-discipline (cut off the hand and foot, pluck out the eye) in view of the eternity of damnation.

7

The Necessity of Sanctification and Good Works

The dispute about the necessity of good works was in part simply a logomachy, the words "necessity" and "free" lending themselves to different meanings. Formula of Concord: "This controversy was originally occasioned by the words *necessitas* and *libertas,* that is, necessary and free, because especially the word *necessitas,* necessary, signifies not only the eternal immutable order according to which all men are obliged and in duty bound to obey God, but sometimes also a coercion, by which the Law forces men to good works" (*Trigl.* 939, Sol. Decl., IV, 4). But in part basic doctrinal differences occasioned the strife. In the words of the Formula of Concord: "But afterwards there was a disputation not only concerning the words, but the doctrine itself was attacked in the most violent manner, and it was contended that the new obedience in the regenerate is not necessary because of the above-mentioned divine order" (939, *ibid.*, 5). The Fourth Article of the Formula of Concord is directed against the errors and incautious statements on this point that had disturbed the peace of the Lutheran Church.[24]

---

23 "The old Adam, as an intractable, refractory ass, is still a part of them, which must be coerced to the obedience of Christ, not only by the teaching, admonition, force, and threatening of the Law, but also oftentimes by the club of punishments and troubles, until the body of sin is entirely put off, and man is perfectly renewed in the resurrection" (*Trigl.* 969, F. C., Sol. Decl., VI, 24). This wording agrees with 1 Cor. 9:27: "I buffet my body and bring it into bondage" (R. V.). The Formula of Concord refers in this connection (*Trigl.* 969, Sol. Decl., VI, 19) to the fact that according to their flesh Christians are not more pious than the ungodly and that in dealing with the old Adam of the Christians only coercive measures are in place.

24 The Leipzig Interim (Melanchthon) states: "It is certainly true that these virtues, faith, love, hope, and others, must be in us and are necessary to salvation" (Gieseler, III, 1, p. 364). — George Major: "I do confess that I have hitherto taught, and still teach, and henceforth will teach all my life: that good works are necessary to salvation. And I declare publicly and with clear and plain words that no one is saved by evil works, and also, that no one is saved without

Scripture teaches that sanctification and good works are not necessary for salvation. It teaches that faith obtains not only the remission of sins, but also salvation without the works of the Law, entirely irrespective of sanctification and good works. The Formula of Concord, quoting Rom. 4:6 and Eph. 2:8, declares: "We believe, teach, and confess also that good works should be entirely excluded, just as well in the question concerning salvation as in the article of justification before God, as the apostle testifies with clear words, when he writes as follows: 'Even as David also describeth the blessedness of the man unto whom God imputeth righteousness without works, saying, Blessed is the man to whom the Lord will not impute sin,' Rom. 4:6 ff. And again: 'By grace are ye saved through faith; and that not of yourselves, it is the gift of God; not of works, lest any man should boast,' Eph. 2: 8-9." (*Trigl.* 799, Epit., IV, 7.) Luther: "Where there is forgiveness of sins, there is also life and salvation."

But also the modified form of Majorism, which holds that good works are necessary not to obtain salvation, but in order to retain salvation, is contrary to Scripture. The texts quoted declare that faith from its very beginning is in full possession of salvation. The assumption that it is the business of the works to preserve salvation for the believer would create the queer situation that, in the words of the Formula, "faith only in the beginning lays hold of righteousness and salvation and then resigns its office to the works as though thereafter they had to sustain faith, the righteousness received, and salvation" (*Trigl.* 949, Sol. Decl., IV, 34). Faith as the means of salvation would be deposed! But "St. Paul, Rom. 5:2, ascribes to faith not only the entrance to grace, but also that we are in grace and boast of the future glory, that is, the beginning, middle, and end he ascribes all to faith alone. Likewise, Rom. 11:20: 'Because of unbelief they were broken off, and thou standest by faith.' Col. 1:22: 'He will present you holy and unblamable and unreprovable in His sight if ye continue

---

good works. Furthermore I say, let him who teaches otherwise, even though an angel from heaven, be accursed." (Reply to the treatise of Niklas of Amsdorf, 1552, c. I. See Gieseler, III, 2, 213 ff.) A year later, in 1553, he declared that good works are not necessary in order to obtain salvation, but they are necessary in order "to retain salvation and not to lose it again." Justus Menius took the same position from 1554 on. On the Majoristic controversies see Salig, I, 628 ff., 637 ff.; Schluesselburg, *Catalogus*, VII; Walch, *Streitigkeiten*, etc., I, 98 ff. and *Bibliotheca Theol.*, II, 617 *sqq.*; Arnold, I, 939 ff.; Frank, *Theol. der F. C.*, II, 216 ff.; Thomasius, *Dogmengesch.*, 2d ed., II, 472 ff.; Seeberg, *Dogmengesch.*, II, 352 ff.; K. Thieme, sub "Gute Werke," R. E., 3d ed., XXI, 110 ff., 120 ff. (See *Trigl.*, Hist. Introd., 107, 115 ff.)

in the faith.' 1 Pet. 1:5, 9: 'By the power of God we are kept through faith unto salvation.' Likewise, 'Receiving the end of your faith, even the salvation of your souls.'" *(Ibid.)* In short, Major, Menius, and the others directly contradict Scripture when they speak of the necessity of good works whether for the obtaining or for the retaining of salvation.

What Major and his adherents really meant by asserting that good works are necessary for salvation was that good works are necessary for the preservation of faith. It was this Semi-Pelagianism or synergism which lay at the bottom of Majorism.[25] Synergism, which holds that conversion, the kindling of faith, is brought about by the proper human conduct, by refraining from willful resistance, will also teach that good works or the abstention from evil works are necessary to preserve faith. It has been correctly pointed out, in the past and also in recent times, that George Major did not invent the theory that good works are necessary for salvation. Already in 1536 and even earlier Melanchthon, the father of synergism in the Lutheran Church, had insisted that good works are necessary for salvation.[26] On account of Luther's strong opposition he refrained for a time from reiterating such a statement, but he again made it in his later writings, particularly in the Leipzig Interim: "It is certainly true that these virtues, faith, love, hope, and others must be in us and are necessary to salvation." That Major was swayed by synergistic considerations becomes particularly evident from his chief argument: "No one is saved by evil works." [27] He was ensnared by the synergistic paralogism: Since evil works entail the loss of faith and consequently the loss of salvation, it must also be said that good works are necessary for the preservation of faith and, consequently, of salvation. This paralogism had also been enunciated by Melanchthon in his *Loci* of 1543. Frank: "Among the reasons why good works are necessary the *Loci* list 'the necessity of retaining the faith' and offer as proof: 'since the Holy Spirit is expelled and grieved

---

25 Major's opponents took him to task for this (Salig, I, 640).

26 Frank (*Theol. der F. C.*, II, 151) adduces the statements in Melanchthon's *Loci* of 1535 as proof of this assertion. — Read the "Disputatio Philippi Melanchthons mit D. Martin Luther, allein gehalten ueber den Artikel von der Rechtfertigung, Anno 1536," in the Erl. ed., 58, 339 ff. Philippus: "Is this proposition true: 'The righteousness of works is necessary unto salvation?'" (P. 353.)

27 Synergists of all times have used this argument. Luthardt, for example, imagines that he has brought Scriptural proof for the co-operation of man in conversion by quoting Matt. 23:37: "Ye would not" (*Dogmatik*, p. 284; Luthardt-Jelke, p. 384).

when a man sins against his conscience'" (*Theol. der F. C.*, II, p. 151).[28]

Scripture, however, clearly distinguishes between the relation of evil works and of good works to the Christian's state of faith. Scriptural teaching on this point may be summarized thus: Evil works destroy faith, but good works do not preserve faith.

Scripture teaches most distinctly that evil works destroy faith. 1 Tim. 1:18-20 and 2 Tim. 2:16-18 state that those who by evil actions thrust aside their conscience have made shipwreck concerning their faith. 1 Cor. 6, 9 ff. warns: "Be not deceived: neither fornicators, nor idolaters, nor adulterers, nor effeminate, nor abusers of themselves with mankind, nor thieves, nor covetous, nor drunkards, nor revilers, nor extortioners shall inherit the kingdom of God." Gal. 5:21, Eph. 5:5, Rom. 8:13, Col. 3:6, make the same statement. Quoting these passages, the Lutheran Confessions declare: "The false Epicurean delusion is to be earnestly censured and rejected, namely, that some imagine that faith and the righteousness and salvation which they have received can be lost through no sins or wicked deed, not even through willful and intentional ones" (*Trigl.* 947, F. C., Sol. Decl., IV, 31—32). Faith cannot endure in the heart which is given to sin because, as Scripture so plainly tells us, the Holy Spirit, who is the *causa efficiens* of faith, is grieved by evil works and will finally depart from the heart. Hence the earnest admonition of Scripture: "Grieve not the Holy Spirit of God, whereby ye are sealed unto the day of redemption" (Eph. 4:30). The Holy Spirit is not only "the Spirit of faith" (2 Cor. 4:13),[29] but also the Spirit of sanctification and good works.[30] He incessantly admonishes and urges believers to avoid the evil and perform the good.[31] And if the Holy Ghost is persistently thwarted in this part of

---

[28] See also *Corp. Ref.* XXI, 775. Menius, too, adduced the fact that "if one, after obtaining forgiveness, sins against conscience, he thereby loses life and salvation" as proving the statement that "new obedience to God . . . also is necessary for salvation." (See Thomasius, *Das Bekenntnis der ev.-luth. Kirche*, p. 103 f.)

[29] Meyer's comment on this passage: "The πίστις which the Spirit works was in the case of David trust in God; in the case of Paul, faith in the salvation provided by Christ," overlooks the fact that David's "trust in God" was faith in the salvation provided by Christ, as David expressly states 2 Sam. 23:1 ff.

[30] Gal. 5:22: "The fruit of the Spirit is love, joy, peace, long-suffering, gentleness, goodness, faith, meekness, temperance."

[31] Though true Christians because of their flesh also continually obstruct the sanctifying work of the Holy Spirit, they do not as a result lose their faith. In "daily contrition" (*poenitentia continuata, quotidiana*) they deplore their *peccata*

His work, He will cease to perform the other part, the preservation of faith. The Christian Church has always taught that evil works destroy faith.

On the other hand, we dare not say that good works preserve faith. True, good works, being effected through faith by the power of the Holy Spirit, assure Christians of their faith, of their state of grace *(tesimonium externum Spiritus Sancti de fide et statu gratiae),* and for this reason Christians should show all diligence in good works.[32] But to say that good works preserve faith and thereby assure Christians of the final salvation, turns everything that Scripture says of the relation of faith to good works upside down. Good works do not sustain faith, but, conversely, faith sustains good works. It cannot be otherwise, since good works, according to Scripture, are in every case only the effect, fruit, and consequence of faith. (See the chapter on "The Relation of Justification to Sanctification.")

It seems incredible that the proposition that good works preserve faith should ever have arisen within the Lutheran Church. Major and his associates were guilty of a glaring self-contradiction when they contended both that good works are solely the fruit and effect of faith and that faith is sustained by good works. They might as well have said that the fruits sustain the tree instead of the reverse. Majorism would make sense only if it were not true that good works are the fruit and result of faith, only if good works were placed ahead of faith. Majorism belongs in the Semi-Pelagianistic-synergistic camp, in the Roman camp. The Formula of Concord puts it there: "The decree of the Council of Trent, and whatever elsewhere is set forth in the same sense, is justly to be rejected, namely, that our good works preserve salvation, or that the righteousness of faith which has been received, or even faith itself, is either entirely or in part kept and preserved by our works" (*Trigl.* 949, Sol. Decl., IV, 35). Without any further ado all should admit that Majorism reproduces the Catholic doctrine.

Any attempted defense of Majorism flouts logic and contradicts the Scripture doctrine of justification. Some theologians of our day have sought to extenuate the error of Major by pointing to his good intention, namely, "to stress the necessity of the renewal and good

---

commissionis and *omissionis* (Paul, Rom. 7:24), by faith appropriate the remission of their sins, and through this forgiveness of sins maintain their dominion over the deeds of the flesh, Rom. 6:14: "Sin shall have no dominion over you; for you are not under the Law, but under grace."

[32] 2 Pet. 1:10. *Trigl.* 947, F. C., Sol. Decl., IV, 33.

works which grow out of faith." [33] There is absolutely no logical connection between "the necessity of the renewal and good works which
grow out of faith" and the assertion that good works sustain faith. On
the contrary, as surely as renewal and good works are only fruits of
faith, so surely they do not sustain faith, but are sustained by faith.
Furthermore, what does Majorism do to the doctrine of justification?
If good works sustain faith and thus preserve salvation, faith is no
longer the sole means of obtaining salvation, but good works take their
place beside faith as the means of obtaining salvation, yea, they take
the place of faith. Then man no longer obtains salvation by faith minus
works, but by faith plus works. And that is exactly the Papistic
doctrine of the *fides caritate formata*. In the words of Luthardt,
Major's teaching "bases the continuance of the communion with God
on both faith and the new obedience" (*Dogmatik*, p. 321; Luthardt-
Jelke, p. 424). Thomasius himself reaches the same conclusion. According to the propositions of Major and Menius, "The salvation of
man still rests on two factors: God's work of grace through Christ
for us and the work of the Spirit in us, the trust in the former and
the obedience toward the latter. Faith does not, in the course of the
Christian life, entirely surrender its position of chief importance to
sanctification, but it does share it with sanctification, and thus after
all loses it." (*Op. cit.*, p. 108.)

Again, in order to extenuate Majorism, it has been urged that
Majorism was far from ascribing any merit to the good works in the
obtaining of salvation. Major himself made much of this point.[34]
It is the same kind of deception which is practiced with regard to
conversion and justification. We are told that conversion does not
depend on the *facultas se applicandi ad gratiam,* the right conduct, etc.,
as a merit, but as a *conditio sine qua non.* Likewise, in justification the
works are said to be required not as a merit, but as that without which
justification cannot come about: *Praesentia bonorum operum ad iusti-*

---

[33] Thus Thomasius, *op. cit.*, p. 105 f., and Seeberg, *Dogmengesch.*, II, 352.

[34] In his reply to Amsdorf he declared: "Though we teach that works are
necessary unto the soul's salvation, such good works nevertheless cannot effect or
merit the forgiveness of sins . . . and the eternal life given to us; for such glorious
heavenly gifts were purchased for us alone by the death of our only Mediator
and Savior Jesus Christ and must be received alone by faith. Still, good works
must also be present, not as a merit, but as the obedience due to God." (Quoted
by Gieseler, III, 2, p. 214.) This plea gained for him the support of the Wittenberg student body (Salig, I, 646). In the *Testamentum Doctoris Georgii Majoris,*
1570, B 2, Major stressed that he did not consider the works as meritorious. (See
Schmid-Hauck, p. 377.)

ficationem necessaria est. We have shown that this is simply a juggling with words (Vol. II, p. 482 f.; 534 f.). They will not call it a merit, but ascribe to it the effect of merit, namely, "that through this trifling thing we obtain righteousness and grace" (Luther, St. L. II:580). And that is precisely what is wrong with Major's statement that good works, while they do not merit salvation, are nevertheless necessary for salvation. One who believes this assertion will not look to the Gospel, which promises salvation "without the deeds of the Law," but will look about for the good works which supposedly are necessary for salvation; he will, in fact, base his salvation on works; he will seek his salvation in the Law. The Formula of Concord emphatically calls attention to this deception. It rejects as "modes of speech that should not be taught, defended, or excused" such statements as the following: "We should not indeed rest faith upon the merit of works, but we must nevertheless have them as things necessary to salvation." Again: "Although we require works as necessary to salvation, yet we do not teach to place trust in works." (*Trigl.* 945, Sol. Decl., IV, 27 ff.) In short, Majorism belongs in the Romish camp. The content of this teaching is Papistic, and the effect on the assurance of justification and salvation is Papistic. If good works are necessary to preserve faith and salvation, "they [these propositions] take from afflicted, troubled consciences the comfort of the Gospel, give occasion for doubt, are in many ways dangerous, strengthen presumption in one's own righteousness and confidence in one's own works" (*Ibid.*, 23).[35]

Majorism to this day seeks cover behind Heb. 12:14: "Follow peace with all men and holiness, without which no man shall see the Lord." But, in the first place, true sanctification presupposes the faith which already possesses salvation (Eph. 2:8: "By grace are ye saved through faith." John 5:24). Because we already have heaven, we lead a holy life (Col. 3:1 ff.; 2 Cor. 7:1). Possessing the treasures of heaven, we turn from the refuse of earthly things. And, in the second place, this passage, as the context shows, warns against carnal security and thus is part of the Law. Because Christians are inclined to carnal security and forget sanctification, these words: "Without

---

[35] The ministry of Luebeck, Hamburg, Brunswick, and Magdeburg declare: "The teaching that works are necessary for salvation adds a condition to the doctrine of faith, makes salvation uncertain, and leads consciences to doubt. If good works are necessary for salvation, the promise is uncertain, salvation is doubtful, and consciences will be filled with insecurity and fear. They will always dispute and ask which, how many, and what kind of works are necessary; have I the works which are necessary unto salvation?" (Quoted in Schluesselburg, VII, 598 *sq.*)

holiness no man shall see the Lord" are also directed to them; for the very next words are: "Looking diligently lest any man fail of the grace of God; lest any root of bitterness springing up trouble you and thereby many be defiled; lest there be any fornicator or profane person, as Esau, who for one morsel of meat sold his birthright." In short, it is clear that these words belong to the preaching of the Law, and it is just as clear that these words have no place in answering the question how the sinner, condemned to hell by the Law, appropriates and keeps God's grace and eternal salvation. That is done by faith without the works of the Law, without the works enumerated Heb. 12:14-16. Here, as Luther often reminds us, one must entirely forget all about the Law and its demands. Also Heb. 12:14-16, like all other passages demanding good works, belongs to the Law (sunt phrases legales), is directed against carnal security (contra fucatam fidem), and must be kept out of the doctrine of justification and the attainment of salvation.

In defending their position Major and Menius mixed Law and Gospel in still another way. They claimed that though the statement concerning the necessity of good works for salvation does not apply in the sphere of justification, it is true in the sphere of the *obedientia* of the new man.[36] That will never do. The new obedience is fulfillment of the Law (Rom. 13:8-10). But since the obtaining of salvation is in no wise dependent on our fulfillment of the Law, it will never do to say that the new obedience is necessary for salvation.

In opposition to Major's claim, Nicholas of Amsdorf asserted that good works are detrimental and injurious to salvation.[37] What he originally meant to say was that to trust in good works for justification and salvation is injurious. Formula of Concord: "If anyone should wish to drag good works into the article of justification, or rest his righteousness or trust for salvation upon them, to merit God's grace and be saved by them, to this not we say, but St. Paul himself says, and repeats it three times, Phil 3:7 ff., that to such a man his works

---

[36] Major: "The good works which God commands and the new obedience are needed by the believers for their salvation, not to purchase it therewith, for they already possess it by grace alone through faith, but as fruit of a true faith." (See Thomasius, *op. cit.*, p. 102.) Menius: "Righteousness and life in the believers, which begins in this life . . . though still very weak and imperfect, is nevertheless necessary for salvation and will be perfected in the future resurrection." (*"Von der Bereitung zum seligen Sterben"*; quoted by Salig, III, 55.)

[37] "That the proposition 'Good works are injurious to salvation' is a correct, true, Christian proposition, taught and preached by St. Paul and Luther. Niklas of Amsdorf, 1559." (Salig, I, 642.)

are not only useless and a hindrance, but also injurious" (*Ibid.*, 37). But the Formula of Concord then rejects the flat statement that good works are injurious to salvation. We are not "to say *simpliciter* and flatly: good works are injurious to believers for or as regards their salvation." They are to be performed with all diligence because 1) they are a "token" (ἔνδειξις) of salvation, Phil. 1:28, 2) they are "God's will and command," and 3) God "promises a glorious reward in this life and in the life to come." Therefore, says the Confession, the proposition that good works are injurious to salvation is to be avoided as false and offensive; it impairs discipline and decency (*Trigl.* 951, *ibid.*, 38 ff.).

Concluding this section, we take note of the offer made by Major in 1558 that "in order not to give anyone a cause for further contention he would no longer employ the words 'good works are necessary for salvation,' because they are liable to be misunderstood." [38] However, this statement must be avoided not because it is liable to be mis-understood, but because it is wrong in itself. The Formula of Concord was right in rejecting the proposition outright: good works are not necessary to obtain nor to preserve salvation, not to procure nor to preserve faith. There is only one cure for Major's proposition, and that is to strike out the words "for salvation." It must be made to read: "Good works are necessary." Majorism can be cured only by elim-inating it.

"Sanctification and good works are necessary." This statement, too, has been violently assailed. But it must stand as a statement of Scripture. Scripture calls the obedience rendered to the government a "necessity" (ἀνάγκη, Rom. 13:5); it declares that we "must" (δεῖ) obey God rather than men (Acts 5:29). The fact that Scriptural terms, such as "necessity" and "must," have been misused by false teachers to hide their error must not induce us to criticize and reject the Scriptural terms. That would be a criticism of the Holy Ghost. The Holy Ghost always uses exact language.

When Scripture speaks of the necessity of good works, it means that we must perform them. It is the clear teaching of Scripture that God has commanded them (*necessitas voluntatis et praecepti sive mandati divini*). We read: "This is the will of God, even your sanc-tification," 1 Thess. 4:3. "This is His commandment that we should . . . love one another, as He gave us commandment," 1 John 3:23. God

---

[38] "Bekenntnis von dem Artikel der Justifikation," B. 3 (see Schmid-Hauck, p. 377).

commands Christians to lead a holy life 1) on His account. He does not want His children to serve sin and Satan. He wants them to serve Him, their rightful Lord, who has created them and then dearly purchased them by the blood of His Son. He redeemed them for this very purpose that they should lead a holy life. Titus 2:12-14: "Christ gave Himself for us that He might redeem us from all iniquity and purify unto Himself a peculiar people, zealous of good works." Eph. 2:10: "We are His workmanship (ποίημα), created in Christ Jesus to good works." [39] 2) Christians should perform good works on their own account. Sanctification and good works are to be for Christians the external testimony *(testimonium Spiritus Sancti externum)* of their state of grace and their possession of salvation. 1 John 3:14: "We know that we have passed from death unto life, because we love the brethren." [40] 3) Christians live a holy life on account of the world. By their holy life they should prove the truth of the Gospel to the unbelievers and thus induce them to hear the saving Word. 1 Pet. 2:12: "Having your conversation honest among the Gentiles," etc. 1 Pet. 3:1-2: Husbands should be won without the Word "by the conversation of the wives." Matt. 5:13-16: "Salt of the earth, light of the world."

This necessity, however, does not imply coercion, compulsion *(necessitas coactionis);* it is a necessity which is coupled with willing-ness, since Christians according to their new man gladly and willingly do the will of God. Rom. 7:22: "I delight in the Law of God after the inward man." The necessity which arises from God's will, precept, and command and the willingness on the part of the Christian go together, because the Gospel has written the Law, i. e., the will, precept, and command of God into the heart of the Christian (Jer. 31:31 ff.). He performs his duty willingly.[41] The Antinomians would

---

[39] Luther: "For this end Christ is Christ, redeeming us from sin and death, that the Holy Ghost might change us from the old Adam into new men, that we should be dead to sin and live unto righteousness, as St. Paul teaches, Romans 6, beginning it and growing in it here and completing it yonder. For Christ gained for us not only *gratiam,* grace, but also *donum,* the gift of the Holy Spirit, so that we should have not only the forgiveness of sins, but should also cease from sins." (XVI:224 f.)

[40] See Apology, *Trigl.* 199, 154 f.; Luther on Matt. 6:14-15, VII:512 ff.; the chapter on "Justification on the Basis of Works" in Vol. II, 541.

[41] Christians perform their duty by "an inner necessity," by "a natural compulsion," just as the tree because of its good nature bears fruit, just as the sun is driven by its nature to shine. See Luther, Erl. ed., 58, p. 350 f. Willingness belongs to the nature of a good work; to the extent that a work is done unwillingly it is not good, but evil. Quenstedt: "A good work must not be done by coercion.

not tolerate the use of the terms "necessary" and "must" because of their mistaken notion that these terms always imply coercion.[42]

On the other hand, the terms "willingness," "free," etc., have been subjected to criticism. Yet Scripture itself uses these terms in setting forth that good works are done without the coercion of the Law. Ps. 110:3: "Thy people shall be willing in the day of Thy power"; 2 Cor. 9:7: "Every man as he purposeth in his heart, not grudgingly or of necessity" (there is to be no compulsion about it); 1 Pet. 5:2: "Not by constraint, but willingly." No man in his right senses will get the impression that Scripture leaves it to the discretion of the individual whether he will or will not do good works.[43]

8

The Imperfection of Sanctification

While justification is always perfect, admitting of no degrees, our sanctification in this life will remain imperfect, sometimes showing a minus, sometimes a plus, but never reaching perfection. Scripture

---

He who does his duty unwillingly does not only deserve no praise, but he cannot even expect his works to pass muster before God. For he himself condemns his action; he could not have performed it if the option had been his" (*Systema* II, 1374). Accordingly, Christians need forgiveness of sins for their good works, since these works are contaminated by the unwillingness of their rebellious flesh. It is only the stupidity of the Papistic theology which condemns such statements of Luther as this: "A pious man sins in all his good works" (St. L. XV:1551 ff.).

[42] Melanchthon states in his Opinion, given to the Senate of Nordhausen (*Corp. Ref.* VIII, 411): "Some object to the statement 'Good works are necessary,' 'One must do good works.' They cannot abide the words '*necessitas*' and '*debitum*.' The court preacher" [Agricola] "played on the word '*muss*' and said: '*Das Muss*' [pap] '*ist versalzen*,' taking '*necessarium*' and '*debitum*' to mean coercion by fear of punishment, '*extortum coactione*' (extorted by coercion). He used high-sounding words and declared that good works are done without the Law" (which is, of course, true of the Christian according to the new man). "Yet the first meaning of '*necessarium*' and '*debitum*' is not '*extortum coactione*,' but the eternal and immutable order of divine wisdom; and the Lord Jesus and Paul themselves employ these words '*necessarium*' and '*debitum*.'" (See *Trigl.*, Hist. Introd., p. 123 f.) Melanchthon says concerning the proposition: "Good works are necessary to salvation" that "this proposition arose from many mischievous statements made during the past twenty years." Yes, indeed, only it was Melanchthon himself who twenty years before advanced that "proposition," moved by his synergistic tendencies.

[43] Formula of Concord: "It is false and must be censured when it is asserted and taught as though good works were free to believers in the sense that it were optional with them to do or to omit them" (*Trigl.* 945, Sol. Decl., IV, 20).

admonishes us to grow, increase, abound, in sanctification, Eph. 4:15; in every good work, 2 Cor. 9:8; in the work of the Lord, 1 Cor. 15:58; in the knowledge of God, in all patience and long-suffering, Col. 1:11; in the love of the brethren and of all men, 1 Thess. 3:12; in the knowledge of what is excellent, Phil. 1:10; in doing what pleases God, 1 Thess. 4:1; and couples these admonitions to grow in holiness with the admonition to keep on putting off the old man, Eph. 4:22. It is clear that the sanctification of even the most earnest Christians remains imperfect in this life.[44] The σάϱξ remains in Christians throughout this life, Rom. 7:14-24; Heb. 12:1,[45] and for this reason their sanctification remains imperfect throughout this life. Paul describes the situation in these words: "So, then, with the mind" (the new man) "I myself serve the Law of God, but with the flesh" (the old man) "the law of sin," Rom. 7:25.[46] The dogmaticians express it thus: *Iustitia fidei sive imputata perfecta sive consummata est, iustitia vitae sive inhaerens imperfecta, inchoata, non consummata.* (Baier-Walther, III, 312.)[47]

Perfectionism, which teaches that complete sanctification is attainable in this life,[48] cannot dwell in the Christian heart, which daily

---

[44] Formula of Concord: "There is a great difference perceptible among Christians not only in this, that one is weak and another strong in the spirit, but each Christian, moreover, experiences in himself that at one time he is joyful in spirit, and at another fearful and alarmed; at one time ardent in love, strong in faith and hope, and at another cold and weak" (*Trigl.* 907, Sol. Decl., II, 68).

[45] Formula of Concord, *Trigl.* 805, Epit., VI, 4; 965, Sol. Decl., I, 7.

[46] Compare Luther, St. L. XV:1552.

[47] The question has been asked why God does not consummate sanctification, just like justification, instantaneously by the complete eradication of evil from our nature. There is no doubt that God could do this by His omnipotence. Since, however, God's revelation in His Word shows that He does not do it, this question belongs to the *quaestiones otiosae et inutiles.* See Carpzov, *Disputatt. isagog.,* p. 1161, in Baier-Walther, III, 312, and Luther, St. L. II:778.

[48] Rome teaches perfectionism. See *Tridentinum,* Sess. VI, can. 11 and can. 18; also the Unitarians, e. g., Socinus in his *Disput.* on Romans 7, p. 56, and W. E. Channing in his *The Imitableness of Christ's Character (The Works of W. E. C.,* p. 316); the Arminians, e. g., Limborch, *Theol. Christ.,* V, 15, 2; "Enthusiasts" such as Schwenkfeld and Weigel (cp. Quenstedt, II, 921 *sq.*); the Methodists, the Evangelical Association, and like bodies, the Inspirationists; Mahan and Finney of Oberlin. See Hodge, *Syst. Theol.,* III, 255 ff.; "Perfectionism" in index of *Popular Symbolics.* Source material in Baumgarten, *Streitigk.,* II, 462–482. On the doctrine of perfectionism among the Methodists consult Schneckenburger, *Kleine protest. Kirchenparteien,* p. 136 ff. — The argument of the perfectionists "God does not command the impossible" is thus disproved by Baumgarten: "The admonition of God to be zealous in sanctification proves the very opposite of the contention of the perfectionists, for it presupposes that there is still much

asks for the forgiveness of sin. Rome goes so far as to teach that certain individuals merit more holiness than they need for themselves, the surplus going to those who need it.[49] Scripture denounces perfectionism as a lie. 1 John 1:8, 10: "If we say that we have no sin, we deceive ourselves and the truth is not in us. . . . If we say that we have not sinned, we make Him a liar and His word is not in us." See also Prov. 20:9; Job 14:4; Eccl. 7:20; Rom. 7:18-24; Matt. 6:12. 1 John 3:9: "Whosoever is born of God doth not commit sin; for His seed remaineth in him" — the favorite prooftext for perfectionism — describes the Christian according to the new man who maintains the dominion over the old man. The Apostle distinguishes between "committing sin" (ἁμαρτίαν ποιεῖν, 1 John 3:9) and "having sin" (ἁμαρτίαν ἔχειν, 1 John 1:8). Christians do not "commit sin," that is, they do not permit sin to rule over them, to give it free reign; they "have sin," but in the power of the new man, the offspring of God, they control sin. Speaking of the same matter, Rom. 6:14 declares: "Sin shall have no dominion over you; for ye are not under the Law, but under grace."

---

room for improvement, not only for the beginners, but for all, unto the final consummation" (II, 479). A compilation of the alleged reasons of the perfectionists is found in Baumgarten, II, 468 ff.; 478 ff. It is characteristic of all the various species of perfectionism, from Rome down to Mahan and Finney, that they deny the perfectness demanded by the divine Law in direct opposition to Gal. 3:10, and thus perfectionism, where it is consistently held, does away with faith in Christ. Strong (*Syst. Theol.*, p. 877 f.): "This view reduces the debt to the debtor's ability to pay — a short and easy method of discharging obligations. I can leap over a church-steeple if I am only permitted to make the church-steeple low enough." Rome and Wesley obtain their "perfection" by lowering the standard of the divine Law, denying the sinful character of innate lust and involuntary transgressions. Wesley: "I believe a person filled with love of God is still liable to involuntary transgressions. Such transgressions you may call sins if you please; I do not." (See Strong, *loc. cit.*) Rome, *Trid.*, Sessio V, "*Decretum de peccato originali*": "This concupiscense, which the Apostle sometimes calls sin . . . the Catholic Church has never understood it to be called sin."

[49] These are the so-called *opera supererogationis*, produced by monks and others, who are so pious that beyond performing what God has commanded they also fulfill what God has only recommended (*consilia evangelica*, particularly the three great virtues of monkery: poverty, obedience, and celibacy). See Bellarmine, Lib. 2, "*De Monach.*," c. 7. 8. Gerhard aptly characterizes the *opera supererogationis* by this play upon words: "Correctly are such works called *supererogationis* because huge sums of money are expended (*erogata*) for them, since these works are sold to others. More correctly, however, they should be called *opera superarrogantionis*, since it is certainly arrogance for anyone to claim such things for himself and make promises to others on that basis." Gerhard gives Bellarmine's and Thomas' definition of the *consilia evangelica*. The *opera supererogationis* are described as *opera superarrogantiae* in the Augsb. Confession, *Trigl.* 83, XXVIII, 62, and in the Apology, *Trigl.* 219, III, 239; 257, XII, 14; 295, VI, 45—47.

The fact that sanctification in this life will always be imperfect must not be put forward as an excuse for the neglect of sanctification. On the contrary, it is God's will and the will of the Christian that he strive after perfection; [50] he wants to be fruitful, not only in some, but in all good works.[51] It is characteristic of the true Christian life and the will of the new man that he refrain from every sin. The Christian is eager to serve God in all good works. "I delight in the Law of God after the inward man," Rom. 7:22. And when Scripture calls Christians "perfect" also with regard to their life ("Let us, therefore, as many as be perfect," Phil. 3:15), it takes "perfection" in the sense of "striving after perfection," Phil. 3:13-14: "Forgetting these things that are behind and reaching forth unto those things that are before, I press toward the mark." [52]

The Christian who does not strive to serve God alone is perilously close to losing his Christianity. "Ye cannot serve God and mammon," Matt. 6:24; "So likewise, whosoever he be of you that forsaketh not all that he hath, he cannot be My disciple," Luke 14:33 (the entire passage, Luke 14:25-35, belongs here). Unsparing self-denial marks the Christian life. "If any man will come after Me, let him deny himself and take up his cross and follow Me," Matt. 16:24. The way to heaven leads through "the strait gate" and the "narrow way," Matt. 7:13-14. Only he can go this way who is willing to cut off his hand and foot and pluck out his eye, Matt. 18:8-9. The Apostle Paul describes the Christian as one who exercises self-control in all things, πάντα ἐγκρατεύεται, 1 Cor. 9:25, and points to himself as an example: "I keep under" (ὑπωπιάζω — buffet, maul) "my body and bring it into subjection, lest that by any means, when I have preached to others, I myself should be a castaway," 1 Cor. 9:27.[53]

---

[50] 2 Cor. 7:1: "Having therefore these promises, let us cleanse ourselves from all filthiness (ἀπὸ παντὸς μολυσμοῦ) of the flesh and spirit, perfecting holiness in the fear of God." 1 Pet. 2:1: "Laying aside all malice and all guile," etc. 1 Pet. 1:15: "Be ye holy in all manner of conversation."

[51] Col. 1:10: "That ye might walk worthy of the Lord unto all pleasing, being fruitful in every good work." Phil. 4:8: "Whatsoever things are true, whatsoever things are honest, whatsoever things are just, whatsoever things are pure, whatsoever things are lovely, whatsoever things are of good report; if there be any virtue and if there be any praise, think on these things." Meyer: " Ὅσα, whatsoever, nothing excepted, is said asyndetically six times, with great emphasis."

[52] See Luther, St. L. VII:489 ff.; Quenstedt, II, 924.

[53] Wahl on ὑπωπιάζω: "I hit someone in the face so that he receives brown and blue marks under the eyes." The word occurs also in Luke 18:5. See Meyer on both passages, also Winer, *Grammatik*, 6th ed., p. 42.

CHRISTIAN DOGMATICS

3

In view of the Scriptural requirement of perfect sanctification, the Christian will ask: "Who, then, can be saved?" Christ tells him: "With men this is impossible, but with God all things are possible," Matt. 19:25-26. Nothing makes Christians so conscious of their daily deficiencies as the earnest striving for perfection. And when they acknowledge and confess their daily shortcomings before God, they flee for refuge to divine grace, knowing that the grace of God takes no account of the Law and human works, of our daily success or failure in sanctification and good works. Only by keeping Law and Gospel separate could the Apostle, on the one hand, be fully assured of grace and salvation, Rom. 8:37-39, and, on the other hand, require unsparing self-denial, 1 Cor. 9:27. The whole life of the Christian thus becomes a daily repentance. The more sincerely Christians daily endeavor to rid themselves of all they have and to serve God alone in all their works, the better they learn to know the abysmal sinful depravity which clings to them, and the more earnestly they will daily implore the free grace of God in Christ. And since they are no more under the Law, but under grace (Rom. 6:14), they daily begin anew their struggle to attain perfect sanctification, deploring their many failures ("O wretched man that I am! Who shall deliver me from the body of this death?"), but, at the same time, being assured of their ultimate victory ("I thank God through Jesus Christ, our Lord," Rom. 7:24-25). Striving after perfect sanctification, the Christian thus leads a life of daily repentance (*poenitentia quotidiana, poenitentia stantium*).

Which is the greater evil, perfectionism or indifference to sanctification? A. J. Gordon says: "If the doctrine of sinless perfection is heresy, the doctrine of contentment with sinful imperfection is a greater heresy. . . . It is not an edifying spectacle to see a Christian worldling throwing stones at a Christian perfectionist." (See Strong, *Syst. Theol.*, p. 881.) It is useless to discuss the question which of these two "heresies" is the greater. The Bible says to the "Christian worldling": "This ye know that no whoremonger, nor unclean person, nor covetous man, who is an idolater, hath any inheritance in the kingdom of Christ and of God. Let no man deceive you with vain words; for because of these things cometh the wrath of God upon the children of disobedience. Be not ye therefore partakers with them." (Eph. 5:5-7.) And to the perfectionists the Bible says: "If we say that we have no sin, we deceive ourselves, and the truth is not in us." Again, in still stronger language: "If we say that we have not sinned, we make Him a liar and His word is not in us." (1 John 1:8, 10.)[54] If perfectionists such as Wesley retained their faith, this was due to the fact that for their own persons they did not believe their doctrine.

In the treatise *An Argument in Defense of All the Articles of Dr. Martin Luther Condemned in the Roman Bull* Luther, following Augustine, insisted: "A pious man sins in all his good works," and: "The very best work is a venial sin according to God's merciful judgment, and a mortal sin according to His strict judgment." (St. L. XV:1551, 1554.) Later the Council of Trent repeated the Pope's condemnation of this statement of Luther,[55] which overthrows the foundation of Roman work-righteousness and of the whole Papacy. It is clear that if Christians stand in need of the forgiveness of sins for their good works because of the imperfection clinging to them, they cannot merit the forgiveness of sins by these works. What Luther says in establishing the article which the Pope had condemned is a complete refutation both of Papistic and of "Protestant" perfectionism. Luther writes: "This article (a pious man sins in all his good works) is obnoxious to the work-saints, who place their reliance not upon God's mercy, but on their own righteousness, that is, on sand (Matt. 7:26 f.). But a pious Christian should learn and know that all his good works avail nothing in the sight of God; with all the dear saints he should despair of his own works and rely on the pure mercy of God with all confidence and firm trust. Let us see what the dear saints say about it. Isaiah (64:6) says: 'We are all of us unclean, and all our righteousness is like a filthy, stinking rag.' Observe that the Prophet excepts nobody; he says, 'we are all of us unclean,' and he was a holy Prophet. Again, he says, 'all righteousness,' none excepted. If, then, there is such a thing as a good work, without sin, this Prophet is lying, which God forbid. Is not this passage of Isaiah clear enough? Why, then, do they condemn my article, which states nothing but what this Prophet states? But we shall gladly stand condemned with the holy Prophet. Furthermore, Solomon says (Eccl. 7:20): 'There is no man on earth so righteous that he doeth a good

---

[54] Regarding the perfect tense ἡμαρτήκαμεν, Huther correctly remarks: "The perfect does not prove that ἡμαρτήκαμεν is intended to refer to the sinning before conversion. Rather it is the sinning of Christians that is spoken of here, as in all preceding verses."

[55] *Sess.* VI, can. 25: "If anyone saith that, in every good work, the just sins venially at least, or — which is still more intolerable — mortally, and consequently deserves eternal punishments: and that for this cause only he is not damned that God does not impute those works unto damnation: let him be anathema."

work and sinneth not.' I think this passage covers everything; it states, nearly word for word, what my article states. Well, Solomon here stands condemned. And his father David is in like condemnation. He says in Ps. 143:2: 'Lord, enter not into judgment with me, Thy servant, for in Thy sight shall no man living be justified.' Who is God's servant but he who does good works? How, then, does it happen that he cannot endure God's judgment? Surely God's judgment is not unjust. If a work, then, were altogether good and without sin, it need not flee God's just judgment; the fault must necessarily lie in the work, which is impure. Therefore no man living is justified in God's sight, but all men need His mercy, even when they do good. Here you Papists should exhibit your skill, not by simply fabricating bulls, but by answering these passages. I have already shown, in the first two articles, that all the saints struggle against their sinful flesh and are sinners as long as they live in the flesh, which warreth against the spirit; therefore at one and the same time they serve God according to the spirit and sin according to the flesh. If, then, a righteous man is at the same time justified by reason of the spirit and sinful by reason of the flesh, the work must certainly be as the person, the fruit as the tree. Inasmuch as it is a work of the spirit, it is good; inasmuch as it is a work of the flesh, it is evil. . . . If they say, as they are wont to say, 'Yes, but this uncleanness is not sin, but rather an imperfection, or weakness, or defect,' I answer, It is indeed a defect and weakness, but if that be not sin, then I will say that murder and adultery are not sins, but defects and weaknesses. Who has given you Papists authority thus to tear up God's Word and to call the impurity of a good work weakness and not sin? Where is there a single letter of Scripture for that? Must we believe your poor dreams without Scripture and you will not believe our plain Scripture? . . . If David says (Ps. 143:2) that even God's servants cannot endure His judgment and no man living is justified in His sight, then this defect must certainly be sin. . . . Again, St. Augustine says in his *Confessions* (9): 'Woe unto all human life, though it were most laudable, if it were judged without mercy.' Behold the great heretic St. Augustine speaking against this holy bull so impudently and wickedly that he attributes sin not only to a good life, but even condemns the very best life (which is made up of good works), if judged without mercy, as though it were nothing but mortal sin. O St. Augustine, dost thou not fear the most holy father Pope? Gregory, too, speaks of the holy man Job thus: 'The holy man Job saw that all our good works are nothing but sin if God judge them; he says (Job 9:3): "If anyone will contend with God, he cannot answer

Him one of a thousand." ' What, you, too, Gregory? Dost thou dare to say that all our good works are nothing but sin? Thou art under the Pope's ban and a heretic far worse than Luther. Luther says only that there is sin in all good works; thou makest them sin outright. . . . If these passages do not help my article, then may God help it! I had rather be condemned with Isaiah, David, Solomon, Paul, Augustine, and Gregory than be lauded with the Pope, and all bishops and Papists, though all the world were made up of Pope, Papists, and bishops. Blessed is he that must die for these things." XV, 1551 ff.

9

The Quality and the Quantity of Good Works

In this section the following points will be presented: 1. Good works a) are done according to the norm of the divine Law, and b) flow from a willing spirit. 2. An examination of the good works of heathen and of Christians according to these criteria. 3. God's will as to the quantity of good works and the deficiency in actual practice.

The Norm of Good Works

Perfect conformity to the Law of God is of the essence of good works. First, only that is a good work which agrees with the norm and standard set up by God. Man is not autonomous, but is under God.[56] Neither his own will[57] nor the will of others[58] should determine his actions. Works which are done in obedience to the commandments of men instead of in obedience to the commandments of God lack the quality of good works. "In vain do they worship Me, teaching for doctrines the commandments of men," Matt. 15:9; Mark 7:7.

---

[56] Deut. 5:32: "Ye shall observe to do therefore as the Lord your God hath commanded you: ye shall not turn aside to the right hand or to the left." Matt. 4:10: "Thou shalt worship the Lord, thy God, and Him only shalt thou serve."

[57] Col. 2:23: ἐθελοθρησκεία is prohibited. "Which things have indeed a show of wisdom in will worship." See Luther, St. L. I:866 f. Num. 15:39: "That ye seek not after your own heart and your own eyes, after which ye use to go a whoring." See Lucas Osiander on this passage. The Lord says reprovingly of the time of the Judges: "In those days every man did that which was right in his own eyes" (Judg. 17:6; 21:25).

[58] Ezek. 20:18: "Walk ye not in the statutes of your fathers." Col. 2:16: "Let no man judge you in meat," etc.

Neither can good intention change an evil work into a good work.[59]
The only norm for good works is God's will.

Setting aside the divine norm is, according to Scripture, nothing
less than rebellion against God and idolatry. One who makes his own
will the standard of action is actually deposing God as his Lord and
Master and putting himself in place of God.[60] And if he permits the
commandments of other men to regulate his actions, he *eo ipso* puts
them in place of God. Furthermore, by obeying men rather than God,
man degrades himself; he forgets the glorious dignity for which he
was created and for which he was redeemed — to serve God alone
(Matt. 4:10) and not to become subservient to his fellow creatures.
"Ye are bought with a price; be not ye the servants of men," 1 Cor. 7:23.

Thus Scripture constantly and in manifold ways impresses upon
us the necessity of complying with the command and will of God
in all our activity. Luther urges this necessity by arguing *ab impos-
sibili:* "If you could save the whole world by one sermon and yet
have no call to preach, desist; for you would be breaking the true
Sabbath, and it would not please God" (St. L. III:1090). Even our
cross must not be self-imposed; our suffering is a true cross only when
sent by God (1 Pet. 3:17). The dogmaticians express it thus: "The
directive according to which good works are to be done and evaluated
is the word of the divine Law, which contains the most perfect rule
of divine righteousness and prescribes both that which should be done
and that which should be left undone" (Quenstedt, II, 1387).

The order of God that only His divine will should regulate our
activity is not invalidated by the strict command of Scripture that we
obey our parents (Eph. 6:1 ff.; Col. 3:20) and the civil government
(Rom. 13:1 ff.; 1 Pet. 2:13-14); for in so doing we are not forsaking
God's commandment for the commandments of men. In this case
He has invested the commandments of men with His divine authority.
God has, moreover, commanded that in case the orders given by
parents and civil government conflict with His divine Law, we should

---

[59] 1 Sam. 15:22; John 16:2; Acts 26:9. Brochmand shows that the good
intention does not change the evil nature of a work which departs from the
divine norm, but that the wicked intention turns every work which outwardly
agrees with the divine command into an evil work, e. g., Matt. 6:1 ff. (Quoted
in Baier-Walther, III, 322.)

[60] 1 Sam. 15:22-23. Concerning Saul, who chose to follow his own will
rather than the commandment of God, Luther says: "Scripture calls it the most
abominable witchcraft and idolatry not to listen to God's Word and to resolve to
act without or contrary to God's Word; and this is indeed a most dreadful verdict,
especially when you consider how common and prevalent such behavior is in the
world" (St. L. I:866).

disregard them (Acts 5:29) and refuse to obey (1 Cor. 7:23; 1 Tim. 4:1 ff.; Matt. 10:37): "He that loveth father or mother more than Me is not worthy of Me," etc. The rule that only God's will, God Himself, is the norm of good works remains intact.

How are we to ascertain the will of God which is to be the sole standard of good works for all men unto the end of days? The question is clearly answered in Scripture. The norm binding upon all men is not the natural conscience, for since the Fall the conscience is liable to err (John 16:2; Acts 26:9); not the law of Moses, because this law contains precepts which were intended only for the Jews (Lev. 11; Num. 15:32 ff.; Col. 2:16-17); not the special commandments given to individuals, e. g., to Abraham (Gen. 22:1 ff. — See Luther, St. L. I:1232f.); not the so-called "commandments of the Church," since the Church is given no authority to decree anything which goes beyond the Word of God (Matt. 23:8).[61] We ascertain the norm of good works only from Scripture. It is the Moral Law. Only Scripture tells us which commandments in Scripture were only temporary precepts and which are obligatory for all men in all ages and in all places. (See Luther, St. L. III:1083 ff.)

But while the Christian Church rejects all works which are performed in obedience to any human norm, she must teach with greatest diligence that everything which Christians perform in obedience to God's will is good and great, whether men prize it or not. Nothing is good in itself. Only God is good in Himself. "There is none good but One, that is God," Matt. 19:17. All creatures and everything produced by the creatures is good only *dependenter a Deo*, that is, only in so far as it corresponds to God's will. To say that anything is good independently of God is a form of dualism, of atheism. How frequently this self-evident truth is forgotten! It is forgotten by philosophy and the speculating theologians who place the "idea of good" outside and above God. And theology forgets it when it declares works "good" which are not done according to God's will and command. Only that is good which is performed according to God's will and ordinance. Such works are exalted and ennobled, no matter whether men prize them highly or despise them. Here the saying "In His Majesty's service" receives its true and full meaning. The Apostle reminds Christian servants (δοῦλοι, slaves) to look upon the despised works of their estate in this spirit: "With good will doing

---

[61] Luther: "The Church has nothing to say in this case . . . she is a pupil of Christ, and though she does teach, she teaches nothing but what Christ commands her to teach" (St. L. I:867).

service as to the Lord and not to men." Eph. 6:5-8; Col. 3:22-24.[62]
Christians should "trample under foot the sneers of Satan" and glory
in the Lord in performing the work which the Lord has assigned to
them in their vocation. (St. L. I:867.)

It was Luther who restored the truth that good works must be
performed according to God's command and rule and that thereby
they become noble. Luther not only re-discovered the Gospel for the
Church, but he also showed the right form of the Christian life.
The Pope and his man-made canons and decretals had made a caricature of the Christian life. We quote at some length — and we are
sure that the student of dogmatics will welcome it — from Luther's
sermon "Of Our Blessed Hope" on Titus 2:13 (St. L. IX:952 ff.):
"We did not learn in the Papacy what constitutes a good work. Before
the Gospel came, we were told that the works which we ourselves
devised and chose were good works, such as making a pilgrimage to
St. James or some other place, giving money to the monks in the
cloisters for the reading of many Masses, burning candles, fasting
with but bread and water, praying a certain number of rosaries, etc.
But now that the Gospel is come, we preach thus: Good works are
not those which we choose of ourselves, but those which God has
commanded, those which our vocation calls for. A servant does good
works when he fears God, believes in Christ, and obeys his master.
First he is justified by faith in Christ, then he walks in faith, leads
a godly life, is temperate and well-behaved, serves his neighbor,
cleanses the stable, feeds the horses, etc. In performing such tasks
he does better works than any Carthusian monk. For since he is
baptized, believes in Christ, and in assured hope is waiting for eternal
life, he goes on and obeys his master and knows that what he does
in his calling pleases God. Therefore everything that he does in his
occupation is a good and precious work. It does not look like a great,
fine work when he rides out on the field, drives to the mill, etc.,
but since he has God's command and directive for it, such works,
mean as they seem, are nothing else than good works and a service
rendered to the Lord. In like manner also a maidservant does good
works when she performs her calling in faith, obeys her mistress,
sweeps the house, washes and cooks in the kitchen, etc. Though these
works are not as glamorous as the works of the Carthusian who hides

---

[62] Luther: "Here one is not to regard what is said or commanded, but who
it is that commands it. . . . He who regards Him who is here commanding will
consider the thing commanded as the greatest work, even if it appears to be the
lowliest." (St. L. I:527. See Large Catechism, Trigl. 607, 3d Com., 91–93.)

behind a mask and has people gaping at him, still such works are much better and more precious before God than those of the Carthusian who wears a hair shirt, keeps his vigils, gets up at night and chants for five hours, eats no meat, etc. He does them without God's command and order; how, then, can they please God? Likewise when a burgher or a farmer helps his neighbor, warns him of the danger threatening his body, wife, child, servant, cattle, and goods, etc., such works do not make a great show, but they are nevertheless good and precious works. When the civil government punishes the wicked and protects the virtuous, and when citizens yield obedience to the government and do so from faith and the hope of eternal life, they are performing good works, though they do not shine and glitter in the sight of reason. . . . If you ask reason, the works of a servant, a maid, a master, a mistress, a mayor, and a judge are common, lowly works compared with the Carthusian's keeping his vigil, fasting, praying, abstaining from meat; but if you ask God's Word, the works of all Carthusians and all monks, melted together in one mass, are not as good as the work of a single poor servantmaid, who by Baptism has been brought into the kingdom of God, believes in Christ, and in faith is looking for the blessed hope. These two articles St. Paul would keep alive among Christians: the knowledge of Jesus Christ our Savior, who has called us by Baptism and the Gospel as heirs of eternal life, waiting for that blessed hope and the glorious appearance of our Lord Jesus Christ, and the knowledge that everything we do in our Christian calling and station by faith is altogether a good and precious work; on which account we should be zealous unto good works. . . . Now, therefore, since we have heard what blessed hope we should look for, we should also learn that the works which we do by faith in our appointed calling according to God's command and order are good works. Though such works do not glitter in the sight of reason, they are nevertheless precious before God, while the Carthusian and the monk cannot see and understand these things. For example, I am a preacher; that is my office; if now I believe in Christ and look for the blessed hope and then go and tend to my preaching and perform my calling, even though men hold my office in low esteem, I would not trade my office for all the works that all the monks and nuns do in the cloister. . . . Likewise also that wife is a living saint who believes in Christ, looks for the blessed hope and appearance of our Lord Jesus Christ and in such a faith goes and does what belongs to the calling of a wife. . . . As reason knows nothing of the blessed hope of eternal life, so, too, it does not understand what constitutes truly good works. It reasons thus: This maid milks the cow, this farmer plows the field, they are performing common, lowly works, which also the heathen perform; how, then, can they be good works? But this man becomes a monk, this woman a nun, they look sour, put on a cowl, wear a rough garment: these are exceptional works, they are not performed by the common people; therefore they must be good. Thus reason argues. Thus reason leads us away from the true knowledge of both the blessed hope and the good works." Luther's writings abound in such presentations.[63]

Good Works Flow from a Willing Spirit

Good works must not only conform to the divine Law, but they must also flow from a willing spirit, that is, from the love of God. "Good works," according to the old paradox, "must not only be good, but they must also be well done," *(bene fieri debent).*[64] Whatever is not done from a willing spirit, from the love of God, for the purpose of serving Him, is not a keeping but a transgression of the divine Law, Rom. 13:8-10; Matt. 22:37-40. Luther therefore introduces his explanations of the several Commandments with the words: "We should fear and love God." That is the uniform teaching of Scripture. Only those works are acceptable in the sight of God which are done willingly, from the love of God, Ps. 110:3; 2 Cor. 8:3-4, 12.

To perform works of this nature is an art which only a Christian can accomplish. Non-Christians can do works which conform externally (*"in materia,"* says Luther) to God's Law, but the motives behind these works are at best only those that come natural (the natural inclination to work, the natural love toward parents, wife, children, natural sympathy), or in many cases the love of fame, or even the desire to make amends for sins and to merit salvation by their works. The love of God and the desire to serve Him is found only in those

---

[63] Particularly in his exposition of Genesis, where he presents the lowly works of the patriarchs in their true light: St. L. I:526 ff.; 762; 1161 ff.; 1179 ff.; 1310 f.; 1479 f.; II:704; 847 ff.; 1742 f. Classic passages from his other writings: St. L. III:1086 ff.; IX:1205 ff.; XIII:2216 ff.; XII:568 ff.; 892 ff. On the comfort which flows from the assurance that God has placed us in our station, Luther writes: "Every Christian should accustom himself from his youth to become certain that he is in a God-pleasing calling. He who does that, though he fall down the stairs and die, can nevertheless say: My father, my mother, my master, my mistress, told me to go down; therefore I die in a blessed calling, in the performance of a work that is pleasing to God." (St. L. XIII:2218.) On being satisfied in our earthly calling as chosen for us by God, see Luther, St. L. XIII:194 ff.

[64] Kromayer, *Theol. posit. — pol.,* II, 395, quoted in Baier-Walther, III, 324.

who have come to faith in the Gospel by the operation of the Holy Ghost and as a result of this faith love Him who first loved them. Good works, as Luther reminds us, "are done out of heaven" (St. L. XII:136), that is, are performed by those who through faith in Christ already possess heaven and accordingly bring the works which they do on earth to God as a thankoffering (Rom. 12:1). For this reason, catechisms and works on dogmatics point out, in defining good works, that they can be performed only by believers, the regenerate.[65] Luther continually stresses the axiomatic truth: "The person must in all cases first be good and pious before he can do good works" (St. L. XIX: 1003), and Luther tells us, too, how the person becomes good and pious. "Whoever believes in Christ, believes that He was born for us, died, was buried and raised again from the dead, he is regenerated, or born anew. He is a new man, for now he has thoughts which no Papist or Turk ever had. . . . If you continue in this faith, the Holy Ghost is there and baptizes you, strengthens and increases your faith, puts a new understanding into your heart, and awakens in you holy and new thoughts and affections, so that you begin to love God and refrain from all wicked actions, and do from your heart what God would have you do, and love your neighbor, and shun anger, hatred, and envy." (St. L. VII:1862.)[66]

The Good Works of the Heathen

The foregoing discussion has already answered the question how the good works of the heathen are to be regarded. This question has caused much discussion. By good works of the heathen and unbelievers in general such works are meant as comply externally (in materia) with the norm of the divine Law still written in the heart of fallen man (Rom. 2:15 f.; 1:32). That such works are being done is stated in Rom 2:14: "The Gentiles do by nature the things contained in the Law." Also Luther sets forth that in their external form such works as feeding the hungry, clothing the naked, succoring the dis-

---

[65] Dietrich's Cat., Qu. 142: "What are good works? Good works are actions of the regenerate, performed by the power of the Holy Spirit, proceeding from true faith, conforming to God's Commandments, and designed solely to glorify God and manifest due gratitude."

[66] Luther: "Cursed and damned is every life that aims at selfish gratification and seeks its own gain. Cursed are all works that are not done in love." (St. L. X:407). Formula of Concord: Only the Christians serve God willingly (Trigl. 967, Sol. Decl., VI, 16—17). Apology: "We do not love unless our hearts are firmly convinced that the remission of sins has been granted us" (Trigl. 153, IV, 110; 157, III, 1 ff., etc.).

tressed, laboring diligently in one's profession and trade, etc., are much like the works of Christians, yea, surpass them in the sight of men.[67] How are we to view these works?

It will hardly do to say: "The good works of the unregenerate are indeed properly called sins, but they are not in themselves, not outrightly, sins." The best distinction between the good works of the heathen and those of Christians is made when the Lutheran Confessions assign these works to the wholly different spheres to which they actually belong. The good works of the heathen belong in the sphere of civil righteousness (*iustitia civilis*) or of the State. In this sphere they deserve high praise, and, as the Confession says, God rewards them in this life with temporal blessings.[68] It is God's will that the kingdoms of this world be maintained, namely, as the scaffolding for the building of the Church. And as civil righteousness is the mainstay of the kingdoms of the world, God bestows temporal rewards upon the works of civil righteousness. That is the glory and the value of the good works of non-Christians in the civil domain. But as to their value in the spiritual sphere, they are to be rated as sin, not only *secundum quid* but absolutely, without any limitation. Without any limitations Scripture declares that the heathen are dead in sins (Eph. 2:1), alienated from the life in God (Eph. 4:18), that they have no hope and are without God in the world (Eph. 2:12), are carried away unto dumb idols (1 Cor. 12:2), and that their sacrifices are offered to the devils, not to God (1 Cor. 10:20). Sharply distinguishing between the worldly kingdoms and the Church, we say with the Lutheran Confessions that the works of the heathen are good in the civil sphere but have no spiritual value. That is the consistent declaration of our Confessions; [69] and one cannot understand how the contrary teaching ever dared to raise its head in the Christian Church.

This is the teaching of Scripture, as presented in clear terms by

---

[67] "Alexander the Great, Julius Caesar, and Scipio have performed greater feats than ever any Christian; such prowess in war, such endurance and fortitude in all kinds of adversity and hardship you will not easily discover in any king in Christendom nor among the kings in Israel, such as David and the others" (St. L. II:461 ff.).

[68] Apology: "In this life and in a worldly nature nothing is ever better than uprightness and virtue, and Aristotle says aright: 'Neither the evening star nor the morning star is more beautiful than righteousness,' and God also honors it with bodily rewards." (*Trigl.* 127, IV, 24. Luther makes a similar statement, St. L. II:472.)

[69] See *Trigl.* 51, Augsb. Conf., XVIII; 124, Apol., IV, 16; 883, F. C., Sol. Decl., II, 7; 891, *ibid.*, 26; 905, *ibid.*, 59, 61; 913, *ibid.*, 85; 893, *ibid.*, 28 ff.

the Apology (*Trigl.* 129, IV, 33 f.): "If the carnal mind is enmity against God, the flesh certainly does not love God. . . . The flesh sins even when we do external civil works. . . . It certainly sins even when, according to human judgment, it possesses deeds that are excellent and worthy of praise. . . . Since, therefore, contempt of God, and doubt concerning the Word of God, and concerning the threats and promises, inhere in human nature, men truly sin, even when, without the Holy Ghost, they do virtuous works, because they do them with a wicked heart, according to Rom. 14:23: 'Whatsoever is not of faith is sin.' For such persons perform their works with contempt of God, just as Epicurus does not believe that God cares for him, or that he is regarded or heard by God. This contempt vitiates works seemingly virtuous, because God judges the heart."

Since, according to Scripture, all the works of the natural man are sin, there is no room for the teaching that conversion is effected through human co-operation. "Since outside of Christ sin and death are our lords, and the devil our god and prince, there can be no power or might, no wisdom or understanding, whereby we can qualify ourselves for, or strive after, righteousness and life" (Luther, as quoted in *Trigl.* 897, F. C., Sol. Decl., II, 43). There is no room in the Christian Church for the teaching of the Pelagians, the Semi-Pelagians, and all the various synergists of ancient and modern times, all of whom deny that all works done before faith are sin. In the interest of her work-righteousness the Church of the Pope goes so far as to anathematize all who teach that works done before the sinner is justified are truly *(vere)* sin.[70]

Even conservative modern theologians deny that all works done without faith in Christ are sin before God. Hofmann asserts that on Judgment Day heathen will be justified on the basis of the works done according to the dictates of their conscience.[71] It is only consistent for the Unitarians to ascribe good works to the heathen; they themselves are *extra ecclesiam,* and they certainly would not want to deny their own works the attribute "good." [72]

---

[70] *Trid.,* Sess. VI, can. 7: "If any one saith that all works done before justification, in whatever way they be done, are truly sins or merit the hatred of God . . ., let him be anathema."

[71] *Schriftbeweis* I, 470 f.; see Baier-Walther, II, 230.

[72] The Socinian Valentine Schmalz, in *Disp.* 6, *"De bonis operibus"*: "It is certain that also the non-regenerate man, with nature and reason as his guide, performs good works; of course, not so perfectly as he who is reborn, nor are they so perfect, or so accepted of God, as those are which are performed from the love of Christ." Cf. Schneckenburger, *Kleine protest. Kirchenparteien,* p. 56.

The Quality of the Good Works of Christians

Measured by the standard of the divine Law, the works of heathen do not deserve to be called good. What, then, becomes of the good works of Christians? They, too, do not measure up to the requirements of the divine Law. They show a deficiency, first, as to the requirement that the Law be the only norm of good works. Christians are in daily need of the warning of Scripture against ἐθελοθρησκεία (self-appointed worship, Col. 2:16-23). Scripture also reports, by way of warning, that members of the congregation at Rome mistakenly (Rom. 14:14) regarded abstinence from meat and wine as the proper form of Christian conduct (Rom. 14:1 ff.). And, secondly, the deficiency as to the requirement that all good works must be done in a willing spirit is shown by Paul's confession: "I delight in the Law of God after the inward man. But I see another law in my members, warring against the law of my mind, and bringing me into captivity to the law of sin which is in my members," Rom. 7:22-23. No Christian boasts about the quality of his good works.

And yet the works of Christians are pronounced good. They receive high praise: "Since we heard of your faith in Christ Jesus and of the love which ye have to all the saints," Col. 1:4; Rom. 15:14; 1 Cor. 1:7; Phil. 2:12; 1 Thess. 1:3; 2 Thess. 1:3-4. And the reason for this praise is the fact that Christians, unlike heathen, believe in the remission of sins and through this faith receive forgiveness continually also for those sins which taint their good works because of their imperfect application of the right norm and their lack of perfect willingness. Christ's atoning blood, which cleanses the person of Christians, eo ipso cleanses also their works. Christ's perfect righteousness covers the person of the Christians and so also the imperfection of their deeds. "We have an Advocate with the Father, Jesus Christ, the Righteous; and He is the Propitiation for our sins" (1 John 2:1-2). Baier's (III, 326) definition of good works agrees perfectly with the terminology of Scripture: "The forma of good works, considered in themselves, is their conformity with the Law of God; but when we consider why they please God, though they do not comply perfectly with the Law, their forma is faith in Christ." The Lutheran Confessions and the works of Luther are replete with such statements.[73]

---

[73] Apology: "Well does Augustine say: 'All the commandments of God are fulfilled when whatever is not done is forgiven'" (Trigl. 171, III, 51). "Even though these works are as yet far distant from the perfection of the Law, yet they please on account of faith, by which we are accounted righteous, because we

The Quantity of Good Works

It should not be necessary to discuss at length how many good works are expected of Christians. Since Christ by His blood has purchased them entirely for Himself, it is self-evident that they should place themselves entirely, with everything they have, into His service. That is what Scripture expects of Christians, Rom. 12:1; Is. 60:6, 9,[74] and Christians are minded, according to their new man, to do so, Gal. 2:20; Ps. 110:3.

However, the old man draws them in the opposite direction and, misusing the doctrine of grace, urges Christians to neglect good works. The doctrine of grace was thus misused in the Apostolic Church (Gal. 5:13; 6:6-10; Titus 3:14), in the Church of the Reformation (see Luther, St. L. XI:301; X:456 ff.), and we would be closing our eyes to the facts if we pretended that the Church of our day were free from this abuse.[75] To stem this indolence, Scripture speaks not only of the quality of good works but has also much to say of their quantity. Christians should not be satisfied with having performed this or that good work, but they should become rich in good works (2 Cor. 8:7, 20; 9:8, 11). They should not sit at home and wait to be importuned to do good works, but they should go out and seek opportunities to do good works; they should be "zealous of good works"

---

believe that for Christ's sake we have a reconciled God" (203, Apol., III, 172). Formula of Concord: "Nor is there a controversy as to how and why the good works of believers, although in this flesh they are impure and incomplete, are pleasing and acceptable to God, namely, for the sake of the Lord Jesus Christ, by faith, because the person is acceptable to God" (941, Sol. Decl., IV, 8). "But how and why the good works of believers, although in this life they are imperfect and impure because of sin in the flesh, are nevertheless acceptable and well-pleasing to God, is not taught by the Law, which requires an altogether perfect, pure obedience if it is to please God. But the Gospel teaches that our spiritual offerings are acceptable to God through faith for Christ's sake, 1 Pet. 2:5; Heb. 11:4 ff." (969, ibid., 22.)

[74] Isaiah says: "All they from Sheba shall come; they shall bring gold and incense; and they shall show forth the praises of the Lord. . . . Surely the isles shall wait for me, and the ships of Tarshish first, to bring thy sons from far, their silver and their gold with them." Luther: "Isaiah foretells that the people of this land Arabia will flock to the Gospel and will give themselves to it, with all their goods, camels, dromedaries, gold, frankincense, and all their possessions. Where there are Christians, they will dedicate themselves and all they have to Christ and His Church. It happened so among us that rich endowments were given the Church, and everybody willingly and gladly gives himself with all that he has to Christ and those that are His, as St. Paul also reports of the Philippians and Corinthians, 2 Cor. 8." (St. L. XII:312.)

[75] See Proceedings, Southern Ill. District, 1913, p. 42 ff.

(Titus 2:14; 2 Cor. 8:4), never "weary in well doing" (Gal. 6:9). Serving God should not be their avocation, but their vocation; they should make the very most of their time on earth in doing good works (Eph. 5:16; Gal. 6:10; Col. 4:5). In addition, God has instructed the teachers and watchmen in His Church to give attention not only to the quality but also to the quantity of the works performed by Christians. Titus is to make it his business to "affirm constantly that they which have believed in God might be careful to maintain good works," Titus 3:8.[76] Pastors are to see to it in particular that those who are rich in worldly goods may be "rich in good works, ready to distribute, willing to communicate," 1 Tim. 6:17-19.

In urging Christians to be "rich in good works" the ministers of the Church must begin with themselves. As *ministri Dei et ecclesiae* they must not be content with a minimum, as was the case with the unfaithful teachers and watchmen of Israel, who are described as "sleeping, lying down, loving to slumber" (Is. 56:10), but they must be intent on attaining the maximum in the performance of their duty, following the example of the Apostle and other faithful teachers (1 Cor. 15:10; 1 Tim. 4:15; 2 Tim. 4:2). They should ever bear in mind the words of Luther: "Therefore look to it, ye pastors and preachers, our office is a different thing now from what it was under the Pope; it has now become a serious and salutary work. Hence it involves much more trouble and labor, danger and trial, gaining little reward and gratitude in the world. But Christ Himself will be our reward if we labor faithfully." (St. L. X:5.)

Secondly, in urging the members of their churches to become "rich in good works," pastors should not be deterred from doing this boldly and resolutely, without any fear or faltering, by the thought that this insistence on good works might crowd out of its central position the doctrine of justification without works. Only if one does not know the Scriptural doctrine of justification by faith will he be timid in asking for a multitude of good works. It is therefore impossible to teach a doctrine of sanctification and good works in accord with Scripture without at the same time teaching justification. According to Scripture the only motive for good works is the pure grace of God, which we have experienced in Christ Jesus. St. Paul knew of no other incentive to good works: "I beseech you by the mercies of God

---

[76] "Be careful to," φροντίζωσι, make a point of maintaining good works, καλῶν ἔργων προΐστασθαι (also v. 14), make good works your real business. Luther: "Im Stande guter Werke gefunden werden." See Meyer on this passage.

that ye present your bodies a living sacrifice, holy, acceptable unto God," Rom. 12:1; 2 Cor. 8:9. The more boldly we teach good works in the way Scripture teaches them, the more definitely do we at the same time keep the grace of God in Christ in the foreground. Yea, if we follow this method of teaching good works strictly and persistently, the result as to the quantity of good works produced will, in spite of the deficiency for which the flesh is responsible, often be astounding. Recall Dr. Walther's words: "All true Christians are so constituted that one earnest admonition suffices to induce them to put forth their strongest efforts. Many preachers achieve so little with Christians because, instead of admonishing them ("by the mercies of God"), they attempt to induce them to perform good works and to desist from evil by the demands, commands, threats, and reprimands of the Law. They have forgotten that they possess a mighty weapon, and they are not using it. Sincere Christians, though weak in many respects, do not mean to reject the Word of God; they desire to live unto Him who died for them." *Pastorale,* p. 86. [Fritz, *Pastoral Theology,* 2d ed., p. 441 f.] Walther adduces the words of Luther: "The lawmonger compels with threats and punishments; the preacher of grace persuades and incites men by reminding them of the goodness and mercy of God which they have experienced, for he wants no unwilling works or grudging service; he wants men to render a glad and joyous service to the Lord. Whoever will not let himself be moved and drawn by the consoling and lovely words of God's mercy, granted to and bestowed on us without measure in Christ, so that he gladly and joyfully does all this to the glory of God and the welfare of his neighbor, amounts to nothing and all labor is wasted on him. How can laws and threats soften him to do God's will, whom such fire of heavenly love and grace does not soften and melt? It is not man's mercy but God's compassion that we have received and that St. Paul sets before us to urge and impel us." (St. L. XII:318 f.)

A word on *tithing.* A booklet bearing the title *The Tithe* [77] deplores the fact that Christians in "wealthy America" contribute less than two dollars per person annually for missions at home and abroad, puts the blame for this miserly giving primarily on the theological professors who teach the future pastors "that we laymen and lay women owe everything to God in general, but nothing in particular,

---

[77] *The Tithe.* By Rev. E. E. Stewart. Introduction by Layman. Winona Publishing Co., 1903.

nothing definite; that the time of payment, manner of payment, and even the amount of payment of whatever we owe, or think we owe, or somebody else tells us we owe, is left entirely to our natural disposition to benevolence or stinginess, or to our moods and caprices"; and the layman who wrote the preface of the booklet argues with the best of intentions for the introduction of the tithe, meaning "that the tithe is — not was — God's Law for the human race and that the obligation to pay it is as binding now as it ever was."

Our answer to this: We Lutheran professors deplore and reprove as sin the undeniable fact that New Testament Christians make use of their deliverance from the Old Testament tithe to excuse their indolence in contributing for the purposes of the Church, particularly for missions. Also Luther reproved this sin.[78] But we also know that the Christian Church never commands where Scripture does not command. The obligation to pay the tithe has been abolished in the New Testament. While the New Testament Scripture inculcates the obligation of generous and untiring giving, it leaves the exact amount and the details of the contributions to Christian insight and freedom. Scripture says: "He which soweth sparingly shall reap also sparingly, and he which soweth bountifully shall reap also bountifully. Every man as he purposeth in his heart, so let him give; not grudgingly or of necessity." (2 Cor. 9:6-7.) Again: "See that ye abound in this

---

[78] "This sin [refusal to contribute towards the support of the Gospel] entails the most severe punishments, and I verily believe that for no other reason were the churches in Galatia, Corinth, etc., ruined by false prophets than this that they did not provide for their faithful teachers" (St. L. IX:748). "For what else are the Gospel and the preaching office in our midst than the blood and sweat of our Lord? He won them by His anguished, bloody sweat. . . . And yet, it would seem that by all this suffering He earned from us only this: some persecute this office, and others refuse to support it and give nothing toward the maintenance of pastors and preachers; besides, they turn their children away from this office, so that it will soon go to destruction and Christ's blood and agony be in vain. . . . If this is the way things are to go in Germany, I am sorry that I was born a German or ever wrote or spoke German; and if I could do it with a good conscience, I would give aid and counsel that the Pope and all his abominations should return and oppress, shame, and ruin us worse than ever he did before. Formerly, when people served the devil and put the blood of Christ to shame, all the purses were wide open, and there was no limit to men's giving to churches, schools, and all sorts of abominations; children were driven, pushed, and forced into monasteries, foundations, churches, and schools at unspeakable cost, and all of it was lost. But now, when real schools and real churches are to be founded . . . all the purses are locked with iron chains. I pray that God would graciously let me die and take me hence that I may not see the misery that must come over Germany." (St. L. X:456 ff., cp. IX:1200 ff.; XI:301.)

grace also. I speak not by commandment, but by occasion of the forwardness of others and to prove the sincerity of your love. For ye know the grace of our Lord Jesus Christ, that, though He was rich, yet for your sakes He became poor, that ye through His poverty might be rich. And herein I give my advice" (γνώμην, opinion; opposite of ἐπιταγή, v. 8), 2 Cor. 8:7-10. This "general" admonition will do the work. "In the Old Testament," says Luther, "it was prescribed that in addition to the annual tithe due the Levites the people had to contribute a special tithe every third year for the poor, the widows, and orphans, etc. Now, such amounts are not expressly fixed by specific laws in the New Testament, for it is an era of grace, in which everyone is admonished to do this willingly, as Paul says Gal. 6:6: 'Let him that is taught in the Word communicate unto him that teacheth in all good things.'" (St. L. XII:337.)

We also know the reason why in the New Testament the Christians themselves are to determine the amount of their giving. We read in Gal. 4:1-3: "Now I say that the heir, as long as he is a child, differeth nothing from a servant, though he be lord of all; but is under tutors and governors until the time appointed of the father. Even so we, when we were children, were in bondage under the elements of the world." In the New Testament the sun of God's grace in Christ is shining in full splendor. And it is God's will that Christians be no more children but full-grown men who, prompted by the willing spirit of sonship, will also in financial respects do all and more than was prescribed to the people of the Old Covenant by an express command. If we, then, confine ourselves to persuading and urging Christians unto diligent and untiring giving for the Gospel by presenting to them the wonderful love of God in Christ, we are not employing impotent "generalities," but are urging upon our people the strong divine motives which will always awaken responsive love and fan it to a bright flame. The contemplation of the thorn-crowned head of the Savior (2 Cor. 8:9) will produce the right quality and the right quantity of their gifts for the Gospel.

It is, of course, no legalism when we reprove slothful contributing to the support of the Gospel as earnestly as the Apostle, who addressed these sharp words to his congregations: "Be not deceived; God is not mocked" (Gal. 6:7). We address these words to the old man of the Christians, who must be coerced to outward obedience by the threats of the Law (Formula of Concord, 969, Sol. Decl., VI, 24). But we expect the good works from Christians according to their new man, who, harassed by the flesh, must be strengthened by the message of divine love.

Nor do we practice Old Testament legalism when we voluntarily obligate ourselves to pay the tithe or the quint or, according to the advice of the Apostle in 1 Cor. 16:1-2, adopt the method of systematic giving. This advice of the Apostle is not a command (2 Cor. 8:8).[79]

10

The Reward of Good Works

Scripture teaches that the good works of Christians receive a reward (1 Cor. 3:8), yea, a very great reward (μισθὸς πολύς — Matt. 5:12; Luke 6:23, 35). The false connotations which have been connected with this word "reward" must not deter us from using it. We shall unhesitatingly teach, both publicly and privately, that God rewards the good works of Christians here in time and, particularly, in eternity (1 Tim. 4:8; Luke 14:14). "The world hath not the grace," says Luther, to appreciate and reward the good works of Christians, e. g., their preaching of the Gospel in the world, their prayers, their intercessions.[80] The world hates and persecutes Christians just because of their very best works.[81] But our gracious God makes up for that. He is so pleased with our good works that He rewards us richly for doing them.

But this reward, so Scripture further instructs us, must be regarded strictly as a reward of grace. The kingdom of Christ is the Kingdom of Grace, and he who hands God a bill for his good works places himself outside the Kingdom of Grace. This double truth, namely, that God rewards good works, but that no man may demand this reward as his right, as earned by him, is brought out clearly in Matt. 19:27—20:16. Peter raised the question concerning reward in Christ's kingdom. Reminding the Lord of the fact that the disciples, unlike the young man who would not forsake his goods, had forsaken every-

---

[79] This whole matter regarding contributions of Christians in support of the Gospel is treated in the *Proceedings of the Southern Ill. Dist., 1913,* pp. 37—62. "Thesis II. The Laymen's Movement and the Finances of the Church. 1. How much shall we give? 2. The danger of small contributions. 3. The salary of pastors and teachers. 4. The cause and the cure of financial sluggishness."

[80] On Gal. 3:23. St. L. IX:443.

[81] For preaching the Gospel the Apostles were beaten, Acts 5:40; Rom. 8:36; 1 Cor. 4:13.

thing and followed the Lord, he asks: "What shall we have therefore?"
In response the Lord says two things: 1) All works done for Him,
Christ ("for My name's sake," v. 29) shall be recompensed with a great
reward ("they shall receive an hundredfold and shall inherit everlasting life," v. 29); 2) But a claim of merit because of the works
done would make the first become the last; a child of grace would
thus become a child of wrath, who will receive the just dues of the
work-righteous, eternal condemnation. Gal. 3:10: "As many as are
of the works of the Law are under the curse." [82]

The words: "The last shall be first and the first last" have been
grossly misinterpreted, particularly in recent years. Luther understood
them correctly. He says: "Christ simply desires to show in this parable
that in the kingdom of heaven, that is, in Christendom on earth,
God judges and operates in a strange manner: He makes the first
the last and the last the first; He humbles those who are something,
so that they learn to rely on nothing but the bare mercy and compassion of God, and, conversely, He will not have those who are
nothing despair but have them also rely on God's goodness, just as
well as the first. First, then, He casts down the presumption of those
who strive to gain heaven with works, as did the Jews, who claimed
to be nearest and dearest to God, just as our spiritual orders also did.
These are all working for wages . . . and they despise those who have
done nothing at all. They murmur against the householder because
he takes account of their great trouble and labor no more than of
the idleness and loose life of the others; they consider such a treatment
unjust, they blaspheme the Gospel and become obdurate in their
behavior. So they lose the favor and grace of God; they must take
their temporal reward, go their way with their penny, and be damned.
They did not work because of the eternal favor of God, but in order
to be paid. The others, however, confessing that they have merited
neither the penny nor the favor, are given more than they thought
had been promised them. These remain in grace and are saved, beyond
having enough here in time too. For all depends on the good will of
the householder." (St. L. XI:508 ff.)

If anyone claims any merit on the basis of having performed good
works, he is excluded from the Kingdom of God — a fact which anyone

---

[82] The question whether the words "Many are called, but few are chosen"
belong in the text need not concern us. They are found, by the way, in C, D, It.,
Syr. Also Meyer regards them as genuine, even though he does this on the false
ground that because of their "seeming impropriety" at this place they may have
been omitted by B, L, etc. If these words fit anywhere, they fit in the context
here, as will be shown in what follows.

at all acquainted with the teaching of Christianity will admit at once. Not any kind of faith makes a Christian a Christian, but only that faith which "rests on pure grace," that is, the belief that God gives righteousness, eternal life, and all things by grace, for Christ's sake, without any meritorious work. If a person hands God a demand for wages based on his works, he has abandoned that faith which makes him a Christian. The reward of grace accords well with the faith in God's grace, in fact, strengthens it;[83] but to claim that one is entitled by law to any reward means that such a one has lost his belief in grace. It is impossible for a Christian, according to the new man, to even think of making such a monstrous claim.

Besides, the quality of his good works will not permit him to do so. He sees that his works are tainted with sin [84] and that, unless they are forgiven, they will subject him to damnation. How, then, can he ask for a reward of merit? [85] Nor can he do so in view of the fact that not he, but God is the *causa efficiens* of his good works. These good works, which are done by a Christian, are wrought in him by divine grace and power. What a Christian's own natural mind and heart contribute can only hinder the work or pollute it. If God nevertheless rewards the works, He is crowning His own work. On what, then, will we base our claim that God owes us anything? [86]

But the old man in a Christian puts forward the *opinio legis* against the Christian doctrine of grace and thus endangers the Christian's state of grace and salvation. Therefore Christ admonishes the Twelve and all Christians to be on their guard lest the first become the last. Luther, applying the warning also to himself, has this to say on Christ's admonition: "It is very necessary that this Gospel be preached to those in our day who know the Gospel, to me and others like me, who can teach and train all the world and consider themselves

---

83 Because the reward is given solely by grace for the sake of Christ's merit. See Chemnitz, *Examen,* p. 185. Even when the reward of grace consists in temporal blessings, the grace of God in Christ is not crowded into the background, but is rather brought all the more into view.

84 Chemnitz on Is. 64:6 ("All our righteousnesses are as filthy rags"): "The Prophet is speaking not of misdeeds but of good works" (*Examen,* p. 187).

85 Quenstedt: "Will he who must daily implore God: 'Forgive us our debts' demand of God that He discharge His debt to him? Can he merit an eternal reward who daily asks God to remove eternal damnation from him? Or with what face can he who daily must ask for clemency boast of merit?" (II, 1421.)

86 Chemnitz: "We are not fit of ourselves (2 Cor. 3:5), but it is God who works in us both to will and to do the things pleasing to him (Phil. 2:13) 'If thou didst receive it, why dost thou glory as if thou hadst not received it?' (1 Cor. 4:7). Hence, if God crowns His gifts in us, He does it not because He owes us anything, but because of His mercy and goodness." (*Examen,* p. 188.)

very close to God, as having entirely devoured God's Spirit, with feathers and bones. For why have so many sects now arisen which, in their own separate ways, tamper with the Gospel? Without doubt it is this, that not one of them applies this passage to himself, 'The first shall be the last.' . . . Did not the same thing happen to the Pope? He and his followers believed that he was God's vicar and the very next to Him, and they had also persuaded the world to believe this; but by this very thing he became the vicar of Satan and the very farthest from God, so that no man under the sun ever so raved and raged against God's Word as he does. Enmeshed in this horrible deceit, he became secure and disregarded the sharp, penetrating, mighty judgment: 'The first are the last.' For this judgment strikes at what lies deepest in the heart of man, the spiritual self-conceit, which in poverty, disgrace, and misfortune — and just because of this — regards itself as the first. . . . By telling you that 'the first shall be the last' God takes all arrogance out of you and forbids you to set yourself above any whore, though you be Abraham, David, Peter, Paul. And when He says, 'the last shall be the first,' He checks all despair and forbids you to place yourself beneath any saint, even though you be Pilate, Herod, Sodom and Gomorrah. For just as we have no reason to exalt ourselves, so we have no reason to despair, for this Gospel confirms and preserves the great truth, which lies in the middle, namely, that we should not regard the penny but the goodness of the householder, which extends in one and the same way to the high and the low, the first and the last, to saints and sinners, so that no man has a greater claim on it than another; for He is God not only of the Jews, but also of the Gentiles, the God of all, whoever they may be or whatever they may be called." (St. L. XI:513 f.)

It need not surprise us that the semi-Pelagianistic or synergistic theology cannot accept the plain meaning of the warning words: "The last shall be the first, and the first last." [87] This theology has eliminated the Christian principle of grace as the sole source of faith by teaching that the kindling of faith and the perseverance in faith depend on *aliquid in homine* — on right conduct, self-decision, etc. And so the majority of modern "positive" theologians assign a place to good works in obtaining eternal salvation. Thieme: "The Lutheran

---

[87] Meyer, for instance, finds in the warning words of Christ that only a few in the Kingdom achieve the first-class accomplishment and reward; Lange: that in the Kingdom of God not so much an extensive as rather an intensive activity counts; Noesgen: that the reward depends on faithfulness. All of these interpretations are contrary to the context.

dogma *quod bona opera penitus excludenda sint, non tantum cum de iustificatione fidei agitur, sed etiam cum de salute nostra aeterna disputatur* (*Trigl.* 799, F. C., Epit., IV, 7) is taught today by only a few Lutherans' (R. E., 3d ed., XXI, 120). But if good works are necessary, in addition to God's grace, for the obtaining of salvation, then the doctrine of grace, and therewith also the doctrine of the reward of grace, is eliminated from the Christian doctrine, and the principle of the reward of merit is substituted for it.

The Papists have no use at all for the concept "reward of grace," since they distinctly teach that good works "truly merit *(vere mereri)*" justification and eternal life (*Trid.*, Sess. VI, c. 16, can. 32). They disagree only as to whether the entire salvation or only half of it is "truly" merited by good works. The *Tridentinum* ascribes half of the merit to Christ's work and the other half to good works.[88] But other Romish theologians, particularly the Jesuits, hold that good works alone, and not Christ's merit, truly merit salvation. Andradius, the interpreter of the *Tridentinum,* declares that it is unscriptural and inconsistent to make the bestowal of eternal life dependent equally upon the merit of Christ and the merit of our works, since Paul says: "Now to him that worketh is the reward not reckoned of grace, but of debt" (Rom. 4:4). He insists that Scripture teaches that since the ungodly merit eternal torment by their evil works, just so the pious merit salvation by their good works. The Jesuit Vasquez declares that "the good works of the just derive no worthiness from the merits or person of Christ." [89] Quenstedt here forsakes his habitual restraint and makes bold to say: "Satan so inflates and bewitches these men that, puffed up by their own merits, they forsake the righteousness of Christ and, leaning on a reed for support, collapse" *(loc. cit.).* But this difference of opinion among the Romanists is of no practical importance, since also those who make salvation dependent upon the merit of Christ and good works completely renounce the Christian concept of "grace" and thus also of the "reward of grace." "If by grace, then it is no more of works; otherwise grace is no more grace"

---

[88] Sess. VI, c. 16: "Life eternal is to be proposed to those working well unto the end and, hoping in God, both as a grace mercifully promised to the sons of God through Jesus Christ and as a reward which is, according to the promise of God Himself, to be faithfully rendered to their good works and merits." Chemnitz comments: "The reader will note that the Tridentine fathers refuse to say that we obtain eternal life entirely by our merits. They are more modest, and in order to preserve the glory of Christ they divide eternal life between Christ's merit and the merits of our works." (*Examen,* p. 186.)

[89] See the quotations from the writings of the *modestiores* and *crassiores Pontificii* in Quenstedt, II, 1421 *sq.*

(Rom. 11:6). In dealing with the Romanists we lay greater stress on their contention that these works (whether they earn much or little) are "done in God," performed by "the living members of Christ" (*Trid.*, Sess. VI, c. 16, can. 32). We tell them that they are operating with something which does not exist. Works by which one would "truly *(vere)*" merit salvation are not "done in God," but in opposition to God (Rom. 10:3). Such works are not rewarded by God, but are under God's curse (Gal. 3:10). And such works are not done by "living members of Christ," but by such as either have lost Christ (Gal. 5:4) or have never been members of His body (Rom. 9:31-32).

The long and the short of the matter is this: One who is still *extra muros ecclesiae* and thinks that he must earn his salvation will always, when the reward of good works is mentioned, think of a reward which he has earned. But as soon as the Gospel has taught him the Christian way of thinking, namely, that remission of sins and salvation have been fully and completely gained by Christ and are freely offered in the Gospel, his thoughts concerning reward also assume the Christian form; he will think of the reward only as a reward of grace, as Christ so powerfully presented this truth in the parable of the laborers in the vineyard. Therefore the Apology says: "We are not agitating an idle logomachy concerning the term 'reward.' . . . If the adversaries will concede that we are accounted righteous by faith because of Christ, and that good works please God because of faith, we will not afterwards contend much concerning the term 'reward.' We confess that eternal life is a reward because it is something due *[res debita]* on account of the promise, not on account of our merits. . . . We also confess what we have often testified that although justification and eternal life pertain to faith, nevertheless good works merit other bodily and spiritual rewards, which are rendered both in this life and after this life. . . . But those who merit this are justified before they do the Law." (*Trigl.* 219, III, 241, 246.)

In his exposition of the fifth, sixth, and seventh chapters of Matthew, Luther sets forth the two points that our good works do not earn anything and that God promises us the reward in order to console us in our afflictions. "The blind, false preachers conclude from these passages [such as 5:12: "The reward of those persecuted for His sake shall be great in heaven"] that we get to heaven and are saved by our work and labor, and on this then they found their chapter houses, cloisters, pilgrimages, masses, etc. . . . We must know the difference between grace and merit. Grace and merit do not accord with each other. If one preaches grace, he surely cannot preach merit;

and whatever is grace cannot be merit, else grace, as St. Paul says, Rom. 11:6, would not be grace. Whoever mixes these two confuses the people and leads both himself and his hearers astray. . . . Works have absolutely nothing to do with obtaining God's favor and grace, forgiveness of sins, and eternal salvation. Merit is here altogether excluded. Any attempt to introduce it should be trampled on and consigned to the abominable devil in hell as a thing that destroys my faith and denies Christ. . . . But how, then, do you explain the many passages which speak of reward and merit? Of that we say to the common people that the promises of a reward are mighty consolations to the Christians. For after you have become a Christian and now have a gracious God and the remission of all your sins, both your past sins and those which you daily commit, you will find that you must do and suffer much because of your faith and Baptism. For the abominable devil in company with the world and the flesh will be on your trail and plague you on all sides, as Christ has shown sufficiently throughout these three chapters; you will feel as though there is no room left for you in the world. If, now, He would let us remain without a word of consolation, we would despair because of this persecution and say: Who wants to be a Christian, preach, and do good works? Is this to last eternally? Is it never going to change? Here He steps up to us, consoles, and strengthens us, and says: You are now in grace and God's children; although you must on that account suffer in the world, be not terrified, but be firm, do not permit these things to tire and weaken you, but let every man perform his duty; he may fare badly, but that shall not be his loss; let him know that the kingdom of heaven is his and that he shall be richly repaid for it. What? Repaid? Has it not been given us already, through Christ, without and before all our work? God will repay in this manner that, as St. Paul says, He will make a great, bright star of you and give you particular gifts, already in this life. . . . Not that the works deserve it because of their worthiness, but because He has promised it for our strengthening and consolation, that we might not think that our labor, burden, and misery were in vain and forgotten. . . . To this *Magnam habetis remunerationem,* etc., such fine passages and admonitions as Heb. 10:35 refer: 'Cast not away therefore your confidence, which hath great recompense of reward'; and Christ's promise (Matt. 19:29): 'He shall receive an hundredfold now in time and in yonder world eternal life,' etc. Just so He says here too: *Merces vestra magna est in coelo,* 'Great is your reward in heaven.' Herewith He tells them that they already have heaven, and still they are to have the same more gloriously when it shall be revealed. . . . When Christ says: 'Blessed are the poor in spirit; for theirs is the kingdom of heaven,' and 'Blessed are ye if men persecute you for My sake, for great is your reward in heaven,' etc., He does not teach me to make this the foundation of my salvation, but He gives me a promise, namely, what is to be my comfort in my suffering and Christian life. Here you must not mingle and brew these things together; you must not turn into a merit of mine what God gives me in Christ through Baptism and the Gospel. For it is not stated here that I can merit this and need no Christ and Baptism for it, but rather that Christ's true disciples, to whom He preaches here and who must suffer all manner of things for His sake, should know what is their comfort. Since they are unwelcome on earth, they shall be the more richly rewarded in heaven; he that works and suffers the most will also get the greater reward. For though, as I have said, all are alike in Christ, and grace bestows on each one the whole salvation as the highest good, possessed by all, so that he who has Christ has everything, nevertheless there will be a difference in the brightness and glory with which we shall be adorned. Just as there is a difference in the gifts which we have now, one laboring more and suffering more than the other, so in the future life it will all be made manifest; all the world will see what everyone has accomplished, and he that has accomplished more will receive greater glory to the joy of the entire heavenly host. Let this now suffice. God keep us in His grace which He showed us in Christ! Amen." (St. L. VII:666 ff.)[90]

11

The Great Value of Good Works

After Luther had brought to light the great truth of the Christian doctrine that good works have no value in gaining justification and salvation (Rom. 3:28: "without the deeds of the Law"; Eph. 2:8-9), the pseudo-reformers, in their desire to outdo Luther, claimed that the good works of the Christians had no value whatever. Over against them Luther emphasized the great excellence of the good works. He declared: "Outside the article of justification we cannot sufficiently praise and magnify these works which are commanded by God. For who can sufficiently commend and set forth the profit and fruit of

---

[90] On the reward of good works see Quenstedt, II, 1419 *sqq.*; Chemnitz, *Examen*, "De bonis opp.," 4. *qu.*, *de praemiis et meritis b. o.*, p. 185 *sqq.*

only one work which a Christian does through faith and in faith? Indeed, it is more precious than heaven or earth." (St. L. IX:442 f.)

The Anabaptists declared that good works are worthless. Luther replied: "See what little value they attach to good works — they are ready to sell their good works for a penny! By this they want to ape us and our teaching that good works do not make a sinner pious, do not blot out sins, do not reconcile God. To this the devil adds his bit and so utterly despises good works that he is ready to sell them for a penny. I thank God that the devil in his cleverness here over-reaches himself and so shamefully befouls and befools himself. We teach that to reconcile God, to make righteous, to blot out sin, is so high and great and glorious a work that alone Christ, the Son of God, could do it and that this is indeed such a pure, special, peculiar work of the one true God and His grace that our works are nothing and can do nothing. But that therefore good works should be nothing or be worth only a penny, who ever heard of such a thing, or who could teach such a thing except the lying mouth of the devil? I would not give up one of my sermons, not one of my lectures, not one of my treatises, not one of my Lord's Prayers, nay, whatever small work I have ever done or am doing, for all the riches of the world; yea, I hold my good works dearer than my own life, which certainly should be held more precious than all the world; for if what I do is good, God has done it through me and in me. But if God has done it and it is God's work, what is the whole world over against God and His work? Though it does not make me holy — that must be done before, through Christ's blood and grace, without works — still it is done to the praise and glory of God and for the benefit and welfare of my neighbor, both of which cannot be paid for or equaled by all the world's goods. And this fine rabble would take only a penny for it! Has not Satan here hidden himself well? Who cannot feel him here?" (St. L. XIV:310 f.)

Luther's hymnic praise of good works is entirely Scriptural. 1. Good works have such a great value because they are done according to the norm of God's will. While all works that are not done according to God's will are worthless, all works which flow from obedience to the will of God, the supreme Lord, are great and precious. 2. Good works are God's work. He is the *causa efficiens* of them. While the new man of the Christian co-operates in performing them, this co-operation is so completely subordinate to God's operation that the Christian does the good only so far and so long as God works in and through him. Scripture expressly calls the good works of

Christians God's work, God's operation (Phil 2:13; 2 Cor. 3:5; 1 Cor. 12:6-11; Eph. 2:10). And who will dare to place a low valuation on the works of the great God? Luther indeed would have all works that are mingled with the article of justification trampled under foot as blasphemy (St. L. IX:245). But such works are not God's works but accursed (Gal. 1:8), works of the flesh and the devil. 3. Good works have great value for all Christians because they serve as *testimonia Spiritus Sancti externa* for their state of grace (Luke 7:47; 1 John 3:14). 4. Scripture furthermore declares that they are worth more than heaven and earth in that, while heaven and earth will pass away, the good works of Christians abide. All the earthly possessions of men, of Christians, too, will be consumed by the fire of Judgment Day, but the good works of Christians, also those performed by means of their perishable possessions, will not be consumed, but will follow them into eternity (Rev. 14:13) and will be crowned with an eternal reward of grace (Matt. 5:12; 19:29; 10:42; Gal. 6:9). Why, it is only for the sake of the good works of the Christians, among which the preaching of the Gospel ranks first, that the world is being preserved (Matt. 24:14; 1 Pet. 2:9). 5. Accordingly, the Christians are admonished to make the most of their short stay on earth by performing good works (Gal. 6:10; Eph. 5:16; Col. 4:5), and the pastors are directed to teach good works with all diligence (Titus 3:8, 14; 1 Tim. 6:17 ff.). For what purpose does God leave Christians in this world? As soon as a man comes to faith in Christ, he no longer belongs in this world; his true home is heaven (Phil. 3:20; John 5:24). But God wants him to stay in this world for a while in order to serve Him on earth, particularly in the cause of the Gospel. The ultimate purpose of our life on earth is the performance of good works.

12

The Papacy and Good Works

The Papacy makes the boast before the Church and the world [91] that it is the great protector of sanctification and good works,[92] and its chief charge against the Church of the Reformation is that

---

[91] The world, of course, accepts the claim, for, as the Apology says, "men judge by nature that God ought to be appeased by works. Nor does reason see a righteousness other than the righteousness of the Law, understood in a civil sense." (*Trigl.* 225, III, 273.)

[92] Cf. Cardinal Gibbons, *The Faith of Our Fathers,* ch. 3, p. 35 ff.

its doctrine of grace "possesses no power of moral renovation." [93]
As early as 1521 the Imperial Edict of Worms placed Luther under
the ban because "Luther teaches an unbound, self-willed life, exempt
from all laws, entirely bestial." [94] Luther commented: "It is a disgrace
that the Emperor and the lords thus publicly deal in lies" (St. L.
XV:2275). It is not Luther with his Biblical doctrine of grace, but
it is the Pope's sect with its doctrine of works that does away with
truly good works. By its ban on the Christian doctrine of justification
(*Trid.*, Sess. VI, can. 11-12), the Papacy bans *eo ipso* also good works,
since good works are in every case solely the product of justification
without works (Rom. 12:1; Gal. 2:20; Rom. 7:5-6; 6:4; 8:3-4). The
only reason why men who lead a Christian life are found within the
Catholic Church is that they believe in the Gospel of the remission
of sins without the deeds of the Law in spite of the prohibition of
the Pope. (*Trigl.* 225, Apol., III, 269–271.)

1. The "good works" performed according to the prescription of
the Papacy differ from Christian good works in their nature. The
works of Christians are in every case thankofferings for the remission
of sins already received through faith; but the Papists perform works
in order to gain grace by the *meritum de congruo* and *de condigno*,
as though God had not been in Christ and had not reconciled the
world unto Himself (2 Cor. 5:19; 1 John 2:2; 4:10). Therefore the
works which the Roman Church calls "good works" are a denial and
defamation of Christ's work of redemption; "for if righteousness come
by the Law, then Christ is dead in vain" (Gal. 2:21). And to prevent
the awful calamity that Christ's death should be in vain in the case
of any individual, the Apostle Paul pronounces the curse on all who
teach "good works" according to the formula of the Papacy (Gal. 1:6-9;
5:12) and tells all who follow these directions that they do not enjoy
the favor of God but are under the curse (Gal. 3:10). In short, as the
Papacy in its official declarations destroys the Gospel and the Christian
faith, so by these same official declarations it does away with good
works and the Christian life. When Cardinal Gibbons calls the Roman
Catholic Church with its teaching of work-righteousness "a society . . .
for the sanctification of its members" (*op. cit.*, p. 35), he demonstrates
that his ideas of sanctification and good works are pagan and not
Christian; he does not know that sanctification and good works spring
only from faith in the Gospel. Luther's judgment of the Roman "good

---

[93] See Moehler, *Symbolism*, p. 162 ff.; *The Faith of Our Fathers*, p. 49.
[94] Reprint of the Edict in St. L. XV:2274 ff., 2281.

works" is entirely Scriptural: "Works done without faith, although they
have ever so goodly a show of holiness, are sinful and under the curse.
Wherefore the doers of such works, far from meriting grace, righteousness, and eternal life, rather heap sin upon sin. After this manner
the Pope, the man of sin and the son of perdition, and all that follow
him, do their work. So also work all meritmongers and heretics, who
are fallen from faith." (St. L. IX:443.)

This, then, is the situation: By rejecting the Gospel the Papacy
and its loyal members have rendered themselves incapable of performing good works and are bound to do only evil works. Plug up the
spring, and you can no longer dip water from it. You cannot reject
the Gospel and still do good works. Works are "worthless if detached" — if detached from faith in the Gospel. Where faith in the
Gospel does not dwell in the heart, there the devil rules (Eph. 2:2),
and he incessantly impels to evil works. These are the works performed under the Papacy: Instead of lauding the Gospel, the Papists
curse it (Trid., Sess. VI, can. 11, 12, 20); instead of hearing and honor-
ing the teachers and confessors of the Gospel, as God's Word demands
(Luke 10:16; John 13:20; Phil. 2:29), they revile them as apostates and
heretics;[95] and wherever they are in the ascendancy, they persecute
the Gospel and its confessors with external force.[96]

2. The works enjoined by the Papacy do not belong in the
category of good works because they are performed according to
a false norm. Scripture tells us that only those works are good which
are commanded by God. The Papacy, however, obligates Christians

---

[95] In the Edict of Worms, Luther is declared to be "not a man," but "the
old evil Foe in the form of a man, wearing a monk's cowl" (St. L. XV:2282)
and in the Bull of Excommunication, issued by Leo X, 1520, Luther is called
"a vicious wild boar and a fierce beast," whose "memory is to be entirely
eradicated from the society of believers in Christ" (ibid., 1427, 1452).

[96] In the Papal Bull of Excommunication Leo X "commands" everybody,
from the emperor down to the least citizens, to apprehend, hold, and deliver
to the Pope the person of Martin Luther, and "for such a good work" he
promises "a fit reward and remuneration" (St. L. XV:1453 ff.). In the Imperial
Edict all are commanded to take Luther captive and deliver him to the emperor,
and they are promised a reward "for such a holy work." Luther comments:
"Behold, the murderers call it a holy work to slaughter people" (ibid., 2287).
And such good works the Pope is demanding of authorities and nations up to
this day. The Immortale Dei of Leo XIII, November 1, 1885, requires the
United States to suppress all other "cults." See Lehre und Wehre, 1886, p. 12 ff.
Cardinal Gibbons slanders Luther, classing him with the "pseudo reformers,"
whose "private lives were stained by cruelty, rapine, and licentiousness" (op. cit.,
p. 49). These are samples of the "sanctification of its members" which Rome
accomplishes.

to obedience not only to God's commandments, but also to the commandments of the Church, that is, to man-made precepts.[97] Therefore the "good works" which are peculiar to Rome fall under the verdict of Christ: "In vain they do worship Me, teaching for doctrines the commandments of men" (Matt. 15:9). It has been well said that the flood of man-made Papistical commandments [98] has turned the entire Christian life into a caricature. According to Scripture the life of Christians has this form: They sing and rejoice in the Lord over the grace obtained through faith in the Gospel (Eph. 5:19; Col. 3:16) and then joyfully serve God in the works which their station in life, in the Church, or in the State, or in society, calls for (Rom. 15:16; 1 Cor. 7:20 ff.; Col. 3:23-24; Eph. 6:7; 1 Tim. 2:15).[99] However, where Rome directs lives, these things happen: After Rome has gotten rid of the Gospel of the grace of God by its anathemas, its dupes seek to earn grace and salvation by their personal holiness and good works (*Trid.*, Sess. VI, can. 32). The great mass of its victims grasp the "second plank" (*secunda tabula*), the Sacrament of Penance invented by Rome (*contritio cordis, confessio oris, satisfactio operis* — can. 14)[100] and go on pilgrimages to Rome, Lourdes, etc., to find grace.[101] The elite are assembled in the cloister to earn salvation for themselves by observing the *consilia evangelica,* devised by man, and to obtain a surplus of good works (*opera supererogationis*) for the benefit of others. However, since this process does not give full assurance (*Trid.*, Sess. VI, c. 14, 9), they look to purgatory to complete their "sanctification" (*Trid.*, Sess. VI, can. 30).[102] In short, as Rome's doctrine of justification is diametrically opposed to the Christian doctrine, so also a life directed by Rome is the very opposite of the Christian life delineated in Scripture.

[97] *Trid.,* Sess. VI, can. 20: "If anyone saith that the man who is justified . . . is not bound to observe the commandments of God and of the Church . . . let him be anathema." Also Sess. VII, can. 8.

[98] The rejection of the Gospel inevitably results in man-made commandments. Apology: "Because no works pacify the conscience, new works, in addition to God's commands, were from time to time devised" (*Trigl.* 177, III, 87).

[99] Recall Luther's classic description of the Christian life according to the various estates in his sermon "Of Our Blessed Hope": "If the Christian is a servant, he is joyous and cheerful; when he drives into the forest or rides into the fields, he is singing" (St. L. IX:957).

[100] See Luther, St. L. XIX:54 f.; XI:720 f.

[101] Cf. Luther on the devilishly mendacious, shameful hoodwinking, which they [the Romanists] employ in connection with the relics and pilgrimages" (St. L. XVI:1661).

[102] See Luther on the "blasphemous fraud of purgatory, by which treacherous deception they have made fools of all the world" (St. L. XVI:1653 f.).

Rome's perversion of sanctification and good works reaches its climax in the Order of the Jesuits, which has laid down the rule that sins cease to be sins and become eminently good works when the superior commands these sins and the members of the order perform them in obedience to their superior. The *Institutum* [103] provides: "It has appeared good unto us in the Lord . . . , that no constitutions, declarations, or rules of life can obligate to commit mortal or venial sins except when the superior commands them in the name of our Lord Jesus Christ or on the strength of the obedience. That can happen in those cases where judgment decides what best serves the particular good of the individual or the universal good, and where in place of the fear of offense love and the desire for all perfection should step in and the greater glory and praise of Jesus Christ, our Creator and Lord, be obtained." The *Index generalis* sums it up thus: "The superiors can obligate unto sin by virtue of the obedience, if this confers great benefits." [104]

This rule, by the way, that the members of the Jesuit order must put their conscience into the keeping of the superior, represents no new development in the system of the Papacy. When the Pope denies to the rest of mankind the right to judge for themselves in matters of doctrine and demands the *sacrificium intellectus et voluntatis*,[105] he thereby requires every human being to surrender his own conscience and thus to renounce that faculty which distinguishes man from beast. It has been justly said of the Papacy that it "dehumanizes mankind." The right to be a man has been reclaimed for mankind by the Reformation. Luther demands that all questions of right and wrong be submitted to the conscience of the individual, that the individual Christian decide for himself the questions of doctrine and morals according to God's revealed Word,[106] and that in matters pertaining

---

[103] *Institutum societatis Jesu, auctoritate congregationis generalis 18. auctum et recusum, Pragae 1757.* Vol. I, 414 *sq.*

[104] *Op. cit.,* Vol. II, *Index generalis.* — Cp. the article "Jesuitismus," by Dr. Walther, in *Lutheraner,* 1853, p. 49 ff.

[105] This demand was not first made in the decree of infallibility (see Baier-Walther, I, 81), but the *Tridentinum* already made it, Sessio IV: "Holy mother church — whose it is to judge of the true sense and interpretation of the holy Scriptures." This demand is made wherever the individual Christian is denied the right to judge the doctrine. Cp. Luther, St. L. XIX:341 ff.

[106] Luther speaks of this most powerfully in his exposition of 1 Pet. 3:15: "Behold how Peter here tells us all that we are to give answer and show the basis of our faith. When you are in the throes of death, I shall not be with you, neither will the Pope be there. If you then do not know the foundation of your hope and say: I believe what the councils, the Pope, and our Fathers have

to the State and civil life the individual decides according to the light of reason, or the "natural Law, in which reason appears at its best" (St. L. X:416).[107]

In defense of the Roman demand for the renunciation of private judgment it has been argued that also God demands the *sacrificium intellectus et voluntatis* and that Christians comply with this demand: "We bring into captivity every thought to the obedience of Christ" (2 Cor. 10:5). We answer: God and His Word and the Pope and his word are radically different. By placing his word as authority beside the Word of God and *eo ipso* above God's Word, the Pope demonstrates that he is the Antichrist. Moreover, as Luther reminds us, God deals with us in a manner altogether different from that of the Pope. Certainly, God obligates man to subject his intellect and will to Him, but God brings about this subjection by enlightening the intellect of man and changing his will so that it becomes *ex nolente volens*. In other words, God illumines and corrects the natural conscience, the Pope suppresses it.

It has also been argued that suppression of the conscience is not a specialty of the Pope and of Jesuitism, but is practiced in the world

---

believed, the devil will answer you: Ah, but what if they erred? and thus he will have won and will drag you down into hell. Therefore we must know what we believe, namely, what God's Word says, not what the Pope or the councils have decreed or said. You dare by no means trust in men, but must trust in the bare Word of God. . . . Therefore you should say this: What do I care what this or that man believes or decrees? If it is not God's Word, I do not care to hear it. But, you say, there is such confusion in matters of faith that no one knows what he ought to believe, therefore one must wait until it has been decreed what should be believed. Answer: Then you will in the meantime go to hell. For when death approaches, and you do not know what is your faith, neither I nor anyone else can help you. Therefore you must know personally what to believe and, turning your back to all men, firmly cling to the Word of God if you would escape the devil and hell." (*Ibid.*, 1235 ff.)

107 In accordance with this everyone must carefully examine whether, e. g., a war is justified or not. Cf. Luther, St. L. X:413 ff., 524 ff. Here the conscience of the individual must decide; he cannot permit the State or the Church (pastor, synod) or any other man-made agency to make the decision for him. Therefore Luther stresses the need to investigate the situation, not in a superficial manner, but "with the greatest diligence." That is also the meaning of the 16th article of the Augustana, where among the functions of the government also the right "to engage in just wars" is mentioned. If the government calls its citizens to arms to prosecute an unjust war, the citizens must refuse their obedience, as the end of the article states. Luther states the same in the treatises mentioned above. Only where, after diligent inquiry, a personal decision becomes impossible and the matter remains uncertain, there, according to Luther's opinion, the Christian, when forced to serve in the war, should "not weaken the certain obedience" (to the government) "for the sake of an uncertain right." (*Ibid.*, 525.)

wherever the difference between right and wrong is ignored in the interest of business, of political partisanship, of the family, of the club, etc. This is true. But it simply proves that the Papacy is the *confluxus* of all heresies and abominations to be found in the Church and the world. Moreover, there is a great difference between the wickedness of the world and the wickedness of Rome. The world openly confesses that it is sinning against God when it ignores the distinction between good and evil. Rome, however, hides its wickedness under the name of Christ and of the Christian Church.

13

Modern Protestant Theology and Good Works

Thieme reports that the Lutheran doctrine that good works are not necessary for salvation has been given up by most modern Protestant theologians, including the so-called "positive" theologians; instead, they have generally adopted the "idea of the religion of morality, that the fruit of faith is necessary for salvation" (R. E., 3d ed., XXI, 120). Unfortunately that is true. Modern Protestant theology generally rejects the concept of Christ's *satisfactio vicaria* as being too "juridical"; "it would deepen the concept of expiation by making the transformation of human life into its God-pleasing form a factor in the work of the Atonement." [108] That, however, is fundamentally the Roman doctrine of the meritoriousness of good works and agrees altogether with the *Tridentinum* in its rejection of the doctrine that the Gospel is the absolute promise of the eternal life "without the condition of observing the commandments" (Sess. VI, can. 20).

It follows that the "good works," which modern Protestant theology teaches as necessary for salvation, do not, as little as do the Papistical works, belong in the category of good works. Rather, they dishonor the perfect propitiation of Christ and thereby draw down God's condemnation and curse upon all that teach and do them (Gal. 1:6-9; 5:12; Phil. 3:2; Gal. 3:10). Max Mueller has truly said that such works as are not the grateful offerings of faith, but are done for the purpose of earning salvation, belong in the realm of paganism. See Vol. II, 2, footnote 6. One cannot teach truly good works and at the same time teach that they are necessary for salvation. The latter

---

[108] Thus Kirn, *Dogmatik*, p. 118.

cancels the former. When the adherent of modern theology really performs a good work, he does so because in his heart he has abandoned his theory of the necessity of good works for salvation (the theory that "the transformation of man is a factor in the work of atonement"), and does the good work solely as a thankoffering for the grace and salvation obtained *sola fide*.

14

The Christian Life and the Cross

In their presentation of the Christian life Lutheran teachers, such as Quenstedt and Calov,[109] embody a chapter on the cross (*"De cruce"*). That is in harmony not only with the practical tendency of their dogmatical writings but also and, above all, with Scripture, which has much to say on the cross of Christians. We learn from Scripture, on the one hand, that Christians by their faith in Christ enjoy the full favor of God — God is not against them but for them (Rom. 8:31), they are God's children and heirs of eternal life (John 1:12-13; Gal. 3:26; Rom. 8:17), the angels serve them (Heb. 1:14), etc. —; on the other hand, that God has ordained that the high dignity of Christians should not become manifest in this life, but rather that the same lowliness which characterized the earthly life of Christ should characterize their earthly life (1 Pet. 4:1).[110] And this lowly form of the life of Christians, by which they are conformed to the image of Christ, is called the cross of Christians.[111] What Scripture says of the cross of Christians we shall present under six heads.

---

109 Quenstedt, II, 1431 *sqq.*; Calov, X, 703 *sqq.*

110 "Forasmuch then as Christ hath suffered for us in the flesh [σαρκί, in the earthly life], arm yourselves likewise with the same mind." See Luther on this passage, St. L. IX:1248.

111 Luther describes the contrast between the high dignity of Christians and the lowly form of their life on earth in these words: "We are even now the children of God, and through faith and Baptism have been put into possession of eternal salvation, as is written Mark 16:16 and John 1:12. . . . But who among men recognizes us as children of God? Who will call those men children of God that are thrown into prison and are so tortured and tormented in every conceivable way that they appear to be the children of the devil, condemned and accursed souls? For that reason St. Paul says that the glory of the children of God is now hidden, but shall be manifested in them later (Col. 3:3-4). So long as God's children are here upon earth, they are not clothed with the livery of God, but wear the devil's livery. For the devil's children should be bound in fetters and

1. What constitutes "cross"? The wicked, too, have many sorrows (Ps. 32:10; 16:4; Pharaoh, Exodus 7—11), but only the sufferings of Christians are called a cross.[112] What Christians suffer as Christians, in living their Christian faith in this world, that properly constitutes the cross.[113] If they follow Christ, particularly if they confess the Gospel of Christ Crucified, who is a stumbling block to the Jews and an offense to the Greeks, they will receive the same treatment from the world as Christ received. "If they have called the Master of the house Beelzebub, how much more shall they call them of His household?" (Matt. 10:25.)

It is true, Christians are still sinners after the flesh and in so far they deserve not only their temporal suffering, but also eternal damnation. But since they repent of their sins and by faith in Christ daily appropriate the forgiveness of sins, their suffering is no longer a punishment of sin in the proper sense, because the true punishment of sin is not this or that temporal misfortune, but eternal damnation. Nor do the sins of Christians elicit the hatred of the devil. Luther: "The evil foe and the world hate Christians not because they are sinners and stumble and fall occasionally. No, both the devil and the world could well tolerate that and would be well satisfied with them. But the fact that Christians hold to the Word in faith, that they put their hope in the Son of God, comfort themselves with His death and resurrection, fear God and desire to live according to His will, earnestly desire that through their confession others may come to the knowledge of God and faith, this the devil and the world cannot endure. For this reason they constantly torment the Christians; Satan

---

should suffer all manner of misfortune. But that does not happen to the devil's offspring; they have all the world's pleasures, are wealthy and powerful, enjoy honor and money to the full; withal they put on God's garb and name, as though they were God's favorites. Us they regard as heretics, under God's wrath. The right order is reversed: those who are God's children are called children of the devil, and those who are the children of the devil are called God's children. That hurts the pious; heaven and earth and all creatures cry out in complaining protest, are unwilling to be thus subjected to vanity and to suffer that the wicked abuse them to the dishonor of God" (St. L. XII:729 f.).

[112] See Luther, St. L. XIII:433 f.

[113] Luther: "A Christian, just because he is a Christian, is subjected to the dear cross, so that he must suffer at the hands of men and of the devil, who plagues and terrifies him with tribulation, persecution, poverty, and illness and inwardly, in his heart, with his poisonous darts. The cross is the Christians' sign and watchword in their holy, precious, noble, and blessed calling, which is taking them to heaven. To such a calling we must render full due and accept as good whatever it brings." (St. L. XII:544 f.)

afflicts their bodies with diseases, as St. Paul complains: The messenger of Satan buffets him and impales him, filling his heart and
conscience with sadness, melancholy, terror, and the like; or he
destroys their property by storms, hail, fire, as was the case with
Job. . . . Therefore mind well, you dare not deny that you are a poor
sinner, deserving all punishment; yea, God subjects His children to
punishment for their sins, as Peter says: 'Judgment must begin at the
house of God.' But you should say: Satan and the world do not
hate me on account of my sins. . . . Why, then, do they hate me?
It is on account of this Man [Christ], the Sin-bearer, whom I accept
and confess as my God and Savior." (St. L. XIII:434 ff.) — The confession of Christ entails persecution. To escape this cross, the
antagonists of Paul preached the doctrine of works, which the world
wants to hear (Gal. 6:12), and for the same end many in our day
embrace synergism, which again is the doctrine of salvation by works,
so pleasing to the world.

Furthermore, since the flesh of Christians lusts against God's
Word, will, and order and refuses to submit to suffering, bearing the
cross means self-denial (Matt. 16:24);[114] it means that we must
renounce everything that interferes with our following Christ (Luke
14:33);[115] we must renounce our own wisdom in spiritual matters
(Matt. 11:25-26), our peace and tranquillity (Matt. 10:34; Luke
12:51), honor among men (Matt. 5:11; Luke 6:22; 1 Pet. 4:14), the
friendship of father and mother, son and daughter (Matt. 10:35-37;
Luke 12:52-53), our temporal possessions (1 Cor. 7:30; Matt. 19:
21-22), yea, our own life (Luke 14:26). Bearing the cross means,
finally, that we must crucify all the passions and lusts of the flesh
(Gal. 5:24) and mortify our "members which are upon the earth:
fornication, uncleanness, inordinate affection, evil concupiscence, and
covetousness, which is idolatry" (Col. 3:5); "knowing this, that our
old man is crucified with Him, that the body of sin might be destroyed,
that henceforth we should not serve sin" (Rom. 6:6).

2. *The inseparable connection* (NEXUS *indivulsus*) *between Christianity and the cross.* Bearing the cross is inseparably bound up with
Christianity, so inseparably that he who refuses to bear the cross
can no longer claim to be a Christian; he has renounced the right

---

114 "If any man will come after Me, let him deny himself [ἀπαρνησάσθω
ἑαυτόν] and take up his cross and follow Me."
115 "Whosoever he be of you that forsaketh not all that he hath, he cannot
be My disciple."

to share the glory of Christ.[116] Luther: "Whoever is no *crucianus*, if I may so express it, is also no *christianus*. That is to say, he who does not bear the cross is no Christian; he is not like his Master Christ." (St. L. II:467.)

This does not mean, however, that the Christian may impose a cross upon himself or upon others. He must leave that to God (1 Pet. 3:17; 1:6),[117] for God alone knows which cross is beneficial and only God gives the strength needed to bear the cross (1 Cor. 10:13). Luther calls those who purposely seek a cross "work saints" and "the devil's martyrs." [118]

3. The right view of the cross. The flesh of Christians considers cross-bearing a heavy burden. By their flesh they are led to think that when the world mistreats them they are not receiving what they ought as children of God and members of Christ's body. They may even think at times that God has forgotten them and become cruel to them (Lam. 5:20; Ps. 13:1; Job 30:21). And unless these thoughts are checked, these tempted Christians will lose their faith; "which for a while believe and in time of temptation fall away" (Luke 8:13).

Scripture therefore instructs us, first of all, that the cross, even though by it our sins are judged, does not manifest God's wrath against us, but rather reveals God's love toward us. It marks us as God's children. Scripture assures us that "whom the Lord loveth He chasteneth and scourgeth every son whom He receiveth" (Heb.

[116] Christ impressed this truth on the "great multitudes" which accompanied Him (Luke 14:25-35). It is also set forth in Matt. 10:38-39; Mark 8:34-35; Luke 9:23-24, 57-62; Rom. 8:17, etc.

[117] 1 Pet. 3:17: "If the will of God should so will" (R. V.); 1 Pet. 1:6: "If need be" — when God finds it necessary.

[118] Luther: "Note that the Apostle adds: 'If need be.' Just as he does also in 3:17, saying, 'It is better, if the will of God be so, that ye suffer for well-doing.' For there are many who without necessity impose a cross upon themselves; that is the way of the work saints, who, as St. Paul says, walk in a voluntary humility (Col. 2:18). The Papacy produced many such people. But that is not as it should be, for it is not God's will that you should choose for yourself, from your own devotion, a certain suffering or cross; if you nevertheless do it, you are the devil's martyr, and not Christ's. . . . If, however, it is necessary, that is, if God sends it, then you must endure it for the sake of confessing your faith; accept it, and be comforted by this statement of St. Peter, that the tribulation shall last but a little while; the salvation, however, in which you rejoice, shall last throughout all eternity." (St. L. IX:1130.) — Nor dare we lay a cross on another with the intention of keeping him humble and thus lead him safely to heaven. That is nothing less than meddling with God's business; it is for God to say what cross each one is to bear. And we would be jeopardizing the brother's salvation, since we mortals do not at all know what cross is profitable to him and how much he can bear.

12:6-10), and that "when we are judged, we are chastened of the
Lord, that we should not be condemned with the world" (1 Cor.
11:32). Scripture further instructs us that when we suffer because
of our confession of Christ by word and deed, the cross is for us
a testimony of the Holy Spirit *(testimonium Spiritus Sancti externum)*
that we are not of the world, but belong to Christ, for we then
experience the same treatment which Christ and all witnesses of
Christ experienced. "If ye be reproached for the name of Christ,
happy are ye; for the Spirit of glory and of God resteth upon you"
(1 Pet. 4:14). "For so persecuted they the prophets which were
before you" (Matt. 5:12). Scripture explicitly informs us that the
sufferings of this time, by which we become like Christ, are for us
a pledge of the eternal glory awaiting us. "Heirs of God, and joint
heirs with Christ, if so be that we suffer with Him, that we may be
also glorified together" (Rom. 8:17; 2 Thess. 1:5-7; 2 Cor. 4:7-8). It is
entirely Scriptural to call the cross the "livery" of Christians. They
wear the colors of the King.[119] They should therefore rejoice when,
instead of being praised and honored by the world, they reap abuse
and blows (Matt. 5:12; Luke 6:23). The Apostles took this view of
the cross when they were flogged by the council: "They departed from
the presence of the Council, rejoicing that they were counted worthy
to suffer shame for His name" (Acts 5:41). When Paul and Silas at
Philippi lay in the inner prison, their feet fast in the stocks, they
"prayed and sang praises unto God" (Acts 16:25). And when a Christian is harassed by the thought that God might have miscalculated
the weight of the cross and laid more on him than he can bear,
Scripture assures him that the same gracious God who imposes the
temptation will provide for its happy termination; He "will with the

---

[119] Luther calls the cross "the marks of Christ," which are "not painted on
the wall," but "are branded in the flesh and blood of the Christians." "If you
refuse to suffer with the Lord Jesus Christ and do not desire to become like Him,
He will on the Last Day certainly not acknowledge you as a brother and fellow
heir, but will ask you where your crown of thorns, your cross, nails, and scourge
are. After this manner Paul said to the Galatians, ch. 6:17: From henceforth let
no man trouble me and say anything about teaching that which gains friendship
here on earth, for I bear in my body the marks of my Lord Jesus Christ. He is
here speaking of such marks as are found in ancient paintings of Christ, where
the Savior is represented as bearing His cross upon His shoulders, with the nails,
the crown of thorns, and the scourge. These marks, Paul says, I and all
Christians must exhibit, not painted on the wall, but branded in our flesh and
blood. They are made when the devil inwardly plagues you with terrors and
griefs and the world outwardly slanders you as a heretic and, whenever possible,
takes you by the throat and puts you to death. St. Paul here tells every Christian
that he must show these scars of the Lord Jesus Christ." (St. L. XII:718 f.)

temptation also make a way to escape, that ye may be able to bear it" (1 Cor. 10:13). See Meyer on this passage.

4. *The purpose and profit of the cross.* The cross belongs to the ways and means by which God leads Christians through this world into eternal life. "We must through much tribulation enter into the Kingdom of God" (Acts 14:22); "Our light affliction, which is but for a moment, worketh for us a far more exceeding and eternal weight of glory" (2 Cor. 4:17). The cross renders us humble before God; "Lest I should be exalted above measure through the abundance of the revelations, there was given to me a thorn in the flesh, the messenger of Satan to buffet me, lest I should be exalted above measure" (2 Cor. 12:7). It warns us to place our sole reliance in the grace of God (2 Cor. 12:8-9). It thus exercises and strengthens our faith (1 Pet. 1:6-7),[120] moves us to prayer (Ps. 18:6; Is. 26:16), destroys the body of sin (Rom. 6:6; 1 Pet. 4:1), and in general turns our gaze from the things that are seen and must perish to the things which are not seen and are eternal (2 Cor. 4:16-18).

Christians should bear their cross patiently also for the purpose of setting a good example in patience to the brethren and of encouraging them.[121]

Luther has this to say on the profit of the cross, particularly as it serves to increase faith: "Here [1 Pet. 1:7] the Apostle shows clearly the fruit and benefit of such trials as are inflicted on believers both by tyrants and by sects. These trials, he says, tend to prove your faith and cause it to be found more precious than perishable gold that is proved by fire. For just as the fire does not hurt the gold, does not consume it nor diminish it, but is of benefit to it, for it purges it of all dross, so that it becomes pure and sterling, so, too, the fire and heat of persecution and all sorts of temptations indeed inflict pain and hurt the old man exceedingly, so that those who are tried in them become sad and at times impatient, but their faith is thereby purified and becomes refined like sterling gold or silver. For there is this about the Christian life that it must continue to improve to become holier and purer. First we come to faith through the preaching of the

---

[120] See Luther, St. L. IX:1129 ff.

[121] Paul is the example for the cross-bearers (2 Cor. 1:6); the Thessalonians are examples for all believers. 1 Thess. 1:6-7: "Ye became followers [μιμηταί, imitators] of us and of the Lord, having received the Word in much affliction, with joy of the Holy Ghost, so that ye were examples [τύποι] to all that believe in Macedonia and Achaia." See Walther, *Pastorale*, p. 386, on the duty of the pastor to be an example to his flock as a patient cross-bearer.

Gospel, and by this faith we become righteous and holy before God. But since we still live in the flesh, which is not free from sin, since sin continually is astir in us, holds us back, and prevents us from becoming so perfectly holy and pure as we ought, therefore God casts us right into the fire of affliction, suffering, and distress, which tries and refines us to the end, so that not only the sin in us is killed more and more, but also our faith is proved and becomes stronger, and we from day to day become surer in our conviction, grow in understanding of the divine wisdom and knowledge, and so Scripture becomes all the plainer and clearer to us, enabling us the more powerfully to exhort our people by sound doctrine and to convict the gainsayer. If the devil had not all these years so vehemently attacked us with both force and cunning, we would never have reached this certitude of doctrine, nor would the article of Christian justification and the doctrine of faith have been brought to light with such clarity. On this account St. Paul declares, 1 Cor. 11:19: 'There must be also heresies among you that they which are approved may be made manifest among you.'" (St. L. IX:1131.)

5. *The strength to bear the cross.* Scripture teaches that the strength to bear the cross is derived from the assurance of the forgiveness of sins and salvation. Only he can glory in tribulation, only he will not perish in it, in whose heart the love of God is shed abroad by the Holy Ghost, in whose heart the certitude dwells that "while we were yet sinners Christ died for us" (Rom. 5:5, 8). Only he will disregard the sufferings of this present time who is assured of the glory awaiting him (Rom. 8:18). Only he will mortify his members which are upon the earth who knows by faith that his life is hid with Christ in God (Col. 3:3-5). Amid the hatred and persecution of the world only he will refrain from sorrowing and complaining and, instead, rejoice and praise the Lord who is certain that his reward is great in heaven (Matt. 5:12; Luke 6:22). Whoever, therefore, destroys the assurance of grace and salvation by making grace and salvation depend on human works or moral efforts in any form deprives himself of the strength needed to bear the cross.

In the words of Luther: "Because he is not certain of eternal life and is not awaiting the blessed hope, he cannot be content nor have patience. As soon as the wind changes and things do not go as he would like, he grows impatient and murmurs against God." (St. L. IX:956.) How, on the contrary, the assurance of eternal glory makes one able to bear the cross, Luther presents in these words: "Behold how he [St. Paul] turns his back on the world and looks forward to the coming revelation, as though he saw nowhere on earth misfortune or misery but only unalloyed joy. Verily, though we fare badly, he says, what is our suffering compared with the unspeakable joy and glory which shall be revealed in us? . . . If one could grasp this fully in his heart, he would have to say: Though he were burned or drowned ten times, if that were possible, it were nothing whatever when viewed in the light of the future glorious life; for what does temporal suffering, no matter how long it lasts, amount to in comparison with the eternal life? . . . Thus St. Paul reduces all suffering on earth to a little drop and tiny spark, but of yonder life, for which we are to hope, he makes a boundless sea and a great fire. . . . In calling it a glory to be revealed he indicates why it is that we suffer so unwillingly, namely, that our faith is still weak and hesitates to look into the glory which is hidden and waiting to be revealed in us. For if it were a glory that we could see with our eyes, then indeed we would be fine, patient martyrs! If a man should stand on yonder shore of the Elbe with a chest filled with florins and said: Whoever will dare to swim across shall have the chest filled with florins, how quickly everybody would start to swim across to get the florins that the eye can see! . . . Therefore St. Paul says: I know for certain that a great glory is placed before us, in comparison with which all suffering on earth is as nothing, but this is lacking that it is not yet revealed. If the faith were there, it would be a small matter to us even if such suffering lasted thirty, forty, and more years; yes, we would consider it too small a matter to take account of it if only our Lord God will not take account of our sins. Oh, why will people talk so much of their great suffering or of the merit of their suffering! How little we deserve such great grace and unspeakable glory that through Christ we are made children and heirs of God, brothers and co-heirs with Christ! Therefore we have all reason to say, I will gladly keep silence about my suffering, not boast or brag of it, but patiently bear all that my dear God sends and lays on me, and even thank Him from all my heart that He has chosen me for such a great, surpassing goodness and grace. But, as I have said, it will not sink in because of our miserable, impotent flesh, which is more affected by things present than by things to come. Therefore the Holy Ghost must be our Teacher in this matter and put such comfort into our hearts." (On Rom. 8:18. St. L. XII: 717 ff.)[122]

6. *The cross and the sin of Christians.* The question has been

---

[122] Pastors need to fix their eyes on eternal life so that they do not tire under the cross. See Walther, *Pastorale*, p. 61 f.

debated whether the sin which still cleaves to a Christian forms a part of the cross of Christians. It must be answered in the affirmative. Christians as Christians renounce the sin in their members; they are filled with hatred of it (Rom. 7:15); they deplore the fact that they are "sold under sin" (Rom. 7:14), "into captivity to the law of sin" (Rom. 7:23), as a galling captivity, as a calamity which is inflicted upon them and from which they want to be delivered. Groaning under this captivity, they cry out with the Apostle: "O wretched man that I am! Who shall deliver me from the body of this death?" (Rom. 7:24.) Luther: "Paul, the dear saint, connects the cross with all creation, saying that heaven, earth, and all they contain suffer with us. . . . All creatures are now subjected with us to the tyrants who violate our honor, bodies, and goods according to their malice, just as the devil violates our soul. Such things we must suffer as long as we are captive in the devil's kingdom. . . . With great sighing and longing we pray the Lord's Prayer: 'Thy kingdom come,' that is: Help, dear Lord, that the blessed day of Thy glorious return may soon come, so that we may be delivered out of this wicked world, the devil's kingdom, and be freed from that horrible plague, which we must endure without and within, both from wicked people and our own conscience.[123] Keep on strangling the old sack, that we may soon get a different body which is not full of sin and no longer inclined to all evil and disobedience, as at present, which no more is subject to sickness, persecution, and death but, delivered from all misery in body and soul, will be like unto Thy glorified body, dear Lord Jesus Christ, and we thus may finally come to our glorious deliverance! Amen." (St. L. XII:727, 728, 735.)

15

The Christian Life and Prayer

1. The inseparable connection (nexus indivulsus) between Christian life and prayer. As soon as a Christian has been justified by faith and thus has become God's child, he begins to commune with God.

---

[123] The sins which Christians do against their will are still recorded in their conscience as guilt which merits eternal damnation; and holding them up as such to the Christians, the devil would drive them to despair of God's grace. On account of his sins a Christian is perturbed in his conscience and therefore continually prays the Fifth Petition not merely as a matter of form, but with the inner desire for forgiveness. Cp. Luther, St. L. XV:1551 ff.

This personal conversing of the Christian with God is called prayer. It is altogether Scriptural to define prayer as "the conversation of the heart with God" (Ps. 27:8), whether the heart alone communes with God without clothing the prayer in words of the mouth [124] or whether the mouth utters the prayer of the heart.[125] Prayer, the *consequens* of faith in the remission of sins, is a *continuum*, the continuous longing of the heart for God; the Holy Ghost, who by faith has made His home in the heart and is the *causa efficiens* of prayer, never ceases His activity but unceasingly vivifies and moves the heart.[126]. A Christian prays even when, as often happens while fulfilling his earthly calling, he is not conscious of praying, yes, even when by reason of great sorrow and grief he imagines that he cannot pray. (Luther, St. L. XI:922.)

Prayer has been fittingly compared to the heartbeat of physical life: it never ceases. Luther says: "Where there is a Christian, there is the Holy Ghost, who is always engaged in prayer. For though the Christian does not continually move his lips to utter words, nevertheless the heart is beating and pulsating, like the arteries and the heart in the body, unceasingly sighing: O dear Father, may Thy name be hallowed, Thy kingdom come, Thy will be done among us and all people, etc. And as the attacks, trials, and troubles press and crowd harder, also such sighing and begging becomes more urgent, even audible. So, then, you cannot find a Christian who is not always praying, as little as a living person is without a pulse, which never rests, but beats continuously, though the person may be sleeping or is occupied otherwise, so that he is not aware of its beating." (St. L. VIII:363.) — Dividing prayer into thanksgiving and supplication fully covers the ground.[127]

2. *The requisite for prayer.* Christian prayer does not flow from

---

[124] Rom. 8:26-27: "The Spirit itself maketh intercession for us with groanings which cannot be uttered"; Is. 65:24.

[125] Acts 7:59; 16:25. Luther, St. L. XI:923.

[126] Rom. 8:14-15: Christians "are led by the Spirit of God." Luther: "He is a restless Spirit in the midst of the highest rest, in God's grace and peace, so that He cannot be silent or idle, but is always wrestling and striving with all His energies, as one living for only one purpose, to wit, to spread God's honor and praise among the people" (St. L. VIII:361).

[127] Luther: "With God we cannot deal in more than two ways, namely, thanksgiving and petition. In our thanksgiving we praise Him for the gifts and graces already received; in our petitions we praise Him for the gifts and graces we desire." (St. L. X:2204.) The intercessions for all men and for the government (1 Tim. 2:1-3; Jer. 29:7), for believers (Eph. 6:18) and unbelievers and for enemies (Matt. 5:44; Luke 23:34; Acts 7:59) fall under the head of "supplication."

Schleiermacher's "absolute feeling of dependence upon God" nor from Ritschl's "faith in the divine providence." [128] What is back of this wonderful situation, that a man who is dust and ashes (Gen. 18:27) and — more than that — a sinner, dares to speak with the majestic and holy God as a child talks with his father (Matt. 6:9)? The Holy Ghost has engendered in him the faith that God is gracious to him because of Christ's vicarious satisfaction and both bids him to pray and promises to hear his prayer. In other words, prayer presupposes justifying faith.[129] Only faith in the forgiveness of sins for Christ's sake makes prayer a prayer "in the name of Christ," and only prayer in the name of Christ has God's command and promise (John 16:23; 14:13-14). And it is only because of Christ's work that we have the boldness to approach God in prayer. Luther: "Without communion with Christ no one can pray even one word which would count before God or be pleasing to Him. The prayers of the Turks, Jews, monks, and hypocrites are of that kind." (On John 14:13-14. St. L. VIII:362. See also XI:922 f.)

Men have argued that also such as are ignorant . of Christ's vicarious satisfaction (the heathen) or even reject and attack it (the Unitarians) pray with great fervor or even "by contemplation become absorbed in God." However, all devotion and all prayer which does not flow from faith in the reconciliation effected by Christ is the result of natural emotions. The *causa efficiens* of such praying is not the Holy Ghost, whose work it is to glorify Christ as the only Reconciler (John 16:14), but the devil, who works in all unbelievers (Eph. 2:2). Scripture expressly declares that the things which the Gentiles sacrifice — and that includes their prayers — "they sacrifice to devils and not to God" (1 Cor. 10:20).[130] Ritschl indeed states the correct principle: "Prayer to God as our Father through Jesus Christ distinguishes the Christian religion from all others," but since he denies the *satisfactio vicaria*, the very thing which distinguishes the Christian

---

[128] Ritschl, *Unterricht in der christlichen Religion*, § 54.

[129] Apology: "Prayer relies upon God's mercy, when we believe that we are heard for the sake of Christ, the High Priest, as He Himself says John 14:13: 'Whatsoever ye shall ask in My name, that will I do.' 'In My name,' He says, because without this High Priest we cannot approach the Father." (*Trigl.* 211, III, 212.)

[130] The last words of Socrates made it plain to whom he offered his sacrifices and prayers: "We still owe Aesculapius a cock; be sure to sacrifice it, and do not forget it." Particularly his pride in his virtuous life showed that it was the devil who "was active" in him. Cf. the remarks of Socrates' great admirer, Funke, in *Real-Schullexikon*, V, 374.

religion from all others, his religion lacks the prerequisite for "prayer to God as our Father through Jesus Christ." — The objection that one can conceive of God as being gracious without Christ's vicarious satisfaction carries no weight. The feeling of guilt in man's heart and conscience will not permit man to have such a conception. It is only by inscribing in the heart of man the divine verdict of justification, and thus canceling the divine verdict of condemnation, that the Holy Ghost creates faith in the heart.[131]

Speaking of this prerequisite of prayer, Luther says: "The Spirit of grace brings it to pass that we can and may, yea, must, begin to pray. Hence Christ here means to say: If you believe in Me and have received the Spirit, your hearts having thus become sure of God's grace, as He had said above, 'He that hath seen Me hath seen the Father,' then your prayer will follow as a matter of course. For this is the true and proper work of Christians, and of the Christian only.[132] For before we become Christians and believe, we do not know what and how we should pray. And though a man prays most fervently [as far as the external act is concerned, as in the case of the heathen, the Romanists, the Unitarians, etc.], still the Spirit of grace is not there. The natural heart can only speak thus: Dear Lord, do Thou regard how virtuously I live, how much I suffer; or take into consideration the merit of this and that saint, the intercession and good works of pious people. Here there is no faith in divine grace and mercy for Christ's sake; here the heart always remains uncertain and cannot know that it is certainly heard; it wants to deal with God only on the basis of man's own holiness or that of others, without Christ, as though God ought to humble Himself before such a man and be forced to bestow His grace or help and thus become our Debtor and Servant. Such an attitude does not merit grace, but wrath; it is not prayer, but a mocking of God." (St. L. VIII:361 f.)

The uncertainty about the efficacy of every prayer which does not flow from faith in Christ is evidenced by the battologizing of the heathen and the Romanists: "They think that they shall be heard for their much speaking" (Matt. 6:7).[133]

---

[131] But on their deathbeds Ritschl and Horace Bushnell based their prayer on the *satisfactio vicaria*. See Vol. II, 370.

[132] Augustine: *Si fides in Christum deficit, oratio perit* (quoted in Quenstedt, II, 1438).

[133] *Trigl.* 705, Large Cat., 25. The rosary of the Romanists: the prayer wheels of the Tibetan Buddhists.

The prayers of all saints have ever been based on Christ's right-eousness, on God's grace and mercy in Christ, never on their own worthiness (Dan. 9:18). And so today and to the end of time every Christian, entirely disregarding both his own worthiness and his unworthiness, derives his confidence and boldness to pray solely from the reconciliation effected by Christ and from God's command and God's promise to hear.[134]

3. *The power and effect of the Christian prayer.* Since God preserves this world only for the sake of the Christians, in order that they may execute their Christian calling in the world (Matt. 24:14), and since the will of Christians as expressed in their prayers coincides with the all-sustaining and governing will of God (1 John 5:14),[135] it follows that the Christians' prayer sustains and governs *instrumen-taliter* the whole world. The prayer of Christians has its effect on all occurrences in the Church and the world. Scripture here goes into detail. It is owing to their prayer that the Word of God spreads over the earth in spite of the bitter opposition of the world (2 Thess. 3:1), that, e. g., the Apostle Paul finds an open door and preaches the Word boldly (Col. 4:2-4; Eph. 6:19-20) and is delivered from danger (Rom. 15:30-32). It is owing to their prayer that the State is preserved and prospers (Jer. 29:7), that peace is preserved and restored (1 Tim. 2:1-3; Ps. 76:6), that bloody and deceitful men are destroyed (Ps. 5:6, 10; 55:23). Let us always bear in mind that according to the teaching of Scripture the Christians are doing exactly what Christ does, that whatever Christ does as *causa efficiens* He does through the Christians as *causa instrumentalis.*

Hear Luther's exposition of John 14:12: "Verily, verily, I say unto you, he that believeth on Me, the works that I do shall he do also; and greater works than these shall he do." Luther says: "Do not separate the head from its members, that is, Christ and His Apostles and all Christendom. Every single Christian is such a one as the Lord Christ Himself was on earth and accomplishes such great things

---

134 Quenstedt correctly remarks: "Let those that pray be on their guard that they do not doubt God's power, as though He cannot help even though He wishes; or His benign affection, as though He does not want to help even though He can; but they should firmly believe that God can and will help" (II, 1438). But without the "special faith by which an individual believes that for Christ's sake his sins are remitted him and that for Christ's sake God is reconciled and propitious" (*Trigl.* 133, Apol., IV, 45), no man will believe that the *potentia Dei* is exerted in his behalf nor that the *benevolus Dei affectus* goes out to him.

135 All that the Christians ask is asked "according to His will."

that he can rule the whole world in divine matters, help and benefit everyone, and perform the greatest works that ever were effected on earth. For God thinks more of him than of the whole world; for his sake God gives and preserves to the world all that it has; if there were no Christians on earth, no city or nation would have any peace, yea, in one single day everything on earth would be destroyed by the devil. But that grain is still growing in the fields, that people enjoy health, have their living, peace, and protection, all this they owe to the Christians. We are indeed poor beggars, says St. Paul, 2 Cor. 6:10, but we make many rich; we have nothing and yet possess all things. And this also is true: all that kings, princes, lords, burghers, and farmers possess they have not because of their blond hair, but they owe it to Christ and His Christians. . . . Lords, burghers, and farmers have their land and its inhabitants, their power, honor, and goods because of the Christians living among them, though they do not see it and reward it with evil. . . . Therefore the Christians are truly helpers and saviors, yea, lords and gods, of the world, as God said to Moses (Ex. 7:1): 'I have made thee a god to Pharaoh.' On this account also the 8th Psalm says: 'Thou hast put all things under his feet,' namely, emperors, kings, princes, power, honor, and goods, even the cattle in the fields, oxen, sheep, wild animals, the birds in the air, and the fishes in the waters. Do not overlook these things: God is telling us that whatever the world has and can do it has as a loan from these beggars who have nothing and yet possess all things; all that God gives the world He gives because of these beggars; all these things are declared to be works and miracles of the Christians which they perform until Judgment Day, and when they stop working God will also make an end of the world and burn it all with fire. . . . The world gapes only on what appears high and great, is rich and powerful, and parades in splendor and show; and yet it does not recognize from whom men get these things. But if you are baptized, says Christ, and believe in Me, you are the man who has and can do more and greater things, yea, who does the very works and greater ones than I do" (that is, in the state of exinanition). "For I shall make of you believers lords whose works shall count for more and accomplish more than those of any king or lord on earth; you shall bring about and achieve whatever you desire and shall help Me rule spiritually over souls for their salvation, and also as to material things you shall obtain through your prayer all that there is on earth; men must receive all at your hands and unwittingly live on you." (St. L. VIII:350—356.)

4. Things for which a Christian prays. The Christian is bidden to ask of God everything that is covered by the divine will and the divine promise. And we should note here, first of all, that Christ assures the Christians that they shall obtain everything they ask for. "All things whatsoever [πάντα ὅσα] ye shall ask in prayer, believing, ye shall receive" (Matt. 21:22). See also Mark 11:24; John 14:13-14; 16:23; Matt. 7:7-8. We would not be justified to limit the πάντα ὅσα, which Scripture emphasizes so strongly.

However, we must not forget that the will of Christians, as far as they are Christians, coincides entirely with God's will and that accordingly they ask God to give them not what their whim dictates, but what accords with His command and promise. The Christian disavows in advance all outcroppings of his carnal self-will. The supreme rule regulating his praying is: "Not as I will, but as Thou wilt." Just as the constitutions of some of our congregations contain the provision that any resolution of the congregation is null and void from the outset if it conflicts with God's Word, so every Christian prays with the understanding that wherever his petitions go beyond God's command and promise, they are *a priori* null and void. He prays in submission to God's will. "This is the confidence that we have in Him that, if we ask anything according to His will, He heareth us" (1 John 5:14).

It is therefore perfectly correct when the new Catechism states the case thus (Qu. 205): "What distinction should we make in our prayers? When praying for spiritual blessings, necessary for our salvation, we should ask unconditionally; when praying for other gifts, we should ask that God grant them to us if it be His will." (Dietrich's Catechism, qus. 348, 349). This is correct because the grace of God, that is, forgiveness of sins, life, and salvation, is guaranteed to us under all circumstances by the divine will and promise. We learn this from 2 Cor. 12:9. The Lord refused to relieve Paul of his heavy cross and instead pointed to His never-failing grace as all-sufficient: "My grace is sufficient for thee."

There are cases in which Christians have asked unconditionally for temporal blessings, as, for example, when Luther prayed unconditionally for the prolongation of Melanchthon's life. Luther himself says: "There our Lord God had to give in to me; for I threw down the sack before His door and rubbed into His ears all His promises that He would hear prayer which I could enumerate from Scripture, saying that He would have to hear me if I were to trust His promises." [136] But such cases belong to the domain of the *fides heroica* and are not subject to the general rule. It is the business of the Holy Spirit to direct the prayer of the individual Christian in special, exceptional circumstances. Who will dare to circumscribe His power? [137]

Concerning the Lord's Prayer, taught by Christ Himself, Luther says in his Large Catechism: "Besides this we should be incited and drawn to prayer because in addition to this commandment and promise God anticipates us and Himself arranges the words and form of prayer for us, and places them upon our lips as to how and what we should pray, that we may see how heartily He pities us in our distress, and may never doubt that such prayer is pleasing to Him and shall certainly be answered; which prayer has a great advantage indeed over all other prayers that we might compose ourselves. For in them the conscience would ever be in doubt and say: I have prayed, but who knows how it pleases Him, or whether I have hit upon the right proportions and form? Hence there is no nobler prayer to be found upon earth than the Lord's Prayer, which we daily pray, because it testifies excellently that God loves to hear it, which we ought not to surrender for all the riches of the world." (*Trigl.* 703, Large Cat., Lord's Prayer, 22 f.)

Additional matters. To pray to the departed saints is folly (Is. 63:16; 1 Kings 8:39), idolatry (Matt. 4:10), and a blasphemous insult to the all-sufficient merit of Christ, who has perfectly reconciled God to us (1 Tim. 2:5-6; Rom. 8:34; 1 John 2:1-2; Rom. 8:31-32). — The adoration of angels is expressly prohibited in Scripture (Rev. 19:10; 22:8-9. — See the *locus* on God, Vol. I, 438, and on the angels, Vol. I, 507). — Divine adoration is due also the human nature of Christ. (See the *locus* on the Person of Christ, Vol. II, 215 ff.) — Extempore prayer, *ex corde* prayer, does not in itself rank higher than the set formal prayer. "Mechanical babbling," or battologizing, occurs also in the case of extempore prayers, as revival meetings often demonstrate.[138]

---

[136] See Koestlin, *Luthers Leben*, II, 515.

[137] Cf. Roos, Reformationsgesch., Vol. II, 472, footnote. On the *fides heroica* in healing those bodily possessed, see Walther, *Pastorale*, p. 294 [Fritz, *Pastoral Theology*, 2d ed., revised, p. 210]. Quenstedt: "There are extant heroic examples of prayers of certain men who were impelled by divine zeal; those examples are not rashly to be imitated" (II, 1439). As illustration Quenstedt refers to Elisha's prayer against the children of Bethel (2 Kings 2:23-24).

[138] Reading the prayers in Dr. C. F. W. Walther's *Ansprachen und Gebete in Gemeindeversammlungen* (English: *Church Membership Addresses and Prayers*), one gains the impression that the careful preparation of these public prayers did not do away with their fervor. Hodge on the necessity of carefully preparing for public prayer: "Public prayer, it is often said, is the weak point in the

As to the ceremonies to be observed in prayer, Luther observes: "It is of little importance whether one stands, kneels, or lies prostrate, for these are external matters, neither commanded as necessary nor forbidden, just as other customs, e. g., raising the countenance and eyes to heaven, folding the hands, smiting the breast; only let them not be despised, since Scripture and Christ Himself praise them (Eph. 3:14; 1 Tim. 2:8; John 17:1). On the other hand, it is not wrong if one, while binding sheaves in the field or lying in bed, should pray only in the heart." (St. L. VIII:748).[139]

16

The Christian Life and the Hope of Eternal Life

In his sermon on the Christian hope Luther describes Christians as waiting in this life for the glorious appearance of the Lord Jesus Christ on the Last Day.[140] The thoughts presented are entirely Scriptural. As the believers of the Old Covenant awaited the promised appearance of Christ in the flesh (Zacharias' hymn of praise, Luke 1:67-79; Simeon described as "waiting for the Consolation of Israel," Luke 2:25, and all believers in Israel as "looking for redemption," Luke 2:38), so the believers of the New Testament await the promised second coming of their Lord. Not only when they approach death, but from the moment they became Christians and thus came into possession of their eternal inheritance in heaven they are looking

---

Presbyterian Sabbath service. This is probably true. That is, it is probably true that there are more good preachers than good pray-ers. The main reason for this is that the minister devotes a great part of the labor of the week to the preparation of his sermon and not a thought to his prayers. It is no wonder, therefore, that the one should be better than the other." (*Syst. Theol.*, III, 707.) Likewise the pastor should carefully prepare the prayers he speaks when he is visiting the sick, etc. It is self-evident that he should be able, by the grace of God, to speak an instructive and edifying prayer also *ex tempore*. He will escape the danger of "losing himself in generalities" by turning a fitting Scripture passage into a prayer. Experience shows that the young pastor is frequently afraid to risk an *ex tempore* prayer. The best preparation for praying *ex tempore* is that students in their school days lead a life of prayer and make it their habit to commune with God on their experiences, be they joyful or sad, in short prayers of praise or supplication. They can do this even while strolling.

139 Quenstedt: "Also the posture of the body should be used as an aid; it shows both reverence for the divine will, earnest and true humility before God, and helps to fix the attention of the soul in this sacred exercise" (II, 1440 *sq.*).

140 Luther's guest sermon on Titus 2:13: "Looking for that blessed hope and the glorious appearing of the great God and our Savior Jesus Christ," was preached at Kemberg in August, 1531 (St. L. IX:930 ff.).

forward to the day when their Savior will return visibly and take them with Him into eternal glory. That view characterizes the entire life of a Christian. To the Corinthians who had just come to faith the Apostle writes that they "come behind in no gift" and are now only waiting "for the coming of our Lord Jesus Christ" (1 Cor. 1:7). Again, Titus 2:13: "Looking for that blessed hope and the glorious appearing of the great God and our Savior Jesus Christ." Once more, Phil. 3:20: "Our conversation is in heaven; from whence also we look for the Savior, the Lord Jesus Christ." As Christians are called "beloved of God, called to be saints" (Rom. 1:7; 1 Cor. 1:2), men "that call on the name of the Lord" (Acts 9:14; 1 Cor. 1:2; 2 Tim. 2:22; Acts 9:21), so, too, they are named men that "wait" and "look for" the Lord.

We find not only this general characterization in Scripture, but every phase of the Christian life, all its activities, and all its sorrows are brought into the light of Judgment Day and the glory then to be revealed. Because they are waiting for their Lord, Christians are diligent in good works (Matt. 24:45-51; 25:14 ff.; Luke 12:15 ff.), especially in preaching the Gospel (Matt. 24:14). They keep themselves unspotted from the world (Titus 2:12-14). They guard against the carnal security which characterized the time of Noah (Matt. 24:36 ff.). They remain strangers and pilgrims in this world (1 Pet. 2:11; Heb. 13:14). They use this world without abusing it (1 Cor. 7:31). They do not seek revenge, but leave that to the coming of the Lord (Phil. 4:5). They are like the wise virgins whose lamps were filled (Matt. 25:1 ff.). They regard the sufferings of this present time as light (Rom. 8:18), so light that instead of weeping they rejoice (Rom. 8:18; Luke 6:23; Matt. 5:12; 1 Pet. 4:12). They are confident in the midst of death (1 Thess. 4:13-18). In short, it is the blessed hope of heaven which shapes a Christian's life on earth into the right form. This hope insures the happy life of a Christian; this is the key to a successful ministry.[141]

True, Scripture at times turns the eyes of Christians toward a blessed death (Phil. 1:21-23; Luke 23:43). But primarily and finally the life of every Christian should get its bearing from the dawning of Christ's return.

Luther made this view the theme of his sermon on "the blessed hope." We bring some of his main thoughts. Luther calls it "the fine

[141] For example, in dealing with the troublesome "dance and theater question," which permits of so much theoretic debate, the minister will in practice often settle the matter by asking: Where and in what company would you want to be found at the appearance of your Savior?

art and true masterpiece of Christianity" for the believer "to turn his
back on this transient life and keep his gaze fixed on the future life,
firmly and confidently hoping that it will endure forever and be our
proper home." "The citizenship, the sojourn, and the home of Christians is not in this world but in heaven." Luther reminds us that it is
difficult to put this article of faith into practice: "This is correctly
taught, but not easily learned; rightly preached, but not so soon
believed; correctly impressed upon the heart, but not easily followed;
well said, but poorly practiced. . . . Were we to confess the truth,
we would have to admit that we seldom think of the fact that we
must at last depart and leave this life; and for that reason our mind
is not constantly set on our eternal home. Add to that our faint-
heartedness: we always stand in fear of death, we mourn and tremble
under our misfortunes. All of this shows that we do not look for the
blessed hope as we should." But every Christian needs to learn this
article: "Whoever does not direct and prepare his heart for yonder
imperishable life, but continues to cling only to this temporal,
perishable life, does not understand what Baptism, Gospel, Christ,
faith, mean. We have not been baptized unto this life; we are not
called Christians in order that we might be burghers, peasants, masters,
servants, mistresses, maids, rulers, subjects, laborers, householders. But
for this we are baptized, for this we hear the Gospel and believe in
Christ, that we may set aside all these vocations (though we abide
in these vocations here on earth as long as it pleases God and therein
serve God, each one in his appointed calling) and turn from this
world to another existence and life where there is neither servant nor
master, neither maid nor mistress, neither wife nor husband, but where
we are altogether equal and one in Christ Jesus (Gal. 3:28), which
equality begins here in faith, but yonder is made perfect in sight
(1 Cor. 15:53), where there is no death, but only eternal and imperishable life, no sin, but only righteousness and innocence, no fear
nor sorrow, but only security and joy, no dominion nor authority nor
power, but God alone will be All in All; in short, where God and
Christ Himself is with all His elect and saints. Unto this eternal life
we have been baptized, unto this life Christ has redeemed us by His
blood and death, and to reach this life we have received the Gospel.
As soon as the child is baptized and clothed in the chrisom, he is
from that hour dedicated unto eternal life, so that henceforth throughout his life he is only a pilgrim and stranger in this world, prepared
and ready to leave this temporal life, always hoping and looking for
yonder enduring life." (St. L. IX:930 ff.)

Final Perseverance

(DE PERSEVERANTIA)

T HE subject of a Christian's perseverance [1] in faith is of the utmost importance (Luther, St. L. IX:1807, on Matt. 24:13). When Christ speaks of the trials and tribulations which will come upon the believers, He makes the significant statement: "He that endureth to the end [R. V.: the same] shall be saved" (Matt. 10:22). Christ repeats the same statement in Matt. 24:13. Only he that endureth to the end, "the same" (οὗτος emphasizing the subject of the sentence) shall be saved, he and no other.[2] What Scripture teaches on the final perseverance may be summarized in these two statements: 1. He that perseveres in faith does so only through God's gracious preservation; the believer's perseverance is a work of divine grace and omnipotence. 2. He that falls from faith does so through his own fault; the cause of apostasy is in every case rejection of God's Word and resistance to the operation of the Holy Spirit in the Word. This doctrine the Christian Church must maintain and defend on two fronts: against Calvinism and against synergism.

1

The Calvinistic Doctrine of Perseverance

Consistent Calvinism teaches the inamissibility of faith. It holds that even *peccata enormia* cannot result in the loss of faith; gross sins will destroy the exercise of faith *(exercitium fidei),* but never faith itself.[3]

---

[1] Chemnitz discusses Final Perseverance under *"De iustificatione"* (*Loci,* II, 709) and *"De bonis operibus"* (III, 48 *sqq.*); likewise Gerhard, *Loci, "De iustificatione,"* § 83 *sqq.*, and *De bonis operibus,* § 134 *sqq.* So we, too, have shown in the *locus* on Justification that justifying faith includes the assurance both of forgiveness of sin and of salvation (Vol. II, 406) and in the *locus* on Sanctification that good works do not preserve faith and salvation (Vol. III, 20). We shall treat of it again in the section on Election. Here we are stressing particularly the points that must be maintained against Calvinism and synergism.

[2] Fritzsche says that the "οὗτος is put with great force after ὁ δέ."

[3] For instances from the *Canones Synodi Dortrechtanae* and of the *Confession of Faith* see Vol. II, 468, footnote 24. Calvin: "It must be remembered that however feeble and weak the faith of the elect may be, the Spirit of God is to them a sure pledge and seal of their adoption. The impression once engraven can never be effaced from their hearts." (*Inst.* III, 2, 12.) Heidegger teaches the same thing in *loc.* 24, *De constantia foederis gratiae* (see Baumgarten, II, p. 636 *sq.*).

This false teaching, which Luther and the Lutheran Confessions so emphatically reject,[4] has been invented for the purpose of allaying the uncertainty and doubt which the denial of the *gratia universalis* will necessarily raise in the hearts of sinners seeking assurance of grace. By such denial those who have actually lost their faith and are now again seeking grace are either driven to despair or led to trust in their former faith instead of trusting in the grace of God in Christ. Take the case of Cromwell, of which Strong says: "Cromwell questioned his chaplain as to the doctrine of final perseverance and, on being assured that it was a certain truth, said: 'Then I am happy, for I am sure that I was once in a state of grace.'" Strong criticizes the counsel given Cromwell and declares: "But reliance upon a past experience is like trusting in the value of life insurance upon which several years' premiums have been unpaid. If the policy has not lapsed, it is because of extreme grace." He wants a man like Cromwell to be told: "The only conclusive evidence of perseverance is a present experience of Christ's presence and indwelling, corroborated by active service and purity of life." But Cromwell would have profited nothing by such a counsel. He would have replied that in his case the "present experience of Christ's presence" was lacking.

No, indeed. Christ would have given an altogether different counsel. He did not ask the malefactor on the cross, whose case was similar to that of Cromwell, to rely on "the present experience of Christ's indwelling" and the corroboration of it by a pure life, but told him the objective Word of grace. This is the cure for these cases — the objective, universal, perfect grace of God, which is not based on Christ's indwelling and on the holy life of the suppliant, but has been gained by Christ's vicarious satisfaction for all men, is offered in the Gospel to all, with the object of bringing them to faith in it. Universal grace (which is an objective reality and is offered in the objective means of grace), and not the "Christ in us" and our virtuous life, is "the grace of God that bringeth salvation" (Titus 2:11); and this grace "that bringeth salvation to all men" is to be proclaimed to all the Cromwells and all the malefactors in the world. This grace alone can rekindle lost faith, for "faith cometh by hearing" (Rom. 10:17).

By its denial of universal grace consistent Calvinism is prevented from supplying this cure to those who have actually lost their faith

---

[4] Smalc. Art. (*Trigl.* 491, Part III, Art. III, 42—44); Augsb. Conf. (*Trigl.* 49, Art. XII). See Vol. II, 468, note 25.

or are troubled by the fear of having lost it. The doctrine of the inamissibility of faith is not the remedy. This doctrine will only drive sinners to despair or lead them to trust in their former faith or in their renewal and sanctification of life. As a matter of fact, without the universal objective reconciliation, gained by Christ and proffered in the objective means of grace, the regeneration of a sinner, the perseverance of a believer, or the return of a backslider cannot be achieved. Fortunately many Calvinists, both preachers and hearers, forget about their *gratia particularis* in practice. (Cp. Vol. II, 50, 432.)

2

The Synergistic Doctrine of Perseverance

Synergism contends that the preservation of faith, like the conversion of man, depends not only on God's gracious operation, but also on man's endeavor. It argues that if man's own efforts — call it refraining from willful resistance, personal self-determination, correct conduct, self-decision, exercising the moral qualities of the new life, or other names — do not play the decisive role in the preservation of faith, salvation would rest solely in God's hand, and the whole procedure would be discreditable to man. Unless the "free choice," the "personal self-determination," be postulated, both conversion and perseverance would be effected by coercion, and man's responsibility would be abolished. On account of these "necessary consequences" synergism feels constrained to teach that salvation must be made dependent also on man.

Synergism also misuses Scripture to prove that salvation, conversion, and perseverance do not rest only in God's hands. It makes use of the imperative and conditional statements of Scripture for this purpose. Thus, for example, the *Lutherische Kirchenzeitung* declared: " 'Work out your own salvation with fear and trembling.' Thus the Apostle admonishes us Phil. 2:12. There is no stronger way of stating that the salvation of man does not depend in every respect only on God, for, literally translated, this text says: Effect, or accomplish, your salvation." (Vol. 26, No. 10.)

Again, synergism is wont to argue that guarding against what causes apostasy must also cause perseverance. Thus: if evil works and the evil conduct bring about the loss of faith, it must follow that the perseverance of faith depends on man's abstaining from evil conduct and supplying the right conduct.[5] All the arguments that synergism employs against monergism in conversion reappear in the doctrine of perseverance.

Holy Scripture makes short work of those synergistic arguments and apprehensions. It plainly teaches divine monergism both in conversion and in the preservation of faith. According to Scripture, not only the kindling of faith (Eph. 1:19-20), but also the perseverance in faith is the work of divine omnipotence. St. Peter assures the Christians: "Ye are kept by the power of God through faith unto salvation" (1 Pet. 1:5).[6] Also the words of Christ in John 10:28-30 clearly state that the *causa efficiens* of the constancy of Christians is the divine omnipotence: "Neither shall any man pluck them out of My hand. My Father, which gave them Me, is greater than all [omnipotent]; and no man is able to pluck them out of My Father's hand. I and My Father are One."[7] Paul tells the Christians that it is God who effects the beginning and the consummation of their faith: "He which hath begun a good work in you will perform it until the day of Jesus Christ" (Phil. 1:6). God's faithfulness, not ours, is the guarantee of our perseverance; "Faithful is He that calleth you, who also will do it" (1 Thess. 5:24); "The Lord is faithful, who shall stablish you and keep you from evil" (2 Thess. 3:3).

Finally, why should Christians work out their salvation with fear and trembling? Because, as Scripture tells them, their salvation rests not in their hands, but in God's. "Work out your own salvation with fear and trembling, for it is God which worketh in you both to will and to do of His good pleasure" (Phil. 2:12-13). The synergists are in the habit of quoting only the admonition in v. 12 and entirely dis-

---

[5] Thus Majorism taught that good works are necessary "in order to retain, or not to lose, faith." See Frank, II, 195 ff.

[6] Chemnitz on this passage: "'By the power of God we are kept through faith unto salvation, ready to be revealed in the last times.' You hear that the preservation of salvation up to its revelation at the last is ascribed to the power of God through faith; likewise v. 9: 'Receiving the end of your faith, even the salvation of your souls.' And this is in perfect harmony with Paul's statement, Rom. 4:14, that if the preserving of salvation depends on our fulfillment of the Law, i. e., on our works, then faith is made void and the promise is made of none effect. In order, therefore, that the promise of salvation, not only of the salvation received, but also of the salvation to be conserved, may be reliable, salvation is given without works through faith, by grace." (*Loci,* III, 64 *sq.*)

[7] Here the numerical unity of the omnipotent action of the Father and the Son, which is based on the numerical unity of the divine essence, is predicated. And since this divine omnipotence preserves our faith, the attacks of all hostile powers will prove futile.

regarding v. 13, where the reason for the admonition is given. As we saw in the quotation above, they quote only "Work out your own salvation with fear and trembling" and then assert: "There is no stronger way of stating that the salvation of man does not depend in every respect only on God," simply closing their eyes to the statement: "It is God which worketh in you both to will and to do of His good pleasure."

He who disregards this truth is headed for a fall. There is, in the last analysis, only one thing that causes the loss of faith, and that is self-confidence — the synergistic idea that salvation does not depend solely on God's gracious operation, but also on the "self-determination," the "correct conduct," of man. That brought about Peter's fall. Trusting in his own ability to sustain his faith, he declared: "Although all shall be offended, yet will not I," οὐκ ἐγώ. Others may fall, but I will observe the right conduct! Jesus predicted what the result of this self-confidence would be. "Verily I say unto thee," He said, "that this day, even in this night, before the cock crow twice, thou shalt deny Me thrice" (Mark 14:30). Only a few hours later Peter cursed and swore that he did not know the Lord Jesus. Luther calls this attitude of unwillingness to depend solely on God's grace for salvation the "vicious, insidious deception" which still stirs in the flesh of the Christians and must be suppressed constantly and mercilessly if the first are not to become the last.[8] Against this "insidious deception" Paul is warning the Philippians when, admonishing them to work out their salvation with fear and trembling, he tells them that it is God who works in them both to will and to do of His good pleasure.

And because synergism nourishes, fosters, and strengthens this "insidious deception" by teaching that perseverance depends not only on God's gracious operation, but also on man's proper conduct,

---

8 Recall Luther's remarks on Matt. 20:16: "So the last shall be first and the first last": "It is very necessary that this Gospel be preached to those in our day who know the Gospel, to me and others like me, who can teach and train all the world and consider themselves very close to God, as having entirely devoured God's Spirit, with feathers and bones. . . . For this judgment strikes at what lies deepest in the heart of man, the spiritual self-conceit, which in poverty, disgrace, and misfortune — and just because of this — regards itself as the first. . . . It reaches very high and strikes very fine people; yes, it terrifies the most eminent saints. Christ is here addressing the warning to His Apostles. We see how fear has here gripped the greatest saints, and how many have here fallen from their high spiritual estate. . . . They fell because of the vicious insidious deception by which they became secure and thought: We have become close to God, there is no longer any danger. . . . Behold, how Saul fell! How He suffered David to fall! How Peter had to fall! How several disciples of Paul fell!" (St. L. XI:513 f.).

it constitutes a menace to Christianity. It leads directly to apostasy. As no one was ever converted by following the synergistic prescription, so no one will persevere in faith and obtain the end of faith by doing what the synergist prescribes. Luther says: "By our own strength we can in no wise escape the craftiness by which Satan beguiled Eve. He will corrupt our minds from the simplicity that is in Christ unless the Lord, moved by our humble prayer, sustains our course. For here the 'free will' can achieve nothing; nor does the 'first grace,' as they call it, suffice; perseverance is needed which depends not on the will of man, but on God's preservation *(est non volentis hominis, sed sustentantis Dei)*." (St. L. IV:1008 f.)

When synergists admonish their adherents never to be certain of their final salvation,[9] they are presenting the inevitable corollary of the synergistic doctrine of perseverance. The caution is superfluous because there can be no assurance of salvation if salvation depends on man himself. However, their admonition is not sufficiently comprehensive. To be fully consistent, they should tell their people that they can be sure only of damnation. For even in Christians, apart from the gracious operation of God, there "dwelleth no good thing" (Rom. 7:18). The person who holds, not merely at his desk and in his polemics, but in his heart and before God, that his salvation rests not exclusively with his gracious God, but depends also on his conduct, has lost his faith. It is the nature of Christian faith to "rest on pure grace," and faith ceases the moment a man widens the foundation to include human good conduct (*Trigl.* 163, Apol., III, 33). Such a faith is not the product of the Holy Ghost, but owes its existence to the evil flesh and the archenemy of man, who would destroy the faith of Christians even as he brought about the fall of Peter. Contrariwise the preaching of the truth, revealed in Scripture, that we are kept by the power of God through faith unto salvation is the means employed by the Holy Ghost constantly to create anew and to strengthen and sustain faith. Christian faith comes into being and subsists only vis-à-vis the *sola gratia Dei*.

Another factor in the synergistic teaching on perseverance should be pointed out. Some synergists hold that divine grace and power indeed preserve the believer's faith against all external foes but not

---

[9] Latermann already pointed out this uncertainty. Thesis 43 in his *Disput. de praedestinatione* reads: "Since man is certain that he can lose the hope of salvation, he cannot but doubt as to his final perseverance" (quoted by Quenstedt, II, 819).

against his own evil flesh. Philippi advanced this view.[10] Meyer also operates with this limitation and thus divests the pertinent Scripture passages of their true meaning.[11] Likewise Lyman Beecher seems to have had this limitation in mind when he answered the question whether he believed in final perseverance with these words: "I do, except when the wind is from the East" (Strong, *Syst. Theol.*, p. 883). But Philippi's idea that in our own power we must cope with our sinful flesh is altogether unscriptural. Scripture excepts no enemy. God's promise is unlimited. He promises to keep us against every foe. According to 1 Pet. 1:3-5, God has begotten the Christians "to an inheritance incorruptible, and undefiled, and that fadeth not away, reserved in heaven for you, who are kept by the power of God through faith unto salvation." Here is a declaration, without any reservations or restrictions (1) that the inheritance of Christians is reserved in heaven for them by God, and (2) that they, the Christians, are kept by the power of God through faith for that inheritance so that nothing shall separate the heirs from their inheritance. We note here that "the power of God" operates "through faith," and that means that God's power is exerted through the Gospel as a means of grace, since faith and the evangelical promise are correlatives,[12] and that God's power is exerted upon the soul, the heart and mind, of the

10 Philippi on Rom. 8:35-36: "Though it is true that no one and nothing can pluck us out of the hand of God and Christ, since the omnipotence and grace of God and Christ is stronger than all earthly powers, this does not do away with the fact that we can willfully and voluntarily break away from God. Though tribulation cannot separate us from God, our sin can."

11 Meyer on Phil. 1:6: "The idea of resistance to this grace, as a human possibility, is not thereby excluded, but Paul does not have to fear this on the part of the Philippians, as he feared it in the case of the Galatians." This comment is a direct denial of Phil. 2:12-13. Knowing that the Philippians, like all believers, have to contend with this synergistic "resistance," this self-confidence that their salvation depends not only on God, but also on their own efforts, Paul tells them: "For it is God which worketh in you both to will and to do of His good pleasure."

12 The phrase "through faith" also disproves the Calvinistic error that "efficacious grace," being an exercise of divine omnipotence, cannot be exercised *through means.* Hodge contends that "efficacious grace acts immediately." "Regeneration itself, the infusion of a new life into the soul, is the immediate work of the Spirit. There is here no place for the use of means any more than in the act of creation." (*Syst. Theol.*, II, 682 ff.) Hodge is here separating what according to Scripture belongs together. Scripture teaches, on the one hand, that faith is created and preserved by the divine omnipotence (Eph. 1:19-20; 1 Pet. 1:5), and, on the other hand, that the faith which appropriates and clings to grace is created by the Word of grace and clings to the Word of grace (Rom. 10: 17, 8). See the section on the Means of Grace.

Christians, preserving their faith in the *sola gratia* against the onslaughts of their inherent synergism. Therefore Christians not only pray: "Take not the Word of truth utterly out of my mouth" (Ps. 119:43), but also: "Incline my heart unto Thy testimonies" (Ps. 119:36), and "Create in me a clean heart, O God; and renew a right spirit within me" (Ps. 51:10). God promises to protect us against ourselves, against our own flesh, as we heard from the passages Phil. 2:13: "It is God which worketh in you [ἐν ὑμῖν] both to will and to do of His good pleasure"; Phil. 1:6: "He which hath begun a good work in you [ἐν ὑμῖν] will perform it until the day of Jesus Christ";[13] 2 Thess. 3:3: "The Lord is faithful, who will stablish you and keep you from evil"; 1 Pet. 5:10 f.: "The God of all grace . . . make you perfect, stablish, strengthen, settle you. To Him be glory and dominion forever and ever. Amen." In this doxology Christians already offer thanks for their finished preservation because the Holy Ghost has taught them that it is God Himself — note the emphatic αὐτός — who stablishes and keeps them.

The proof which synergists offer for their queer notion that Christians are indeed "kept by the power of God through faith" from all other hostile powers, but not from their own flesh, does not rest on theological grounds, but is the product of an unwarranted, untheological confounding of Law and Gospel. The warnings against defection (1 Cor. 10:12; Rom. 11:20) which are directed against the carnal security and self-confidence of the old man,[14] they use to restrict

---

[13] Meyer correctly comments: "ἐν ὑμῖν — not *among* you, but *in* you, *in animis vestris*."

[14] Balduin: "The fear which Paul here enjoins upon us is the opposite of (1) Epicurean security, by which faith is suffocated, the Holy Spirit grieved, and the grace of God lost; and (2) spiritual pride and arrogance; we should not become proud on account of our gifts, but depend solely on God's grace and compassion, taking pains lest we lose it. (Quoted in Baier-Walther, III, 598.) Chemnitz: "Looking to God's will in the revealed Word and to Christ, our Mediator, we can and should declare: 'Who shall separate us? I am persuaded that neither things present nor things to come shall be able to separate us,' etc., Rom. 8:35 ff. For we have been called to fellowship with Christ; He will then certainly not reject again those whom He has received. But He is an everlasting Savior, and we are called to have eternal fellowship with Him. The Father is eternal, and 'the gifts and calling of God are without repentance.' 'No man shall pluck them out of My hand.' Hence the perseverance of the pious is certain as far as God is concerned. And because it is so revealed in the Word, faith must believe this. But does not Paul say in Rom. 11:22: 'If thou continue in His goodness,' and Heb. 3:14: 'If we hold the beginning of our confidence steadfast unto the end'? I answer: John says: 'Those things have I written unto you . . . that ye may know that ye have eternal life,' 1 John 5:13. Phil. 1:6: 'I am per-

the Gospel, which, in dealing with the broken, despairing, Paul-like souls (Rom. 7:18), unconditionally promises preservation by the power of God through faith in His grace; and by making final salvation depend on man's efforts, they make of it a matter of the Law. Scripture, however, bids the brokenhearted, who despair of all self-help, to disregard the Law entirely and to look only to the Gospel. And the Gospel, with its present assurance of the grace of God, assures us also of our future salvation. (See Vol. II, 407.) The Formula of Concord says on this point: "Here we must be well on our guard lest works are drawn and mingled into the article of justification and salvation. Therefore the propositions are justly rejected that to believers good works are necessary for salvation, so that it is impossible to be saved without good works. For they are directly contrary to the doctrine *de particulis exclusionis in articulo iustificationis et salvationis,* that is, they conflict with the words by which St. Paul has entirely excluded our works and merits from the article of justification and salvation, and ascribed everything to the grace of God and the merit of Christ alone. Again, they [these propositions concerning the necessity of good works for salvation] take from afflicted, troubled consciences the comfort *of the Gospel,* give occasion for doubt, are in many ways dangerous, strengthen presumption in one's own righteousness and confidence in one's own works; besides, they are accepted by the Papists, and in their interest adduced against the pure doctrine of the alone-saving faith." (*Trigl.* 945, Sol. Decl., IV, 22 f.) — The doubts which arise in a Christian concerning his final salvation arise from his flesh and must be suppressed as sin. (See Saving Faith, Vol. II, 445.)

In the doctrine of perseverance, too, the Christian doctrine and the synergistic teaching are as far apart as the poles. Where one says Yes, the other says No. The Christian doctrine calls for the mortification of the old man. This killing of the old man occurs when the Law hurls him to the ground with all his pretense, including his "correct conduct," his "self-decision," his "personal self-determination," and

---

suaded that He which hath begun a good work in you,' etc. Thus also 1 Cor. 1:8. And so David says, Ps. 31:1: 'Let me never be ashamed.' Therefore we are commanded to pray for perseverance because God has promised it. For a prayer always needs a promise so that it may be said without hesitation. We pray and wrestle that the wantonness of the flesh may not wreck the gift of perseverance. And this distinction will solve this difficulty regarding perseverance." (*Loci,* 1559, II, 709.) "Confusion and perversion of the distinction between Law and Gospel, plainly conflicting with the doctrine of Paul, arises from teaching that our works are necessary for salvation" (*l. c.* III, 63).

drives him to despair (*Trigl.* 479, Smalc. Art., Part III, Art. II, 2), and God then through the Gospel kindles and sustains faith in the grace of God in Christ. Synergism calls for no mortification of the old man, but only for his "renascence"; all that is needed is that the old man be aroused and trained so that he learns to "conduct himself properly" toward grace and observes the correct "personal self-determination." Of course, a more or less vigorous influence of grace is necessary in this training, for "without Me ye can do nothing" (John 15:5), as even Erasmus admitted. But the operation of grace must halt at the boundaries of self-decision;[15] the correct conduct of man also plays a part in obtaining salvation; yes, it plays the decisive part, turning the scales for or against salvation. While those who believe Rom. 7:18 find their consolation in the fact that the power of God keeps them through faith unto salvation, the advocates of synergism — those who practice according to their theory — console themselves with the belief that their salvation depends not only on God's grace but also on their conduct.

Why is it that men whose personal faith one is reluctant to question will defend the synergistic teaching which so directly contradicts Scripture and Christian experience? We can only repeat here what, in the doctrine of conversion, was stated as to "the true reasons" for synergism. Both the *opinio legis,* inborn in all men, and the itch to find an answer to the *crux theologorum:* "Why do some persevere and others not?" motivate the synergistic teaching. Since all Christians are alike in that no good thing dwells in their flesh and since the grace of God is universal and serious, either all should persevere or all fall away. But actually only some persevere, while others lose their faith. Now, whoever has not yet learned with Luther and the Formula of Concord to be satisfied with the *sola gratia* as the only cause of perseverance and with the *sola culpa hominis* as the only cause of defection, that is, whoever will not admit that the question why only some and not all persevere presents a mystery which is insoluble in this life, will land either in the Calvinistic ditch, denying the universality of grace, or in the synergistic ditch, denying the equal guilt. Take to heart the instruction and admonition which the Formula of Concord applies not only to man's conversion, but also to his preservation: "No injustice is done those who are punished and receive the wages of their sins; but in the rest, to whom God gives and preserves His Word, by which men are enlightened, converted, and preserved,

---

15 Thus Luthardt, *Die christl. Glaubenslehre,* p. 442.

God commends His pure [immense] grace and mercy, without their merit. . . . However, as regards those things in this disputation which would soar too high and beyond these limits [namely, whatever goes beyond the *sola culpa* in the case of the one and the *sola gratia* in the other] we should, with Paul, place the finger upon our lips, and remember and say, Rom. 9:20: 'O man, who art thou that repliest against God?'" (*Trigl.* 1083, XI, 61—63.)

Men tell us that it is dangerous to teach the certainty of perseverance because such a doctrine would engender spiritual pride. On the contrary, the conviction that we can persevere only by relying on the promise of God's grace will cause us to despair of our strength and will foster true spiritual humility, while the contrary opinion — that perseverance depends not only on God's power and grace but also on man's own conduct — generates pride, the pride that goes before a fall.

Again, they tell us that the assurance of perseverance through divine grace leads to carnal security and to neglect of sanctification and good works. On the contrary, the assurance that we are kept by the power of God through faith unto salvation cannot but increase our gratitude and love for God and hence strengthen our zeal to shun sin and serve God in good works (2 Cor. 7:1; Gal. 2:20). The more our assurance of gaining the heavenly inheritance grows, the greater will be our patience and our strength to overcome the sufferings of this present time (Rom. 8:18; Luke 12:32), and the more will the things of this world lose their fascination (1 John 2:16-17; 1 Cor. 7: 29-31). On the other hand, where the assurance of salvation is lacking, the gratitude toward God and the strength to resist the allurements of the world and the desires of the flesh will also be lacking (Matt. 6:21). Luther says on this point: "If a person could with firm and constant faith hold to this, and comprehend the magnitude of this gift, that he is a child and heir of God, he would regard all that there is of power and treasures in all nations in the world as filth and dung in comparison with his heavenly inheritance. He would turn with disgust from all that the world considers high and glorious; the greater the glory and pomp of the world is, the more he would hate it; in short, all that the world most admires and praises to the sky would be ugly and worthless in his sight. For what is the whole world with its power, riches, and glory compared with God, whose heir and child he is? . . . But the law in my members, warring against the law of my mind, will not permit faith to become perfect." (St. L. IX:516.)

Two more points need to be noted: (1) the realization of the truth of Rom. 7:18, that utter despair of our own strength will impel us to diligent use of God's Word, of the means through which God will complete the good work begun in us, as He has promised John 8:51: "If a man keep My saying, he shall never see death" (cp. *Trigl.* 901, F. C., Sol. Decl., II, 50—56); (2) the realization of the truth that our salvation is entirely in God's hand will drive us humbly to petition and implore God for His gracious help. Such a prayer has never remained unanswered; God has promised unconditionally to fulfill it (John 6:37: "Him that cometh to Me I will in no wise cast out"; Ps. 10:17: "Lord, Thou hast heard the desire of the humble"; Matt. 11:28; Ps. 31:22; Is. 57:15).

The Means of Grace

(DE MEDIIS GRATIAE)

IN reconciling the world unto Himself by Christ's substitutionary satisfaction, God asked no one's advice concerning His singular method of reconciliation. In like manner, without asking any man's advice, He ordained the means by which He gives men the infallible assurance of His gracious will toward them; in other words, He both confers on men the remission of sins merited by Christ and works faith in the proffered remission or, where faith already exists, strengthens it. The Church has appropriately called these divine ordinances the means of grace, *media gratiae, instrumenta gratiae;* Formula of Concord: *"Instrumenta sive media Spiritus Sancti"* (*Trigl.* 903, Sol. Decl., II, 58). They are the Word of the Gospel, Baptism, and the Lord's Supper, as will be shown more fully on the following pages.

According to Scripture, a twofold power inheres in these means: first, an exhibiting and conferring, or imparting, power *(vis exhibitiva, dativa, collativa),* and, secondly, as a result of this, an efficacious, or operative, power *(vis effectiva sive operativa).* The conferring, or imparting, power consists in this, that these means offer men the forgiveness of sins, supplied through Christ's work of reconciliation, hence God's grace *(favor Dei).*[1] In other words, through the means of grace God reveals and declares to men that He is fully reconciled through Christ, that because of Christ's work He loves them and would have them believe it. The efficacious, or operative, power of the means of grace consists in this, that through them the Holy Spirit works and strengthens faith, faith in the very forgiveness, God's love and grace, which these means declare and reveal.[2]

One would think that men would not take exception to the means of grace, ordained by God Himself. But history reports the opposite. As critics have declared God's method of reconciling the world unworthy of God and man, so they have also taken exception to the means of grace ordained by God. Some, for instance Zwingli, have

---

[1] Formula of Concord: "Christ . . . offers to all men His grace [*clementiam*] in the Word and holy Sacraments" (*Trigl.* 903, Sol. Decl., II, 57).

[2] Formula of Concord: "The Word of God preached and heard is [truly] an office and work of the Holy Ghost, by which He is certainly efficacious and works in our hearts" (*Trigl.* 903, Sol. Decl., II, 56). Augustana: "That we may obtain this faith, the ministry of teaching the Gospel and administering the Sacraments was instituted. For through the Word and Sacraments, as through instruments, the Holy Ghost is given, who works faith, where and when it pleases God [Vol. II, 401, footnote 9], in them that hear the Gospel." (*Trigl.* 45, V, 1, 2.)

argued strongly that it does not befit God to bind His revelation and operation to such external means as the Word and the Sacraments, that for His work the Holy Ghost does not need a vehicle.[3] In other words, Zwingli and his numerous adherents declare that the means God has ordained are unnecessary and hinder true piety. Others, particularly the Papists, create their own means of grace and "improve" those which God has ordained.[4] On this account a manual of Christian dogmatics must devote considerable space to a presentation of the Christian doctrine of the means of grace. The study will also show that the rejection and every alteration of the divinely appointed means of grace impairs the core and center of the Christian faith, the article of justification by faith without the deeds of the Law. When the means of grace are rejected or impaired, human works regularly take the place of Christ's substitutionary satisfaction as the basis of salvation.

1

The Means of Grace in General

Seeberg correctly writes: "The doctrinal understanding of the means of grace begins with the relation of these means to the work of Christ."[5] Unfortunately the term "work of Christ" has, in both the past and the present, been given widely different connotations, and this ambiguity lessens the value of the statement. Some do not regard the work of Christ as perfect in extent, for they let it count only for a part of mankind. This is done by the Calvinists. Others refer Christ's work of reconciliation to all men, but deny its perfection in value by asserting that His work is insufficient for man's actual salvation and must be supplemented by *aliquid in homine* — some achievement of man, an innate goodness in man, faith as a moral achievement, the free choice of man, faith as the germ of good works, the new life and the good works themselves, etc. Without this complement the work of Christ or the grace earned by Christ could not secure man's salvation. Where such warped conceptions of the "work" of Christ prevail, almost anything except the Scriptural concept of the means of grace can be the outcome. The means of grace do not remain means dispensing grace, but become means of prodding man to virtuous endeavors, variously named and of various grades.

---

[3] *Fidei Ratio*, ed. Niemeyer, p. 24; Jacobs, *Book of Concord*, II, 168.
[4] More on the Roman sacraments and the denial of the cup later.
[5] R. E., 3d ed., VI, p. 726.

The starting point in presenting the doctrine of the means of grace must be the universal objective reconciliation or justification. This is the procedure of Scripture. What it says of the divine transmission of the grace which Christ has gained for all men it joins immediately to the objective reconciliation or justification of sinful mankind. We here repeat and expand the thoughts we touched upon in the Preliminary Survey of the Application of Salvation, or Soteriology, in Volume II. The reconciliation which Christ brought about is history, a finished event lying in the past (θεὸς ἦν ἐν Χριστῷ κόσμον καταλλάσσων ἑαυτῷ) that pertains to all mankind and is of an entirely objective character. For it does not consist in a change of mind or "moral transformation" on the part of man, but in a change in God; God in His heart is not imputing their trespasses unto men, but forgiving them (μὴ λογιζόμενος αὐτοῖς τὰ παραπτώματα αὐτῶν, 2 Cor. 5:19). To the report of the finished universal objective reconciliation the Apostle immediately adds that God has committed unto us the Word or news of this complete reconciliation (καὶ θέμενος ἐν ἡμῖν τὸν λόγον τῆς καταλλαγῆς) in order that men may share in the finished reconciliation.

Hence the first means of grace is "the Word of Reconciliation," the Word of the Gospel. The Law of God, which is also contained in Scripture, must be excluded from the concept "means of grace," because the Law does not assure those who have transgressed it — and all men have transgressed it — of the remission of their sins, or God's grace, but on the contrary proclaims God's wrath and damnation. For this reason the Law is expressly called ἡ διακονία τῆς κατακρίσεως, "the ministration of condemnation," [6] whereas the Gospel is ἡ διακονία τῆς δικαιοσύνης, "the ministration of righteousness" (2 Cor. 3:9).[7]

Two things must here be kept in mind. The Gospel is means of grace not only in the sense that it tells of a readiness on the part of God to forgive, but in the sense that whenever we hear the Gospel, we hear God pronouncing absolution upon us, forgiving our sins. Luther: "The Gospel is in itself a general absolution, for it is a promise

---

[6] Luther: "*das Amt, das die Verdammnis predigt*"; Meyer: "the office transmitting condemnation."

[7] Luther: "*das Amt, das die Gerechtigkeit predigt*"; Meyer: "The office transmitting righteousness." That "righteousness" must here be understood juridically as acquittal or justification is evident from its antithesis to "condemnation." Meyer: "Observe the antithesis of κατάκρισις and δικαιοσύνη. The former is an *actus forensis*, hence the latter, too, is founded on imputation. This against Hofmann, *Schriftbeweis*, I, 627 f."

which all and everyone in particular should appropriate on God's command" (St. L. XXIb:1849).

Furthermore, the Gospel is such a means of grace in every form in which it reaches men, whether it be preached (Mark 16:15-16; Luke 24:47),[8a] or printed (John 20:31; 1 John 1:3-4),[8b] or expressed as a formal absolution (John 20:23),[8c] or pictured in symbols or types (John 3:14-15),[9] or pondered in the heart (Rom. 10:8),[10] and so forth. Some recent Lutheran theologians, too, have assailed the inspiration of Scripture with the strange contention that not the read, but only the preached Word is a means of grace.[11] But Scripture equates the

---

[8a] Mark 16:15-16: Κηρύξατε τὸ εὐαγγέλιον . . . ὁ πιστεύσας . . . σωθήσεται. Luke 24:47: ἔδει κηρυχθῆναι . . . ἄφεσιν ἁμαρτιῶν.

[8b] John 20:31: Ταῦτα γέγραπται, ἵνα πιστεύητε ὅτι Ἰησοῦς ἐστιν ὁ Χριστός. 1 John 1:3-4: "That which we have seen and heard declare we unto you . . . and these things write we unto you, that your joy may be full."

[8c] John 20:23: Ἄν τινων ἀφῆτε τὰς ἁμαρτίας ἀφέωνται αὐτοῖς. The term "whosesoever" indicates that Christ here has in mind the application of the Gospel to definite persons, hence the absolution pronounced on an individual.

[9] E. g., by a crucifix or some picture. Luther often recalls that in the Papacy many, when in the throes of death, were reminded of Christ's substitutionary satisfaction by means of a crucifix held before their eyes and thus died a blessed death. St. L. XIII:2575: "Thus I believe that our dear Lord preserved many of our forefathers in the gross darkness of the Papacy. In that blindness and darkness so much still remained that a crucifix was held before the eyes of the dying and that some laymen would urge them: 'Behold Jesus, who died for you on the Cross!' This induced many a dying man to turn again to Christ, though previously he, too, believed the lying wonders and was given to idolatry." Similar statements: St. L. VIII:183; XI:528; XXII:471.

[10] Here the Word of the Gospel is meant, in contrast to the Word of the Law (vv. 5-7). He who ponders a Gospel statement in his heart has in that word the divine absolution from all his sins (Vol. II, 509 ff.), and no more is necessary than that he appropriate the absolution by faith. That the Word of God, when pondered in the heart is a means of grace, the Formula of Concord, too, teaches in the words: "Through the preaching and consideration [*meditatione*] of the holy Gospel concerning the gracious forgiveness of sins in Christ a spark of faith is kindled in him, which accepts the forgiveness of sins for Christ's sake, and comforts itself with the promise of the Gospel, and thus the Holy Ghost (*who works all this*) is sent into the heart, Gal. 4:6" (*Trigl.* 903, Sol. Decl., II, 54).

[11] Thus particularly the theologians of Dorpat in the early eighties of the last century. Volck of Dorpat, for example, says in "*Die Bibel als Kanon*," p. 14: "What is it that brings the individual to faith in Christ and thus makes him a Christian? Is it perhaps his reading of the Bible? No, it is rather the Church's testimony of Christ that approaches him in this or that form. 'Faith cometh by hearing,' says Paul. If it were engendered by the reading of the Bible, the task of missions would be a simple one. They would then merely have to send Bibles to the various peoples in their native tongue, provided, of course, that they were literate." A number of Baltic pastors wrote against these Dorpat professors, e. g., F. Neerling, *Die Bibel als Heilsoffenbarung*, 1886.

read and the preached Word of God as it pertains to the conferring of grace and the working of faith. This fact is evident from the passages cited above. To the appeal to Rom. 10:17 Gerhard has given the sufficient answer: "The statement (Rom. 10:17) that 'faith cometh by hearing,' is not to be understood as excluding the written Word, but as including it, as meaning that God works faith and salvation not only through the oral Word but also through the written Word, since it is and remains one and the same Word whether it is preached and heard or written and read. On this account John significantly states of the written Gospels, and hence of the entire Scriptures of the Old and the New Testament: 'These are written that ye might believe,' John 20:31, and: 'These things write we unto you that your joy may be full,' 1 John 1:4. Accordingly, faith and spiritual joy, and consequently also salvation, can be obtained from the written Word of God, too, when it is put to use by reading and pondering it." (*Loci*, "De Scriptura," § 365.) To the opinion that "the Word of Scripture, when multiplied by printing, takes on the character in the case of ever so many thousands of people of a remote or weak action *(actio in distans)* as to space and time," [12] we reply: That is not occasioned by Scripture, but is the fault of the readers who do not recognize the Word of Scripture as the Word of God, and particularly the fault of those theological professors who spread such erroneous thoughts about Scripture among the people. He, however, who considers Scripture to be the very Word of God, as Scripture itself demands (2 Tim. 3:16; 2 Pet. 1:21;[13] 1 Cor. 14:37), does not think of a "remote action as to space and time," but as he reads his Bible, he is aware that God Himself is speaking to him, that through the Word of the Law He is convincing him of his sin and just condemnation and that through the Word of the Gospel He is assuring him of the forgiveness of his sins and salvation and inviting him to believe this Word of the Gospel. So Christ instructs us to recognize the demands of the Law from the written Law: "What is written in the Law? How readest thou?" (Luke 10:26-28; Matt. 22:35-40.) And so Christ teaches us to know Him as our Savior from the written Gospel: "Search the Scriptures, for in them ye think ye have eternal life; and they are they which testify of Me" (John 5:39), and: "Had ye believed Moses, ye would have believed Me; for he wrote of Me" (John 5:46). Just so the Formula of Concord equates the heard and

---

[12] A. v. Oettingen, *Luth. Dogmatik*, II, 2d ed., 335.
[13] The προφητεία γραφῆς is spoken of.

the read Gospel: "And by this means, and in no other way, namely, through His holy Word, when men hear it preached, or read it, and the holy Sacraments, when they are used according to His Word, God desires to call men to eternal salvation, draw them to Himself, and convert, regenerate, and sanctify them" (*Trigl.* 901, Sol. Decl., II, 50, 53).

Furthermore God has attached the promise of the forgiveness of sins to certain external acts which He has ordained (*actiones circa elementum quoddam externum et visibile occupatae*), namely, Baptism and the Lord's Supper. Scripture says expressly that Baptism takes place "for the remission of sin," or "to wash away sins" (Acts 2:38; 22:16).[14] In the Lord's Supper Christ likewise bestows His body as given (διδόμενον) and His blood as shed (ἐκχυννόμενον) "for the remission of sins" (Luke 22:19-20; Matt. 26:26-28). For this reason also Baptism and the Lord's Supper are means of grace. Because the actions with which the forgiveness of sins is connected are visible, these rites, in distinction from the mere Word of the Gospel, have been called "*verbum visibile*" and "Sacraments." [15]

2

All Means of Grace Have the Same Purpose and the Same Effect

According to Scripture, all means of grace have the same purpose and the same effect, namely, the conferring of the forgiveness of sins and the resultant engendering and strengthening of faith. We are not to imagine that each one of the three means transmits one third of the forgiveness. We saw before that Scripture ascribes the forgiveness of sins without reservation to the Word of the Gospel, to Baptism, and to the Lord's Supper. Therefore all means of grace have also the

---

[14] Meyer on Acts 22:16: "Here, too, Baptism is the means through which the sins which were committed before conversion are forgiven. See Acts 2:38; Eph. 5:26; 1 Cor. 6:11. Calvin employs restrictions in order to sever grace from the Sacraments."

[15] Apology: "But just as the Word enters the ear in order to strike our heart, so the rite itself strikes our eye in order to move the heart. The effect of the Word and of the rite is the same, as it has been well said by Augustine that a Sacrament is a *visible Word*, because the rite is received by the eye and is, as it were, a picture of the Word, signifying the same thing as the Word. Therefore the effect of both is the same." *Trigl.* 309, XIII, 5.

vis effectiva, the power to work and to strengthen faith.[16] And where there is forgiveness of sins, there is also life and salvation, with the full measure of divine gifts.

Modern theologians in particular have the idea that a different effect must be attributed to each means of grace. Baptism, they say, differs from the Word of the Gospel in working regeneration, and the Lord's Supper differs from both Word and Baptism by a special physical effect, for example, the implanting of the resurrection body.[17]

---

[16] Augsb. Conf., Art. V, XIII.

[17] R. E., 2d ed., XIII, 298 f. Luthardt reviews briefly the recent attempts to find a different purpose for Baptism and for the Lord's Supper (*Dcgmatik,* 11th ed., pp. 373, 386 f.; cp. Nitzsch-Stephan, *Ev. Dogmatik,* p. 646 ff.). In his edition of Baier's *Compendium* (III, 526 f.) Walther adduces a longer quotation from Georg Koenig (d. 1654) which shows that also the old Lutheran theologians gave considerable thought to the question whether a physical effect is to be ascribed to the Lord's Supper. Koenig denies this and thereby opposes not only men like Weigel, but also a few *"ex nostratibus"* (of our own men). Koenig writes in *Casus consc.,* p. 484 ff., 494 ff.: "May one correctly hold that the reception of Communion effects an essential union of Christ with us? We here do not desire to contend with anyone but Weigel, who believes that from Communion, that is, from the use of the Lord's Supper, in which with the bread the body of Christ and with the chalice His blood is distributed, there follows an essential union of our body and blood with Christ's body and blood. Be pleased to hear his very words. . . . Most clearly he sets forth his meaning in Part I of his postil, p. 214: 'Christ,' he says, 'gives us the bread from heaven not only in faith, spiritually, without bread and wine, but also in the Supper with bread and wine; not that the visible bread and wine is Christ's body and blood perceptibly, but in it He is given to us. For the bread from heaven is His Word, and He is the Word, and the Word is in the bread, and this invisible Bread from heaven, or the Word, becomes flesh and blood in us and is joined to our flesh and blood. On this account we are, when we receive this memorial food, united with Christ's crucified body and are bodily united with Him.' . . . This assertion of Weigel is of such a nature that we cannot assent to it with a good conscience for the following reasons: 1. It has no foundation at all in Scripture. . . . For where did Christ say: 'Take and drink so that My body and blood may be transformed into a common substance with you'? Where did He say: 'Take, eat and drink; this, when it is eaten and swallowed, works in you a common essence with Me'? Where did He say: 'Eat; this is the invisible Bread from heaven which becomes flesh and blood in you and is closely united with your flesh and blood'? Where did He say: 'Eat, in order to be made one in substance with My crucified body'? . . . . 2. The Sacrament confers upon us what is promised in the Word. For the Sacraments are seals of the Word; but seals do not confirm more than the writing to which they are appended contains. But nowhere is it promised to us in the words of Scripture that either in Communion or outside it Christ should be essentially united with us. . . . 3. If the communicants are united essentially with Christ by the mere [*nudo*] use of the Supper of our Lord, also the unbelieving should be acknowledged participants in this union, because they, too, use the Lord's Supper, and this uncorrupted. For what he who receives the Sacrament believes, or with what sort of faith he is imbued, makes no difference when we deal with the integrity and sanctity of

But this is taught without Scripture basis. As surely as Baptism is a means of regeneration (λουτρὸν παλιγγενεσίας καὶ ἀνακαινώσεως πνεύματος ἁγίου, Titus 3:5), so surely the Word of the Gospel works regeneration (ἀναγεγεννημένοι . . . διὰ λόγου ζῶντος θεοῦ, 1 Pet. 1:23).

---

the Sacrament. Of course, it makes a great difference in regard to the way of salvation, but as to the nature of the Sacrament it makes no difference. For it can happen that a man has the Sacrament uncorrupted, but has a perverted faith, says Augustine 1, 3, *contra Donat.*, c. 14; see him 1, 4, c. 24. But the afore-mentioned conclusion is absurd. For in this manner would be united the purest and the most impure essence, the Son of God and the child of the devil, Christ and Belial, contrary to the manifest Scriptures, 2 Cor. 6:15. . . . You say: 'Then, beside the spiritual, there is not to be placed a certain sacramental union between Christ and the believers, flowing from participation in the body and blood of Christ? Are there not such among us, too, who believe that there is such a sacramental union which flows from the power and efficacy of the Communion and is equally common to both the worthy and the unworthy'? . . . I judge that this cannot be asserted or defended without injury to the truth: I. Because in this manner the term 'union' is plainly misused. Now the *unio sacramentalis*, simply spoken of so far, is that which takes place between the earthly and the heavenly element; from this then are to be deduced the sacramental propositions, as the personal from the personal union. Now, however, a new sacramental union is added. But of it Scripture is entirely unaware; nor does it furnish any foundation for it. Paul in 1 Cor. 10:16-17 indeed mentions an at least twofold communion which occurs by virtue of the Eucharist: 1. the sacramental, per-taining to the Eucharistic symbols united with the heavenly element; 2. the mystical, which pertains to the mystical body of Christ and its members. Since, however, hypocrites are not members of that mystical body, except by sham, it is not to be believed that any union, properly so called and derived from the Eucharist, pertains to them or occurs between them and Christ, whether through the one usually called sacramental or otherwise. II. This other sacramental union, if it can trace its origin to anything, occurs only through the eating of the body and drinking of the blood. But it is one thing that the godless eat Christ's body and drink Christ's blood, and another that they are mystically united with Christ by virtue of the Sacrament. The former we necessarily grant because of the true sacramental union, which takes place between the earthly and the heavenly element and results from the authority of the Institutor, not from the condition of the eater. The latter, on the contrary, we necessarily reject because of the absence of the condition required of him who eats and drinks, namely, faith. He, therefore, who has no faith can by no means experience the salutary effect of the Sacrament, the circle of which must also include union with Christ. Unless this is conceded, any salutary effect attributed to the Sacrament would have to be *ex opere operato sine bono motu utentis.* But this sentence of the old Scholastics is for the most part given up also by the modern Jesuits. III. A comparison made with the Baptism of adults also opposes the alleged sacramental union. What spiritual effect, pray, has Baptism that is common to believers and hypocrites? None evidently as regards salvation; merely external communion with the Church because both by Baptism were received into the periphery [*pomoeria*] of the Church. The same reasoning applies here, and no other. We must indeed admit that the fathers at times have spoken a trifle strongly regarding the effect of the Sacrament . . . for many statements have been furnished which can easily be twisted in favor of those hypocrites, but such utterances should be read *cum grano salis.*"

And as certainly as Christ gives His true body and blood, and not mere symbols of His body and blood, in the Lord's Supper, so sure it is also that He names as purpose of this wonderful gift not a special physical effect, but merely the assurance and attestation that God is graciously disposed toward those who eat and drink, because of the body given and the blood shed by Christ. That is the only possible meaning of the words: "This is My body, which is given for you; this do in remembrance of Me" (Luke 22:19)[18] and: "This is My blood of the new testament, which is shed for many for the remission of sins" (Matt. 26:28).[19]

We find the same teaching in our Lutheran Symbols. They stress emphatically that the Sacraments have no other purpose than the Word of the Gospel, namely, the attestation and conferring of the forgiveness of sins and the engendering and strengthening of faith in this forgiveness. Listen to the Apology: "Therefore Baptism, the Lord's Supper, and Absolution, which is the sacrament of Repentance, are truly Sacraments. For these rites have God's command and the promise of grace, which is peculiar to the New Testament. For when we are baptized, when we eat the Lord's body, when we are absolved, our hearts must be firmly assured that God truly forgives us for Christ's sake. And God, at the same time, by the word and by the rite, moves hearts to believe and conceive faith, just as Paul says, Rom. 10:17: 'Faith cometh by hearing.' But just as the Word enters the ear in order to strike our heart, so the rite itself strikes the eye, in order to move the heart. The effect of the Word and of the rite is the same, as has been well said by Augustine that a Sacrament is a visible Word, because the rite is received by the eye and is, as it were, a picture of the Word, signifying the same things as the Word.

---

[18] Luther: "I hope it is not necessary to say much as to what the remembrance of Christ might be. In other places we have often and amply explained this term. It is not such a contemplation of the suffering as some practice, hoping by such a good work to render service to God and to obtain grace by occupying themselves in sorrowing over the bitter sufferings of Christ, etc. The remembrance of Christ rather consists in teaching and believing the power and fruit of His suffering; accordingly, that our works and merit are worthless, that the free will is dead and lost, that, on the contrary, we are absolved from our sin and become righteous solely through Christ's suffering and death; hence that the remembrance consists in teaching or recalling the grace of God in Christ and not in a work done by us." (St. L. X, 2188.)

[19] Luther: "Therefore this Luther has correctly taught that he who has an evil conscience because of sin should receive the Sacrament and get consolation, not from the bread and wine, not from the body and blood of Christ, but from the Word which in the Sacrament offers, presents, and gives to me Christ's body and blood as given and shed for me" (St. L. XX:275).

Therefore the effect of both is the same." (*Trigl.* 309, XIII, 4 f.) Just so the Augsburg Confession declares that the purpose of the Sacraments is "to be signs and testimonies of the will of God toward us, instituted to awaken and confirm faith in those who use them" (*Trigl.* 49, XIII). This terminology of the Augsburg Confession, that the Sacraments are "signs and testimonies of the [scil., gracious] will of God toward us" and therefore awaken and strengthen faith, rests on the universal objective reconciliation and deserves to be called classic.

The objection of modern theologians that the Sacraments are diminished in value if the conferring and confirming of the forgiveness of sins is taught as their one purpose is out of place entirely. For one thing, determining the purpose of the Sacraments is God's business, who instituted them, and it is decidedly improper for men to presume to improve on the divinely determined purpose. Moreover, is not the forgiveness of sins the real and chief good (*Hauptgut*), "the new testament," so that he who has remission of sins forfeits nothing? Scripture presents all other spiritual gifts and activities as resulting from the forgiveness of sins: the state of grace, the indwelling of the Holy Spirit, the *unio mystica,* sanctification, the love of God and the neighbor, membership in the Christian Church and all privileges which this includes.[20] If, therefore, we content ourselves with the purpose of the Sacraments as God determined it, namely, that they are means of transmitting the forgiveness of sins and for this reason also means of creating and strengthening faith, the reception of all remaining goods and gifts is guaranteed us. Specifically, the resurrection of the body on the Last Day is then also provided for. The notion that the resurrection body is implanted through the receiving of Christ's body and blood in the Lord's Supper is superfluous. The divine promise guarantees the resurrection of the body to all who believe that they have the forgiveness of their sins in Christ,[21] even if, due to certain circumstances, they have not eaten and drunk Christ's body and blood in the Sacrament, as, for instance, in the case of believing children in the Lutheran Church and of believers in Christ in the Reformed bodies.

Some theologians who teach a physical bestowal of the resurrection body on the communicants claim Luther as their champion. Luther does indeed teach that the hope of the resurrection of the body is strengthened by partaking of the Lord's Supper. But he does not

---

[20] See the Survey of Soteriology, Vol. II, 406 ff.
[21] See Luther, St. L. XVII:2212.

teach it as a physical result in the body of Christians because of their bodily eating, but as the effect of the spiritual eating which a Christian combines with the bodily eating, of his faith in the word of absolution "Given and shed for you for the remission of sins." The Reformer writes (St. L. XX:831): "Of course, nobody can force the words down his throat into his stomach, but through his ears he must take them to heart. But what is it that he takes to heart through these words? Nothing else than what the words say: 'the body given for us.' This is the spiritual eating. And we have added that he who receives the Sacrament orally without these words or without this spiritual eating not only has no benefit from his eating, but even experiences harm, as St. Paul says 1 Cor. 11:27: 'Whosoever shall eat this bread unworthily shall be guilty of the body of the Lord.' Hence there was no reason for you to instruct us that bodily eating does not profit." To these words Luther then adds the comment that a Christian may entertain the hope that Christ on the Last Day will raise the body which He deigned to honor here on earth by a union with His body through the oral eating in the Lord's Supper. "The mouth, which eats Christ's flesh bodily, does of course not know what it is eating or what the heart is eating; nor would it have any benefit from it because it cannot grasp or perceive what the words say. But the heart is well aware of what the mouth is eating. For it understands the words and eats spiritually what the mouth eats bodily. Since, however, the mouth is a member belonging to the heart, it [the mouth and accordingly the whole body] must in the end live eternally by reason of the heart which receives eternal life through the Word, because the mouth in a bodily manner eats the same eternal food which its heart eats spiritually."

Moreover, ascribing a physical effect to the Sacraments is by no means a harmless speculation. Thereby we fall into the Romanist error of an operation of the Sacraments *ex opere operato sine bono motu utentis*, by the mere performance of the act without participation of the heart, an imparting of grace without faith as the receiving hand of man. Saving grace is then no longer conceived of as the forgiveness of sins, or the *favor Dei propter Christum*, but as the infusion of a grace substance. The remission of sins and faith, or, in other words, justification by faith, is thereby set aside and the foundation of Christianity impaired.

For this reason our Lutheran Confessions so stress the *idem effectus* of the Word and the Sacraments, emphasizing that the offer of the favor of God and the engendering and strengthening of faith must be maintained. The Confessions add the following critical remarks: "Here we condemn the whole crowd of scholastic doctors, who teach that the Sacraments confer grace *ex opere operato* (through the act performed), without a good disposition on the part of the one using them, provided he does not place a hindrance *(obicem)* in the way. This is absolutely a Jewish opinion, to hold that we are justified by a ceremony, without a good disposition of the heart, i. e., without faith. And yet this impious and pernicious opinion is taught with great authority throughout the entire realm of the Pope. Paul contradicts this and denies, Rom. 4:9, that Abraham was justified by circumcision, but asserts that circumcision was a sign presented for exercising faith. Thus we teach that in the use of the Sacraments faith ought to be added, which should believe these promises, and receive the promised things, there offered in the Sacraments. . . . The promise is useless unless it is received by faith. . . . And here we speak of special faith which believes the present promise, not only that which in general believes *[fides generalis]* that God exists, but which believes that the remission of sins is offered. This use of the Sacrament consoles godly and alarmed minds. Moreover, no one can express in words what abuses in the Church this fanatical opinion concerning the *opus operatum,* without a good disposition on the part of the one using the Sacraments, has produced. Hence the infinite profanation of the Masses. . . . Yea, Augustine says the contrary, that the faith of the Sacrament, and not the Sacrament, justifies." (*Trigl.* 313, Apol., XIII, 18 ff.)

Also the objection that there is no need of offering and confirming to Christians one and the same forgiveness of sins in several ways betrays an astonishing ignorance. Both Scripture and experience teach that men who feel the weight of their sins find nothing harder to believe than the forgiveness of their sins. Hence repetition of the assurance of the forgiveness of sins in various ways through the means of grace meets a practical need of Christians. This need Luther, too, pointed out in the Smalcald Articles: "The Gospel not merely in one way gives us counsel and aid against sin; for God is superabundantly rich [and liberal] in His grace [and goodness]. First, through the spoken Word by which the forgiveness of sins is preached in the whole world; which is the peculiar office of the Gospel. Secondly, through Baptism. Thirdly, through the holy Sacrament of the Altar. Fourthly, through the power of the keys, and also through the mutual conversation and consolation of brethren, Matt. 18:20: 'Where two or three are gathered together,' etc." (*Trigl.* 491, Part III, Art. IV.)

3

The Number of Sacraments

Arguing about the number of sacraments is pointless until agreement is reached on the definition of a sacrament. The action of the Council of Trent in anathematizing all who teach "more or less than seven" sacraments is both wicked and foolish.[22] How many sacraments we enumerate depends on the definition adopted. If we describe a sacrament as an act ordained by God to which He has attached the promise of the forgiveness of sin and for which He has prescribed a visible element, then there are but two Sacraments, Baptism and the Lord's Supper.

Omitting the visible element in its definition, the Apology counts absolution, too, a sacrament: *"Ritus, qui habent mandatum Dei, et quibus addita est promissio gratiae"* (*Trigl.* 309, XIII, 4). Absolution conforms to that description. But elsewhere the Apology, employing a stricter definition, names but two Sacraments, Baptism and the Lord's Supper.[23]

The Roman Catholic Church and the Eastern Catholic Church enumerate seven sacraments, adding to Baptism and the Lord's Supper

---

[22] *Trid.*, Sess. VII, can. 1. The Apology speaks in a sensible Christian manner of the number of the sacraments: "For no prudent man will strive greatly concerning the number or the term, if only those objects still be retained which have God's command and promises" (*Trigl.* 313, XIII, 17). But just this — the abolition of the divine Word and command and the establishment of its own authority — is the aim of Rome in decreeing that there must be seven sacraments, as will be demonstrated. On the use of the term *sacrament* in *various* meanings in the State and in the Church see Gerhard, *Loci,* "De Sacramentis," § 3 ff.; Baier-Walther, III, 402. The study of the etymology and of the various meanings in which the term *sacrament* has been used among Gentiles and Christians contributes nothing, of course, toward answering the question whether, and in what respect, Baptism and the Lord's Supper are means of grace. Since *sacrament* is not a Biblical, but an ecclesiastical term *(vox ecclesiastica),* we use it in Christian liberty to designate such acts as have God's command, divinely appointed visible elements, and the promise of the remission of sins. In this sense we call only Baptism and the Lord's Supper Sacraments of the New Testament. Gerhard, *Loci,* "De sacramentis," § 5: "Though the term *'sacramentum'* occurs in the Latin version of the Bible, it is there not used properly and specifically of those external and visible signs of invisible grace of which we are treating here, but was first transferred to these by the ecclesiastical writers." On the variant use of the term see Luthardt, *Dogmatik,* 11th ed., p. 387 ff. Cf. Hauck, R. E., 2d ed., XIII, 264 ff.; Kattenbusch, R. E., 3d ed., XVII, 349 ff.; Nitzsch-Stephan, *Ev. Dogmatik,* p. 642 ff.

[23] Luther, Large Cat., *Trigl.* 732, De Baptismo, 1.

Confirmation, Penance, Extreme Unction, Order, Matrimony. What
these church bodies mean by Confirmation,[24] Penance,[25] Extreme
Unction,[26] and Ordination of Priests [27] lacks the *mandatum Dei.*
Matrimony, it is true, is of divine institution, but its promise is not the
forgiveness of sins, but the propagation of the human race.[28]

4

False Teachings on the Means of Grace

We reiterate: The teaching of church bodies and theologians on
the means of grace always corresponds to their teaching on Christ's
work of reconciliation. If they mutilate the Scripture doctrine of the
perfect reconciliation of all men by the substitutionary satisfaction

---

[24] *Trid.,* Sess. VII, *"De confirm.,"* can. 1-2. On the puerile notion of a
spiritual affinity "contracted between the person baptizing and the baptized"
(prohibiting their marriage) see Sess. XXIV, *"De reform. matrimonii,"* cap. 2.
On the *character indelebilis,* Sess. XXIII, *"De sacramento ordinis,"* cap. 4. On
confirmation as a praiseworthy church custom, but not a divine ordinance see
Walther, *Pastorale,* p. 261 ff. (Fritz, *Pastoral Theology,* p. 127).

[25] By *Penance* the Papists do not mean the repentance commanded in
Scripture, consisting of contrition and faith, but a threefold work of men,
embracing the *contritio cordis* (a man-made meritorious sorrow), the *confessio
oris* ("confessing secretly to a priest alone"), and the *satisfactio operis* (works of
penance enjoined by the priest). On this Antichristian abomination, the Roman
Penance, cp. Vol. II, 470, 503; Vol. III, 192.

[26] *Trid.,* Sess. XIV, *"De sacr. extr. unct.";* *Smets,* p. 75 f. The anointing with
oil of which Mark 6:13 speaks was a miraculous gift for healing physical sick-
nesses. James 5:14 refers to the common custom of anointing the sick to refresh
and strengthen the body and ascribes the healing not to the anointing, but to
the prayer of faith.

[27] *Trid.,* Sess. XXIII, *"De sacr. ordinis."* The "sacred ordination" is asserted
to be a rite which only the bishops may perform, which imprints an indelible
character and confers the power to sacrifice the body and blood of Christ. —
It is Christian teaching that God has commanded the calling of men apt to teach
into the public ministry which Christ instituted. But the public ordination of
these men according to a formal ritual is no more than an ecclesiastical arrangement which is based on the example of the Apostles. Apology: "The adversaries
understand *priesthood* not of the ministry of the Word and administering the
Sacraments to others, but they understand it as referring to sacrifice. . . .
But if ordination be understood as applying to the ministry of the Word, we are
not unwilling to call ordination a sacrament. For the ministry of the Word has
God's command and glorious promises." (*Trigl.* 311, XIII, 7—13.)

[28] Apology: "But if marriage will have the name of sacrament for the
reason that it has God's command, other states or offices also, which have God's
command, may be called sacraments, as for example, the magistracy" (*Trigl.*
311, XIII, 115).

of Christ, they cannot correctly present the Scripture doctrine of the means of grace. These cease to be *media iustificationis* and become no more than means of stimulating such changes of mind and conduct as would make man completely, or at least decisively, his own savior.

Romanism on the Means of Grace

The Roman Church still teaches that Christ has merited grace for men; the teaching that man is justified and saved "without the grace of God through Jesus Christ" is expressly condemned (*Trid.*, Sess. VI, can. 1—3, 10, 22). She also anathematizes Calvinism with its teaching that the grace of God in Christ is limited to a part of mankind (*Trid.*, Sess. VI, can. 17). But Rome would have us believe that the grace won by Christ moves God to infuse into man so much grace (*gratia infusa*), that is, sanctification and good works — and this, let it be noted, with man's constant *co-operation* (Trid., Sess. VI, can. 4) — that he is enabled truly to merit (*vere mereri, Trid.*, Sess. VI, can. 32) justification and salvation, either *de congruo* (according to fairness or liberality) or *de condigno* (by actual merit). According to Rome, Christ has merited only enough grace to enable men to merit salvation for themselves.

Therefore the *media gratiae* in the papistic sense are not means through which God offers to faith the complete forgiveness of sins and the salvation merited by Christ, and through that offer also works faith in man or strengthens the faith already present, but they are means to incite and aid him to such virtuous endeavors, under Roman direction, as can gradually and in constantly increasing measure (*Trid.*, Sess. VI, cap. 16, can. 32) win God's grace for him.

Rome itself points out that these virtuous efforts of men, except in the case of a small elite, remain piecemeal; yet it makes the forgiveness of sins depend on them. By such teaching the means of grace are debased to means of keeping man in uncertainty as to the possession of God's favor. The Council of Trent calls it a part of true piety that a Christian remain in doubt whether or not he has obtained the grace of God, unless he has received a special revelation from God (Sess. VI, c. 9, and can. 13). But since doubt is the opposite of faith and deprives man of the forgiveness of sins, the Papacy is actually perverting the means of grace into means effectually barring man's access to the grace and salvation provided by Christ.

Instead, men are chained to the ordinances of the Papacy, which represents itself with its devices as the one institution dispensing grace. The scandalous crusades, pilgrimages, indulgences, monasticism, and the like, were devised, and are still serving, to keep men away from the grace provided by Christ and now bestowed through the means of grace. For the same purpose Rome has multiplied the number of sacraments. By means of its many sacraments, not all of which are indeed of equal worth, but which are nevertheless "necessary unto salvation" (*Trid.*, Sess. VII, "Of Sacr. in General," can. 3–4), the Papacy in many ways places the forgiveness of sins which Christ has purchased for men securely under lock and key; for when it speaks of saving grace, as Winer correctly notes, it does not mean the grace of God's forgiveness, which man appropriates by faith and of which he thus becomes certain, but it has in mind the infusion of good qualities, on which man — as even Rome tells him — dare not depend after all.[29]

That the Papacy, when it speaks of grace which the Sacraments confer, is thinking of the infusion of a grace substance is apparent from its assertion "that grace is conferred through the act performed [*ex opere operato*]," without "faith in the divine promise." All conferring of grace by the Sacraments *sine bono motu utentis,* as claimed by Romanists, is of course hallucination; in any case not a part of the Christian religion, because Scripture teaches all Christian virtues as the result and effect of the faith which appropriates the forgiveness of sins gained only by the merit of Christ.

Calvinism on the Means of Grace

Because saving grace is particular, according to the teaching of the Calvinists, there are no means of grace for that part of mankind to which the grace of God and the merit of Christ do not extend. On the contrary, for these people the means of grace are intended as means of condemnation. Calvin teaches expressly: "For there is a universal call, through which, by the external preaching of the Word, God invites all, indiscriminately, to come to Him, even those for whom He intends it as a savor of death and an occasion of heavier con-

---

[29] Winer, *Kompar. Darstellung,* 3d ed., p. 117: "Though the Sacraments are regarded as means of grace by both the Roman and the Evangelical Church, still the two Churches differ in their definition of the grace which the Sacraments transmit. The Evangelical Church teaches that the grace which consists in the forgiveness of sins is imparted through the Sacraments. At the same time she designates as their effect the engendering and strengthening of faith." (That this is true only of the Lutheran, and not of the Reformed Church, will presently become evident.) "The Roman Church, on the contrary, regards all Sacraments as canals conveying the purifying and sanctifying grace [i. e., the *gratia infusa*] in its rich variety."

demnation" (*Inst.* III, 24, 8). In spite of this, Calvin speaks of means
of grace in relation to the reprobate, declaring that they merit double
condemnation because they despise the grace offered also to them.
This is one of the self-contradictions of which Calvinistic theology
becomes guilty in its teaching regarding the appropriation or rejection
of salvation.[30] With their teaching Calvinists cannot consistently speak
of a contempt of grace by the reprobate because they hold that no
saving grace is provided for these unfortunates. Hence there would
be no grace which could be despised by them. This manifest self-
contradiction has been called to the attention of the Calvinists in times
past and present.[31] To speak of means of grace in connection with
the *reprobi* and *impii* and to charge them with contempt of the grace
of God is obviously a concession to the language of Scripture and
the Christian Church that is indefensible as long as men cling to
the teaching of a particular grace.

But neither do the Calvinists have means of grace for the elect.
Believers are expressly directed by Calvin not to ascertain their
predestination from the external Word, that is, from the universal call
(*universalis vocatio*) which occurs through the outward Word (*per
externam praedicationem*), but from the special call (*specialis vocatio*),
which consists in an inner illumination by the Holy Spirit. And that
is entirely consistent from Calvin's standpoint. It is impossible for
believers to know their election from the external Word of the Gospel
because through that Word, according to Calvin's view, God invites
not only the elect, but also "those to whom He intends it as a savor
of death and an occasion of heavier condemnation." So the *pii* and
electi have no choice but to relinquish the external Word of the
Gospel, since its invitation may be meant unto damnation instead of

---

30 For proofs see Vol. II, 24 ff.

31 For instance, by Gerhard, *"De elect.,"* § 68 (quoted Vol. II, 47, footnote 88). Steitz-Hauck, R. E., 2d ed., XIII, 294: "According to Calvin's system,
the elect, or predestinated, are the believers. Only these experience (*Inst.* III,
24, 15 and especially *Consens. Tigur.,* c. 16) the internal power of the Spirit and
receive, besides the signs, also the *res* or *virtus sacramenti.* For this reason it is
actually nothing but vacuous talk when he says that the promise is offered also
to the disbelieving; in fact, it sounds like irony when he addresses them: 'You
need merely in faith take hold of the word that is placed into the sign, in order
to have with the sign also the substance [the effect].'" When Steitz-Hauck
elsewhere opine that Calvin teaches an "objectivity of the means of grace" because
his determinism leaves no place at all for "subjectivity," it should be recalled
that by "objectivity" of the means of grace we usually mean this, that by the
means of grace God offers the remission of sins without distinction to all who use
them and is active in all for the purpose of working or strengthening faith.

salvation, and to place their trust in the special call or the inner illumination of the Spirit *(interior Spiritus illuminatio)*.

But according to the teaching of Calvinism this "inner illumination" is not brought about through the means of grace; it is worked immediately by the Holy Ghost. Modern Reformed, too, teach this very emphatically. Hodge, for example, says: "In the work of regeneration all second causes are excluded. . . . Nothing intervenes between the volition of the Spirit and the regeneration of the soul. . . . The infusion of a new life into the soul is the immediate work of the Spirit. . . . The truth (in the case of adults) [that is, the setting forth of the truth of the Gospel through the external Word] attends the work of regeneration, but is not the means by which it is effected." *(Syst. Theol.* II, 634 f.)

Consistent Calvinism therefore has no means of grace for the elect either, no means that offer the gracious will of God to man, and for that reason also no means that work saving faith and effect a regeneration. And how could faith, and with it regeneration to spiritual life, be effected by a Word that is, according to the Calvinist, equivocal in the extreme, perhaps intended by God to transmit wrath instead of grace? One cannot so gravely mutilate divine revelation, as by the denial of universal grace, and yet retain the means of grace as instituted by God. Denial of the *gratia universalis* nullifies the means of grace. The existence of means of grace, which are "signs and testimonies" *(signa et testimonia)* of the gracious will of God toward us, through which the Holy Ghost also awakens and strengthens faith, necessarily presupposes that all men without a single exception are reconciled to God through the vicarious satisfaction of Christ. When the Calvinists, therefore, follow us in calling the Word and the Sacraments "signs, symbols, seals" *(signa, symbola, tesserae, sigilla)* of the grace of God, they are simply accommodating themselves to the usage of Scripture and their Christian environment.[32] If they actually maintain the *gratia particularis*, they lack all justification for the use of these terms, because then the Word and the Sacraments may be signs

---

[32] *Conf. Helvet.* II, c. 19: "The Sacraments are mystical symbols. Through them [God] seals His promises and externally represents what He Himself works internally in us and sets them, so to say, before our eyes to contemplate and thus strengthens and augments our faith, worked in our hearts by the Spirit of God. Through them He finally separates us from all other peoples and religions and consecrates and obligates us solely to Himself and signifies what He requires of us." — *Conf. Belgica,* Art. 33: "The Sacraments are visible signs and symbols of internal and invisible things. Through them, as through means, God Himself operates in us by the power of the Holy Spirit."

of wrath as truly as signs of grace. Ambiguous signs are no signs at all, for they fail to direct properly. Nor can the Word and the Sacraments be signs of the *interior illuminatio* of the Holy Spirit, because He is alleged to work this inner illumination not by external means, but immediately.

Moreover, when universal grace is denied and in consequence faith is said to be engendered by an immediate operation of the Spirit, also the Scriptural concepts of saving faith and of saving grace are lost. A faith that is not created by the outward Word of the Gospel is not the faith of Holy Writ. The faith of which Scripture speaks always begins and continues only vis-à-vis its correlative, the Word of the Gospel (Rom. 10:14; Mark 1:15; 16:15-16). A faith that is torn from its correlative, the Gospel, and is supposed to be the product of an immediate exertion of divine omnipotence, is only a feeling infused into man. And saving grace no longer is the gracious disposition of God in Christ (*favor Dei propter Christum*), but becomes *gratia infusa,* a good quality implanted in the heart.

Hence, while to all appearances they are heading in different directions, Romanists and Calvinists concur in the *gratia infusa.* Rome conceives of saving grace as a current which flows into man by way of the many Papistic means of grace if man "does not place an obstacle in its way" *(obicem non ponit),* while Calvinism thinks of saving grace as a current which, like lightning, strikes immediately and hence irresistibly *(gratia irresistibilis).* Both take saving grace *(gratia salvifica)* to mean, not the mercy or favor of God in Christ, but a good quality implanted in the heart of man. At the outset Calvinists often give a perfectly correct definition of saving grace, namely, God's gracious disposition in Christ or the forgiveness of sins (see Vol. II, 12, and footnote 21); but by their denial of universal grace, and the resultant denial of the appropriation of grace through the Word of the Gospel and the Sacraments, they are carried into the Roman current of "infused grace" as the basis for the remission of sins.

For this reason they have the same difficulty with their "grace" as do the Romanists. In practice the *gratia infusa,* or the "inner illumination," proves to be imperfect and fluctuating. Recall the case of Oliver Cromwell, adduced above (p. 90). Because of its imperfection, the infused grace does not put an aroused conscience at rest, but perturbs it. In this dilemma the theory of the inamissibility of faith was added to the Calvinistic system. But this again severs faith in the gracious disposition of God from the means of grace and founds faith on faith, that is, on its presumed or actual earlier existence.

It is, therefore, a fact that consistent Calvinism with its denial of the universal objective reconciliation has no room for the Scripture doctrine of the means of grace.

But here, fortunately, an inconsistency appears in the *practice* of the Calvinists inasmuch as they found their faith, in spite of Calvin's remonstrance, on the universal call and thus on the external Word, which assures all men of God's grace. This has been pointed out before. Schneckenburger, too, has called attention to the fact that, especially in counseling persons who fear that they have committed the sin against the Holy Ghost, the practice of the Reformed, to be effectual, must take its stand on Lutheran ground. (*Vergleich. Darstellung* I, 260 ff.)

The Synergists on the Means of Grace

The denial of the *gratia universalis* by the Calvinists abolishes the Biblical doctrine of the means of grace. The same thing happens through the denial of the *sola gratia* by the synergists, who teach that faith in the Gospel, or conversion to God, is not entirely God's gracious work, but depends also on the right conduct of man. All who attribute to man a co-operation in his conversion, or his coming to faith, by teaching that faith is brought about through man's "free choice, self-determination, self-decision, correct conduct, omission of willful resistance, neutral attitude," etc., do not conceive of the means of grace as instruments through which God offers to man the grace which Christ merited, or the forgiveness of sin, and calls forth faith in man without his assistance. Rather, these synergists regard them as means by which man is stimulated (*excitatur*) to contribute something on his part toward his salvation, such as his personal choice or determination, his right conduct, his neutral attitude, his right use of "the freedom left him by grace," his "own decisive choice," his exercise of his "free moral agency," etc. In short, for synergists of all shades the means of grace are not merely channels of the grace merited by Christ's *satisfactio vicaria*, but generators of the human activities, variously named, by which man really can and should come to possess God's grace.

We find both Reformed and Lutheran synergists actually saying that the means of grace are not sufficient to obtain grace and salvation. The Arminians, who are typical of the Reformed synergists, expressly call the grace offered and operating in the means of grace a "partial power" (*vis partialis*) which cannot be effective without the co-operation of the free will of man (*non posse exire [vim gratiae] in actum sine co-operatione liberae voluntatis humanae ac proinde ut effectum habeat pendere a libera voluntate).*[33] The same thing was taught by Melanchthon in his later years and by his followers. Not content with two causes of conversion, namely, the Word of the Gospel and the Holy Ghost, that is, with the means of grace, they added as a third cause "man's assenting, non-resisting will." (*Loci,* ed. Detzer, I. 72 ff.) American synergists have expressed their conviction that the grace offered and operative in the means of grace is not sufficient for conversion and salvation in these words: "According to the revealed order of salvation the actual final result of the means of grace depends not only on the sufficiency and efficacy of the means themselves, but also upon the conduct of man in regard to the necessary condition of passiveness and submissiveness under the Gospel-call" (*Luth. Standard,* February 28, 1891). Thus synergism actually degrades the means of grace, the very nature of which is that they offer God's grace gratis, χωρὶς ἔργων νόμου, and thus create and strengthen faith, into mere means to spur man to furnish the thing that will allegedly induce God to grant forgiveness of sins to man.

Of course, not all synergists will go as far as Luthardt (*Dogmatik,* 11th ed., p. 284) who expressly calls faith the work of man. Not all will speak with Seeberg (R. E., 3d ed., II, 544) of a "free choice" (*"persoenliche Selbstsetzung"*) or with Keyser (*Election and Conversion,* p. 67) of an exercise of the "free moral agency" to bring man under the grace of God. Among synergists the most popular way of stating the co-operation of man is the formulation that the obtaining of God's grace depends on the "dissimilar," or "right" conduct of the individual. To be effective the means of grace must be supplemented by merely "the necessary condition of passiveness and submissiveness" on the part of man. But whatever way they may choose, the meaning always is that the grace which is offered and operating in the means of grace is not adequate in itself actually to endow man with the grace of God. "If man's conversion were to depend in no sense on anything else than grace and thus . . . on the *means of grace,* all men would be converted and saved" (*Kirchenzeitung,* April 18, 1891).

The denial of the *sola gratia* has an effect similar to the denial of the *gratia universalis.* So grave an alteration of the Biblical doctrine as the denial of the *sola gratia* cannot be perpetrated without the loss of the means of grace ordained by God. If the *sola gratia*

---

[33] *Apol. Conf. Remonstr.,* p. 162; Winer, *Kompar. Darstellung,* 3d ed., p. 81 f.

disappears, Scripture's means of grace disappear too. Hence it is only an accommodation to the language of the Church when proponents of synergism still speak of means of grace.

As to their nature we must maintain: The means of grace which God ordained are not Law, but Gospel, pure, unconditional Gospel, which calls for no good work or good quality in man. Therefore they do not demand of man free choice, self-determination, neutral attitude, personal decision for or against grace, right conduct, or any other human deed, but simply faith. Luther: "*Evangel* is Greek and means glad tidings, for it brings us the saving doctrine of life by God's promise and offers us grace and forgiveness of sins. Therefore its correlative is not performance, for it is not Law, but solely faith, for it is absolutely nothing more than promise and proffer of divine grace. Now, he who believes the Gospel receives the grace and the Holy Spirit." (St. L. XI:84.) And this faith, which is simply the receiving hand (*medium* ληπτικόν) and the correlative of the Gospel, is engendered by the Holy Ghost through the Gospel itself, without man's assistance, "in them that hear the Gospel" (*Trigl.* 45, Augsb. Conf., V); for "faith cometh by hearing" (Rom. 10:17).

The synergistic concept of the means of grace is also very dangerous. A "Gospel" conditioned upon a man's personal decision, right conduct, self-determination for or against grace, is no glad tidings, no true Gospel, and hence does not create the Christian faith "which builds on grace alone." Instead it fosters a reliance on one's own power and ability which effectually shuts out the grace that is offered in, and operates through, the means of grace. As long as man labors under the delusion that he can or must do something to obtain grace, he will not obtain grace (Luther, *Opp. v. a.,* VII, 154). Faith in God's grace is not a thing a person carefully considers before closing the deal, carefully weighing the pros and cons, and deciding his attitude toward grace accordingly. But faith in God's grace is worked by the Holy Ghost "where and when it pleases God in them that hear the Gospel" (*Trigl.* 45, Augsb. Conf., V), and this in the midst of "*terrores conscientiae*," which consume all thoughts of "personal choice," "free moral agency," "dissimilar conduct," etc., as fire does straw (*Trigl.* 125, Apol., IV, 20).

In our study of the doctrine of conversion (Vol. II, 454 f., 457 f.) we have shown that synergism does not consider the return of man to God as consisting in faith in the Gospel, or in the forgiveness of sins won by Christ and offered to man in the Gospel, but thinks of conversion as an "ethical act" or a moral self-arousing. Thus synergists transfer conversion to the domain of the Law. This fact becomes apparent again in their teaching on the means of grace, which are said to make such moral demands as "right conduct" and "personal choice." But the very essence of conversion to God is conversion to the Gospel. Conversion consists in faith in Christ (Acts 11:21). Accordingly Luther tersely states: "To be converted to God means to believe in Christ . . . the Mediator" (St. L. XIII:1101). Conversion to God-pleasing works, or to the Law, which is inseparably connected with conversion to the Gospel, is, properly speaking, a result of faith in the Gospel, as our Confessions remind us (*Trigl.* 259, Apol., XII, 28).

Behind the synergists' teaching regarding the means of grace, which makes room for assistance by man, lurks the denial of the perfection of the reconciliation effected by Christ's work of redemption. If a man really believes that he must assist the grace offered in, and operative through, the means of grace to attain its "final result," he certainly has forgotten the perfect reconciliation of the world by the blood of the Son of God. Luther: "These words, 'The Son of God . . . gave Himself for me,' are nothing else than thunderclaps and flashes from heaven against the righteousness of the Law and the doctrine of works. So great an iniquity, so great a perversion, darkness, and ignorance was there in my will and intellect, that I could be redeemed only through so unspeakably great a ransom. . . . Therefore it is an unspeakable and horrible blasphemy if you invent any work whereby you undertake to reconcile God, since you see that He could not be reconciled otherwise than through this immeasurable and infinite treasure, namely, through the death and blood of His Son." (St. L. IX:236 f.)

Means of Grace According to the Deniers of the Vicarious Satisfaction

Scripture teaches that the Word of the Gospel and the Sacraments are means of grace solely because they assure men that God in His heart (*in foro divino*) forgives their sins for the sake of Christ's *satisfactio vicaria*, without making any ethical demands and because they, through this declaration, engender and strengthen faith (Vol. III, 105ff.). Obviously, then, all who deny the *satisfactio Christi vicaria* deny also the means of grace in the Biblical sense. If they still speak of means of grace, they merely accommodate themselves to the terminology of the Church. They regard the means of grace merely as stimuli to such moral endeavors as either supplant or supplement the *satisfactio Christi vicaria*.

Thus the Unitarians of ancient and modern times candidly reject both the essential deity of Christ and the vicarious satisfaction and define Christianity as human morality inspired by Christ's teaching and example.[34] The endeavor to lead "a life at one with God" or "to keep the commandments" in response to the intellectual, psychological, and moral influence proceeding from Christ ("moral-influence theory") replaces the means of grace, which as *media remissionis peccatorum sive iustificationis* are thus entirely abolished.[35]

Likewise some modern theologians [36] propose merely to "deepen the conception of satisfaction" of the Church of the Reformation by making the transforming or recasting of the life of men, hence sanctification and good works, a part of the reconciliation of men with God. If these theologians actually hold with Kirn that "We find it imperative to make the transformation of men a part of our concept of Christ's work of reconciliation" (R. E., 3d ed., XX, 574), the means of grace are for them no longer media that transmit the forgiveness of sin, but only aids in effecting "the transformation of men."

This is clearly the effect also of the "guaranty theory," substituted for the *satisfactio vicaria Christi*. This amazing theory claims that Christ by His work of reconciliation "guaranteed" or promised the Father that "in the Church ruled by God which Christ would found" men would studiously practice moral rectitude or lead "a life at one with God." In other words, Christ reconciled the world with God by giving God a note in mankind's name which men will have to pay. For the proponents of the guaranty theory the means of grace are therefore not signs and testimonies of the God gracious in Christ, signs testifying to the fact that God for Christ's sake has nothing against us any more, but they are means of collecting a note that is due, a notice and summons to men to pay what Christ has failed to pay or paid only in part.

It is obvious that means of grace of such a nature are not able "to awaken and confirm" (*Trigl.* 49, Augsb. Conf., XIII) faith in the remission of sins which Christ secured for men. Such means rather belong in a class with the Papistico-pagan error of which Scripture says: "Christ is become of no effect unto you, whosoever of you are justified by the Law; ye are fallen from grace" (Gal. 5:4).

---

[34] See R. E., 3d ed., XX, 573 and Harnack, *Wesen des Christentums*, 3d ed., p. 92.

[35] The *Racovian Catechism* therefore explicitly denies (Qus. 337—338) that sin is remitted and faith strengthened through the Lord's Supper. Its purpose is said to be not to receive something, but to render service to God.

[36] See Vol. II, 361 f.

This verdict applies to every theory of reconciliation which in any way detracts from the *satisfactio vicaria* and therefore also to Hofmann's theory. Instead of Christ's substitutional obedience and the forgiveness of sins resulting from it, Hofmann proposed the inauguration of a new humanity in the Person of Christ. But the fact that in the Person of Christ a new, holy humanity appeared, and that through Christ a new, holy humanity was to come into being in the future, works no Christian faith. Christian faith must needs have as its correlative the forgiveness of sins which Christ gained and dispenses in the Gospel. Eph. 1:7: "In whom we have redemption through His blood, the forgiveness of sins." See *Trigl.* 55, Augsb. Conf., XX, 23.

The Means of Grace According to the "Enthusiasts"

The Christian doctrine of the means of grace is abolished by all "enthusiasts," all who assume a revealing and effective operation of the Holy Spirit without and alongside the divinely ordained means of grace. We have noted above that the Calvinists, because they deny the *gratia universalis,* have means of grace neither for all men nor for the elect — not for all men because there is not grace for all; not for the elect because the grace provided for them works directly and not through means.

Zwingli is a good example of those who separate grace from the means of grace. His assertion that the Holy Ghost needs no vehicle *(vehiculum)* is well known. And this rule he applies not only to the Sacraments,[37] but to the Word of the Gospel as well. Zwingli asserts emphatically that faith does not come through the outward Word, but through the immediate operation of the Holy Spirit: *ipse tractus internus* (through which we are converted to God) *immediate operantis est Spiritus.*[38] In their phraseology the later Reformed teachers adopt terms employed by Lutherans in setting forth the doctrine of the means of grace, without, however, giving up Zwingli's teaching.[39] Recent Calvinists, too, insist that God's grace does not operate efficaciously through the means of grace (see p. 118 ff.).

Most consistent of all in applying the principle of separation are the Quakers. They teach that on the day of visitation appointed by Him the Holy Ghost illumines man immediately, without the Word,

---

[37] *Fidei Ratio,* ed. Niemeyer, p. 24; Jacobs, *Book of Concord,* II, 168.

[38] *Zwingli, Opp.,* ed. Schulthess, IV, 125.

[39] Winer, *Kompar. Darstellung,* 3d ed., p. 117. For further material see p. 142 ff.

and by this illumination enables man to understand the Word of Scripture, which before was a dead letter to him. The Quakers therefore hold so-called "silent meetings." Their theologian Robert Barclay (d. 1690) reports: "In these meetings everyone's great task should be to await God and, withdrawing from his own thoughts and ideas, to feel the presence of God. . . . There no one confines the Spirit of God, nor does he set forth material he has memorized and assembled, but everyone reports whatever the Lord puts in his heart. It may happen among us, and often has happened, that numerous meetings were held without a word being said, and still our souls were much edified and refreshed, and our hearts were overwhelmed by the hidden feeling of God's Spirit and power passing from vessel to vessel without words." (Guenther, *Symbolik*, 4th ed., p. 273.) Still, even the Quakers are not entirely consistent in the matter of these silent meetings. Schneckenburger remarks correctly: "According to Quaker principles one could properly expect no common worship of God at all, since the very appointing of time and place is human interference" (*Kleine protest. Religionsparteien*, p. 90).

All modern theologians who, like Ihmels, deny that faith in Christ is worked solely through the Word of Christ and assert that faith is produced in man by the Person of Christ, the historical activity or appearance of Christ, etc., also belong to the "enthusiasts." Ihmels says: "Today also only that is real faith in Christ which is thrust upon man by the appearance of Christ Himself" (*Zentralfragen*, p. 89).

In listing the arguments by which men seek to prove an efficacious operation of the Holy Spirit without the divinely ordained means of grace, we find them to be principally the following: 1. The means of grace are superfluous because the Holy Ghost can work without means (*vehiculum*). 2. It does not befit the Spirit to bind His gracious revelation and operation to external means of grace. 3. The fact that not all hearers of the Gospel come to faith warrants the conclusion that the Holy Ghost keeps His faith-creating activity separate from the Word.[40]

But all these arguments are based on rationalistic human considerations. Against the argument that the means of grace are superfluous we must maintain: we are not concerned with the question

[40] Zwingli already used this argument: "That this is so [namely, that faith is engendered by an immediate working of the Spirit] is observed also in practice [*usu*], for we daily see that some indeed hear the preaching of the Gospel, but none the more believe."

whether God could not also operate in the spiritual sphere without means. The issue solely is whether God says in His revealed Word that He wants to work through certain means appointed by Him and has therefore directed us to these means. In theology it is out of place to urge possibilities against the facts revealed by God in His Word. Zwingli's contention that the Holy Spirit needs no vehicle is already in principle a denial of the Scripture principle. The same holds true of Ihmel's declaration: "It cannot be affirmed too earnestly that if Jesus actually is what the Church confesses Him to be, He Himself must also be able to convince men of this reality by the reality of His own Person" (Vol. II, 368).

Also the second argument, that an operation through external means is beneath the dignity of the Holy Ghost is thoroughly untheological. We mortals do not know *a priori* what is seemly or unseemly for God, but we can know this only *a posteriori* from God's revealed Word; for *a priori* we are not sufficiently at home in the code of the divine ethics (1 Tim. 6:16).

The deduction that the Holy Spirit's activity must be dissociated from the external Word because not all hearers of the Word become believers rests on the error of the *gratia irresistibilis*. Scripture teaches that there is a divine operation through the Gospel aiming at faith and salvation also in those who remain unconverted and are lost (Matt. 23:37; Acts 7:51; 13:46). Because this activity does not take place in unveiled divine majesty, but through means, it is resistible.[41]

It also directly contradicts Scripture to assert that the Word of the Gospel comes into consideration in regeneration only as "an attending circumstance," that what precedes or follows regeneration is indeed worked through the Word, but not regeneration itself. (Hodge, *Syst. Theol.*, II, 685). When Scripture says: "Being born again . . . by the Word of God" (1 Pet. 1:23); "which shall believe on Me through their Word" (John 17:20); "faith cometh by hearing" (Rom. 10:17), it declares the Word to be not "an attending circumstance," but the instrumentality through which regeneration is wrought or faith worked. Besides, these Scripture texts speak not of things preceding or following regeneration, but of regeneration itself.

The "enthusiasts" appeal to John 3:8: "The wind bloweth where it listeth, and thou hearest the sound thereof, but canst not tell whence it cometh, and whither it goeth; so is everyone that is born

---

[41] See the chapter "Man Can Prevent His Conversion," Vol. II, 464 f.

of the Spirit."[42] Here Christ indeed describes regeneration as a mysterious process which we neither have produced nor can "comprehend and explain rationally." But at this very place it is expressly stated that man is born again "of [ἐξ] water and of the Spirit." It is therefore a misuse of the text to try to prove by it an immediate working of regeneration.[43]

But as the *extra enthusiasticum* is contrary to Scripture, so it is also devoid of all good reasoning. It suffers from a manifest self-contradiction. Luther's description of it in the Smalcald Articles aptly says: "All this is the old devil and old serpent, who also converted Adam and Eve into enthusiasts, and led them from the outward Word of God to spiritualizing and self-conceit, and nevertheless accomplished this through other outward words. Just as also our enthusiasts [at the present day] condemn the outward Word, and nevertheless they themselves are not silent, but they fill the world with their pratings and writings, as though, indeed, the Spirit could not come through the writings and the spoken word of the apostles, but [first] through their writings and words He must come. Why [then] do they not also omit their own sermons and writings, until the Spirit Himself come to men, without their writings and before them, as they boast that He has come into them without the preaching of the Scriptures?" (*Trigl.* 495, Smalc. Art., Part III, Art. VIII, 5—6.)

But the chief damage caused by this separation of the gracious revelation and operation of God from the outward Word is that it carries one irresistibly into Papistic error, for it founds the *certitudo gratiae* on the *gratia infusa* instead of basing it on the gracious disposition of God, won for us by Christ and pledged to us in the means of grace. Thus it supplants faith's certitude of justification by a forced, man-made assurance based on "feelings," which fail when terrors of conscience assail man. By separating grace from the means of grace all "enthusiasts" fall into the error of interpreting saving grace as a spiritual infusion, for the appropriation of which faith as an apprehending act *(actualis apprehensio gratiae)* on the part of man is not necessary. Teaching such infused grace, the Synod of Dort could assert that saving grace can remain in a man even when through grievous sins he loses the *exercitium fidei*. Saving grace and saving faith are taken to be a good quality inhering and resting

---

[42] Zwingli, too, adduces this passage to prove an immediate operation of the Holy Ghost; cf. *Fidei Ratio,* ed. Niemeyer, p. 25, Jacobs, *Book of Concord,* II, 168.

[43] Hengstenberg is right in pointing out that the *tertium comparationis* in this text is the incomprehensibility of regeneration.

in man. Rome and the "enthusiasts" differ only as to the process of infusion. According to the "enthusiasts," it takes place without the means of grace ordained by God; according to Papists, it takes place principally through the means of grace invented by the "Church."

Denial of the Means of Grace in the Personal Life of the Christians

To remain properly humble while firmly rejecting all erroneous teachings regarding the means of grace, we should remind ourselves how even Christians who teach and, as a rule, also believe, the correct doctrine of the means of grace, in their personal practice very often lose sight of the means of grace. This is done whenever they base the certainty of grace, or of the forgiveness of sin, on their feeling of grace or the *gratia infusa,* instead of on God's promise in the objective means of grace. All of us are by nature "enthusiasts." Instead of listening to and believing God's declarations of love in the Gospel, in the means of grace given by Him, or, in other words, instead of fixing our gaze on God's reconciled heart which — thanks be to God! — is a present reality through Christ and is revealed and offered to us by God in the Gospel and the Sacraments, we look into our own heart and seek to gauge God's feelings toward us by the thoughts and moods we find in our heart. But that amounts to a practical denial of the fact that God has reconciled us to Him through Jesus Christ, and hence to a practical denial of the means of grace, in which God acquaints us with this completed reconciliation.

This feature of our Christian life must occupy us as long as we live. Christianity is an absolutely unique religion. It completely transcends human horizon and our inborn conception of religion. Native to us is the *opinio legis,* the religion of the Law. When we observe virtue in ourselves, we regard God as gracious. When we discover sin in us and our conscience condemns us because of it, we fear that God is minded to reject us. But the Christian religion teaches that God is gracious for Christ's sake "without the deeds of the Law," hence without regard to our keeping or transgressing of His Law. The righteousness that avails before God lies outside ourselves (*Trigl.* 935, F. C., Sol. Decl., III, 55). It is the acquired righteousness of Christ; in other words, the forgiveness of sins, which God pledges to us for Christ's sake in the means of grace. Therefore our spiritual life is lived on the right basis and in agreement with the unique character of the Christian religion only when we — to express it in the words of Luther — "soar above ourselves" and base our faith in God's grace on the means of grace lying outside us, the Word of the Gospel and its seals, Baptism and the Lord's Supper.

The *gratia infusa* — in its good sense as true Christian sanctification, or holy living — is, of course, also intended to be a *signum et testimonium* of divine grace (*Trigl.* 199, Apol., III, 154 f.). But the *gratia infusa* is always imperfect. It does not stand the test before man's conscience or the revealed Law of God. Our practice therefore must remain as Luther describes it: "There is no good counsel other than to disregard your own feelings and all human solace and to rely only on His Word" (St. L. XI:455). More on this in the following chapter.

5

The Importance of the Christian Doctrine of the Means of Grace

Adolf Harnack felt he could justly say in criticism of Luther: "The Christian lives, as Luther knew better than anyone, not by the means of grace, but through the personal communion with God which he experiences in Christ" (*Dogmengesch., Grundriss,* 1905, p. 431). These words show that Harnack sets the life of a Christian derived from the means of grace in opposition to his personal communion with God. Harnack is of the opinion that he who wants to experience personal communion with God in Christ, that is, wants to become sincerely or inwardly pious, must, above all, shun the thought that the means of grace convey to him the grace of God. This method of experiencing God in Christ, Luther is alleged to have disregarded, though he really knew better, and on that account to have misdirected the Reformation. In this way, says Harnack, "Luther retrograded to the constricted medieval thought pattern which he had left."

Harnack merely reiterates the criticism which Carlstadt, Zwingli, and their confederates voiced against Luther. They, too, never tired of exposing Luther's "aberrations" in the doctrine of the means of grace. By his urging of the external Word and the Sacraments as means of grace Luther is supposed to have injured personal piety and to have hindered the Spirit, because Spirit and personal piety are not given through such external things. Zwingli said: "I believe, yea, I know, that all the Sacraments are so far from conferring grace that they do not even convey or distribute it. In this, most powerful

Emperor, I may perhaps appear too bold to thee. But I am firmly convinced that I am right. For as grace is produced or given by the divine Spirit (I am using the term 'grace' in its Latin meaning of pardon, indulgence, gracious favor), so this gift reaches only the spirit. The Spirit, however, needs no guide or vehicle, for He Himself is the Power and Energy by which all things are borne and has no need of being borne. Nor have we ever read in the Holy Scriptures that perceptible things like the Sacraments certainly bring with them the Spirit." (*Fidei Ratio,* ed. Niemeyer, p. 24; Jacobs, *Book of Concord,* II, 168.) In agreement with Zwingli more recent Reformed theologians emphatically assert that "efficacious grace acts immediately" and that in regeneration the outward Word is indeed an "attending circumstance," but not the means through which regeneration is wrought.

Indeed, many modern theologians, including those calling themselves Lutherans, take the position of Harnack and Zwingli. They teach that faith is engendered not only by the Word of Christ, but also by the "living Person of Christ," by "the historical reality of Christ," and offer the justification that in this way "intellectualism" or formalism is prevented and an inward "experience" of God in Christ is safeguarded.

What do we answer to this persistent criticism of Luther and the Lutheran Church? Two things Luther knew better than many others. First, that a Christian indeed lives only through the personal communion with God as He has revealed Himself in Christ. For that reason Luther fought Rome's teaching that the means of grace put one in possession of grace *ex opere operato,* without a personal faith that appropriates the pledge of grace in the means of grace. Secondly, Luther knew better than many that every "personal communion with God" which does not come about by way of the means of grace, or, in other words, is not faith in the forgiveness offered for Christ's sake in the Word of the Gospel and in the Sacraments, is a delusion and self-deception. In the Smalcald Articles he says: "And in those things which concern the spoken, outward Word, we must firmly hold that God grants His Spirit or grace to no one, except through and with the preceding outward Word, in order that we may thus be protected against the enthusiasts, i. e., spirits who boast that they have the Spirit without and before the Word. . . . All this is the old devil and old serpent, who also converted Adam and Eve into enthusiasts, and led them from the outward Word of God to spiritualizing and self-conceit [*proprias opiniones*]. . . . In a word, enthusiasm inheres in

Adam and his children from the beginning [from the first fall] to the end of the world, [its poison] having been implanted and infused into them by the old dragon, and is the origin, power [life], and strength of all heresy, especially of that of the Papacy and Mahomet. Therefore we ought and must constantly maintain this point, that God does not wish to deal with us otherwise than through the spoken Word and the Sacraments. It is the devil himself whatsoever is extolled as Spirit without the Word and the Sacrament." (*Trigl.* 495, Part III, Art. VIII, 3—10.)

Men have felt offended by these unvarnished words of Luther and the Lutheran Confession. But they do not exceed the bounds of truth. In nature, it is true, God operates everywhere. By Him all things consist (Col. 1:17). Specifically, in the case of men God is the *causa efficiens* of the natural life of all in all climes. God "giveth to all life and breath and all things" (Acts 17:25). In Him they live and move and have their being (Acts 17:28). He gives to all men everywhere the things needed for this physical life. He provides "rain from heaven, and fruitful seasons, filling our hearts with food and gladness" (Acts 14:17). But the remission of sins for Christ's sake and faith in this remission, regeneration unto spiritual life and all the spiritual gifts connected with it, God will give only through the means of grace He has ordained, through the Word of the Gospel and the Sacraments. To this fact Scripture bears witness by saying that all members of the Church "shall believe on Me through their [the Apostles'] Word" (John 17:20), are regenerated by the Word and by Baptism (1 Pet. 1:23; Titus 3:5). Hence Christ commissions His Church not to remain at home, but to go into all the world with the preaching of the Gospel (Mark 16:15-16), to preach repentance and remission of sins among all nations (Luke 24:47). Hence also the description of the nations who lack the Gospel as people who sit in darkness and in the shadow of death (Luke 1:78-79; Is. 9:2; 60:2), though they have the light of the material sun and though they have the witness of God in His giving them the things needed for this temporal life (Acts 14:17). The personal communion with God is so inseparably bound up with the means of grace that those who are still outside the Church are described as people who "obey not the Word" (1 Pet. 3:1), and that the Apostle Paul charges everyone who "consents not to the wholesome words, even the words of our Lord Jesus Christ," with conceit and ignorance, τετύφωται, μη ἐπιστάμενος (1 Tim. 6:3-4). This Scriptural term "conceited, knowing nothing" vindicates the similarly sharp language of the Smalcald Articles:

"It is the devil himself whatsoever is extolled as Spirit without the Word and Sacraments."

The "good intention" of the people who refuse to found faith on the external means of grace has been urged in their defense. They want to prevent "formalism," mere "head knowledge," "intellectualism," and foster a "Christianity of the heart," an inward "experience" of the saving truths. From this point of view recent histories of dogma have conceded a partial justification to such fanaticism as, for instance, that of Andrew Osiander. See Seeberg, *Dogmengesch.*, II, 360 ff. But even if we do not question the "good intention," Scripture obliges us to maintain that in the case of all who want to detach God's gracious revelation and operation from the means of grace we are dealing with ignoramuses (μὴ ἐπιστάμενοι, 1 Tim. 6:4) and quacks, who do not realize what they say or set down, and with might and main work for exactly the opposite of what they purpose to do. "Communion with God," "inward experience" of Christ, "fervor in Christianity," can always be achieved in only one way, namely, by faith in the Word of grace, in the forgiveness of sins provided through Christ's *satisfactio vicaria* and pledged to us by God in the means of grace. Whoever detaches this "experience" from the Word of grace, the λόγος τῆς χάριτος, falls prey in every respect to his own flesh. The true knowledge of spiritual matters, which is derived from continuing in the Word of Christ, he supplants with the "swell head" of his own wisdom, τετύφωται. Faith in the grace of God, which comes solely from the Word of grace and is God's work through the Word (Rom. 10:17; 1 Cor. 2:4-5),[44] is supplanted by "autosuggestion" — to use a modern term — by an "illusory and self-produced enthusiasm."[45] The modifiers "illusory" and "self-produced" fit the case perfectly because Scripture leaves no doubt that an "enthusiasm" or "illumination" or "regeneration" of immediate origin cannot be shown to have the Holy Spirit as *causa efficiens*. Except in cases reserved for Himself and not of our concern (Luke 1:15), the Holy Ghost does not concern Himself with immediate operations in the Kingdom of Grace.

Scripture binds all knowledge of Christian truth to the Word of Christ, who says: ἐὰν ὑμεῖς μείνητε ἐν τῷ λόγῳ τῷ ἐμῷ . . . γνώσεσθε τὴν ἀλήθειαν (John 8:31-32). Faith and regeneration is effected by

---

[44] Luther: "Even as it is God who gives the Word, which is not ours, but His, so it is God who gives faith in the Word, so that both are God's work, the Word and faith, or forgiveness of sins and faith" (St. L. XIII:2440).

[45] Von Oettingen, *Luth. Dogma.*, 11th ed., II, 333.

the Holy Ghost through the Word (1 Cor. 2:4-5; 1 Pet. 1:23). The Spirit is received through the hearing of faith (Gal. 3:2, 5). The Word of the Cross (ὁ λόγος ὁ τοῦ σταυροῦ) is the power of God to those who are saved (1 Cor. 1:18). Hence actually everything that is regarded as brought about by the Holy Ghost without the Word is fictitious, "illusory," "self-produced." The experience one has, or imagines, without the means of grace is not the product of the Holy Ghost, but is "man-made." [46] Here the trails of "enthusiasm" and Rome merge. Whether one supplants the means of grace with the "Spirit," or "the Person of Christ," or "the historical reality of Christ," or something else, every divorce of the divine revelation and operation of grace from the means of grace forces one into an "autogeneration," which supplants the *favor Dei propter Christum* with a spurious *gratia infusa* as the grounds for the forgiveness of sins and salvation. Justification by grace, for Christ's sake, through faith, without the deeds of the Law, is surrendered, and the assurance of grace and salvation is undermined. It is quite impossible to perform so radical an operation on the body of the Christian doctrine as to sever grace from the means of grace and still retain the Christian faith unimpaired.

Such, then, are the evil consequences when grace is consistently divorced from its means in practice. Frequently, however, the false principle is shelved in practice for the simple reason that every false doctrine proves unworkable when matters become serious, i. e., when the conscience is thoroughly aroused. We have already pointed this out regarding the Calvinistic thesis of a *gratia particularis*. It sounds very plausible when men argue for it in this fashion: "It cannot be supposed that God intends what is never accomplished, that He adopts means for an end which is never to be attained" (Vol. II, 26 f.), and then take the liberty of deducing that God's grace and Christ's merit cannot possibly extend over all men. But when the assaults of doubt become heavy and terror seizes the conscience, the champions of a *gratia particularis* themselves console the terrified sinner with the *gratia universalis*. See Vol. II, 50. Also against the *satisfactio vicaria* numerous objections are raised which sound plausible; for example: God as supreme Judge can forgive sins without any substitutional satisfaction by virtue of His omnipotent power, and this method would be far more becoming to God and more beneficial for men in ethical respects. But when anguish of conscience seized them, antagonists

---

[46] Aptly J. Gottschick remarks (R. E., 2d ed., XVII, 335): "Where the pretended immediate communion is really independent of the outward Word, it is simply mental preoccupation with a God and Christ of fantasy."

of the *satisfactio vicaria,* such as Bushnell, Ritschl, Hugo Grotius, returned to this doctrine. See Vol. II, 370.

A similar situation prevails in regard to the means of grace. In one's study or in other safe retreats one can marshal arguments for a separation of grace and the Spirit from the external Word that make one appear in one's own estimation and in the eyes of others as very pious and withal scientific. But when the terrors of conscience strike, then those who got along on an immediate grace realize that they must either despair or cling to the immovable rock of the objective promise of grace in the means of grace. As in the case of the denial of universal grace and the vicarious satisfaction, the fact remains that in time of crisis the error of severing grace from the means of grace refutes itself.

It is a fact that some who taught an immediate illumination without the Word exhibited a great assurance of grace, but two things should here be remembered. First, an apparent assurance may be a delusion and self-deception. Secondly, such as theoretically detach grace from the means, may in their heart actually, by an unrealized inconsistency, be relying on God's pledge of grace in the outward Word of the Gospel. With regard to this inconsistency on the part of synergists Mead writes: "The most ardent champion of the doctrine of free will may be found supplicating the Lord to give him those graces which, according to his theory, he ought to obtain and cultivate for himself" (*Irenic Theol.,* Chas. Marsh Mead, 1905, p. 161).

In short, Luther and the Lutheran Church are the mouthpiece of the Church Universal in their teaching of the means of grace. All men who — to use Harnack's expression — are in personal communion with God, experience this communion through the means of grace and not without them.[47] Only this method of attaining communion with God is taught in Scripture. Only by this method is the cardinal Christian doctrine of the forgiveness of sins through faith without the deeds of the Law left intact. And only by this method can be attained the *certitudo gratiae et salutis,* which the Christian religion aims to impart. Rom. 4:16: "It is of faith . . . to the end the promise might be sure to all the seed."

No other human writer has so forcefully as Luther set forth the nature of the divinely ordained means of grace, their importance for faith and life, and the destructive effect of severing grace from the

---

[47] Gottschick (R. E., 2d ed., XVII, 334): "While one entertains this notion [of an immediate communion with God], one's need of personal assurance of salvation remains unsupplied."

means of grace. For Luther was trained in the school of the terrors of conscience for the work of reforming the Church, while Zwingli's reformation and theology sprang largely from the soil of Humanism and bears a speculative stamp throughout. Calvinistic theology from Calvin down to our day teaches not so much the God who has revealed and given Himself to us in His Word, but at the critical points substitutes speculations regarding the absolute God for what the divine Word teaches. Of this fact we have taken note in the section of God's Grace, of Christ's Person and Work, and we must refer to it here. Let us quote Luther at some length.

He teaches: In the realm of nature, Christ is present and rules everywhere, but as to ruling the heart and conscience, i. e., conferring and certifying the remission of sins, He wants to operate through His Word. Hence everyone should learn to judge of God's feelings toward him only from God's Word. Luther writes: "What is the meaning of this, 'I must be about My Father's business'? Are not all creatures His Father's? Everything is His; but He has presented the creatures to us for our use, to make use of them in this earthly life as best we know. But one thing He has reserved for Himself, which is His sacred property and which we must receive separately from Him. That is His holy Word, by which He rules hearts and consciences, sanctifies and saves. On this account, too, the Temple was called His sanctuary and holy dwelling, because in it He revealed His presence and was heard through His Word. In like manner Christ is in His Father's sanctuary when He speaks to us through His Word and thus brings us, too, to His Father. Behold, for this reason He now chides His parents that they wander about confused and seek Him in other, worldly and human, affairs and activities, among their acquaintances and friends, and do not give it a thought that He must be in that which is His Father's. By this saying He would indicate that His rule, and the whole Christian religion, is to be found solely in the Word and in faith, not in other, external things (like the external sanctimoniousness of the Jews), nor in temporal, worldly doings or secular rule. . . . Now this is what I have said: God will not have us rely on anything else, or trust with our heart in anything that is not Christ in His Word, no matter how sacred and full of Spirit it may be. Faith has no other foundation on which it can endure. . . . We must seek Christ in that which is the Father's, that is, we must simply and solely cleave to the Word of the Gospel, which shows and reveals Christ aright to us. If you would effectively comfort others and yourself, then learn in this and other spiritual temptations to say with

Christ: Why are you running to and fro, tormenting yourself with fearful and distressed thoughts, as though God had no more grace for you and as though Christ were not to be found, and refuse to be satisfied unless you find Him in yourself and feel holy and without sin? That will get you nowhere; it is all toil and labor lost. Don't you know that Christ is minded to be present and to be found nowhere but in that which is His Father's and not in that which you or all men are or have? The fault does not lie with Christ and His grace; He indeed is and remains unlost and can always be found; the fault lies in you, that you do not seek Him right, namely, where He is to be sought, because you are judging according to your feelings and expect to seize Him with your thoughts. But you must come here, where there is neither yours nor any man's, but God's business and rule, namely, where His Word is. There you will meet Him and hear and see neither wrath nor displeasure, as you fear, but only grace and cordial love toward you. . . . But it means a struggle for the heart to get there and take hold of this; first it must crash and experience that all our notions of seeking Christ are futile and in vain and that in the end there is no other choice than to turn away from oneself and all other human consolation and trust only in His Word." (St. L. XI:452 ff.)

Luther shows that it has always been God's manner to deal with us through external means and signs and thus to impart His grace to us. Accordingly, we have God's gracious countenance in the New Testament wherever we have the Word of the Gospel and the Sacraments. He writes: "God has always followed this custom of giving a visible sign, a person, place, or spot, where He could certainly be found. For if we are not bound and held by a physical, external sign, every one of us will seek God wherever he pleases. For this reason the holy Prophets wrote much of the Tabernacle, the dwelling place and tent where He willed to be present. Thus God has always done. In a like manner He has built us Christians a temple where He would dwell, namely, the spoken Word, Baptism, and the Lord's Supper, which also are perceptible things. But our false prophets, factious spirits, and 'enthusiasts' despise it and cast it aside, as though it were worthless, and say: Truly, I will sit and wait until a flying Spirit and revelation comes to me from heaven. But beware of that! Of course, we know well that water, bread, and wine do not save us. But what do you say to this, that in the Lord's Supper there is not mere bread and wine, and so in Baptism not just simple water, but God promises that He will be in Baptism and it shall cleanse and wash us of our sins? And in the Lord's Supper the body and blood of the Lord Christ is given us under the bread and wine. Will you here willfully despise God and His sign and view and regard the water in Baptism like water flowing in the Elbe or you cook with? Will you regard the Word of the Gospel as on a level with the word or remarks of peasants at a fair or in taverns? God has said: When the Word of Christ is preached, I am in your mouth, and I go with the Word through your ears into your heart. So, then, we have a sure sign and know that when the Gospel is preached, God is present, there He would be found by us; at that place, then, I have a perceptible sign by which I can perceive God's presence and find Him. And so He also is in Baptism and the Lord's Supper, for He has bound Himself to be there. If I, however, go on a pilgrimage to St. James or to Grimmetal, enter a cloister, or seek God at other places, I shall not find Him. When now those factious spirits preach on this wise: Just as monasticism, invocation of saints, masses, and pilgrimages are nothing, so, too, Baptism and the Lord's Supper are nothing, that does not fit together by a long shot. For there is a big difference, whether God appoints and institutes something or men institute it. Truly, you should believe God's ordinances and institutions, hold them sacred and highly regard them. In like manner He gave Moses commandment: Bring them into the Land, that is, appoint and designate a certain place, so that whoever cannot in person worship Me there, at least turn his body toward it and face in that direction and pray. Thus I also have God at a certain place, namely, here in the Word and Sacraments, so that though one be at Rome, or wherever he may be, if he turns his face toward Word and Sacrament and worships, he there finds our Lord God; and though it were in a straw that He willed to be found, there we should then seek and honor Him." (St. L. III: 924 f.)

To the accusation that he binds grace to definite external and apparently lowly things — Harnack, too, repeats this complaint — Luther answers: "If God were to bid you pick up a straw or strip a feather, and with it command, order, and promise that through this act you should have forgiveness of all your sins, grace, and everlasting life, should you not accept that with great pleasure and gratitude, love it, praise it, and esteem that straw or feather a higher and holier possession than heaven and earth? For however insignificant the straw or feather is, by it you get so precious a gift as neither heaven nor earth, nor all the angels, can give you. Why are we such shameful folk that we do not esteem the water of Baptism, the bread and wine which is Christ's body and blood, the spoken

Word, and the laying on of hands for the forgiveness of sins to be as precious and sacred a thing as we would hold such a straw or feather to be? For in these things, as we see and hear, God Himself wills to work, and they are to be His water, Word, hand, bread and wine, whereby it is His will to sanctify and save us in Christ, who has obtained this salvation for us and sent His Holy Spirit from the Father to apply this to us. On the other hand, even though you were to go on a pilgrimage in heavy armor to the shrine of St. James, or let yourself be killed by the severe life of the Carthusians, Franciscans, or Dominicans in order to be saved, and God had not commanded or instituted this, what good would it do you? He doesn't know of these things, but the devil and you have devised them, like the special sacraments and the orders of priests. Even though you were able to carry heaven and earth on your shoulders in order to be saved, it would be labor lost, while he who picked up the straw (if God commanded it) would do more than you, even if you could carry ten worlds." (St. L. XVI:2296.)

Luther explains that the practical result can only be despair if we do not learn, and daily learn anew, to cling to the external Word of the Gospel against all our feelings and perception. He says: "Over against all that reason suggests or would measure and fathom, yes, all that our senses feel and perceive, we must learn to cling to the Word and simply judge according to it. . . . For if you insist on judging according to what you see and feel and, when you are told God's Word, urge your opposite feelings and say: You have good talking, but my heart talks quite another language, and if you felt what I feel, you, too, would talk differently, etc.: then God's Word is not in your heart, but by your own thoughts, reason, and musings you have smothered and extinguished it. In short, if you will not esteem the Word above all your feelings, eyes, senses, and heart, you will inevitably be lost, and there is no help for you. . . . I also feel my sin, and the Law, and the devil on my neck, that I lie prostrate under it as under a heavy load. But what should I do? Were I to judge according to such feelings and my strength, I and all men would have to despair and perish. But if I desire to be helped, I must verily face about and look at the Word and learn from it to say: I indeed feel God's wrath, the devil, death, and hell; but the Word says otherwise, namely, that I have a gracious God through Christ, who is my Lord, superior to the devil and all creatures." (St. L. VIII:1102.)

Luther stresses in particular that the written Word of God is a means of grace. He comments on 1 John 5:13: "In order that nobody may deceive us, John says it once more against the 'enthusiasts' that he writes these things: 'These things have I written unto you.' For them the letter is a dead thing on paper. But John says: 'I write you,' since the writing should serve to make the Epistle a means by which one receives faith and eternal life. In the twentieth chapter of his Gospel John says: 'These are written that ye might believe that Jesus is the Christ, the Son of God; and that, believing, ye might have life through His name.' Therefore we should know that the testimony of God comes to us in no other way than through the human voice or Scripture. 'All Scripture is given by inspiration of God and is profitable for doctrine, for reproof, for correction, for instruction in righteousness, that the man of God may be perfect, thoroughly furnished unto all good works.' 2 Tim. 3:16 f. Likewise in the preceding verse of the chapter cited: 'And that from a child thou hast known the Holy Scriptures, which are able to make thee wise unto salvation through faith which is in Christ Jesus.' Again, 1 Tim. 4:13: 'Till I come, give attendance to reading, to exhortation, to doctrine.' Why does God command to read the Scriptures if written matter is a dead thing? Why do the "enthusiasts" write and publish books if the letter is powerless and useless? Why do they seek to instruct us and others by their writings? If they say that the Spirit is there before the writing, and they first had the Spirit, and then they wrote: that is no argument. For, then, Scripture would be good for nothing but for show. Hear what Christ says: 'Neither pray I for these alone, but for them also which shall believe on Me through their Word,' John 17:20. 'Through their Word' certainly means their word of mouth or the written word, not the 'inner word.' For that reason one must above all things hear and read the Word, which the Holy Ghost uses as His means. When one reads the Word, the Holy Spirit is there, and on that account it is impossible to hear or read Scripture without benefit." (St. L. IX:1514 f.; VIII:829 ff.)

6

Comprehensive Characterization of the Reformed Teaching of the Means of Grace

Though we may be accused of unnecessary repetition and prolixity, several reasons prompt us to add here a comprehensive characterization of the Reformed teaching of the means of grace.

Zwingli's doctrine of an immediate operation and communication of the Spirit caused a schism in Protestant Christendom at the time of the Reformation. To this day that schism exists, and it constitutes a constant offense to the unbelieving world and offers Rome the welcome opportunity to deride the disunity of Protestantism.

Furthermore, it must be admitted that the Reformed teaching of the means of grace filtered, particularly through Pietism, also into the Lutheran Church. And the entire modern so-called "theology of experience" in principle has obviously gone over into the Reformed camp, since it bases faith in Christ not merely on the Word of Christ, but, in distinction from the Word, also on the "living Christ," "the Person of Christ," "the historical appearance" and "operation" of Christ.

Finally — and this reminder bears constant repetition — we are here dealing with a matter which no Christian can ever finish learning in this life. The finding of the correct position over against the Reformed, Pietism, and the "experience theology" is indeed facilitated by the clarity of Holy Writ, but to cling to the true doctrine in practice is a difficult task. To take the right position in practice transcends the ability of man and is solely the gracious work of the Holy Ghost through the Word. By our natural powers we are capable not only of opining that faith and regeneration are the immediate work of the Holy Spirit, but also of calling forth in ourselves moods and states which we may regard as the work of the Holy Ghost. But in true faith to cling to the external means of grace as sure "signs and testimonies" of the gracious will of God toward us, particularly when harassed with doubts, to cling with all our heart to the external Word of the Gospel against all our feelings and perceptions, against the condemnatory verdict of the Law and of our own conscience, that is something we can do only if the Holy Ghost works it and helps us suppress and mortify our flesh, to which Christ Crucified, that is, the Christ for us and outside us, is an offense and foolishness.

The question has been raised whether the distinctively Reformed teaching of the means of grace can still be called Christian. In answering this question we face the same situation which confronted us in the Reformed teaching of Christ's Person and work. Where Reformed Christology consistently follows through its fundamental principle that the finite is not capable of the infinite *(finitum non est capax infiniti)*, it forsakes Christian ground and is crowded onto Socinian (Unitarian) territory, that is, it is driven to a denial of the incarnation of the Son of God. Reformed theology, however, returns to Christian ground when it becomes inconsistent, namely, when in the stress of practical Christian life it forgets its *finitum non est capax infiniti,* allows the real communion of the divine and human natures *(realis communio naturarum)* to stand and teaches that the divine nature communicates infinite value to the suffering of the human nature (cp. Vol. II, 129, 271). This two-sided character, consistency and inconsistency, confronts us also in the Reformed teaching of the means of grace. In so far as Reformed theology actually teaches and applies its basic principle that the grace which really saves is given without the means of grace or alongside them ("Efficacious grace acts immediately"), it forsakes Christian ground. In so far as it in practice abandons its basic principle, it returns to Christian territory.

Let us once more recall the *status controversiae.* The question is not whether God could work immediately if He willed so to work. Nor is the question whether God has not in fact reserved for Himself cases of immediate operation; this, too, is granted (Luke 1:15). Nor is the question — this we emphasize against modern "experience theologians" — whether a perceptible operation of the living and exalted Christ does not confront us in world and church history, which likewise is granted. The question is solely whether, when our conscience is terrified by God's Law and we need reliable information on God's feelings toward us, God then has directed and bound us to the objective Word of His grace in Christ, the Gospel, and to the Sacraments of Baptism and the Lord's Supper as objective *signa et testimonia* of His gracious will, or whether in this situation, *scil.,* in asking for assurance of God's grace, we are to be referred to an immediate operation of God, an *interior Spiritus illuminatio,* an "immediate agency of the Spirit." [48] The Lutheran Church teaches the former; the Reformed denominations teach the latter wherever they apply their Reformed principle.

There is no Scripture proof for the Reformed teaching of the means of grace. We have demonstrated above (pp. 104ff., 108ff.) that according to Scripture the Word of the Gospel and the Sacraments were given and instituted by God for the very purpose of offering the remission of sin secured through Christ's *satisfactio vicaria* and that from these means and through them (ἐϰ and διά) faith and regeneration might come and the Holy Ghost be received.

To this we now add that the Apostolic practice, too, agrees with this Scriptural doctrine, while the Reformed practice is contrary to

---

[48] Calvin, *Inst.,* III, 24, 8; Hodge, *Syst. Theol.,* II, 685.

the Apostolic. Where Reformed theology actually practices its teaching of an immediate operation of the Holy Spirit, it warns men against seeking grace and salvation in the means of grace. Thus Calvin, as we saw, cautions against seeking to discern one's election from the universal call, that is, from the Word of the Gospel (*Inst.* III, 24, 8). Likewise the *Consensus Tigurinus* (c. 20) warns against the thought that "the visible sign [the Sacraments], in the same moment when it is being offered, brings with it the grace of God" (*Niemeyer,* p. 195). The *Geneva Catechism,* too, enjoins ["*De Sacramentis*"], that salvation must not be sought in the visible signs.[49]

The Apostles take exactly the opposite course. Paul does not warn against trusting in the external Word, but decidedly enjoins it when, in parting, he says to the elders at Ephesus: "And now, brethren, I commend you to God, and to the Word of His grace" (Acts 20:32). Peter, too, on the Day of Pentecost does not warn against the *visibile signum* of Baptism, but directs the men who ask, "Men and brethren, what shall we do?" to Baptism, informing them that Baptism is performed "for the remission of sins" (Acts 2:38). And to answer immediately the objection of the Reformed that many misuse their Baptism as a ground for carnal security, Peter after the first Pentecost lived to see much misuse of Baptism on the part of such as either never believed in the baptismal grace or fell away from it, Acts 5:1 ff. (Ananias and Sapphira); 8:13 ff. (Simon). Nevertheless Peter does not go over into the Reformed camp. He does not say with Boehl (*Dogm.,* pp. 558, 560) and all the old and modern Reformed: "Baptism does not wash away sins and does not save." Peter rather continues to teach of Baptism also in his First Epistle: "Baptism doth also now save us" (1 Pet. 3:21). The other Apostles, too, had the sad experience that not all hearers of the Word became believers. Paul expressly reports: "All men have not faith" (2 Thess. 3:2). Nevertheless the Apostles do not separate the working of faith and regeneration from the outward Word. They do not say with Zwingli: "*Tractus internus immediate operantis est Spiritus*" (Opp. IV, 125), nor with Shedd: "The influence of the Holy Spirit is directly upon the human spirit and is independent even of the Word" (*Dogm. Theol.* II, 501). They rather continue to teach that faith, regeneration, and the Spirit are given through the external Word (Rom. 10:14-17; 1 Pet. 1:23; Gal. 3:2). In short, as the Apostles teach that the outward Word

---

[49] Niemeyer edition, p. 161: "Why do you say that Christ is to be sought there [in the Sacraments]? I understand that one is not to cling to the visible signs in order to seek salvation there."

of the Gospel and the *visibilia signa* of the Sacraments bring to us the grace of God, or the remission of sins, so also in their practical application of this doctrine they point those seeking grace to these external things as the divinely ordained means to which faith must cling. Therefore we must judge that the Reformed theology and confessions misdirect souls by directing them not to seek grace and salvation in the Word and in Baptism.

Its teaching of the means of grace creates a very strange situation for the Reformed theology. By teaching an immediate communication of saving grace it declares that the entire method of communicating salvation as taught in Scripture is a blunder on the part of God. Reformed theology finds itself in a similar situation when, in discussing Christ's Person and work, it asserts that the human nature of Christ could not be the organ for the acts of the divine nature. As to the instrumental function of the human nature of Christ, Scripture teaches that the Son of God came in the flesh, i. e., assumed a human nature, for the purpose of destroying the works of the devil through the works performed by the Son of God in His human nature (1 John 3:8). In God's judgment, then, the human nature of Christ is a very fitting means for the accomplishment of the divine work of world redemption. But the Reformed theology denies this fitness. It asserts that the human nature of Christ can by no means be the organ for divine acts and operations and that therefore the action, or operation *(actio, operatio)*, of the divine nature of Christ must be kept separate from His human nature. We heard: "Omnipresence and omniscience are not attributes of which a creature can be made the organ" (Hodge, *Syst. Theol.*, II, 417). These words actually declare that the assumption of a human nature by the Son of God was a mistake. The Reformed teaching of the means of grace amounts to a similar criticism of a divine provision. Scripture teaches that God, having reconciled the world unto Himself through Christ, now ordained that His Word be proclaimed in the world and that men be baptized in order that they may become believers or regenerate through these means and thus possess the grace procured by Christ. In God's judgment, therefore, Word and Baptism are very fitting means for the communication and operation of grace. Reformed theology is of the opposite opinion, declaring: "There is here no place for the use of means." "Nothing intervenes between the volition of the Spirit and the regeneration of the soul" (*Ibid.*, 685, 684). "*Tractus internus immediate operantis est Spiritus*" (Zwingli, *Opp.* IV, 125). "*Dux vel vehiculum Spiritui non est necessarium*" (Zwingli, *Fidei Ratio* [ed. *Niemeyer*, p. 24]; Jacobs,

Book of Concord, II, 168). "The Sacraments do not work in us the grace signified by them. Only the Spirit of God can communicate grace." (Boehl, *Dogm.*, 550.)

What is wrong here? How does Reformed theology get into this unenviable situation that it opposes the Yes of Scripture with a direct No? It is due to the fact that Reformed theology in its teaching of the means of grace, even as in its Christology, is dominated by the idea of an absolute God who cannot be bound to means. Behind the Reformed teaching of the means of grace looms the rationalistic thought, foreign to Scripture, that divine omnipotence, which is needed to bring about faith and regeneration, cannot be exercised through means. Among the modern Reformed theologians this thought is stressed particularly by Charles Hodge. He says: "If this one point be determined, namely, that efficacious grace is the almighty power of God, it decides all questions in controversy on this subject" (*op. cit.*, 683). On this basis he claims: "Regeneration itself, the infusion of a new life into the soul, is the immediate work of the Spirit. There is here no place for the use of means" (*ibid.*, 685). He holds that it is a waste of time to write books against this fact. All that is necessary to find one's way in the doctrine of the means of grace is to cling to this one fact, that regeneration is a work of divine omnipotence. He says: "Volumes have been written on the contrary hypothesis; which volumes lose all their value if it be once admitted that regeneration, or effectual calling, is the work of omnipotence." In answer we say: Christian faith, or regeneration, is of course wrought by the exercise of divine omnipotence. Scripture so teaches. Luther, too, teaches this very earnestly. "When God creates faith in a man, that is verily so great a work as if He created heaven and earth anew" (St. L. IX:972). This must be maintained also against all forms of synergism. But that faith and regeneration must for this reason be wrought without means is purely a man-made idea. Scripture teaches both that faith and regeneration are the work of divine omnipotence and that this divine power is exerted through the outward means of the Word and Baptism.

But now an immediate grace has become a fixed idea of Reformed theology, the πρῶτον ψεῦδος, by which all that Scripture says of the means of grace is perverted. When Scripture says διά and ἐκ, through the Word and out of the Word, through Baptism and out of Baptism, then "through" does not mean "through," and "out," not "out," but "without," at best, "besides," "the attending circumstance." And when Scripture makes the Word or Baptism directly the subject, e. g., when it says: The Word shall "accomplish that which I please, and it shall prosper in the thing whereto I sent it" (Is. 55:11); the Word "is like as a fire and like a hammer that breaketh the rock in pieces" (Jer. 23:29); the Word is "a light that shineth in a dark place, until the day dawn and the daystar arise in your hearts" (2 Pet. 1:19); "Thy Word is a lamp unto my feet and a light unto my path" (Ps. 119: 105); the Word is "the sword of the Spirit" (Eph. 6:17); and "Baptism doth also now save us" (1 Pet. 3:21), then these statements must merely mean: Word and Baptism outwardly symbolize what the Spirit works inwardly without means, before or beside them, namely, the immediate inner illumining of the Spirit, the immediate inward cleansing of the soul by the Spirit and the blood of Christ.

There is not even the semblance of Scripture proof for the Reformed teaching of the means of grace. Examination of the Scripture proof these men attempt to adduce reveals that the proof is nothing but a *petitio principii,* that from the outset they always assume as proved and certain that the Holy Ghost needs no *vehiculum,* yes, that God's honor is assailed if His "efficacious grace" is bound to the means of grace. This man-made postulate is then used to misinterpret the Scripture texts. Where a working of the Holy Ghost or God is mentioned in Scripture, the Reformed promptly conclude that it must be an immediate operation, even if the text or context states that the operation proceeds through the Word or through the water. Furthermore, wherever Scripture states that no man can work faith, because natural man is dead in sin, and that therefore his conversion consists in a regeneration, a resurrection from spiritual death, by the working of divine omnipotence, they again promptly insert the "immediate." And in this method of bringing "Scripture proof" all opponents of the doctrine of the means of grace agree, no matter whether we turn to the Zwickau prophets, or Zwingli, Calvin, Beza, or Boehl, Hodge, Shedd, and Macpherson.

In Alexander Hodge's *Outlines of Theology,* p. 338 f., we find the Reformed Scripture proofs assembled. He puts the question: "What arguments go to show that there is an immediate influence of the Spirit on the soul besides that which is exerted through the truth?" [50] and answers with the following six Scripture proofs:

---

[50] By "truth" the Reformed understand the Word of truth, the Word of the Gospel. Thus Shedd uses the term (*Dogm. Theol.* II, 509), as is evident from his added comment that regeneration does not occur through the Word of truth. Barnes, however, correctly observes on 1 Pet. 1:23: "It is the uniform doctrine of the Scriptures that divine truth is made the instrument of quickening the soul

"1. The influence of the Spirit is distinguished from that of the Word." To prove that this is taught in Scripture, he refers *primo loco* to John 6:45, 64-65. But there it is merely said that man has no strength to come to Christ (v. 44), that all who actually come to Christ are "taught of God" (v. 45). The same thought is expressed in v. 65: "No man can come unto Me except it were given unto him of My Father." Not a word is said here of the point Hodge wants to prove, namely, an "immediate influence of the Spirit" and an operation "beside" that of the Word. But the opposite, the operation through the Word, is taught very definitely. Christ expressly declares (v. 63): "The words that I speak unto you, they are spirit, and they are life." And Peter correctly understood the Lord to mean that the operation of the Holy Ghost proceeds through the Word. To the question of Christ (v. 67): "Will ye also go away?" Simon Peter responded (v. 68): "Lord, to whom shall we go? Thou hast the words of eternal life."

"2. A divine influence is declared to be necessary to the reception of the truth." Ps. 119:18 is referred to: "Open Thou mine eyes that I may behold wondrous things out of Thy Law." Here it is indeed taught that the opening of eyes to the truth of the divine Word is God's work. But nothing is said of an immediate working of God. On the contrary, in the same Psalm we are instructed that the opening of eyes for the understanding of the Word is worked through the Word itself (vv. 104-105): "Through Thy precepts I get understanding. . . . Thy Word is a lamp unto my feet and a light unto my path."

"3. Such an internal operation on the heart is attributed to God." Again the same situation. Phil. 2:13 is cited: "It is God which worketh in you both to will and to do of His good pleasure." To be sure, this passage teaches very definitely that "to will and to do" is the work of God. But nothing is said of such an immediate operation as Hodge would prove by that text. On the contrary, also in the Epistle to the Philippians St. Paul binds the divine saving operation so fully to the Word that he rejoices if only Christ is preached, even though it be "of envy and strife" (ch. 1:15 ff.).

"4. The gift of the Spirit is distinguished from the gift of the

---

into spiritual life." Shedd, however, at the place quoted, offers the indefensible exegesis that when James 1:18 and 1 Pet. 1:23 say that regeneration takes place "through the Word of truth" and "through the Word of the living God," this phrase merely means "under the Gospel dispensation" or "under the Christian dispensation." In commenting on 1 Pet. 1.23 he says specifically: "The 'Word of God' here is not 'the incorruptible seed' itself from which the birth proceeds. The Holy Ghost is this."

Word." Again the same misuse of a Scripture statement. We are referred to the words of Christ, John 14:16: "And I will pray the Father, and He shall give you another Comforter, that He may abide with you forever." But here Christ calls the Holy Ghost "another Comforter" in distinction from His, the Son's, Person, not in distinction from His Word. Christ, on the contrary, says in the same discourse that the Holy Ghost will execute His office as Comforter through the Word of Christ (v. 26): "He shall teach you all things and bring all things to your remembrance, whatsoever I have said unto you."

"5. The nature of this influence is evidently different from that effected by the truth (Eph. 1:19; 3:7). And the effect is called a 'new creation,' 'new birth,' etc., etc." In the first passage adduced we are indeed told that we believe "according to the working of His mighty power," hence through a creative act of God. But what we do not read there is that this creative act of God is performed without the Word or beside the Word. This thought Paul once and for all thrusts aside when he says: "How shall they believe in Him of whom they have not heard? And how shall they hear without a preacher? . . . So, then, faith cometh by hearing." (Rom. 10:14, 17.) In the second passage (Eph. 3:6-7) it is expressly added that the sharing of the Gentiles in Christ and His kingdom is mediated "by the Gospel," of which Paul was made a minister.

"6. Man by nature is dead in sin and needs such a direct intervention of supernatural power." Here no Scripture is adduced. We are referred to Turretin. But Turretin, too, cannot save the situation. Man is indeed dead in sin, and only through a supernatural power is he brought to faith in the Gospel. But that this power is exercised "directly" or "immediately" is a human notion, conceived without Scripture and clung to in spite of Scripture on the basis of the rationalistic canon that a "vehicle" is neither necessary nor proper for the Holy Ghost in His work of saving men.

The Reformed are simply deluding themselves in claiming Scripture support for their teaching regarding the means of grace. Their teaching is not derived from the Bible. "Faith cometh by hearing," "through their [the Apostles'] Word," and: "born again by the Word of God," "of water and the Spirit," "God saved us by the washing of regeneration," "Baptism doth also now save us," "Christ sanctifies and cleanses the Church with the washing of water by the Word," "Ye received the Spirit by the hearing of faith" — these Scripture statements call forth in no man's mind, hence neither in the mind of the

THE MEANS OF GRACE

Reformed, the idea that faith, regeneration, the Spirit, are given or received immediately, independently of the Word and Baptism. The Reformed arrived at such teaching because here, as in Christology, they fell into the hands of a powerful tyrant. The tyrant in Christology is the man-made axiom: "*Finitum non est capax infiniti.*" Here, in the doctrine of the means of grace, the tyrant is the axiom: "Nothing intervenes between the volition of the Spirit and the regeneration of the soul." Dominated by this despot, they misinterpret Scripture. The inevitable result is that all attempted proofs are hollow proofs, paralogisms.

The same holds true of the analogy, used by Calvin as proof, that a blind man's sight is not improved by the light of the sun. This fallacious proof has passed from one generation to another of Reformed theologians like a hereditary disease. Calvin (*Inst.* III, 1, 4) says: "In vain would the light present itself to the blind unless this Spirit of understanding would open their mental eyes, so that He may be justly called the key with which the treasures of the kingdom of heaven are unlocked to us; and His illumination constitutes our mental eyes to behold them" (Allen, Transl., I, 488). This proof by analogy appeals also to modern Reformed theologians. Macpherson (*Chr. Dogmatics,* p. 425) quotes these words of Calvin and declares "the position taken by Calvin a most reasonable and thoroughly consistent one." And Hodge repeatedly returns to this proof for the immediate operation of the Holy Ghost. He says: "We may admit the value and absolute necessity of light, while we deny that light can open the eyes of the blind," and: "Men see by the light. Without light, vision is impossible. Yet the eyes of the blind are not opened by means of the light." (*Syst. Theol.* II, 700, 685; likewise, 703, 714.) Shedd, too, uses this argument (*Dogm. Theol.* II, 506 f.).

Still, this proof taken from the power of natural light is a delusion. Of course, natural light shining on a physically blind man does not improve his situation. He can't see the light. But if in the case of the physically blind there were a light which, though approaching him from without, would work the power to see, or sight, such a light would really be a help to him. And such a light the Word of grace is, as Holy Writ consistently teaches. Christ was "to preach . . . recovering of sight to the blind" (Luke 4:18), and Paul is sent among the Gentiles "to open their eyes" (Acts 26:18). When the heart has come to faith, the spiritually blind man has recovered his sight. But faith is created through the Word of God heard (John 17:20; Rom. 10:15-17; John 20:31) or read (John 20:31; 1 John 5:13). Calvin and all who have adopted his proof without investigating its validity are therefore deceiving themselves by a *petitio principii*. They were to prove, and set out to prove, that the spiritual illumination of the spiritually blind cannot be wrought through the Word of truth, the Gospel. Their proof consists in the unwarranted sequence: As natural light does not restore the sight of the physically blind, even so the spiritual light of the Word of God does not give sight to the spiritually blind. In other words, they take for granted what they are to prove, namely, that the spiritual illumination cannot be effected through the Word of the Gospel. If this persuasion had not *a priori* controlled their thinking, they would never have thought of using such an analogy. Other arguments advanced for an operation of the Spirit apart from the means of grace we have reviewed above (p. 128 ff.). At this point we summarize the chief points of Calvinists to show that their arguments beg the question and are, accordingly, deceptive.

Our opponents hold that saving faith must be founded on Christ Himself, not on the means of grace. This reasoning, common to the Reformed, the "enthusiasts" of all shades, and modern "experience" theologians, assumes that faith can and should be based on Christ to the exclusion of the means of grace. But faith in Christ, according to Scripture, is possible only through faith in the Word of Christ (John 8:31-32; 17:20), and any faith that does not depend on the Word of Christ is illusory (1 Tim. 6:3 ff.). The reproach heaped upon us for clinging to a "dead letter" does not change the fact that one either believes in the Word of Christ or does not believe in Christ at all, but in oneself and one's own speculations.

A further argument: God's glory must be safeguarded; it is intolerable to have an effect which unquestionably is God's work alone attributed to the means of grace or even to stewards of the means. This reasoning is general among the Reformed from Zwingli to our day and is made the basis for the accusation that the Lutheran doctrine of the means of grace robs God of His gracious and omnipotent work and transfers it to outward means, at least in part. In describing the Lutheran doctrine as binding the activity of the Holy Ghost to the Word of God, Charles Hodge ventures to remark: "This theory cuts us off from all intercourse with the Spirit and all dependence upon Him as a personal voluntary agent." "God has given opium its narcotic power, and arsenic its power to corrode the stomach, and left them to men to use or to abuse as they see fit. Beyond giving them their properties, He has nothing to do with the effects which they produce. So the Spirit has nothing to do with the conviction, conversion, or sanctification of the people of God, or with illuminating, consoling, or guiding them, beyond once for all giving His Word divine power. There it is: men may use or neglect it as they please. The Spirit does not incline to use it. He does not open their hearts, as He opened the heart of Lydia, to receive the Word. He does not enlighten their eyes to see wondrous things out of the Law." [51] That is indeed a grave accusation, and Hodge seems to raise it in good faith. But also here the *spiritus enthusiasticus* engages in a *petitio principii*. It assumes as *a priori* certain that the Holy Ghost, if He desires to maintain His divine dignity and retain His divine functions, must not use the *vehiculum* and dare not bind His activity to the means of grace. To be more exact, Reformed theology assumes that the Spirit of God cannot so work through means that the work remains His own. But Scripture teaches that the gracious and omnipotent operation remains solely God's, though the entire divine activity proceeds through the means of grace. It is not detached from God, nor divided between God and the means of grace. God works all of it, and the means of grace work all of it. Scripture says this by declaring: God saves (2 Tim. 1:9), and the Word and Baptism save (Acts 11:14; James 1:21; 1 Pet. 3:21); faith is wrought by God's omnipotent operation (Eph. 1:19) and through the preached Word (Rom. 10:17); the Spirit quickens (John 6:63), and the words that Christ speaks are spirit and life (John 6:63); the Christians are born of God (John 1:13), and Paul has begotten Onesimus and the Corinthians through the Gospel (Philem. 10; 1 Cor. 4:15).

It amounts to a begging of the question, too, when the Reformed theologians point to the fact that not all hearers of the Word come to faith and imagine thereby to have proved that the divine working of faith must be conceived as detached from the Word. [52] This takes for granted that the unbelief of the hearers who remain unbelieving must be traced to an absence of divine gracious activity through the Word. Scripture, however, teaches very definitely that God's effort to work faith includes also those who, though they hear the Word, remain unbelieving. Matt. 23:37: "How often would I have gath-

---

[51] *Syst. Theo.* III, 482; also II, 656 f. Hodge incidentally ascribes to the Lutheran Church the synergistic doctrine: "The reason why one man is saved and another not is simply that one resists the supernatural power of the Word and another does not." "The difference is in the moral state of those to whom the Word is presented."

[52] Zwingli, *Opp.*, IV, 125; Calvin on the *Consens. Tigur.* (ed. Niemeyer, p. 209).

ered . . . and ye would not"; Acts 7:51: "Ye do always resist the
Holy Ghost: as your fathers did, so do ye." When the truth is studied
in the "light" of Scripture and not under the Reformed bias of an
immediate and irresistible working of the Spirit, the fact that many
hearers of the Word remain unbelieving proves, not the detachment,
but the union of the efficacious grace with the outward Word of God.

This is perhaps the best place to recall that the whole terminology
of the Reformed which distinguishes between "common grace" and
"efficacious grace" has the tendency to conceal the truth in this matter
from themselves and others. To the question: "How does common
grace differ from efficacious grace?" Alexander Hodge answers very
definitely: "1. As to its subjects. All men are more or less the subjects
of the one; only the elect are subjects of the other." (*Outlines*, p. 337;
so also Chas. Hodge, II, 675, 683 ff.) But if we test this terminology
by the Scriptures, we find it disallowed. Scripture does not restrict
"efficacious grace" to the elect, but expressly extends it to include
those who reject it (Acts 13:46; 7:51; Matt. 23:37). — Again, we are
told by the Reformed that the effects of "common grace," which are
imparted also to the lost, never transcend the natural powers of man.
"The moral and religious effects ascribed to it [*scil.*, to common grace]
never rise above, so to speak, the natural operations of the mind.
The knowledge, the faith, the conviction, the remorse, the sorrow,
and the joy, which the Spirit is said to produce by these common
operations, are all natural affections and exercises, such as one man
may measurably awaken in the minds of other men." [53] But this
assertion again contradicts Scripture. Holy Writ says also of some
who are lost that they had received the knowledge of the truth and
had been sanctified by the blood of the Son of God (Heb. 10:26, 29).
It should also be noted that all who, like Hodge (*Syst. Theol.* II, 323),
expressly confine the merit of Christ to the elect deceive themselves
and others in speaking of "common grace." If the ransom paid by
Christ and accepted by God is not of sufficient value to cover all men,
there can be no "common grace" at all, that is, a grace embracing
all men. It is evident, therefore, that the differentiation between
"common grace" and "efficacious grace" is not Scriptural instruction,
but human self-deception. It is simply playing with words.

A comprehensive characterization of the Reformed teaching
regarding the means of grace should point out also the pernicious
consequences which inevitably follow when men seek to become

---

[53] Chas. Hodge, II, 674; Alexander Hodge, *Outlines*, p. 337.

independent of the divinely instituted means of grace, that is, when they assume a divine revelation and operation of saving grace without or alongside the means of grace. In the following we shall draw together some matters already mentioned and enlarge on some points.

Neither in the realm of nature nor in the Kingdom of Grace can men disregard the divine order with impunity. As to the realm of nature, it is recognized that every infringement of the "laws of nature" carries with it its punishment. In the Kingdom of Grace the effort to free ourselves from the divinely ordained means of grace turns everything topsy-turvy. All Christian concepts relevant to the faith and life of a Christian (saving grace, saving faith, assurance of grace and salvation, communion with God and Christ, the testimony of the Holy Ghost) are perverted into their opposites. The saving grace of God, that is, the gracious disposition of God in Christ, *favor Dei propter Christum,* is supplanted by an immediate working of grace in man, a *gratia infusa,* which is an illusion, since the Holy Spirit will have nothing to do with an immediate infusion of grace. The place of saving faith, which can exist and subsist only vis-à-vis the Word of the Gospel, is taken by a man-made enthusiasm based on an imaginary immediate operation of the Spirit. Faith's assurance of grace and salvation, which the Holy Ghost always works only by way of faith in the remission of sins offered in the means of grace, is displaced by the human resolve — one might say, doggedness — to claim sonship with God because of some illusory inner operations of divine grace, a resolve which breaks down lamentably and becomes evident as self-deception as soon as man is brought to a real knowledge of his sin with its accompanying *terrores conscientiae.* Likewise, a genuine personal communion with God is supplanted by a human delusion. Communion with Christ and God is mediated, according to Scripture, only by faith in the Word of Christ. Therefore a so-called fellowship with God resting on a purported immediate working of the Spirit is certainly no dealing with God, but a communing with oneself and a playing with fantasies of one's own creation. Similarly, the theory of immediate operation substitutes for the testimony of the Holy Ghost a *quid pro quo.* The internal testimony of our sonship with God, of which the Spirit of God bears witness to our spirit *(testimonium Spiritus Sancti internum),* consists in this, that the Spirit works in our heart faith in God's witness of His Son, i. e., faith in the external Word of God. 1 John 5:9-10: "This is the witness of God which He hath testified of His Son. He that believeth on the Son of God hath the witness in himself [ἐν ἑαυτῷ]; he that believeth not God hath made Him a liar, because he believeth not the record [the external Word is meant] that God gave of His Son." In him who rejects God's record of His Son, that is, the external Word of the Gospel, there is no testimony of the Holy Ghost, but such a person is himself forging the testimony of his state of grace and sonship with God. With the loss of the internal testimony of the Holy Ghost, which consists in faith in the Word of the Gospel wrought by the Spirit, also the external testimony of the Holy Ghost (*testimonium Spiritus Sancti externum*), which consists in our good works, is lost. Good works are in every case the fruits only of that faith which owes its existence and subsistence to the Word of the Gospel ("through their Word," *scil.*, the Apostles', John 17:20). There is no such thing as a faith created without and beside the Word; accordingly, neither any fruit of such a faith. — In short, if we abandon the divinely appointed means of grace and look for an immediate inner illumination and operation of grace, Christianity is converted into unstable subjectivism. Instead of planting man firmly on the immovable rock of the Word of God, we teach him to rely upon himself. Instead of lifting him to a height lying outside and above him, we crowd him back upon his own ego. Instead of helping him to come to a real communion with Christ and, through Christ, with God, we direct him to commune with himself and his own thoughts, moods, and endeavors. This subjectivism has been accurately and subtly and graphically described.[54]

Another species of self-deception needs to be pointed out in this connection. We meet it in the Reformed theologians of every era and also in their confessions. We are thinking of their endeavor to assign to the means of grace the function of externally expressing, confirming, and sealing what the Holy Ghost works immediately and internally. Even though saving grace, "efficacious grace" say the Reformed, does not come through the means of grace, still these means, especially the Sacraments, are valuable, because they certify to those immediately regenerated or converted that the immediate gift and impartation of

---

[54] For example, it has been said: To the extent that men cut loose from the outward Word, they never rise above communing with their own "fanciful notions about God and Christ," their "autosuggestions," the "projections of their own Ego." Some have likened the subjectivist to the man who raised himself by his own bootstraps, or the kitten that amuses itself with its own tail, or Muenchhausen, who lifted himself and his mount out of the morass by his hair. Luther, too, says of those who would separate the Spirit from the outward Word: "*Sie fuehren mich auf den Affenschwanz*" (they want me to mount a monkey's tail).

the Spirit is genuine.[55] The Reformed theologians have never been slack in praising this feature of the means of grace. They have even waxed eloquent in its praise. Though Zwingli has "never read in the Scriptures" that the Sacraments confer grace and the Spirit, he is very willing to grant (he says: *volens ac libens admitto*) "that the Sacraments are given for a public testimony *(testimonium publicum)* of the grace which every individual already possesses" (*Fidei Ratio*, ed. *Niemeyer*, p. 24 f.). Calvin chimes in with him. Though averse to the teaching that grace and the Spirit are conferred through the Sacraments as vessels and vehicles *(ceu vasculis et plaustris)*, he makes much of the fact that the Sacraments as "earnests and pledges *[arrhae et tesserae]* ratify" as genuine the grace which the Holy Ghost confers on the elect by an inner operation; and he holds that if one thus teaches of the Sacraments, "their dignity is duly recognized, their use plainly indicated, their usefulness extolled." (*Inst.* IV, 14, 17; Allen Transl. II, 468.) Boehl, too, speaks thus. He first assures us categorically that such an institution as Baptism cannot wash away our sins and work regeneration. He says: "The water cannot do such great things" (*Dogm.*, p. 560). But then he emphasizes just as decidedly that Baptism is a "sign," yea, "a clear proof," for this, that God is ready to wash us inwardly of our sins through Christ's blood and Spirit. Baptism is called a *"signum ablutionis."* "As the water cleanses us of external filth, so Christ's blood and Spirit cleanse us of all our sins." [56] (*Ibid.*, p. 558.) Nor will Boehl permit the Word of the Gospel to be the means of the remission of sins and of the operation of the Spirit, but he makes it a sign of the piety previously and immediately worked. He says: "Only to those whom the Holy Ghost has quickened do the assurances of Jesus apply that the Word cleanses them"; "where it [the Word] meets kindred personalities,

---

[55] Thus the Reformed confessions (the pages according to Niemeyer) call the Sacraments (*Heidelb. Cat.*, p. 407) "visible holy signs and seals"; (*I. Helvet.*, 111): "signs of divine grace"; (*Cat. Genev.*, 160): "external testification of divine good will toward us, which pictures spiritual graces by a visible sign, for the purpose of sealing to our hearts the promises of God"; (*Consens. Tigur.*, 193): "pledges, portrayals, and seals." The chief purpose of the Sacraments is "that God by them pledges to us His grace, portrays, and seals it."

[56] Here Boehl cites Acts 22:16; Eph. 5:26; Titus 3:5 without printing out the passages, which really disprove his theory of mere signification. The texts do not say that the water of Baptism removes external uncleanness, but that it washes away sins, cleanses of sins and saves. Acts 22:16: "Be baptized, and wash away thy sins"; Eph. 5:26: "That He might sanctify and cleanse it with the washing of water by the Word"; Titus 3:5: God "saved us by the washing of regeneration and renewing of the Holy Ghost."

whom the Holy Ghost has [immediately] illumined in regeneration, the Word of Scripture cannot fail to impress them." (*Ibid.*, p. 445 f.) In short, the Reformed seek to compensate for the defects in their doctrine by declaring the divinely appointed means, particularly the Sacraments, to be external signs, symbols, and therefore seals, attesting the genuineness of the internal grace obtained immediately.

But this is mere self-delusion. The means of grace certainly do not know an immediate grace, but only a grace which they themselves transmit, that is, bring, offer, and give. Remission of sins and salvation are not signified, or symbolized, by the Gospel, but are proclaimed and promised by it in order that they may be believed by the hearers (Luke 24:47; Acts 13:46). Neither is faith symbolized, or signified, by the Gospel, but springs from, or is generated through, the preaching of the Gospel (John 17:20; Rom. 10:17). Nor is regeneration outwardly symbolized by the means of grace, but is wrought through the Word and Baptism (1 Pet. 1:23; Titus 3:5). And as to the Spirit, He, too, is received through the preaching of faith (Gal. 3:2, 5), not signified or externally represented. It is a fact, therefore, that the means of grace, far from "picturing and confirming" immediate grace, label as spurious every "grace," every "faith," every "regeneration," which anyone claims to have received before, beside, or apart from the means. Accordingly, inasmuch as they teach an immediate revelation and operation of grace, the Reformed are not privileged to call the Sacraments signs and seals of grace. Their use of these terms again proves that certain terms are passed on for generations without men's taking account of their exact meaning. Also the "histories of dogma" which do not object to the use of the terms "signs," "seals," etc., by the Reformed thereby betray their lack of sound judgment. Only the Lutheran Church, since it teaches that there is remission of sins for all men through Christ's substitutional satisfaction, and that God pledges this forgiveness of sins through the means of grace to all who use them, has the right to call the Sacraments "signs and testimonies of the [gracious] will" of God, as is done in the Augsburg and the other Confessions.[57a]

[57a] The declaration of Article XIII of the Augsburg Confession that the Sacraments are "signs and testimonies of the will of God toward us, instituted to awaken and confirm faith in those who use them" (*Trigl.* 49) must be acknowledged and maintained as classic and entirely fitting. This terminology is based on the universal and complete reconciliation of the world, which is an accomplished fact through Christ. As divinely ordained signs of this fact the Sacraments are never "empty signs," but announce unequivocally and infallibly to everyone using them that God is gracious to him, on which account faith on the

Some may regard as a "hard saying" our verdict that the Reformed doctrine of an immediate operation of the Spirit reduces personal Christianity to human subjectivism and what amounts to self-deception. For this reason we begin our reply with a concession. We grant that from a solely natural or human standpoint all endeavors and struggles to gain the grace of God, the Holy Spirit, and personal communion with God apart from the divinely appointed means of grace, are respectable as an earnest expression of natural religion. One can hardly help respecting monks who, like Luther, strive whole-heartedly for an inner communion with God according to the rules of monasticism. Similarly, one naturally respects earnest Quakers, with their "silent meetings." Nor can we find it in our hearts to ridicule the revival meetings of Negroes who seek to attract the Holy Ghost by turbulent shouting and repulsive movements. The ridicule poured out on revival meetings by irreligious reporters and editors is offensive to us.

But our natural respect for these earnest endeavors to obtain the Spirit dare not blind us to the Scriptural verdict that all purported personal communion with God apart from the means of grace is self-

---

part of man is necessary for the salutary use of the Sacraments. As the divinely appointed signs they are the giving hands of God from which faith, as the receiving hand, should and can take the remission of sins. As Luther says in the Large Catechism: "Everything, therefore, in the Christian Church is ordered to the end that we shall daily obtain there nothing but the forgiveness of sin through the Word and signs, to comfort and encourage our consciences as long as we live here" (*Trigl.* 693, Art. III, 55). Accordingly, to characterize the Sacraments, our Lutheran Confessions often repeat the expressions "signs of grace," "signs of the New Testament," "signs of the remission of sins," etc. Apol.: "For these are signs of the New Testament, i. e., signs of the remission of sins" (*Trigl.* 261, XII, 42). "Which [the two Sacraments] are properly signs of the New Testament and testimonies of grace and the remission of sins" (*Ibid.*, 311, XIII, 14). "The Sacrament was instituted for the purpose of being a seal and testimony of the free remission of sins, and that, accordingly, it ought to admonish alarmed consciences to be truly confident and believe that their sins are freely remitted" (*Ibid.* 401, XXIV, 49). "The Sacraments are signs of God's will toward us, and not merely signs of men among each other; and they are right in defining that Sacraments in the New Testament are signs of grace" (*Ibid.* 409, XXII, 69). It is inaccurate to say that the difference between the Lutheran Church and the Reformed denominations consists in this, that for the Reformed the Sacraments (and the means of grace in general) are merely signs of the divine grace, while according to the Lutheran doctrine the means of grace also offer and convey what they signify. Because of their teaching of a *gratia particularis* and an immediate communication of grace, the means of grace are for the Reformed not signs and testimonies of God's gracious disposition, but question marks, causing uncertainty and doubt. When particular grace and an immediate operation of the Spirit are assumed, the means of grace can be for the recipient signs of wrath as much as signs of grace.

deception. Scripture establishes the fact that the Holy Ghost does not commit Himself to working faith immediately. The Holy Ghost does not take as His guide Zwingli's *Fidei Ratio,* with its reminder that the Holy Ghost needs no vehicle. The Holy Ghost insists on His *vehiculum,* because He has declared through His organ, the Apostle Paul, that He is received through the preaching of faith. Nor does the Holy Spirit conform to the views of Shedd, Hodge, and Boehl, who instruct Him that "efficacious grace" does not work through the means of grace, but without means. The Holy Ghost also does not avail Himself of the "silent meetings" of the Quakers, because He has willed to work, not through silence, but through the preaching of the Gospel. But He immediately becomes active when the Quakers, contrary to their own principle, diligently read the Bible, the external Word. The Holy Spirit is not impressed by the often very boisterous meetings of the revival preachers. Shouting and uproar are not His vehicle. Drums and flags, too, leave Him cold. But He immediately responds when Christ, crucified for the sins of the world, and faith in Him as the way to salvation, is proclaimed in these meetings. In short, the Holy Ghost insists upon His *vehiculum.* When this vehicle is pushed aside, the Holy Ghost is absent, and men mistake the product of another spirit and of man's own spirit for the work of the Holy Ghost and for the Holy Spirit Himself. Luther's verdict on the striving of all who assume an immediate activity of the Holy Spirit is Scriptural: "They say, You must have the Spirit; but the way in which I can receive the Spirit they want to block for me. How can I get the Spirit and believe if the Word of God is not preached to me and the Sacraments given me? I must have the means; for faith cometh by hearing and hearing by the oral Word, Rom. 10:17." (St. L. III:1695 f.)

But a comprehensive review of the Reformed teaching of the means of grace should also contain a reference to the fact that fortunately, though inconsistently, the Reformed restore in practice what they disavow in theory. This happens in more than one way. For one thing the Reformed teachers themselves do not keep silence, but preach and write a great deal about God's mercy in Christ, Christ's reconciling sacrifice for men, the necessity of hearing and reading God's Word, etc. (*Trigl.* 495, Smalc. Art., Part III, Art. III, 6.) This is, of course, inconsistent with their position that the Spirit, faith, and regeneration are not given through the external Word. But God is very gracious and the Holy Spirit very faithful. Though men in their blindness speak of Him as working immediately whatever really saves a person (efficacious grace), still He uses their preaching, as far as it is the Word of God, as a means whereby He works faith and regeneration.

Furthermore, the reminder is in place that the Reformed teachers are not even consistent in what they teach regarding the means of grace. On the one hand, Calvin warns against the endeavor to determine one's eternal election from the external Word of the Gospel (*Inst.* III, 24, 8), and the *Geneva Catechism* enjoins not to seek salvation in the Sacraments (*Niemeyer*, p. 161). On the other hand, one finds both in Calvin's writings and in the *Geneva Catechism*, as well as in the other Reformed Confessions, that they call the external Word the foundation of faith, admonish to hear and read it, and even declare Word and Sacrament to be the means through which faith is engendered and strengthened (Calvin, *Inst.* III, 2, 6).[57b] Now, whoever sets aside the erroneous statements and accepts only the correct — a thing many no doubt do — remains in the realm of truth.

The Reformed capitulate entirely when it is a matter of delivering souls from anguish of conscience caused by doubts concerning their election. Then they keep quiet about particular grace and immediate operation and point the terrified to the objective statements of Scripture that assure all men without exception of the grace of God in Christ. This, of course, is again very inconsistent. But inasmuch as this inconsistency makes room for the divine truth, the Holy Spirit is given the opportunity to perform His work of kindling faith in the Gospel.

This circumstance should, of course, not induce us to become indifferent to the Reformed errors in the doctrine of the means of grace. We are confident that we have amply shown their unscripturalness and the complete revolution they cause in the relation God has ordained between Himself and men, because they do not place man on the Word of grace and thus on Christ and God Himself, but direct man to take his stand on himself and his own product. Hence indifferentism here is surely not in place. On the contrary, we must

---

[57b] "The divine Word is the footing on which faith is sustained and supported, from which it cannot be moved without an immediate downfall. Take away the Word, then, and there will be no faith left." *Thirty-Nine Art.*, XXV: "Sacraments ordained by Christ be not only badges or tokens of Christian men's profession, but rather they be certain witnesses, and effectual signs of grace, and God's good will towards us, by the which He doth work invisibly in us, and doth not only quicken, but also strengthen and confirm our faith in Him." In its wording this article is leaning strongly on Art. XIII of the Augsburg Confession.

challenge the teaching of any operation of the Spirit independently of the Word within the Christian Church and combat it as a foreign element that has penetrated into the Christian doctrine and as a deadly enemy of living personal faith.

Moreover, the advocates of this error are by no means always irenic people. Rather, they go on the warpath and malign the Biblical truth in many ways. They assert, as we repeatedly had occasion to point out, that to teach that the divine revelation and operation of grace proceeds only through the divine Word and the Sacraments fosters a superficial Christianity, that it involves a "cession" of the Spirit's divine power to the Word (Boehl, *Dogmatik,* p. 440), and that in general it transfers to men what is manifestly God's alone.[58] In addition, their polemics often are of an unsavory character. They use the unethical method employed in the *Tridentinum* (Sess. VI, can. 10). They lump the Biblical truth with a manifest error, e. g., with the Roman doctrine of an effect of the Sacraments *ex opere operato,* and condemn both together, the truth with the error. Thus Beza, for example, proceeds and calls it "a palpable error, scooped out of the malodorous puddles of the Scholastics, when the power to communicate grace is ascribed to God indeed as Author, but to the Sacraments as instruments" (Quenstedt, II, 1131).

Another very repulsive concomitant of the Reformed false teaching is spiritual pride. Because those who harbor the conception of an activity of the Holy Ghost apart from the means of grace are dealing in an illusory, man-made quantity, they regard themselves, as experience amply proves, as the truly spiritual people and first-class Christians, while they consider those who in simple faith abide by the divinely appointed means of grace, "intellectualists," having a mere Christianity of the head; at best, second-rate Christians. Zwingli displays his low regard for Luther's Christianity in the words: "I am going to show you [Luther] that you have never grasped the vast and marvelous glory of the Gospel; and if you have once known it, you have forgotten it" (St. L. XX:1131). The same pride we meet among "enthusiasts," past or present, who arose in the Lutheran Church. Cf. Vol. II, 527 ff. This great self-esteem lasts as long as there is no anguish of conscience. But when the *terrores conscientiae* set in, pride ends in despair, unless there is a conversion to true Lutheranism,

---

58 Calvin: "Here also it must be remarked that God accomplishes inwardly what the minister represents and testifies by the external act, that we may not attribute to a mortal man what God claims exclusively for Himself" (*Inst.* IV, 14, 17; Allen Transl. II, 468).

that is, unless faith is founded on the external Word, which heretofore was despised.

Is there an essential difference among the advocates of an immediate operation of the Spirit? A great deal has been written to prove such a difference between Zwingli and Calvin. Histories of dogma incline toward assuming an essential difference between the two. Thus we read in the third edition of Winer's *Komparative Darstellung* (p. 117): "The older Reformed Confessions, written by Zwingli, teach differently of the Sacraments. Zwingli's *Fidei Ratio* says: 'I believe, yes, I know, that all the Sacraments are so far from conferring grace that they do not even convey or distribute it.' The doctrine of the later Reformed theologians, influenced by Calvin, might be comprehended under the following aspects: 1. *Symbola mystica;* 2. They are signs of God's grace appointed by Him, accordingly, more than mere moral representations of heavenly matters; for mere symbols could be introduced by the Church, too; 3. They are signs of what the Holy Ghost is working internally; sign and effect synchronize." This statement is misleading. Zwingli, too, claims to teach that the Sacraments are divinely appointed signs or symbols of what the Spirit works inwardly, and that sign and action synchronize, in this sense, that the signs in the case of the elect picture and symbolize what the Spirit is working in them immediately.[59] Beyond that Calvin does not go either.

In fact, there is no basis for a real disagreement between Zwingli and Calvin. The situation here is analogous to the one that obtains in the doctrine of Christ's Person and Work and the doctrine of the Lord's Supper. In these doctrines Zwingli and Calvin and all Reformed will agree as long as they all teach that Christ's body can possess only a local and visible mode of subsistence or presence. Similarly Zwingli and Calvin cannot differ materially in their teaching on the means of grace because they agree, first, that Christ's merit and saving grace do not apply to all who use the means of grace; secondly, that saving grace is not bound to the means of grace. Therefore the "signs" and the "effect" are for them never joined as cause and effect. According to Scripture, the signs are signs of grace for all; according to

---

[59] Of this fact we can convince ourselves by reading just a few pages in Zwingli's *Fidei Ratio*. For example, "De Sacramentis": "I believe therefore, O Emperor, that a Sacrament is a sign of a sacred thing, that is, of grace that has been given. I believe that it is a visible figure or form of invisible grace, which has of course been provided and given by God's bounty, that is, a visible example which presents an analogy to something done by the Spirit." (Jacobs, *Book of Concord,* II, 169.) For this reason the Sacraments are "to be religiously venerated, that is, to be greatly valued."

Zwingli and Calvin, only for the elect. According to Scripture, the saving operation of the Spirit proceeds through the Word and the Sacraments; according to Zwingli and Calvin, this operation is not bound to the means of grace. The sign and the effect will coincide only if we cling to the Scripture doctrine that God's grace in Christ is not particular but universal and that the Holy Ghost is active through the means of grace in all for the purpose of engendering saving faith in the proffered grace. Guericke points to Calvin's definition of the Sacraments [60] as sounding more complete than Zwingli's, but adds: "Really it is so more in appearance than in essence. Also according to Calvin's teaching, and that of the Reformed Symbols shaped by Calvinistic influences, the visible signs in the Sacraments do not as such communicate an invisible divine thing, but merely symbolize it somehow, and in addition perhaps seal it; when the Sacrament is partaken of, according to Calvin, a communicating activity of the Holy Ghost occurs, but only incidentally, entirely independent of the external signs (Calvin: "It is distinguished from the external ministry," *Inst.* IV, 14, 17; Allen Transl. II, 468), and not for all partakers, but only for the believers, for the predestinated; for all others the Sacraments in themselves are nothing but dead, wholly ineffectual signs. Sanctifying and saving power is and remains sharply detached from the Sacrament as the perceptible sign, according to Calvin's teaching as well as Zwingli's." (*Symbolik,* 2d ed., p. 437 ff.)

There is no actual reason at all to assume an essential difference between the advocates of an immediate operation of the Spirit, no matter who they are and whether they are of the 16th or of the 20th century. Luther has been reproached for putting all who teach an operation of the Spirit "without, and previous to, the Word" into one class. Modern Lutherans have particularly deplored that Luther saw the same "enthusiast" (*Schwarmgeist*) in Zwingli as in Carlstadt and the Zwickau prophets. See Meusel, VII, 403. But though we grant a dissimilarity — in truth, a pronounced dissimilarity — in their public demeanor, we cannot fail to see, for example, that Zwingli

---

[60] *Inst.* IV, 14, 1: "In the first place, it is necessary to consider what a Sacrament is. Now, I think it will be a simple and appropriate definition if we say that it is an outward sign by which the Lord seals in our consciences the promises of His good will toward us, to support the weakness of our faith; and we, on our part, testify our piety toward Him, in His presence and that of the angels as well as before men. It may also be briefly defined in other words by calling it a testimony of the grace of God toward us, confirmed by an outward sign, with a reciprocal attestation of our piety toward Him." (Allen Transl. II, 453 f.)

agreed with Thomas Muenzer in the following three points: 1. In the teaching that the Holy Spirit must contact the spirit of man without means. 2. In the accusation that Luther, because he would not hear of a revelation and operation of the Spirit without and beside the external Word of the Gospel, did not really grasp the Gospel and was wrecking the true reformation of the Church. Both were convinced, too, that they had been called by God as reformers just as well as, or even rather than, Luther. Muenzer called himself "Martin's rival with the Lord." Zwingli reminded Luther that he was but "one sincere Ajax or Diomedes" among many heroes in the Greek camp (St. L. XX:1134). 3. Both were determined to reform also the State and social conditions with the Gospel, that is, their strange interpretation of the Gospel.

Nor would we be evaluating the facts objectively if we did not list under the general classification of "visionaries" and "enthusiasts" also the more recent Reformed dogmaticians and the "experience theologians" who claim the name Lutheran. As Muenzer wanted to lead "without any means in the Spirit and to God," as Zwingli claimed that the Holy Spirit gets *"ad solum spiritum"* "without a vehicle," so also Hodge declares: "Nothing intervenes between the volition of the Spirit and the regeneration of the soul" (*Syst. Theol.* II, 684), and Shedd: "The influence of the Holy Spirit is directly upon the human spirit and is independent even of the Word itself" (*Dogm. Theol.* II, 501); and Ihmels: "Today also only that is real faith in Christ which is thrust upon man through the appearance of Christ Himself" (*Zentralfragen*, p. 89). In short, all who espouse the πρῶτον ψεῦδος that the Holy Ghost works faith and regeneration apart from the external Word do belong in one class. What differences there are among them will be found to result from the stricter or laxer application of the basic false principle.

The Reformed teaching and the Lutheran doctrine of the means of grace are direct opposites. The Reformed aver that the efficacious operation of the Holy Spirit must not be bound to the means of grace. The Lutherans declare that a purported activity of the "Spirit" without the Word and the Sacraments is a delusion and deception of the evil spirit. Zwingli represents the former, Luther the latter.

Whence this difference between Luther and Zwingli? Whence, in the case of Luther — to use the words of a recent Reformed theologian (E. F. Karl Mueller) — "his type of faith, resting directly on the Word and the Sacraments," while Zwingli warns against relying on such outward things as Word and Sacrament? The reason for the difference is this: Luther was prepared for his reformative work by a deep realization of his sinfulness and under dreadful anguish of conscience lasting for years and thus had learned in God's school that a conscience smitten by the Law can become sure of the grace of God in no other way than by taking hold by faith of the grace pledged us in the objective Word of the Gospel and in the objective Sacraments. This realization accounts for "Luther's type of faith, resting directly on the Word and the Sacraments." Over and over Luther declares: "*Experto crede Ruperto!*" "If you do not seek the forgiveness in the Word, you will stare heavenward in vain for grace or, as they say, for the inner remission" (St. L. XIX:946). But Zwingli's "reformation" did not at first grow from any terrors of conscience, but sprouted from the soil of Humanism. Zwingli's prime purpose was not to bring peace through preaching the Gospel of the remission of sins to a conscience smitten by the Law of God, but to reform the corrupt morals of the community, as this was the program of Humanism and particularly also of Erasmus. Because Zwingli had not, like Luther, come to despair of himself and all his own efforts in *terrores conscientiae*, he had also not experienced the truth that nothing whatever will deliver from doubt and despair but trusting in the objective divine promise of grace contained in the external Word of the Gospel and in the Sacraments. From this sprang Zwingli's lack of appreciation, yes, disdain, of the objective means of grace as the answer to the question how man receives, and becomes assured of having, grace and the Spirit.

The humanistic origin of Zwingli's reformation is quite generally acknowledged in recent histories of dogma. Seeberg says (*Dogmengesch.* II, 294): "Luther was then [when Zwingli began his ministry in Glarus in 1506] seeking 'a gracious God' in the cloister. When Luther in 1517 began the great struggle, Zwingli 'at Einsiedeln in the Black Forest' was searching Scripture for the true philosophy of Christ. The former entered on the great struggle of the Church from the solitude of inner struggles; the latter had learned to know men and their life while devoting himself to his studies in solitude. The religious need of his own heart guided Luther. The personal experience of faith made him the Reformer. Zwingli followed the advice of Erasmus and the humanistic trend of his day when he turned to the 'very purest sources.' He had a starting point different from Luther's, namely, the humanistic critical frame of mind over against the Church and the doctrine, the return to the sources, or the persuasion that only the teaching of the Bible is truth. These were ideas which Erasmus championed, which were hailed with joy by the greater part of the intelligentsia." Seeberg later adds (*ibid.*, p. 304), that the "undeniable difference" between Zwingli and Luther "is explained by the fact that Zwingli owed the impetus that gave rise to his ideas to Erasmian rationalism. . . . In all spheres we meet the medieval and humanistic limitations in Zwingli's teaching and activity, and in so pronounced a fashion that they account for the difference between his and Luther's views. Capito in 1536 wrote to Bullinger that he (Capito) and Zwingli, prior to Luther's emergence (*antequam Lutherus in lucem emserserat*), had taken their reformatory ideas "*ex Erasmi consuetudine*" (Gieseler, III, 1, p. 138). That Zwingli never got rid entirely of the Erasmian ideas is also evident from the fact that shortly before his death, in his *Christianae Fidei Expositio,* he ranks Hercules, Theseus, Socrates, Aristides, Numa, *et al.,* with the saints of the Old and New Testaments, with Isaiah and Elijah, with Peter and Paul, among the saints in heaven (St. L. XX:1767). From the colloquy at Marburg Luther had formed a good opinion of Zwingli and his associates for the reason that they "agreed to so many good items." He was, therefore, much perturbed when he got to see the work in which Zwingli placed these heathen among the Christian saints in heaven. It was then that Luther wrote the words which have been taken amiss by many because of the circumstances in which they were written: "Tell me, you who would be a Christian, what need is there of Baptism, the Sacrament, Christ, the Gospel, or the Prophets, and Holy Scripture, if such godless heathen, Socrates, Aristides, even the dreadful Numa, who through the devil's instigation was the first to institute the idolatry of all nations at Rome, as St. Augustine reports in *De civitate Dei,* and Scipio, the Epicurean, are blessed and saints with the patriarchs, Prophets, and Apostles in heaven, though they knew nothing of God, Scripture, the Gospel, Christ, Baptism, and the Sacrament, or the Christian faith? What can such a writer, preacher, and teacher believe of the Christian faith other than that it is on a level with all religions and that everyone can be saved by whatever he believes, even an idolater and epicure like Numa and Scipio?" (*Ibid.,* 1767.) Luther therefore repudiates the assertion of some that Zwingli died as a Christian martyr, especially since he also "had an evil score according to worldly standards, for he had acted maliciously against the other part by blocking the roads." [61] Luther adds, however:

---

[61] By blocking the roads to the five Catholic cantons the Reformed cut off their supplies; this induced the cantons to declare war against the Reformed of Zurich (St. L. XX:1777, note 3).

"From my heart I wish that he [Zwingli] had fared according to these texts (1 Cor. 5:5; 11:32: 'chastened of the Lord, that we should not be condemned with the world'); for I was very sorry, and still am, that this ill-fortune befell him" (*Ibid.*, 1777). Though Zwingli very decidedly — in fact, in a morbid manner — stressed his independence of Luther,[62] still he embodied in his writings much of the evangelical truth that Luther had brought to light.[63]

But even if we disregard the Erasmian origin of Zwingli's reformation, the fact remains that the Reformed doctrine, because it supposes an immediate operation of the Spirit, teaches man to rely on his own works and effort. It is quite generally admitted that the Reformed teaching, in distinction from the Lutheran, bears a "legalistic stamp." The Reformed Schneckenburger says (*Vergleichende Darstellung*, p. 160) that in the Reformed teaching of soteriology "an approximation to the Catholic doctrine" is noticeable. The Reformed Seeberg remarks (*Dogmengesch.* II, 299): "Zwingli does not perceive that the Law gives expression to another world view; imperceptibly the Gospel becomes for him 'a new Law.'" Seldom, however, do theologians today point out that this "legalistic stamp," or this "approximation to the Catholic doctrine," is a necessary consequence of the Reformed teaching of the means of grace. — We must, to be factual, render an even sharper judgment as to this "legalistic character." We must say that the Reformed teaching of the means of grace, where it is not neutralized by inconsistency, makes man take his stand not in part, but entirely on his own efforts and works. This judgment must be true because the immediate working of the Spirit, insisted on by the Reformed theologians from Zwingli to our day, is non-existent, except in the human imagination. But if, as is very evident from Scripture, the Holy Ghost has nothing to do with such an immediate operation we are forced to conclude that man himself produces such internal states, moods, changes, and works as bear an external resemblance to the genuine product of the Holy Ghost. Thus the Reformed teaching

---

[62] *Opp.* I, 253: "Prior to and before ever any man in our neighborhood knew anything of Luther's name, I had begun to preach the Gospel of Christ in the year 1516." P. 254: "For who has taught me to preach the Gospel and to preach an entire Evangelist serially? Was it perhaps Luther? But indeed I began such preaching before ever I had heard Luther mentioned." By "preaching the Gospel" Zwingli meant preaching on the "Gospel written by Matthew," instead of the pericopes. "Luther's writing helped me little at that time toward the preaching of Matthew."

[63] Seeberg, too, insists on this: "Zwingli found Luther's ideas in Scripture after he had learned them from Luther" (*Dogmengesch.* II, 294f.).

of the means of grace naturally and inevitably leads to the papistic doctrine of works.

Lately some have indeed argued that in its doctrine of predestination Reformed theology has an antidote against the Roman teaching of salvation by works. Seeberg remarks (*ibid.,* pp. 300, 304): "To counteract the Roman teaching of merit and works, Zwingli developed his dogma of predestination"; and of Zwingli's "determinism" he judges that "it has proved its worth as a weapon against the Roman teaching of salvation by works." Schneckenburger, too, sees in the Reformed dogma of predestination the factor that keeps Reformed theology out of the Roman camp and secures for it a place "in the realm of evangelical Protestantism." He says: Reformed teaching "remains within the bounds of evangelical Protestantism only through its concepts of predestination and the irresistible operation of grace" (*op. cit.,* p. 160). Even more extravagant as to the supposedly anti-Roman character of the Reformed doctrine of predestination is the assertion in Meusel: "There can be no question that Zwingli's dogma of predestination thoroughly did away with the synergism of the Roman Church" (*Handlexikon* VII, 405).

This is a fallacy. The very opposite actually happens. The predestination taught by the Reformed is, just like the "immediate operation" of the Spirit, nothing more than a chimera, because the immediate operation of the Spirit is a part of it. But an imaginary factor can produce no genuine activity of grace. There is, of course, an eternal election. This eternal election, however, did not take place immediately, but through the means of grace (2 Thess. 2:13). And so its realization in time does not come to pass without means, but through the means of grace (2 Thess. 2:14; 2 Tim. 1:9-10). The truths, already outlined (Vol. II, 418), will be more extensively treated in the section on Election. The election taught by the Reformed, which includes an illusory immediate operation of the Spirit, cannot, for that very reason, "counterbalance" the Roman doctrine of salvation by works, but must drive men all the more into efforts of their own. It becomes necessary by one's own efforts to produce such moods, changes, and works as seem to be marks of eternal election.

There is but one way by which the Reformed theology can escape the doctrine of works — by accepting Lutheranism. And the Reformed actually take this step when they, including Calvin, at the last direct those who are troubled by grave doubts of their election to the universal grace as it is attested in the means of grace. Schneckenburger, too, acknowledges this fact. After he has pointed out the various means by which Reformed theologians vainly endeavor to remove a man's doubt of grace and election, he continues: "Hence the admonition to appropriate the universal promises of God, to view one's election only in Christ, the Mediator of its execution, not to offend God by distrust of His grace, etc. But all these things, strictly speaking, can be said only from the Lutheran point of view, and practical considerations will compel one to take the Lutheran stand. For [according to Reformed doctrine] the universal grace of God and the merit of Christ may not be for me." (*Op. cit.*, p. 260 ff.)

We have repeatedly referred to Schneckenburger's "*Vergleichende Darstellung des lutherischen und reformierten Lehrbegriffs.*" He errs in a number of points; we have already taken note that in his presentation he treats the predestination taught by the Reformed as real, while in fact it is entirely illusory. Still, Schneckenburger's book is worth perusing. For that reason we quote another passage (I, 233 ff.; 265 ff.), in which he treats of two things: 1. Reformed theology seeks to console those harassed by doubts as to grace and election by urging contemplation of their sanctification and good works; but the gravity of the practical situation forces a transition to Lutheran ground; 2. Within the Lutheran Church, Pietism prepared the way for a shift to Reformed territory, and the modern "theology of experience" is walking entirely in Reformed paths. Schneckenburger says: "In Reformed congregations the fear of having committed the sin against the Holy Ghost is found much more frequently than in Lutheran. This is due to the [Reformed] dogma that a complete fall from faith is impossible in the case of the truly regenerate [64] and to the admission that one may be mistaken as to one's religious state.[65] Formerly feeling that he had a right to regard himself as regenerate, the sinner is now gripped by a genuine knowledge of his sin, overcome by the feeling of guilt, bereft of all hopeful feelings.[66] Then, his confidence shaken, the desperation of being a *reprobus* sets in; his former experiences seem to have been mere illusions, or rather he seems to have tasted of the heavenly gift, but only tasted and never possessed it. The more pronounced his former experiences were, the more reason he may have to accuse himself of having misused the grace bestowed, the more keenly he now feels the disparity, and the sin against the Holy Ghost, leaving no room for repentance, excluding his return, appears to have

---

[64] See the Canons of the Synod of Dort (Niemeyer, p. 716), quoted in Vol. II, 468, footnote 24. Calvin, *Inst.*, III, 2, 12.

[65] Calvin, *Inst.*, III, 24, 8, quoted in Vol. II, 47.

[66] Cromwell, see p. 90.

been committed. 1. To reassure people in this situation, they are regularly told that this fear itself is proof of the contrary and an indication of the presence of a spark of faith.[67] But this procedure seldom suffices; for the fear is there, gripping the heart,[68] all the more since, according to the [Reformed] system, it can always be argued with good reason that this fear may just as likely be the presentiment of hell as salutary sorrow.[69] For even the positive feeling of possessing grace may be fraudulent; then how much more this fear? Besides, since the immediate self-assurance, which is to be propped up by the idea of predestination, fluctuates, the fear of reprobation, more germane to the depressed consciousness, is frequently coupled with it. Under these conditions it becomes difficult to console, and of the *periculosissima praedestinationis tentatio* even the Symbols have much to say. 2. Now one must show that no one can be certain either of his election or of his reprobation, that therefore a person is committing an error if, without further ado, he regards himself as a castaway. Nevertheless, the possibility ever remains that the alarmed person may really be a *reprobus,* the very thought of which has a paralyzing effect on any effort of restoration. 3. Hence the admonition to take advantage of the universal promises of God, to view one's election only in Christ, the Mediator of its execution, not to offend God by distrust of His grace, etc. But all these things, strictly speaking, can be said only from the Lutheran point of view, and practical considerations will compel one to take the Lutheran stand. The universal grace of God, the merit of Christ, as you know [according to Reformed doctrine], may apply not at all to me, because I am a reprobate. Still, to encourage the soul against such thoughts, I must ever and again seek to find positive reasons for my not being a reprobate, but, of course, only reasons that lie in my subjective state as a person under the influence of God's grace. 4. For this purpose all sorts of former experiences of grace are again called to mind which may have been genuine, though there can be no absolute dependence on the truth of these inner experiences. 5. One is told to consider that the elect are the very ones whom God leads, like Christ, into grave fears, and how this trial bespeaks their sonship with God. 6. But finally, of course,

---

[67] This course, in itself, is not wrong. When a terrified sinner has a desire for the grace of God in Christ, faith itself is present, and the distressed individual is to be told this fact.

[68] See Vol. II, 444 f. for Scriptural treatment of the case.

[69] According to Calvin (*Inst.* III, 24, 8; see the words, p. 118f.), the Gospel is preached to some as "an occasion of heavier condemnation."

with the question returning again and again whether it is merely a trial or incipient condemnation, nothing is left but to direct attention to that subjective behavior which alone has the marks of truth and is the true token of election. One admonishes unto active obedience, the practice of piety, diligence in good works; in other words, activity is called for, which alone can produce a result satisfying the consciousness. But in most cases also this proves to be an insufficient means of consolation, since it bids man refute his inner doubt by his own activity regardless of his feelings and ignores the fact that just this doubt enervates any real activity. But by all means to stimulate action the inducements just mentioned are employed, and the admonitions to godly activity are used, e. g., those drawn by Hyperius from eternity, notwithstanding the danger of still being condemned, since in this case the damnation would at least be mitigated. In short, it all has this one end in view, never to let the thought of being rejected take root, but by one's conduct continually to seek to establish whether one is not, after all, one of the elect, always to live as if one really is elect, and to that end also to believe oneself elect, after one's condition has shown at least the possibility of it. 7. That alone is said to befit our relation to God, whose grace we would be despising if we distrusted his willingness to accept us. The promising will of God addressed to all must also be regarded by all as pertaining to them individually. As faith in general, so also this special confidence of one's election comes under the law of duty. You must permit yourself to be influenced by the promises and the will of God and, accordingly, believe that divine grace is for you, too, that is, forget that the grace may indeed be merely apparent and not real.[70] Always the fundamental thought is that the energetic resolve of one's own will, one's own internal self-assertion *(Selbsttat)*, courageous self-vindication is — since saving grace alone makes it possible [71] — the most dependable sign of this grace and therefore, above all, to be stimulated. Such is the position of old teachers, faithful to the system. Recent teachers, however, e. g., Schaff, though they cling to the thesis which causes all this trouble, know of no other answer to allay the doubt of the soul as to whether one really is regenerate than simply to take the Lutheran stand; in offering this solution, they drop the dogma of reprobation.

---

[70] That is, that God may be presenting the Gospel to you not to give you salvation, but to make you deserve a "heavier condemnation."

[71] "Saving grace," however, is active only through the means of grace. When an immediate operation is assumed, there is no working of God's grace, but a product of one's own ego.

Yes, even the *Confessio Helvetica (Conf. Helvet. posterior* is meant, ed. Niemeyer, p. 481, c. 10), as a last resort against the *periculosa tentatio praedestinationis,* points to the Sacraments, which are to give the sufferer the desired confidence; but in giving this counsel, the Confession entirely disregards the fact that the Sacraments can impart such confidence only if they are used in faith, therefore in just the spiritual state of which the person is uncertain." In these words Schneckenburger shows correctly that through the Reformed *gratia particularis* and through the consequent separation of grace from the means of grace man, in his search for the grace of God, is thrown back on himself, on his subjective condition and his own works.

How Lutherans came to take the Reformed position Schneckenburger (p. 254) describes thus: "As the Reformed doctrine is *in praxi* always driven toward the Lutheran position, so the Lutherans, once they have forsaken the old Lutheran way of viewing things . . . in theory immediately succumb to the abstract consistency of the Reformed doctrine, which we see ruling in modern theology today." Farther on (p. 282) he says: "The individual's assurance of his sonship with God and salvation, a primary need of the Reformed, could not come into question at all for a Lutheran while orthodoxy was in bloom in his Church. In penitential faith he took the assurance of forgiveness out of the absolution, which was for him the absolute truth and the consolation of the Holy Spirit; and where there is forgiveness of sins, there is also life and salvation. Only when Pietism arrived, there was introduced a reflection on one's inner status. Unrestrained subjectivity operated entirely apart from the objective acts of the Church, which no longer gave full satisfaction. Thus gradually an approach to the Reformed way of viewing things begins to appear even among the orthodox."

A few annotations should be appended to these words of Schneckenburger. The question: "Can I be sure that I am a child of God?" confronts, of course, an orthodox Lutheran, too, and that daily, because he recognizes, like David (Ps. 143:2) and Paul (Rom. 7:18), that he deserves damnation. But while really orthodox, he does what God would have every poor sinner do, i. e., he looks upon the gracious countenance of God in Christ, "the glory of God in the face of Jesus Christ" (2 Cor. 4:6), which shines on him from the Word of grace and the Sacraments as the divine means for remitting sins. — Again, for orthodox Lutherans absolution is but one form among several of God's pledge of grace. In the Smalcald Articles we read: "The Gospel not merely in one way *(non uno modo)* gives us counsel and aid against sin; for God is superabundantly rich (and liberal) in His grace (and goodness). First, through the spoken Word by which the forgiveness of sins is preached in the whole world; which is the peculiar office of the Gospel. Secondly, through Baptism. Thirdly, through the holy Sacrament of the Altar. Fourthly, through the power of the keys, and also through the mutual conversation and consolation of brethren, Matt. 18:20: 'Where two or three are gathered together,' etc." (*Trigl.* 491, Part III, Art. IV.) The orthodox Lutheran knows, as Luther expresses it in his Large Catechism: "Everything, therefore, in the Christian Church is ordered to the end that we shall daily obtain there nothing but the forgiveness of sin through the Word and signs [Sacraments], to comfort and encourage our consciences as long as we live here." (*Trigl.* 693, Art. III, 55.) — "Reflection on one's own inner status" in seeking assurance of the forgiveness of one's sins the orthodox Lutheran correctly regards as superfluous because he knows well that the remission of sins is entirely independent of his own subjective status. The fitting "subject" for the remission of sins, or justification, is in every case "the ungodly" (Rom. 4:5).

As for "Pietism," it has been said with good reason (R. E., 2d ed., XI, 672 ff.) that the term has not always been employed in the same sense. With Schneckenburger we understand it to mean the unhealthy phenomenon which appeared within the Lutheran Church toward the end of the 17th century and was prominent in the first half of the 18th century. The essence of this Pietism was that it led men to base their state of grace before God on inner experiences of the human heart, contrition, "faith," internal renewal, etc., instead of basing it on the grace earned by Christ and offered by Him in the objective means of grace. Schneckenburger rightly sees in this subjectivity a transition to Reformed territory. Some of the Pietists plainly had a good intention. With a "heartfelt," "living" Christianity they wanted to oppose the externalism which unfortunately had become rampant in the Lutheran Church and made an *opus operatum* of the use of the divinely appointed means of grace. But unhappily they belonged to the class of reformers who do not know how to bring about a true reformation of the Church. Instead of confining themselves to condemning the misuse of the means of grace on the part of the carnally secure, they impugned also the right use which the contrite sinners were to make of those means. Every poor sinner who, with a heart terrified by the Law, seeks for the grace of God is to be guided directly to the Word of the Gospel and the Sacraments, in which God proffers the forgiveness of sins earned by Christ to the sinner without attaching any subjective condition, i. e., a stipulation as to man's inner state. In so far as Pietism did not point poor sinners directly to the means of grace, but led them to reflect on their own inward state to determine whether their contrition was profound enough and their faith of the right caliber, it actually denied the complete reconciliation by Christ (the *satisfactio vicaria*), robbed justifying faith of its true object, and thus injured personal Christianity in its foundation and Christian piety in its very essence. The reflection on their own inner state, to which the carnally secure are to be admonished and which belongs to the preaching of the Law, the Pietists enjoined upon the poor, terrified sinners, to whom the Gospel is to be preached. Thus Pietism turned into the channel common to the Reformed and the Papists.

Of greatest importance to us, however, is the fact that all modern "experience theologians," who want to base faith not merely on the Word of Christ, but also on the "historical appearance" of Christ, on the "historical impressions" of Christ, on the "Person" of Christ in distinction from the Word of Christ, manifestly have deserted Lutheranism and gone over to the Reformed. This defection to the Reformed is found even in the most conservative advocates of the "experience theology." Only that is supposed to be "real faith in Christ" which is "thrust upon man through the appearance of Christ Himself" (Ihmels, *Zentralfragen*, p. 89).

In defense of the "experience theology" men have asked: Can one not gain the "impression" that there is a gracious God also from the history of God's guidance and government of the Church Universal or of the lives of individuals? In reply we say that two things must not be forgotten: 1. There are, indeed, in the life of the Church and of individuals events in which we can see the strong and gracious hand of God. But as there appear in the realm of nature, along with the signs of God's goodness, along with sunshine, growth and prosperity, peace and protection, etc., also terrifying signs of God's wrath, such as thunder and lightning, earthquakes, floods, epidemics and hard times, wars and destruction: so, too, we have in history this double manifestation of grace and wrath in the life of the Church and of individuals. Our eye meets, on the one hand, the multitude of false teachers and their overwhelming number of adherents; on the other hand, the small number of Christians and their cross. And these historical phenomena are felt also by Christians as manifestation of God's wrath and at times make so profound a "historical impression" on the children of God as to make them imagine that the devil and not Christ rules all things, and that not the pious, but the ungodly enjoy the favor of God. Read, for example, the 73d Psalm. Then our only help is to flee with Asaph into the "sanctuary of God" and get our bearings as to these "historical phenomena" from God's Word alone. Without such Biblical orientation we must fall a prey to doubt and despair.

2. But also when we have gotten our orientation from God's Word regarding the historical phenomena in our and the Church's life and realize that all things, also the manifestation of God's wrath, work together for good to them that love God (Rom. 8:28), we must still maintain on the basis of Scripture that these historical phenomena should not be made the basis of saving faith. The correlative of saving faith is that grace of God, that remission of sins, which Christ earned for us some 1900 years ago by His *satisfactio vicaria*, which is dispensed and deeded to us in the Word and the Sacraments. Whoever makes what God graciously works in the Church or the individual the foundation of his faith in the gracious God, is *eo ipso* deserting Christ. He is founding grace with God on his contrition, his faith, his renewal, his being "implanted into Christ," his inclusion in "the new humanity," "in the Church," etc., instead of founding it on Christ's perfect reconciliation of sinful mankind. Luther is not exaggerating when he calls the man who founds his faith in a gracious God on his "experiences," particularly on his possession of faith, an "idolatrous, apostate Christian," for this reason: "For he trusts and builds on his own, namely, on a gift which God has given him, and not on God's Word alone" (which promises us God's grace for the sake of Christ's work), "just as another builds and trusts in his strength, riches, power, wisdom, holiness, which as well are gifts given him of God" (St. L. XVII:2213). Thus it is clear as day that Schneckenburger is right when he says that modern theology is standing not on Lutheran, but on Reformed ground, that is, knows only a faith that in the quest for God's grace ponders itself and its subjective nature. Thus Kirn (*Dogm.*, p. 118) expressly declares that reflective faith trusts in the recasting of the life of mankind, since this contributes to the redemptive value of the work of Christ. Other "experience theologians" prefer other ways of stating it. For the Christian faith that seizes the divine remission of sins in the means of grace they substitute reflection on one's ingrafting into the new humanity of Christ, on one's membership in the Kingdom of God and one's activity in it, etc.

The close relation between the "experience theology" and the Reformed also explains the odd appraisal of Zwingli's and Calvin's theology by "experience theologians," e. g., Seeberg. We should like to preserve the Lutheran Church of America from bewilderment by such untrustworthy appraisals. On the one hand the Erasmian source of Zwingli's reformation is conceded; it is granted that Zwingli unwittingly changes the Gospel to a "new Law"; that Zwingli does not, like Luther, lead us to know God in Christ, but bids us to know God before we learn to know Christ; that Zwingli's Christianity is a sort of "philosophy" distilled from the Bible. On the other hand it is contended that there is this striking essential agreement between Zwingli and Luther, that both have "a common understanding of the Gospel," that there is an "essential agreement" between Calvin's and Luther's "type of Protestantism." According to this appraisal it would be irrelevant to a true understanding of the Gospel and Christianity in general whether Christ redeemed all men or only some, whether grace and the Spirit were given only through the God-appointed means of grace or apart from them! We repeat, the kinship of the "experience theology" with the Reformed theology accounts for this strange finding. Both kinds of theology deny that mankind is reconciled to God by Christ's *satisfactio vicaria*. The Reformed theology limits the extent, the "experience theology" the intrinsic value, of the reconciliation accomplished by Christ. Both theologies further deny that saving faith is generated solely through the means of grace and has the means as its object (the thing believed). Both therefore are standing on Roman ground in soteriology, that is, they both agree in this, that man must become sure of his being in grace by reflection on his subjective state, on his experiences, his renewal and God-pleasing life, etc. Truly, an unbiased study of the situation created by the assumption of an operation of grace divorced from the Word of Christ always leads to Luther's verdict that in practice Papist and "enthusiast" are one.

But though we adhere to this judgment of Luther, we have no cause to exalt ourselves before God above any "enthusiast." We rather remind ourselves again that because of our innate *opinio legis* our flesh, too, is inclined to that "enthusiasm" which we condemn in others. Luther, too, confesses again and again that in answering the question whether God is gracious to him he has not yet finished learning to disregard himself entirely or to turn his back on himself and against all his feelings and own sensations to cling to nothing but the Word of promise. But the difference that does remain between Luther and the Lutheran Church on the one hand and Calvin, the Reformed Church, and the "experience theologians" on the other hand is that the Lutherans reject all "enthusiasm" as error, while the others defend "enthusiasm" as the truth.

In a discussion of the means of grace also the separation of Church and State must be dealt with because the question is being asked whether also the State with its laws and powers is to be employed as a kind of auxiliary means of grace for the building of the Church. — Rome's position is familiar. Both pre-Reformation and post-Reformation Rome demands two things of the State. First, it declares that it is the duty of the State to serve the Church with its power, even with fire and sword if necessary. Secondly, it declares that it is the duty of the State to order its affairs in accordance with the decrees of the Church.[72] — What position did the 16th-century Reformation take on this question? Here also recent histories of dogma point out a difference between Reformed and Lutheran teaching. While Luther lays down the principle that the State is not to be governed with God's Word, but by human reason [73] and that, accordingly, it is not the business of the government "to prevent anyone from believing and teaching what he will, be it Gospel or lies" (St. L. XVI:50), Zwingli vigorously inculcates the principle that the State must be ruled with the Word of God and that the government, if found lax in this respect, "could be deposed with God's approval." See *Opp.* I, 369 ff., 524. And while the Augsburg Confession restricts the authority of the government, as not concerned with the protection of the souls, to the protection of "bodies and bodily things against manifest injuries," and to the restraining of men "with the sword and bodily punishments" (*Trigl.* 85, XXVIII, 11), Calvin contrariwise — most likely with a frown at the Augsburg Confession — points to the folly (*stultitia*) of people "who would wish magistrates to neglect all thoughts of God and to confine themselves entirely to the administration of justice among men (*ius inter homines*); as though God appointed governors in His name to decide secular controversies (*terrenae controversiae*), and disregarded that which is of far greater importance — the pure worship of Himself according to the rule of His Law" (*Inst.* IV, 20, 9; *Allen Transl.* II, 641). — Schneckenburger therefore judges: "The affinity of Reformed piety with the Catholic appears in general also from this, that both aim to set up a theocracy (divine government) by men over the State and secular matters in general

---

[72] Both demands are definitely enunciated in the encyclical *"Immortale Dei"* of Nov. 1, 1885. See *Lehre und Wehre,* 1886, p. 12 ff.

[73] St. L. X:382 ff., 417. See also *Lehre und Wehre,* 1896, 193 ff.: "Sind politische Pastoren ein Unding?"

and demand that the positive divine Law be applied as the direct norm of all social relations. . . . Both forms of piety [the Catholic and the Reformed], because of their active social trend, are definitely different from the Lutheran." (*Vergl. Darstell.* I, 161.)

Of course, the Lutheran Church has an "active social trend," too, in so far as it very energetically directs Christians to serve their fellow men in their social relations. Well known is the dictum of Luther: "Cursed be the life wherein a man serves only himself and not his neighbor; and, again, blessed be the life wherein a man lives not for himself, but for his neighbor!" (St. L. XI:747.) The Lutheran Church more than any other directs Christians into the social relations with all their works by teaching emphatically that works do not belong to the relation toward God, that is, are not necessary to obtain or preserve salvation. "Look to it," says Luther, "that the works which you do are not directed toward God, but toward your neighbor! Let him who is a sovereign, a lord, a mayor, a judge, not imagine that he is a sovereign to merit heaven with it, or to seek his own gain by it, but rather that he thereby serve the community. And so it is with all other works, which I undertake for my neighbor's good." (*Ibid.*) — But the Lutheran Church, so far as it remains true to its principles, teaches no social activity aiming at the establishment of a theocracy by demanding, for instance, that the State embody the Christian religion in its Constitution and attend to its enforcement. On the contrary, the Lutheran Church warns against this mingling of Church and State. The Augustana says: "Let it [the Church] not break into the office of another; let it not transfer the kingdoms of this world; let it not abrogate the laws of civil rulers; let it not abolish lawful obedience; let it not interfere with judgments concerning civil ordinances or contracts; let it not prescribe laws to civil rulers concerning the form of the Commonwealth." "For civil government deals with other things than does the Gospel. The civil rulers defend not minds, but bodies and bodily things against manifest injuries, and restrain men with the sword and bodily punishments in order to preserve civil justice and peace." (*Trigl.* 85, XXVIII, 13, 11.) Making religion a concern of the State, as is done in a theocracy, agrees with Roman and Reformed teaching, but is contrary to the Lutheran doctrine. That is Schneckenburger's meaning when he at this point affirms a difference between the Lutheran Church on the one hand and the Roman and Reformed Churches on the other.

Seeberg describes Zwingli's conception of the relation of Church and State in this way: "The theocratic idea which guided Zwingli

permitted neither the Church nor the State to come into its own.
For, on the one hand, the civil government exercises church discipline,
so that the tenets of the Church actually become the law of the State;[74]
on the other hand, this government is entirely under the authority of
Holy Scripture; its laws and ordinances are valid only in so far as
they agree with Scripture. When the government acts contrary to
Scripture, it is to be deposed.[75] The subjection of the Church to the
State is not an actuality, for the laws of the State are valid only when
they match the Law of the Church or of the Bible. This is a genuinely
medieval thought complex. The execution of Zwingli's reformation
embraced both a new system of doctrine and new rules of life, both
of which were to be enforced by the powers of the State. Christianity
is a concern of the State, but the State is the organ of the Church.
Like Savonarola, Zwingli sought to reform his city according to the
divine code of the Bible with the help of the civil government. . . .
In all spheres we therefore meet the medieval and humanistic limitations in the teaching and activity of Zwingli, and in so pronounced
a fashion that they account for the difference between his and
Luther's views." (*Dogmengesch.* II, 305.)

Seeberg (*ibid.*, p. 400 f.) states that Calvin "assigned to the
State the duty as a servant of God to enforce the ideals of the Church
also with worldly measures. . . . The State has the duty to punish
every insubordination to the established religion and to see to the
enforcement of the Commandments not only of the Second, but also
of the First Table. This duty is said to be evident not only from the
history of Israel, but also from the views of the heathen, who all
make the *cura pietatis,* the promotion of piety, the first object of the
State. (*Inst.* IV, 20, 3. 9.) In such promotion the State may, of course,

---

74 Second Disputation at Zurich (*Opp.* I, 524): "My lords are also to enact
no law other than from the holy, infallible Scripture of God. Should they become
negligent in this and pass opposing laws, contrary to my hope, I shall promptly
preach against them with the Word of God."

75 In his explication of Art. XLII, *Opp.* I, 369, he says of the government:
"If, however, they are unfaithful and deviate from the plumbline of Christ, they
may be deposed with God's sanction." At the end of this section Zwingli explains
how it happens that a tyrannical government is not unanimously deposed. It is
due to the fact that piety and righteousness are not yet general enough. He says:
"Because we are so lukewarm in our love of common righteousness, we overlook
all the wicked deeds of the tyrants and are deservedly rent by them and at last
punished with them. So, then, it is not counsel or way of getting rid of the
tyrants that is lacking, but general piety is lacking. Beware, you tyrants! The
Gospel will train pious people. Become pious, too; then you will be borne up
on hands. If, however, you do not do that, but rage and storm, you will be
trodden under foot."

not alter the divine Law. In reality it will therefore only have to execute what the clergy prescribe. From this viewpoint one can comprehend the position which Calvin claimed for himself in Geneva as well as also the Draconian severity of the legislation and administration of justice directed by him. Since every sin is a revolt against the divine Majesty, the severest civil punishments must be inflicted on the sinner. Calvin's reformation was therefore executed in the manner of a theocracy. God is the Lord, service of whom the Church demands and the State enforces. Since, however, civil authority is closely related to the Church through the church office endowed with divine authority, the connection of Calvin's ideal of the Church with the medieval ideas is far clearer in his than in Zwingli's case. . . . This persuasion [of Calvin] explains his procedure against Servetus." [76]

Schneckenburger regards this Reformed mingling of Church and State as a valuable supplement to Luther's Reformation. He thinks the difference between the Catholic and Reformed piety on the one hand and the Lutheran on the other hand "is so great that one can question whether it would have been possible at all to achieve and maintain the Reformation in its purely Lutheran form against the more forceful, regimenting principle in Catholicism if the specifically Reformed reformation had not been allied with the Lutheran. How long they hesitated in Saxony, though many years had passed after the first preaching of the Gospel, to alter even the least thing in the cultus, until Carlstadt made things fly in Reformed style, which, however, made it impossible for him, as a heterogeneous element, to hold out here indefinitely. . . . In Zurich, on the other hand [under Zwingli] a beginning was immediately made to abolish everything improper, radically to change the cultus, to improve the morals and the police." (*Vergl. Darstell.* I, 161 f.)

But this Reformed reformation of Church and State, which Schneckenburger and others [77] regard as a valuable addition to the faith and life taught by Luther, actually constitutes a continuance in the teaching and practice of Rome and tends to convert Christianity into work-righteousness trimmed with Christian frills. Both the assumption of an immediate operation of the Spirit and the mingling

---

[76] Michael Servetus was burned at the stake in Geneva on October 27, 1553, for his heresy (Antitrinitarianism). Too bad that Melanchthon, too, condoned this act. Cf. Melanchthon's letter to Calvin of October 14, 1554, in *Corpus Ref.* VIII, 362 f.

[77] Schneckenburger mentions Ranke, *Reformationsgesch.*, III, 89. But regarding Ranke see *Lehre und Wehre*, 1868, 119 f.

of Church and State crowd the Reformed Church into the doctrine of works. The assumption of an immediate operation of the Spirit has this effect because there is no such immediate operation and man is therefore left to his own efforts, which he then mistakenly regards as the product of the Holy Ghost. Seeking to build the Church by the use of the powers of the State leads to work-righteousness because the powers of the State, even with rigorous enforcement, never transmit the grace of God in Christ, faith, and the Holy Spirit, but at best achieve an outward piety that does not rise above the province of the Law and externalism. Luther writes: "Therefore it is useless and impossible to command or compel anyone by force to believe one thing or another. A different method must be used; force cannot accomplish it. . . . Faith is a voluntary thing, to which no one can be forced. Nay, it is a divine work in the soul, certainly not a matter which outward authority could compel or create. . . . The blind, wretched folk do not see how utterly hopeless and impossible a thing they are attempting. For no matter how sternly they command and how hard they rave, they can only force the mouth and hand of the people to comply; the heart they cannot compel, though they wear themselves out trying. . . . In this way they compel weak consciences to lie, to deny, and to say what they do not believe in their hearts, and thus they load themselves down with the dreadful sins of others." (St. L. X:397 f.)

In spite of the warnings of Luther and the clear presentation of the doctrine in Article XXVIII of the Augustana, the mingling of Church and State, sad to say, crept into the Lutheran Church, too. This confusion, however, is not to be considered a complementing or perfecting of the Lutheran doctrine and position, but it is to be adjudged a trespassing on Reformed-Roman territory, with the same evil consequences which result wherever the false principle prevails.[78]

----

[78] Subject to historical investigation is the question whether Luther did not in specific cases transgress the correct principle taught by him. Such a thing happens also to eminent people. Peter on one occasion acted contrary to the correct principle he himself taught, even after Pentecost (Gal. 2:11 ff.). On Luther's sharp distinction in principle between Church and State on the one hand and his accommodation to the prevailing confused conditions on the other hand compare Walther, *Pastorale*, p. 368 ff.; Koestlin, *Luthers Theol.*, 2d ed., II, 274 ff. In the St. Louis edition of Luther's works, in the historical introduction to the section *Against the Jews*, disapproval is expressed of Luther's writing of 1543 *"Von den Juden und ihren Luegen,"* in so far as Luther, after the Jews had misused his former protection, here advises the use of the power of the State against them (cf. St. L. XX, Introduction, p. 63, note 1). Luther makes it the duty of the authorities "to force the Jews to labor, to forbid them to charge

There is no choice: If we desire to retain the Christian doctrine, namely, the doctrine that we are justified and saved by God's grace through faith without the deeds of the Law, we must, for one thing, hold to the divinely ordained means of grace; and, secondly, we must be content with these means and refrain from employing the powers of the State to build the Church. We shall revert to this subject, the separation of Church and State, in the doctrine of the Church.

7

The Relation of Luther's Doctrine of the Means of Grace to the Medieval and Reformed Teaching.

Some have asserted an affinity between Luther's doctrine of the means of grace and the medieval doctrine. Recall Harnack's opinion referred to before: "By singling out certain action as 'means of grace' Luther harked back to the constricted medieval range of ideas which he had left" (see p. 132). However, the truth is that there can be no affinity between Luther's doctrine and the medieval teaching of the means of grace because Luther and the medieval theology held diametrically opposite views of saving grace. According to the teaching of the Middle Ages, saving grace is a good quality infused into man, *gratia infusa*, and the purpose of the means of grace is to infuse such a measure of "grace" into man that by co-operating with this "grace" man can earn the remission of sins and salvation first *de congruo* and then also *de condigno*. According to Luther's doctrine, saving grace is not something that adheres to, or inheres in, man, but is God's gracious disposition for Christ's sake, *favor Dei propter Christum*, or the forgiveness of sins for Christ's sake, and the purpose of the means of grace is to offer to man the remission of sins provided by Christ and through this offer to work, or to strengthen, faith in man.

Luther was fully aware of this radical difference between him and the Scholastics. In opposition to the Scholastic concept of "grace"

---

interest, and to restrain them from blasphemy and cursing" (XX:1997). But even here Luther's refrain recurs: "Though they do not believe as we do, for that we cannot be blamed, and no one is to be forced to believe"; and the admonition is addressed to the preachers: "Not as though they are to curse them much or do them bodily harm" (1997, 1996). Compare Luther's letter of December 10, 1537, addressed to "Jesel, Jude zu Rossheim, *warum er ihm schriftliche Fuerbitte versage.*" The letter begins: "To the prudent Jesel, Jew of Rossheim, my good friend."

as held by Latomus he writes: "God's grace is a treasure outside us, God's gracious disposition, the opposite of God's wrath. . . . Grace I take in its proper sense for God's favor, as it ought to be taken, not as a quality of the [human] spirit, as our recent theologians [the Scholastics] have taught." [79] Melanchthon, too, had early grasped this dissimilarity between the medieval and the Lutheran concept of grace. He reveals this fact by stating in the first edition of his *Loci:* "Justly we raise the complaint against the Scholastics that they have shamefully misused the sacred word 'grace' by taking it to mean a quality in the spirit of the saints; plainest of all the Thomists. . . . Away with the Aristotelian delusion of qualities (in the soul of man)! . . . The term 'grace' does not connote a quality in us, but rather God's will itself or God's good will *[benevolentiam]* toward us." [80] — So fully aware was Luther of the dissimilarity between his and the medieval concept of grace that he keeps reiterating the dictum in one or the other form: "On this doctrine the whole Papacy is founded: that grace is infused into man by a secret operation" (St. L. XIII:917).

Luther's and the Scholastics' conflicting concepts of grace beget another dissimilarity, namely, that while the Scholastics teach that the Sacraments communicate grace *ex opere operato,* Luther calls this a vicious notion and in every case demands faith on the part of man for a salutary use of the Sacrament. "For if the Sacrament for my receiving it imparts grace to me, then I am in fact obtaining grace through my work and not through faith. . . . Here you see clearly how completely the Sacraments were misunderstood by the sentence writers [Scholastics] because they entirely disregarded faith and the promise in dealing with the Sacraments. . . . For that reason they have not only shackled the Sacraments *[captivaverunt],* but have, as far as lay in their power, entirely abolished them *[aboleverunt]."* [81]

---

[79] *Opp. v. a.* V, 489. In the preface to his commentary on Romans: "Grace properly means God's favor or good will, which He bears in His heart toward us" (St. L. XIV:98). Cp. the extensive discussion of the meaning of "grace" (Vol. II, 7 ff.).

[80] *Loci,* ed. Kolde, 1890, p. 168 f. With this compare Kolde on Thomas Aquino's concept of grace (p. 168, note 1). Thomas teaches: "Grace is infused into man, and because of it man is then a *homo gratus* before God, is loved of God."

[81] *Opp. v. a.* V, 64 f.; St. L. XIX:62 ff. Properly Luther will here grant no difference among the Scholastics. Luther occasionally praises the Scholastics as "brainy men" (*"gute Koepfe"*). But they "imagined things" and taught "monstrosities" because they did not understand the fall of Adam and knew not that the Law is spiritual. Hence they had also no correct comprehension of the Gospel, of grace, and of faith. Saving grace they understood to be a quality in man's

It is, then, a fact that no affinity whatever is possible between Luther's doctrine of the means of grace and that of the Middle Ages, but that rather they are the very opposite of each other. Seeberg says correctly: Luther "felled the medieval semi-Pelagianism, its teaching of grace, all its teaching of the Sacraments, its hierocracy, its doctrine of works and of merit. In addition, the fanatic notions of an immediate operation of the Spirit tumbled because of the driving force of the fundamental principle of the Reformation." (*Dogmengesch.* II, 284.)

This last remark of Seeberg leads to another question: Is there any affinity between Luther's doctrine of the means of grace and that of the Reformed? Here again some have sought to prove not only similarities, but even complete agreement, e. g., Boehl and Macpherson.[82] As proof of this agreement they bring the statements of Luther in which he distinguishes between the "external Word" and the operation of the Holy Ghost "within the heart." This distinction is actually common in Luther's works. — But while so distinguishing, Luther most clearly and emphatically rejects every separation of the working of the Spirit from the "external Word" and teaches that the Holy Ghost always exerts His influence "within the heart" through the outward Word. Luther says in his treatise *Against the Heavenly Prophets:* "Now that God has sent forth His holy Gospel, He deals

---

heart, toward the attainment of which man co-operates. Cf. St. L. IV:1836, 633; XVIII:840; XXII:1402; V:574. Well-compiled material on medieval theology and specially on its teaching of the Sacraments is contained in Schmid-Hauck, *Dogmengesch.*, p. 275 ff.

[82] Boehl, *Dogm.*, p. 440 f.; Macpherson, *Chr. Dogmatics*, p. 4224 f. Present-day Reformed often assert that the Reformed teaching indeed differs from the later Lutheran theologians, but not from Luther. Boehl says *(loc. cit.):* "On the one side we have the Lutheran Church, which in its later dogmatic development assumed a *vis conversiva et regenetrix Scripturae inhaerens*. . . . That was something entirely different from Luther's remark that whatever is professed to be the Spirit without the Word is purely diabolical. Here he was entirely right, and in this particular the Reformed Church, too, followed him." Boehl accuses the later Lutheran theologians of departing from Luther's position, "especially since the controversy with Rathmann." But somewhat cautiously he adds: "Though the Formula of Concord (*Trigl.* 903, Sol. Decl., II, 55) already makes a start of chaining the Holy Ghost to the letter of the Bible." When Lutheran theologians, in opposing Rathmann, used the expression that God's Word has divine power also *extra usum*, they directed this expression against the error of the "enthusiasts" that the Word of Scripture acquires life-giving power only through believing use of it (which amounts to the immediate illumination). But the expression [power *extra usum*] is not to be recommended for general use, since it demands added explanations if it is to be understood correctly.

with us in a twofold manner: the one is external, the other internal. Externally He deals with us through the preached Word of the Gospel and through perceptible signs, that is, Baptism and the Sacrament. Inwardly He deals with us through the Holy Ghost and faith and its gifts. But all this in this manner and order, that the external parts should and must come first, and the internal follow and come through the external, so that He has determined to give no man the internal parts unless it be through the external parts; for it is His will to give no man the Spirit or faith without the external Word and sign." (St. L. XX:202.) On Ex. 15:16 Luther remarks: "God has said: When the Word of Christ is being preached, *I* am in your mouth, and with the Word *I* go through your ears into your heart" (St. L. III:925). And on John 6:63: "God has established this order regarding His Holy Spirit, that ordinarily He is to come through the Word. Christ Himself says this at this place. . . . He will not have it that you fly to and fro to seek or to imagine a 'Spirit' so that you might say: I have received it through the 'inner voice' *[Einsprechen]* of the Holy Ghost. . . . Christ will not accept such inner voice, but binds us to His Word only; He does not want the Spirit separated from His Word. Therefore, if you hear some one boasting that he got something by inspiration or inner voice of the Holy Spirit, and it lacks God's Word, be it what it may, then declare it to be the abominable devil" (St. L. VII: 2389, 2388). Still more brusquely Luther says it in the following words: "Do you there see the devil, the enemy of divine order? How by the words 'the Spirit, the Spirit, the Spirit!' he gets you to stand there spellbound, and meanwhile he upsets the bridges, path and way, ladder and everything, by which the Spirit is to come to you, namely, through the external ordinances of God in bodily Baptism, His pledges, and the preached Word of God! He wants to teach you not how the Spirit comes to you, but how you should reach the Spirit; you should learn to fly with the clouds and ride on the wind." (St. L. XX:203.) Seeberg says of Luther's teaching regarding the Word and the operation of the Holy Spirit: "Luther distinguishes the purely human effect of the Word from the operation of the Spirit occurring 'in,' 'with and through,' 'therewith and thereunder,' but distinguishes so, that the latter absolutely ensues only by virtue of the former" (*op. cit.*, p. 267). In short, as surely as Zwingli and Calvin and also recent Reformed theologians, such as Boehl, Hodge, Shedd ("Efficacious grace acts immediately"), teach an immediate operation of the Spirit, while Luther contrariwise rejects every immediate working of the Spirit as delusion and diabolical deception, so surely no likeness, but only unlikeness between Luther's teaching and that of the Reformed can be proved.[83]

But to this dissimilarity another is joined, namely, the disparity in the concept of grace. The Reformed often correctly define saving grace as God's favor, God's gracious disposition, etc. But when you ask to whom this gracious disposition of God applies, they begin to hedge, to limit its application. The gracious disposition and the resultant working of the Spirit, we are told, applies only to those who are immediately illuminated or regenerated. This is the teaching of both the older and the modern Reformed theologians. Boehl, too, takes pains to inculcate: "Only to these who have been quickened by the Holy Ghost do the assurances of Jesus apply that the Word cleanses them" (*Dogm.*, p. 445 f.). Thus we find the Reformed agree-

---

[83] We add another quotation from Luther in which he points out the causal relation between the "outward Word" and "faith in the heart." Luther says on the words John 17:20: "Neither pray I for these alone, but for them also which shall believe on Me through their Word": "Christ extols and praises the preaching of the Apostles, that through it we must come to Christ and to faith. This is today attacked by Satan through factious spirits of his who instruct people to despise the outward Word and who pretend that the Spirit by Himself must do all; outward things, signs, and oral preaching are said to help nothing toward faith in the heart; the inner man needs an inner Word. Before the nose of these lying spirits write in large letters merely this text: 'which shall believe on Me through their Word,' and ask them whether the word 'believe' pertains to the inner or outer man or whether the Apostles preached an outward or an inner Word. Then they will not be able to deny that this word 'believe,' which pertains alone to the heart and the inner man, and 'through their Word' belong together and make an inner man. Faith is of the innermost bottom of the heart. Since, now, Christ says that they shall believe, that is, become inner or spiritual people, through the Word of the Apostles, it certainly follows undeniably that such Word is of service not to the outer, but to the inner man; and there is surely nothing to it when they fume that oral Word or preaching is useless except as an external testimony or confession of the inner man. If they retort, however: 'If the outward Word accomplished such things, why, all who hear it would have to come to faith and be saved,' answer: Thanks to them for that! For that is already half a confession, which they cannot deny, that some nevertheless believe. For that is what we, too, say: Though not all believe, many do come to faith. Christ, too, does not say that all will believe. What sort of talk is it, therefore, when they deduce and conclude: Not all believe, hence faith does not come through the Word? Suchwise I could also deduce and juggle: Not all are obedient to lords, magistrates, or parents, hence government, lords, and parents must be useless or needless and God's command vain. Therefore we invert it and say instead: We know that some who hear the Word believe and can prove it by many passages and examples of Holy Writ; therefore we conclude that the Word must be useful and needed, not merely for the ears, but also for the heart or inner man. That some, however, do not believe though they hear the Word does not rob the Word of anything; it still remains true that the Word is the means through which faith enters the heart, and that without it no man can believe." (St. L. VIII:829 f.)

ing with Rome that the forgiveness of sins is granted only to those who can show an "infused grace" in themselves. This consensus is not disproved by the fact that the Papists teach an infusion of grace with human co-operation, the Reformed, however, an immediate infusion without any human co-operation. Since the immediate operation of the Spirit exists only in their imagination, the Reformed, too, are, in fact, entirely dependent on their own efforts. For this reason Luther's opinion is fully warranted, that through their teaching of an immediate operation of the Spirit the "enthusiasts" become entangled in the Roman doctrine of works and "lose Christ, the Cornerstone," because they seek to come to God not by faith in the remission of sins earned by Christ and offered in the means of grace, but through a grace infused into and innate in them.

A result of these differences between Luther and the Reformed is the difference in their practice. While the Reformed warn against relying on the external means of grace, and are in constant fear that God might be supplanted by the means of grace and the administrants of the means,[84] Luther feels he cannot stress enough that in the means of grace and in the persons administering the means God Himself is dealing with us and that we are never to conceive of God otherwise than we hear and see in the means of grace (St. L. XIII:2438 ff.). This is the touchstone by which every Christian can and should test himself whether he holds to the Christian doctrine of the means of grace and practices it. We are foolishly living far away from God instead of in His presence graciously granted us if our heart does not feel: God is speaking to me in His Word, which passes from mouth to mouth among men and I am told by men; God is addressing me in His Word as I read it; Christ Himself is absolving me in the Word which He has committed to men; Christ Himself is baptizing; Christ Himself forgives my sins by imparting to me His body and blood in the Holy Supper. This is the "type of faith resting immediately on Word and Sacrament," which E. F. Karl Mueller praises in Luther (R. E., 3d ed., XV, 599); and herein this Reformed theologian sees a difference separating Luther from Calvinism. But the same thing must be said of the whole Lutheran Church wherever it clings to the doctrine of the means of grace as taught by Luther and our Lutheran Confessions. As far as the doctrine of the means of grace is concerned,

---

[84] Cf., e. g., *Consens. Tigur.* XI, XII, XIII, XV; *Niemeyer,* p. 194. With it Calvin's *Expositio,* p. 208. Here there is no real difference between them and Carlstadt, who, too, asserted: "This is a common and horrible fault, that our Christians seek remission of sins in the Sacrament." See Carlstadt's essay "*Von dem widerchristlichen Missbrauch,*" etc., St. L. XX:94.

only extreme need brings about an agreement in practice among Lutherans and Reformed. Because the *gratia particularis* and the immediate operation of the Spirit fail to console in the terrors of conscience and the anguish of death, the Reformed in such cases themselves direct the terrified sinner to the universal promises of God and thus to the objective means of grace. The demands of practical life crowd the Reformed into the Lutheran position, as Schneckenburger expressed it (*Vergl. Darstell.*, I, 261 f.)

Fault has been found with Luther because of the strong language he uses against the "enthusiasts." Luther himself is aware of his harsh language and in a manner begs pardon for it by explaining (St. L. XX: 204 f., 201 f.) that he has in mind not so much the persons of the "enthusiasts" as rather the archenemy of the Church, the devil, whose intention is to draw the Christians off the rock of the objective Word of God by the delusion of an immediate operation of the Spirit and thus actually to rob them of the Gospel, just brought to light again by the Reformation. Every man who does not base his state of grace before God on the remission of sins signed over to him in the outward Word of the Gospel is deceiving himself as to his communion with God.

8

The Means of Grace in the Form of Absolution

We shall discuss absolution in a separate section because this doctrine tests one's knowledge of Christianity. The general use of such terms as "Gospel" and "reconciliation by Christ" harbors much unclear thinking. This haziness reveals itself in the objections brought against absolution.

The Gospel in all its forms pronounces the remission of sins purchased by Christ and is therefore absolution, as we have repeatedly shown. However, Luther and the Lutheran Church in her Confessions reserve the name "absolution" for a special form of proclaiming the Gospel, namely, the announcing of the forgiveness of sins to one or more persons upon their confession of sins, either by a public servant of the Church or by a lay Christian. Besides the spoken Word, Baptism and the Lord's Supper, the Smalcald Articles name, under the general heading "Gospel," also absolution as a way "that gives us counsel and aid against sin" (*Trigl.* 491, Part III, Art. IV). Furthermore, we read there, in the Article "Of Confession," that "Confession or Absolution ought by no means to be abolished in the Church," because "Abso-

lution or the Power of the Keys is also an aid and consolation against
sin and a bad conscience, ordained *[instituta]* by Christ Himself in
the Gospel" (*Trigl.* 493, Part III, Art. VIII, 1). In an opinion of theirs
Luther, Melanchthon, and Bugenhagen say: "The consoling, free
Gospel, too, must be given free course, that it may be told individuals
as well as groups. But what else is absolution than the Gospel told
a single person that through it he may receive consolation for his
confessed sin? Thus, among other examples, there is that of Christ,
who (Matthew 9) absolved the man sick of the palsy, and (Luke 7)
of Mary Magdalene." [85]

This absolution was and is offensive to many. Zwingli's antagonism to Luther was directed specifically against absolution, which
Luther taught and prized highly.[86] Zwingli's rejection of absolution is
easily understood in view of his πρῶτον ψεῦδος. Since Zwingli asserted
in general that the Spirit needs no vehicle, he felt impelled to scoff
in particular at Luther's finding a source of consolation for the consciences of sinners even in an absolution pronounced by men. Zwingli
writes: "From the Spirit our spirit derives its assurance that we are
the sons of God, not from the pronouncing absolver." (Zwingli jeer-
ingly substitutes "*Achselvierer*" for "*Absolvierer.*")[87] This opposition
and scoffing has continued to our day. Within the Lutheran Church,
too, men have sought to abolish, along with the abuse, also the right
use of confession and absolution. Evidence of this attempt is the
dictum of the leftists among the Pietists: "*Beichtstuhl, Satansstuhl,
Hoellenpfuhl*" (confessional, Satan's throne, bottomless pit).[88] Here
in America not only leaders of the Reformed denominations, but also
Lutherans spoke of "papistic leaven" when the fathers of our Synod
taught and practiced confession and absolution (*Lutheraner*, 1850,
p. 113 ff.). The former Norwegian Synod, in its controversy with the
Augustana Synod on the objective reconciliation or justification, had
to set forth also the Christian doctrine of absolution.[89]

---

[85] *Ratschlag auf die Handlung zu Schmalkalden*, 1531 (St. L. XVI:1795).

[86] Luther: "Because of this part (absolution) most of all do I use confession
and will not and cannot get along without it, for it often, yes, daily, greatly
consoles me when I am sad and downcast" (St. L. XVII:2021).

[87] Zwingli's *Answer That These Words, This Is My Body,*" etc. (St. L.
XX:1131 f.).

[88] Kaspar Schade, Th. Grossgebauer, etc. — H. Schmid, *Gesch. des Pietismus,*
p. 259 ff.

[89] *Lehre und Wehre*, 1872, p. 161 ff.: "*Ein Aktenstueck, den Lehrstreit unter
den skandinavischen Lutheranern ueber die Absolution betreffend.*" *Lutheraner,*
1850, p. 113 ff.: "*Wie gross und verderblich der Irrtum derjenigen sei, welche den
Predigern des Evangeliums die Macht absprechen, auf Erden Suenden zu ver-*

From John 20:23 Luther, our Lutheran Symbols, and also later dogmaticians have cogently proved that absolution is a Scriptural mode or form of proclaiming the Gospel. The words "Whosoever sins ye remit, they are remitted unto them," clearly state three things: (1) Those who have received the Holy Ghost, namely, all Christians, shall remit sins, or absolve; (2) this remission, or absolution, pertains to definite persons (individuals), "whosoever"; (3) this absolution pronounced by men ends the matter before God: "they are remitted unto them." [90]

To circumvent the sense of Scripture, Zwingli took the same liberty here as in the doctrine of the Person of Christ and practiced *alloeosis*, substitution *(permutatio)* of the subject. In the Scripture text the disciples, hence men, are mentioned as the persons who remit the sins: "Whosoever sins ye remit." Zwingli, however, asserts that one must substitute the Holy Ghost for the disciples; Christ "from divine friendship" ascribed to the disciples what really was the sole work of the Holy Ghost. He writes: "Though Christ attributes the binding and loosing to the disciples, it nevertheless belongs only to the operative Spirit. They merely preached what the Spirit before [that is, previously, without the Word, immediately] had brought to life in them,[91] and at all times He vivifies wherever He pleases; hence from divine friendship what is only the Spirit's is connected with the name of the disciples." (St. L. XX:1132.) And Zwingli does

---

geben." Proceedings of the 10th Convention of the Missouri Synod, 1860, p. 34 ff.: "Discussion of the Doctrine of Absolution." The theses were formulated by Pastor Brohm. From the *Proceedings* it is evident that agreement in the Biblical doctrine was reached only through thorough discussion. In *Lehre und Wehre,* 1874, p. 138 ff., Prof. F. A. Schmidt (then at the Seminary in St. Louis) furnishes a fine presentation of the doctrine of absolution and defends the doctrine as taught by the Norwegian Synod as Scriptural and Confessional against the attacks of the Swedes and the Iowans. Testimonies of the old Norwegian Synod regarding justification and absolution: Tract Number 4: *"Om Retfaerdiggjoerelsen."* Decorah, Iowa, 1872. — V. Koren, *"Samlede Skrifter,"* III, 45—74, Decorah, 1911. — H. A. Preus, *"Wisconsinisme,"* pp. 65—95, Decorah, Iowa, 1875. — E. Hove, *"Retfaerdiggjoerelsen," Synodalberetning,* 1901, Decorah. — J. B. Frich, *Festskrift,"* Decorah, 1903, pp. 250—258.

[90] Perhaps the reading ἀφέωνται (perfect) is preferable. But also if we read ἀφίενται (present), the translation "they are remitted unto them" can stand, since according to the context the present tense ἀφίενται expresses simultaneousness with the ἐὰν ἀφῆτε. On the perfect ἀφέωνται see Winer, 6th ed., p. 74.

[91] What the Spirit had "before" brought to life in the disciples He had also called forth in them through the Word, as Christ expressly declares (John 17:8): "For I have given unto them the words which Thou gavest Me; and they have received them and have known surely [scil., by faith in the Word] that I came out from Thee."

not stand alone. In the Reformed camp the rejection of absolution is general.[92] It is the inevitable result of teaching a *gratia particularis* and an *immediata Spiritus Sancti operatio.* If divine grace is limited, the absolution, in spite of being general, would apply only to the elect; and if the Holy Ghost works immediately, the Word of the Gospel could, of course, not be the bearer of the absolution, which therefore could not be communicated by the preachers of the Word.

But opposition to absolution, open as well as veiled, has penetrated also into the Lutheran Church chiefly for two reasons (cf. Caspari, R. E., 3d ed., II, 538 f.). First, in general because of a lack of understanding of the Gospel of God; for example, among the Pietists; secondly, as an inevitable concomitant of synergism. Like Calvinism, synergism, too, makes the remission of sins subject to something good in man. For Calvinism this *aliquid in homine* is whatever the Spirit has worked immediately, either previously or concomitantly. For synergism it is the *facultas se applicandi ad gratiam,* "right conduct," "personal choice," etc. In both cases neither the absolver nor the absolved knows whether the absolution applies. But let us turn to the principal objections raised against absolution and see what, in general and in particular, a large part of the religious public finds offensive in absolution.

A general objection advanced against absolution is that the practice of absolving sinners upon their confession of sins is a remnant of "papistical leaven." [93] This objection is attributable to ignorance of both the Roman and the Christian doctrine of absolution. Rome teaches that absolution is an act (a) that can be performed only by a priest ordained by the Pope, in graver cases only by the bishop, and in the gravest cases only by the Pope himself;[94] (b) that is conditioned on three works of men: contrition, a full confession, and the rendering of an imposed satisfaction;[95] (c) in all of which the priest decides whether the requirements have been sufficiently fulfilled or

---

[92] Heppe, *Dogm. der ev.-ref. K.,* pp. 486, 502. Cp. also G. Plitt, *Grundriss der Symbolik,* 3d ed., p. 131 ff.

[93] Because of its doctrine of absolution the Norwegian Synod was accused of both "theoretical Catholicism" and "practical Catholicism," because it was allegedly espousing a doctrine "that aims at the establishment of the cornerstone in the Papacy, the Sacrament of Order," "an Antichristian trend which, supported by a papistical principle, tends to transmute Christianity into Universalism and hierarchy." Cf. *Lehre und Wehre,* 1874, p. 140 f.

[94] *Trid.,* Sess. XIV, c. 4, 6, 7, can. 10—11.

[95] *Trid.,* Sess. XIV, c. 4, can. 5. -- Sess. XIV, c. 5, can. 6—8. — Sess. XIV, c. 8, can. 13—14.

not; accordingly he grants or denies absolution.[96] With this Roman abomination [97] the Christian doctrine of absolution has nothing in common.

According to Scripture, the power to absolve, or the power of the keys *(potestas clavium)*, belongs not to one person or to a few persons in the Church, but to all who have received the Holy Spirit, hence to all Christians without exception. This is clearly taught not only in John 20:23 and Matt. 18:18, but also in Matt. 16:19.[98] These

---

[96] *Trid.,* Sess. XIV, c. 5, 6, 8, can. 9.

[97] The most powerful description of this abomination, denying Christ's perfect satisfaction and making grace uncertain, is Luther's in the section "Of the False Repentance of the Papists" (*Trigl.* 481, Smalc. Art., Part III, Art. III, 10 ff.). See *Lutheraner,* 1850, p. 116 f. Also Cardinal Gibbons of Baltimore clings to the Roman abomination in its full extent in *The Faith of Our Fathers,* ch. 26, p. 385 ff.

[98] All restriction of John 20:23: "Whosoever sins *ye* remit," to the persons of the Apostles, or to the persons of the Apostles and the New Testament public ministry, is an imposition. Only Luther's explication agrees with the text. See St. L. XI:745 f.; XIX:845 f.; *et al.* This right understanding Adolf Spaeth (d. 1910, General Council) reproduces in his *Annotations on the Gospel According to St. John:* "On whom is this power here conferred? Is it on a special class or order of men, the clergy, as Rome and all Romanizers teach? But when this power was conveyed by the Lord, the Apostles were not all present; nor were those present on this occasion all Apostles. John clearly distinguishes between the Twelve (v. 24) and the disciples (v. 19). And Luke tells us distinctly that others were gathered with the disciples (Luke 24:33) on that evening. Luther therefore is right in saying: This power is given to all Christians. Whosoever hath the Holy Spirit, to him this power is given, that is, to him who is a Christian. But who is a Christian? He that believeth. He that believeth hath the Holy Spirit. Every Christian, therefore, has the power, claimed by Pope and bishops, of forgiving or retaining sins. Well, then, some might say, we can pronounce Absolution, baptize, preach, administer Communion. No, indeed! St. Paul says: 'Let all things be done decently and in order' (1 Cor. 14:40). We all have this power, but let no one presume to exercise it publicly, except he be called and chosen for this office by the congregation. But in private we may use this power. If, for instance, my brother comes to me, saying: 'Dear Brother, I am vexed in my conscience, give me a word of absolution,' I am free to do this and tell him the Gospel, how that he should take hold of Christ's work, believing that the righteousness of Christ is truly his own and that his own sins are truly Christ's. This is indeed the greatest service I may do to my fellow man."

In the words Matt. 18:18: "Whatsoever ye shall bind on earth shall be bound in heaven; and whatsoever ye shall loose on earth shall be loosed in heaven," Christians are addressed. This is evident both from the words preceding ("If he neglect to hear the church") and from the words following ("Where two or three are gathered together in My name").

And as to Matt. 16:19, "I will give unto thee the keys of the kingdom of heaven," one cannot but be astonished that not merely Romanists, but even Protestants (e. g., Meyer in his *Commentary*) find it possible to interpret these words of a prerogative of Peter, whether it be as an Apostle, or as the head of the Apostles, or as a representative of the Apostles. According to the whole context (vv. 13-17) these words describe not the prerogative of an Apostle, but of a person who has come to faith in Christ.

passages of Scripture show that every Christian, yes, every child, can pronounce as valid and effective an absolution as any pastor, bishop, archbishop, etc.[99]

And as to the conditions on which absolution is said to depend we must say: the absolution rests neither on self-aroused contrition nor on true contrition worked by the Holy Ghost through the Law; neither on the confession of all sins before men nor on any sort of human satisfaction. Absolution is based solely on the fact of world reconciliation by the perfect satisfaction of Christ and on the divine command (John 20:21; Luke 24:47) in Christ's name to proclaim the remission of sins provided by Him. And this proclamation of forgiveness for Christ's sake, in no wise affected by human worthiness or unworthiness, the hearers are to believe. But these points will be amplified as we proceed with the objections.

Among these is the criticism of absolution, current in all ages, that to forgive sins is universally acknowledged to be a prerogative of God. Therefore to concede to men the power and authority to absolve other sinners would be a wrong, yea, blasphemous, transfer to men of a prerogative actually belonging only to God. The answer to this objection is (Luther, St. L. XI:758 f.; XIII:2438): To remit sins is, of course, a divine prerogative. Only God, whose Law has been transgressed, can pardon the transgressor. No creature in heaven or earth, no mundane monarch, not even an angel or archangel, can forgive sin. The sins of the sinner whom God does not forgive remain unforgiven, though all creatures in chorus, *unisono*, pronounced absolution. But at this point one must ask: Does God exercise this prerogative immediately or mediately? Scripture answers: God exercises this power mediately, through the Word of the reconciliation brought about by Christ, through the Word of the Gospel. God has commissioned men, His Church to proclaim this Gospel. It is men to whom Christ says (Mark 16:15): "Go ye into all the world, and preach the Gospel to every creature." Accordingly men are also told by Christ (John 20:23): "Whosesoever sins *ye* remit, they are remitted unto them." So, then, two things are certain: Only God can remit sins, and God does so through His Gospel, which men are enjoined to proclaim. And even if a sinner reads his absolution in a text of Scripture — it surely is contained in every evangelical passage — he still receives absolution through men, namely, through a word of the

---

[99] Smalcald Articles, *Trigl.* 523, "Power and Primacy of Pope," 67—69; *Lutheraner,* 1850, p. 117; Luther, St. L. X:1235, 1243, 1579, 1590.

Prophets or Apostles, and not through an immediate *interior Spiritus illuminatio.*

Not quite so far-reaching is the objection that absolution can easily lead to carnal security on the part of the absolved and to "clerical pride" on the part of the pastor. In regard to the first part of this criticism we grant that absolution, and with it confession, has been and will be used by many to hide their inward defection from grace by an external show of piety. But all other forms of the Gospel (preaching, Baptism, the Lord's Supper) have been and always will be subject to the same abuse. — The danger that "clerical pride" will be fostered in the confessor obtains in the Roman caricature of absolution, practiced by a special priesthood instituted by the Pope and invested with the power to absolve to the exclusion of the Christians in general. The Christian power to absolve, however, is an authority given by Christ to all believers, and in the public administration of it the officiants are merely servants *(ministri)* and delegates of the Christians.

It remains for us to consider the last and at the same time the most widespread and plausible objection against absolution. It is couched in the words: "No man is a searcher of hearts or omniscient. No man can therefore know whether the sinner seeking absolution is truly contrite and has true faith in his heart. Therefore no man should arrogate to himself the right to pronounce absolution." The underlying thought is that absolution is based on the contrition and the faith of the one asking absolution. Against this erroneous thought the truth must be upheld that absolution is not based on the state of man's heart, but entirely on the state of God's heart. And as to God's heart we are well informed, not as though we were omniscient, but because God has bared His heart to us in the Gospel. From it we know most certainly that, before contrition and faith, God is fully reconciled to each and every man through Christ, does not impute the sinners' trespasses to them, but remits their transgression; and that all Christians, also their public servants, have God's command to reveal God's reconciled heart, to proclaim the remission of sins in all the world, proclaim it particularly also to those who expressly confess their sins and desire absolution. Accordingly, the absolution is, as Luther often says, in no case a *"Fehlschluessel"* [a wrong key], that is, spurious. Among all nations and in all climes not a single person can be found whom we would be deceiving if we not only assured him, but affirmed it with an oath in the name of God: "Through Christ God is reconciled to you, does not impute your sins to you, but forgives them." If he fails to believe us, it is his loss. But true it nevertheless remains that God is reconciled to him through Christ and that he is to believe the finished reconciliation on the strength of the divinely enjoined announcement. The thoughts of a "wrong key" [*Fehlschluessel*] are, as Luther correctly points out, the result of our founding absolution on our contrition, our faith, our renewal, in short, our subjective state and worthiness, instead of Christ's perfect work of reconciliation.

It is therefore evident where the trouble lies. The Biblical idea of the universal and plenary reconciliation of the world by the vicarious satisfaction of Christ is disregarded by those who take offense at absolution. They will indeed speak in a general way of Christ as the Reconciler of men. They also credit Christ's work of reconciliation with a "great" effect on God. Christ, they like to say in our day, has indeed "effectually" prepared the way for a new "relation" between God and man. Nevertheless, they entertain the false view that God is fully gracious to men only after a change has taken place also in men. In other words, they believe that Christ's work of reconciliation indeed effected an inclination, a readiness, in God to remit sin; but this inclination develops into actual remission of sins in God's heart only after men, too, have changed their mind toward God. The human change of mind which is to consummate the change in God's heart is, for some, contrition and faith; for others, who have wandered a little farther from the Christian faith, it is renewal and at least the beginning of sanctification. Implied is the further error that the Gospel is not the proclamation of forgiveness for Christ's sake, but the promulgation of a divine "plan of salvation," or a proclamation of conditions by the fulfillment of which man may obtain forgiveness of sins. Thus Kirn speaks of a "historically finished" reconciliation by Christ, but then limits the "finished" reconciliation by stating that "the pardoning of sinners has for all time been made ethically possible." The pardon becomes a fact when "the foundation of salvation laid by Christ is efficacious toward recasting the life of mankind into its God-pleasing form." (*Grundriss der Dogmatik*, p. 118.)

But all these restrictions of the reconciliation of mankind to a mere inclination or a mere possibility on the part of God to forgive fail to do justice to the statements of Scripture that the "historically finished" reconciliation of some 1900 years ago consists in the divine remission of sins itself. The words of 2 Cor. 5:19, "not imputing their trespasses unto them" are the authentic exegesis of the words, "God was in Christ, reconciling the world unto Himself," and express not merely a possible but an actual remission of sins in God's heart which has been taking place ever since God was in Christ reconciling the world unto Himself. Therefore the Gospel, too, is not the proposal of a mere "scheme of how to achieve salvation," or the statement of the conditions through the fulfillment of which man finally obtains the forgiveness of sins, but the Gospel is an absolution, addressed to the whole world, which men should believe. There is not only to be preaching about the forgiveness of sins among all nations, but the very "remission of sins should be preached in His [Christ's] name among all nations" (Luke 24:47). Luther therefore says of a Gospel preacher that he cannot open his mouth without continually re-mitting sin.

And when men have arrived at this understanding, when they look at absolution from the Biblical viewpoint of world reconciliation and the Gospel, their antagonism against absolution ceases. Without the right understanding of these cardinal Biblical truths the open or veiled opposition to absolution will not subside. This fact we should remember for our practical ministry. Experience has taught us two things: 1. Among us, too, there is veiled and public antagonism against the use of general and private absolution. 2. This public or veiled opposition is overcome if by public instruction from the pulpit or in voters' meetings we bring home to our people the Biblical doc-trine of the perfect reconciliation of the world by Christ and thus demonstrate that the Gospel is nothing less than the divine tender of the remission of sins, which one and all are to appropriate by faith.[100]

It is of the greatest practical importance for every Christian to understand well and hold fast the relation of faith to absolution. And what has been said of absolution is true of every form of the Gospel. It applies to Baptism, for Baptism, too, is absolution, even private absolution, since the individual (ἕκαστος) is baptized "for the remission of sins" (Acts 2:38). Likewise, the Sacrament of the Altar is private absolution, because the communicants as individuals receive

---

[100] Luther, St. L. XXIb:1849. Luther comments on Luke 24:47: "Absolution is nothing else than the preaching and publishing of the forgiveness of sins, which Christ here commands both to preach and to hear. But because such preaching must be preserved in the Church, absolution, too, should be retained; for between the two there is only this difference that while through preaching the Gospel this forgiveness is published everywhere and told to all in general, in absolution it is told specifically to one or more desiring it. So Christ has ordained that this preaching of remission of sins should go on and be heard everywhere and always, not only in general before assemblies, but before individual persons, too, wherever there are people who need it; as . . . He says: 'Whosesoever sins ye remit, they are remitted unto them.' " St. L. XI:721.

Christ's body, which is given for them, and Christ's blood, which is shed for them, "for the remission of sins" (Matt. 26:27-28).[101] Now, every Christian must understand well and hold fast the truth that faith is indispensable for a salutary use of absolution and of the means of grace in general. God does not want His forgiveness to be despised, but He wants it to be accepted by faith. Secondly, however, the Christian should not let himself be misled to think that absolution, and the means of grace in general, are based on his faith or anything whatever in him; for by such a misconception he would deny Christ's perfect work of reconciliation and would turn everything upside down in soteriology. Such a false foundation would convert Christianity into an unstable subjectivism. Luther calls the faith that makes itself its own object or cause of confidence apostasy from Christianity. He writes: "It is certainly true that one should have faith for Baptism, but one is not to base his Baptism on his faith. There is a very great difference between having faith and relying on one's faith and thus being baptized on it. Whoever bases his Baptism on his faith is not only uncertain, but an idolatrous, apostate Christian, for he trusts and relies on what is his, namely, on a gift given him of God and not alone on God's Word, just as another trusts and relies on his strength, wealth, power, wisdom, sanctity, which indeed also are gifts, given him of God." (St. L. XVII:2213.) Luther voices the same thought on Baptism as well as on the Lord's Supper in his Large Catechism: "For I myself also, and all who are baptized, must speak thus before God: I come hither in my faith and in that of others, yet I cannot rest in this that I believe and that many people pray for me; but in this I rest, that it is Thy Word and command. Just as I go to the Sacrament trusting not in my faith, but in the Word of Christ; whether I am strong or weak, that I commit to God. But this I know, that He bids me go, eat, and drink, etc., and gives me His body and blood — that will not deceive me or prove false to me. . . . Therefore they are presumptuous, clumsy minds that draw such inferences and conclusions as these: Where there is not the true faith, there also can be no true

---

101 Luther on the nature of Baptism and the Eucharist as private absolution: "To preach forgiveness of sins has no other meaning than to absolve and acquit of sin. This also takes place in Baptism and the Sacrament, which both have been instituted to show and assure us of such remission of sins. So that being baptized or receiving the Sacrament is also an absolution, where forgiveness in the name and command of Christ is awarded and adjudged to each one individually; this absolution you are to hear where and whenever you need it and to accept and believe it as though you heard it from Christ personally." (St. L. XI:722.)

Baptism. Just as if I would infer: If I do not believe, then Christ is nothing. . . . . My dear man, just invert the argument and rather draw this inference: For this very reason Baptism is something and is right, because it has been wrongly received. For if it were not right and true in itself, it could not be misused nor sinned against. The saying is: *Abusus non tollit, sed confirmat substantiam,* Abuse does not destroy the essence, but confirms it." (*Trigl.* 747, Inf. Bap., 56 ff.) And of absolution in particular Luther writes: "Then remember that the key, or the remission of sins, is not founded on our contrition and worthiness, as they teach and pervert it, for that is entirely Pelagianistic, Turkish, pagan, Jewish, Anabaptist, 'enthusiastic,' and Antichristian; but, contrariwise, that our contrition, work, heart, and what we are, is to be founded on the keys and with full confidence to rely on them as on God's Word. . . . . True, you should have remorse, but that this should make certain the remission of sins and confirm the work of the keys is a forsaking of faith and denial of Christ. He is minded to forgive and pardon your sins not on your account, but for His sake, from sheer grace, through the key." (St. L. XIX:943.) It will not do to assume that Luther is exaggerating when he calls it a denial of Christ and applies the predicates "pagan," "Turkish," etc., in case we base the remission of sins on our contrition and our faith. For this doctrine, that God is already reconciled to all men through Christ and in the Gospel distributes the forgiveness of sins, with faith here coming into consideration as nothing more than the means of reception, *medium* ληπτικόν, is the characteristic which distinguishes the Christian religion from all heathen religions. The remission of sins, long ago provided by Christ and offered in the means of grace, is the correlative or foundation of faith. Whoever inverts this relation and founds forgiveness on contrition and faith certainly harbors the thought that God becomes fully gracious only because of man's contrition and faith. But that places the Christian religion in one class with the pagan work religions.

These facts we must keep in mind in answering the much-discussed question whether absolution is to be pronounced conditionally or unconditionally. The question has repeatedly been touched upon in other connections. Cf. Vol. II, 35 f., 540, 551. At the outset it must be recalled that the term "conditional absolution," just like the term "conditional will of grace," is susceptible of several meanings. Even Luther says in an opinion addressed to the Nuernberg Council: "Every absolution, both general and private, has the condition of faith." But, as Luther immediately adds, here the part of faith is

"only this much, that it takes the absolution and says Yes to it."
(St. L. XXIb:1847 ff.) In other words, faith is necessary on the part
of man *(ex parte hominis)* for the acceptance or reception of absolution.
But the term "conditional absolution" has also been used in the sense
that absolution has contrition and faith as its cause. Luther is at a loss
for words adequately to reject a conditional absolution in this sense,
as his words just quoted show. Among Lutherans Paul Tarnov, for
example, asserted that absolution must be pronounced hypothetically.
Christian Chemnitz firmly opposed him.[102] His forceful refutation of
Tarnov Dr. Walther reported in *Lehre und Wehre* (1876, 193 ff.) under
the title: "Is Absolution to be Pronounced Categorically or Hypothetically?" Christian Chemnitz' argument is summarized in the statement: "As Baptism and the Lord's Supper are given to everyone
categorically on his outward confession by mouth and actions, and no
one says conditionally to an adult: 'If you have true contrition and
truly believe, I baptize you,' or, 'Then take, this is Christ's body,'
so also absolution is to be given categorically, and not conditionally,
to him who by mouth and actions outwardly confesses true repentance.
For even though a man, as occasionally may happen, be a hypocrite
and only simulate repentance, nevertheless the absolution on the part
of God would remain valid, and it begins to become efficacious to
salvation as soon as that simulation has given way to a sincere confession. For 'the gifts and calling of God are without repentance'
(Rom. 11:29); 'Let God be true but every man a liar' (Rom. 3:4)."
Walther classes "conditional absolution" with the "covert deviations"
from the Christian doctrine of justification. He says: "If the pastor
strongly doubts the repentance and sincerity of a person confessing
to him, without, however, being able to convict him of it and refuse
absolution, he dare not salve his own conscience by adding all sorts
of conditions, or even warnings and threats, to the absolution" (*Pastorale*, p. 164) [Fritz, *Pastoral Theology*, 2d ed., p. 115].

Tarnov defended his espousal of conditional absolution with the
argument: "Also in the general and public sermon the forgiveness of
sins is proclaimed to no one but to the truly believing" (*Lehre und
Wehre*, 1876, 195). According to this statement, faith in the remission
of sins would have to precede the pronouncing of the forgiveness.
Tarnov and all who have so argued did not perceive that they were

---

102 Deyling reports (*Institutiones prud. pastoralis*, III, 4, 38, p. 447) that it
is "the nearly unanimous opinion" of our old Lutheran theologians that the
formula of absolution should properly have the categorical or indicative form.

taking for granted an impossibility. Faith is a correlative concept. It rises and lives only when rooted in its already existing foundation. As we can believe other unknown facts only after we have been told them, so, too, faith in the wonderful fact that God graciously for Christ's sake, without the deeds of the Law, forgives our sins can come into being only if we have first been told, not as a probability, but as a fact, that God does forgive us by grace, for Christ's sake, without any regard to our subjective condition (Rom. 10:14). To create this faith, Christ wants both repentance and remission of sins proclaimed in His name (Luke 24:47). For that reason Scripture says that faith cometh by hearing (Rom. 10:17), and the Apology teaches with Scripture: *Fides concipitur et confirmatur per absolutionem, per auditum evangelii,* "Faith is conceived and strengthened through absolution, through the hearing of the Gospel" (*Trigl.* 263, XII, 42). The statement that remission of sins may be proclaimed or affirmed only to those who already believe is one of the assertions that pass from mouth to mouth and from generation to generation, without anyone's awaking to their absurdity. It is at home in the camp of the Reformed, men who teach a distribution of grace without means and a Gospel that comes into being only through faith. It is foreign to the Lutheran Church, which teaches that in every case faith rests on the means of grace, that is, is born of the remission of sins bequeathed to us in these means. Wherever so-called Lutherans seriously speak of a forgiveness resulting from faith, the underlying thought certainly must be that the Gospel is merely an announcement of the conditions by the fulfillment of which man can in part earn the forgiveness of sins.

Our own mode of pronouncing absolution has also been urged against the categorical form of absolution. But when prior to the absolution we ask those desiring it whether they sincerely repent of their sins, believe in Jesus Christ, and have the good and earnest purpose henceforth to amend their sinful life, we do not mean to imply that the remission of sins is based on contrition, faith, and improvement of life. Why, this view would conflict with the very confession of the penitents, for they base their plea for grace on God's "boundless mercy and the holy, innocent, bitter suffering and death of His beloved Son Jesus Christ." Our one aim in asking those questions before pronouncing absolution is not only to keep secure sinners from becoming fortified in their carnal security, but to console poor, brokenhearted sinners. Any other interpretation of our form of absolution would contradict the Gospel of grace and, instead of consoling burdened consciences, would drive them into the sea of doubt.

Three groups are a unit in asserting that the promise of the Gospel or the forgiveness of sins is contingent upon a good quality in man: the Papists, the Calvinists, and the synergists. They differ merely in their designation of the conditions. The Papists base their absolution on the *contritio cordis, confessio oris, et satisfactio operis.* The efficacy of the Sacraments they make contingent on this, in particular, that man remove the impediment to the operation of the Sacraments *(obicem non ponit).* The Calvinists make the promise of the Gospel contingent on immediate illumination or regeneration, the synergists on right personal conduct: man's own choice, omission of willful resistance, lesser guilt, etc. Accordingly, these three parties describe the Gospel not as the proclamation of the remission of sins for Christ's sake, addressed to all men, but as the announcement of a set of conditions which man must fulfill before the promise of the Gospel concerns him. Rome in the *Tridentinum* (Sess. VI, can. 20) anathematizes everyone who defines the Gospel "as if indeed the Gospel were a bare and absolute promise of eternal life, without the condition of observing the commandments" (*Waterworth,* p. 47). Just as decidedly Calvinists and synergists stress that the Gospel calls for an accomplishment of man. The Calvinist Charles Hodge says of the Gospel: "Being a proclamation of the terms on which God is willing to save sinners, and an exhibition of the duty of fallen men in relation to that plan, it of necessity binds all those who are in the condition which the plan contemplates. It is in this respect analogous to the moral Law." Again: "This general call of the Gospel" is "a general amnesty on certain conditions." (*Syst. Theol.* II, 642 f.)

Theodore Zahn, a recent synergist, has this to say of the remission of sins through the Gospel: "The Gospel . . . announces a general amnesty of God to men and offers them remission of their guilt by God, but does this from the outset and always only under the condition of μετάνοια and πίστις, that is, repentant faith on the part of the hearers. Since, however, penitent faith, just like the sinning that burdens man with guilt, is a personal behavior toward God . . . the forgiveness of sins offered by the preachers of the Gospel does not from the outset hold good for all in spite of the universality of the saving intention of God and Jesus, but . . . always only for some men, that is, for those who are minded to fulfill the condition imposed." (*Commentary,* John 20:23.) Other synergists call the imposed condition *facultas se applicandi ad gratiam,* self-decision, man's own choice, necessary point of contact, receptivity to the Gospel, etc.

In short, Romanists, Calvinists, and synergists agree in making the promise of the Gospel contingent on some human accomplishment; that is, they pervert the Gospel into a teaching of salvation by works. The Calvinists indeed contend energetically that they teach an immediate and irresistible regeneration for the very purpose of excluding from the outset all human co-operation in obtaining salvation. We saw, too, that they impress recent historians with their emphatic assertion (see p. 169). But just as firmly we must reiterate that this is a case of self-deception. Since the immediate operation of the Spirit is no reality, but hallucination, every alleged immediate operation of the Spirit in reality and in every actual case amounts to a product of man's own ego, a teaching and seeking of salvation by works, as in the case of the Romanists and the synergists.

Hence it is inexact to say that the difference between the Reformed and the Lutherans is this, that for the Reformed the Gospel, or absolution, is merely news of a remission, while for the Lutherans the Gospel, or absolution, is the remission itself. In fact, for the Reformed the Gospel is not even the news of a remission, but merely a proclamation of the conditions under which man can secure for himself the remission of sins. Only those Lutherans are entitled to call the Gospel an "announcement of the forgiveness of sins" who teach and maintain that through Christ's substitutionary satisfaction forgiveness has been provided for all men without exception, and that, accordingly, the Gospel offers and assures the forgiveness of sins to all men without exception and without any regard to their subjective condition. The dogmatician, Lutheran or Reformed, owes it to his hearers or readers to clear away all misleading terminology.

9

Addenda on the Means of Grace

We should like to single out or reiterate the following points.

I

In the study of the means of grace, specifically in answering the question whether absolution is to be pronounced conditionally or unconditionally, we encounter the fact that one and the same text of Scripture is understood quite differently by two groups, depending upon whether the Biblical concept of the Gospel is adhered to or not observed. We have in mind the evangelical conditional and imperative clauses, such as "He that believeth and is baptized shall be saved"; "Believe on the Lord Jesus Christ, and thou shalt be saved and thy house"; "If thou shalt . . . believe in thine heart that God hath raised Him from the dead, thou shalt be saved." (Mark 16:16; Acts 16:31; Rom. 10:9.)

If the Law predominates in the heart of the readers of these evangelical statements, they will teach and practice as if man, before he can claim for himself the remission of sins purchased by Christ, must make sure that he has faith. In other words, they want to make the Gospel result from faith, instead of basing faith on the Gospel. They make faith cling to faith in justification. Wittingly or unwittingly they entertain the thought that God becomes fully gracious toward man only after man has fulfilled the condition of faith. On the basis of this teaching they regard themselves as the people who "duly emphasize" faith and really "let it come into its own." The effect of this mode of teaching "Gospel" is that the sinner stricken by the Law now searches in his heart for this faith, but never finds it there, because faith is always created and sustained only by the prevenient forgiveness of sins, effected through Christ's work and given to man in the Gospel prior to all faith.

Entirely different is the teaching and practice of those who have and hold to the Biblical concept of the Gospel. When they are asked: "What must I do to be saved?" they do not use such evangelical statements as "He that believeth shall be saved," etc., to announce conditions that must first be fulfilled, but use them as what they are meant to be, namely, as means urgently to invite and persuade men to believe the Gospel message: "You need do nothing to be saved; just believe; do not at all regard yourself, your worthiness or unworthiness, not even your faith;[103] God graciously receives you for Christ's sake without any work of yours." In other words, the true Gospel teachers do not direct the grace seeker to his faith, but to the object of faith, namely, to Christ's perfect reconciliation or, expressed differently, to the objective promise of grace. In this way the evangelical conditional and imperative clauses are used aright, that is, in the sense Christ put into the words: "Come unto Me, all ye that labor and are heavy laden, and I will give you rest" (Matt. 11:28). "Him that cometh to Me I will in no wise cast out" (John 6:37). Only this

---

[103] As Luther says that, to free himself from the Law, he conceives of the thing "as though there were no such quality in his heart called faith or love" (*Corpus Ref.* II, 502 f.).

modus docendi, since it is the only one which suits the nature of the Gospel, works faith in hearts stricken by the Law, or strengthens faith where it is already present. The other method does not call forth faith, but makes faith impossible, because faith is denied its correlative.

Here Schneckenburger sees an essential difference between Lutheran and Reformed teaching. He asserts that this idea of placing faith ahead and first ascertaining one's state of faith before daring to regard God as gracious is not native to the Lutheran, but to the Reformed Church. He says: "The Lutheran Christian does not make his faith itself the object of reflection, namely, as a believer, but all the immediate activity of faith is for him activity toward the object clung to by faith, toward the divine promise, toward the grace in Christ. A member of the Reformed Church reflects on his faith itself as his state, his proof of life." "A member of the Reformed Church regards faith as a quality, as a habitude, of which one can become certain only by way of reflection, namely, by considering the actions to which it gives birth." "For the troubles of a weak faith the orthodox Lutherans have as the last restorative always and only the Word and Sacrament and not an inner activity and reflection." (*Vergl. Darstell.* I, 51, 57, 50.) That statement is correct.

But it must be added that the Reformed spirit also at this point has always sought entrance into the Lutheran Church. When Paul Tarnov, as we saw (see p. 200; Vol. II, 551), contended that absolution must be pronounced conditionally, he, too, was seeking to found faith on faith, instead of basing it on the Gospel. Carpzov was opposing that same error when he pointed out that the object of justifying faith is not the remission of sins already appropriated, but the remission to be appropriated.[104] And here in America, against members of other Scandinavian synods, the Norwegian Synod had to defend the truth that the right use and benefit, but not the essence of absolution depends on the faith of man (*Lehre und Wehre,* 1872, 101 ff.; 1874, 138 ff.).

Finally we do well to recall that also sound teachers of the Gospel are still in practice forever tempted to base faith on faith. When we feel our faith, we regard God as gracious and are ready to leap over all obstacles. But when the feeling of faith disappears, and instead we feel in our conscience the accusations of the Law,

---

[104] *Isagoge in libr. symb.*, p. 208 f.; quoted Vol. II, 541, footnote 75. Cf. also the warning of Hoenecke (*Dogm.* III, 404, quoted Vol. II, 540, footnote 72).

we imagine God to be angry and are ready to despair, just as though there were no Gospel that promises us forgiveness of sins entirely for the sake of Christ's righteousness. Here the religion of the Law, innate in all men, is asserting itself in us. This religion inclines us to build our trust that God is gracious not on the "Christ outside us," but on the "Christ in us," on *aliquid in nobis,* and particularly on faith as a good quality dwelling in us. In spite of our theoretical orthodoxy we then do not conceive of the Gospel as an absolution that is pronounced upon all sinful mankind and that presents itself to our faith as its proper correlative, but we imagine it to be a proclamation of conditions, "a general amnesty on certain terms," which we must first fulfill if God is to be fully gracious toward us. In short, we change the evangelical conditional and imperative clauses into conditions and imperatives of the Law, and, all our talk about Gospel and faith notwithstanding, we lock the door to God's grace in Christ. This tendency explains the drastic words with which Luther (St. L. XVII: 2213) contends for the objective validity of Baptism, the Lord's Supper, and absolution: "There is a very great difference between having faith and relying on one's faith and thus being baptized on it. Whoever is baptized on his faith is not only uncertain, but an idolatrous, apostate Christian, for he trusts and relies on what is his, namely, on a gift given him of God, and not solely on God's Word [the promises of grace for Christ's sake], just as another trusts and relies on his strength, wealth, power, wisdom, sanctity, which indeed also are gifts, given him of God."

Against this position of Luther the objection has always been raised that Scripture itself expressly demands reflection on our faith and the fruits of faith, that the Bible enjoins: "Examine yourselves whether ye be in the faith; prove your own selves. Know ye not your own selves how that Jesus Christ is in you, except ye be reprobates?" (2 Cor. 13:5.) Indeed, this preaching, too, ever is to be heard in the Church until Judgment Day. But at the same time, as Christian teachers we should know that with such preaching we are in an entirely different domain. Then we are not proclaiming the Gospel to terrified sinners by inviting and persuading them to believe, but we are warning against incipient carnal security and against self-deception. In other words, we are then engaged in the preaching of the Law by reprimanding unbelief. "The Gospel is such a preaching as shows and gives nothing else than grace and forgiveness in Christ" (*Trigl.* 955, F. C., Sol. Decl., V, 12). Conversely, reproof and warning against unbelief belong to the Law. "The Law reproves unbelief [namely] when men do not believe the Word of God" (*Trigl.* 957, F. C., Sol. Decl., V, 19). "Now, him who is adept at this art of properly dividing Law and Gospel set at the head of the table and declare him a Doctor of the Holy Scripture" (Luther, St. L. IX:802).

II

Luther holds that all who deny that the Word and the Sacraments dispense the forgiveness of sins, who therefore find it particularly offensive if men remit sins, do not actually take God's Word to be God's Word, but regard it as merely the word of men. See St. L. XIX: 945; XIII:2441, etc. At first sight this verdict of Luther might appear unfair in view of the fact, for example, that the Reformed strongly stress the inspiration of the Bible. But on closer examination Luther's conclusion proves to be right. For to teach that the Scriptures are the Word of God and consistently to practice this truth are certainly two different things. When the Reformed, Calvin included, caution men against seeking to become certain of the gracious will of God from the outward Word of the Gospel, the thought underlies this warning that the outward Word of the Gospel as it is contained in the Scriptures, is not the Word of God. He who really considers Holy Writ to be God's voice will surely not assert that the gracious will of God cannot be definitely ascertained from it. Again, when the Reformed deny the forgiveness of sins through Baptism, the thought at the bottom of this denial is that the Word of God connected with Baptism and expressly predicating the remission of sin (εἰς ἄφεσιν ἁμαρτιῶν) is not God's Word. Again, when the Reformed accuse the Lutherans of robbing God of what is His by their doctrine of a remission of sins pronounced by men, the thought latent in this accusation is that God's Word is no more God's Word when men utter and circulate it, but merely the word of man. So we shall have to grant that Luther gauges the situation aright when he says: "Such thoughts of two kinds of keys [to wit, that the declaration of forgiveness by men in the name of Christ is not God's forgiveness] arise because they do not take God's Word to be God's Word, but, because it is spoken by men, they look upon it as being merely words of men and think that God is high above, and far, far, far from such Word that is on earth, and they gape up to heaven and invent additional keys." (St. L. XIX:945.)

Thus our attitude toward the means of grace reveals whether we really take the Word God has given to His Church to be God's Word. This is the case only if we believe and maintain that God the Holy

Spirit Himself is always present in His Word and is Himself dealing with us, no matter how and through whom His Word approaches us. "Even though the Word is uttered by men," says Luther, "it is not their word, but the Word of God. . . . Hence there is no need of climbing up into heaven to obtain remission of sins. God has put the forgiveness of sins into holy Baptism, into the Lord's Supper, and into the Word. Yes, He has put it into the mouth of every Christian when he comforts you and assures you of the grace of God through the merit of Jesus Christ, so that you should accept and believe it just as if Christ Himself had with His own mouth assured you of it. . . . Because they [the sectaries and visionaries, Zwingli, Oecolampadius, and their tribe] sweep away the Word of God, they rob themselves and others who permit themselves to be persuaded by them of all blessings, the remission of sins, Baptism, the Sacrament, the Lord Christ, and retain nothing of Baptism and the Sacrament but the empty hulls." (St. L. XIII:2439 ff.)

Of course, here again we must recognize and acknowledge that the "enthusiast" is still hiding in all of us. Really to regard God's Word as God's Word, no matter where and how and through whom it approaches us, is an art we must daily learn anew. How entirely different and altogether more spiritual a form would our Christian life assume if we always regarded God's Word, which approaches us in manifold ways (through the reading of the Scriptures and Christian books, through public preaching, through conversation with fellow Christians), in full earnest as God's Word! We see this deficiency as a vestige of our estrangement from God and deplore it. The express direction, however, not to take the external Word of God to be the Word of God, but instead to judge of God's will toward us according to the purported *interior Spiritus illuminatio,* is a seduction which the Enemy of the Church has circulated and still is circulating through Zwingli, Calvin, Andrew Osiander, Weigel, and their followers.

III

In discussing the doctrine of absolution the question *Cui bono?* is again and again asked, also within the Lutheran Church. Why add absolution when we teach very definitely that through this special form of proclaiming the Gospel nothing more and nothing else is given than every believer already has through the general preaching and promise of the Gospel? [105] The objection is of a kind with several

---

[105] *Proceedings of the 10th Convention of the Missouri Synod,* 1860, p. 4.

others, such as, What can Baptism and the Lord's Supper benefit, since by faith in the mere Word of Christ the Christian already has the remission of sins and, with it, all spiritual treasures obtained by Christ?

The objectors forget two things. First, they do not take into consideration that the preaching of the Gospel in the particular form of absolution is Christ's ordinance (John 20:23). For this reason our Lutheran Confessions correctly say that "it would be wicked [*widei Gott*] to remove private absolution from the Church" (*Trigl.* 281, Apol., VI, 3). Secondly, they do not take into consideration that this institution of Christ springs from a need of the souls and is by no means intended to make the divine ordinance of the means of grace complicated or to place a legalistic yoke on the necks of the disciples. Remember, it is difficult to lead a man to a true knowledge of his sin. Equally difficult it is to bring a heart terrified by the Law of God to a knowledge of the grace of God in Christ and to sustain it in this faith. Therefore the Smalcald Articles say that God, because He "is superabundantly rich [and liberal] in His grace," gives us counsel and aid against sin, not merely in one way (*uno modo*), but in various ways: through the preaching of the forgiveness of sins in the whole world, through Baptism, through the Sacrament of the Altar, and also through the Power of the Keys, as also through the mutual conversation and consolation of Christians among each other (*Trigl.* 491, Part III, Art. IV). — *The Proceedings of the 10th General Convention of the Missouri Synod,* 1860, set forth two things at some length: (1) that through absolution nothing else and nothing better is given than through the preaching of the Gospel; (2) that through absolution, and especially through private absolution, the appropriation of the forgiveness of sins to himself is made easier for the terrified sinner.[106]

---

[106] P. 34 f., 37. And on p. 54 ff. we read: "A parable will make clear the relation of private absolution to the general absolution in the sermon. The general absolution through the sermon is like a rich man throwing a large number of gold coins into a crowd with the intention of having everyone get a coin; now, whoever grasps one has one. But private absolution is like a rich man sending his servant to a timid soul who dares not seize a piece and having him press the coin into his hand. As that person has no more valuable a coin than the others, so through private absolution nothing different or better is given than through the sermon. It is a mistaken distinction, frequently made, that in the sermon the treasure of the forgiveness of sins is merely advertised, or perhaps offered, but that in private absolution it is really dealt out. When Luther speaks of a greater certainty of forgiveness obtained in private absolution, he merely means: It is more difficult for a believer to appropriate the consolation from the general sermon than from private absolution. . . . Also the Sacraments are nothing more than a visible Word; their content is, therefore, identical with that of the Word. In ordaining, along with the Word, the Sacraments, in which He deals with the individual, God has considered the condition of believers; for, since the believer

The same *Proceedings*, however, also point out that private confession as well as the joining of confession and absolution with the
Lord's Supper is only a church custom and not a divine order.[107]

---

finds it more difficult because of the infirmities of his present life to appropriate
consolation when it is simply proclaimed in general to an assembly, God, as
Luther says, does not act niggardly, but has ordained that the consolation be
imparted to believers in various ways. We see here, therefore, God's marvelous
condescension to the infirmity of His believers. Because He knows how difficult
it is for them to take hold of the general consolation contained in the sermon,
He has instituted private absolution, Baptism, and the Lord's Supper for the
individuals so that everyone may be assured: Here *I* am the person with whom
He deals and speaks. . . . To the objection that it is beyond understanding why
private absolution is so stressed; that he must be a dull sort of a fellow who
cannot just as well apply the public sermon to himself and take comfort from it,
the answer was given: Then one can also not comprehend why Christ, beside
preaching, also instituted Baptism and the Lord's Supper; for there is no
essential difference between them and the sermon. Then one must also be
astonished to hear Christ say after His resurrection: 'Tell His disciples *and Peter*'
(Mark 16:7); then one would also have to say: Peter must have been stupid
if he could not appropriate the consolation sent to the Apostles in general,
to whom he plainly belonged. But Peter thought: You are no longer an Apostle.
Therefore the Lord had the consolation brought to him personally. Our old
theologians say: The anxiety of a Christian is not whether the world is redeemed,
but whether he himself is redeemed, that is, whether the universal redemption
applies also to him personally."

    107 *Op. cit.*, pp. 55, 57. *Trigl.* 281, Apol., VI, 5: "But in reference to the
enumeration of offenses in confession, we have said above that we hold that it is
not necessary by divine right." In the same connection the Roman "Scripture
proof" is investigated and correctly declared to be "ridiculous and puerile."
Cp. also Gibbons, *The Faith of Our Fathers*, p. 393 ff. — Luther's clear presentation of "three kinds of confession" in his sermon on "Confession and the Sacrament," St. L. XI:582 ff.: "1. Confession before *God*. This is so highly necessary
that it may not be omitted even for a moment, but must go on through the
entire life of a Christian. It consists in this, that we condemn ourselves as
deserving death and the fire of hell. With this confession we anticipate God,
so that He can no more condemn us, but must be gracious to us; for if we judge
and condemn ourselves (1 Cor. 11:31), God will no more judge and condemn us.
2. Confession before the *neighbor*. By this is meant, if one has done his neighbor
harm, he should confess it before him. This confession, too, is needful and
commanded. If this fruit is not there, one's faith and first confession also are
not honest. 3. The confession 'commanded by the *Pope,* which is made privately
into the ears of the priests.'" This confession has no divine command. To rescue
their confession, Papists had claimed also Luther as their champion because "also
that man Luther himself extols and praises confession." Luther replies in a letter
to the congregation at Esslingen (St. L. XXIa:562 f.): "I have indeed said that
confession is a good thing. Likewise I prevent no one from fasting, making
a pilgrimage, eating meat, observing days, etc., if only it is done of one's own
accord, and not done as though he had to do it in conscience and as though
omitting it would be mortal sin, as the Pope with his blind leaders raves. . . .
Confess undisturbed, fast cheerfully if you care to, but do not imagine that you
must and that you commit a sin if you omit it." Yes, says Luther (St. L. XI:722):
"To desire absolution is in itself sufficiently confessed," because desiring absolution
is already as much as "acknowledging one's guilt and confessing oneself a sinner."

And as to the relation of general confession to private confession these *Proceedings* aptly say: "Also in the general confession, as customary among us before partaking of Communion, there is in a certain sense a personal confession and a personal appropriation; for one is there dealing with a definite number of Christians who confess their sins, desire grace, and receive absolution; in regard to the personal appropriation, therefore, this absolution is somewhat more than the public sermon, and one must be cautious in preaching of it not to impair God's sacred ordinance. To speak slightingly of general confession is dangerous; I must not depreciate the one to make much of the other; rather let both be esteemed as of high, glorious value." (*Ibid.*, p. 58.)

10

The Means of Grace in the Old Testament

The Gospel of Christ, the divine message of the remission of sins by faith in Christ, was the means of grace for the whole era of the Old Testament. So the Scriptures themselves inform us, declaring: "To Him give all the Prophets witness that through His name whosoever believeth in Him shall receive remission of sins" (Acts 10:43). Abraham believed in Christ: "Your father Abraham rejoiced (ἠγαλλιάσατο) to see My day: and he saw it and was glad" (John 8:56).[108] Moses wrote of Christ (John 5:46). The Christians of the New Testament have the same faith as Abraham and for that reason, even when they are no natural descendants of Abraham, are called "the children of Abraham" (υἱοὶ Ἀβραάμ), Gal. 3:7, and "Abraham's seed" (τοῦ Ἀβραάμ σπέρμα), Gal. 3:29. The New Testament Scriptures state explicitly that the Christian doctrine of justification, justification by faith in Christ without the deeds of the Law, is witnessed in all the Scripture of the Old Testament, μαρτυρουμένη ὑπὸ τοῦ νόμου καὶ τῶν προφητῶν (Rom. 3:21). The entire Fourth Chapter of the Epistle to the Romans is devoted to proving in particular that the New Testament doctrine of justification is no *novum*, but taught also in the Old Testament. Even under the Mosaic covenant of the Law the promise of

---

108 Luther, St. L. XI:573: "Where and when did he see it? Not with bodily eyes, as the Jews understand the words, but with the sight of faith he recognized Christ when it was told him Genesis 22: 'In thy Seed shall all the nations of the earth be blessed.' . . . The day of Christ is the era of the Gospel [the New Testament times]." Thus also Luthardt comments correctly. But his remark on "and he saw it and was glad" is an imposition: "This joy in reference to the day of Christ was realized only after the death of Abraham."

Christ remained in force as means of grace. Gal. 3:17: "The covenant
that was confirmed before of God in Christ, the Law, which was
430 years after, cannot disannul, that it should make the promise of
none effect." When Christ appeared in the fullness of time, the Jews
did not believe in Him. But Christ Himself traces their unbelief back
to their refusal to believe Moses' Scriptures (John 5:45-47). And the
reason why also His disciples found it difficult to reconcile Christ's
death and resurrection with their faith is revealed by Christ in the
words: "O fools, and slow of heart to believe all that the *Prophets*
have spoken" (Luke 24:25). For the same reason, namely, disregard
of the words of Scripture, some theologians past and present have
been blind to the fact that ever since the Fall, throughout the entire
Old Testament era, the Gospel of Christ has been the divinely appointed means of communicating grace to men and that faith in this
Gospel made men the children of God.

Modern theologians, conservative as well as radical, here put on
a pretense of theological superiority. They charge all who understand
the Old Testament as did Christ and the Apostles with a lack of
"historical understanding" of the Old Testament revelation in general
and with exegetical obtuseness in particular. But the fact is that this
modern rationalistic theology violates history, because it transfers its
own deficiency in understanding the Messianic prophecies to the
children of God in the Old Testament.

This becomes painfully patent in the interpretations they have
labored to give to the first Gospel (Gen. 3:15). The "Seed of the
woman" is supposed not to be a designation of the one person, Christ,
but "impersonally" to connote all mankind. That this interpretation
will not fit the text has been shown (Vol. II, 516, footnote 19). Here
let us merely add that we certainly have no right to believe Adam
and Eve capable of such folly as the impersonal interpretation of the
"Seed of the woman" reveals. When our first parents heard what
a powerful deed God ascribed to the Seed of the woman, namely,
that He would crush the head of the serpent (הוּא יְשׁוּפְךָ רֹאשׁ), they
could not possibly think of an "impersonal subject." Impersonal subjects — we can trust Adam and Eve to have known this — do not
accomplish such deeds. Particularly would Adam and Eve not have
gotten the idea that the "descendants of the woman" or mankind
collectively would achieve this mighty work. The true history is this:
Adam and Eve knew by their own sorry experience that the devil
had vanquished them when they still were perfect and in the state
of integrity. The thought, therefore, that mankind, guilty and sinful

and doomed to die, or in general any mere man, would blot out the guilt of sin and overcome death must have seemed preposterous to them. Modern theology can entertain this thought and trust fallen mankind to perform such heroic deeds as the blotting out of man's guilt and victory over death only because they disregard the "historical situation" created by the Fall. But what right have men to antedate this disregard of the actual facts and to ascribe to Adam and Eve the opposite of what their own experience taught them? We certainly remain with a true "understanding of history" when we assume that Adam and Eve were very attentive listeners to the promise of the Seed of the woman, who would remedy their terrible misfortune, and that they therefore also took note that God Himself is the acting subject in the promise. It is not a man nor mankind, but God Himself who puts enmity between the devil and his seed and the woman and her Seed. Eve reveals her belief that the Seed of the woman would not be a mere man, but Jehovah Himself, by exclaiming at the birth of Cain: "I have gotten a man, Jehovah" (Gen. 4:1).[109]

Accordingly we shall have to agree with Luther when he calls this first promise after the Fall both "very lucid and clear," as also "very dark."[110] Very dark it is as to the accompanying circumstances, since as yet it says nothing of Abraham's Seed, David's Branch, Mary's Son, etc. Very clear it is, inasmuch as it promises a Woman's Seed, in whom God Himself is the acting subject and who will make an end of the devil in his work of destroying mankind, that is, will abolish the guilt and death of men. In Gen. 3:15 we have the substance of 2 Cor. 5:19: "God was in Christ, reconciling the world unto Himself."[111] Luther says: "Look at Adam and Eve; they are full of sin and death; nevertheless, because they hear the promise of the Seed of the woman

---

[109] Luther: "Although Eve was mistaken in this hope [that Cain was the promised Seed of the woman], her words nevertheless reveal that Eve was a holy woman and believed the promise of the future salvation by the blessed Seed" (St. L. I:296). Again: "When Eve had given birth to her first son, Cain, she of course supposed this child to be the man whom the Lord had promised and announced to her who would avenge her on that serpent. On that account she exclaims: 'I have gotten a man, the Lord,' the God Jehovah, the Woman's Seed." (St. L. III:653.)

[110] Luther, St. L. I:240 ff.; see also on Gen. 3:15 Luther's sermon of the year 1526 (St. L. III:650 ff.).

[111] Luther, St. L. III:66: " 'The Seed of the woman shall bruise thy head.' This passage is the absolution whereby God acquitted Adam and Eve and all of us. For if the Seed is so strong that He crushes the head of the Serpent, then He also crushes all its power; then the devil is overcome and all the loss made good which Adam had incurred, and he is again placed in the state he was in formerly."

who shall crush the head of the Serpent, they hope for the same thing that is our hope, namely, that death will be abolished, sin eradicated, and righteousness, life, and peace be brought back. In this hope our first parents live and die, and because of this hope they verily are holy and righteous." (St. L. I:241.) Luther, therefore, will grant no difference whatever between the faith of Adam and Eve and the faith of New Testament Christians as pertains to the way of salvation (St. L. III:661; XII:494 ff.). Quenstedt expresses the same opinion in these words: "Substantially the same Gospel which today is preached in the whole world stood in full vigor and freshness and was promulgated also in the Old Testament, and indeed from the earliest times of the fallen human family, through which the grace of God, the remission of sins, and one and the same salvation in Christ, the Redeemer of the world, was announced and offered to all; and all in the Old Testament, as many as were justified and saved, were justified and saved by faith in the merit of Christ, which benefited before it existed [*quod profuit, antequam fuit*]" (*Syst.* II, 1013 f.). Whoever has not arrived at this understanding of the Old Testament revelation of salvation ought to admit, at least, that it is the understanding of Christ and the Apostles. As to the clarity of the revelation of the Gospel, Luther and our old theologians acknowledge a difference in degree, as they frequently state.[112]

Also circumcision and the Passover were, ever since their institution, means of grace for the period of the Old Testament. Regarding circumcision we read in Gen. 17:7: "I will establish My covenant between Me and thee and thy seed after thee in their generations for an everlasting covenant, to be a God unto thee, and to thy seed after thee," that is, to be your gracious God, assuring you of the remission of sins by this rite of circumcision. Therefore Paul, in Rom. 4:11, calls circumcision "a seal of the righteousness of the faith." [113]

And as concerns the Passover, Ex. 12:21 ff. shows that the Children of Israel were exempted from the punitive judgment of God not because they were Jews, but because of the blood of the paschal lamb. Vv. 23-24: "For the Lord will pass through to smite the Egyptians;

---

[112] Luther, St. L. I:236 ff., 1008, 1092, 1526, 1585. Quenstedt says: "The Gospel is presented sufficiently clearly in the Old Testament, but not with that degree of clarity in which it shines in the New Testament" (*Syst.* II, 1014).

[113] Baier-Walther, III, 426: "*Finis cuius proximus* and therefore *principalis* of the Sacrament of circumcision was the confirmation of the covenant grace for the forgiveness of sins. In Gen. 17:7 God promises that He will be the God of circumcised Abraham and of his circumcised seed, which should first of all be explained as pertaining to . . . adoption into the covenant [*foedus*] of grace."

and when He seeth the blood upon the lintel, and on the two side posts, the Lord will pass over the door and will not suffer the destroyer to come in unto your houses to smite you. And ye shall observe this thing for an ordinance to thee and to thy sons forever." On this account Luther says: "It is not true that the Sacraments of the New Testament differ from the Sacraments of the Old Testament as to their signification" [namely, as God-appointed signs of the *grace* of God]. . . . "Both our and the fathers' signs or Sacraments have a word of promise attached which calls for faith and can be fulfilled by no other work. Therefore they are signs or Sacraments of justification." (*Opp. v. a.* V, 62.) Both through the Word about the coming Messiah and through circumcision and the Passover, the Sacraments of the Old Testament, the remission of sins was given and, by the believers, appropriated.

11

The Means of Grace and Prayer

The main points of Scripture's teaching regarding prayer were presented in the section on sanctification and good works (p. 76 ff.). Here we shall consider the further question whether prayer should be placed beside Word and Sacrament as a means of grace. This is done, for example, by Hodge (*Syst. Theol.* III, 466, 708) when he says: "The means of grace, according to the standards of our Church, are the Word, Sacraments, and prayer." Shedd (*Dogm. Theol.* II, 561) quotes from the Larger Catechism, Qu. 154: "The outward and ordinary means whereby Christ communicates to His Church the benefits of His mediation are all His ordinances, especially the Word, Sacraments, and prayer; all which are made effectual to the elect for their salvation." The Methodists enumerate as their "special means of grace" their "love feasts and class meetings." As means of grace instituted by God they mention "prayer, searching the Scriptures, the Lord's Supper, fasting, Christian conference." See Guenther, *Symbolik*, 4th ed., p. 272 for quotations (*Pop. Symb.*, p. 285).

In contrast to this view we read in Meusel (*Handlexikon* III, 5, *sub* "Means of Grace"): "It is confusing and to be rejected when recent theologians, following Schleiermacher . . . classify also prayer in the name of Jesus with the means of grace. Things objective and subjective, divine and human acts, must not be co-ordinated and confounded in this way." This objection is in place. Though we list the term "means of grace," like the term "Sacrament," with the ecclesiastical terms, in the use of which a certain latitude must therefore be granted,[114] it certainly is no commendable *modus docendi* to place prayer on a level with the Word and the Sacraments as a means of grace, since that is co-ordinating incongruous things. Word and Sacrament are the means through which God deals with us men, that is, imparts to men the remission of sins earned by Christ and through this bestowal creates and strengthens faith in them. Word and Sacraments are, as Luther was accustomed to say, something God does to us. By prayer, on the other hand, the believers are doing something toward God. Prayer is an exercise of the faith of Christians. If now we co-ordinate prayer with Word and Sacraments as a means of grace, it can easily be regarded as a complement of the grace of God, as if God became fully reconciled and ready to forgive men their sins by their work of prayer. Men are led to believe the widely prevalent error that God has not fully reconciled the world unto Himself by Christ, and that to become reconciled to God men need more than faith in the reconciliation Christ achieved for them. The co-ordination of prayer with the means of grace can easily be made to serve the pernicious practice of directing souls terrified by God's Law to prayer for grace, instead of to the Word and Sacrament, thus creating the impression that forgiveness of sins is obtained by prayer as a work performed by man.

Here the objection is voiced that in Scripture an obtaining of forgiveness of sins through prayer is clearly taught; not only is it stated in general, "Ask, and it shall be given you" (Matt. 7:7), but we are also in particular taught to pray for the remission of sins in the Fifth Petition, "Forgive us our sins" (Luke 11:4); thus Christ not only instructs us to ask for forgiveness, but at the same time promises that through such prayer we shall obtain forgiveness of sins. — The answer is: True, we obtain also remission of sins through prayer; however, not inasmuch as prayer is a work performed by man, but rather inasmuch as there is present in the prayer "Forgive us our sins" a divinely wrought yearning for the grace of God in Christ, a *velle*

---

[114] Cf. *Trigl.* 311, Apol., XIII, 16—17, and Hollaz' distinction between means of grace in the narrow and in the wider sense: "Means strictly so called, the giving means on the part of God, or those imparting the salvation, are the Word of God and the Sacraments; on our part the receiving means, or the one apprehending the proffered salvation, is faith which relies on the merit of Christ. Means of grace in the wider sense are those that are introductory or executive or leading into the Kingdom of Glory, *scil.*, death, resurrection, final Judgment, and the end of the world." *Examen, "De mediis salutis in genere,"* qu. 2.

remissionem peccatorum, hence faith in the Gospel. Th\
Fifth Petition upholds the doctrine that a man is justifie
works by faith alone.

Furthermore, it has seemed strange to some that, on
hand, prayer, according to Scripture, presupposes trust in tl ˛ grace
of God ("Our Father"), while, on the other hand, the forgiveness
of sins is still to be obtained or asked for in prayer. The seeming
contradiction disappears if we remember the true inner state of a
praying Christian. Because Christians still sin, and this sin registers
in their conscience as guilt, the faith still present in their heart reacts
against this feeling of guilt by fleeing to the gracious promise of
the Gospel.

Observe carefully what relation faith, as it prays for forgiveness
of sins, assumes toward the completed propitiation of Christ and
toward the means of grace. It does not want to be a complement
to Christ's work of reconciliation. It does not ignore the means of
grace, nor does it displace them, but on the contrary it makes Christ's
perfect merit and the means of grace the grounds on which it stands.
The Christian prays that God would remit his sins for Christ's sake
according to His gracious promise in the Word.

The moment one's prayer ignores Christ's completed acquisition
of grace and its bestowal through the promise of the Gospel, the
prayer takes on the following unchristian features: It is no longer
a prayer in the name of Jesus, but in opposition to the name of Jesus;
it is no longer an exercise of faith, but of unbelief toward the Gospel;
it becomes in itself a work whereby man hopes to be able to earn
God's grace and thus becomes an abomination to God. And the more
fervent this prayer becomes, while ignoring the plenary grace acquired
for us by Christ and its presentation in the Word of the Gospel, the
greater an abomination it is. Christ characterizes such prayer in
Matt. 6:7: "But when ye pray, use not vain repetitions, as the heathen
do; for they think that they shall be heard for their much speaking."
Chemnitz writes: "The Augsburg Confession earnestly reproves [*serio
improbat*] those who seek or teach men to seek reconciliation with
God and the remission of sins outside the ministry of the Word and
the Sacraments" (*Examen,* "De poenitentia," p. 370).

Calvinists such as Hodge do not by chance count prayer, with
Word and Sacraments, as a means of grace. Because of their rejection
of universal grace and their assumption of an immediate communication of grace and operation of the Spirit they cannot direct men to the
promise of grace in the objective Word of the Gospel. They must

rather refer sinners who are terrified by God's Law and are seeking
grace to prayer and other human endeavors and by these activities
induce in them such moods and feelings as can perchance (as long as
they are not aware of their utter sinfulness) be regarded as marks
of sonship with God. Likewise one can understand why synergists,
whether they call themselves Reformed or Lutheran or otherwise,
like to refer to prayer as a means of grace, or employ it as such,
since they teach that the gift of divine grace depends also on what
man does, *scil.*, on personal self-determination, on right conduct, etc.
It is a well-known fact that the run of the revival preachers among
the sects point the soul seeking grace to prayer for grace instead of
to the Word and the Sacraments. Lutheran Pietists, even a man like
Fresenius, have done the same thing.[115] Underneath this practice

---

[115] See Dr. Walther's report on his own sad experiences in using Fresenius'
Book on Confession and Communion in *The Proper Distinction Between Law
and Gospel*, translated by Dr. W. H. T. Dau, p. 140 ff. Also Fresenius' first rule
for a "thorough" conversion "in a short time" reads: "Pray for grace!" "You enter
your closet, as the Savior advises in Matt. 6:6, or wherever you can speak to God
in private, bow your knees, and with all your might cry for grace; not only for
the grace that God may forgive your sins, but also for the grace that your heart
may be changed and the love of sin destroyed in you." "This prayer you should
offer, not once or twice, but you must continue offering it daily with sighs and
strong crying until you obtain grace, which assures you from your own experience
that your heart has been truly changed." Against this Walther sets the thesis:
"The Word of God is not rightly divided when sinners who have been struck down
and terrified by the Law are directed, not to the Word and the Sacraments, but
to their own prayers and wrestlings with God in order that they may win their
way into a state of grace." Walther shows by three examples from Apostolic
practice that terrified sinners were pointed to the Word of the Gospel and Baptism
(Acts 2:16, 22); then, that three errors lie at the base of the opposite practice
of the Reformed sects and of Lutherans given to Reformed practices: 1. They do
not believe and teach a real, complete reconciliation of man with God through
Christ's vicarious satisfaction. 2. They teach falsely on the Gospel. They do not
regard the Gospel as a proclamation of the remission of sins, but as a primer for
human endeavors toward meriting God's grace. Individual preachers among the
sects are sometimes an exception due to some Lutheran influence. 3. The sects
teach falsely on faith. They regard the faith through which men are justified and
saved as a quality in man. "The doctrine of infused grace is the whole mystery
of the Papacy and the sects." However, Walther does not fail to point out that
also Lutherans who confess the correct doctrine are only too often papistic and
sectarian in practice because every man by nature "is minded to base his
redemption not on something outside him, but entirely on himself" (*Die luth.
Lehre v. d. Rechtfertigung*, p. 64). Of the nature of modern theology Walther
says (*ibid.*, p. 69): "All modern Christendom refuses to trust God on the basis
of His mere Word — will believe God only if grace is felt in the heart and imagines
that one can become certain of grace by his own efforts (basing faith on the
regenerate ego, the Christian consciousness). That indeed amounts to nothing
else than a shipwreck of faith. . . . They are minded to seek Christ only in
themselves and not to be content until they have supposedly found Him there.

there always lies the conscious or unconscious denial of the complete reconciliation of the whole world by Christ's *satisfactio vicaria* and the denial of the truth that Word and Sacraments are the divinely ordained means through which God both proffers the remission of sins won by Christ and calls forth and strengthens faith.

We must add a few words on the modern "theology of experience." These theologians aim to base their entire theology, including prayer, on their "experience." W. Herrmann [116] says very correctly that true prayer must not be "a cry of distress projected into uncertainty," but must be a "real approach to God." It is also correct that man can address only the God who has revealed Himself to man personally. But of what kind must the revelation be actually to create confidence in man to "approach" God for the forgiveness of sins? It is not sufficient, as Herrmann imagines, that we recall some experience in which God noticeably intervened in our life and thus made us feel His "presence." Every man experiences a revelation of God's presence in his soul, in the realm of nature, and in history (Acts 17:24-28). But this revelation is so far from filling man with the confidence to ask God for the forgiveness of sins that it rather prompts him strongly to flee from God, because his feeling of guilt fills him with fear. This guilty feeling can be dispelled by no human endeavor, whether it take the form of a "vigorous exercise of one's own spiritual powers" or of man-devised worship and sacrifices. The recollection of some divine intervention in our life is, therefore, not a sufficient basis for our petition for the forgiveness of sins. Here the recollection of that great occurrence in the life of Christ is necessary — the event that concerns the whole world and therefore also every single human being, that is, the recollection of the phenomenon that God was in Christ, reconciling the world unto Himself, and that God has committed unto us the Word of Reconciliation for us to believe. Any appeal for forgiveness that sets aside Christ's *satisfactio vicaria* and the means of grace is not a prayer in the sense of the Fifth Petition, but rises out of self-deception. And if a person comes to a true knowledge of his sin, the self-deception will also be recognized for what it is.

Their custom is to ask: 'Have you Christ in the heart? Do you feel that He is working in you,' If the answer given is Yes, then, and not till then, is there cause for comfort and hope; then are they ready to believe. But what is thus imagined to be faith is not true faith but pure illusion or, at best, a fruit of faith. Woe to him who relies on it! To do that means to make a false Christ for yourself and to reject the Christ who hung on the Cross and gives Himself to us in the Gospel."

[116] R. E., 3d ed., VI, 386 ff. See the same author's *"Verkehr der Christen mit Gott."*

LAW AND GOSPEL

(DE DISCRIMINE LEGIS ET EVANGELII)

Because Scripture divides doctrinally into Law and Gospel, one cannot but treat constantly of Law and Gospel and their mutual relation in presenting the Christian doctrine on the basis of Scripture. Already in the very Prolegomena, in distinguishing the Christian religion from pagan religions, we had to demonstrate that the Christian religion is a religion of the Gospel, while all non-Christian religions bear the stamp of the religion of the Law. In describing theology as fitness for the office of public teaching in the Church (ἡ ἱκανότης ἡ ἐκ τοῦ θεοῦ, *facultas docendi*), we had to include in our definition of the theological aptitude also the ability to discern and teach both in what sense Law and Gospel are one and in what sense they are opposites. In the doctrine of God (*De Deo*) we distinguished between the natural concept and the Christian concept of God and pointed out that the Triune God revealed in the Scriptures is the God gracious to sinners, or the God of the Gospel, while the natural concept of God never rises above the Law, and for this reason may indeed produce an evil, but never a good conscience. Because sin is discord with, or departure from, the divine Law (ἀνομία), we had to set forth under the doctrine of sin (*De peccato*) that the divine Law always and everywhere obligates all men. In the doctrine of grace (*De gratia Dei salvifica*) we had to make clear that saving grace is the *favor Dei propter Christum,* is proclaimed in the Gospel, and is the direct opposite of the *iustitia inhaerens vel vitae,* which the Law demands. The doctrine of the procurement of grace by Christ (*De opere Christi*) adds up to this, that in the stead of men Christ took upon Himself both the obligation and the punishment of the Law which God had given to men. In soteriology (*De gratia Spiritus Sancti applicatrice*) the Law was excluded from the means of grace, and the Gospel shown to be the only means of grace because it alone bestows the remission of sins earned by Christ and through such bestowal works and strengthens faith. Conversion of man to God (*conversio*) consists in man's turning from the Law, from his innate *opinio legis,* to the Gospel. The Christian doctrine of the justification of man before God (*De hominis iustificatione coram Deo*) is taught correctly only when the *particulae exclusivae* are meticulously observed, that is, when everything that is Law and work of the Law is carefully weeded out. In the doctrine of sanctification and good works (*De sanctificatione*

220

et bonis operibus) it was necessary to emphasize that not the Law, but only the Gospel produces sanctification and good works.

In proceeding now with a fuller discussion of "Law and Gospel," we can therefore only assemble materials already familiar. Such a compilation, however, is highly necessary and profitable in our day. Though the older Lutheran theologians dealt extensively with *De lege et evangelio* or *De discrimine legis et evangelii*, in newer dogmatic works this topic is either entirely missing, or hardly more than casually mentioned. Among recent theologians also Frank has called attention to this defect. He says: "In our Evangelical Church hardly any other doctrine has been more constantly maintained and elaborated as to both subject matter and practice than the doctrine of Law and Gospel. It was connected so intimately with the way God led Luther, with the cardinal doctrine of the Evangelical Church, justification by grace through faith, with the shaping of the Confessions, with the formulation, in Article V of the Formula of Concord, of the result of the controversy with Agricola and of later related controversies, that one can hardly imagine a continuity of the *publica doctrina* without this doctrine. The relation between the First and the Second Chief Part of the Catechism ever anew leads one to dwell on the difference and the connection between Law and Gospel. Indicative of present-day trends is the fact that also this piece of our evangelical heritage (*paradosis*) is deemed unsuited and declared to conflict with true evangelical knowledge. . . . Many deny that man's original relationship to God is a legal one, with the requirement: 'This do, and thou shalt live,' but that God has now appointed grace and the Gospel to save the transgressors of this Law. . . . Attention may therefore well be called to this point, in which the practical theologian is deeply interested for the spiritual guidance of every evangelical Christian." (*Dogm. Studien*, 1892, p. 104 ff.) Modern theologians have no use for the article "Law and Gospel," more particularly, Law and Gospel look alike to them, because they renounce *satisfactio vicaria* and thus inevitably discard the Gospel, however much they use the term "Gospel" and hold that they have a deeper understanding of the Gospel than former ages.

What we wish to add regarding Law and Gospel and their mutual relation, we shall assemble under the following heads: 1. The Terms Law and Gospel. 2. What Law and Gospel Have in Common. 3. Law and Gospel as Opposites. 4. Their Mutual Relation and Joint Use in Practice. 5. The Difficulty of Properly Distinguishing Between Law and Gospel. 6. The Importance of This Distinction. 7. The Confounders of Law and Gospel.

1

The Terms Law and Gospel

We differentiate between Law and Gospel when both terms are used in their proper sense. The Law in the proper sense (*lex proprie accepta*) is the Word of God in which God demands of men that in their nature and in their thoughts, words, and acts they conform to the standard of His commandments and pronounces the curse on those who fail to comply.[1] The Gospel in the proper sense (*evangelium proprie acceptum*) is the Word of God in which God makes no moral demands whatever on men, hence reproves no transgressions, but, on the contrary, promises His grace for the sake of Christ's vicarious satisfaction to such as have not kept the divine Law.[2]

The term "Law" is used in its proper, i. e., primary, sense in Scripture when it refers to what does not bear on faith, but demands perfect observance on the part of man (Gal. 3:12), pronounces the curse on all transgressors (Gal. 3:10), stops the mouth of all the world (Rom. 3:19), and therefore transmits the knowledge of sin (Rom. 3:20). The term "Gospel" is used in its proper sense in Holy Writ when it refers to what does not call for works, but for faith (Rom. 1:16-17), hence does not condemn sinners, but assures them of grace (Acts 20:24), peace (Rom. 10:15; Eph. 6:15), and salvation (Eph. 1:13).

The term "Law" is used in Holy Writ also in a wider, or general, sense to designate all the divine revelation and, moreover, the divine

---

[1] Formula of Concord: "The Law is properly a divine doctrine in which the righteous, immutable will of God is revealed, what is to be the quality of man in his nature, thoughts, words, and works, in order that he may be pleasing and acceptable to God; and it threatens its transgressors with God's wrath and temporal and eternal punishments" (*Trigl.* 957, Sol. Decl., V, 17). Shorter in the Epitome: "We believe, teach, and confess that the Law is properly a divine doctrine which teaches what is right and pleasing to God and reproves everything that is sin and contrary to God's will" (*Trigl.* 801, V, 2).

[2] Formula of Concord: "The Gospel is properly such a doctrine as teaches what man, who has not observed the Law and therefore is condemned by it, is to believe, namely, that Christ has expiated and made satisfaction for all sins, and has obtained and acquired for him, without any merit of his, forgiveness of sins, righteousness that avails before God, and eternal life" (*Trigl.* 801, Epit., V, 4). Luther: "The Gospel is such a doctrine or Word of God as does not demand our works nor enjoin us to do something, but bids us simply to receive the offered grace of the remission of sins and eternal salvation and accept it as a present" (St. L. IX:803).

revelation κατ' ἐξοχήν, the Gospel, as in Is. 2:3: "For out of Zion shall go forth the Law (תּוֹרָה)." [3] The term "Gospel," too, is used in Holy Writ to designate the whole body of Christian doctrine. In this case it is a synecdoche, denominating by its principal part all that is to be taught in and by the Church. *Denominatio fit a parte potiori. Ex parte digniori et potiori totum intelligitur.* Thus Mark 1:1 says of the whole Gospel according to St. Mark, in which also the preaching of repentance by John the Baptist is recorded (v. 4 ff.): "The beginning of the Gospel of Jesus Christ." But the term "Gospel" is never used to designate the Law in the proper sense.[4]

This use of the term "Gospel" in the wider and in the proper, or narrower, sense is noted in the Formula of Concord too. A controversy had arisen as to the question whether the Gospel also may be called a preaching of repentance and judgment, more particularly, whether it is correct to say that the Gospel reproves the sin of unbelief. The Formula of Concord answers yes if the term "Gospel" is used in the wider sense (*late*), and no if the term is used in the proper sense (*proprie*). The Formula says: "Now, when we consider this dissent [whether the Gospel should be called a preaching of repentance] aright, it has been caused chiefly by this, that the term "Gospel" is not always employed and understood in one and the same sense, but in two ways, in the Holy Scriptures, as also by ancient and modern church teachers. For sometimes it is employed so that there is understood by it the entire doctrine of Christ, our Lord, which He proclaimed in His ministry upon earth, and commanded to be proclaimed in the New Testament, and hence comprised in it the explanation of the Law and the proclamation of the favor and grace of God, His heavenly Father, as it is written, Mark 1:1: 'The beginning of the Gospel of Jesus Christ, the Son of God.' And shortly afterwards the chief heads are stated: 'Repentance and

---

[3] There can be no doubt that תּוֹרָה here signifies the Gospel, for it is the designation of that Word of God by which the Gentiles are gathered into the Christian Church. Luther: That the Law goes forth out of Zion "is the cause of the increase of the Church and of the expansion of the kingdom of Christ, namely, the preaching of the Gospel. For He here promises a new Word . . . since He adds, 'out of Zion,' as though He would say: Previously I have given the Law on Mount Sinai; now I will give another Word on Mount Zion, which is not to be a doctrine of works, but of faith, not of laws, but of grace, not an accusing Word, but one conferring remission of sins." (St. L. VI:35; *Opp. exeg.* XXII, 42 *sq.*)

[4] Quenstedt (II, 1027) remarks: "In Scripture the designation 'Law' is, indeed, given a number of times to the Gospel, but the appellation 'Gospel' is never given to the Law."

forgiveness of sins.'" (*Trigl.* 953, Sol. Decl., V, 3 f.) This is "the description of the word 'Gospel' when employed in a wide sense and without the proper distinction between the Law and the Gospel." In this "wide sense" the Gospel may be called a preaching of repentance. "Furthermore the term 'Gospel' is employed in another, namely, in its proper sense, by which it comprises not the preaching of repentance, but only the preaching of the grace of God, as follows directly afterwards, Mark 1:15, where Christ says: 'Repent, and believe the Gospel.'" (*Trigl.* 953, *ibid.*, 6.)[5]

2

What Law and Gospel Have in Common

First, both Law and Gospel are the Word of God. "Thou shalt love the Lord, thy God, with all thy heart," and, "Thou shalt love thy neighbor as thyself," including the curse, "Cursed is everyone that continueth not in all things which are written in the Book of the Law to do them" — these words of the Law are as much God's Word and will as the word of the Gospel with which Paul and Silas saved the jailer at Philippi from despair: "Believe on the Lord Jesus Christ, and thou shalt be saved and thy house."

Furthermore, both Law and Gospel apply to all men. As the Word of the Law, "Ye shall be holy, for I am holy," imposes a duty on the king and the beggar, the cultured man and the barbarian, so, too, there is not a man in all the world for whom the Word of the Gospel, releasing all men from guilt and damnation, is not intended.

Finally, both Law and Gospel are to be taught side by side in the Church and by the Church up to the Last Day.[6] The necessity

---

[5] Baier says of the difference in the use of the terms Law and Gospel: "At times the terms are understood in a wider sense, so that Law in this meaning includes the Gospel, and the latter in a measure the former, for example, when the Law is used for the entire Scriptures, Ps. 1:2, or more especially for the Scriptures of the Old Testament, John 15:25; 1 Cor. 14:21, and lastly in particular for the Mosaic Scriptures, Luke 24:44. Gospel is also at times understood in a wider sense for the entire doctrine of the New Testament, delivered by Christ and the Apostles, Mark 1:14; 16:15; Luke 9:6. Here, however, the terms Law and Gospel are understood in so far as they stand in full contradistinction to each other." (Baier-Walther, III, 342.)

[6] Thus Paul in his Epistle to the Romans thoroughly teaches both side by side, first the Law (ch. 1:18—3:20), and then the Gospel (ch. 3:21—5:21 ff.). The Formula of Concord comments: "From the beginning of the world these

of preaching particularly also the Law must be maintained against Antinomianism, which at the time of the Reformation sought to invade the Lutheran Church through Agricola and his followers.[7] Antinomianism is basically the theory that the knowledge of sin must be taught not from the Law, but from the Gospel, and that accordingly the Law does not belong in the Church, but "in the courthouse," in the sphere of the State.[8] The Lutheran Church disowned this error in all its forms in Art. V and VI of the Formula of Concord. See *Trigl.*, Hist. Introd., pp. 161–172.

Nothing can be said, either from a theological angle or from the viewpoint of natural reason, in favor of the position of Agricola and

---

two proclamations [kinds of doctrine] have been ever and ever inculcated alongside of each other in the Church of God, with a proper distinction" (*Trigl.* 959, Sol. Decl., V, 23).

[7] John Agricola, b. 1492 at Eisleben, 1525 pastor of Nicolai Church at Eisleben, 1536 in Wittenberg, 1540 court preacher in Berlin, d. 1566. — In the Majoristic controversy (see p. 20 ff.) regarding the necessity of good works for salvation the pastors Andrew Poach of Erfurt and Anton Otto of Nordhausen defended antinomistic principles.

[8] Agricola and his followers declared: "Repentance is to be taught not from the Decalog or from any Law of Moses, but by means of the Gospel from the wounding of the Son of God." "Christ says in John that not the Law, but the Spirit reproves sin." "Any matter by which the Holy Ghost is not given or men justified need not be taught, neither at the beginning, nor middle, nor end of justification." "Those who teach that first the Law and then the Gospel must be preached pervert the words of Christ." "The Gospel teaches the wrath of God from heaven and at the same time the righteousness of God, Rom. 1." "The Law does not deserve to be called God's Word." "The Decalog belongs in the courthouse, not in the pulpit." — Agricola first (1527) attacked Melanchthon's *Articles of Visitation*, then, ten years later (1537), also Luther. He says against Melanchthon: "In the Saxon *Visitation* [this is impure]: Because Christ commands to preach repentance and remission of sins, the Decalog must be preached." Agricola even names Luther in his attacks: "In his commentary on the Epistle to the Galatians, Luther says that it is the proper office of the Law to plague and terrify the conscience, in order that it might the easier recognize Christ. There are many such passages in this commentary, which we reject as erroneous in order to preserve purity of doctrine." — Agricola's *Positiones inter fratres sparsae* ("Theses Circulated Among Brethren") and other antinomistic propositions advanced by him or his adherents are found in St. L. XX:1624 ff. Luther's six disputations against the Antinomians are also offered (*ibid.*, 1628 ff.). For the Latin see *Opp. v. a.* IV, 424 ff. In addition, Luther's essay "*Wider die Antinomer*" (1539) and "*Luthers Bericht von M. Joh. Eislebens falscher Lehre und schaendlicher Tat*" (1540) pertain to this matter (St. L. XX:1610 ff., 1649 ff.). Also Luther's sermon on the Fifth Sunday after Trinity in his *Gospel Postil* (see *Trigl.* 955, Sol. Decl., V, 12) offers a clear analysis of Agricola's Antinomianism (St. L. XI:1328 ff.). In Schluesselburg's *Catalogus*, Volume IV pertains to this matter. Sufficient material properly to judge the controversy is to be found in Gieseler, III, 2, 137 ff.; Schmid-Hauck, *Dogmengesch.*, 4th ed., p. 360 ff.

his adherents. They did not want the Law taught in the Christian Church. But what they sought to get rid of, they retained under another name. They injected the Law into the Gospel. They made God's wrath an appendix of the Gospel. Luther exactly describes the logical and theological folly of the Antinomians when he says: "They want to abolish the Law and nevertheless teach the wrath, which is exclusively the office of the Law. Therefore all they do is, they throw these letters '*L-a-w*' away, confirm, however, the wrath of God, which is indicated and understood by these letters, not to mention that they attempt to wring the neck of St. Paul and to make the head the tail." "They have invented a new way of putting it, that one is first to preach grace, then the revelation of wrath, in order that one might not be obliged to hear or utter the word 'Law.' That is a handy footstool which pleases them highly, and they hope to draw all of Scripture in and out of it and thus to become *lux mundi.* They make St. Paul teach this in Romans 1. But they do not see that Paul uses exactly the opposite manner of presenting it. He begins with and shows first the wrath of God from heaven and proves all men sinners and guilty before God; then, after they have become sinners, he teaches them how to obtain grace and become righteous. This the first three chapters mightily and clearly show. Moreover this, too, is an exceptional blindness and folly, that they think the revelation of wrath is something else than the Law, which is impossible; for the Law is revelation of wrath wherever it is understood and felt, as St. Paul says: *Lex iram operatur.* Now, didn't they do a perfect job by banning the Law and then reinstating it by teaching the revelation of wrath? Only they wear the heel in front and teach us the Law after the Gospel and wrath after grace!" (St. L. XX:1618 f.)

Just as foolish is the argument of Agricola that the Law is not to be taught because it does not justify.[9] Inverted, the argument makes sense: Because the Law does not justify, but condemns, it must be preached before the Gospel in order that the damnation pronounced by the Law may be canceled by the Gospel. Justification presupposes condemnation by the Law. Luther therefore asked Agricola to consider: "Is not this blindness without measure that he does not want to preach the Law without or before the Gospel? Why, that is an impossible thing. How is it possible to preach of forgiveness of sins if one has not first established the sins? How can one proclaim

---

[9] *Positiones inter fratres sparsae* 6—9; St. L. XX:1625.

life without death being there?" "For grace must war and win in us against the Law and sin that we may be kept from despair." (St. L. XX:1659, 1656.) Luther is therefore not stretching the truth when he claims that Agricola's objection to the preaching of the Law must as a natural result do away with the Gospel, with Christ and His active obedience to the Law, and thus with the whole Christian faith.

Furthermore, Agricola wants contrition or repentance taught from the Gospel and not from the Law, because a contrition or repentance from love of God can come only from the Gospel. The last part of this sentence is true, of course. But when he then says of the contrition which flows from love of God: This is "the first rung of the new birth, the real blowing and breathing upon by the Holy Spirit; after that the heart gains the sincere confidence in God that He will overlook its foolishness," [10] he is actually making trust in God, or faith in the remission of sins, follow on the contrition which proceeds from love of God, hence dependent on renewal and sanctification. With his new "*methodus*" he is not saving the doctrine of justification, but has turned his steps toward Rome.

Taking into account the further fact that Agricola, in spite of his logical and theological fogginess, presented himself as the savior of the purity of the Christian doctrine [11] and rejected as false the teaching of the Wittenberg faculty, and particularly of Luther, one easily understands why Luther at times employed strong language against Agricola and listed his advent with the "tempests" by which the devil was forever trying to extinguish the restored light of the Gospel. Other details of Antinomianism will be found in the next chapters.[12]

---

[10] *Kurze Summarien*, p. 304; in Schmid-Hauck, p. 361; The "*Kurze Summarien*" of Agricola appeared 1537, but were suppressed because they had been published without being censored; G. Plitt, R. E., 2d ed., I, 452.

[11] *Positiones*, etc., 13: "In order to keep the Christian doctrine pure those must be opposed who teach that the Gospel should be preached only to those whose hearts have previously been terrified and crushed by the Law."

[12] *Wider die Antinomer* (St. L. XX:1619—1623). — A short biography and a striking description of his character by Gustave Plitt is to be found in R. E., 2d ed., I, 214. There, too, the true motive of his attack on Melanchthon is noted. Agricola "was a gifted and not unintelligent man. . . . But all his good sides were nullified by his boundless vanity. Luther, who knew his character well, wrote Dec. 6, 1540: 'If you want to know what vanity itself looks like, you can learn to know it by no better image than that of Agricola.' This character trait made him unfit for service in the Church. Agricola belongs to those assistants of the Reformers who have done more harm than good." The letter mentioned by Plitt is addressed to Jacob Stratner, court preacher in Berlin, and can be found in De Wette, V, 319 f.; St. L. XXIb:2535 ff.

3

Law and Gospel as Opposites

There is no need to apologize for Luther, much less to admit that Luther used language liable to be misunderstood,[13] when he described Law and Gospel as perfect opposites. Indeed, Luther's language in this matter is unequivocal. He says of Law and Gospel that they "differ most widely from each other and are separated farther than opposites" (*inter se longissime distincta et plus quam contradictoria separata sunt, ad Gal.*, St. L. IX:447). And he is entirely right. In content Law and Gospel are actually, like yes and no, perfect opposites. While the Law demands that man perfectly comply with its precepts in his nature and his conduct and proclaims God's wrath to all delinquents, the Gospel makes no moral demands whatever on man and therefore reproves no transgressions — not even the sin of unbelief [14] — but rather, without regard to any good quality or works on their part, promises God's grace for Christ's sake to all transgressors condemned by the Law. We must by all means maintain what a synergistic theology has lost sight of, namely, that the very persons whom the Law pronounces guilty and sentences to death the Gospel acquits of guilt and frees from condemnation. In its promise of grace the Gospel knows of no difference between great and little sinners, between such as conducted themselves properly and such as did not conduct themselves properly, between the more guilty and the less guilty. Rather, there being "no difference, for all have sinned and come short of the glory of God," the Gospel justifies all "freely, by His grace, through the redemption that is in Christ Jesus" (Rom. 3:22 ff.). Men falsify the Gospel through an admixture of Law as soon as they say that the grace promised by the Gospel pertains to other and different, relatively better or less guilty persons than those to whom the Law's verdict of condemnation applies.

The Gospel indeed demands faith. This is the Bible's way of speaking (1 John 3:23) and therefore not to be criticized. But the faith demanded by the Gospel in no wise is a good quality in man or a human accomplishment (*Leistung*), but the very opposite of any accomplishment of man, since "by faith" (διὰ τῆς πίστεως) is tanta-

---

13 Against Thomasius, *Das Bekenntnis d. ev.-luth. K. in d. Konsequenz seines Prinzips*, p. 47 f.; also *Dogmengesch.*, 2d ed., II, 425.

14 The Gospel indeed demands faith, but does not reprimand unbelief. More on this at the end of this chapter.

mount to *"not of works"* (οὐκ ἐξ ἔργων), Eph. 2:8-9. God's demand, or command, that the sinner believe proves how earnestly God's Gospel offer of grace is meant. Cf. Vol. II, 441. Moreover, the Gospel itself, without the assistance of man, kindles the faith it demands. This faith is, as Luther says, no "work enjoined" in the Law, such as love, obedience, etc., but a product of the promise (*opus promissionis*). The Gospel imperative: "Believe on the Lord Jesus Christ," breathes faith into the heart, as, for instance, it made a believer of the jailer at Philippi. (Erl. 58, 353 f.)

To show and maintain the complete dissimilarity of Law and Gospel in content, our old theologians have also pointed out the essential difference between the promises of the Law and the promises of the Gospel, calling the former conditional (*promissiones conditionales*) and the latter pure promises of grace (*promissiones gratuitae*). Some Antinomians denied that any promises were added to the Law.[15] But with Scripture we must maintain that the Law promises life to those who keep it. Gal. 3:12: "The man that doeth them [the things written in the Law] shall live in them." Hence the promises of the Law and those of the Gospel in their nature are opposites. Scripture, as we have seen, makes it very clear that the Law promises life only to those who have actually and in all respects kept the Law. Note the character of the promises of the Law by observing how emphatically Christ pointed those who aimed to inherit eternal life by way of the Law to the need of really keeping the Law. "This do," He said (Luke 10:28), "and thou shalt live." On the other hand, if we scrutinize what Scripture has to say of the promises of the Gospel, we note how persistently Scripture stresses the truth that the Gospel promises righteousness and life to those who have not kept the Law. Scripture multiplies the *particulae exclusivae:* "without the Law," "without the deeds of the Law," "not of works," "not by the works of the Law" (Rom. 3:21, 28; Eph. 2:9; Gal. 2:16). In other words, if we compare the promises of the Law with the promises of the Gospel, we find: The Law pronounces the righteous man righteous; the Gospel, however, pronounces the unrighteous man righteous. Faith in the Gospel is faith in the God "that justifieth the ungodly [τὸν ἀσεβῆ]" (Rom. 4:5).

Finally, we must here again keep in mind the fact that the term

---

[15] Andrew Poach of Erfurt and Anton Otto of Nordhausen contended that the Law contained no promise of salvation at all. Schluesselburg, *Catalogus*, IV, 276; Schmid-Hauck, p. 363; *Trigl.*, Hist. Introd., p. 170.

"condition" is susceptible of different interpretations. We may not forbid anyone to designate the promises of the Gospel "conditional promises," because the evangelical promises, too, frequently have the grammatical form of conditional statements. Rom. 10:9: "If thou . . . shalt believe in thine heart . . . thou shalt be saved." But the teachers who understand and maintain the difference between Law and Gospel point out that in legal conditional clauses the term "condition" actually denotes a human accomplishment, e. g.: "If you keep the Law, you will obtain life"; but in evangelical conditional clauses, e. g.: "If you believe, you will be saved," "believing" does not denote a product or work of man, but merely the mode and manner of appropriation (*modus applicationis*). The sense of the sentence: "If you believe, you will be saved," is not: "If you furnish the faith, you will be saved," but rather: by way of faith, without any goodness or accomplishment of your own, you will be saved.[16] Quenstedt devotes a special section to the discussion of the question: *An promissiones evangelicae sint conditionales* (*Syst.* II, 1018 ff.).

If, however, we must maintain with Luther that Law and Gospel are *contradictoria* in content, then an insurmountable difficulty seems to arise. When God in the Law sentences sinners to death for their sins, and in the Gospel absolves and awards life to the same sinners — for there is no difference among them — it would seem to follow that neither do the hearers of the Word of God know whether the Word of death or the Word of life applies to them, nor does the minister know whether in applying the Word to individual persons he should say to the individual, "Thou shalt surely die" (2 Sam. 12:5), or, "The Lord also hath put away thy sin; thou shalt not die" (2 Sam. 12:13). To solve this puzzle men have at times resorted to the expedient of announcing the consolation of the Gospel only to those who had apparently mended their ways. We learned above that this is not the solution. To become clear in this matter, we must let Scripture instruct us with regard to a further distinction between Law and Gospel, namely, that each has its separate, sharply defined sphere within which it functions in the order of salvation (οἰκονομία).

The Law is certainly to be preached without diminution (Matt. 5:17-18; Gal. 3:10; Rom. 1:18; 3:9-19), but solely for the purpose of bringing man to a realization of his sinfulness and deserved condemnation. As soon as this purpose is attained, as soon as man asks

[16] See the quotations from Heerbrand, Seb. Schmid, and Gerhard in Vol. II, 35, footnote 71.

in contrition, "What must I do to be saved?" the preaching of the Law should cease. It is a divine requirement, and not merely a church regulation, that terrified hearts should hear not the Law, but only the Gospel, which for Christ's sake assures them just as they are ("Just as I Am") of remission of sins and salvation, without the Law and the works of the Law. The Catechism sums up the matter in this fashion: "The Law is to be preached to secure, the Gospel to terrified sinners." In the words of Scripture (Rom. 10:4): "Christ is the end of the Law for righteousness to everyone that believeth," the boundary between Law and Gospel is sharply defined, and Christ asserts the sole authority of the Gospel in the area of broken and humbled hearts when He declares the purpose of His mission to be "to preach the Gospel to the poor, to heal the brokenhearted," (Is. 61:1; Luke 4:18). This line of demarcation between Law and Gospel is clearly fixed in the Scriptures of both the Old and the New Testament, particularly by the practice of Christ and the Apostles.[17] Luther: "The Law has its end, how far it is to go and what it is to achieve, namely, 'unto Christ,' to terrify the impenitent with God's wrath and disfavor. Likewise the Gospel has its peculiar office and function, namely, to preach remission of sins to the troubled consciences. . . . Now, when the conscience is truly smitten, so that it duly feels its sin, experiences the terrors of death, is weighted down with war, pestilence, poverty, shame, and similar misfortune, and the Law then says: You are a dead man and doomed because you have not complied, nor been able to comply, with anything of all that I demanded of you — when the Law, I say, thus crashes down on man and terrifies him with the anguish of death and hell and with despair, it is then high time to know how to separate Law and Gospel from each other and to confine each to its place. Here let him separate who knows how to separate; for here there is occasion and need of separation. To this matter St. Paul's words pertain: 'But before faith came, we were kept under the Law, shut up unto the faith' (Gal. 3:23). . . . Therefore, when the Law accuses me of not having done this or that, of being unrighteous and listed in God's record of debtors, I must confess, it all is true. But the deduction: Therefore you are lost, I must not concede, but in strong faith struggle against it and say: According to the Law, which imputes my guilt unto me, I am

---

[17] Nathan and David (2 Sam. 12:13); Christ and the harlot (Luke 7:47); Peter on Pentecost (Acts 2:37-39); Paul and Silas and the jailer at Philippi (Acts 16:27-31); the congregation at Corinth and the man living in incest (1 Cor. 5:1-5 and 2 Cor. 2:6-8).

indeed a poor, lost sinner, but I appeal from the Law to the Gospel; for God has given another Word over and above the Law, called the Gospel, which makes a gift to us of His grace, remission of sins, eternal righteousness and life, also acquits and delivers me from all your terrors and condemnation and hands me the consolation that all my debt is paid by the Son of God, Jesus Christ Himself. Therefore it is most necessary to know well how to direct and handle both these Words and constantly to take heed that one does not mix them up." (St. L. IX:798 ff.)

It is therefore a part of the proper distinction between Law and Gospel that the Gospel be recognized as the "higher Word," which is to be God's final Word for the terrified sinner. Luther adds: "Now, when both Law and Gospel meet, and the Law declares me a sinner, accuses and condemns me, the Gospel, however, says (Matt. 9:2): 'Be of good cheer; thy sins be forgiven thee,' 'thou shalt be saved,' and both are God's Word, which am I, then, to follow? St. Paul tells you. 'But after faith is come,' he says, 'we are no longer under a schoolmaster,' the Law has come to an end. For as the lesser Word it should and must give way and place to the Gospel. Both are God's Word, the Law and the Gospel, but the two are not equal. One is lower, the other higher; one is weaker, the other stronger; one is lesser, the other greater. When now they wrestle with each other, I follow the Gospel and say, Good-by, Law!" [18]

Law and Gospel differ also as to the sources from which they are known. While natural man still knows the Law, no thought of the Gospel has ever come of itself to even the wisest and civilly most righteous among men. Solely through God's revelation of it in the Word has the Gospel become known among men. Scripture takes great pains to call attention also to this difference between Law and Gospel. Rom. 2:14-15 says of the Law that the Gentiles, who have not the written Law, are a law unto themselves because the work of the Law, that is, the things demanded by the Law, is written in their hearts. But of the Gospel 1 Cor. 2:6 ff. states: "Not the wisdom of this world, nor of the princes of this world, that come to nought but we speak the wisdom of God in a mystery, even the hidden wisdom which God ordained before the world unto our glory, which none of the princes of this world knew; for had they known it, they would

---

[18] Luther's manner of speaking of a "lesser" and a "higher" Word in reference to the sphere of authority of Law and Gospel within the divine order of salvation is Scriptural, as can be seen from passages such as Rom. 10:4; 5:20-21; 2 Cor. 3:7 ff.; Deut. 18:15 ff.; Jer. 31:31 ff.; Heb. 8:6-13.

not have crucified the Lord of Glory. But as it is written: Eye hath not seen, nor ear heard, neither have entered into the heart of man, the things which God hath prepared for them that love Him. But God hath revealed them unto us by His Spirit." [19]

For this reason all pagan religions, being religions of the Law, have no resemblance whatever to the Christian religion. As a rule, modern studies of comparative religion assert a similarity between, or even a basic identity of, the pagan religions and the Christian religion.[20] They arrive at this conclusion by eliminating the Gospel of Christ Crucified from the Christian religion as unessential, as is done, for example, by Pfleiderer [21] and Frank B. Jevons.[22] Actually, however, the difference between Law and Gospel, in respect to the sources from which they are known, becomes antipodal because natural man insists on opposing the Gospel with his innate religion of the Law. The Gospel of the grace of God in Christ is to him an offense and foolishness (1 Cor. 1:23; 2:14), until the rule of the *opinio legis* in his heart is overcome by the Gospel (*Trigl.* 197, Apol., III, 144).

In considering in what respects Law and Gospel are opposites, theologians have studied the special question whether the Gospel or the Law reproves the sin of unbelief. The Formula of Concord teaches, as stated above (p. 223), that reproof of unbelief is to be regarded as Law and not Gospel if the term "Gospel" is taken in its proper sense. Against this finding it has been and is argued that it is inconceivable that the Law can reprove unbelief, since it knows nothing of faith. Accordingly, the reproof of unbelief necessarily had to belong to the Gospel. This was, as Gerhard remarks upon occasion, the chief argument (*palmarium argumentum*) also of the later Philippists, or crypto-Calvinists.[23] Frank, too, inclines to this view.[24]

---

[19] We have repeatedly pointed out that according to the context these words speak not of heaven, but of the Gospel.

[20] Max Mueller of Oxford takes a wholly different position. See Vol. I, 15 f.

[21] *Religion und Religionen*, 1906, p. 215 ff.

[22] *An Introd. to the Study of Compar. Rel.*, 1908, p. 69.

[23] Gerhard, *Loci*, "De ev.," § 105, points to the fact that Agricola's theses regarding the Gospel as a preaching of repentance were zealously defended by the crypto-Calvinists, "as is apparent from the catecheses and theses published in the year 1570 and 1571 at the same place" (Wittenberg). Cp. Muenscher, *Dogmengesch.* (Neudecker), III, 576.

[24] *Dogm. Studien*, p. 114: "The difficulty is that the censuring and reproving function of the Law is nothing more than the reverse side of its demanding and commanding function; in the nature of the case the former cannot extend farther than the latter."

To answer the question, we need but heed two things: 1. According to all that Scripture tells us of the Gospel in its proper sense, one cannot by the remotest chance come to the conclusion that the Gospel reproves the sin of unbelief. 2. According to all that we know of the Law from Scripture, the Law, reproving, as it does, all other sins, surely cannot fail to reprove the sin of unbelief.

Concerning the first point, we recall the exceedingly close relation of the Gospel to the merit of Christ. The Gospel distributes what Christ has merited. But Christ has purchased the remission of all sins for all men, accordingly remission of the sin of unbelief too. The Gospel therefore distributes with the forgiveness of all sins also forgiveness of the sin of unbelief. How, then, could the Gospel, which remits the sin of unbelief, come to reprove it? We should have to disavow Christ's merit and the very essence of the Gospel if we insisted on making reproof of unbelief a part of the Gospel in its proper sense. Moreover, if the Gospel reproved unbelief, it would continually be condemning also the believers, because believers, too, always harbor considerable unbelief along with their faith — a fact that certainly troubles their conscience much. Hence where could we flee with our guilt of unbelief, which we must daily confess? where find consolation if the Gospel reproved the sin of unbelief, instead of forgiving it? Furthermore, if the Gospel reproved the sin of unbelief, no man could ever come to faith in the Gospel, that is, become a Christian, since every man is an unbeliever before he comes to faith. Therefore we shall have to concur in this judgment of the Formula of Concord: "Accordingly we reject and regard as incorrect and injurious the dogma that the Gospel is properly a preaching of repentance or reproof, and not alone a preaching of grace; for thereby the Gospel is again converted into a doctrine of the Law, the merit of Christ and Holy Scripture are obscured, Christians robbed of true consolation, and the door is opened again to [the errors and superstitions of] the Papacy" (*Trigl.* 805, Epit., V, 11. See also 961, Sol. Decl., V, 27).

And now the other point — how the Law comes to reprove unbelief toward the Gospel, whereas the Law by itself knows nothing of Gospel and faith. Here we must recall that Law and Gospel are not abstract concepts suspended in space, but both are God's Word addressed to men. The Law is *Deus propter peccata damnans,* and the Gospel is *Deus propter Christum absolvens sive iustificans.* Now, what should prevent God from extending His punitive activity as

Deus propter peccata damnans also over the sin of despising His grace, that is, over unbelief? The Formula of Concord states the case in this way: "Thus the Law reproves unbelief, [namely,] when men do not believe the Word of God. Now, since the Gospel, which alone properly teaches and commands to believe in Christ, is God's Word, the Holy Ghost, through the office of the Law, also reproves unbelief, that men do not believe in Christ, although it is properly the Gospel alone which teaches concerning saving faith in Christ." (*Trigl.* 957, Sol. Decl., V, 19.) We fully realize that this does not explain how there can be both Law and Gospel simultaneously in God. But our limitation is due to the fact that our mundane knowledge of God bears the stamp: "Now I know in part" (1 Cor. 13:12).

Men have thought to prove that the Gospel is a preaching of repentance and reproof also by pointing to the suffering and death of Christ. The argument took about this form: Christ's suffering and death certainly belongs to the Gospel. But sin is reproved by Christ's suffering because only from His suffering do we learn fully how great God's wrath and man's guilt are. Therefore the Gospel must be a preaching of repentance and reproof. In answer we say: Of course the wrath of God over the sin of men can and should be taught also from the suffering and death of Christ. Christ Himself makes this use of His suffering and death.[25] But in so far as it is thus used, not Gospel, but Law is being preached, both terms taken in their proper sense. This fact, too, the Formula of Concord clearly sets forth in Luther's words: "Anything that preaches concerning our sins and God's wrath, let it be done how or when it will, that is all a preaching of the Law. . . . Yea, what more forcible, more terrible declaration and preaching of God's wrath against sin is there than just the suffering and death of Christ, His Son? But as long as all this preaches God's wrath and terrifies men, it is not yet the preaching of the Gospel nor Christ's own preaching, but that of Moses and the Law against the impenitent. For the Gospel and Christ were never ordained and given for the purpose of terrifying and condemning, but of comforting and cheering those who are terrified and timid." (*Trigl.* 955f., Sol. Decl., V, 12.) In the Epitome terrifying with Christ's suffering and death is called "a foreign work [*alienum opus*] of Christ, by which He arrives at His proper office [*proprium suum officium*], that is, to preach grace" (*Trigl.* 803 V, 10).

---

[25] Luke 23:27 ff. V. 31: "For if they do these things in a green tree, what shall be done in the dry?"

4

How Law and Gospel Are to Be Joined in Practice

While the theologian must differentiate sharply between Law and Gospel, yet he must in practice join them most intimately. This necessity Luther expresses in these words: "Though these two in content [*re ipsa*] are very far apart [*remotissima*], they are at the same time most intimately joined in one and the same heart. Nothing is linked more closely than fear and confidence, Law and Gospel, sin and grace. For they are so bound together, that the one is swallowed by the other (*absorbeatur*). Therefore there can be no mathematical combination that equals this." (St. L. IX:454.)

This intimate connection sets in at conversion, which takes place in the moment when the first ray of faith in the Gospel lights up the heart (Acts 11:21; Col. 2:12; etc.). But only that sinner whom the Law has brought to a knowledge of his deserved condemnation will in faith accept the remission of sins offered in the Gospel. Whoever therefore refuses to preach the Law prevents the Gospel, or Christ in His redemption, from taking effect. This is the theme which Luther developed and thoroughly presented from many angles in his offensive against Antinomianism.

But also objectively, or in regard to content, there is a connection between Law and Gospel inasmuch as the Gospel furnishes and presents man with the very fulfillment which the Law demands. The Gospel of course tells of the redemptive work of Christ, who in the stead of men by His perfect obedience kept the Law given to men (Gal. 4:4-5; Matt. 5:17) and bore the punishment for man's transgression of the Law (Gal. 3:13; Is. 53:4-6). Luther therefore rightly asserts that by their demand that the preaching of the Law be banished from the Church the Antinomians are doing all they can to rob the Church also of the Gospel and Christ. Luther writes: "If the Law is removed, no one knows what Christ is, or what He did when He fulfilled the Law for us." Again: "What will you retain of Christ when the Law, which He fulfilled, has been removed, and you do not know what He has fulfilled?" Again: "Whence shall we learn what Christ is, what He has done for us, if we are not to know what that Law is which He has fulfilled for us, or what sin is, for which He has atoned?" [26]

---

[26] *Fifth Disputation*, Theses 61, 67 (St. L. XX:1646). — *Wider die Antinomer* (*ibid.*, 1616); *Second Disputation Against the Antinomians*, Theses 25—26 (*ibid.*, 1634).

And turning to the mutual relation of the effects of the Law and of the Gospel in the heart of man, we note that the Gospel with its verdict of justification must supersede or "devour" the Law with its verdict of condemnation. "For grace [pledged to us in the Gospel] must war and win in us against the Law and sin, that we may be kept from despair" (St. L. XX:1656). For this reason it is a factual verdict on Antinomianism "that by this 'spiritism' ['*Geisterei*'] the devil does not mean to take away the Law, but Christ, who fulfilled the Law." [27]

But also after a man has become a Christian, Law and Gospel are still joined for him; more exactly, there is still a use of the Law for him, for he cannot do without the preaching of the Law. To be sure, as far as he is a Christian or new man, he no longer needs the Law. This is the clear teaching of Scripture. 1 Tim. 1:9: "The Law is not made for a righteous man, but for the lawless and disobedient, for the ungodly and for sinners." For the Christian according to his new man the Law is superfluous not merely in part, but in its every use. Without the recorded Law, the new man in him knows both what is sinful and what is good; and since the Christian is entirely godly according to the new man, he does not need the Law to keep him in check outwardly by its threats and scourges. According to the new man, the Law is written in the heart of the Christian (Jer. 31:33), even as the first men before the Fall were created with God's Law in their hearts. (*Trigl.* 963, F. C., Sol. Decl., VI, 5.) The Formula of Concord states this truth repeatedly and lucidly. It says: If the Christians had only their new man, "they would do of themselves, and altogether voluntarily, without any instruction, admonition, urging or driving of the Law, what they are in duty bound to do according to God's will; just as the sun, the moon, and all the constellations of

---

[27] *Wider die Antinomer* (*ibid.,* 1614). Chemnitz (*Loci,* "*De iustif.,*" II, 228) says of the natural connection between Law and Gospel in spite of their divergence: "Two things are to be considered: that there is a difference between Law and Gospel and that Law and Gospel are so joined that there can be no mathematical conjunction like air, as Luther says in his commentary on the third chapter of Galatians. Law and Gospel come together above all in this, that the benefits of Christ of which the Gospel preaches are nothing less than satisfaction for the guilt and punishment which we incurred by transgressing the Law and for the most perfect righteousness of the Law by obedience, and that these two things which the Law requires and vehemently demands are given the believers and imputed unto righteousness. Nor can the magnitude of the benefits of Christ be understood unless one is strictly held in this manner to the rigor and severity of the Law."

heaven have their regular course of themselves, unobstructed, without admonition, urging, driving, force, or compulsion, according to the order of God which God once appointed for them." [28]

But the Christian, considered *in concreto*, as he exists in this world, is not yet entirely a new man; he still has the old man dwelling in him. And in this respect, according to his old man, the Christian still needs the Law in all its uses, no matter how these uses are divided or designated.[29] It is no contradiction, therefore, when Paul, on the one hand, says that "the Law is not made for a righteous man" (1 Tim. 1:9), and, on the other hand, as pointed out by Luther (St. L. IX:880 f.), in that very chapter (v. 18) begins to give commandments, saying: "This charge I commit unto thee, son Timothy." This is no contradiction, because in the one case the Christian comes into consideration according to his new man; in the other case, according to the old man still dwelling in him. Luther asks: "Are, then, Paul and Timothy or the Christians not pious? Or how can Paul say, 'The Law is not made for a righteous man' and then proceed to give Timothy a law?" Luther answers: "According to the spirit the believer is righteous, without any sin, has need of no law whatever; according to his flesh he still has sin. . . . There all manner of filth still clings to him, and evil concupiscence, worry about his daily bread, fear of death, avarice, anger, hatred; the filth always remains beside his faith, for him to contend with it and sweep it out. Now, because this is still in us, Scripture in this respect rates us as of a kind with the unrighteous and sinners, so that according to our flesh we need the Law as much as do they." (St. L. IX:881.) Luther gives it this turn too: "A Christian is in two realms at once. So far as he is flesh,

---

[28] *Trigl.* 965, Sol. Decl., VI, 6; 967, *ibid.*, 17. St. L. IX:879.

[29] Nitzsch-Stephan, *Dogmatik*, p. 509: "In agreement with the doctrine of the Formula of Concord the elder dogmaticians, too, assert some a threefold, some a fourfold *usus* of the Law: (1) an *usus politicus seu civilis*, (2) an *usus elenchticus*, (3) an *usus paedagogicus*, (4) an *usus didacticus seu normaticus*. At times numbers two and three are combined. Where they are distinguished, the distinguishing mark of the *usus elenchticus* is *"peccati manifestatio et redargutio"* (the revealing and refuting of sin); the mark of the *usus paedagogicus* is the *compulsus indirectus ad Christum*, according to Gal. 3:23 f." One need not feel alarmed either at the threefold nor at the fourfold division, so long as the thoughts brought out correspond to Scripture, as in fact they do. When the *usus paedagogicus* is further distinguished from the *usus elenchticus*, this distinction is acceptable because the Law by itself does not lead to Christ, but does so only when Christ takes it in hand. By itself the Law leads only to despair. The Holy Ghost must establish the right, divinely intended connection of Law and Gospel in the heart of man.

he is under the Law; so far as he is spirit, he is under grace." (St. L. IX:452.) But, of course, in such a manner that in the struggle of the two with each other the reign of grace or of the Gospel remains victorious: "When the Law has terrified you, say: Madam Law, you are not alone; and so you are not everything, but besides you there is something still greater and better, namely, grace and faith." But the victorious reign of the Gospel always presupposes the succumbing reign of the Law. Luther: "Therefore the teaching of the Law is necessary in the Church and by all means to be retained, since without it Christ cannot be retained." [30]

And this is what the Formula of Concord confesses on the basis of Scripture over against the current error and doubt: "We believe, teach, and confess that the preaching of the Law is to be urged with diligence, not only upon the unbelieving and impenitent, but also upon true believers, who are truly converted, regenerate, and justified by faith," and it gives this reason: "For although they are regenerate and renewed in the spirit of their mind, yet in the present life this regeneration and renewal is not complete, but only begun." (*Trigl.* 805, Epit., VI, 3–4.)

In addition, the Formula of Concord shows in detail how Law and Gospel are joined in the case of a Christian. First, since the Christian, according to his flesh, still sins daily, but at the same time, according to the same flesh, is inclined not to see the gravity of his sin, rather to imagine "that his work and life are entirely pure and perfect" (*Trigl.* 969, Sol. Decl., VI, 21); and since, as a result, the Christian is in constant danger of falling from faith, the Law must continually reveal and reprove the sin in him, while he, on the other hand, must daily appropriate from the Gospel the consolation that for Christ's sake his sins are remitted unto him. The Formula refers to this process in these words: "Therefore, as often as believers stumble, they are reproved by the Holy Spirit from the Law, and by the same Spirit are raised up and comforted again with the preaching of the Gospel" (*Trigl.* 967, *ibid.*, 14).

Secondly, since the Christian because of his flesh is inclined to err in regard to the good works desired of him by God, he must daily learn from the Law, as the unchanging norm of a God-pleasing life, what God would have him do. "So, too, this doctrine of the Law is

---

[30] Luther, *Fifth Disputation,* Thesis 66 (St. L. XX:1646). See in the same disputation Theses 40—45.

needful for believers, in order that they may not hit upon a holiness and devotion of their own, and under the pretext of the Spirit of God set up a self-chosen worship, without God's Word and command, as it is written Deut. 12:8, 28, 32: 'Ye shall not do . . . every man whatsoever is right in his own eyes,' etc., but 'observe and hear all these words which I command thee. Thou shalt not add thereto, nor diminish therefrom.'" (*Trigl.* 969, *ibid.*, 20.) The Gospel, however, must continually be employed in this matter of good works in order to work the will and the strength to comply with the divine will which is known from the Law. This fact, too, is sedulously stressed by the Formula: "But we must also explain distinctively what the Gospel does, produces, and works towards the new obedience of believers, and what is the office of the Law in this matter, as regards the good works of believers. For the Law says indeed that it is God's will and command that we should walk in a new life, but it does not give the power and ability to begin and do it; but the Holy Ghost, who is given and received, not through the Law, but through the preaching of the Gospel, Gal. 3:14, renews the heart." (*Trigl.* 965, *ibid.*, 10—11.)

Finally, an application of the Law to the Christian according to his flesh is necessary to keep his flesh outwardly in check. It is no rhetorical overstatement when Luther and the Formula of Concord (*Trigl.* 969, *ibid.*, 19) say that the flesh of the Christians never becomes pious in this life, but retains throughout its characteristic of "enmity against God" (Rom. 8:7). Negatively the Scriptures say of the flesh of the Christian that in it dwells no good thing (Rom. 7:18); and positively, that it wars against the new man (Rom. 7:23). This being the nature of the flesh also of Christians, no more can be achieved than to force the flesh externally to obey the will of God. And this coercion is applied to it both by the threatening of the Law (Mark 9:43 ff.) and by the infliction of punishments (*praedicatio verbalis et realis;* 2 Cor. 12:7 ff.; 1 Cor. 9:27). Formula of Concord: "For the old Adam, as an intractable, refractory ass, is still a part of them, which must be coerced to the obedience of Christ, not only by the teaching, admonition, force, and threatening of the Law, but also oftentimes by the club of punishments and troubles, until the body of sin is entirely put off, and man is perfectly renewed in the resurrection, when he will need neither the preaching of the Law nor its threatenings and punishments, as also the Gospel any longer; for these belong to this [mortal and] imperfect life" (*Trigl.* 969, *ibid.*, 24).

5

The Difficulty of Properly Distinguishing Between Law and Gospel

Properly to distinguish between Law and Gospel is a difficult art. Of course, not in theory, for it is easy to say what is Law and what is Gospel; but in practice the difficulty is present, particularly in one's own heart and conscience. Luther wisely reminds us again and again that the proper differentiation between Law and Gospel exceeds the powers of natural man and is achieved only through the action of the Holy Ghost. The reason lies in man's natural condition. Natural man seeks grace and salvation through the Law, that is, he strives to secure through the Law what can be obtained only through the Gospel. This *opinio legis* is an obsession with him, and continues to be an obsession, until God's grace and power turns his heart from the Law to the Gospel. (*Trigl.* 197, Apol., III, 144 f.)

Also from this standpoint — the discriminating use of Law and Gospel — it again becomes evident that man's conversion, or coming to faith, is solely a work of divine grace and omnipotence, without any assistance on the part of man. In the psychology of conversion the divine verdict of condemnation, spoken by the Law, is replaced by the divine verdict of justification, pronounced by the Gospel. But the conscience-stricken sinner can believe the Gospel verdict only by God's gracious and mighty operation. Therefore Christ says (John 6:44): "No man can come to Me except the Father which hath sent Me draw him," and St. Paul reminds the Christians that their faith in Christ is a gift of grace (Phil. 1:29: "For unto you it is given to believe on Him") and an effect of the same divine power that raised Christ from the dead (Eph. 1:19-20; Col. 2:12). To come to Christ, or to believe in Christ, is in fact nothing else than properly to distinguish between Law and Gospel in one's heart, to believe the verdict of the Gospel over against the contrary verdict of the Law. Men have deemed it incongruous that Christ describes the entrance into the Kingdom of God, which always takes place solely by faith, with the words: "And from the days of John the Baptist until now the kingdom of heaven suffereth violence, and the violent take it by force" (Matt. 11:12). They consider it inappropriate to think of faith, which does not lie in the power of man and is no coercion either, as a "heaven-storming" act of violence. But such people forget that "believing" means, in the face of the condemnatory verdict of the Law, to seize and claim the amnesty proclaimed in the Gospel. Since this is a feat exceeding human powers and always a work of the creative power of God, faith is described as a βιαστής, a man of violence. For this reason Luther, Chemnitz, and other old theologians of ours regard it as self-evident that the words "The kingdom of heaven is gotten by force" refer to faith. Cf. Vol. II, 435, footnote 66. To them this interpretation is obvious because they correctly hold that the faith which makes man a member of the Church is not a dormant quality in the heart (*otiosa qualitas*), but *fides actualis*, the divinely wrought act of distinguishing between Law and Gospel, that is, claiming as one's own the justifying verdict of the Gospel in the face of the condemning verdict of the Law.

And as the first separation of Law and Gospel, making man a Christian, is so difficult that it can be brought about only by divine operation, so, too, the continued lifelong separation, by which man remains a Christian, lies entirely beyond the reach of human ability. Therefore Scripture says of the Christians that they are kept by the power of God through faith unto salvation (1 Pet. 1:5). For thus to be kept is in fact nothing else than, by the power of God, perpetually to distinguish between Law and Gospel, to oppose the condemnatory sentence of the Law, assailing us because of present and past sins, with the acquitting sentence of the Gospel. Luther says: "It is not in the power of man to shake off this frightful terror caused by the Law or any other sorrow of the heart" (St. L. IX:446). Therefore he regards it wise for a Christian not to be alone, but to seek the companionship of a Christian brother, so that, when the reign of the Law and the reign of the Gospel begin to struggle in his heart, the Christian brother is at hand with a word of Gospel to set in motion the divine power of the Gospel against the condemnation of the Law. (*Ibid.*, 421.)

To the difficulty experienced by the pastor in properly differentiating between Law and Gospel Luther's well-known word pertains: "Now, him who is adept at this art of properly dividing Law and Gospel set at the head of the table and declare him a Doctor of the Holy Scriptures" (*ibid.*, 802). The task is so to teach what Law and Gospel have in common, in what they are opposites, and how they are to be joined in use that secure sinners become frightened and the terrified take comfort. To this end the preacher dare not deduct aught from either the Law or the Gospel, dare not rob the Law of its severity by an admixture of Gospel nor the Gospel of its consolation by an admixture of Law. He must know how to keep both within the sphere in which they are to apply according to God's will and order, as we have shown above. Facing this duty, the pastor will despair of his own wisdom and ability [31] and will agree with Luther, who says: "Without the Holy Spirit it is impossible rightly to divide Law and Gospel. I experience it in my own case, also daily observe it in others, how difficult it is to separate the doctrine of the Law from that of the Gospel. The Holy Ghost must here be pedagog and teacher, or no man on earth will ever have the knack of it or be able to teach it. . . . The theory is easy; quickly we can explain how the Law is another Word and doctrine than the Gospel; but to divide them *practice* and to apply the art to life, that is trouble and toil. St. Jerome, too, has written much about it, but like a blind man about colors." [32]

6

The Importance of Proper Discrimination

The importance of properly discriminating between Law and Gospel appears, as we have seen, from the fact that through such discrimination man becomes a Christian and remains a Christian. In other words, without a discriminative use of Law and Gospel there can be no personal or subjective Christianity. Luther places

---

[31] The context indicates that the words in 2 Cor. 3:5 pertain specifically to the proper discernment and application of Law and Gospel. A truly Christian sermon, which properly divides and properly joins Law and Gospel, is in every case a gift from above and must be obtained by prayer. It is very advisable that a pastor subject his carefully prepared sermon to a final review to see whether it applies Law and Gospel correctly, namely, in such a manner that the secure are terrified and those that labor and are heavy laden are consoled.

[32] St. L. IX:802, 806 ff. In this connection a question is occasionally raised about the pastoral activity and success of a man who himself is unbelieving. A preacher who has no personal faith, who in his own heart does not distinguish between Law and Gospel, may nevertheless through his ministry convert other people, that is, teach them to divide Law and Gospel in their heart. This is due to the fact that the efficacy of the Word of God does not depend on the personal state of faith of the preacher. Of course, a preacher who has not learned to divide Law and Gospel in his own heart will in his public preaching, and still more in caring for the individual soul, encounter great difficulty in properly preaching Law and Gospel. Yet such instances are conceivable and *do occur* in which an unbelieving pastor so presents Law and Gospel according to Scripture, from correct theological instruction received and from sound postils, that his hearers come both to know their sin and to believe in the Gospel.

this fact at the head of his sermon of 1532 on "The Difference Between Law and Gospel" (*ibid.*, 798 ff.): "This distinction . . . is the highest art in Christendom, which each and all who pride themselves on or appropriate the name 'Christian' should know and be able to practice. For where there is a lack of this art, one cannot tell a Christian from a heathen or Jew; so absolutely everything depends on this discrimination."

Furthermore, the objective teaching of a theologian is Christian only in so far as the distinction between Law and Gospel is observed in it. See the full discussion of this truth in the chapter "The Doctrine of Justification and the Separation of Law and Gospel," Vol. II, 545 ff. The Christian doctrine of justification is virtually identical with the discrimination between Law and Gospel. Moreover, the elimination of the Law from the article of justification must be absolute. Justification, as Luther reminds us, may not be made to hinge on even one devout Lord's Prayer (Luther is cited in Vol. II, 546, footnote 84) if our teaching is to retain its Christian and consoling character. See Walther's exposition of the thesis "Purity of doctrine also includes that the Word of truth be 'rightly divided,' which means, that Law and Gospel be properly distinguished." (2 Tim. 2:15.) For our warning Walther proceeds to enumerate the most common ways of mixing Law and Gospel. He writes: "Whoever uses the Gospel to deprive the Law of its severity, or the Law to deprive the Gospel of its sweetness; whoever so teaches that secure sinners are comforted and terrified sinners are still more frightened; whoever fails to direct those who have been terrified by the Law to the means of grace and instead directs them simply to pray for grace; whoever explains the demands and threats of the Law to mean that if a Christian do as much as he can, God will be satisfied and overlook the sins of weakness, and so preaches the Gospel as to make it seem to give comfort only to such as already in their life show a change of heart; whoever tries by the demands, threats, and promises of the Law to persuade the unregenerate to do good works, and demands that those who are no Christians (still being without faith) shall desist from sin and love God and their neighbor; whoever demands a certain degree of contrition and comforts only such as have already undergone a change for the better; whoever confounds not being able to believe with not being permitted to believe; and the like: such a one does not rightly divide the Word of Truth, but presents the Law and the Gospel in a tangled and mixed form; even though he otherwise preach the Law and the Gospel and even define it correctly, yet he is guilty of preaching false doctrine." (*Pastorale*, p. 79 f. [Fritz, *Pastoral Theology*, p. 69].)

Furthermore, as mentioned above, it must be stressed particularly that only a precise distinction between Law and Gospel preserves the consoling character of the Christian religion. As an admixture of Law to the Gospel involves a denial of Christ's substitutional fulfillment of the Law and therefore of Christ's merit (Gal. 4:4-5; 2:21), so the same confused and Antichristian procedure also abolishes the certainty of God's grace for men (Gal. 3:10). Thus Christians are robbed of the comfort they sorely need in life and death. There can be no thought of the *certitudo gratiae et salutis,* which Christians should have (Rom. 4:16), till man in his conscience before God is completely free from the Law, that is, by the Holy Spirit's working in the Gospel believes that God does not demand of him even a single work to secure grace and salvation, but for Christ's sake receives him as he is, without regard to what he did or omitted to do. Of this necessary expulsion of the Law from the conscience in the matter of grace and salvation Luther says: "It is impossible that Christ and the Law should dwell together in one heart; either the Law or Christ must give place. But if thou thinkest that Christ and the Law can dwell together, then be thou sure that Christ dwelleth not in thy heart; but the devil, in the likeness of Christ, accusing and terrifying thee, and straitly exacting of thee the Law and the works thereof; for the true Christ (as I have said before) neither calleth thee to a reckoning for thy sins, nor biddeth thee to trust in thine own good works. And the true knowledge of Christ, or faith, disputeth not whether thou hast done good works to righteousness, or evil works to condemnation; but simply concludeth after this sort: If thou hast done good works, thou art not therefore justified; or if thou hast done evil works, thou art not therefore condemned." (St. L. IX:619; *Middleton Transl.,* p. 430.)

Finally it must be pointed out that the differentiation between Law and Gospel is necessary in order to correctly *understand the Scriptures.* The Formula of Concord calls on us to "guard with especial care" this distinction between the Law and the Gospel because it "is a special brilliant light, which serves to the end that God's Word may be rightly divided, and the Scriptures of the holy prophets and apostles may be properly explained and understood" (*Trigl.* 951, Sol. Decl., V, 1). This statement of the Confession is no overstatement. Scripture on the one hand says: "This do, and thou shalt live"; on the other hand: "He that believeth on the Son hath everlasting life."

How can we arrive at a harmonization of these words of Scripture, whose relation is as yes and no? It may not be achieved in the manner of the Antinomians, who relegate the Law to the courthouse. Christ forbids that course when He says: "Whosoever therefore shall break one of these least commandments, and shall teach men so, he shall be called the least in the kingdom of heaven" (Matt. 5:19). Nor may we say, like the Unitarians and modern theologians, that the Gospel, which tells us of Christ's *satisfactio vicaria* and of justification by faith without the deeds of the Law, originated in the Middle Ages or a period of imperfect development of Christian doctrine. Christ's Apostle forbids that, too, when he says: "But though we, or an angel from heaven, preach any other Gospel unto you than that which we have preached unto you, let him be accursed" (Gal. 1:8-9), for the Gospel Paul preached was the Gospel of Christ's substitutional satisfaction and of justification by faith without the deeds of the Law (Rom. 3:23-24, 28). Likewise, we may not harmonize the words of the Law and the words of the Gospel by agreeing on a compromise between them and declaring: "Man is justified and saved in part by grace for Christ's sake, in part by his own works." Scripture rejects this compromise when it says: "And if by grace, then is it no more of works; otherwise grace is no more grace" (Rom. 11:6). There remains but one way of understanding Scripture: We must let both the words of the Law and the words of the Gospel remain in full force, but distinguish between Law and Gospel in this manner, that we confine each to the realm assigned to it by God. The Law is given to reveal sin, not to forgive sin. For the latter purpose the Gospel is given. When therefore the Law has revealed sin, it is to be muzzled, and only the Gospel is to have and hold the floor, as we have shown at length above. Thus, and thus only, will Scripture be understood.

A few details in closing. From Scripture passages such as 1 Cor. 10:12: "Let him that thinketh he standeth take heed lest he fall," and Rom. 8:38 f.: "I am persuaded that neither death nor life . . . shall be able to separate us from the love of God," both Romanists and Protestant synergists of all shades compound a *tertium* and then teach in all seriousness that a Christian may not be certain of his salvation, but must waver between fear and hope. He who knows how to divide Law and Gospel lets both classes of Scripture passages stand in their full import. But he applies the Scripture passages which warn of backsliding to the Christian according to his carnally secure old man, who is to be reproved with the Law. And the Scripture passages asserting the certainty of salvation he applies to the Christian according to the new man, inasmuch as the Christian as a poor sinner should believe and actually believes the Gospel. Cf. Vol. II, 547 f.; Vol. III, p. 96, footnote 14. — Also the text (Heb. 12:14): "Without holiness no man shall see the Lord," has been given most surprising and impossible interpretations to make it harmonize with those Scripture passages that guarantee salvation to faith without the deeds of the Law. The correct exposition (p. 26f.) recognizes these words as Law, as a warning against carnal security, which must be spoken to Christians in so far as they are in danger of succumbing to carnal security. In so far, however, as Christians are of a terrified, humbled spirit and believe the Gospel of salvation for Christ's sake, those threatening and reprimanding words do not at all concern them.

7

The Chief Confounders of Law and Gospel

The distinction between the Law and the Gospel is abolished:

1. *By the Romanists.* The *Tridentinum* demands very firmly that the Law be mixed into the Gospel. It anathematizes the doctrine "as if indeed the Gospel were a bare and absolute promise of eternal life, without the condition of observing the commandments" (Sess. VI, can. 20; Waterworth, p. 47). Rome must mix Law and Gospel to prevent the assurance of grace and salvation and also the destruction of the dominion of the Pope.

2. *The Calvinists.* Because the Calvinists teach particular grace and an immediate operation of grace, they must lead sinners smitten by the Law to base the favor of God on *gratia infusa,* on an internal change, i. e., on sanctification and good works, instead of on the means of grace. Far from safeguarding the Gospel against the "ergism" (salvation by works) of Rome, i. e., against the perversion of the Gospel into Law, Calvinism rather regularly and necessarily embraces this perversion.[33] Since there is no immediate operation of the Spirit, as Calvinism assumes, the purported experience of the Spirit's operation must be man's own product. This is the reason why Calvinists, like all other teachers of the doctrine of works, construct definitions of the Gospel which make it Law. The Calvinists define the Gospel as a mere "plan of salvation," i. e., as a proclamation of the terms

---

[33] Against Seeberg, *Dogmengesch.,* II, 304, 300.

upon which man may share in divine grace. Alexander Hodge thus answers the question "What is included in the external call?": "1. A declaration of the plan of salvation. 2. A declaration of duty on the part of the sinner to repent and believe. 3. A declaration of the motives which ought to influence the sinner's mind, such as fear or hope, remorse or gratitude. 4. A promise of acceptance in the case of all those who comply with the conditions." (*Outlines,* p. 333 f.) For the Calvinists the Gospel is anything but the proclamation and gift of the remission of sins purchased by Christ. Charles Hodge agrees with his son Alexander, for he says of the "universal call": "Being a proclamation of the terms on which God is willing to save sinners, and an exhibition of the duty of fallen men in relation to that plan, it of necessity binds all those who are in the condition which the plan contemplates. It is in this respect analogous to the moral law." (*Syst. Theol.* II, 642.)

Incidentally, this supposedly necessary conception of the Gospel explains in what sense even strict Calvinists occasionally speak of a "general offer of the Gospel." [34] In spite of their doctrine of particular grace they can so speak because they do not understand the Gospel to be the proclamation of the forgiveness of sins which actually has been provided by Christ for all men and every man, but the proclamation of a general principle or of a number of duties and conditions; and these, moreover, are not addressed to certain persons, but acquire significance for individuals only if they have undertaken these duties and fulfilled the required conditions.

3. *The Synergists.* Because the synergists let the promise of grace apply only to those who in distinction from others cultivate the proper conduct (make the right choice, take the right attitude toward God's grace, refrain from willful resistance, make the possible faith actual, etc.), they abolish the difference between Law and Gospel. For them, too, the Gospel has the condition of human performance. Therefore they do not conceive of the Gospel as a general amnesty embracing every person on earth, but as the proclamation of a scheme of salvation or of a fundamental rule which stipulates that God is willing to be gracious to those who make the right choice, practice the proper behavior, etc. In other words, from the outset the synergists add

---

[34] Charles Hodge: "If anyone holds any views of the decrees of God, or of the satisfaction of Christ, or of any other Scriptural doctrine, which hampers him in making this general offer of the Gospel, he may be sure that his views or his logical processes are wrong" (*ibid.,* p. 648).

some deed of man, variously named, to the Gospel as a condition. They think, with Theodore Zahn, that the Gospel from the outset is not meant for all, but always for only some men, specifically for those who are minded to comply with the fixed condition, "the personal conduct" (cf. p. 202). The synergists falsify both the Law and the Gospel, since neither the Law nor the Gospel admits a difference in men in their relation to God. The Law condemns all without exception, and the Gospel assures all without exception of grace. Rom. 3:23-24: "For there is no difference, for all have sinned and come short of the glory of God, being justified freely by His grace through the redemption that is in Christ Jesus."

4. *All Who Deny the Satisfactio Vicaria.* The Scriptural doctrine of the substitutional satisfaction of Christ rests — to speak in modern terms — on a "twofold attribute" (*"zweifache Bestimmtheit"*) in God: (1) God's trait of inviolable holiness and righteousness, according to which He demands that men keep the Law He has given them and is wroth with transgressors; (2) God's trait of a most wonderful love, which prompted God to give His Son to the world and through His obedience and suffering to reconcile the world to Himself. Hence all who deny the vicarious satisfaction of Christ are actually abolishing both Law and Gospel and therefore also the distinction between the two. What Frank says against Ritschl in particular is true of all deniers of the *satisfactio vicaria:* "It is all so designed and shaped that the detested doctrine of satisfying the just demands of the Law . . . and with it the doctrine of 'Law and Gospel' be excluded" (*Dogm. Studien,* p. 129). This applies also to Ihmels and Frank himself, inasmuch as both misinterpret the vicarious satisfaction of Christ.[35]

5. *The Proponents of the "Higher Unity" of Law and Gospel.* Ever since theology abandoned Scripture as the sole source and norm of Christian doctrine, it has adopted the technique of making the so-called "uniform conception" of all parts of the Christian doctrine, the "harmonization free of all discord," etc., the criterion of truth. This technique has been tried also on the doctrine of Law and Gospel. There is talk in our day of the need of seeking a "higher unity" (*"hoehere Einheit"*) of Law and Gospel. The idea is, of course, that

---

[35] On Ihmels cf. Vol. II, 366 ff.; on Frank, Vol. II, 354; on modern theology in general, the chapter "Some Modern Theories of the Atonement Examined," Vol. II, 361 ff.

Law and Gospel cannot be antithetical in content, but differ merely in degree. Both are said to demand moral accomplishments of man — only that the works demanded by the Gospel are different in quantity and quality. The Gospel is taken to be a modified Law. At least the later Luther is not reputed to have seen and clung to this higher identity of Law and Gospel. On the other hand, Zwingli as over against Luther asserted the complete identity in essence of Law and Gospel.[36]

In answer we say: One could, of course, speak in a correct sense of a "higher unity" of Law and Gospel, inasmuch as both are the Word of God, or to express it more concretely, inasmuch as it is one and the same God who in the Law demands and accuses but in the Gospel drops all demands as well as all accusations and only absolves. Lutheran theologians say with Luther: *Lex est Deus accusans et damnans; evangelium est Deus absolvens et iustificans.* But this "higher unity," that both are the Word of God and in both one and the same God deals with men, is the very thing these modern theologians reject. They assert that this concept of God and God's actions lacks "unity of thought," is "fragmentary," "stratified," unsatisfactory to man as a rational being. Therefore they endeavor to subordinate Law and Gospel to the common higher principle in such a way that not only the promises of the Law, but also the promises of the Gospel are conditioned on an action of man, right conduct, man's free choice, etc. But in this way, as demonstrated above, the Gospel is converted into Law. And Luther and our Lutheran Confessions are to be lauded rather than criticized for shunning this higher identity and adhering to Law and Gospel in their proper sense, as complete opposites in content, *plus quam contradictoria,* since the Law demands

---

[36] Thus Schenkel, *Wesen des Protestantismus,* I, 173 ff.; in Frank, *op. cit.,* p. 115. In regard to Zwingli it is indeed true that he makes the Gospel Law. Seeberg (*Dogmengesch.* II, 299) admits: "Zwingli does not sense that the Law is the embodiment of another world view; imperceptibly the Gospel becomes 'nueves gesatz' (new Law; I, 311)." We have shown above that the assumption of particular grace and an immediate operation of the Spirit, persistently followed through, destroys the Gospel. Luther's judgment is right that the "enthusiasts" "under Christ's name teach their dreams, under the name of the Gospel only laws and ceremonies. Hence they are, and always remain, what they were before, that is, monks, taskmasters, teachers of the Law and ceremonies, only that they invent new names and works." (St. L. IX:414.) That Zwingli and Calvin bring much Gospel, too, is due to the powerful influence Luther's reformation exerted on them. But the Gospel does not really fit into the system of doctrine characteristic of Zwingli and Calvin, for the essential parts of this system are particular grace and an immediate operation of the Spirit.

and condemns, while the Gospel demands nothing and therefore condemns no one, but only pledges and tenders grace and salvation for Christ's sake, without any contribution on the part of man.

Admitting the "fragmentary" or "stratified" character of our knowledge of God if we take Law and Gospel as *contradictoria* in content, we recall again the Scriptural *ceterum censeo* that in this life we have only a piecemeal, or fragmentary, knowledge of God. 1 Cor. 13:9, 12: "We know in part, and we prophesy in part. . . . Now I know in part." Men, including the theologians, do not know in this life what is in God. In other words, in this life we have no "unified conception" of God's essence, attributes, and works. The unified conception belongs to the "high school" above. For our knowledge of God here below we are dependent on God's revelation in His Word. This revelation, in condescension to our weakness, is "piecemeal," that is, it discloses attributes that differ, as far as our understanding is concerned.

This truth must be applied also in the case of Law and Gospel. God's justice sentences sinners to hell; His grace declares the same sinners in the same condition heirs of salvation. How both properties, or "traits," form a "higher unity" in the one indivisible God exceeds our comprehension. Scripture does not elucidate the matter beyond saying that the gracious verdict of the Gospel upon the sinners condemned by the Law is mediated in God (*in Deo, apud Deum*) through the redemption (ἀπολύτρωσις, ransoming) which is in Christ Jesus. Let us, then, beware of making the Gospel's promise of grace dependent upon something in man (*aliquid in homine*), such as correct conduct, personal free choice, etc. We would, indeed, thus gain a "higher unity" for Law and Gospel, namely, the higher unity of human efforts, but we would thereby lose the *differentia specifica* of Christianity, the Gospel, which alone can save our souls.

Here in the doctrine of Law and Gospel we again meet the *crux theologorum*. Following Scripture, our teaching and faith must be "fragmentary" and "stratified," i. e., without any rationalizing attempt to harmonize the two facts that those who are saved are saved by God's grace alone, and that those who are lost are lost solely by their own fault. We could easily arrive at a "higher unity" between these two statements by assuming with the synergists a lesser guilt, or a "different," that is, a better conduct on the part of those who are saved in comparison with those who are lost. But then we would collide with the Scriptures, which — like it or not — teach equal guilt and equally wicked conduct on the part of the saved. Therefore here, too, in the doctrine of Law and Gospel, we must desist from attempting, by adding the condition of a human accomplishment to the Gospel, to arrive at a "higher unity" between them.[37]

---

[37] The most powerful book ever written on the doctrine of Law and Gospel as well as on the doctrine of justification is Luther's comprehensive commentary on the Epistle to the Galatians. The Latin: Erl., *curavit* Irmischer, 3 vols.; the German: St. L. IX:9 ff. On the French and English translations compare Hoppe, St. L. IX:2, note, and Walch, *Bibliotheca Theol.*, IV, 696 ff. The treatises of Luther directed specifically against Antinomianism were mentioned in note 8 above. All Luther's writings are characterized by their clear distinction of Law and Gospel. For this reason Dr. Walther used to say that no writer makes one so certain of God's grace as does Luther. In the 17th century the material on the doctrine of Law and Gospel was compiled in the best manner and richest measure, we would say, in Gerhard's *Loci*, "De lege" and "De evangelio." In the Missouri Synod the doctrine of the difference between Law and Gospel has been dealt with repeatedly in periodicals, synodical essays, and special treatises. We mention Walther, *Gesetz und Evangelium*, 1878; *Gesetz und Evangelium*, 1897; done into English by W. H. T. Dau: *The Proper Distinction Between Law and Gospel*, 1929; F. Bente, *Gesetz und Evangelium*, 1917; F. Pieper, *Der Unterschied von Gesetz und Evangelium, Iowa District Proceedings,* 1880; F. Pieper, *Die praktische Wichtigkeit der rechten Scheidung von Gesetz und Evangelium, Kansas District Proceedings,* 1892; G. Stoeckhardt, *Die unterschiedlichen Wirkungen von Gesetz und Evangelium, L. u. W.* 1887, 154 ff.

HOLY BAPTISM

1

Baptism a Divine Ordinance

Baptism is not merely an ecclesiastical custom, but a divine ordinance (*institutio divina*), in force to the Last Day and ordained for all nations. It is no less a divine ordinance than preaching the Gospel and teaching God's Word in general. Christ groups them together in His command: "Make disciples of all nations, baptizing them in the name of the Father and of the Son and of the Holy Ghost, teaching them to observe all things whatsoever I have commanded you, and, lo, I am with you alway, even unto the end of the world!" (Matt. 28:19-20.) The divine institution is evident, too, from the Apostolic practice. The Apostles practiced Baptism immediately on the first Pentecost, and that not merely as a thing suggested, but as a thing enjoined and necessary for all who had come to faith. Peter's words are: "Repent, and be baptized every one of you in the name of Jesus Christ for the remission of sins" (Acts 2:38). Likewise we read of Peter in the home of Cornelius: "He commanded them to be baptized in the name of the Lord" (Acts 10:48).

The rejection of Baptism by the Quakers (*Pop. Symb.*, pp. 83, 85, 384) is but a part of their rejection of the means of grace in general. For the water Baptism they substitute the "Baptism of the Spirit and fire." The Socinians grant in the later editions of the Racovian Catechism that Baptism was ordained by Christ, but, they say, merely for His day. The Salvation Army takes a similar position. It puts Baptism in the same category with circumcision, clipping the hair, footwashing, and rejects Baptism together with these "abrogated Jewish ceremonies that were never intended to bind our consciences." [1]

Recent theologians, and especially those of radical bent, strive with all their might to prove that Christian Baptism cannot be traced back to a specific command of Christ to baptize. Though admitting that Baptism was in common use in the Apostolic Church, they assert that the Apostles and the churches devised Baptism themselves,

---

[1] See Guenther, *Symb.*, 4th ed., p. 294 [*Pop. Symb.*, p. 329].

prompted perhaps by similar Jewish or pagan rites or by the Baptism of John. Holtzmann, for example, grants (*Neutest. Theol.* I, 452) that "the Christian custom of baptizing is an original possession of the whole primitive Church," but at the same time he asserts that "an actual institution by the historical Jesus" cannot be established. He grants that Matthew (28:19) attributes the command to baptize to the resurrected Christ. But, although one would have to concede that faith in a resurrected Christ was also "common property of the primitive Church" (*ibid.*, p. 433), this faith did not spring from an actual resurrection of Christ, but from the wish, particularly of Peter and Paul, to have a risen Savior. Thus Holtzmann "proves" that there can be no "actual" command of Christ to baptize. Of course, if Christ did not rise, the command to baptize, reported by Matthew, cannot have been given by the risen Lord.

Holtzmann complains (*ibid.*, p. 450, note) that "such a representative Lutheran theologian as A. v. Oettingen" accuses him of "dogmatic bias" in his argumentation. Von Oettingen might have used much stronger language without exceeding the facts. To Holtzmann the entire Christian doctrine is *terra incognita*. Nevertheless, he correctly reproduces some parts of the Christian doctrine in an objective manner, e. g., the doctrine of the *satisfactio vicaria* in Paul's Epistles, as we have acknowledged before. But in the doctrine of Baptism, and particularly in regard to Christ's command to baptize, his animosity against the Christian religion trips him up repeatedly. For instance, he maintains that the Apostles could not have known a command of Christ to baptize because Paul personally baptized very infrequently (1 Cor. 1:14) and that though Peter in the home of Cornelius commanded to baptize, yet Peter did not perform the Baptism himself.[2] He also claims that the Evangelist John knew of no command of Christ to baptize, since he reports (ch. 3:22; 4:2) that Christ indeed baptized, but did not "personally" administer Baptism. Whoever indulges in such absurdities and even utters them with an air of superiority, amply demonstrates his inability to be factual with regard to Baptism and its institution.[3]

Against the "historicity" of the baptismal command in Matt. 28:19

---

[2] Similarly P. Feine in R. E., 3d ed., XIX, 397.

[3] As men who "proved the mythical character of the command in Matthew to baptize" Holtzmann enumerates, among others, de Wette, Scholten, Hilgenfeld, Lipsius, Juelicher, Weizsaecker, Pfleiderer, Harnack. "The formal authenticity of the words of institution, particularly of the Trinitarian formula, also Bossert, Beyschlag, B. Weiss, A. and R. Seeberg, and Feine deny."

the objection has been raised — and not merely by those whose faith in Christ stops with the "dead and buried" — that the early Christians could not have been so advanced in theology as the words "in the name of the Father, the Son, and the Holy Ghost" would indicate. But such objectors very unhistorically impute their own poor knowledge of the Christian doctrine to the primitive Christian Church. From what the Gospels and the Epistles of the Apostles have to say regarding the state of knowledge of the early Christians, it is very evident that the knowledge of the Father, the Son, and the Holy Ghost belonged to the ABC of Christian faith. We are not surprised, therefore, to find that as early as in the *Teaching of the Twelve Apostles* (A. D. 120) and in Justin (A. D. 100—166)[4] Baptism in the name of the Father, the Son, and the Holy Ghost is mentioned as something self-evident and generally known.

When modern "positive" theologians acknowledge Baptism as a divine ordinance to be observed in the Church until Judgment Day by God's will and command, and yet, in contrast to our traditional theology, decline to ascribe to Baptism the character of a "statutory order,"[5] their meaning is not clear. Since Baptism is proclamation and application of the Gospel, the command to baptize can be legalism no more than can the command to preach the Gospel. Lutherans also do not teach an absolute necessity of Baptism, but hold that a person can possess grace and salvation without Baptism,[6] because already the Word of Christ transmits not only a part, but the whole salvation earned by Christ. However, the possibility of salvation without Baptism no more militates against Baptism as a divine ordinance than the Lord's Supper ceases to be a divine ordinance because there can be faith in the remission of sins without the Lord's Supper, purely through the Word of the Gospel. "For God is superabundantly rich (and liberal) in His grace" (*Trigl.* 491, Smalc. Art., Part III, Art. IV) and therefore, to meet our practical needs, "not merely in one way gives us counsel and aid against sin." This point will be given further consideration under "The Necessity of Baptism."

---

[4] *Didache*, ch. 7, 1, ed. Harnack, p. 22: Βαπτίσατε εἰς τὸ ὄνομα τοῦ πατρὸς καὶ τοῦ υἱοῦ καὶ τοῦ ἁγίου πνεύματος. Justin, *Apology*, I, 61 (St. L. ed., p. 65): "Upon the name of the Father of all things and Lord God, and of our Savior Jesus Christ, and of the Holy Ghost the water Baptism is then performed."

[5] Cf. F. Kattenbusch in R. E., 3d ed., XIX, 423.

[6] This objection is always raised by "enthusiasts" against the divine institution or at least against Baptism as a means of grace.

2

The Material of Baptism

Our theologians used to speak of a material of Baptism (*materiale Baptismi*), meaning the water and the application of the water. This is a commendable *modus docendi* (Baier-Walther, III, 443). For Baptism water is essential; Scripture acknowledges no substitute for water. The use of another element is therefore inadmissible, and one so "baptized" is to be regarded as not baptized.[7]

Baptism can be performed by immersion, pouring, or sprinkling, because βαπτίζειν merely denotes the application of water, without any implication as to the way it is applied.[8]

---

[7] See Walther's *Pastorale*, p. 113 ff. [Fritz, *Past. Theol.*, 1932, p. 103.] Cp. the opinion rendered by Luther and Bugenhagen on a Baptism performed without water (St. L. X:2128 ff.): "She [the midwife who has performed the "Baptism"] says: 'I baptized without water, solely with the word of God, in the name of the Father, and of the Son, and of the Holy Ghost,' First of all it is a mocking lie to say: 'I baptized,' and then add, 'without water.' The term 'baptize' implies water, for it means to bathe or immerse or wet with water. Christ has commanded us to baptize with water, John 3:5; Eph. 5:26, and the Apostles and others, too, baptized with water, as is seen in the Acts of the Apostles. Secondly, it is a satanic falsehood when she says, 'solely with the word of God.' Christ's command in Baptism is God's word; now, Christ has commanded to baptize with water; hence this alleged Baptism does not take place with God's word, but without God's word, yea, directly against God's word, that is, Christ's command. Thirdly, that she adds to such blasphemy and lie, 'in the name of the Father,' etc., is a horrible misuse of God's name contrary to the Second Commandment. Therefore such infants should, as not yet baptized, be baptized in the manner commanded by Christ." Beza's remark in a letter (*Opp. III*, p. 196; in Gerhard, *"De bapt.,"* § 72) expressing confidence that in case of need he could baptize as validly with any other fluid as with water makes light of God's word. Boehl (*Dogm.*, p. 553), too, is satisfied to say: "If at all possible," water ought to be used in Baptism and bread and wine in the Lord's Supper. But Luther is right: "If you were to use for it anything else than the appointed substance or the substance named [*scil.*, water], and still pronounce the right words: 'I baptize thee in the name of the Father, Son, and Holy Ghost,' that would be no baptizing, but cheating and a mockery of the Sacrament by one who willfully ignores the ordinance and command in which the substance is clearly named." (St. L. X:2068.)

[8] According to Luke 11:38 the Pharisee was astonished that Jesus did not first "baptize" (ἐβαπτίσθη) Himself before eating. Νίπτεσθαι and βαπτίζεσθαι are manifestly used as synonyms in Scripture. Mark 7:3 we read: "For the Pharisees and all the Jews, except they wash their hands oft [ἐὰν μὴ νίψωνται τὰς χεῖρας], eat not." But in the next verse "baptizing" is substituted for "washing": "Except they baptize [ἐὰν μὴ βαπτίσωνται], they eat not." And here it is added that the Jews practiced "the baptizing of cups, and pots, brasen vessels, and of tables." Cremer agrees: "According to Mark 7:4; Luke 11:38 . . . βαπτίζειν seems at that time to have been the technical term for these [Levitical] ablutions."

3

What Makes Baptism a Sacrament (Forma Baptismi)

Essential to Baptism, as we noted, is water and the application of the water. But this washing becomes Christ's Baptism by the addition of His word to the water applied, the word of command and the word of promise, a fact well stated in the oft-quoted words of Augustine: *"Accedit verbum ad elementum et fit sacramentum."* [9] Hence the essentials of Baptism are (a) water, (b) the application of the water, (c) Christ's word.

Which word of God is to be added to the water applied is not left to our fancy, since Christ, besides commanding to baptize, specifies: "in the name of the Father, and of the Son, and of the Holy Ghost." Luther says in regard to the word of God that must be added to the application: "If you were to baptize a child with water and say a Lord's Prayer or other passage from Scripture and word of God over it, that would not be a true Baptism, and it will not suffice that you say: I am using water, essential to Baptism, and a word of God;

Fritz reproduces a word of Walther (*Pastorale* 115 f.), which presents practically everything that can be said in this matter: "The usage of the word βαπτίζειν in the New Testament must determine its meaning in the Lord's baptismal command. From Mark 7:4, cf. Luke 11:38, it is evident that the word βαπτίζειν does not limit the use of the water to any specific method of application, but simply refers to a liberal use of water, a liberal application of water in any form. If such a text as Rom. 6:3-4 ('buried with Christ by Baptism into death') be explained to refer to the mode of Baptism, then such texts as Acts 22:16 ('be baptized, and wash away thy sins'), Titus 3:5-6 ('by the washing of regeneration and renewing of the Holy Ghost, which He shed on us abundantly'), and Heb. 10:22 ('having our hearts sprinkled from an evil conscience and our bodies washed with pure water') (cf. Ex. 24:8; Heb. 9:19; Eph. 5:26) would, by a like hermeneutical rule, have to be explained to refer to the mode of Baptism and accordingly various modes of Baptism would be taught in such texts. But all these texts speak not of the mode, but of the benefit of Baptism. It is, however, true that the manner in which they speak of the benefit may well indicate also the mode of Baptism. The purpose of the Sacrament of Baptism is not 'the putting away of the filth of the flesh,' 1 Pet. 3:21, but the saving of the soul, its cleansing from sin; neither is the power of Baptism in the water itself (wherefore much water has no more power than little water); therefore, in whichever way the water is applied in the act of baptizing (by immersing, pouring, or sprinkling), provided that it is applied in the name of the Father and of the Son and of the Holy Ghost, it is in every case a true Baptism. The Christian pastor of the orthodox Lutheran Church should conform to the usage of his Church in reference to the mode of Baptism, as a testimony against the Baptists, who even today insist that immersion is essential to a valid Baptism. According to the Word of God the particular mode of baptizing is in itself a matter of Christian liberty. Gal. 2:4-5." (*Pastoral Theology,* p. 103 f.)

[9] *In Joh. Tractatus* 80: *Opp.* IX, 303.

for the third piece is missing; God has not commanded you to speak those words. Here in Baptism we can prove that He gives us command and tells us to baptize, that is, plunge a man into water, and with it say the words 'in the name of the Father, the Son, and the Holy Ghost.' For neither I, nor any man, have decided upon such baptizing with water, after the fashion of the sorcerers and Papistic consecrators of the host [*Fladenweiher*], nor have I devised the words myself or spoken them from my own devotion, but both water and word are clearly and plainly told me and comprehended in His command and thus secured." (St. L. X:2068, 2067; also 2065.)

Unfortunately we must say more on "formulas of Baptism." Modern theologians have succeeded in spreading a dread of all "formulas," in particular of the formula of Baptism "In the name of the Father and of the Son and of the Holy Ghost." Also Noesgen (in his commentary on Matt. 28:19) is evidently infected with this fear, for he says that in Matt. 28:19 there is "indeed no formal command of a formula of Baptism in the strict sense." But Noesgen recovers himself and adds: "But materially the formula of Baptism is all the more contained in those words because the historical occurrence of many kinds of βαπτίσματα made it necessary from the outset in every case [*scil.*, when a new baptism was instituted] to announce to what purpose and end the βαπτίζειν was being performed. The use of the formula εἰς τὸ ὄνομα τοῦ πατρὸς καὶ τοῦ υἱοῦ καὶ τοῦ ἁγίου πνεύματος, moreover, makes the neophyte certain that by his Baptism he is brought into communion with the God known through His name, according to His essence, as the Triune God." Noesgen thus correctly recalls that there were many kinds of βαπτίσματα in the name of gods or men among the Gentiles and that on this account Christ gave instruction to perform His Baptism among all nations, in distinction from all other baptisms in use, "in the name of the Father and of the Son and of the Holy Ghost." [10]

But what has been urged against Matt. 28:19 as the prescribed formula of Baptism? The fact that Peter on Pentecost admonished

---

[10] Tertullian (*De bapt.*, c. 5) points to the same fact: "Also (foreign nations) are through a bath initiated into certain mysteries of Isis, for example, or Mithras; they also praise these their gods in their washings. Again, they everywhere deliver farm homes, houses, temples, and whole cities from evil by sprinkling water round about; in the Apollinarian and Pelusian games they are certainly immersed. And this they presume works in them regeneration and freedom from punishment for their perjuries. Likewise, among the ancients whoever had stained himself with homicide purified himself with cleansing water." Cf. Bretschneider, *Dogmatik*, 4th ed., II, 626 (text and note 501).

the novices to be baptized "in the name of Jesus Christ [ἐπὶ τῷ ὀνόματι Ἰησοῦ Χριστοῦ]," Acts 2:38, and that also in other passages of Scripture Baptism is simply described as Baptism "in the name of the Lord Jesus [εἰς τὸ ὄνομα τοῦ Κυρίου Ἰησοῦ]," Acts 8:16; or "in the name of the Lord [ἐν τῷ ὀνόματι τοῦ Κυρίου]," Acts 10:48; or still more briefly, as Baptism "into Christ [εἰς Χριστόν, εἰς Χριστὸν Ἰησοῦν]," Gal. 3:27; Rom. 6:3. — But these texts present no real difficulty. There are no grounds whatever to regard such "shorter expressions" as baptized "into Christ" or "in the name of the Lord" as formulas of Baptism employed by the Apostles contrary to Christ's command to baptize in the name of the Triune God. Very correctly Meyer states that Peter's command (Acts 10:48) to baptize " 'in the name of the Lord,' 'does not affect the formula of Baptism.' " [11]

The Apostles' Baptism according to Christ's instructions, "in the name of the Father and of the Son and of the Holy Ghost," was *eo ipso* baptizing in the name (ἐν τῷ ὀνόματι), upon the name (ἐπὶ τῷ ὀνόματι), and also into connection with the name (εἰς τὸ ὄνομα) of Christ. Since Christ had commanded Baptism in the name of Father, Son, and Holy Ghost, this Baptism is a Baptism "in [ἐν] the name of Christ." This Baptism is also founded upon the name of Christ (ἐπὶ) because it was purchased by Christ's vicarious satisfaction, as Eph. 5:26 expressly teaches: "Christ also loved the Church and gave Himself for it [*satisfactio vicaria*], that He might sanctify and cleanse it with the washing of water by the word." And as to Baptism εἰς τὸ ὄνομα τοῦ Κυρίου Ἰησοῦ, into the name of the Lord Jesus, we must remember that confessing the name of Christ always includes confessing the Holy Trinity, as Scripture clearly teaches. For instance, those who "confess that Jesus Christ is Lord" (Phil. 2:10 f.) worship God the Father ("to the glory of God the Father") and likewise adore the Holy Spirit, without whom "no man can say that Jesus is the Lord" (1 Cor. 12:3). Following the example of the Church Fathers, Scherzer correctly says: "To confess Christ is to confess the whole Trinity." [12]

---

[11] By this statement, it is true, Meyer seems to contradict himself, since (in connection with Matt. 28:19) with the "concise expression" to baptize "into Christ," "into the name of Christ," he opposes the formula of Baptism given Matt. 28:19.

[12] *Systema,* "De baptismo," p. 356. Cf. the quotations from the Church Fathers in Gerhard, *Loci,* "De bapt.," § 91. R. E., 2d ed., XV, 242 ff. The usual explanation of the difference between the prepositions is: εἰς expresses the relation into which the baptized are placed; ἐπί and ἐν designate the foundation on which Baptism takes place (Cremer). Or εἰς, into, unto communion, unto ownership; ἐν, ἐπί, on the basis of (Ebeling). But it is self-evident that such general expressions as "in relation to," "on the basis of," and, above all, the popular

Why, then, misuse the shorter expressions ("in the name of Jesus Christ," etc.) to nullify the baptismal formula?[13] Besides, the Apostles themselves would not have baptized one who was ready to be baptized in the name of Christ, but not at the same time in the name of the Father and of the Holy Ghost; for throughout they teach that one cannot know the Father without simultaneously knowing the Son and the Holy Ghost; e. g., 2 Cor. 13:14: "The grace of the Lord Jesus Christ and the love of God and the communion of the Holy Ghost be with you all."[14]

It has also been argued that the texts cited bring new and additional thoughts not contained in Matt. 28:19, that, e. g., Acts 2:38 speaks of Baptism in the name of Christ "for the remission of sins." However, the Triune God of Matt. 28:19 is gracious to sinners, and therefore Baptism in His name is always Baptism "for the remission of sins." Heathen, indeed, aware of God's existence, but ignorant of the Triune God, revealed in God's Word, regard God as angry and think they must placate Him with worship and sacrifices. Christians, however, clinging to the Christian concept of God, think always of the Triune God as graciously disposed toward men for Christ's sake, that is, as forgiving their sins.

Within the Lutheran Church, too, the question has been discussed whether the Holy Trinity must always be confessed in the very words of Matt. 28:19 if the Baptism is to be valid. Brenz comments: "If a minister, after the applicant's recitation of the Apostles' Creed, performed the Baptism with these words: 'I have now heard from thee thy profession of faith, viz., that thou believest in God the Father

---

"in the sphere of," etc., derive their specific meaning only from the context. When Baptism on the basis of the name of Jesus Christ is modified by the phrase "for the remission of sins," εἰς expresses the purpose or effect; Baptism is a means of transmitting remission. Ebeling very correctly says that εἰς also in 1 Cor. 12:13 designates the effect: "By one Spirit are we all baptized into one body"; because Baptism is a means of remitting sin, it also implants into the spiritual body of the Church.

[13] Zoeckler, too, says of Acts 2:38 in his *Commentary:* "The formula of Baptism employed by the Apostles in baptizing certainly was the Trinitarian formula prescribed by the Lord in Matt. 28:19 (for proof see also *Didache* 7, 2. 3), and not the mere mentioning of the name of Jesus, a notion for which the ἐπὶ τῷ ὀνόματι I. Χǫ., v. 38, is misapplied by some."

[14] Thus Peter's sermon on Pentecost Acts 2:14 ff. is itself a mighty testimony regarding the Father, the Son, and the Holy Ghost. Cf. also 1 Cor. 8:4 ff.; 12:3 ff.; Gal. 4:4-7; Eph. 1:11-14; 3:2-5; 4:3-6; Titus 3:4-7; 1 Pet. 1:10-12; 2 Pet. 1:16-21; 1 John 2:22-24; 3:23-24; 4:2-3; 5:6-12 (even with the omission of the disputed 7b and 8a).

Almighty, Creator of heaven and earth, and in His only-begotten Son, Jesus Christ, and in the Holy Ghost; accordingly, upon this thy profession and faith, I baptize thee with water in order that thou mayest be assured that thou hast been grafted into Christ and the communion of all His blessings. Go in peace!' such a Baptism would certainly be a true Baptism because it contains the essentials of Baptism and because the sense of the words of Christ has been publicly expressed, though the sound itself of the words seems to have been a little changed." All will agree with Brenz that with such a pronounced confession of faith in the Holy Trinity a Baptism should be acknowledged as valid.

But such a case will rarely occur, particularly since Brenz sounds the following prefatory warning as to practice: "It must be stated that in baptizing the usual words: 'I baptize thee in the name of the Father and of the Son and of the Holy Ghost,' are by all means to be retained and that no one should be permitted capriciously to change these words and use other words in baptizing. For there are the most weighty reasons [*gravissimae causae*], the enumeration of which is superfluous here, why the use of these words should diligently be retained [*diligenter retinendus sit*]." *Catechismus pia et utili explicatione illustratus*, 1551, p. 56. Just imagine what thoughts of a more complete and less complete, of a "better" or "poorer," Baptism are apt to arise if, in baptizing, the words are changed *ad libitum*. Yet we, too, grant that a Baptism performed in the manner described by Brenz would have to be acknowledged as a true Baptism. We agree with those theologians who hold that the Matt. 28:19 formula of Baptism is the most fitting, the simplest, and the safest. "No doubt Christ had important reasons," says Deyling, "why He expressly mentioned the individual Persons in this formula of initiation and desired that we do so likewise" (*Prudentia Pastoralis*, p. 366). Nevertheless we acknowledge as valid a Baptism performed "in the name of Jesus Christ" if the baptizers are known as Trinitarians and confess their faith in the Holy Trinity at the Baptism in some such manner as suggested by Brenz.[15]

---

[15] This is the opinion of Brenz, Scherzer, Deyling. See the quotations in Walther's *Pastorale*, p. 110 ff. Gerhard discusses the entire matter very sensibly and calmly (*Loci*, "*De bapt.*" § 91—93). In 1520 Luther in *De captivitate babylonica* (St. L. XIX:61) expressed the opinion that such words as Acts 2:38, "in the name of Jesus Christ," stated the Apostles' manner (*ritus*) of baptizing. To this Walther remarks (*Pastorale*, p. 111): "This opinion, that the Apostles baptized in this manner, Luther seems later to have given up." Walther's judgment is confirmed

But what shall we say of the Baptism of anti-Trinitarian bodies employing the Trinitarian formula in the rite? This is an entirely different case. St. Augustine notes that one will find few heretics who do not use the words of Matt. 28:19. In many places the Lutheran Church in America found that Free Protestant Churches (German Unitarians) baptized in the name of the Father and of the Son and of the Holy Ghost, but publicly taught (also in their catechisms) that Christ is an excellent man, not the Son of God, and that the Holy Ghost is not God, but the spirit of culture, etc. In such cases we did not accept their Baptism as Christian, the orthodox formula notwithstanding, because of the express public declaration that it was not their intention to perform the Baptism Christ instituted in Matt. 28:19. In such a Baptism God's Word is not being added to the water (*ad elementum*), but a man-devised caricature of the words of Christ. We accept the principle set up by Walther (*Pastorale*, p. 121): "If a heretical pastor baptizes with the very same sounds as an orthodox pastor but publicly teaches with his whole church body that by Father he understands a god who is not three Persons, that the Son is a mere man, that the Holy Ghost is the spirit of our age and of enlightenment, or at most an alleged power or operation of God, that he therefore with those sounds is not baptizing into the most holy Trinity, such a heretical pastor is not only baptizing without faith,[16] but also without God's Word; the sound of it he indeed keeps, but to express an entirely different sense. For this reason the purported Baptism of all preachers of anti-Trinitarian communions can be acknowledged as

---

by the words of Luther of 1535 quoted p. 256, footnote 7. Moreover, Luther's remark of 1520 was directed against the erroneous view of those who did not recognize Baptism as God's own work (as a Baptism "by the Holy Trinity through men"), but regarded Baptism as an operation in which a man "pours grace" into the baptized by the use of certain words of God. Therefore, in the same connection, Luther attacks the notion of some Scholastics "as though there were a hidden spiritual power [*vis magica*] in the words and water that works the grace of God in the soul of him who receives Baptism," even without faith on the part of the baptized. True, Luther's remark in *De captivitate babylonica* gave the Romanists the welcome opportunity to accuse Luther even of Arianism. Thus Bellarmine. Gerhard (*Loci*, "*De bapt.*,"§ 90) meets the attack of Bellarmine with the fact that Church Fathers, Roman teachers, and even Pope Nicholas I spoke just as Luther had spoken, yet are exonerated by Bellarmine. Luther, too, in all his various baptismal formularies gives no other direction than to baptize in the name of the Father and of the Son and of the Holy Ghost. See the baptismal formularies, St. L. X:2134—2149.

16 Walther, *loc. cit.*, p. 121: "Neither the faith nor the right intention of either the officiant or of the applicant for Baptism (Rom. 3:3), belong to the essence of Baptism, but solely Word and water."

valid as little as a Baptism in sport and mockery, and those who have received such a spurious Baptism are still to be baptized."

Various reasons have been adduced why a Unitarian "Baptism" might possibly be a true Baptism, particularly if Christian parents unwittingly have their child baptized by a Unitarian. But to rely on possibilities here will not do. Baptism is too serious a matter. It is intended for practical use. A Christian desires to derive comfort from his Baptism, but he can do so only if his Baptism is not in doubt. At best a Baptism administered by Unitarians, also in the instance assumed, is an uncertain Baptism. All uncertain Baptisms, however, must be held to be invalid. In the nature of the case, any uncertainty as to the fact of my Baptism makes its consolatory use impossible for me.[17]

4

Baptism a True Means of Grace

(Baptismal Grace)

Above all, we must clearly recognize and maintain that Baptism is a means of grace. Baptism is no more and no less than a divinely ordained means whereby God in a special manner conveys and imparts to the person baptized the remission of sins provided for him by Christ's *satisfactio vicaria.* In other words, Baptism is a means of justification, *medium iustificationis sive remissionis peccatorum.* Baptism is not a work that we offer to God, but one that God does to us and by which "God offers and presents the remission of sins" (*Trigl.* 389, Apol., XXIV, 18).[18] Baptism does not belong to the Law, but to the Gospel (*Trigl.* 491, Smalc. Art., Part III, Art. IV), as we have set forth earlier under the doctrines of grace, of faith, of justification, and more extensively under the doctrine of the means of grace. We now summarize and add some further details.

---

[17] For further information on uncertain Baptisms see Walther, *Pastorale,* p. 124; [Fritz, *Pastoral Theology,* p. 106 ff.]. See the opinions of Luther on the Baptism of foundlings and private Baptisms without witnesses (St. L. X:2130 ff.). The Baptisms performed by the Roman Catholic Church and the Reformed denominations are not to be considered uncertain Baptisms, since both bodies baptize with water in the name of the Father, the Son, and the Holy Ghost, therefore alter nothing in the things which make up the essence of Baptism.

[18] Apol., *Trigl.* 389, XXIV, 18: "*Baptismus est opus, non quod nos Deo offerimus, sed in quo Deus nos baptizat, videlicet minister vice Dei, et hic offert et exhibet Deus remissionem peccatorum.*"

What has Baptism in common with the Word of the Gospel? This must be clearly understood. Like the Word of the Gospel, Baptism is a means imparting the remission of sins, for Scripture declares that Baptism is to be used for the remission of sins (Acts 2:38), washes away sins (Acts 22:16), that Christ cleanses His Church by Baptism (Eph. 5:26), etc. Through the bestowal of the remission of sins the Word of the Gospel calls forth faith, or strengthens it, and thus is a means of regeneration (1 Pet. 1:23); even so Baptism, imparting the same grace, is a means to awaken and strengthen faith and therefore also a washing of regeneration and renewing of the Holy Ghost (Titus 3:5).[19]

Wherein does Baptism as a means of grace differ from the Word of Christ? Not in an individual bestowal and assurance of the remission of sins; such a bestowal we have also in private absolution. The distinctive characteristic of Baptism is rather that the promise of grace given to a single person becomes a "visible Word," *verbum visibile*. As the Apology says: "And God, at the same time, by the Word and by the rite, moves hearts to believe and conceive faith, just as Paul says, Rom. 10:17: 'Faith cometh by hearing.' But just as the Word enters the ear in order to strike our heart, so the rite itself strikes the *eye* [*incurrit in oculos*] in order to move the heart." (*Trigl.* 309, XIII, 5.)

It is therefore an error when the grace-bestowing nature of Baptism is rejected. The chief offenders in this respect are the Ro-

---

[19] The assertion that regeneration is worked only by Baptism and not by the Word of the Gospel we had to reject as unscriptural above (p. 110 f.). — Some have found it difficult to see how Baptism could be a washing of regeneration in the case of adults who have come to faith and by faith have been regenerated. The difficulty is no greater than it is with the Word of the Gospel. As the Word of the Gospel keeps and exercises its regenerating power when preached to the regenerate, so, too, Baptism regenerates when it is performed on such as are already believers and regenerate. The preservation and strengthening of regeneration demands the same divine power as working regeneration initially. The dogmaticians concerned themselves with this question because the Reformed raised the objection: "At times some are baptized who were already regenerated through the Word and the Holy Ghost, for example, the Ethiopian eunuch (Acts 8:38) and those who had already received the Holy Ghost (Acts 10:47). Since Baptism was no means of regeneration for these, it dare not be assumed that Baptism has this purpose in the case of others." Gerhard (*Loci*, "De sacram.," § 123) replies: "Though these and many others were truly regenerated before they received Baptism, that fact does not deprive Baptism of any of its efficacy, namely, that it is and is called a washing of regeneration, as can be clearly seen from the example of the divine Word, which is heard by many who are already regenerated; still the Word is the salutary means whereby we are born again as of the incorruptible seed" (1 Pet. 1:23; James 1:18).

manists, the Romanizing Lutherans, the Reformed, and modern theologians who walk in Reformed paths.

The Romanists teach that Baptism imparts grace *ex opere operato*, that is, even though the person baptized does not have faith, the hand which lays hold of the forgiveness of sins offered in Baptism. Of this teaching the Apology says: "This is absolutely a Jewish opinion [*Iudaica opinio*], to hold that we are justified by a ceremony, without a good disposition of the heart, i. e., without faith. . . . Thus we teach that in the use of the Sacrament faith ought to be added, which should believe these promises, and receive the promised things, there offered in the Sacrament." (*Trigl.* 313, XIII, 18 f.) The Council of Trent not only subscribed to the Scholastic doctrine, but also rejected the Christian doctrine with an anathema. It decreed: "If anyone saith that by the said sacraments of the New Law grace is not conferred through the act performed [*ex opere operato*], but that faith alone in the divine promise suffices for the obtaining of grace; let him be anathema" (Sess. VII, can. 8; *Waterworth,* p. 55).[20]

The Roman teaching on Baptism has the specific purpose of separating the baptized from their Baptism. This end Rome attains in two ways. 1. By its doctrine that Baptism works *ex opere operato*, without the faith which appropriates the remission of sins, Rome makes personal Christianity impossible, which is, fundamentally, faith in the remission of sins for Christ's sake. The teaching that Baptism *ex opere operato* totally eradicates original sin, the remaining evil lust (*concupiscentia vel fomes*) being no more sin, has the same tendency.[21] 2. Rome does not permit the lapsed to return to the grace of Baptism, but refers them to the "second plank," the Roman Sacrament of Penance (*contritio cordis, confessio oris, satisfactio operis*).[22] All this serves to keep alive the *monstrum incertitudinis gratiae*, which is the foundation of the dominion of the Papacy over the souls.

But there are also later Lutherans who speak in Roman fashion of a communion with Christ, even of a regeneration through Baptism, without the simultaneous presence of faith in the forgiveness of sins.

---

[20] The *Tridentinum* (Sess. VI, c. 7) is misleading when it calls Baptism "the Sacrament of faith." Its next words show that by "faith" it does not understand the faith which apprehends the remission of sins proffered in Baptism, but a counterfeit faith, namely, a faith to which love, hence sanctification and good works, must have been added in order to unite with Christ or make one a member of the Church.

[21] *Trid.*, Sess. V, *De pecc. orig.*, 5. — *Cat. Rom.* II, 2. 32.

[22] *Trid.*, Sess. VI, c. 14; Sess. XIV, can. 2.

They imagine the effect of Baptism to be some sort of physical action (*Naturwirkung*), or the infusion of a substance, for the experience or reception of which, they say, no faith is necessary. Proponents of this theory assert that apostates among the baptized remain members of Christ,[23] or that unbelievers among the baptized nonetheless carry within them the Spirit of Christ, "deposited in them as a dowry for their whole life." [24] Kattenbusch is right in calling this view a "theosophical speculation" (R. E., 3d ed., XIX, 422). Scripture knows of no regeneration without faith in the remission merited by Christ. Scripture recognizes as regeneration only that change in man effected by faith in the Christ-wrought remission of sins (John 1:12-13; 3:5, 14-15; 1 John 5:1). Furthermore, Baptism is a means of regeneration only because it bestows the remission of sins and by this bestowal generates, or strengthens, faith.

Intrinsically Roman is also the notion, popular today, that Baptism first makes man a member of the Church, or grafts him into the "new humanity," and then, through his membership in the Church, or this ingrafting into the "new humanity," gives him a share in the forgiveness of sins. This idea is papistical because it bases the remission of sins, or justification, on membership in the Christian Church or participation in the "new humanity," instead of basing it on the promise in Baptism. Here Dorner's remark against Hofmann holds true: "Therefore at least by an incipient sanctification we have reconciliation" (*Glaubenslehre* II, 587). Holy Writ reverses the matter. Baptism, in the order of cause and effect, mediates first the remission of sins, or justification, therefore communion with God by grace, and then, as a result, membership in the Christian Church. In short, when we discuss Baptism as a means of grace or, in other words, when we answer the question: "What does Baptism give or profit?" we must firmly maintain that the proffer of the remission of sins and the accompanying generation or strengthening of faith is the first effect of Baptism, in relation to which all other effects of Baptism, such as membership in the Christian Church, the state of being dead to sin and alive to God, are solely fruit and consequence. This relation we dare not invert, lest we be mixing sanctification into justification. When we discussed justification (Vol. II, 410, 412), we observed that the *unio mystica*, membership in the Church, sanctification, etc., do not precede justi-

---

[23] Thus Franz Delitzsch, *Vier Buecher v. d. K.*, p. 43 f.; in Baier-Walther, III, 482.

[24] Thus Thomasius, *Dogm.* IV, 9.

fication, but follow it. These blessings follow also Baptism, since Baptism is *primo loco* a medium of justification, or of imparting the remission of sins (Acts 2:38).

The difference between the old Lutheran doctrine of Baptism and the teaching of modern Lutherans can be defined thus: According to the doctrine of Luther and our Lutheran Confessions, the remission of sins is the true "chief thing" in Baptism, and for this reason they repudiate a saving effect of Baptism without faith on the part of the baptized. Hence Luther once remarked that he, too, would omit Infant Baptism if he felt constrained to hold that children could not themselves believe (St. L. XI:490). Many recent Lutherans, however, eliminate from Baptism both the remission of sins and faith, the means of receiving this remission. They teach that Baptism communicates psychic (or "psychophysical") powers and gifts which the baptized do not receive with the hand of faith. This is the Romanizing element in their teaching.

The Reformed teach that Baptism is not at all a medium or *vehiculum* of the remission of sins or of God's gracious operation, but only a symbol or image of the forgiveness of sins and of regeneration, which the Holy Ghost is alleged to work without the use of the external Word and Sacraments or, at least, independently of such use, that is, immediately. To this day Lutheran doctrine is expressly rejected by the Reformed. Asking, "What is the Lutheran doctrine on this subject?" Alexander Hodge answers: "The Lutherans agreed with the Reformed churches in repudiating the Romish doctrine of the magical efficacy of this Sacrament as an *opus operatum.* But they went much further than the Reformed in maintaining the sacramental union between the sign and the grace signified. Luther in his Small Catechism says Baptism 'works forgiveness of sins, delivers from death and the devil, and confers everlasting salvation on all who believe,' and that 'it is not the water indeed which produces these effects, but the word of God which accompanies, and is connected with, the water, and our faith, which relies on the word of God connected with the water. For the water without the word is simply water and no Baptism. But when connected with the word of God, it is a Baptism, that is, a gracious water of life and a washing of regeneration.'" (*Outlines,* p. 500 ff.)

To understand the controversy between the Lutherans and the Reformed we must clearly recognize the motives or reasons underlying both positions. The pivotal point of controversy is raised in Luther's question in his Small Catechism: "How can water do such great things?" All Reformed, from Zwingli down to Boehl, deny that Baptism forgives sins and works regeneration, because Baptism cannot do or work these great things. Boehl says: "The water cannot do such great things" (*Dogm.*, p. 560). The position of Luther and the Lutheran Church is presented in Luther's well-known words: "If God bade you pick up a stalk of grain or strip a feather, and, with His command, promised that through this act you should have forgiveness of all your sins, grace, and everlasting life, should you not accept that proposal with great pleasure and gratitude, love it, praise it, and esteem that stalk or feather a higher and holier possession than heaven and earth?" The issue is not whether water is water, which Luther and all Lutherans have always conceded. The question solely is (a) whether God has commanded Baptism with water, (b) attached to it His promise of the remission of sins, and (c) thus made it a medium of the forgiveness of sins and a washing of regeneration and renewing of the Holy Ghost. Luther's way of saying it in his Small Catechism is a sufficiently exact dogmatic formulation too of the Scripture doctrine of Baptism. To the question: "What is Baptism?" Luther answers: "Baptism is not simple water only, but it is the water comprehended in God's command and connected with God's word." And after Luther has quoted the divine command, Matt. 28:19: "Baptize them in the name of the Father and of the Son and of the Holy Ghost," and the divine promise, Mark 16:16: "He that believeth and is baptized shall be saved," he asks: "How can water do such great things?" and answers: "It is not the water, indeed, that does them, but the word of God which is in and with the water, and faith which trusts such word of God in the water. For without the word of God the water is simple water, and no Baptism. But with the word of God it is a Baptism, that is, a gracious water of life and a washing of regeneration in the Holy Ghost." The position of Luther and the Lutheran Church in the doctrine of Baptism is therefore clear. It can readily be seen why the Lutheran Church asserts these great things of Baptism: "It works forgiveness of sins, delivers from death and the devil, and gives eternal salvation to all who believe this, as the words and promises of God declare."

Zwingli, however, claims never to have read in the Holy Scriptures (*neque unquam legimus in Scripturis sacris*) that the Sacraments — and he refers particularly to Baptism — bring and confer grace (*Fidei Ratio, Niemeyer*, p. 24 f.; Jacobs, *Book of Concord*, II, 168). But Zwingli is deceiving himself. Zwingli, like Luther, has read in the

Scriptures that Baptism is for the remission of sins, washes away sins, that Christ cleanses His Church by Baptism, that Baptism is a washing of regeneration, that Baptism saves, etc. But Zwingli refuses to believe these statements of God. With him it is a clear case of not believing the clear Word of God. His real and only reason is that he regards the matter as incredible; he is simply opposing the authority of God's Word with his Zwinglian ego. The same thing all Reformed, Boehl, too, do to this day. Boehl exhibits a certain naiveté and frankness. He calls attention to the Scripture passages which declare that Baptism washes away sin, cleanses of sin, and works regeneration (Acts 22:16; Eph. 5:26; Titus 3:5), but then he adds: "Water cannot do such great things" (*Dogm.*, pp. 558, 560). He simply opposes the words of Scripture with his own "Impossible!"

The difference between the Lutheran Church and the Reformed in the doctrine of Baptism is fully and adequately defined by saying that the former believes God's Word regarding Baptism, the latter not. Refusing to believe the clear Word of God, Zwingli and his co-laborers invented the Reformed teaching of Baptism, and Calvin propagated it. For the Reformed doctrine that Baptism is merely a symbol, image, emblem, etc., of the remission of sins and regeneration there is not a shred of proof in Scripture. P. Feine correctly declares: "Everywhere Baptism is presented as effecting real, objective results; it is not a mere emblem or a dramatic symbolic action. The concepts of justification and the remission of sins are clearly and firmly connected with Baptism. Likewise Baptism is firmly connected with the doctrine of faith, of communion with Christ, and of the gift of the Spirit." (R. E., 3d ed., XIX, 400.) Feine cites the same Scripture passages which Luther and the early dogmaticians adduced to prove the Lutheran doctrine of Baptism: Eph. 5:26; Titus 3:5;[25] Acts 22:16; 2:38; 1 Pet. 3:21.

Observe also that even as the remission of sin and regeneration

---

[25] The first edition of *Meyer's Commentary* remarks on Titus 3:5: "Baptism is considered as the inner regeneration of men, which is disclosed through the external act of washing." This Huther disavows in the third edition with the comment: "The term τὸ λουτρὸν παλιγγενεσίας has been given very arbitrary meanings by some exegetes; for they take λουτρόν to be a figurative connotation of the *regeneratio* itself, or of the *praedicatio evangelii*, or of the Holy Ghost, or of His rich outpouring. On the authority of Eph. 5:26 the term can mean nothing else than Baptism. According to the context, Paul calls Baptism the washing of regeneration not because it makes regeneration obligatory (Matthies), nor because it symbolizes regeneration (de Wette), for in neither of these meanings could it be effectual as a means of salvation (ἔσωσεν ἡμᾶς διά), but by that name he characterizes it as the washing by means of which God actually brings about the regeneration of man."

are bestowed through Baptism as a means (*medium remissionis peccatorum et regenerationis*), so also the implantation into the body of Christ, viz., into the Church, is wrought, and not merely portrayed, by the Holy Ghost through Baptism. We are told (1 Cor. 12:13): "For by one Spirit are we all baptized into one body." [26]

Also sanctification, the death of the old man and the resurrection to a new life, is not only typified by Baptism, but actually effected. In Rom. 6:1-11 Paul teaches that the Christians are dead unto sin, but alive unto God. This, however, is an effect of Baptism (διὰ τοῦ βαπτίσματος). Sanctification according to both its negative (dead unto sin) and its positive side (alive unto God in Christ Jesus) is a *status quo* created through Baptism. Amazing is Boehl's notion that in Baptism the old man is mortified only symbolically, *"in effigie"* (*Dogm.*, p. 556 ff.), although this statement agrees with Boehl's teaching that Baptism also remits sins only *in effigie*. Baptism, he says, is only *signum absolutionis peccatorum*. However, Holy Writ says that Baptism is not merely an image, *effigies*, but a means of forgiving sin. Likewise the mortification of the old man and the resurrection of the new, holy man is not only typified, but effected in Baptism. The Bible certainly teaches no other means of mortifying the old man or of causing the Christian to die to sin than the remission of sins, or the Gospel. By the Law sin is not mortified, but mobilized (Rom. 7:5-6). But believers in the Gospel, or the forgiveness of sins, are told: "Sin shall not have dominion over you; for ye are not under the Law, but under grace" (Rom. 6:14). Now, just as surely as Baptism belongs to the Gospel, that is, is a means of forgiving sins, of washing away sins, of cleansing from sin, etc., the old man himself is put to death in Baptism, not merely an effigy of him. And that is the very thing Paul asserts when he says that we are "buried with Christ by Baptism [διὰ τοῦ βαπτίσματος] into death" (Rom. 6: 3 ff.)

In his Small Catechism Luther, too, speaks of a signification of Baptism, but not in the sense of the Reformed. He teaches that Baptism itself also works what it typifies, namely, the drowning of the old man and the coming forth of the new. Luther writes of Baptism that it "not only signifies such a new life, but also produces, begins, and exercises it. For therein are given grace, the Spirit, and power to suppress the old man, so that the new man may come forth and

---

[26] As the εἰς in Acts 2:38 designates the purpose and effect of Baptism: "Be baptized every one of you . . . for [εἰς] the remission of sins," so also here: "We are all baptized into one body [εἰς ἕν σῶμα]."

become strong." (*Trigl.* 751, Large Cat., Inf. Bap., 75.)[27] When A. v. Oettingen (*Luth. Dogm.* II, 2d ed., p. 431) says of Baptism that it, as it were, includes the "death verdict" over the old man, the "as it were" must be struck out. In the midst of Christendom we must ever and again remind men that sanctification always appears solely as a result of the remission of sins, or justification, and that therefore a sanctifying power of Baptism may be asserted only if Baptism actually, and not merely "*in effigie*," forgives sins, or justifies. We can depend on it that wherever God, as in Baptism, promises His grace, that is, the remission of sins, and faith seizes this promise, there *eo ipso* the old man is put to death, and the new man is called forth and arises. The reason for the daily repetition of this process is, that faith is not yet perfect, but throughout his whole life some unbelief is still to be found in the Christian along with his faith. Hence, to secure the practical benefit of Baptism, it is imperative that we do not regard Baptism as an image, or "*effigies*," of grace, but as a means of grace.

Moreover, the Reformed have no right to call Baptism a "symbol" or "seal" of grace. The only grace Baptism knows is the grace which Baptism itself offers and imparts. Baptism therefore does not seal and confirm a grace which allegedly is given and wrought immediately, but rather declares it to be counterfeit. Cf. The Means of Grace, in General, p. 104 ff. We have seen, p. 163 f., that an essential difference between Zwingli and Calvin does not and cannot exist. To sum up: All who deny that Baptism is a means of the forgiveness of sins and regeneration must, with Zwingli, conceive of Baptism as a "symbol of duty." If some Reformed take a different course in practice, they are, fortunately, inconsistent."

Another thing. Though the Reformed teaching of Baptism manifestly contradicts the Word of God, we must not close our eyes to the seductive power of the objection: "Water is water and cannot possibly do such great things." Not to believe God's Word and work is natural to all men. Consequently man looks upon the water of Baptism, though God has united His word with it, as simple water (Luther, drastically: "with the eyes of a cow," i. e., without understanding; St. L. VII:702). That is, man perversely ignores the word joined to "the washing of water" (Eph. 5:26). For this reason the axiom of

---

[27] Again, *Trigl.* 749, Large Cat., Inf. Bap., 65: "These two parts, to be sunk under the water and drawn out again, signify the power and operation of *Baptism* [*virtutem et opus baptismi*], which is nothing else than putting to death the old Adam, and after that the resurrection of the new man, both of which must take place in us all our lives."

unbelief, "Baptism with water cannot wash away sins; the Spirit must do it," finds fruitful soil among the unchurched as well as among Christians in so far as they follow their natural bent.

The denial of Baptism as a means of grace is abetted by the baptized who do not lead a Christian life. This ungodliness, men say, warrants the conclusion that Baptism is no medium of the remission of sins and regeneration. Very persistently, as we have often noted, the argument is repeated: Many who hear the Gospel do not believe and are not saved, and many who are baptized live wickedly and are lost. Therefore the external Word of the Gospel and Baptism with water cannot be means of grace; on the contrary, "efficacious grace acts immediately," "nothing intervenes between the volition of the Spirit and the regeneration of the soul." That is, of course, a foolish argument. People who reason thus ought, above all, themselves refrain from preaching and writing, for if the Holy Spirit does not come through God's Word and through the divine ordinance of Baptism, far less will He come through the word of Muenzer, Zwingli, Calvin, "Gypsy" Smith, etc., or through the human ordinances of class meetings and revival camp meetings. But to think and act consistently is not man's strong point since the Fall. Such inconsistency is due to his conceit and the influence of the archenemy of the Church, who would bring God's ordinance, the means of grace, into disrepute and induce man to base the remission of sins and salvation on man-made products falsely labeled "Spirit," instead of on the grace of God in Christ. For this reason the opposition to Baptism as a means of grace makes such a profound impression on the public in and outside the Church; therefore we must, in home and Church, continually teach the saving character of Baptism, and stress it particularly, both thetically and antithetically, in our theological instruction.[28]

----

[28] Some years ago a newspaper in St. Louis published the following report on the activity of a revival preacher: "Baptism won't save you. Evangelist says being among God's people is not enough. 'You are not going to be saved by joining the Church, by being baptized, or by taking the Lord's Supper, or by doing anything of this sort,' Evangelist W. R. Newell declared yesterday morning at the Century Theater noonday service. 'If you become a Christian, you will want to do these things, but goats get in among the sheep. It does not save you to get in among God's people.'" Hence we have today all about us the same situation which Luther (St. L. X:2060 ff.) describes: "It is the miserable devil's deception, who makes monkeys and fools of the people by clamoring and shouting: Don't you see that water is water? How can water, which also the cow drinks, benefit the soul and wash away sins? Such language makes the pert rabble gape, that they promptly fall for it and exclaim: That is most certainly true! My, how the devil has fooled me that I did not see and take note of that! This they then call a precious instruction and the high art of the Spirit, merely that they can say:

Within the Lutheran Church the question has been discussed whether there is a heavenly element (*materia coelestis*) in Baptism. Baier inserted a lengthy historical study of the question in his *Com-*

Water is water. And still the pitiable folks are so easily deceived by such gibberish because these fellows adorn their babbling with many smooth words and powerful shouting, pretending that we teach that water as water bathes the soul. My friend, they say, by no means believe that; for here you see how they are trying to deceive you, that you are to put your trust in mere water, which is a created thing. But such fellows deserve to be called desperate traitors and miscreants, who tear Baptism apart, sever and cut off from it the two best and chief parts, namely, God's Word and command, and leave us nothing but the empty shell or hull. They do not want to hear or see that we always and primarily stress the two elements named, with and besides the water. But they claw at us with that lone, single piece and bellow of this as a special art and the Spirit. Friend, so sage and learned as that I fancy I could also be, yes, every peasant behind the plough, without any skill, if that rule were to obtain, that we may arbitrarily sever and tear apart what belongs together and is one thing. . . . For this you must grant, that Christ Himself has instituted such Baptism and adds His Word or command to it when He enjoins us to baptize in the name of the Father, the Son, and the Holy Ghost and adds His promise: He that is thus baptized and believes, shall be saved. This you dare not teach us to ignore nor tear it away as though it were not meant and accomplished nothing, while you meantime point us to Utopia [*Schlaraffenland*] and plead your own fantastic 'promptings of the Spirit [*Geisterei*].' For what the Holy Spirit works in us we, too, know and teach, thanks to God, even more and better than they. But we should not permit Him thus to be torn from Baptism and the Sacrament and made to stand in an empty corner, as they stare into space for the Spirit and seek private revelations apart from the Word and God's order. For we know that He wants to be active in us through the very Word and Sacrament and in no other way. For this reason there is no need of searching further for the Spirit if we have this Sacrament of Baptism; because we hear from Christ's Word and institution that the name of the Holy Ghost, as of the Father and of the Son, i. e., the name of the whole divine Majesty, is present there. Since, however, God's name and Word is there present, you must not regard it as simple and plain water, accomplishing no more than bathing water, but you must regard it as a water that washes us of our sins and Scripture calls a washing of regeneration, by which we are born again into eternal life. Of this matter we shall hear more later. Let these remarks suffice to answer those who regard Baptism as merely a physical water bath and take note neither of the word nor of the divine command. . . . So far sufficient has been said both of what Baptism is and of what power and benefit it has. Now something must be said also of its use or of those who receive it. For here the break comes and the disparity begins, that not all receive the same power and benefit of Baptism though they all receive the same Baptism. For two kinds of people come to Baptism and receive it: some with faith, some without. For this reason, though the Baptism is correct in itself and remains holy and divine in the one case as well as the other, for the unbeliever as well as the believer, still this great difference appears among them that the unbeliever cannot enjoy its power and benefit. This is not the fault of Baptism, but his own fault because he does not receive and use it as he should; the vessel is not fitted to receive the gift; for the heart is locked, so that the power of Baptism cannot enter it and work in it because it [the heart] does not long for and desire that."

pendium (Baier-Walther, III, 447 ff.). Quenstedt reports that there is no *consensus* among the Lutheran theologians as to the *materia coelestis,* for as such they mention God's Word, the Holy Ghost, the blood of Christ, the Holy Trinity. For himself Quenstedt adds: "We hold with Menzer, Meisner, Affelmann, Gerhard, Brochmand, Calov, and others that the heavenly thing [*res coelestis*] is the Holy Trinity" (*Syst.* II, 1085). Now, the persons or things mentioned are indeed present in Baptism, though their relation to this Sacrament varies. God's Word, the word of command and the word of promise, is present as the element which makes the application of water a Baptism (*forma Baptismi*). The Holy Ghost is present, for it is He who works regeneration through Baptism. The blood of Christ is there, for the remission of sins imparted by Baptism was not purchased with gold or silver, but with the blood shed by Christ. The Holy Trinity is present, for not only is Baptism performed in the name of the Holy Trinity, but Father, Son, and Holy Ghost are present in a special manner wherever the means of grace are administered. In fact, Scripture teaches that all three Persons of the Holy Trinity make Their abode in the heart of every man who has come to faith. But, in spite of all this, it is inadvisable to speak of a *materia coelestis* in Baptism for the reason, first of all, that the Holy Ghost, the blood of Christ, and the Holy Trinity are connected in the same way with the preaching of the Gospel.[29] These things, therefore, are not peculiar to Baptism. Accordingly Hollaz remarks that here the term *materia coelestis* is taken in a "wider sense": "Properly speaking [*stricte loquendo*],

---

[29] When Luther said that Baptism "is a water mixed with the blood of Christ," or that in Baptism "appears and is seen the crimson, innocent blood of Christ" (St. L. VII:707), he was by no means thinking of an *unio sacramentalis* between the water and the blood of Christ like the sacramental union between bread and wine and body and blood of Christ in the Lord's Supper; but Luther meant to convey the truth that the fruit of the shedding of Christ's blood, the forgiveness of sins, is given us through Baptism. This is his own explanation of his words, for he says: "This holy Baptism has been purchased for us through the blood that was shed for us and paid for our sins. . . . For we do not obtain remission of sins through our works, but through the Son of God's dying and shedding of His blood. This remission, however, He lays and places into Baptism." In the same connection Luther also says that the blood of Christ is united with the preaching of the Gospel: "The sprinkling [with the blood of Christ] is nothing else than preaching. The holy or sprinkling water is the Holy Scripture. The tongue of the preacher or the Christian is the holy-water sprinkler [*Sprengwedel*]. This he dips into the Lord Christ's crimson blood and therewith sprinkles the people, that is, he preaches the Gospel to them, proclaiming that Christ has purchased forgiveness of sins by His precious blood, which He shed on the Cross for the sins of all mankind. He who believes it has been sprinkled with it."

neither the Holy Ghost nor the Holy Trinity can be, or be called, a *causa materialis*" (*Examen*, "*De baptismo*," qu. 7). In view of these considerations it is advisable to say with Baier and others: "We refrain from speaking of a *materia coelestis* in this Sacrament."

5

The Use of Baptism

Though administered only once, Baptism is to be used by Christians throughout their whole life. Nowhere do the Apostles call on Christians to repeat Baptism; however, they frequently recall to their minds the Baptism once received.[30] This reminder is intended both for consolation and for admonition. In Gal. 3:26-27 Paul reminds the Christians that by their Baptism they put on Christ, that is, became God's children, without the Law, by faith in Christ.[31] In Rom. 6:3 ff. Paul employs Baptism for admonition, instructing Christians that by their Baptism they have become dead unto sin, but alive unto righteousness. Peter strikingly sets forth the consolation of Baptism. He says (1 Pet. 3:21) that as Noah and his family were saved by the water of the Flood, even so the water of Baptism now saves us (σῴζει βάπτισμα), and the reason he gives is that Baptism is "not the putting away of the filth of the flesh, but the covenant of a good conscience toward God [συνειδήσεως ἀγαθῆς ἐπερώτημα εἰς θεόν]."[32] Baptism,

---

[30] 1 Cor. 1:13; 6:11; 12:13; Rom. 6:3 ff.; Eph. 4:5; Col. 2:12; Titus 3:5-6; 1 Pet. 3:21.

[31] Regarding the "evangelical putting on" of Christ by faith in distinction from the putting on of Christ by imitation of His life ("ethical putting on") see Luther, St. L. IX:464 f.; also Meyer on the passage.

[32] The meaning of ἐπερώτημα is in dispute. In the New Testament the word occurs only here. Profane Greek furnishes two meanings. Its first and original meaning is "question, inquiry, *interrogatio*." From this its forensic use in later Greek for "covenant, *stipulatio*," is derived. Cp. Cremer's Dictionary. Those who here render ἐπερώτημα as "interrogation" understand the passage to say, with some shadings of the thought, that in Baptism the baptized appeal to God or pray for a good conscience. This meaning is excluded here, since according to the context the statement here concerns what Baptism itself is, and not what the candidates for Baptism or the baptized do in Baptism. For this reason one has to retain Luther's rendering: Baptism is the covenant of a good conscience toward God or over against God (εἰς θεόν). To the point is the comment of Stoeckhardt: "The first part of the apposition: Baptism 'is not the putting away of the filth of the flesh' demands a continuation such as this: but Baptism is rather an inward cleansing of man, a cleansing, or washing, of the conscience of sin. In other words, it procures a good conscience before God for him who has himself baptized." Baptism is represented here, as in Acts 2:38; 22:16; Eph. 5:26, as a means transmitting the remission of sins. This appears also from the addition:

then, involves the establishment of a covenant of grace between God and the person baptized. With good reason, therefore, the daily repentance of Christians (*poenitentia stantium*) is called a daily return to Baptism, or to the covenant of Baptism, inasmuch as the believers daily confess their transgressions, by faith seize the remission of sins guaranteed by Baptism, and, thus consoled, strive for fruits worthy of repentance in a new life.

Also the repentance of backsliders (*poenitentia lapsorum*) does not consist in seizing the "second plank" (*secunda tabula*), the Roman Sacrament of Penance, but in a return to Baptism (*reditus ad baptismum*), namely, in a return to the grace of which Baptism assures us.[33]

We must beware of supplanting Baptism with confirmation. There is a trend in our day, also among Lutherans, to exalt confirmation at the expense of Baptism. Dr. Walther (*Pastorale*, p. 266) issues this caution: "The pastor must guard against representing confirmation as a complement or supplement of Baptism received in infancy, as though, e. g., the confirmand now for the first time makes the confession and pledge given by his sponsors his own. Rather the rite of confirmation should primarily serve vividly to recall to the confirmands, as well as to the entire congregation present, the glory of their Baptism, received in infancy. To invest confirmation with a sacramental character is one of the aberrations so prevalent today, particularly among those who want to be regarded, above others, as strictly Lutheran and churchly. See the review of an article in Vilmar's *Pastoraltheologische Blaetter*, which was reprinted in *Lehre und Wehre* VIII, 110—116, from the *Erlanger Zeitschrift.*"

"by the resurrection of Jesus Christ." Baptism applies the remission of sins, which God actually, through the resurrection of Christ from the dead, declared available for all men.

[33] Luther (*Trigl.* 751, Large Cat., Inf. Bap., 79): "Repentance, therefore, is nothing else than a return and approach to Baptism, that we repeat and practice what we began before, but abandoned. This I say lest we fall into the opinion in which we were for a long time, imagining that our Baptism is something past which we can no longer use after we have fallen again into sin. The reason is, that it is regarded only according to the external act once performed [and completed]. And this arose from the fact that St. Jerome wrote that repentance is the second plank by which we must swim forth and cross over after the ship is broken, on which we step and are carried across when we come into the Christian Church. Thereby the use of Baptism has been abolished so that it can profit no longer. Therefore the statement is not correct or at any rate not rightly understood. For the ship never breaks, because (as we have said) it is the ordinance of God, and not a work of ours; but it happens, indeed, that we slip and fall out of the ship. Yet if anyone fall out, let him see to it that he swim up and cling to it till he again come into it and live in it, as he had formerly begun."

6

Who Is to Be Baptized

Both adults and children are to be baptized.

Scripture expressly points out that only such adults are to be baptized as have previously come to faith in Christ. Of those baptized on the First Pentecost we read: "Then they that gladly received his word were baptized" (Acts 2:41); and when the eunuch, having been instructed by Philip, desired Baptism, his wish was granted after he had confessed his faith in Christ (Acts 8:36-38).

We do not venture to snatch infants away from their parents in order to baptize them secretly against their parents' will.[34] But children brought to us by their parents or guardians we baptize.[35]

The *Scripturalness of Infant Baptism* is established by Scripture passages such as Mark 10:13-16 and Col. 2:11-12. In the first text two things are evident: (1) Also little children (Luke calls them τὰ βρέφη, infants, 18:15) are to be brought to Christ; (2) Infants, too, are able to receive spiritual blessings and actually are members of the Kingdom of God. Theirs is not a potential but an actual faith, that is, one they have now as children (Matt. 18:6; 1 John 2:13), and they not merely expect to be members in the Church, but are members (Mark 10:14). Col. 2:11-12 states that Baptism has supplanted the Old Testament Sacrament of Circumcision. It is therefore the means of grace for children. Calov comments: "*Sacramentum baptismi Christus surrogatum voluit circumcisioni.*"

At the bottom of the opposition to Infant Baptism is usually the singular notion that adults indeed can believe, but not children (Matt. 18:3; Mark 10:14-15). Cf. "The Faith of Infants" (Vol. II, 448 f.) and "Baptismal Customs" (Vol. III, 282 ff.).

Again, the objection is raised that Infant Baptism is nowhere expressly mentioned in Holy Writ and that therefore Infant Baptism cannot have been practiced in the Apostolic Church. But by the same token we may argue: Infant Baptism is not expressly mentioned in Holy Writ because it was a common practice. Scripture lends at least some support to this view, reporting, as it does, that entire families — some of which, at least, would normally include children — were bap-

---

[34] That is known to be the practice of Rome. Cf. Baumgarten, *Theol. Streitigk.*, III, 311.

[35] For a full discussion regarding parental authority over the children see Walther's *Pastorale*, p. 125 ff. [Fritz, *Pastoral Theology*, p. 109].

tized (1 Cor. 1:16; Acts 11:14; 16:15,33). Furthermore, Holy Writ declares that Christ cleanses "His Church," of which children are a part (Matt. 18:6; Mark 10:13-16), "with the washing of water by the Word" (Eph. 5:26). Again, Paul declares Baptism to be the anti-type of circumcision (Col. 2:11-12). Besides, from church history it can be proved that Pedobaptism was commonly practiced in the second century. Hase (Ev. Dogm., p. 432): "Tertullian bears witness to its prevalence by his disapproval of it." Origen (Epistola ad Rom. V) declares: "The Church has accepted from the Apostles the tradition of giving Baptism also to the little children." [36]

Are children of Christians who die without Baptism saved? There is some basis for the hope that God has a method, not revealed to us, by which He works faith in the children of Christians dying without Baptism, as certainly He did in the case of girls in the Old Testament (Mark 10:13-16). For children of unbelievers we do not venture to hold out such a hope. We are here entering the field of the unsearchable judgments of God (Rom. 11:33).

The "baptism" of bells and other res inanimatae is, of course, a mockery of Christian Baptism.[37] A baptism of the living "for the dead" seems to have been customary among some heretics.[38]

---

[36] In his critique of "the ecclesiastical doctrine of Infant Baptism" even the rationalist Bretschneider finds "more than one thing which induces us to think that Infant Baptism conforms to Jesus' will and the spirit of His religion. The command in Matt. 28:19 is most general. . . . Moreover, the Apostles could refer the command of Jesus to the children with all the more reason because also in the old economy the rite of initiation, circumcision, was performed on infants. When entire families (Acts 16:15, 33; 18:8; 1 Cor. 1:16), and all indeed who belonged to them (Acts 16:33), were baptized, it is probable that if there were a number of children in these families, the Apostles did not exclude these. . . . Jesus Himself, according to Mark 10:14 f.; Matt. 19:15 f.; Luke 18:15 f., blessed the children by the laying on of hands and declared them suited to become members of the Kingdom of God. We shall therefore always be surer of fulfilling Jesus' will if we receive the children by Baptism into the communion of the Christian Church than if we do not. Also the primitive Church, as we learn from Tertullian, had the custom of baptizing the children, a thing they would not have done if the Apostles had denied Baptism to the children." (Dogm. d. ev.-luth. K. II, 649 ff.)

[37] Quenstedt, II, 1092. Luther: "Friend, where is this instituted and who has commanded you to do this? Have you a word or command of God which says: You should consecrate salt or water and speak such words over it? Where such word (of command) is absent, there you have nothing and accomplish nothing, no matter what other signs and words you may use; even Baptism would be no Sacrament without this word of command, though both water and a word spoken over it were there. Thus the Papacy makes a fool of itself by such a lying, false Baptism, when they consecrate and baptize inanimate bells, where they also use both water and Word, as in a true Baptism. What, then, is lacking? Nothing else

7

The Administrants of Baptism

Like all spiritual gifts the means of grace, including Baptism, are given by God directly to the believers, all Christians. The believers do not get them from the pastors, but vice versa. Pastors administer Baptism in their public office only as the called servants (*ministri*) of the believers. If the public servants are not available, every Christian has the right, yea, is in duty bound, to administer Baptism. Our St. Louis hymnal therefore contains several formularies (longer and shorter) for a so-called "lay Baptism." [39]

The Calvinists, following their teacher, entirely reject "lay Baptism," [40] and particularly Baptism by women, and assert that Baptism may be performed only by duly called pastors.[41] The true reason for this odd position Alting reveals when he says that women who perform an emergency Baptism arrogate to themselves the public ministry (*involant in ministerium ecclesiasticum*), and then adds: "They make

than this, that there is no institution and command of God for such baptizing, but men have introduced it of their own will and pleasure, just as the whole Papacy is nothing but doctrines of men and their own stuff and nonsense. Therefore such baptizing is no Sacrament, but purely a perversion, yea, a derision and desecration of Baptism. (St. L. VII:704.)

[38] Cp. Gerhard, *"De bapt.,"* § 165, and Cremer, *sub* βαπτίζειν. On 1 Cor. 15:29 ("baptized for [ὑπέρ] the dead") consult *L. u. W.*, 1884, 413 f. [*Pop. Symb.*, pp. 89, 326]; also Gerhard (*ibid.*) and Cremer (*ibid.*). On the local meaning of ὑπέρ see Winer, *Gramm. d. neutest. Sprachidioms*, 6th ed., p. 342.

[39] But a Christian ought to be able to baptize without using a printed formula by memorizing the few words needed to baptize: "I baptize thee in the name of the Father and of the Son and of the Holy Ghost."

[40] Calvin, *Inst.*, IV, 15, 20: "Christ never commanded women, or men in general, to baptize; He gave this charge to those whom He had appointed to be Apostles." Allen Transl. II, 491, 20. His limitation of the command to baptize to the Apostles is contrary to v. 20: "I am with you alway even unto the end of the world." Furthermore, Calvin proves too much. If the command to baptize was given only to the Apostles, then also the administration of Baptism, and teaching in general, would have to be limited to the persons of the Apostles, a limitation which, of course, Calvin himself would not accept.

[41] For quotations see Heppe, *Dogm. d. ref. K.*, p. 446; Quenstedt, II, 1115 ff.; Guenther, *Symb.*, p. 295 f. Also the *Second Helvetic Confession* rejects lay Baptism: "We teach that Baptism should not be administered in the Church by women, or by midwives. For Paul separates women from the ecclesiastical offices. But Baptism belongs to the ecclesiastical offices." Schaff, *Creeds*, III, 291. *The Confession of Faith* of the Presbyterians of 1646 says: "There be only two Sacraments ordained by Christ . . . neither of which may be dispensed by any but a minister of the Word, lawfully ordained" (Chap. XXVII, 4).

salvation dependent on an external thing because they imagine that the child is lost eternally if death occurs before the Baptism with water has taken place; they do not know that the salvation of the children depends on the grace of election and of the covenant." [42] Their true reason, therefore, is the rejection in general of the means of grace as "external things" and the fiction of an election independent of the means of grace. By the way, when Calvinists assure us that a Baptism performed by laymen can have no power whatever (*baptismi nullam vim esse*),[43] we recall that, according to the Calvinistic doctrine, consistently adhered to, there is no power in any means of grace, Baptism included. These means merely picture what the Holy Ghost works immediately in the elect.

8

The Necessity of Baptism

Baptism is not a matter of choice (an *adiaphoron*), but a divine ordinance; still one may not assert an absolute necessity of Baptism or say that no one can obtain remission of sins and be saved without Baptism. We observed above (p. 108 ff.) that all means of grace have the same purpose and the same effect, namely, the imparting of remission of sins to the sinner and, through this, the generating and strengthening of faith. "We are not to imagine," we said above, "that each one of the three means transmits one third of the forgiveness." We noted that "Scripture ascribes the forgiveness of sins, without reservation, to the Word of the Gospel, to Baptism, and to the Lord's Supper." Whoever, therefore, comes to faith in the Gospel, has remission of sins and salvation, even though circumstances prevent his being baptized. This is the teaching of Luther and our Lutheran theologians.[44] Quenstedt writes at some length against an absolute

---

[42] *Syllabus controversiarum*, etc., p. 263; in Quenstedt, II, 1115.

[43] Thus Chamier, *De baptismo*, V, 14, 8; in Quenstedt, II, 1116.

[44] Luther: "Christ is content to have stated in the first part of this passage, 'He that believeth and is baptized,' and in the second part, 'He that believeth not,' without again mentioning Baptism. He has done this because He has sufficiently directed attention to Baptism in the first part and in addition commanded it in other passages, e. g., Matt. 28:19. However, it does not follow that one might omit Baptism or that it were acceptable if someone pretended he needed no Baptism because he had faith. For anyone who becomes a Christian, or comes to faith, surely will gladly receive also this sign in order that he may have as his own the divine testimony and seal of his salvation, derive strength and consolation from them during his whole life, and make this his public profession before all the world. . . . It may, however, happen that one has faith without

necessity of Baptism as taught by the Church Fathers, the Scholastics, and the later Roman teachers.[45] To soften somewhat the cruel nature of their error the Papists teach only a negative punishment (*poena damni*), not a positive punishment (*poena sensus*) of those children that die without Baptism; that is to say, they assume that infants dying without Baptism are deprived of the beatific vision of God, but subjected to no torment.

Those who teach an absolute need of Baptism quote John 3:5 as proof: "Except a man be born of water and of the Spirit, he cannot enter into the Kingdom of God." But the scope of this passage is reproof of the Pharisees and scribes, who rejected God's counsel of salvation appointed for their day and despised the Baptism of John, while the publicans repented and were baptized.[46] This is what Luke reports (7:29-30): "And all the people that heard him [John], and the publicans, justified God, being baptized with the Baptism of John. But the Pharisees and lawyers rejected the counsel of God [τὴν βουλὴν τοῦ θεοῦ] against themselves, being not baptized of him." In view of this contempt for the Baptism of John as well as for God's counsel of salvation, Christ says to Nicodemus, who was "a man of the Pharisees": "Except a man be born of water and of the Spirit, he cannot enter into the Kingdom of God." We, too, would have to tell a despiser of Christ's Baptism: "Except a man be baptized, he cannot enter into the Kingdom of God." Luther and the Lutheran theologians appropriate Augustine's word: "*Contemptus sacramenti damnat, non privatio.*" They teach that while faith in the remission of sins purchased by Christ, or regeneration, is absolutely necessary, Baptism is not absolutely necessary, since this faith, or regeneration, can be brought about also by the Word of the Gospel alone.

---

having been baptized; and, again, some may receive Baptism who do not truly believe. Hence this text must be understood so as to enjoin and confirm Baptism as a thing not to be despised, but to be used, as we have stated; and yet it must not be explained so narrowly that a person not able to obtain Baptism stands condemned by it. . . . The consensus of opinion has always been that if a person dies a believer but lacks Baptism, he would not be condemned; for it might happen that a person is a believer and, though desiring Baptism, is overtaken by a sudden death." (St. L. XI:984.)

[45] *Syst.* II, 1166 f. Alexander Hodge (*Outlines*, p. 502) is mistaken when he asks: "What is the Romish and Lutheran doctrine as to the necessity of Baptism?" and answers: "They hold that the benefits conveyed by Baptism are ordinarily conveyed in no other way, and consequently, Baptism is absolutely necessary . . . to salvation, both for infants and adults."

[46] Dannhauer in particular sets this forth (*Hodosophia, Phaen.* X, 504): "The particular scope of the talk of Christ is the reproof of a Pharisee who despised the counsel of God in Baptism."

9

Baptismal Customs

In the course of time a number of customs have been introduced in connection with the baptismal rite for the purpose of explaining and portraying both the nature and the effect of Baptism (Luther, St. L. X:2138). Gerhard (*Loci,* "De baptismo," §§ 254—255) divides the usual "ceremonies and customs" at a Baptism into three classes: (1) Those enjoined by God, (2) those free but used by the Apostles, (3) those added by church dignitaries. Better, however, is the division into two classes. And actually Gerhard makes one class of classes two and three when he says that only the ceremonies enjoined by God (the application of water in the name of the Triune God) are binding on the Church, but that those freely observed by the Apostles rest as much on the Christian liberty of the Church as those added by the later Church. We include under baptismal customs all ceremonies and customs not prescribed by God and here make mention of such as were received into the Lutheran baptismal formularies, though perhaps not in all places. Walther (*Pastorale,* p. 130 f.) enumerates the following: (1) the reminder of original sin; (2) the giving of a name; (3) the so-called "small exorcism"; (4) the sign of the cross; (5) a prayer and the *devotum Davidicum;* (6) the "great exorcism"; (7) the reading of Mark 10:13-16; (8) the laying on of hands; (9) the Lord's Prayer; (10) the *abrenuntiatio* and the *confessio* (the Apostles' Creed); (11) the use of sponsors; (12) the covering of the child with a chrisom; (13) the votum.[47]

Christians should, on the one hand, bear in mind that these customs are *adiaphora* (not prescribed by God), so that Baptism loses none of its validity if several or even all of these ceremonies are not used. Gerhard says: "In the customs neither commanded nor forbidden by God (*in ritibus adiaphoris*) the liberty must be guarded which Christ has dearly purchased and conferred on His Church, namely, by observing them freely, without the notion that they are necessary. They may be abrogated or altered according to the regulation and with the consent of the Church. particularly if they cease to be of benefit, do not achieve their salutary purpose, are misused, or degenerate into a superstition."

---

[47] Gerhard's enumeration of the customs common in the Lutheran Church in "*De bapt.,*" §§ 258—269; in the Catholic Church, § 257.

On the other hand, Baptism being a public function, the customs connected with it should not be left to the option or caprice of any individual, not even of the pastor. The Formula of Concord properly defines where authority lies to decide on, or change, the baptismal customs. In Article X, on "Church Rites or Adiaphora," it says: "Therefore we believe, teach, and confess that the congregation of God of every place and every time has, according to its circumstances, the good right, power, and authority (in matters truly adiaphora) to change, to diminish, and to increase them, without thoughtlessness and offense, in an orderly and becoming way, as at any time it may be regarded most profitable, most beneficial, and best for [preserving] good order, [maintaining] Christian discipline [and for εὐταξία—*christlicher Wohlstand* — worthy of the profession of the Gospel], and the edification of the Church" (*Trigl.* 1055, Sol. Decl., X, 9). Self-evidently a local congregation will, as far as feasible, conform to the customs in surrounding congregations of the true faith in order thus to confess outwardly the agreement in doctrine and to avoid confusing members who transfer from one congregation to another.

We add a few remarks on the baptismal customs in vogue in the Lutheran Church. The reference to original sin, with which also the baptismal formulary in our Agenda begins, has the purpose of pointing out the need for Baptism, since "from the fall of Adam we are all conceived and born in sin." — The giving of a name in Baptism serves as a reminder that the person baptized has in his Baptism been given a guarantee of grace, executed in his name, that is, for his personal possession, and valid for his whole life.[48] — How exorcism came to be added to the baptismal customs and in what sense the Lutheran Agendas adopted it, Walther relates (*Pastorale*, p. 133 ff. [Fritz, *Pastoral Theology*, p. 113]). Walther, following Chemnitz, Hutter, and Gerhard, voices the opinion: "Exorcism was indeed not abolished in our German Lutheran Church in the manner which Hutter correctly calls the only correct one; rather this ceremony was dropped in a most irregular manner when indifferentism and rationalism became rampant in the Church. However, since this ceremony manifestly belongs to those that must constantly be explained to avoid misunderstanding, it is, indeed, where still in use, not to be abolished in haste, still less, however, would it seem advisable to strive for its reintroduction."

---

[48] Framed certificates of Baptism are very fitting "diplomas" for display on the walls of a Christian home, particularly, too, in the studies of theological students.

The misunderstanding to be feared is that people think of a bodily possession of the child in connection with exorcism, while it refers only to a spiritual captivity in the kingdom of the prince of darkness.

A matter that often causes trouble for pastors is the choice of sponsors. Walther gives this good advice: "A pastor should use his influence to have only fellow Lutherans chosen as sponsors and, in order to bring this about, should accustom his congregation to announce any approaching Baptism to him before securing sponsors. However, if well-meaning members of other denominations have already been approached, or are already coming to the baptismal font, the pastor will not turn them away, thus publicly shaming them and arousing in them a lasting antipathy against our Church and its ministry. For though it is wrong for a Lutheran to assume the obligations of sponsorship in a heterodox church and thus practice unionism, it certainly is no sin against conscience if, in the case assumed, sincere but heterodox individuals are permitted to be witnesses at a Baptism properly administered by us." (*Pastorale,* p. 136 f. [Fritz, *Pastoral Theology,* p. 114]). Our formulary for Baptism, pledging the sponsors, in case of the death of the parents, to give the child a Christian training in the true faith, presupposes orthodox sponsors. It would be unethical for a pastor to require such a pledge from persons of another faith or for the latter to give it. The heterodox will readily see this point. If they serve not as sponsors, but merely as witnesses, there will be no difficulty. In this case the pastor will know what to omit from the baptismal formulary to make it fit the circumstances.

The renunciation and the profession of faith express the fact that by Baptism the child is transferred from the kingdom of Satan to the Kingdom of Christ. Since this transfer can be made only through the child's own faith, the child is asked whether he believes, the sponsors answering in the stead of the child. It is assumed as certain, of course, that the child has a faith of his own in Baptism and is not being baptized on the faith of the sponsors, or of the Christian Church, or even on his own future faith. The personal faith of the child must by all means be upheld. Any doctrine that would put the child in possession of the blessing of Baptism without faith (*opus operatum*) as the receiving hand on the part of the child is anti-Christian;[49] for the blessing of Baptism consists in the remission of sins, and this can be appropriated through no other means than faith. "Now this [namely, "to receive in the water the promised salvation"] the fist

---

[49] That is the *Iudaica opinio* of the Scholastics, Apol., *Trigl.* 313, XIII, 18 ff.

cannot do, nor the body; but the heart must believe it" (*Trigl.* 741, Large Cat., Bap., 36).

The question whence the child acquired a faith of its own need not seriously trouble us. Since we know that Baptism has taken the place of circumcision and is thus the means of grace for the children, and since Christ commands us to bring the children to Him that He may bless them, and since He declares the kingdom of heaven to be theirs, we can rest assured that Christ will provide the children with the *medium* ληπτικόν, faith, by which alone they can accept the blessing and the kingdom of heaven. Moreover, we know that Baptism as Gospel itself has the power to *work* the faith it calls for. As the Word of the Gospel by imparting the forgiveness of sins also works faith in the proffered remission of sins, even so Baptism works and strengthens faith, not because of a physical or magical power communicated to the water, but by reason of the promise of the remission of sins united with the Baptism with water. Luther: "We say, therefore, that children are brought to Baptism by the faith and work of others; but when they get there and the pastor or baptizer deals with them in Christ's stead, He blesses them and grants to them the faith and the kingdom of heaven; for the word and deed of the pastor are the Word and work of Christ Himself" (St. L. XI:492). "For what else is Baptism but the Gospel to which they are brought? Though they hear it only once, they hear it more effectively, because Christ, who has commanded to bring them, receives them." (*Ibid.*, 497.) We are in fact more certain of faith in the Baptism of a child than in the Baptism of adults. In the Baptism of adults we must accept their word in answer to our question whether they believe, and we should accept their word. If they deceive us or themselves, that is their own lookout. "You are excused and baptize aright," says Luther (*ibid.*, 495). But in the Baptism of a child we have Christ's Word for it that the children believe, since He directs us to bring them to Him that He may bless them, and accordingly He sees to it that they are equipped with faith, the means of reception. Referring to Mark 10, Luther says: "I think, if any Baptism is certain of success, the Baptism of children is most certain because of the Word of Christ in which He commands to bring them to Him, whereas the adults come of themselves; and because in adults there may be deception because of their mature reason; but in children there can be no deception because of their slumbering reason. In them Christ works His blessing, even as He has bidden them to be brought to Him. It is a glorious word, and not to be treated lightly, that He commands us to bring the children to

Him and rebukes those who forbid such bringing. . . . In short, the
Baptism and consolation of children have their root in the word:
'Suffer the little children to come unto Me, and forbid them not;
for of such is the Kingdom of God.' This was said by Him and therefore cannot be a lie. Therefore it must be right and Christian to bring
little children to Him. There is no other way of doing this than in
Baptism. Then it must also be certain that He blesses them and
bestows the kingdom of heaven upon all who come to Him, as He says:
'Of such is the Kingdom of God.' " (*Ibid.,* 495.)

Some still say that our practice of questioning the child about
his faith while expecting the sponsors to answer is a rather queer
procedure. However, the reason for it is obvious. Since infants cannot
as yet speak, but, as we know from God's Word, in Baptism have
personal faith, we utter what they for the time being cannot express.
At the same time we grasp the opportunity to confess the Christian
teaching regarding the faith of infants, which is being denied in the
midst of Christendom. In view of these facts the procedure in question
is not at all strange, but sensible.

This also is the answer to the question whether perhaps our
Church has somewhat thoughtlessly assigned the formulary for the
Baptism of adults to Infant Baptism. Evidently this is not the case.
On the contrary, the question as to faith is no less appropriate in
Pedobaptism than in the Baptism of adults, since we know of children,
and that more certainly than of adults, that in or at their Baptism
they do believe. Then, too, it is expedient to retain this interrogation
to forestall the notion "that the Christian Church has two kinds of
Baptism, or that children have not the same Baptism as adults.
St. Paul says that there is only 'one Baptism, one Lord, one faith,'
Eph. 4:5" (*ibid.,* 490).

But at what point in the baptismal act are we to assume that faith
is generated? Luther is not particularly concerned about establishing
that moment. He says that faith is present "before or certainly in the
Baptism" (*ibid.,* 489). The one important thing for Luther is that the
child has a faith of its own and is not being baptized on the faith of
the sponsors, or of the Christian Church, or on its own future faith.
It is safest, however, to assume that faith is engendered in the moment
when water and Word are applied to the child. We repeat Luther's
words adduced above: When the children have been brought to Baptism by the faith of others "and the pastor or baptizer deals with them
in Christ's stead, He blesses them and grants to them faith and the

kingdom of heaven; for the word and deed of the pastor are the Word and work of Christ Himself" (*ibid.*, 492). We bear in mind always that everything except the application of water in the name of the Father, the Son, and the Holy Ghost can in case of need be omitted, and it still remains a true Baptism.

This gives rise to still another question: How may one call for a confession of faith by the child before the essential part of the baptismal act has occurred? It has been suggested that the question be placed after the application of Word and water. But to this arrangement it might again be objected that this is chronologically incorrect and may call forth the erroneous thought that faith was not present in and during Baptism. We shall therefore have to content ourselves with a sequence of events in the formulary which are synchronous with Baptism itself, because we are so constituted that we cannot think or say everything at once.

Finally it behooves all of us to make a confession about "infant faith." If we look at the matter without God's Word, infant faith appears improbable to us. Our psychological knowledge fails us here. We, too, are apt to pity the poor children because of their rudimentary intelligence, and regard them as capable neither of faith, nor of the kingdom of heaven, nor of Baptism. The disciples had similar thoughts. When the children were brought to Jesus that He might touch them, the disciples rebuked, scolded (ἐπετίμων), those who brought them. The disciples also thought: *Cui bono?* The entire association of the children with Christ could amount to nothing but make-believe. But the Lord checks these thoughts of His disciples. "He was much displeased [ἠγανάκτησεν, R. V.: "moved with indignation"], and said unto them, Suffer the little children to come unto Me, and forbid them not; for of such is the Kingdom of God." At the same time Christ instructs His disciples and all of us what this reason, which we grownups developed in the course of years, actually contributes toward entrance into the Kingdom of God. He says: "Verily I say unto you, Whosoever shall not receive the Kingdom of God as a little child [ὡς παιδίον], he shall not enter therein." The Lord therefore reverses the judgment of the disciples. The disciples hold that children are not the fitting *subjectum quod* for Christ's blessing, but Christ informs them that adults will have to become like the children if they would participate in the kingdom of heaven. Thus also we shall have to desist from our own calculations and learn how to think correctly, by faith in the words of Christ, about the faith and salvation of children.

10

The Baptism of John the Baptist

Thomasius faults Lutheran theologians for "claiming the essential and complete identity of the Baptism of John with Christian Baptism." [50] However, according to Scripture, the Baptism of John actually was a means of grace with *vis dativa* (power to give remission) and *vis effectiva* (power to effect faith). As the Baptism of Christ, which the penitent received on the first Day of Pentecost, was a Baptism "for the remission of sins [εἰς ἄφεσιν τῶν ἁμαρτιῶν]," so, too, the Baptism of John is expressly described as a "Baptism of repentance for the remission of sins [βάπτισμα μετανοίας εἰς ἄφεσιν ἁμαρτιῶν]" (Mark 1:4; Luke 3:3). And as Christian Baptism is called a "washing of regeneration and renewing of the Holy Ghost" through which "He saves us [ἔσωσεν ἡμᾶς διὰ λουτροῦ παλιγγενεσίας καὶ πνεύματος ἁγίου]," and this in contrast to a salvation based on our work (οὐκ ἐξ ἔργων τῶν ἐν δικαιοσύνῃ ὧν ἐποιήσαμεν ἡμεῖς), Titus 3:5, so the Baptism of John is likewise described as a means through which the Holy Ghost works regeneration and a "man of the Pharisees" gets into the Kingdom of God: "Except a man be born of water and of the Spirit [ἐξ ὕδατος καὶ πνεύματος], he cannot enter into the Kingdom of God" (John 3:5).

A correct understanding of John's Baptism is, of course, no longer of immediate practical value inasmuch as no one today receives that Baptism.[51] But such as refuse to acknowledge the Baptism of John

---

[50] *Dogmatik* III, 2, 10. Thomasius attacks in particular Chemnitz, Gerhard, and Aegidius Hunnius.

[51] Chemnitz, *Examen*, "De bapt.," p. m. 230; Calov, *Syst.*, I, 953. In Chemnitz (*ibid.*, p. 233 ff.), there is a carefully compiled list and review of the various interpretations of Acts 19:1-6. Of the opinion that the words of v. 5, "When they heard this, they were baptized in the name of the Lord Jesus," are the words not of Luke, but of Paul, he holds: "The Greek text easily suffers and admits of this explanation." But he does not wish that anyone be anathematized for holding that the twelve disciples of John were baptized at Ephesus into the name of Christ. The interpretation given that historical report Acts 19:1-6, he declares to be a matter for itself. That John's Baptism was a means of grace is certain, he says, from the descriptions Scripture gives of it. Of the notion that John's rite was a Baptism unto repentance "without faith in Christ and without remission of sins" Chemnitz judges: "Such a Baptism is certainly simply pagan (*res ethnica*). Paul, too, in Acts 19 expressly states that John baptized with the Baptism of repentance in such a manner that he at the same time taught those whom he baptized to believe in Christ. Also Mark and Luke assure us that John preached of his Baptism as a Baptism not only of repentance, but

as a means of grace reveal faulty conceptions of the remission of sins and of salvation, as, for instance, Thomasius, who says: "The remission of sins granted in John's Baptism was of a somewhat external and preparatory nature, similar to the effect of the Old Testament sacrifices. It did not make the baptized person a member of the kingdom of heaven, but prepared him for it. Thus it was a type of the Baptism of Christ, the place of which it, therefore, could not take. In the case of the disciples of Christ the outpouring of the Spirit on Pentecost served to compensate for the deficiency." A remission of sins of a "somewhat external and preparatory nature" makes no sense. You either have remission of sins or have it not. Again, the Old Testament sacrifices, inasmuch as they were types of the propitiatory sacrifice of Christ, offered the actual remission of sins for Christ's sake, and the believing Israelites, who were waiting for the Consolation of Israel, also appropriated it through faith.[52] Thomasius' remark that John's Baptism did not make one "a member of the kingdom of heaven" contradicts Christ's declaration (John 3:5) that such men as Nicodemus could enter the "Kingdom of God" through the Baptism of John. But "kingdom of heaven" and "Kingdom of God" are synonyms. Again, Thomasius speaks as if the outpouring of the Holy Spirit on the disciples had been a means of grace, needed to put them into complete possession of the remission of sins and membership in the Kingdom. But, in point of fact, the outpouring of the Holy Ghost on the Day of Pentecost had the purpose of equipping the disciples for their calling as witnesses of Christ in the world: "But ye shall receive power after that the Holy Ghost is come upon you; and ye shall be witnesses unto Me both in Jerusalem, and in all Judea, and in Samaria, and unto the uttermost part of the earth" (Acts 1:8).[53]

---

of repentance for the remission of sins. Also the expression 'for the remission of sins' does not divorce John's Baptism from the remission of sins. . . . The same expression is used of the Baptism of Christ (Acts 2:38): 'Repent and be baptized every one of you . . . *for* the remission of sins.' "

[52] Acts 10:43. Cf. the chapter "The Sacrifice of Christ and the Sacrifices of the Old Testament," Vol. II, 378 f.

[53] Also Luke 24:46-49. Lutheran theologians accordingly distinguish *baptismus sanguinis*, or martyrdom (Matt. 20:22), and *baptismus flaminis*, or the outpouring of special gifts of the Holy Spirit (Acts 1:5), from *baptismus fluminis*, or the Baptism with water, which is a Sacrament for the remission of sins. Cf. Quenstedt, II, 1080.

THE LORD'S SUPPER

(DE COENA SACRA)

1

The Divine Institution of the Lord's Supper

The Lord's Supper is not merely a church custom, but, like preaching the Gospel and Baptism, a divine ordinance (*institutio divina*). It was instituted by our Lord Jesus Christ, who at the same time enjoined that it be observed in His Church to the end of time, a command which the Apostle Paul reiterates. Luke 22:19; 1 Cor. 11:25: "This do ye . . . in remembrance of Me." And thus the first Christians understood Christ's instruction. We find the Lord's Supper, like Baptism, in common use in the Apostolic Church (1 Cor. 10:16-22; 11:17-34).

Consistent "enthusiasts," such as the Quakers, reject the Lord's Supper as well as Baptism as a permanent divine ordinance. In this matter they are more consistent in abolishing "useless external things" than most of the Reformed, who put a figurative interpretation only on the words which refer to Christ's body and blood and reject only the oral eating (*manducatio oralis*) of Christ's body and blood, but practice the oral eating of bread and wine. The Quakers, however, interpret also the bread and wine figuratively and therefore expect Christians who are truly spiritually minded to eat the bread and wine, too, only by faith, and not with the mouth. For this they also claim "Scripture proof." As most of the Reformed support their rejection of the oral eating and drinking of Christ's body and blood by the words, "The flesh profiteth nothing" (John 6:63), so the Quakers appeal to such texts as Rom. 14:17: "The Kingdom of God is not meat and drink, but righteousness and peace and joy in the Holy Ghost"; Col. 2:16: "Let no man therefore judge you in meat or in drink . . . which are a shadow of things to come, but the body is of Christ." Rev. 3:20 ("If any man hear My voice and open the door, I will come in to him and will sup with him, and he with Me") is alleged to teach that a true celebration of the Lord's Supper must take place in the heart. The external action, which Christ at one time performed with his disciples "for the sake of the weak," is no more binding for the later Church than foot-washing, anointing the sick with oil, and abstaining from blood and things strangled.[1]

In recent years radical theologians (B. Weiss, Juelicher, Spitta) have denied that our Lord instituted the Supper and commanded a continued observance of it. Cremer answers them: "No fact could ever be better attested than the ordination of the Lord's Supper for His Church by Jesus Himself."[2]

The relation of the Lord's Supper to Baptism is correctly defined

---

[1] Extensive proofs from Barclay's *Apologia* are furnished in Baumgarten, *Theol. Streitigkeiten*, III, 362 ff. Guenther, *Symbolik*, 4th ed., p. 318, quotes from Barclay's *Catechism*: "Which other Scripture texts show that it is not necessary that the commandment of bread and wine continue in force? The Kingdom of God is not meat and drink. . . . Let no man therefore judge you in meat or in drink." As to value and meaning of the act which Christ once performed with His disciples, which then also became usage in the Apostolic Church, Barclay says (*Apol.*, thesis 13): "The breaking of the bread by Christ with His disciples was a figure [namely, of the spiritual and *inner* reception of Christ's body and blood], which they who received the symbolized thing at times used in the Church because of the weak, just as abstaining from things strangled and from blood, washing one another's feet, anointing the sick with oil. All these things were commanded with no less an authority and solemnity than those first two [Baptism and the Lord's Supper], but, because they merely were the shadow of better things, they were no longer binding for those who attained the substance [the essence, the Lord's Supper in the heart]."

[2] R. E., 3d ed., I, 33. These radical theologians refer to the fact that only the reports of Paul and Luke have the words, "This do in remembrance of Me." But, according to both divine and human order, two witnesses suffice to prove a thing. However, even if we disregard the direct command reported by Paul and Luke, it is unreasonable to suppose that the meal in which Christ gives His body, given into death as ransom for the sins of mankind, and His blood, "the blood of the new testament, which is shed for many," was appointed only for the Apostles and not for the entire Church. Cremer, too, points out this fact. He says (R. E., 3d ed., I, 33 f.): "Besides, it is not true that there is no indication in Mark and Matthew of an institution for posterity. Both designate the contents of the cup as τὸ αἷμά μου τῆς διαθήκης, Matt. 26:28; Mark 14:24; moreover, Mark adds, τὸ ἐκχυνόμενον ὑπὲρ πολλῶν, and Matthew, τὸ περὶ πολλῶν ἐκχυνόμενον εἰς ἄφεσιν ἁμαρτιῶν. But when Christ distributes His 'blood of the covenant' to the disciples His thought cannot possibly have been to limit this distribution to the disciples, as is further proved by the mention of the 'many' (πολλοί) in the clause added." Correctly Cremer adds that the true reason for the rejection of the Lord's institution of His Supper is to be sought elsewhere than in the alleged discrepancy of the reports. "While Rueckert finds the difficulty in the danger of externalism undeniably connected with the 'ritus,' which, he thinks, certainly cannot have been hidden from Christ [the rationalists battle just as valiantly as the "enthusiasts" against all "legalistic externalism"], Spitta in particular rejects the institution as an ordinance for the Church because he regards the reference in the Lord's Supper to Christ's death as impossible." The underlying reason is the denial of Christ's deity and of the *satisfactio vicaria* by these theologians.

by the old theologians when they call Baptism *sacramentum initia-tionis* and the Lord's Supper *sacramentum confirmationis*. A person must have been baptized before he may partake of the Lord's Supper. On the Day of Pentecost the converts were called on to accept Baptism, not to receive Communion. This rule we must observe in our practice. If it appears that persons desiring the Lord's Supper have not yet been baptized, we first baptize them.[3]

Some of the names used for this Sacrament are supplied in Scripture (1 Cor. 11:20: "Lord's Supper"; 1 Cor. 10:21: "the Lord's Table"), church usage has coined others from the words, the nature, or the circumstances of the Lord's Supper.[4] Acrimonious arguments about the names for this Sacrament — even about the name "Mass" (*missa*) — are improper as long as no unscriptural teaching is introduced with the name.[5] In our day the name "Lord's Supper" is perhaps the most common among Protestants. Modern theologians of various schools favor the term *"Herrnmahl."* [6]

---

[3] Walther, *Pastorale*, p. 190. Walther also refers to the "analogy of the Passover." According to Ex. 12:48 only those who had been received into the covenant of grace by circumcision were permitted to join in the Passover.

[4] *Eucharist* is derived from εὐχαριστήσας (Mark 14:23; Luke 22:19; 1 Cor. 11:24); *Communion* from κοινωνία (1 Cor. 10:16); *Supper* from 1 Cor. 11:23: ὁ Κύριος ᾿Ιησοῦς ἐν τῇ νυκτί κτλ. Gerhard (*Loci*, "De s. coena," §§ 3—9) distinguishes between Biblical and ecclesiastical names. As Biblical names he enumerates *coena dominica* (the Lord's Supper), the Table and Cup of the Lord, the Communication of Christ's Body and Blood (with the remark: "where rather a proposed definition of the thing than a name can be spoken of"), the New Testament ("because it was instituted by Christ immediately before His mortal agony and so to say *in memoriam* of the death of the testator"), Breaking of Bread (with the remark: "But because it cannot be demonstrated evidently and indisputably that it is necessary by 'breaking of bread' to understand the administration of the Supper in Acts 2:42; 20:7, some explain the phrase of ordinary meals, in which sense it is used Luke 24:35; Acts 27:35, and many others"). As ecclesiastical names he mentions εὐχαριστία (Thanksgiving); σύναξις (Assembly); ἀγάπη (Love Feast); λειτουργία (Public Service); θυσία (Sacrifice); προσφορά (Offering); μυστήριον (Mystery); *sacramentum altaris, missa*. A wealth of historical material is offered by Gerhard in explanation of these names.

[5] Luther: "Carlstadt scolds us because of the name — that we call the Sacrament a Mass — and calls us hangmen, murderers of Christ, and more such abusive names, even worse than the names the Papists give us, all because Mass means a sacrifice in Hebrew, and he will not let it count in our favor that we battle and campaign so earnestly and fearlessly for this, that *the Mass is no sacrifice*. But now even before the world it is a disgraceful, childish, unmanly thing to wrangle about words if there is agreement in the matter. This thing Paul forbids and calls such people λογομάχους, wranglers about words and quarrelers." (St. L. XX:174 ff.)

[6] Holtzmann, *Neutest. Theol.*, II, 200; Noesgen, *Neutest. Off.*, I, 545.

2

The Relation of the Lord's Supper to the Other Means of Grace

Like the Word of the Gospel and Baptism the Lord's Supper is a medium of justification (*medium iustificationis sive remissionis peccatorum*). The Lord's Supper is no more and no less than a means ordained by Christ to offer and impart to all who partake of this meal the forgiveness of sins which Christ secured for men. In other words, the Lord's Supper is not Law, but pure Gospel, is not a work that we do for Christ, but a work that Christ does to us. It is a work through which He assures us that by His reconciling death we have obtained a gracious God. This is clearly the sense of the words Christ used at the institution of His Supper. When He says: "Take, eat; this is My body, which is given for you," and: "This is My blood, which is shed for you," these words can have no other meaning than that we ourselves no longer have to pay for our sins, but that our sins have already been expiated by Christ's body, given for us, and His blood, shed for us. Hence Luther is right when he insists: "The Mass [the Lord's Supper] is no work or sacrifice [of men], but a Word and rite of divine grace, which God uses to establish and strengthen our faith in Him" [namely, that He is gracious to us] (St. L. XIX:346). In the Apology: "The Sacrament . . . was instituted for the purpose of being a seal and testimony of the free remission of sins, and that, accordingly, it ought to admonish alarmed consciences to be truly confident and believe that their sins are freely remitted" (*Trigl.* 401, XXIV, 49). Hence the Smalcald Articles properly class "the holy Sacrament of the Altar" with "the Gospel" and enumerate it with the spoken Word of the Gospel and Baptism as "a counsel and aid against sin" (*Trigl.* 491, Part III, Art. IV).

Again, like private absolution and Baptism, the Lord's Supper is a pledge of the remission of his sins given to an individual.

On the other hand, Scripture very clearly indicates the *differentia specifica*, that which is peculiar to the Lord's Supper. The Lord's Supper confirms and seals the private absolution to the individual by making him the recipient of the very body of Christ which was given for him and of the very blood which Christ shed for him. This is the feature distinguishing the Lord's Supper from the other means of grace.

But Christ has fared badly with this wonderful means of grace in the very midst of Christendom. Rome cuts the Sacrament of the Altar in half by depriving the laity of the cup; and the body of Christ which it pretends to leave, is, if the Roman doctrine is taken literally, not the body that was given for us, but a body that came into being by the transubstantiation of the bread into the body of Christ (*Trigl.* 493, Smalc. Art., Part III, Art. VI; Luther, St. L. XIX:1303). To this Rome adds the abominable sacrifice of the Mass, wherein the body of Christ is not given and received as a pledge of the remission of sins, but is made an "unbloody" immolation for the living and the dead, offered by the priest to the disgrace of the one, perfect propitiatory sacrifice of Christ and for the suppression of the faith that Christ's one sacrifice has provided all forgiveness needed.

The Reformed church bodies exclude Christ's body and blood from the Lord's Supper entirely and convert the Lord's Supper into a solemn observance in which they distribute bread and wine as symbols of the absent body and blood of Christ. They declare the oral eating of Christ's body and blood in the Sacrament of the Altar to be utterly impossible, and some of their foremost teachers — after the example of the early pagans — go so far as to call Christ's Supper, in which we orally receive His body, given for us, and His blood, shed for us, cannibalism, a Cyclopean meal, a Thyestean banquet, and a satanic lie. See p. 327.

Neo-Lutheran theologians are not satisfied with the doctrine that Christ's body and blood are received for the remission of sins, but feel called upon to "enrich" the old Lutheran doctrine of the Lord's Supper by ascribing to the Sacrament also a physical effect ("*Naturwirkung*"). All these and other perversions of this doctrine call for an extended presentation of the Scripture teaching of the Lord's Supper.

3

The Scripture Doctrine of the Lord's Supper

Three radically different beliefs regarding the Lord's Supper are held among the Churches of Christendom.

1. The belief that only the body and blood of Christ are in the Sacrament of the Altar, in other words, that the bread and wine are transformed or converted into Christ's body and blood. Since the Lateran council of 1215,[7] this dogma (*transubstantiatio*) is the official

---

[7] Mansi, XXII, 982: "Christ's body and blood are truly contained in the Sacrament of the Altar under the species of bread and wine, the bread having been by divine power transubstantiated into the body and the wine into the blood. . . . This Sacrament no one can in any case effect save a properly called priest."

teaching of the Roman Catholic Church, reaffirmed by the Council of Trent.[8]

2. The belief that there is nothing but bread and wine in the Lord's Supper; in other words, that bread and wine are only symbols of the absent body and blood of Christ. This is the position not only of Zwingli, but also of Calvin and all Reformed, including all Reformed minor sects. That Calvin "deepened" Zwingli's view of the Lord's Supper and held a middle position between Zwingli and Luther [9] is a favorite contention of modern histories of dogma, but a thoroughly incorrect opinion. In the *Consensus Tigurinus,* edited by Calvin according to his theology,[10] it is asserted that the body of Christ "is distant [from the Lord's Supper] as far as heaven is from earth," [11] and the literal understanding of the words of institution is judged to be a "preposterous" interpretation.[12]

3. The doctrine that both bread and wine and the body and blood of Christ are present in the Lord's Supper, that, in other words, with the bread Christ's body is received, and with the wine Christ's blood; and that this is a union occurring only in the Lord's Supper. To distinguish this union from the *unio personalis,* obtaining only between the divine and human natures in the Person of Christ, and from the

---

[8] The Council of Trent (Sess. XIII, can. 2) pronounces the curse on all who deny transubstantiation: "If anyone saith that in the sacred and holy sacrament of the Eucharist the substance of the bread and wine remains conjointly with the body and blood of our Lord Jesus Christ, and denieth that wonderful and singular conversion of the whole substance of the bread into the Body, and of the whole substance of the wine into the Blood — the species only of the bread and wine remaining — which conversion indeed the Catholic Church most aptly calls Transubstantiation; let him be anathema." (Waterworth, p. 82.) The material on the development of this teaching (by Paschasius Radbertus, d. ca. 865; Lanfrank, d. 1089), in spite of opposition (from Rhabanus Maurus, d. 856; Ratramnus of Corbie, d. after 868; Berengar of Tours, d. 1088) can be found in Schmid-Hauck, 4th ed., pp. 234—252, 287 ff. Cf. Seeberg, *Dogmengesch.,* II, 10 f., 21 ff., 58 ff., 113 ff. Hase, *Ev. Dogm.,* 3d ed., p. 446 ff.

[9] Loofs, e. g., opines (R. E., 3d ed., I, 68) that, as to its origin, Calvin's "view can be understood more easily and correctly as a modification of Luther's rather than of Zwingli's view."

[10] Schmid-Hauck, *Dogmengesch.,* 4th ed., p. 405.

[11] *Consens. Tigur.,* XXV: "Because Christ's body, since it has the nature and mode of being of a human body, is finite and contained in heaven as a place, it necessarily follows that it is distant from us by as great an interval of space as heaven is from the earth" (Niemeyer, p. 196).

[12] *Consens. Tigur.,* XXII: "We repudiate as preposterous interpreters those who in the solemn words of the Supper, 'This is My body, this is My blood,' urge a precisely literal sense, as they say. For we hold it to be indisputable that these words are to be accepted figuratively, so that bread and wine are called that which they signify." (Niemeyer, p. 196.)

unio mystica, obtaining between Christ and believers, we call it the *unio sacramentalis.* This is the teaching of the Lutheran Church, as it is set forth in all brevity in Luther's Small Catechism. To the question "What is the Sacrament of the Altar?" the answer is given: "It is the true body and blood of our Lord Jesus Christ, under the bread and wine, for us Christians to eat and to drink, instituted by Christ Himself." Likewise Article X of the Augsburg Confession names both bread and wine and body and blood of Christ as present: "Of the Supper of the Lord they teach that the Body and Blood of Christ are truly present, and are distributed to those who eat in the Supper of the Lord; and they reject those that teach otherwise" (*Trigl.* 47).[13] In Article VII of the Formula of Concord we read: "We believe, teach, and confess that in the Holy Supper the body and blood of Christ are truly and essentially present, and are truly distributed and received with the bread and wine. We believe, teach, and confess that the words of the testament of Christ are not to be understood otherwise than as they read according to the letter [*ad literam*], so that the bread does not signify the absent body and the wine the absent blood of Christ, but that, on account of the sacramental union [*propter sacramentalem unionem*], they [the bread and wine] are truly the body and blood of Christ." (*Trigl.* 809, Epit., 6–7.)

Which of these three tenets is taught in Holy Writ?

The Roman dogma of transubstantiation is excluded by the fact that also after the "blessing" (consecration) of bread and wine those elements are still mentioned as present, e. g., 1 Cor. 11:27: "Whosoever shall eat this bread, and drink this cup of the Lord, unworthily, shall be guilty of the body and blood of the Lord." The Roman remonstrance that only the external form or semblance ("*species*") of the bread remains contradicts the words of Scripture, which specify not semblance of bread, but bread. We subscribe to Luther's verdict in the Smalcald Articles: "As regards transubstantiation, we care nothing about the sophistical subtlety by which they teach that bread and wine leave or lose their own natural substance, and that there remain only the appearance and color of bread, and not true bread. For it is in perfect agreement with Holy Scriptures that there is, and remains, bread, as Paul himself calls it, 1 Cor. 10:16: 'The bread which we

---

13 "*Unter der Gestalt*" in the German text does not mean "under the semblance of," but, as the Apology explains it, "with those things which are seen" (*cum illis rebus, quae videntur*) Christ's body and blood are tendered and received (*Trigl.* 247, X, 54). Cf. Bente, *L. u. W.,* 1918, p. 385 ff.: "Does the 10th Art. of the Augustana and the Apology Romanize?"

break.' And 1 Cor. 11:28: 'So let him eat of that bread.'" (*Trigl.* 493, Part III, Art. VI.) The Roman tactic of substituting semblance of bread for bread is so arbitrary that if one granted its validity, all of Scripture could be interpreted as meaning a mere external appearance or semblance.[14] Linked to the dogma of transubstantiation are the numerous abominations which the Roman Church perpetrates with its "Sacrament": the sacrifice of the Mass, in which purportedly the sacrifice of Christ on the Cross is continually being repeated in an unbloody manner; also the reservation of the host; the host "proposed [elevated] publicly to the people to be adored"; the adoration of the host; the host "solemnly borne about in processions" (Corpus Christi festival); the denial of the cup to the laity, defended with the dogma of concomitance. These points will be elaborated later.

The Reformed teaching of the absence of the body and blood of Christ from the Sacrament is not the doctrine of Scripture, because Holy Writ states that the body and blood of Christ are present not merely for the faith, but for the mouth of the communicants. With the words "Take, eat" Christ calls upon us to eat with the mouth, and asserts that what He puts into our mouth and we receive orally is His body and blood. The contention of the Reformed that Christ's body and blood are present not for the mouth, but only for our faith, robs the verbs "eat" and "drink" of the thing Christ connected with them. Chemnitz remarks: "When Christ says, 'Eat, drink,' He is prescribing the mode and manner of taking [*modum sumptionis*], namely, that we are to eat with the mouth [*ore sumamus*] what is present and given in the Lord's Supper. That the words 'eat' and 'drink' are to be understood of such an eating, no one can deny, unless he is also ready to abolish and subvert the entire external act of the Lord's Supper. . . . As to what is present in the Lord's Supper, what is given, what those receive with the mouth who eat, He declares and says expressly: 'This is My body, which is given for you; this is My blood, which is shed for you for the remission of sins.'" (*Fundamenta sanae doc-*

---

[14] Luther calls transubstantiation a "monk's dream, affirmed by Thomas Aquino and ratified by Popes," and adds: "Because they so insist on it from their own effrontery without Scripture, we will do nothing but oppose them and hold in spite of them that true bread and wine remains besides the body and blood of Christ . . . for the Gospel calls the Sacrament bread, thus: the bread is the body of Christ. By that we abide; it is sufficiently sure against all dreams of sophists that what it calls bread is bread. We are ready to risk being deceived by Scripture." (St. L. XIX:1320.) A few other utterances of Luther on transubstantiation: XIX:25 (copious); XIX:1302 ff. (a collation address "delivered impromptu on the contemptible article of transubstantiation"); XIX:1306 (letter to George of Anhalt).

trinae, etc., 1623, p. 12.) Of course, the words of institution contain also a very clear invitation to believe, or to eat spiritually. But this invitation follows on the oral eating and is based on it. The summons unto faith is contained in the words with which Christ describes the body given us to eat as the body "which is given for you." While receiving the body of Christ with their mouth, the disciples are to believe that through this body, given into death for them, they have a reconciled God, or the remission of sins. The summons unto faith is contained also in the words: "This do in remembrance of Me." Also this will be presented more fully later, particularly in the chapter on the purpose of the Lord's Supper (p. 373).

The Lutheran teaching of the Lord's Supper is the doctrine of Scripture, because it accepts at full value both the words pertaining to the presence of the bread as also the words pertaining to the presence of the body of Christ, without subtracting from them or adding to them. To state the matter antithetically: The Lutheran teaching does not, like Rome, make the bread imaginary bread ("species of bread"), nor does it, like the Reformed denominations, make the body of Christ an imaginary body, that is, an emblem or symbol of the absent body of Christ. It teaches a true, essential bread and the true, essential body of Christ in the Sacrament because the words of institution state both. But because of the opposite teaching of Rome and the Reformed we must enter upon this more fully.

First it is necessary to inquire: What manner of speech is Christ using when He gives the bread to His disciples and says of this bread, which they are to eat: "This is My body"? The classification of this remark has called forth much dispute. Prior to all popular or learned investigation it is certain that it must be easy to understand the words used by Christ. There can be no question of this because Christ at the institution and first celebration of the Supper adds no commentary whatever to His words. Had His words been at all difficult to understand, or had there been even the mere possibility of misunderstanding, Christ would have added the necessary exegesis. The omission of any commentary shows definitely that in the words: "Take, eat; this is My body, which is given for you," we are dealing with a mode of speech that will be understood without commentary at the mere hearing or reading. Christ here in the Lord's Supper uses a form of speech commonly employed by all normal people in passing objects to one another. This form of speech has therefore briefly and fittingly been termed *locutio exhibitiva.* When presenting an object, though it be complex, i. e., joined to another object, we mention only the object about which we are concerned and to which we would direct attention.

This *locutio exhibitiva* is in general use both in our daily intercourse and in Holy Scripture. Properly our Lutheran theologians remind us that in tendering food or drink in a vessel we do not mention both the vessel and the food or drink, but only the contents of the vessel. We would be regarded as eccentric and would arouse astonishment, were we to say in our daily life, e. g., in tendering water in a glass: Here is (1) a glass, (2) water. Everybody expects us to make mention only of the water in the predicate, saying: "Here is the water." [15] This is exactly how Christ is speaking when, in the words of institution: "Take, eat; this is My body," He does not mention in the predicate the bread that He took from the table and which His disciples saw with their eyes, but rather His body, which the disciples could not see, but to which He would direct their attention.

When Kirn (*Ev. Dogm.*, p. 130) makes the remark that Luther's "interpretation" of the words of institution "will always remain fanciful," he merely reveals that he has lost sight of the common usage prevalent among all normal people and also in his own home. The same is true of all theologians who declare Luther's "synecdoche" impossible and therefore abandon it.[16] This "synecdoche" practically amounts to what we have just said of the *locutio exhibitiva*. The mother at home, the merchant, the children outdoors and at play, in short, all normal people, in their intercourse with others are constantly employing the "synecdoche," though very few of course know the term. Luther's explanation of this form of speech in the words of institution is in brief: Bread and body are and remain distinct in essence or substance in the Lord's Supper. The changing of the bread into the body of Christ is a dream of the monks and sophists. But by Christ's word and institution the bread and the body of Christ are in the Lord's

---

[15] Thus, e. g., Haffenreffer (*Loci*, Tubing., 1606, p. 628): "It is a well-known usage not only in the Holy Scriptures, but in all tongues, that when two particular things which are joined are held out and shown, the total thing indeed, consisting of two, is held out and shown, yet the second one of them, which is not so exposed to the senses, is actually named; so that in handing a purse I say: Here are one hundred florins, or in pointing to a keg: This is Rhine wine, this Italian, this red wine, or in touching a glass I say: This is water, this beer, this salve, etc. All these examples show that the demonstrative pronoun 'hoc' embraces both, in fact, the vessel and the drink, and that because of the true union in that complex thing which is shown, the one part which is not so obvious to the senses can most truthfully be mentioned, while it can most truthfully be shown and exhibited by means of the other part united and joined with it."

[16] Meyer on Matt. 26:26 ff.; Loofs, R. E., 3d ed., I, 65—66.

Supper united with each other, a union that one may call *unio sacra-mentalis*. Because of this union we say of the bread in the Lord's Supper, as it is offered for eating: This is Christ's body. We are not denying that there is bread, but we name only the one part, the body of Christ, which is our chief concern, just as we do not say of a purse filled with one hundred florins: This is a purse and one hundred florins, but we merely name the one part, the hundred florins.

But let Luther himself tell us of his "synecdoche." He writes: "This manner of speaking of distinct substances as of one thing the grammarians call synecdoche, and it is very common, not only in Scripture, but in all languages. For instance, when I show or tender a pouch or purse, I say: This is a hundred florins. My showing of it and the word 'this' point to the purse; but since purse and florins are in a certain respect one essence, or one complex, my words refer also to the florins.[17] In the same manner I touch a cask and say: This is Rhine wine, this is French wine, this is red wine. Likewise I touch a glass and say: This is water, this is beer, this is salve, etc. In all these expressions you see how the word 'this' points to the vessel and still, because the drink and the vessel are in a way a unit, it pertains at the same time, yea, even principally, to the drink. . . . If now a sharp Wycliffite or sophist would laugh and say: 'You show me the purse and say: This is a hundred florins; how can a purse be a hundred florins?'; again, if he said: 'You show me a cask and say: This is wine. Friend, a cask is wood, and not wine, and a purse is leather, and not gold'; then even the children would laugh at him as a fool or a clown. For he tears the two united substances apart and insists on speaking of each one separately, while we are now in that manner of speech where two substances have become one thing. For the cask is now no longer simple wood or cask, but it is a cask of wine, and the purse is now no longer mere leather or purse, but a purse of gold or money. Of course, if you insist on separating the whole thing into its parts, disconnect gold and leather, then each piece is for itself, and we naturally will have to speak of it in a different manner, as, e. g.: This is gold, that is leather; this wine, that a cask. But if you let the two substances remain a unit, then you must also speak of it as a unit, point to the barrel or purse and say: That is gold, that is wine, because

---

17 When Luther in this connection speaks of "one essence" which bread and body of Christ become in the Lord's Supper, he of course has in mind not "one essence" by transubstantiation — for this you see him expressly reject here, too — but "one essence" in this respect that by Christ's Word and ordinance bread and body of Christ in the Lord's Supper are united unto "one complex," a unit. Hence also the added limitation "*aliquo modo*," in a certain respect one essence.

of the unity of the thing. For one should not listen to the cunning words of these sharp sophists, but observe the language, what manner, usage, and custom of speech prevails there.

"Now, since this mode of speech is common both to Scripture and all languages, the *praedicatio identica* [18] presents no difficulty in the Lord's Supper. There is none, in fact, but Wycliffe and the sophists have dreamed it. For although body and bread are two distinct natures, each taken by itself, and when they are separated, neither of course is the other, nevertheless, when they are united and become an entirely new thing, they lose their distinction as far as that new unity is concerned and in so far as they become and are one thing. Therefore they are also called and spoken of as one thing, without one of the two having to perish and cease to be, but both bread and body may remain; and because of the sacramental union it is right for Christ to say: 'This is My body,' while pointing with the word 'this' to the bread; for now it is no more common bread in the oven, but flesh bread or body bread, that is, bread which has become a sacramental substance and a unit with the body of Christ. And so it is right to say of the wine in the cup: 'This is my blood,' pointing with the word 'this' to the wine; for it is no longer mere wine in the cellar, but blood wine, that is, wine which constitutes a sacramental unit with the blood of Christ." (St. L. XX:1034.)

Therefore the criticism that if the words of institution, "This is My body, this is My blood," be taken literally, this must result in the Roman doctrine of transubstantiation because Christ mentions in the predicate not bread and body of Christ, or wine and blood of Christ, but only Christ's body and Christ's blood, is entirely unsound. This criticism of the Lutheran doctrine of the Lord's Supper is voiced not only by rationalists,[19] but also by Reformed theologians past and present. Hodge, too, says: "If the words of Christ are to be taken literally, they teach the doctrine of transubstantiation" (*Syst. Theol.* III, 662, note). How baseless this criticism is, becomes evident if we apply it to other Scripture statements in which the *locutio exhibitiva* is used. Thus Peter (Matt. 16:16) says of the Son of Man: "Thou art the Christ, the Son of the living God," and in Luke 1:35 the angel says to Mary: "That Holy Thing which shall be born of thee shall be called the Son of God." As the Son of Man and the Son of Mary is the Son of God, not through transubstantiation of the Son of Man into the

---

[18] Luther's full presentation of the *praedicatio identica* (St. L. XX:1026 ff.).

[19] Also by Meyer in his *Commentary*, on Matt. 26:26 ff. In the doctrine of the Lord's Supper Meyer did not shed his rationalism.

Son of God, nor through symbolization of the Son of God by the Son of Man, but through union — in this case through the *unio personalis* — so in the Lord's Supper the proffered bread is the body of Christ, not through transubstantiation of the bread into the body, nor through symbolization of the body of Christ by the bread, but through the union of the bread with the body of Christ, through the *unio sacramentalis*. Hence Hodge blunders in giving us the following instruction in logic and language: "If the bread is literally the body of Christ, it is no longer bread; for no one asserts that the same thing can be bread and flesh at the same time." Hodge himself furnishes the proof that his rule is faulty. He is known to maintain against the Unitarians that the Son of Mary is "literally" the Son of God, is "at the same time" both the Son of Mary and the Son of God. He correctly will *not* concede that a literal understanding of the sentence: "The Son of Mary is the Son of God," assumes a transubstantiation of the Son of Mary into the Son of God.

But there is another point regarding the Reformed antithesis in the doctrine of the Lord's Supper that should be ventilated. Today the cause of the schism of the Protestant Church at the time of the Reformation is usually laid to the disagreement between Luther and Zwingli in their teaching of the Lord's Supper. The Reformed teaching of the Lord's Supper has been called difficult to present. Hodge, e. g., opines: "It is a very difficult matter to give an account of the Reformed doctrine concerning the Lord's Supper satisfactory to all parties." On the causes of this difficulty amongst the Reformed Hodge reports: "They did all they could to conciliate Luther. They adopted forms of expression which could be understood in a Lutheran sense. So far was this irenical [?] spirit carried that even Romanists asked nothing more than what the Reformed conceded. Still another difficulty is that the Reformed were not agreed among themselves. There were three distinct types of doctrine among them, the Zwinglian, the Calvinistic, and an intermediate form, which ultimately became symbolical, being adopted in the authoritative standards of the Church." (*Syst. Theol.* III, 626.) But the disagreement among the Reformed in their teaching of the Lord's Supper must also not be unduly magnified. Shedd correctly remarks: "The difference between Zwingli and Calvin upon sacramentarian points has been exaggerated" (*Dogm. Theol.* II, 569). It is rather a disagreement in the expressions used, and particularly in the attempted proof of their teaching, than in the teaching itself.

In the main points one can easily prove a great unanimity among the Reformed. All agree that Christ's body and blood are not present in the Lord's Supper, but as far removed from it as is heaven from earth. There is general agreement also in their ultimate proof for the absence of Christ's body, namely, that Christ's body can at all times possess only a local and visible presence, that is, a presence not extending beyond the stature of man (*mensuram corporis, dimensionem corporis*). All therefore agree in this, too, that the words of institution cannot be taken literally, but must be understood figuratively. Hodge himself shows convincingly that Calvin and the Confessions influenced by him teach "a Real Presence" in the sense of the Lutheran Church just as little as did Zwingli (*Syst. Theol.* III, 628 ff.). Shedd furnishes the same proof (*Dogm. Theol.* II, 569 ff.; III, 464). Also the Formula of Concord declares that the Reformed agree in their views in spite of all divergences in their expressions (*Trigl.* 971, Sol. Decl., VII, 1—8). Calvin, it is true, at times says "that the Spirit really unites things separated by space" and *transfuses* into the believers Christ's "flesh and blood, just as if He actually penetrated every part of our frame" (*Inst.* IV, 17, 10, and often; Allen Transl. II, 533 f.). But this is no approximation to the Lutheran doctrine, for Lutherans know of no such "transfusion." It is (1) an intensified "enthusiasm," since Calvin has in mind an operation that is wholly imaginary, namely, an immediate operation of the Spirit; (2) an intensified endeavor to accommodate himself to the Scriptural and Lutheran manner of speech and to create the impression, as though he, too, were teaching a real, objective presence of the body and blood of Christ in the Lord's Supper.[20] In spite of what he says, Calvin declines to teach the "Real Presence" in the Lutheran sense, as Hodge correctly states.

But this is true: Though all Reformed agree in teaching the absence of Christ's body and blood, and accordingly permit bread and wine in the Supper to be only symbols of the absent body and blood of Christ, there is disagreement among them as to where in the sentence, "This is My body," the symbolism is located, whether in the "This," or in the "is," or in the words "My body."

Carlstadt tried his luck with the subject of the sentence, with the "This." Christ, he holds, with the "this" (τοῦτο) did not refer to the bread He gave to be eaten, but to His body seated at the table.[21] Luther reports: "Carlstadt made this of the text: 'This is My body,'

---

[20] Read, for instance, *Inst.* IV, 17, 19.
[21] Carlstadt's *"Dialogus oder Gespraechbuechlein"* (St. L. XX:2325). Peter, the layman, who plays the role of Carlstadt: "I have always imagined it in this manner, that Christ pointed to His body and said: This is that body of Mine which is given for you. For Christ did not point to the bread." Again col. 2328.

meant as much as: Here My body is seated. And the text should then read: He took the bread, gave thanks and brake it, and gave it to His disciples and said: Here My body is seated, which is given for you." (St. L. XX:1771 f.)

Zwingli is dissatisfied with Carlstadt's exegetical manipulation. He declares his dissent rather vigorously. He indeed praises the pious intention which Carlstadt's interpretation of the "this" manifests; however, he adds that this interpretation appeared to be "thoroughly preposterous," since Christ manifestly is not speaking of His body seated at the table, but calling what He is giving His disciples to eat His body. Zwingli therefore advises us to let go of the "this," and instead to take hold of the "is" immediately following it, particularly since it, too, has only three letters [*hoc — est*], hence the difference in this respect would not be great. "Is" stands for "signifies," meaning: The bread that I give you to eat signifies (*significat*) My body. Zwingli writes: "Therefore the whole burden does not lie on this demonstrative 'this,' but on another, which in the number of letters is no greater, namely, on the little word 'is,' which is used for 'signifies' in not a few places of Holy Writ." [22]

Oecolampadius and Calvin, however, prefer to take the predicate noun "My body" in a figurative sense, meaning: The bread that I give you to eat is *signum corporis,* an image, or symbol, of My body.

Carlstadt with his "Tuto," as Luther tersely calls this opposition, found few followers. Schenkel (R. E., 1st ed., I, 35) is quite angry at Carlstadt. He is of the opinion that Carlstadt's "absurd contention" so roiled and embittered Luther that he could no more weigh the position of his other opponents fairly. Schenkel writes: "It was a misfortune that a man like Carlstadt had to irritate Luther to the utmost and embitter him by his absurd contention that with the words of institution Jesus pointed to His body then locally present. By this interpretation Carlstadt managed to explain away entirely the presence of the body and blood of Christ in the Sacrament of the Altar. . . . For this reason the terrific anger of Luther . . . and his vehement utterances in his book *Against the Heavenly Prophets.*" Carlstadt's reference of the words, "This is My body," to Christ's body, seated at the table, is indeed bald arbitrariness. Cf. Luther, St. L. XX:210 ff.

But it is no less arbitrary when Zwingli interprets "is" as "signifies," because in no human tongue can the copula "is" have this meaning. Luther (XX:909 ff.) is entirely right in saying: "This is a sure rule in

---

[22] Zwingli's *Meinung vom Nachtmahl Christi* (St. L. XX:470). Latin in *De vera et falsa religione, Opp.* III, 255.

all languages: Where the little verb 'is' is used in speaking, there the true nature of the thing is certainly spoken of, and not what it may symbolize." In other words, where the verb "is" is employed, men are always speaking of what the thing really is and not what it is a figure of. The human tongue would cease to be a medium for the exchange of thoughts if "is" were not to mean "is," but something else. "Language itself would commit suicide if it could tolerate the idea that the substantive verb shall express not substance, but symbol" (Krauth, *Conserv. Reformation*, p. 619).[23] The view, held by many in the past and in the present, that the copula "is" means "signifies" is a consequence of the intellectual weakness of man since the fall into sin. That fall has exerted a baneful influence also on man's logic. In fact, all of us, as members of sinful mankind, have every reason constantly to test our logic. But if we by God's grace use that remnant of logic which God's goodness has salvaged for us from the Fall, we can still recognize that "is" is not used in the sense of "signifies" in those Scripture passages which the Reformed adduce as their principal proofs in the controversy on the doctrine of the Lord's Supper. Even some of the Reformed grant this, as we shall see.[24]

However, from Zwingli on to our day a longer or shorter catalog of Scripture texts has been compiled in which "is" is supposed to stand for "signifies." [25] The principal passages adduced are: John 10:9: "I am the Door"; John 15:5: "I am the Vine"; 1 Cor. 10:4: "That spiritual Rock that followed them . . . was Christ." Especially also Luke 8:11: "The seed is the Word of God"; Matt. 13:38: "The field is the world"; Matt. 11:14: "This [John the Baptist] is Elias"; Gal. 4:24: "These are the two covenants." Zwingli even holds that one becomes a blasphemer (*blasphemus*) if he does not take "is" to mean "signifies" in these passages.[26]

But Zwingli's ardor is far greater than the quality of his logic. The very texts he adduces prove that "is" does not stand for "signifies." When it is said: Christ is the Door, the Vine, the Rock, etc., there is in these sentences, of course, a figurative expression (*tropus*).

---

[23] Hollaz: "*Copula verbalis 'est' non est capax tropi*. For if the copula *est* lost its signification of connecting or uniting the predicate with the subject and assumed another meaning, also the proposition would be destroyed, so that it is no longer a proposition" (*Examen, De euchar.*, qu. 7).

[24] Also Meyer, though from rationalistic principles he adopts the Reformed teaching, says *ad* 1 Cor. 10:16: "ἐστί never means anything else than *est*, never *significat*; it is the copula of essence."

[25] Zwingli's catalog, *Opp.* III, 256 ff.

[26] *Ad Joh. Bugenhagii Pomerani epistolam responsio, Opp.* III, 606.

However, it is not in the copula "is," but in the predicate noun "Door," "Vine," "Rock." Christ does not signify the door, but really is the Door. Of course, not an ordinary door leading from a St. Louis street into a home on that street, but a spiritual Door, namely the Door by which men enter into the Kingdom of God. As Christ Himself immediately explains His words: "I am the Door: by Me, if any man enter in, he shall be saved." The word "door," as Luther expresses it, has become a "new word." Meanwhile, however the copula "is" retains its first and only meaning: it expresses the essence, what Christ actually is, the spiritual Door into the Kingdom of God. The same thing holds true of the other examples adduced. Christ does not signify a vine, but is the spiritual Vine, on which the spiritual branches, the Christians, are growing by faith. Again Christ did not typify the rock, but really was the spiritual Rock (πνευματικὴ πέτρα) that accompanied Israel through the desert.[27]

Also when we are dealing with pictures "is" remains is. True, we say, pointing to a picture of Peter: "That is Peter." But our words do not mean: This picture signifies Peter; they rather mean: The object portrayed is Peter, or, This is a painting or portrait of Peter. (Luther, St. L. XX:988, 990.) Here, too, Peter has become a "new word," i. e., the trope is in the word "Peter." Moreover, all Scripture passages which bring parables or allegories belong to the category of pictures. Christ spoke to the people in parables (ἐν παραβολαῖς, διὰ παραβολῆς, Matthew 13; Luke 8), and Christ parabolizes, or says figuratively: "The seed is the Word of God" (Luke 8:11), and: "The field is the world" (Matt. 13:38). Here, too, the sense is not: Natural seed is an image of God's Word, but: The thing pictured in the parable as natural seed is the Word of God. Likewise a field does not typify the world, but the thing pictured as a field in the parable is the world. "Seed" and "field" have become "new words," i. e., contain the trope.

In Gal. 4:22 ff. St. Paul says of Hagar, the bondwoman, and her son, and Sarah, the freewoman, and her son: "These are the two covenants," the covenant of the Law from Mount Sinai and the covenant of promise. But thus Paul speaks of Hagar and Sarah, etc., allegorically or figuratively: "Which things are an allegory."[28] Here, too, the

---

[27] Meyer on 1 Cor. 10:3-4: "That ἦν here means 'significabat,' as also Augustine, Bengel, and others assume, is an entirely arbitrary assumption."

[28] Gerhard, Loci, "De coena," § 95: "The trope is not in the copula, but an allegorical use of the story is indicated." Stock in his Commentary on the passage: "By this story the Holy Ghost wanted to describe something in a more sublime manner." The historical facts to which reference was had were types of other things.

sense is: The thing portrayed, or typified, by Hagar, the bondwoman, is the covenant from Mount Sinai with its bondservants, and the thing portrayed, or typified, by Sarah, the freewoman, is the covenant of promise, or of the Gospel, which does not give birth to servants, but to children.

Luther (St. L. XX:905 ff.) discourses on the question whether "is" means "signifies," as follows: "Further to instruct you who are on our side, you should know that it is pure fiction, no matter who says it, that the little word 'is' means as much as 'signifies.' Nobody can ever prove this to be the case in even one place of Scripture; yes, I shall go farther: if the 'enthusiasts' bring a single sentence from all languages on earth in which 'is' has the meaning 'signifies,' they shall have won. But they simply can't. Those high spirits fail to consider properly the rhetoric, grammar, or, as they call it, the tropes, as taught in the elementary school. This art teaches a boy how to make two and three words out of one word, or how he may give one and the same word a new use and more meanings. For instance, to prove it by a few examples: The word 'flower' according to its first and old meaning means a rose, lily, violet, and the like, growing out of the earth and blooming. If now I desire to praise Christ with a fine compliment and take note how He comes from the Virgin Mary so pretty a child, I may take the word 'flower' and make a trope, or give it a new meaning and use, and say: 'Christ is a Flower.' Here all grammarians or teachers of speech say that 'flower' has become a *new* word and has a new meaning and now no longer means a flower in the field, but the Child Jesus, and that one must here not claim a figurative sense for the word 'is'; for Christ does not signify a flower, but He is a flower, though a different flower than the natural one. For so says the poet Horatius: '*Dixeris egregie, notum si callida verbum reddiderit iunctura novum*' (*De arte poetica*, vv. 47, 48), that is, It is choice speech when you can give a fine new sense to a common word. From this we have the rule that a word becomes two or many words if, in addition to its common meaning, it gets another, a new meaning. For example, flower is one word when it means Christ, and another when it means a natural rose or such, again another when it means a golden, or silver, or wooden rose. So, when you say of a stingy man: He is a hound, here 'hound' is used as name for a niggardly skinflint, and the old word has become a new word according to the teaching of Horace, and one must not make 'signifies' out of 'is'; for the miser is not a figure of a hound. In this manner people speak in all languages and give words a new meaning, as when we say: Mary is an aurora; Christ is a fruit of the womb; the devil is the god of this world; the Pope is Judas; St. Augustine is Paul; St. Bernard is a dove; David is a little grub, and so on; Scripture is full of such speech. It is called trope or metaphor in grammar when one gives two different things one and the same name because of a similarity in the two; and though that name then is in appearance only one word, it is *potestate ac significatione plura,* according to the strength, use, meaning, two words, an old and a new, as Horace says and the children well know. We Germans are accustomed to add to such new words 'real' or 'another' or 'new' and to say: You are a real hound, the monks are real Pharisees, the nuns are real daughters of Moab, Christ is a real Solomon. Again, Luther is another Huss, Zwingli is another Korah, Oecolampadius is a new Abiram. In such expressions, as all Germans will bear me out and acknowledge, there are new words, and it makes no difference how I say it: Luther is Huss, or Luther is another Huss, or Luther is a real Huss, or Luther is a new Huss. Thus one feels how a new word is made of the former according to the teaching of Horace, for it neither fits nor sounds right [*es klappt noch klingt nicht*] if I say: Luther signifies Huss, but: he is a Huss. One is speaking of the essence in such statements, what one is, and not what he signifies, and one makes a new word to fit his new essence. Thus you will find it in all languages, of that I am sure, and so all grammarians teach and the boys in school know, and you will nevermore find that 'is' may mean 'signify.' Now, when Christ says: John is Elias, no one can prove that John signifies Elias; for it would also be ridiculous that John should signify Elias, since Elias could much rather typify John. And to follow Zwingli's art, Christ would have to invert it and say: Elias is John, that is, he signifies John. However, Christ wants to say what John is, not what he signifies, but what sort of nature or office he has, and so He says, he is Elias. Here Elias has become a new word, and does not mean the old Elias, but the new Elias, as we Germans say: John is a true Elias, John is another Elias, John is a new Elias. In like manner it is said: Christ is a Rock, that is, He has a nature like, and truly is, a Rock, nevertheless a new Rock, another Rock, a true Rock. Again: Christ is a true Vine. My friend, what sense would it make were you to interpret this according to Zwingli's notion, thus: Christ signifies the true vine? Who, then, is the true vine of which Christ is the image? So I really hear that Christ is supposed to be a sign or type of the wood in the vineyard? My, that would be a fine thing! Why, then, did not Christ rather say it this way: The true Vine is Christ, meaning: the wooden vine signifies Christ? It certainly is more fitting that a thing should be an emblem of Christ than that He should be a symbol of a thing, since the thing that symbolizes always is lowlier than the thing of which it is a symbol, and all signs are less than the thing they point to, as even fools and children know very well. But Zwingli does not take note of the word '*vera*' in this passage: Christ is the true Vine. If he would consider that word, he could not have made 'signify' out of the 'is.' For neither language nor reason would suffer one's saying that Christ signifies the true vine. For no one would think of saying that in this passage the true vine is the wood in the vineyard. So the text simply forces us to take 'vine' here as a new word, meaning another, a new, a true vine, and not the vine in the vineyard. Accordingly 'is' can here not be 'signifies,' but Christ really is, and has the nature of, a true, a new vine. Though, even if the text read: Christ is a Vine, it would make no good sense to say: Christ signifies a vine, but rather the vine ought to signify Christ. Again, the passage: Christ is the Lamb of God, John 1:29, cannot be understood to say: Christ signifies the Lamb of God, for then Christ, as the sign, would be less than the Lamb of God. But what, then, would be the Lamb of God signified by Christ? Perhaps the paschal lamb? But in that case, why does he not invert it and more fittingly say: The Lamb of God is Christ, that is, the paschal lamb signifies Christ, as Zwingli interprets? Now, however, since the phrase 'of God' is added to the word 'Lamb,' it forces one to admit that 'Lamb' here is another, a new word, means another, a new, and the true Lamb, which Christ really is, and not the old paschal lamb. And so on, whatever more examples they bring, as: The seed is the Word of God, Luke 8:11 ff.; the field is the world, etc., Matt. 13:38; they cannot on good grounds make 'signify' out of the 'is,' but the children in school will say, that 'seed' and 'field' are *tropi*, or new words by metaphor. For *vocabulum simplex* [original meaning] *et metaphoricum* [derived meaning] are not one word, but two. Thus 'seed' here does not mean corn or wheat, but God's Word, and 'field' means the world, for Christ, the text itself says, is speaking in parables, and not of natural corn or wheat. But whoever speaks in parables, is making of simple words nothing but *tropos*, new and other words; else they would not be parables, if He used the simple words in their original meaning. He is an insane, irrational spirit who would take the words in parables in their common meaning, contrary to the nature and character of parables; he must then, of course, seek to make the thing work by subtilization and delusion."

When the *Apologete* of the Methodists here in the United States became very aggressive in its figurative interpretation of the words of institution, Walther in 1848 wrote in *Der Lutheraner,* p. 93 f.: "In Holy Writ certain things or persons are frequently given names which in their original meaning do not fit them. To people who are ignorant of the rules of language it seems at first sight, therefore, that the little word 'is' very often is used for 'signifies.' And sad to say, since the days of Zwingli even many scholars who know the rules of language well have deceitfully taken advantage of the ignorance of people and as proof for a figurative meaning of 'is' have adduced such passages as: 'I am the Vine, I am the Door, the Rock was Christ, John is Elias,' etc. They have said: Everyone knows, of course, that Christ is not really a vine, not really a door, not really a rock, and that John the Baptist was not really the old prophet Elias; they were this only figuratively; therefore in all these, and similar, passages 'is' must stand for 'signifies.' But this deduction is a paralogism. The words 'vine,' 'door,' 'rock,' 'Elias,' and such, have two meanings, namely, their literal meaning and a figurative or tropical meaning. First, then, vine means a climbing plant, on which shoots and branches grow, which it bears, supplies with sap, and on which it produces grapes, from which the refreshing wine is made. Secondly, one also calls such things a 'vine' with which other things are so intimately united that they are borne by them, draw their life from them, and by them are made fruitful. Now, when Christ says: 'I am the Vine,' He does not mean to say: 'I signify a vine' — it would be blasphemy to assert that Christ is the symbol of an ordinary vine, therefore less than an ordinary vine — no, Christ rather means: I am the true Vine, not such a one as you find in the garden, but the one that is come from heaven; for with Me My believers are so intimately united that they draw their life from Me and by Me are filled with fruit.

"Furthermore, the word 'door,' too, has a twofold meaning. First, of course, it means the opening through which one enters a house. But, secondly, it also means everything through which one enters into something. Now, when Christ says: 'I am the Door,' He does not mean, 'I signify a door,' but I am He through whom alone one can enter into the Kingdom of Grace and Glory; I am not the symbol of this door, but actually am the true, the real Door into heaven.

"Again, the word 'rock' first of all means a large, firm, solid mass of stone. The second meaning of this word is everything that stands without wavering, on which one can therefore firmly build and trust. When, then, Paul writes: 'That spiritual Rock that followed them . . . was Christ,' he does not want to say that a rock followed them which signified Christ, but that the fathers in traveling through the wilderness had a Companion on whom they could rely as on a true, solid Rock and out of whom, as out of a rock, the true, crystal-clear, refreshing water gushed to refresh them, and this very Rock was Christ; on which account Paul calls Christ not merely a rock, but 'the spiritual Rock.' But who would say that Christ *is* not the spiritual Rock, but merely signifies a spiritual rock?

"Finally, the word 'Elias' first of all stands for the well-known prophet of the days of King Ahab. In its second sense, however, it means in general a man who with burning zeal and unusual intrepidity condemns all sin and all error. When now it is said of John the Baptist, 'He is Elias,' this is not to mean, he signifies Elias, but he is a real Elias, that is, a man who with burning zeal and unusual intrepidity reproves sin and error.

"These our remarks, we hope, have clearly shown our readers that one cannot prove from such (and similar) passages as 'Christ is the Vine,' etc., that the word 'is' in Holy Writ ever means 'signifies.' The chief reason, to state it briefly once more, is this: Those passages do not speak of a material vine, or rock, or door, or the first Elias, but all these terms are used in a new, altered, tropical, figurative sense. Now, as certainly as Christ, of course, is not a vine, rock, or door in the first or original sense of these words, so certainly Christ really is, and does not merely signify, what these words mean in their tropical, or figurative, sense; that is, Christ really is the divine Vine, the Door to heaven, the spiritual Rock, and John a second Elias (that is, as Luke 1:17 explains, a man 'in the spirit and power of Elias').

"The little word 'is' therefore always keeps its first and only meaning in Holy Scripture. Hence, whenever Holy Scripture says that a thing is this or that, we can firmly and without doubting rely upon that fact. Consider how worthless the Bible would be if one could not depend upon this little word? Then none, not even one, of the truths revealed in Holy Writ would be stable; in vain we would then read in our Bible: There is a God, there is a Judgment, there is a hell, there is a heaven, Christ is God's Son, etc. For if 'is' could be taken to mean 'signifies,' who could then prevent an unbelieving exegete from making of God, Judgment, hell, heaven, Son of God, etc., nothing but empty signs?"

In a similar vein another Lutheran theologian of America, Krauth (*The Conservative Reformation,* p. 618 f.), wrote: "A more dangerous falsity in interpretation than the assumption that the word 'is' may be explained in the sense of 'signify' or 'be a symbol of' is hardly conceivable. Almost every doctrine of the Word of God will melt under it. 'The Word was God,' would mean: 'The Word signified, was a symbol of God.' 'God is a Spirit,' would mean: 'God is a symbol of the Spirit.' When it is said of Jesus Christ: 'This is the true God,' it would mean that He is the symbol or image of the true God. By it Christ would cease to be the Way, the Truth, and the Life, and would be a mere symbol of them; would no longer be the Door, the Vine, the Good Shepherd, the Bishop of souls, but would be the symbol of a door, the sign of a vine, the figure of a shepherd, the representation of a bishop. This characteristic use of 'is' is essential to the very morality of language, and language itself would commit suicide if it could tolerate the idea that the substantive verb shall express not substance, but symbol. Creation, redemption, and sanctification would all fuse and be dissipated in the crucible of this species of interpretation. It would take the Bible from us, and lay upon our breasts, cold and heavy, a Swedenborgian nightmare of correspondences. The Socinian and the Pelagian and all errorists of all schools would triumph in the throwing of everything into hopeless confusion, and the infidel would feel that the Book he has so long feared and hated, deprived, as it now would be, of its vitality by the trick of interpreters, could henceforth be safely regarded with contempt. Well might Luther write upon the table at Marburg: 'This is My Body'; simple words, framed by infinite wisdom so as to resist the violence and all the ingenuity of men. Rationalism in vain essays to remove them with its cunning, its learning, and its philosophy. Fanaticism gnashes its teeth at them in vain."

It is evident, then, that Zwingli and all his followers deceive themselves and others when they hold that "is" "is used in numerous places for 'signifies.' " [29] A number of the older Reformed theologians

---

[29] Even in the passage Gen. 41:26: "The seven good kine are seven years," this meaning cannot be established. Correctly Luther and the Lutherans have contended that, even if somewhere in Scripture the copula "is" were used for "signifies," this use would still be no proof that the same thing must hold true in the words of institution of the Lord's Supper. Luther, St. L. XX:576 f.: "For there is a world of difference whether I say, This may have that meaning, or say, This must have that meaning and cannot have another. On the former my conscience cannot rely, on the latter, however, it can rely." But for good reasons *significat* is declined as the meaning of *est* also in Gen. 41:26. Do not forget that also this passage belongs to the category of pictures. We are here concerned with a vision in a dream, hence with a picture that Pharaoh saw in a dream. Now, as we say of a picture of Luther: "That is Luther," not in the sense: This picture signifies Luther, but in the sense: What is portrayed in that picture is Luther, or: That is a portrait of Luther, so we also say of the picture of the seven years, namely, the seven kine, that they are seven years, namely in the sense: The thing portrayed by the seven kine are seven years. Luther, *ibid.*,

have therefore rejected the interpretation of *est* as *significat*. Thus Keckermann (d. 1609) says: "Others are of the opinion that the trope is in the copula. But this, too, cannot be substantiated." [30] A greater sensation it was when the more prominent Herborn theologian, John Piscator (d. 1625), came out against interpreting *est* with *significat*. Piscator had previously fought very determinedly for *est* in the sense of *significat*. He had written: "The metonymy is either in the subject, or in the predicate, or in the copula of the sentence. Now it is neither in the subject nor in the predicate. Therefore it is in the copula." (Scherzer, *op. cit.*, p. 574.) But when Piscator had read the refutation of Daniel Hofmann of Helmstedt (d. 1611), he frankly admitted that he had been in error, and he declared "that in the copula 'is' there can be no trope" (*in copula est non posse esse tropum*), that he was therefore retracting his former opinion before continuing the struggle, though he felt plainly (*persentisco*) that he was hurting himself somewhat for further combat by this retraction. Schenkel holds that Zwingli correctly recognized "the figurative sense" ["*das Tropische*"] of the words of institution, but that "he connects it somewhat clumsily exclusively with the copula and illustrates it with Biblical examples which in part were very unsuitable" (R. E., 1st ed., I, 26).

But also the third view, which placed the trope in the predicate noun "body," taking "body" to mean "symbol of My body," is entirely

---

XX:909: "Thus, too, the passage from Genesis, 'The seven good kine are seven years; and the seven good ears are seven years.' Because the text itself says that it is speaking of a dream, of a parable or figure of seven years, we, too, must here let the words 'seven kine, seven ears' be *metaphorae* and new words and mean the identical thing as the words 'seven years,' so that the term 'seven years' according to its ordinary meaning and the term 'seven kine' according to its new meaning mean the same thing. For these 'seven kine' are not merely a symbol of seven years, but are themselves really and truly the seven years; for they are not natural cows, eating grass in the meadow, which of course in the old, common meaning of the term would be called 'seven kine.' But here it has become a new word, and they are seven kine of famine and of plenty, that is, seven years of famine and of plenty. In short, they may indeed adduce passages and assert: Here there is a figurative meaning ["*Deutelei*"] in the copula; but they will never in one instance prove it." Rodatz, in the *Zeitschrift* of Rudelbach-Guericke, 1843, p. 77: "In the matter under consideration parables, visions, and dreams manifestly come under one heading. . . . Living, natural cows cannot, it is true, be years; however, dream cows, dream pictures of cows, can very well. What Pharaoh saw performing in a dream were in appearance cows, in reality years symbolized by that image, since periods of time as such cannot be envisioned by the imagination. The 'seven kine' indeed were not natural years already passed, nevertheless certainly years symbolized through a prophetic vision; such years they actually were, and this, first of all, that expression 'Seven kine are seven years' states."

[30] *Syst. Theol.* III, 8, p. 444; in Scherzer, *Collegium Anti-Calvinianum*, Leipzig, 1704, p. 573; in Gerhard, *Loci*, "*De coena*," § 76.

arbitrary. For one thing, Christ does not say: Take, eat; this is the symbol of My body, but "This is My *body* (τὸ σῶμά μου)." This is the unanimous report of all the holy writers who record the institution of the Holy Supper. Matthew: τοῦτό ἐστι τὸ σῶμά μου; Mark: τοῦτό ἐστι το σῶμά μου; Luke: τοῦτό ἐστι τὸ σῶμά μου; Paul: τοῦτό μου ἐστὶ τὸ σῶμα. Not one of them substitutes "symbol of body" for body. Luther certainly is right in urging this fact, when he writes: "Since all the Evangelists so harmoniously use these words 'this is My body' in all simplicity, one can see that there indeed can be no figurative speech or any trope in them. For if there were any sort of trope in them, someone of the holy writers certainly would have indicated by at least one letter that it might have another wording or meaning. Just as they are known to do in other matters, where one states what the other omits." (St. L. XX:1046 f.) Secondly, Luke describes the body which Christ gives us to eat in the Lord's Supper more definitely by the relative clause "which is given for you." It was not a symbol of His body, but Christ's body itself, the very body He assumed from the Virgin Mary, which was given for us.[31]

Here again there are some Reformed who declare the interpretation of "body" as "symbol of body" to be utterly impossible. Even "the second Calvin," Beza, publicly opposed Oecolampadius' and Calvin's "symbol of the body." He says that if "body" were to be taken in the sense of "symbol of the body," mention of this by the writers would have been necessary to avoid deceiving the readers.[32] Beza here argues just like Luther and the Lutherans. He says expressly that "body" could not stand for "symbol of the body," but had to mean the true, substantial, or essential body, because the "body" was more closely defined in the words of institution themselves as the body "which is given for you," and likewise the blood is defined more closely by the clause "which is shed for you." Beza also opposes those — to add this fact immediately — who, like Calvin and other Reformed theologians, make free to substitute "the fruit and effect of the death

[31] Hollaz, *Examen*, qu. 7: "Neither does the trope lie in *corpus* or *sanguinem* because of the definition 'which is given for you.' For by the term 'body and blood' this is designated which was given into death for us and shed for us for the remission of sins. Now, certainly not a sign of a body, a tropical or figurative body, but the real and true body of Christ was given into death for us; and not a tropical or figurative blood, but the real and true blood of Christ was shed for us for the remission of sins."

[32] Beza, *Hom. 2. de coena* (in Gerhard, *Loci*, "De coena," § 76): "I grant that here there is no trope, because it was imperative that the sign be properly *explained* if we were not to be deceived."

of Christ" for Christ's "body" and "blood." Hodge, too, takes this liberty: "Therefore, to receive the body and blood as offered in the Sacrament . . . is to receive and appropriate the sacrificial virtue or effects of the death of Christ on the cross" (*Syst. Theol.* III, 646). Of this substitute, too, Beza remarks: "It would certainly be absurd to interpret the words 'body' and 'blood' as the fruit and effect of the death of the Lord." The absurdity of this interpretation Beza strikingly demonstrates thus: "Well, let us substitute that interpretation for the words 'body' and 'blood' and say: This is the effect of my death, which is given for you, and this is My Spirit, which is shed for you! Can there be anything more absurd [*ineptius*] than such talk? For the words 'which is given for you' certainly impel [*adigunt*] you of necessity to understand these words of the substance of the body and blood of Christ." [33]

Nevertheless, probably a majority of the Reformed teachers are convinced that it is an indubitably correct usage to substitute the figure, or symbol, for the thing symbolized or signified, and that one might practice this trope (*signum pro signato,* or *signatum pro signo*) without arousing the suspicion of seeking to deceive. They do not agree with Beza when he says that if "body" were to mean "symbol of body," this fact should have been stated; otherwise the statement would amount to a deception. Boehl calls upon Oriental usage for help. He says: "The Oriental treats the image, or symbol, just like the thing represented by it. The symbol is alive for him, and there is no such sharp distinction between the symbol and the thing symbolized as there is for an Occidental." (*Dogmatik,* p. 568.) But Boehl is unfair to the Oriental. As fertile an imagination as the Oriental may have, he will substitute the image for the thing itself as little as will the Occidental or the rest of mankind. If someone said to an Arab, for example: "This is a date," this Oriental would think of a real, substantial date, since he, like all other people, always takes the words of human speech first in their original meaning. If one, after uttering the words "This is a date," shows him a picture of a date, he would immediately see, and most likely also say, that that is something entirely different from what was told him first. And if, with Boehl, one sought to make him believe that "the Oriental treats the image,

[33] *Epist. 5. ad Alemannum,* p. 57, ed. Genev. (in Gerhard, § 76). Cf. Heppe, *sub* Beza, R. E., 2d ed., II, 363, and *Dogmatik d. ref. K.,* p. 469. In his treatise against Flacius (*Adv. Illyricum,* p. 127) Beza says: "We doubt not that by the appellation 'body' that very body assumed for us and crucified is meant." Gerhard adds, *loc. cit.:* "The same thing Zanchius, Grynaeus, Pezelius, Sadeel, Crellius, and Paraeus acknowledge."

or symbol, just like the thing represented by it," he would take that to be either a witticism or an insult. He would say that we, either in play or in earnest, sought to deceive him. We must, then, if we would not deceive ourselves and others, maintain: In content these are two entirely different statements, if I indeed twice use the same words: "This is a date," but the first time by "date" mean a real date, the second time the image of a date. This is what Luther gave Oecolampadius to consider when he wrote: "Therefore Oecolampadius cannot pass muster with his trope, that these two statements should amount to the same thing: 'This is My body,' and: 'This is My body's symbol'; for that no language will permit" (St. L. XX:990).

Here the Reformed have argued that it is not necessary in order to avoid misunderstandings, always to announce that one is speaking figuratively or tropically.[34] And to substantiate this assertion they add: If we show someone the picture of a certain person, for example of "Charles," and in doing it say: "This is Charles," everyone immediately knows that we are not concerned with Charles in person, but with a representation of Charles.[35] Now, it is true, in that case a misunderstanding is excluded. But why? Because we display Charles' picture and so, by showing the picture, from the outset announce that we have in mind a picture of Charles and not the real Charles. If the exhibiting of the picture did not show that we have in mind a picture or portrait of Charles, everyone, on hearing the words: "This is Charles," would think first of Charles in person. Hence, when the Reformed teachers, as they all do, come with the example of pictures (e. g., "This is Peter") and operate against the literal understanding of the words of institution, "This is My body," with Scripture passages that speak in parables, type, and allegories (as: "The field is the world"), they are attempting to prove their point in a manner that is 100 per cent illusion and deception. They are perpetrating

---

[34] Thus Zwingli in his *Answer to Bugenhagen* (*Opp.* III, 606). Bugenhagen had called attention to the fact that in the words of institution we are not dealing with a vision or a parable.

[35] Thus Zwingli says in his *Subsidium* (*Opp.* III, 345): Though we say of a picture or statue of Peter: "That is Peter," everyone immediately is aware that it is not the real Peter, but a picture of Peter. And Zwingli regrets that this argument did not occur to him sooner, that is, when he was writing his *Commentarius*. He imagines that if he had embodied this argument in his *Commentarius*, he would have made such an impression with it that the controversy would have ended and he been acknowledged as victor. "These are things which either escaped us when we hurried with the *Commentarius*, or came into our mind later. If they had been added at that time, they would perhaps so have furthered the attack that, the war being ended, we would now pass the time tranquilly."

a *petitio principii,* that is, they take for granted that in the Lord's Supper we are concerned with nothing but a symbol of body and blood. They take for granted what they are to prove and promise to prove.[36]

To expose this delusion our Lutheran teachers call to mind the following hermeneutical rule, a reminder which some call tiresome, but which is nevertheless very necessary: Every word must be taken in its first, that is, its proper meaning, until circumstances contained in the context or an express declaration of the writer compel one to substitute the figurative or symbolic meaning for the natural. If this principle were not observed, human language would cease to be a medium of intercourse. We would forever be in doubt whether a statement is to be taken literally or figuratively, that is, we would not know what the speaker or writer actually means. As the interchange of "signifies" and "is," so also the interchange of the sign and the signified (*signum pro signato,* or *signatum pro signo*) results in "suicide" of language. Therefore Luther objected to Oecolampadius' substitution of *signum corporis* for *corpus:* "Furthermore it is not true that this trope of Oecolampadius obtains in any common speech or language of the whole world; and him who can furnish me a positive example of such a trope, I'll give the right to behead me" (St. L. XX:988).

All men, the Oriental and the Occidental, actually deal with one another according to the rule that every word must be taken in its first or proper sense until plainly manifest circumstances or an express declaration demand the figurative meaning. When we hear the word "door," we think of an opening leading into a house. But if we hear Christ say of Himself: "I am the Door," then we know from Scripture

---

36 Thus Riissen says (*Turretini compendium auctum et illustratum* XVII, 51; in Heppe, *Dogm. d. ref. K.,* p. 468): "A mode of speaking that is very common in all languages is to ascribe the signified to the sign (*signatum praedicatur de signo*) and to give the name of the former to the latter." And then he adduces nothing but Scripture texts in which Scripture speaks in pictures and parables and imagines thus to have proved that also the words in the Lord's Supper, "*Hoc est corpus meum, hic est sanguis meus,*" must be taken figuratively. He adduces the examples commonly current among the Reformed: "Seven kine are said to be seven years (Gen. 41:26). The bones are called the house of Israel (Ezek. 37:11). The four beasts are four kings, and the ten horns are ten kings (Dan. 7:17, 23, 24; 8:20-21). Thus Matt. 13:38-39 the field is the world; the good seed are the children of the Kingdom, the enemy is the devil, the harvest is the end of the world, the reapers are the angels, etc. And Rev. 1:20 the seven stars are seven angels, the seven candlesticks are seven churches, and ch. 17:9 seven heads are seven mountains, ten horns are ten kings (v. 12). The woman whom you saw is a great city (v. 18), etc."

that Christ is not a natural door leading into a house, but the spiritual Door, through which men are to enter the Kingdom of God. The same holds true of all Scripture texts in which Christ is called the Vine, the Rock, the Way, the Light of the world, etc. Again, if we hear the word "temple," we think of a building of stone, wood, etc. When Christ, however, says to the Jews, "Destroy this temple, and in three days I will raise it up," Scripture itself adds the declaration: "He spake of the temple of His body" (John 2:19-22). When we hear the words "seed," "field," "harvest," etc., we first think of natural seed, a natural field, a natural harvest. But when Scripture tells us, that Christ spoke in parables of seed, field, harvest, etc., we have the declaration of Scripture that these words are used as images, or signs, to represent other things than they ordinarily mean.

Applying this to the doctrine of the Lord's Supper, one must say: The words of Christ, "This is My body, which is given for you," must be understood in their proper sense of Christ's body and not of a symbol of the same, unless Scripture itself tells us that here in the Lord's Supper we are not to think of the actual body of Christ, but of a symbol of His body; but Scripture nowhere does. On the contrary, as we have seen: 1. All Biblical writers who report the institution of the Lord's Supper call the thing that Christ tenders in the Lord's Supper for eating and drinking with the mouth Christ's body and blood; none speaks of an image, or symbol, of Christ's body and blood. 2. In addition, Scripture contains an authentic Apostolic declaration on this point, whether the words of institution are to be taken literally or figuratively. The Apostle Paul, like Matthew, Mark, and Luke, reports the institution of the Lord's Supper and the words used by Christ in this rite. But St. Paul tells us more. Reprimanding the frivolity that had crept into the Corinthian celebration of the Lord's Supper, and admonishing them to observe due reverence and solemnity in their observance of this Sacrament, he powerfully confirms the fact that the terms "body of Christ" and "blood of Christ" are to be taken in their proper and first sense. He calls "the cup which we bless" not the symbol, or image, but "the communion of the blood of Christ," and "the bread which we break" not a symbol, or image, but "the communion of the body of Christ." Furthermore, he says of everyone who "shall eat this bread and drink this cup of the Lord unworthily" that he "shall be guilty of the body and blood of the Lord" and "eateth and drinketh damnation to himself, not discerning the Lord's body" (1 Cor. 10:16; 11:27, 29). In view of this declaration of the Apostle as to what is given us in the Lord's Supper, the Reformed can save their teaching of emblems only by insisting that here, too, the symbol must be substituted for the thing mentioned, namely, for the communion of the body and blood of Christ the communion of the symbol of the body and blood of Christ or the communion of the virtue and effect of the body and blood of Christ.

Zwingli's defense is: "The tropes must be recognized by the light of faith," *tropes fidei lumine deprehendi oportet* (*Opp.* III, 606). But "faith" in spiritual matters is a relative term. As correlative it must always have a word of God. Where this is missing, we have not Christian faith, but only human fiction. What sort of faith, originating entirely in their ego, induces Zwingli and all Reformed teachers to assume tropes in the words of institution, though the Scriptures nowhere indicate tropes in them, ought now to be shown in order to see clearly in the matter.

But before we enter on this, let us, for the sake of completeness, point out that there have also been a number of champions of the Reformed teaching of the Lord's Supper who reject the figurative interpretation of any one word, be it "this" or "is" or "body," but who expect of us kindly to interpret the whole statement symbolically, or to put a figurative meaning into the whole sentence. Thus Keckermann was of the opinion that in the sentence, "This is My body," every word had to be taken in its proper sense and still the whole sentence taken figuratively or as symbol.

That, for one thing, is expecting the impossible in point of logic. If every word of a statement is to be taken in its natural meaning, if "bread" is bread, and "is" means is, and "Christ's body" is Christ's body given into death for us, then no man, Keckermann included, will succeed in taking the entire statement figuratively.[37] Furthermore, on closer inspection it soon becomes apparent that Keckermann is not much in earnest with his demand that every part of the sentence be taken literally. For Keckermann at the same time speaks of a "union of signification" (*unio significationis*), obtaining between the bread and the body of Christ. So he is actually either taking "is" for "signifies" or "body" for "symbol of the body"; else his "union of signification" or symbolization would not result. Here the reminder is in place that Luther is right when he says (St. L. XX:782 f., 1086): "It is certain

---

37 Cf. Dannhauer's criticism of the Keckermann trope in Quenstedt, II, 1197: "Finally, Keckermann's trope of the whole statement, so, however, that all the single words keep their proper sense (which is repeated by Combachius, *De euch.* c. 11), is absurd; the whole (*totum*) statement is tropical, all (*totum*) that is stated is literal (*proprium*); such a monstrosity has never been heard of in any rhetorica (compend of logic)."

that Zwingli and Oecolampadius are agreed as to the meaning, though
they differ in their words. For Zwingli's saying, 'This signifies My
body,' is tantamount to Oecolampadius' saying, 'This is a symbol of
My body.' The German tongue shows it, too, and all languages, that
it is one and the same, whether I say: Laughter signifies joy, or
laughter is a sign of joy; so there can be no question or doubt that
'signify' or 'be a symbol of' mean the same thing." "Oecolampadius
has *figuram corporis,* Zwingli has *significans corpus;* that is one and the
same thing." This certainly is true. Also those among the Reformed
who say with Oecolampadius and Calvin that the trope does not lie
in the copula, but in the predicate noun, who therefore declare that
one must not take "is" for "signifies," but "body" for "symbol of the
body," mean the identical thing that Zwingli and his followers meant.
Both parties, in spite of the difference in words, imagine the relation
between the bread and the body of Christ to be this, that the bread
is an image, or symbol, of the body of Christ.

In general it must be said that all Reformed pay homage to the
so-called *"subject* trope" (*"Subjekts*tropus"), irrespective of where they
nominally place the trope, whether into the subject "this," or the
copula "is," or the predicate noun "body," or the whole clause "This
is My body." All, in fact, take the bread as sign, or symbol, of the
absent body of Christ. In spite of their argument among themselves,
they ultimately agree also in the words. As Zwingli gives this explanation of his *significat: symbolum est, figura est,*[38] namely, the bread is
a symbol, a figure, of the body of Christ, so also Calvin says that the
bread is called the body of Christ because the bread is a sign, or symbol
(*signum aut symbolum*), of the body of Christ.[39] Also those who, like
Keckermann, Zanchi, Bucanus, and others, make the whole sentence
a trope, expressly declare as their meaning: *Panis est symbolum sive
signum corporis Christi.* This is very evident in the case of Bucanus.
He remarks: "The figurative language is found not in the single words,
separated and considered by themselves. For the 'bread' is bread in
the proper sense, and the 'body' is not an allegorical, not a tropical,
not a figurative, much less a pretended body or phantom, also not
a mystical body, which is the Church, also not a sign of the body,
also not the merit of Christ, but 'body' designates the true body of

[38] *Opp.* III, 607: "So we have shown that *'est'* stands here for *'symbolum
est, figura est, significat.'* "

[39] In his *Commentary* on 1 Cor. 11:24: "Why should we here deny the
similarity between a metonymy and giving the name 'body' to bread, since it is
the sign and symbol of it?" Calvin also adduces the same Scripture texts for his
"*signum corporis*" with which Zwingli proves his "signifies" (*Inst.* IV. 17, 21-22).

Christ (*proprium Christi corpus*); certainly the true body of Christ is being asserted of true bread. But the figurative speech is to be found in the whole assertion (*attributione*), since the copula unites two essentially disparate things (*disparata*). And this assertion one can solve in this wise: The bread is a symbol, or emblem, of the body of Christ (*panis est symbolum seu signaculum corporis Christi*)." [40]

To this we merely add that the demand kindly to take the whole sentence, "This is My body," figuratively makes futile all further discussion, for this request is a *petitio principii*. The thing to be proved is assumed as already proved. And again the question arises, touched upon before: Why, if it is permissible to interpret a part of the words of institution figuratively, and what is surely the most important part at that, "This is My body" — why then halt midway and not understand all the words and the entire action of the Supper figuratively? Why not do away with the bread and the eating of it and the wine and the drinking of it as a material substance and an external act and, like the Quakers, merely let the inward, spiritual enjoyment of Christ in the hearts of believers be typified by that first external celebration of the Supper? See the chapter "The Divine Institution of the Lord's Supper," p. 290 ff.

Here we merely add that Luther already pointed out this inconsistency. He says: "Friend, why are not the other words also taken figuratively, and why is there a trope only in the word 'is' or 'body'? Or where is there here a rule teaching us which words must be taken figuratively and which not? For according to their method I can make tropes also of the words, 'Take, eat; this do in remembrance of Me,' and say: 'Take' means hear, 'eat' means believe, 'this do' means ponder it in your heart." (St. L. XX:1006.) Krauth, too, points out this inconsistency: "The Word TAKE these interpreters [the Reformed] have usually construed literally, though why an imaginary body or the symbol of a body might not be taken mentally, they cannot say. . . . The Word EAT they have interpreted literally, though why the eating ought not to be done symbolically or mentally, to correspond with the symbolical or mental character of the body, they cannot say. Certainly there are plenty of instances of a figurative use of the word 'eat,' while there are none of such a use of the word 'is.' The Quakers are more consistent." (*Op. cit.*, p. 608 f.)

But let us now turn our attention to the "faith" which causes the Reformed to deny the presence of Christ's body and blood in the Supper and accordingly to interpret the words of institution figura-

---

[40] Bucanus, *loc. 48*, p. 693; in Gerhard, *Loci*, "De coena," § 85.

tively. The Reformed are profoundly deluding themselves and deceiving others when they assert that their teaching of the Lord's Supper is based on Scripture. The Reformed teaching of the Sacrament is not rooted in Scripture, but in a fixed human idea. It is the fixed notion, held fast in spite of the clear testimony of Scripture to the contrary,[41] that Christ according to His human nature, hence also according to His human body, can possess no other than the local and visible presence (localis et visibilis praesentia). Luther says: "Their whole argument rests on this, that Christ's body can be at only one place, in a physical and tangible manner," "as a peasant fills out jacket and breeches" or "straw the sack" (St. L. XX:950, 953, 1776). And Calvin avers over and over that the reason for his dissent from Luther has been correctly defined by Luther. Thoroughly to refute Luther's doctrine of the Lord's Supper, Calvin would, above all, refute "this ridiculous notion" [stultum illud commentum], that the body of Christ possesses, beside the visible and local, also an invisible, illocal, and supernatural presence. He says that the Lutherans "chatter [garriunt] about an invisible presence" (Inst. IV, 17, 30) and claims most earnestly that one dare not ascribe to Christ's human nature a presence which exceeds His "corporeal dimensions" (mensuram corporis, dimensionem corporis) and represents "His body as in different places at once [pluribus simul locis distrahit]." (Inst. IV, 17, 19, Allen II, 543.) For such teaching would lead to a catastrophe. The true humanity of Christ would inevitably be lost. Calvin: "It is essential to a real body to have its particular form and dimensions and to be contained within some certain space. Let us hear no more, then, of this ridiculous notion which fastens the minds of men, and Christ Himself, to the bread. For what is the use of this invisible presence," etc. (Inst. IV, 17, 29; Allen III, 426.)

To see clearly in this controversy between the Lutheran Church and the Reformed we must constantly bear in mind that precisely in the chief doctrines of Holy Writ there appear in Reformed theology man-made principles, foreign to Scripture, according to which the Scripture statements are "explained." This faced us in the doctrine of the grace of God. Reformed theologians from Calvin down to Hodge and Boehl answer the question whether God desires to save all men or only part of them according to the principle that God's intention regarding the salvation of men must be determined from the result. They argue: From the fact that not all men are saved one must conclude that God does not intend to save all men and that Christ's

---

41 Cp. the full presentation in the Doctrine of Christ's Person, Vol. II, 166 ff.

merit does not extend over all men.[42] According to this human notion they then explain all Scripture texts teaching the *gratia universalis.* The same thing holds true in Christology. They decide the question whether there can be real communion (*realis communio*) between the divine and the human natures of Christ according to the principle *Finitum non est capax infiniti.* According to this maxim they misinterpret all Scripture passages that teach a communion of natures and communication of attributes. The same thing they do in the doctrine of the means of grace. They decide the question whether God works faith in the Gospel, or regeneration, through the means of grace ordained by Him, or without them and alongside them, according to the rule: Since regeneration is effected by divine omnipotence, there is in regeneration "no place for the use of means." Thus we were told by Hodge: "Volumes have been written on the contrary hypothesis; which volumes lose all their value if it be once admitted that regeneration, or effectual calling, is the work of omnipotence" (*Syst. Theol.* II, 683). Applying this false principle, they pervert the Scripture texts which declare faith or regeneration to come through the means of grace or from the means of grace, to mean: without the means of grace or alongside them.

Now, the same thing they do here in the doctrine of the Lord's Supper. The despot which the Reformed theologians use to tyrannize the Scriptures and themselves is their fixed notion that always only a visible and local presence may be ascribed to the human nature of Christ and that therefore the body of Christ cannot be present in the Lord's Supper invisibly and illocally. All objections of the Reformed to the presence of Christ's body and blood, as it is stated in the words of Christ, are in the last analysis based on this preconceived notion. Because of this foregone conclusion Carlstadt held that Christ, in uttering the words, "This is My body," could not have done otherwise than point to His body sitting visibly at the table. Because of this predetermined notion Zwingli thought that in the words of institution "is" could not be "is," but would have to mean "signifies." Because of this fixed idea Oecolampadius and Calvin were convinced that "body" could not be "body," but necessarily would have to be taken for "symbol of the body." And when the Reformed theologians talk of "Christian faith" as not permitting the substantial presence of Christ's body and blood in the Sacrament, they always mean their article of faith regarding only a visible presence of Christ's body as possible. Oecolampadius writes against Luther: "How dare you ascribe many

---

[42] Calvin, *Inst.* III, 24, 15; Hodge, *Syst. Theol.* II, 323.

heads to us because of this explanation [namely, "that one so interprets the *hoc* ('this'), the other takes *est* to mean 'signifies,' and a third seeks another way"]? As far as is known to me, all of us have but one basic principle, namely, that Christ ascended to heaven with His true body." "Our first principle is that the body of Christ is in heaven; this foundation is sure and will not fail us." "The Christian truth is that the body of Christ is in heaven in honor and glory." [43] In other words, all arguments of the Reformed against the true presence of Christ's body and blood in the Lord's Supper finally simmer down to this "one fundamental principle" that only a local and visible presence is possible for Christ according to His human nature.

Dominated by this obsession, Calvin mercilessly slaughters those Scripture passages that confound his notion, as we noted already in the doctrine of Christ's Person. Thus he claims that Christ (John 20) did not come to the disciples through closed doors, but through some opening (*Inst.* IV, 17, 29; Allen II, 559). Again, he claims that when Luke reports (24:31) that Christ "vanished" out of the sight of the disciples of Emmaus, this means: "He assumed no new appearance in order to conceal Himself (*non factus est invisibilis*), but 'their eyes were holden, that they should not know Him'" (*ibid.*). At the same time Calvin in this connection makes short shrift of a number of Scripture doctrines. The right hand of God, to which Christ was exalted according to His humanity by His ascension, is interpreted as a circumscribed place, where Christ according to His humanity is shut off from His Church alway, even unto the end of the world.[44] That perverts the Scripture doctrines of the ascension of Christ and His session on the right hand of God into their very opposite. See Vol. II, 324 ff. Besides, Calvin is indirectly ascribing infinity to the world and local extension to God (*Trigl.*, Hist. Introd., 188). Only if he so conceived of it could Calvin so persistently claim that Christ's body is made "infinite" [45] through the Lutheran doctrine of the real presence

---

[43] His *Answer to Luther's Preface to the Syngramma* (St. L. XX:591 ff.).

[44] Calvin: "The body of Christ was, like other human bodies, circumscribed by certain dimensions; and its ascension to heaven made it evident that it was not in all places, but that it left one place when it removed to another. Nor is the promise, 'I am with you alway, even unto the end of the world,' to be applied, as they suppose it should be, to His body." (*Inst.* IV, 17, 30; Allen II, 560.)

[45] *Inst.* IV, 17, 30: "Though we should grant them [the Lutherans] what they contend for [*garriunt*] respecting its invisible presence, still this would be no proof of its infinity [*immensitas*], without which it will be a vain attempt to enclose Christ under the bread" (Allen II, 560). Luther protests: "Why, even the universe itself is not infinite or without end; how, then, does it follow that Christ's body would have to be infinite to be everywhere?" (St. L. XX:965.)

and is assigned "an immensity diffused through heaven and earth." [46]
Yes, even the greatest and highest thing in the Christian faith, the
incarnation of the Son of God, is sacrificed to the preconceived notion
of nothing but a local and visible presence of the body of Christ.
This becomes particularly pronounced in the case of Calvin. In order
to justify the exclusion of Christ's body and blood from the Lord's
Supper, he declares it to be a most horrible doctrine that the Son of
God everywhere has His human nature present with Him.[47] This is
a transition to Unitarianism, since it reduces the unique union between
God and man in Christ, the *unio personalis*, to the level of the *unio
mystica* obtaining between God and the believers.[48] Because of this
reduction of the *unio personalis* to an *unio mystica*, Calvin, in combatting the Lutheran doctrine of the Sacrament of the Altar, constantly
indulges in the following argument: As the body of other men cannot
at once be at several places, neither may this be conceded of the body
of Christ. Calvin actually declares it an axiom — misapplying such
passages as Heb. 2:14; 4:15 — that, with the exception of sinlessness,
nothing else or more may be asserted of the human nature of Christ
than of any other man. If more were asserted, the human nature of
Christ would be destroyed. Calvin writes: "It pleased God for Christ
to become in all respects like His brethren, sin excepted. What is the
nature of our body? Has it not its proper and certain dimensions?
Is it not contained in some particular place and capable of being felt
and seen? And why, say they (the Lutherans), may not God cause
the same flesh to occupy many different places, to be contained in no
particular place, and to have no form or dimensions? But how can
they be so senseless [*insane*] as to require the power of God to cause
a body to be a body, and not to be a body, at the same time? . . .
Therefore body must be body, spirit must be spirit, everything must

---

[46] *Inst.* IV, 17, 19 f.; Allen II, 542 f. Luther, on the contrary, says: "Oecolampadius spins the very same coarse yarn as Zwingli, namely, that Christ's body
would have to be as big as heaven and earth. . . . Why, God Himself, though He
truly is everywhere, is not so big and broad [i. e., by local extension]." [St. L.
XX:1009]. See the full discussion in the chapter "The Mode, or Manner, of
Christ's Omnipresence According to His Human Nature," Vol. II, 173 ff.

[47] *Inst.* IV, 17, 30: "Some [the Lutherans] are so carried away with the
heat of contention, as to affirm that, on account of the union of the two natures
in Christ, wherever His divinity is, His flesh, which cannot be separated from it,
is there also" (Allen II, 569).

[48] Compare what is said on the christological "suicide" committed by Reformed theology through its denial of the communion of natures and the communication of attributes, particularly the communication of divine omnipresence to
the human nature of Christ, Vol. II, 166 ff., 118 ff., 138 ff., 152 ff.

be subject to that law, and retain that condition which was fixed by God at its creation. And the condition of a body is such that it must occupy one particular place and have its proper form and dimensions." (*Inst.* IV, 17, 24; Allen II, 550 f.) So energetically does Calvin insist upon it that nothing else and nothing more be ascribed to Christ's human nature than to any other man!

Thus the incarnation of the Son of God and the entire work of redemption surely is thoroughly done away with. According to this maxim of Calvin, we should now have to continue the argument in this manner: No other man is God; hence also not the Son of Mary. No other man is the Mediator between God and men; hence also not the Man Christ Jesus. No other man has redeemed mankind by the giving of his body and the shedding of his blood; consequently also not the Man Christ. So thoroughly Calvin's principle, if consistently followed, does away with Christ's Person and work. And thus he rationalizes, as stated, solely to keep Christ's body and blood out of the Lord's Supper. For it is this purpose he has in view in setting up and seeking to bolster the principle that at all times only a local and visible mode of presence may be ascribed to the body of Christ.[49]

The same principle of a solely local and visible mode of presence results in a polemic against the Lutheran doctrine of the Lord's Supper on the part of the Reformed which is untruthful through and through. Because the Reformed, the moment they hear of a true presence of Christ's body and blood in the Sacrament, always visualize only their visible and local presence, "as the peasant fills out jacket and breeches,"

---

[49] Cremer is right when he remarks (R. E., 3d ed., I, 37): "If Christ is nothing more than any other man, differing from other men only in His calling and work, there can of course be no sacramental presence of His body and blood, and the view presented in all reports regarding the Lord's Supper is untenable." But the "view" changes radically if the incarnation of the Son of God is really maintained. If Christ is indeed, on the one hand, like every other man because He has and keeps a truly human nature, but, on the other hand, is something more than every other man, namely, the man who is God, who is united with God unto one ego, in whom the fullness of the Godhead dwells bodily, whose body is God's own body, whose blood is God's own blood, whose blood has the unique virtue of being the ransom for the sins of the whole world — if this is the case, if we must ascribe to the Man Christ, and particularly also to His body and His blood, the above-mentioned predicates (and they are stated of Him in Holy Writ), then the Reformed claim that the Son of God cannot be present in the Lord's Supper with His body and blood is plainly a preposterous assertion. It can be accounted for only by the "theologizing subject's" losing sight of the incarnation of the Son of God, his separating the Man Christ in His Person and work from the Son of God, as Calvin does when he asserts of Christ's merit (*Inst.* II, 17, 1) that it cannot, as the merit of a man, have all-sufficient value, but obtains this rating only by predestination.

they ascribe to us Lutherans a local inclusion (*localis inclusio*, Hodge, *Syst. Theol.*, I, 83) of the body of Christ in the bread, or a local consubstantiation (*consubstantiatio*), or even a physical compounding (*permixtio*) of bread and body of Christ. Because of the same bias they apply to us Lutherans the titles "carnivorous beasts," "blood guzzlers," and "cannibals," [50] and call the Supper instituted by Christ, with the real presence of the body and blood of Christ which is given and shed for us, a "Cyclopean meal" and a "Thyestean banquet." [51] All this is the result of their adoption of the thesis that Christ's body can have only a visible and local mode of presence as their principle of Scripture interpretation.

We would be flying in the face of the facts if we considered the unfortunate disagreement prevailing in regard to the Lord's Supper as caused by any obscurity of the words of institution. These words are of such a nature that they call forth in every man hearing them, "whether Christian or pagan, Jew or Turk," the identical thought. (Luther, St. L. XX:1005.) They are just as clear to the Reformed as to the Lutherans. Christ's words: "Take, eat; this is My body, which

---

[50] Zwingli is one of the coarsest blasphemers, as his *De vera et falsa religione* (*Opp.* II, 555), shows. He proves the absence of Christ's body and blood from the Sacrament not merely with the words (John 6:63), "The flesh profiteth nothing," but also with the words of Peter at the miraculous draught of fishes (Luke 5:8), "Depart from me . . . O Lord." These words of Peter, flowing from his realization of his sinfulness, induce Zwingli to give the following instruction on the Lord's Supper: "And we are to have appetite to eat Christ in a natural manner, as cannibals (*anthropophagi*) do? As though somebody could so love his children that he would wish to devour (*devorare*) them! Or as though among all men those who devour human flesh were not regarded as the most savage." Also Oecolampadius, whom the Reformed praise for his dignified manner of fighting Luther (R. E., 2d ed., X, 722), uses the above expressions in his answer to Luther's preface to the *Syngramma* (St. L. XX:588 ff.). The coarsest Reformed opponent was perhaps Beza. Even Heppe, a great admirer of Beza, concedes (R. E., 2d ed., II, 361): "Beza in 1560 opposed Tilemann Hesshusius, a defender of the Lutheran doctrine, with two dialogues, of which he called the one 'Cannibalism' or 'The Cyclop,' the other 'The Scolding Ass' or 'Sophist,' both of which unfortunately were overflowing with boundless scorn and ridicule." It is principally Beza whom the Formula of Concord has in mind in pointing out "how unjustly and maliciously the Sacramentarian fanatics (Theodore Beza) deride the Lord Christ, St. Paul, and the entire Church in calling this oral partaking, and that of the unworthy, *duos pilos caudae equinae et commentum, cuius vel ipsum Satanam pudeat*, as also the doctrine concerning the majesty of Christ, *excrementum Satanae, quo diabolus sibi ipsi et hominibus illudat*, that is, they speak so horribly of it that a godly Christian man should be ashamed to translate it" (*Trigl.* 997, Sol. Decl., VII, 67).

[51] The legendary Cyclopes were pictured as cannibals (cf. Homer, *Od.* IX, 287 ff.; Virgil, *Aen.* III, 623 ff.). Thyestes ate the flesh of his own son, served him by his brother Aetreus (cf. Cicero, *Tusc.*, III, 12, 26).

is given for you," evoked not only in Luther's mind, but also in that of Zwingli, Oecolampadius, and Calvin the thought, not of a symbol of the body of Christ, but of the true, substantial body which Christ gave into death. The difference between Luther, on the one hand, and Zwingli and his followers, on the other, was solely this, that the former gave assent to Christ's words, while the latter dissented. And as reason for their dissent they allege the impossibility of a presence of the body of Christ in the Sacrament. And the impossibility they base on their notion, begotten not by Scripture, but by rationalism, that the human nature of Christ can possess only a local and visible presence. The same thing holds true of modern theologians because their teaching of the Lord's Supper is essentially Reformed. Meyer, too, sides with the Reformed [52] because he is convinced that the giving and receiving of the substantial body and blood of Christ in the first Lord's Supper posits the "utterly impossible." After he has decided the matter on the basis of its "impossibility," "is" must submit to the "symbolical interpretation."

By the way, the Reformed themselves actually concede in more than one way that they did not get their teaching regarding the Lord's Supper from Scripture. This admission appears, first, in their avowal that the words of institution must be interpreted according to John 6.[53] Since John 6, however, does not pertain to the Lord's Supper at all, as perhaps most of the Reformed grant,[54] the use of this passage to determine the doctrine of the Lord's Supper is actually an admission that the teaching so arrived at is not the doctrine of Scripture, but the product of human ingenuity. This is obvious. Since nothing regarding the Sacrament is taught in the texts which do not treat of the Lord's Supper, the thoughts regarding the Lord's Supper which we conceive on the basis of such texts are solely our own thoughts. And if we put these thoughts into the Scripture passages which actually

---

52 Cp. his *Commentary* on Matt. 26:26 f. Another is Nitzsch-Stephan, *Ev. Dogmatik*, p. 668.

53 Also Hodge (*Syst. Theol.* III, 622) adduces John 6 to explain 1 Cor. 10:16, which treats of the Lord's Supper, and then continues to cite only such Scripture texts as treat of the spiritual union (*unio mystica*) of the believers with Christ, and not of the Lord's Supper.

54 See Strong, *Syst. Theol.*, p. 965; David Brown in *Comm. Crit. and Explan.* on John 6; Calvin in his *Comm.* on John 6:54. Zwingli, *Opp.* III, 241: "We find those entirely mistaken who believe that Christ in this whole chapter says anything about the Sacramental food." But he insists upon it that the words of institution must be explained according to these words that do not speak of the Lord's Supper. This he does as early as 1524 in the letter to Matthew Alberus, often referred to, *Opp.* III, 593, especially, however, *Opp.* II, 1, 447.

treat of the Lord's Supper, we are in fact displacing the doctrine of Scripture with our own thoughts. And if we nevertheless allege that what we are presenting is the doctrine of Scripture, we are not abiding by the truth, but deceiving ourselves and the public.

Attention has rightly been called to the fact that the process of deriving one's teaching from Scripture texts which do not deal with the matter must be classed with the temptations of the devil, as the tempting of Christ by Satan (Matthew 4) clearly shows. The issue between Christ and Satan was whether it would be in accord with Scripture if Christ cast Himself down from the pinnacle of the Temple (Matt. 4:6, "Cast Thyself down"). The devil affirmed it, and as Scripture proof adduced Ps. 91:11: "It is written, He shall give His angels charge concerning thee; and in their hands they shall bear thee up, lest at any time thou dash thy foot against a stone." Christ answered No to the question, and proved His No by citing Deut. 6:16, "It is written again, Thou shalt not tempt the Lord, thy God." The difference between Satan's and Christ's Scripture proof is that Christ cites a text covering the case in hand, while the passage adduced by Satan does not pertain to any plunge from the Temple, but speaks of walking in the divinely appointed paths of duty.

Since such prominence has been given to John 6 in the controversy on the Lord's Supper, a few additional remarks on this passage may be appropriate.[55] Text and context make it utterly impossible to refer John 6 to the Lord's Supper. The entire apparatus of the Lord's Supper, so faithfully described by all four writers, Matthew, Mark, Luke, and Paul, in their report on the Sacrament, is here missing. In John 6 Christ does not take bread, give thanks, break it and give it to the people, and say: "Take, eat; this is My body, which is given for you." Just as little does John 6 mention a cup which Christ takes, gives thanks over, gives to the people, and says: "Drink ye all of it; this is My blood of the new testament, which is shed for many for the remission of sins." The reason, however, why Christ speaks with such emphasis of the eating of His body and the drinking of His blood in John 6 is evident from the context. Christ had fed the populace, the five thousand, with five barley loaves and two fishes. Such a Messiah attracted the Jews. They desired to make Him king. And when He withdraws from them, they follow Him to the western shore of the Sea of Galilee. They are seeking earthly bread from Christ. For this

---

[55] The exegetical history of this passage in Zoeckler's *Commentary;* also see Keil on the text, Harless in *Zeitschrift fuer luth. Theol.*, 1867, p. 115 ff., Calov in *Biblia Illustr*

Christ reproves them: "Verily, verily, I say unto you, Ye seek Me, not because ye saw the miracles, but because ye did eat of the loaves and were filled." He urges them to seek "that meat which endureth unto everlasting life." Then He very definitely declares Himself to be the Bread "which cometh down from heaven and giveth life unto the world." And faith in Him ("that ye believe on Him whom He hath sent") He designates as the thing God would have all men do above all. This faith in His Person Christ then pictures as eating and drinking: "He that cometh to Me shall never hunger; and he that believeth on Me shall never thirst." The Jews find the thought repulsive that "this Jesus, the Son of Joseph, whose father and mother we know," should be the "Bread which came down from heaven." But Christ does not take back what He said; He rather intensifies it by saying that His flesh, which He will give for the life of the world, is the life-giving bread. When this makes the Jews murmur all the more and argue, "How can this Man give us His flesh to eat?" Christ climaxes His statement, saying: "Except ye eat the flesh of the Son of Man and drink His blood, ye have no life in you." Thus He impresses on the mind of the Jews, and us all, the very necessary truth that He is the Savior of the Jews and the world, not by the gift of perishable food and temporal gifts in general, but by His suffering and dying to wipe out the guilt of mankind. John 6 belongs to the most impressive passages of Scripture teaching faith in Christ's *satisfactio vicaria* as necessary for salvation. In closing Christ reverts to His first way of expressing this truth: "This [namely, Christ in His vicarious satisfaction] is that Bread which came down from heaven; not as your fathers did eat manna and are dead. He that eateth of this Bread shall live forever."

Luther (St. L. XI:1143) comments "that these words (John 6) are not to be made to refer to the Sacrament of the Altar; whoever so interprets them does violence to this Gospel text. There is not a letter in them that refers to the Lord's Supper.[56] Why should Christ here have in mind that Sacrament when it was not yet instituted? The whole chapter from which this Gospel is taken speaks of nothing but spiritual eating, namely, faith. When the people followed the Lord, merely hoping again to eat and drink, as the Lord Himself charges them with doing, He seizes the opportunity from the temporal food they sought to speak throughout the entire chapter of a spiritual food.

---

[56] It is an entirely useless question whether Christ in John 6 did not at least think of the Lord's Supper (Bengel, etc.). We can judge of Christ's thoughts only if He reveals them to us in His Word.

He says: 'The words that I have spoken unto you are spirit and are life.' Thereby He shows that He fed them with the object of inducing them to believe on Him, and that as they partook of the temporal food, so should they also partake of the spiritual." What Christ says John 6 of the eating of His flesh and the drinking of His blood should move us to believe this, "that this Bread, His flesh and blood, born of the Virgin Mary, was given because He had to pay the penalty of death and in our stead suffer the torments of hell and, besides, suffer the guilt of sins He never committed, as if they were His own." "The whole New Testament treats of this spiritual supper, and especially does John here," Luther adds. But this fact does not make unnecessary the Sacrament of the Altar, as Oecolampadius in particular thought. On the contrary, in a special manner the Lord's Supper serves to further this spiritual eating by faith. In the Sacrament of the Altar Christ strengthens the faith of the Christian that Christ's body was given also for him and Christ's blood shed also for him by giving him His body and blood also to eat and drink with the mouth.

It is part of the untruthful polemics of the Reformed that they represent the matter as if the Lutherans sidetracked the spiritual eating by emphasizing the oral eating of Christ's body and blood. The direct opposite is true. Lutherans teach the oral eating all the more to awaken and strengthen the spiritual eating. As Luther in his Small Catechism, in reply to the question, "How can bodily eating and drinking do such great things?" answers: "It is not the eating and drinking indeed that does them, but the words here written, 'Given and shed for you for the remission of sins'; which words, beside the bodily eating and drinking, are the chief thing in the Sacrament; and he that believes these words [i. e., eats Christ spiritually] has what they say and express, namely, the forgiveness of sins." In the "Christian Questions with Their Answers" Luther puts the question: "Why do you wish to go to the Sacrament?" And his answer is: "That I may learn to believe that Christ died for my sin out of great love, as before said; and that I may also learn of Him to love God and my neighbor." [57]

---

[57] Shedd (*Dogm. Theol.* III, 464), however, supposes that Luther's energetic stressing of faith in the words, "Given and shed for you for the remission of sins," in his Small Catechism is a proof that Luther and the earlier Lutheran Confessions "substantially adopted this spiritual view of the Supper," namely, the notion of a merely spiritual sumption of Christ's body and blood in the Sacrament. Not till a later day — the Saxon Articles of Visitation of 1592 are mentioned — was the Real Presence so strongly emphasized and the merely spiritual eating by faith rejected. This idea of Shedd proves that his conception of Luther's position in this doctrine and the historical reality have nothing in common.

The fact that their teaching regarding the Lord's Supper does not come from Scripture is revealed even more plainly by those Reformed theologians who declare that the words of institution need not be specially weighed in determining the doctrine of the Lord's Supper, or even assert that the words of institution should not at all be used as proof for the correct doctrine of the Lord's Supper because they are in controversy. Thus Zwingli, after he has toiled to inject the absence of Christ's body and blood into the words of institution, says: "We here desire, however, that no one should permit the anxious searching of the words [namely, the words of institution] to raise scruples in his mind; for we do not base our doctrine on them, but on the one word 'The flesh profiteth nothing'; which word by itself is stout enough to compel one to admit, that 'is' at this place stands for 'signifies,' or 'portrays,' or 'is a symbol of.'" [58] But John 6 does not speak of the Lord's Supper at all, and specifically the words v. 63: "The flesh profiteth nothing," are not spoken of the body of Christ in the Lord's Supper. Therefore Zwingli's affirmation that he does not base his doctrine on the words of institution, but on the words "The flesh profiteth nothing" amounts to a declaration that his doctrine is not taken from Scripture, but is the product of his own imagination.[59]

---

[58] Zwingli's *Opinion Regarding Christ's Supper* (St. L. XX:477; Latin, *Opp.* III, 260).

[59] In regard to the words John 6:63: "It is the Spirit that quickeneth; the flesh profiteth nothing," Beza in a sort of desperation says: "How much this passage has been tortured by a variety of interpretations is hardly believable!" But that is not the fault of the words of Christ, the meaning of which certainly is clearly defined by both wording and context. In this text "flesh" cannot mean the flesh of Christ, since the contrast in which it stands to "spirit" establishes it as referring to the "carnal mind" of man; and in the words immediately following, unbelief over against the words of Christ is described as a manifestation of the flesh: "The words that I speak unto you, they are spirit, and they are life. But there are some of you that believe not." Moreover, referring the words to the flesh of Christ conflicts with the wider context, since Christ previously had declared His flesh to be so profitable that He called it "meat indeed" (v. 55), without which no one could live forever. Cf. also Hengstenberg on the passage.

Men who think of Christ's flesh when hearing the words, "The flesh profiteth nothing," show a fanatic party spirit which disregards all rules fundamental to the understanding of human speech. Luther (St. L. XX:823, 824, 826): "Now, then, their second-best proof is the text John 6:63: 'The flesh profiteth nothing,' of which Oecolampadius brags that it is his iron wall. . . . As often as Christ in Scripture speaks of His flesh, or body, He adds the little word 'My' and says: 'My flesh,' 'My body,' as He says in this very chapter, John 6: "My flesh is meat indeed.' Again: 'Except ye eat the flesh of the Son of Man,' etc. . . . So, then, the iron wall lies blown over by a little word called '*Mea, My.*' For since here we do not read: *My* flesh profiteth nothing, but simply: 'Flesh profiteth nothing,' we have, first, won this, that it may not be understood of Christ's body. For since

The same admission we have in the confession of Zwingli that he entertained the opinion of a figurative understanding of the words of institution before he knew to which word of the sentence to attach the trope.[60]

Finally it should be mentioned here that Zwingli appeals to a celestial vision for his *est* in the sense of *significat* (*Subsidium de euch., Opp.* III, 341 ff.). He reports that he could find no illustrations for "is" in the sense of "signifies" except the parables. "There still remained," he says, "the most difficult undertaking of furnishing illustrations not connected with a parable.[61] We therefore began to reconsider everything, to weigh everything anew. Still no new examples turned up but what had already been offered in the commentary [*Commentarius de vera et falsa religione*]; or whatever presented itself was similar to that. But when the thirteenth day came — I am relating facts, and so truly that if I tried to conceal them, my conscience would force me to reveal [*effundere*, pour out] what the Lord communicated to me, though I am not unaware to what great insults and derision I am exposing myself — I say, when the thirteenth day of April broke, I seemed in my dream to be contending anew with great chagrin with a hostile writer and to have become so dumb that I could not utter what I knew to be true, because my tongue refused to serve me. . . . Then there appeared, as out of a machine [*ex machina*, ἀπὸ μηχανῆς, a contrivance used on a theater stage], a counselor — whether he was black or white, I do not recall, for I am telling a dream — who said: Weakling [*ignave*], why do you not answer him what is written Ex. 12:11: It is Passover, that is, the passing over of the Lord [*est enim Phase, hoc est transitus Domini*]. At this apparition I promptly awoke and jumped up from my couch. First I thoroughly examined that passage in the LXX and preached with power [*pro virili*] on it before the whole congregation. This sermon . . . dispersed all fog among the candidates of Holy Scripture [theological students] who still doubted because of the difficulty caused by the parable, and it came about

---

He Himself does not add it and say: '*My* flesh,' it is forbidden to improve on His words and add something, and we are certain and safe in not referring it to His flesh. Secondly, this have we won, that they cannot prove by a single letter that 'flesh' here means Christ's flesh."

[60] *Opp.* III, 606: "*Videbam* τροπικῶς *dictum esse:* '*Hoc est corpus meum*,' *sed in qua voce tropus lateret, non videbam.*" He got the notion of "this precious pearl [*est pro significat*]," he tells us, from the Dutchman Honius. Only that it was not yet clear to him to which word to attach this pearl.

[61] In parables it is stated from the outset that the language is figurative. "The kingdom of heaven is *likened* [ὡμοιώθη] unto a man," etc., Matt. 13:24.

that . . . the number of those who longingly looked back to the garlic and the fleshpots of Egypt became, I surmise, much smaller." These closing words disclose why Zwingli deceived himself anew. He was scouting for ammunition against Luther. For when he speaks of people hankering for the garlic and fleshpots of Egypt, he is deriding Luther's alleged Roman leaven in the doctrine of the Lord's Supper. So God suffered Zwingli's imagination, or his black or white visitor, to deceive him. Zwingli is inserting his *significat* in Ex. 12:11 just as arbitrarily as in the other texts already discussed.[62]

And as to the contention that the words of institution cannot be used to arrive at the correct doctrine of the Lord's Supper because

---

[62] The words Ex. 12:11 are a part of the record of the divine institution of the Passover. The words read: "And thus shall ye eat it: with your loins girded, your shoes on your feet, and your staff in your hand; and ye shall eat it in haste; it is the Lord's passover [פֶּסַח הוּא לַיהוָה]." Zwingli refers the "it" to the paschal lamb; פֶּסַח to the angel's merciful passing over of the houses of the Children of Israel (a meaning it can have), and thus obtains the sentence: "The paschal lamb is the (sparing) passover of the Lord," and then practices imposition: The paschal lamb signifies the sparing passing over of the Lord. (*Opp.* III, 343: "*Est* cannot be understood otherwise than was said, namely, for *symbolum est aut figura*. So that the sense is: Eat it in haste! For it is a symbol or emblem of the passing of the Lord.") Luther remarks on the same passage (St. L. XX:786): "When Moses says: 'Eat it in haste; it is the Lord's passover,' then Zwingli cannot prove that 'it' refers to the paschal lamb. For he has quickly been given the answer: 'Eat in haste; it is the Lord's passover,' is like our German: Eat meat, for it is Sunday; drink water, for it is Friday. Here no one will press out this sense, that meat signifies Sunday or water signifies Friday. Similarly here: 'Eat in haste; it is the Lord's passover,' that is, it is the day when the Lord went into Egypt," etc. Krauth, too, remarks to the words "It is the Lord's passover": "The 'it' does not refer to the lamb, but to the whole transaction which takes place with girded loins and the eating of the lamb. The 'it' is used indefinitely, as we would say, 'Let us gather round the cheerful hearth, let us light up the children's tree, for it is Christmas.' The reason for the name 'passover' follows in the twelfth verse: 'It is the Lord's passover. For I will pass through the land.'" (*Conserv. Ref.*, p. 617.) Thus Keil, too, among recent exegetes explains the text in his *Commentary*.

But even if with Zwingli we do not refer the statement "It is the Lord's passover" to the feast, or the Passover festival, but to the paschal lamb, that reference still does not result in Zwingli's *significat*. The expression "The paschal lamb is the (sparing) passing over of the Lord" is then analogical to John 11:25: "Christ is the Resurrection and the Life." Christ does not signify the Resurrection and the Life, He actually is the Resurrection and the Life. In Christ, or wherever Christ is, there is resurrection and life for men so that whoever believes in Christ lives and does not die. Thus in Ex. 12:11 we would have the declaration: The paschal lamb is the sparing, or passover, of the Lord. The sense then would be: In the paschal lamb there was present for the Children of Israel sparing, exemption from God's righteous judgment, so that when God saw the blood of the paschal lamb on the huts of the Israelites, He passed by with His vindictive judgment.

they are the point in controversy (τὸ κρινόμενον),[63] one can hardly believe anyone to be serious in saying such a thing. Even if we disregard the fact that it amounts to the demand that the Christians give up all of Scripture as source and norm of doctrine, since all pertinent Scripture passages in every doctrine have been contested, just imagine a number of theologians wanting to ascertain the true doctrine of the Lord's Supper, but from the outset binding themselves not to adduce as proof for the correct doctrine those texts of Scripture which treat of the Lord's Supper! That surpasses even the Pope, who, though he has all doctrines "in the shrine of his heart," still for appearance' sake appeals to Scripture. By ruling that the texts treating of the Lord's Supper are not to be adduced as proof for the doctrine of the Lord's Supper one abandons even the pretense that the resulting doctrine is the teaching of Scripture. That rule is rather a direct demand to set aside the Scriptures entirely and to take one's teaching of the Lord's Supper solely out of one's ego, the *"Inwendigkeit"* of man, as Luther terms it. Luther sets forth the naive character of the demand to give up the texts pertaining to the Lord's Supper in the following likeness: The words of Scripture, which treat of a particular doctrine, are for the Christian both the only source of knowledge of this doctrine and his only weapon in combatting the false prophets. If now the Christian in the controversy on the Lord's Supper is not to use as proof those Scripture passages which treat of the Lord's Supper, that is as if in a secular war the opponent asks me before the beginning of the battle first to surrender my weapons to him.[64]

---

[63] Cp. the quotations in Gerhard, *Loci,* "De s. coena," § 79: "Bullinger and Tigurinus demand in their book against Jacob Andreae, fol. 45, that the words of institution no longer be adduced as basis because they are contested [τὸ κρινόμενον]. The same thought is repeated by Calvin in his *admonitio ult.,* p. 240, *consid. commonef.* pp. 15 and 188; *Witakerus, De script.,* qu. 5, c. 9, *Orthod. consensus,* c. 7, f. 161: 'Manifest is the misuse of the words of institution toward proving what in these words is questioned or controverted.' Daniel Burenus, consul at Bremen, said *anno* 1560 in a public convention, 'that the Lutherans could bring forward for their opinion nothing at all but three impotent words.' A thought which the consul no doubt learned from Peter Martyr, who in *dialogo de natura humana,* p. 127, addresses us with these words: 'Always you see less than befits a wise man, because you labor so hard for an absurd and useless dogma, for the defense of which you have nothing at all but the word of Christ: "This is My body." ' "

[64] Luther writes (St. L. XX:780, 782): "It is the arrogance of the wicked devil, who makes sport of us in this great matter through these "enthusiasts," when he pretends to be ready to be instructed by the Scriptures if only he be permitted first to get rid of Scripture or twist it to suit his fancy. Just as if I would deprive my opponent of his weapons by cunning words and give him in place thereof painted paper weapons — just like his — and then would dare him to

Lastly, the following fact, too, should be remembered. Though the Reformed, Zwingli and Calvin included, declare the Lutheran doctrine of the Lord's Supper to be a horrible and pernicious abomination — as we reluctantly had to record (pp. 294, 327 ff.) — and call us Lutherans cannibals, etc., and though Calvin asserts of the Lutherans, "the devil has blinded them by his delusion [*diaboli incantatio*]," [65] nevertheless they have always offered to unite with Luther and the Lutheran Church even without removal of the doctrinal discord. This fact proves incontrovertibly that they have no assurance from Scripture that their doctrine is true. They lack this assurance, moreover, because they do not base their doctrine on Christ's words, but on a human "exegesis" of them. Melanchthon reports on the colloquy at Marburg: "The opponents would not recede from their preconceived faith [in the doctrine of the Lord's Supper], desired, however, that Dr. Luther should accept them as brethren. To this Dr. Martin would in no wise agree, said sternly to them that he was astonished how they could regard him as a brother if they actually regarded their doctrine as the truth; that it was an indication of how little they thought of their own faith." (St. L. XVII:1949 f.; *Corp. Ref.* I, 1102.) His own opinion Melanchthon expresses in the words: "They tried hard to induce us to acknowledge them as our brethren. Imagine the folly! While they condemn us, they nevertheless desire of us to regard them as brethren. We refused to accede to their wishes in this matter. I am firmly of the opinion, if they had not already gone so far, they now would not think of putting on so great a tragedy." (St. L. XVII:1956; *Corp. Ref.* I, 1107.)

---

vanquish me with them and fight me off. Oh, that would be a daring hero — fit to be spit upon and driven out of the village with shouts if he meant that in earnest, or he would cause a good carnival laugh if he did it as a jest. Now, in like manner these "enthusiasts" deal with us, first want to twist the natural statements and sense of Scripture to their thoughts and intent and then glory that we have no Scripture proof, so that the devil may hold us in derision or rather safely murder us while we are defenseless. But to oppose this scheme there is a little word that serves us exceedingly well, namely, No! As a result they stand as butter in the sun. Here now let not only the Christians, but also the heathen, the Turks, the Tartars, the Jews, the idolaters, and all the world be judge between us, which one of us ought to prove his understanding of Scripture. . . To sum up: We have the clear, bare Scriptures on our side, which read: 'Take, eat, this is My body,' and there is no necessity nor obligation on our side to furnish other Scripture proof (though we could abundantly do it) besides this text; but they owe us a Scripture text that reads: This signifies My body, or: This is a symbol of My body.'

[65] *Inst.* IV, 17, 23; likewise IV, 17, 19: "Satan has deranged their minds by horrible bewitchment."

4

A Survey of the Relation of the Various Doctrines of the Lord's Supper to the Words of Institution

People are wont to say that the differences between the churches in their teaching of the Lord's Supper arise from their different "interpretations" of the words of institution. This is not a precise statement. The truth is that Luther does not "interpret" the words of institution at all, but takes them as they read. The Roman and Reformed teachings, however, rest on extensive and copious "interpretation" of the words of institution.

Let us picture to ourselves how much "exegesis" Christ and the Apostle Paul would have had to use to arrive at the Roman teaching. They would have had to devote extensive exegesis to the word "bread." Christ would have had to say approximately: "I indeed take bread, as you see, bless it, and give it to you to eat. Also My Evangelists and Apostles will later expressly mention the bread as present in My Sacrament. But do not understand My words or theirs as they read. Do not think that bread remains real or substantial bread in this Supper. Merely the external appearance of bread remains. The whole substance of the bread has been converted into My body.[66] Furthermore, I indeed say: 'Take, eat; this is My body.' This might cause you to think that My body really is only to be eaten in the Sacrament. But that would be a misunderstanding. My body should not merely be eaten, but should also be reserved in the *sacrarium,* 'proposed' (exhibited) publicly to the people to be adored, and particularly be solemnly borne about in processions.[67] Again, I indeed say: 'Drink

---

[66] *Trid., De s. euch. sacram.,* can. 2: "If any one saith that, in the sacred and holy sacrament of the Eucharist the substance of the bread and wine remains conjointly with the body and blood of our Lord Jesus Christ, and denieth that wonderful and singular conversion of the whole substance of the bread into the Body, and of the whole substance of the wine into the Blood — the species only of the bread and wine remaining — which conversion indeed the Catholic Church most aptly calls Transubstantiation; let him be anathema." Waterworth, p. 82.

[67] *Trid., loc. cit.,* can. 7, 4, 6: "If any one saith that it is not lawful for the sacred Eucharist to be reserved in the sacrarium, but that, immediately after consecration, it must necessarily be distributed amongst those present; . . . let him be anathema. . . . If any one saith that, after the consecration is completed, the body and blood of our Lord Jesus Christ are not in the admirable sacrament of the Eucharist, but (are there) only during the use, whilst it is being taken, and not either before or after; and that, in the hosts, or consecrated particles, which are reserved or which remain after communion, the true body of the Lord remaineth not; let him be anathema. . . . If any one saith that in the holy

ye all of it.' From that people may get the idea that I want also the
cup passed to all who partake of this Supper ordained by Me. But
that again would be a misunderstanding. For the common Christians
'Communion in one form [*sub una specie*]' is enough. Remember, too,
that there is such a thing as 'concomitance,' by which My blood is
already contained in the body given you, so that the cup really
becomes superfluous.[68] Finally, I would by all means not have you
forget the most important thing in the Sacrament: I indeed say, 'This
is My body, which is given for you,' and, 'This is My blood, which is
shed for you for the remission of sins.' This must, if you took My words
literally, lead you to think that you are fully reconciled to God by
the giving of My body and the shedding of My blood, and that the
main object of giving you this My body and blood in the Sacrament
is to assure you of the forgiveness of your sins and to call forth and
strengthen in you faith in My reconciling sacrifice offered on the Cross.
But thus you would again be putting an entirely wrong construction
on My words. Mark well, and do not forget, that the principal purpose
of My Supper is not to be a remembrance of My reconciling sacrifice
and a means of distributing the remission of sins purchased by Me.
On the contrary, My Vicar on earth, the Pope, will ordain priests, and
these priests will — and they alone have this power — continually sacrifice My body and My blood 'in an unbloody manner'·in the Eucharist,
thus offer to God for you a 'true and proper propitiatory sacrifice,' and
thereby provide for those present and the absent, the living and the
dead, remission of sins and assist them in 'other necessities.'"[69] These,

---

sacrament of the Eucharist Christ, the only-begotten Son of God, is not to be
adored with the worship, even external, of latria; and is, consequently, neither
to be venerated with a special festive solemnity, nor to be solemnly borne about
in processions, according to the laudable and universal rite and custom of holy
church; or, is not to be proposed publicly to the people to be adored, and that
the adorers thereof are idolaters; let him be anathema." Waterworth, p. 83.

68 *Trid., loc. cit.,* c. 3: "Wherefore it is most true that as much is contained
under either species as under both . . . can. 3: If any one denieth that in the
venerable sacrament of the Eucharist the whole Christ is contained under each
species, and under every part of each species, when separated (when a separation
has been made); let him be anathema." Waterworth, p. 78, 82 f.

69 *Trid., loc. cit.,* can. 5: "If any one saith, . . . that the principal fruit of the
holy Eucharist is the remission of sins, . . . let him be anathema." . . . *De sacrificio
missae,* can. 1: "If any one saith that in the mass a true and proper sacrifice is
not offered to God, . . . let him be anathema." . . . Can. 3: "If any one saith that
the sacrifice of the mass is only a sacrifice of praise and of thanksgiving; or, that
it is a bare commemoration of the sacrifice consummated on the cross, but not
a propitiatory sacrifice; or, that it profits him only who receives; and that it ought
not to be offered for the living and the dead for sins, pains, satisfactions, and
other necessities; let him be anathema." Waterworth, p. 83, 158 f.

and still more, "interpretations" would have been necessary to present the Roman conception of the Lord's Supper.

Also the Reformed doctrine of the Lord's Supper demands a great amount of "exegesis." Christ would have had to give approximately this commentary on His words: "True, My words, 'Take, eat; this is My body,' sound as if I were calling on you to eat with your mouth. But don't imagine that My body is here on earth in the Sacrament of the Altar and is intended to be eaten with the mouth (*oralis manducatio*). As distant as heaven is from the earth, so far is My body removed from this Supper and your mouth. What I really mean to say with the words 'Take, eat; this is My body' is this: With the mouth of your faith you are to ascend into heaven and there by faith eat My body spiritually.[70] Furthermore, when I say to you, 'Take, eat; this is My body, which is given for you,' this indeed sounds as though you were receiving that body which is given for you into death and not a symbol or image of My body. However, you must interpret My words according to the axiom that a body always can possess only a local and visible presence and does not extend beyond the natural dimensions of a human body. Since, now, you cannot see My body in My Supper, nor take hold of it with the hands, you must, when you hear the term 'My body,' think only of an 'image of My body.' "[71]

The Apostle Paul, too, would have had to add an extensive commentary to his statements on the Lord's Supper if his purpose had been

---

[70] *Consensus Tigurinus*, cap. 25: "Though philosophically speaking, there is no 'place' above the heavens, nevertheless, because the body of Christ, as the nature and mode of a human body calls for, is finite and is contained in heaven, as in a place, it is necessary that it be distant from us by so great an interval of space as heaven is removed from the earth. . . . For since the signs are here on earth, are observed with the eyes, softly touched by the hands, Christ, as far as He is man, is to be sought nowhere else than in heaven and not otherwise than with the mind and the intelligence of faith."

[71] Calvin: "It is necessary for us to establish such a presence of Christ in the sacred Supper, as neither . . . to deprive Him of His corporeal dimensions, nor to represent His body as in different places at once, nor to assign it an immensity diffused through heaven and earth, which would be clearly inconsistent with the reality of His human nature." (*Inst.* IV, 17, 19; Allen II, 542 f.) — *Confess. Anglicana* (Niemeyer, p. 598): "Since the reality of a human nature requires that the body of one and the same man cannot be at numerous places at once, but must be in one place, somewhere and definite, therefore the body of Christ cannot be present in numerous and diverse places at one and the same time. And since, as the Sacred Scriptures report, Christ has ascended into heaven and there is to remain to the end of time, none of the believers should either believe, or profit from, a presence in the Eucharist of His real and corporeal (as they call it) flesh and blood."

to call forth Reformed conceptions of the Sacrament in his readers. He would have had to add the following or a similar explanation: "I indeed say, the cup is the communion (κοινωνία) of the blood of Christ, and the bread is the communion (κοινωνία) of the body of Christ. As these words sound, they might lead you to think that Christ's body is present in the Lord's Supper besides the bread, and Christ's blood besides the wine, and that all who partake of this Supper receive with the cup Christ's blood and with the bread Christ's body. This communion between the bread and the body of Christ, and between the wine and the blood of Christ, you might also find in my later statement: 'Wherefore whosoever shall eat this bread, and drink this cup of the Lord, unworthily, shall be guilty of the body and blood of the Lord' (1 Cor. 11:27). But to arrive at the proper understanding of my words you must grant room to thoughts foreign to, and independent of, My words, such as: 'The flesh profiteth nothing.' [72] Moreover, why should there be any need at all of the presence of Christ's body and blood in the Sacrament, since the believers by faith already possess everything and since the Church of the Old Covenant also had only symbols of the sacrifice of Christ and of God's grace? [73] It would furthermore plainly detract from Christ's celestial glory if He were to 'fasten to the element of bread' His body and thus forsake heaven.[74] Also we must not overlook the consternation which would have filled the disciples if they had not immediately applied the needed exegesis and substituted 'symbol of the body' for 'body.' [75] At the same time the general rule must always be adhered to that Christ's body under all circumstances can have but

---

[72] Thus Zwingli in the words adduced above (page 332): "We do not base our doctrine on the words of institution, but on the single statement: 'The flesh profiteth nothing.' " (St. L. XX:477).

[73] Thus Hodge (*Syst. Theol.* III, 647) summarizes Calvin's position in these words: "To preserve the consistency of the great Reformer, his language must be interpreted as to harmonize with the two crucial facts for which he so earnestly contends; first, that believers receive elsewhere by faith all they receive at the Lord's table; and, secondly, that we Christians receive nothing above and beyond that which was received by the saints of the Old Testament, before the glorified body of Christ had any existence."

[74] Calvin, *Inst.* IV, 17, 19: "It is necessary for us to establish such a presence of Christ in the sacred supper, as neither, on the one hand, to fasten Him to the element of bread, or to enclose Him in it, or in any way to circumscribe Him, which would derogate from His celestial glory" (Allen II, 542 f.).

[75] Calvin, *Inst.* IV, 17, 23: "For if it had not been understood by the Apostles that the bread was called His body in a figurative sense, because it was a symbol of His body, they would undoubtedly have been disturbed about so monstrous a declaration." Allen II, 549.

a local and visible presence.[76] Bearing all this in mind, you will understand all my statements which speak of a presence of Christ's body in the Lord's Supper to mean an absence of that body and will believe present in the Sacrament only a symbol of Christ's body." [77] — The quotations adduced prove that the Reformed teaching of the Lord's Supper actually rests on these "interpretations."

Contrariwise the Lutheran doctrine of the Lord's Supper rests on the bare words of institution, and not on added "exegesis." It permits "bread" to be bread, and "is" to be is, and "body" to be Christ's body "which is given for you." To this acceptance of the words the Reformed take exception (Calvin, too; *Inst.* IV, 17, 20) and assert that Luther, the Lutheran Confessions, and the Lutheran teachers in their teaching of the Lord's Supper speak of a "sacramental union" (*unio sacramentalis*), which obtains between the bread and the body of Christ, the wine and the blood of Christ, that Scripture, however, speaks of no *unio sacramentalis*. True, the term *unio sacramentalis* is not in Scripture. But the thing so named is clearly taught in Holy Writ, as clearly as, e. g., the ὁμοούσιος. Christ calls the bread which He distributes in the Sacrament His body, which is given for us. Since the bread, however, is not changed but remains bread, as the Scriptures state, and since the unchanged bread is also the body of Christ, as Scripture likewise states, the Scriptures do teach a union of the body of Christ with the bread; and this union Luther and the Lutherans call *unio sacramentalis* because it is peculiar to the Sacrament of the Altar. The term is entirely adequate. It is not "accessory" to the words of institution in meaning, but expresses very exactly the thought of the words of institution. "This union," says Majus, "is unique, and has its unshakable foundation in the words of institution, when Christ distributes the bread and says, 'Eat, this is My body,' and passes the cup and says, 'This is My blood'" (*Synopsis Theol. Christ.*, 1708, p. 185). On the one hand, this term "sacramental union" excludes the Roman teaching of transubstantiation, which substitutes for "bread" the mere semblance of bread, and on the other hand, the Reformed symbolism, which substitutes for "body" the symbol of the

---

[76] Calvin, *Inst.* IV, 17, 29: "But it is essential to a real body to have its particular form and dimensions and to be contained within some certain space. Let us hear no more, then, of this ridiculous notion, which fastens the mind of men, and Christ Himself, to the bread." Allen II, 559.

[77] Calvin in his explanation of the *Consens. Tigur.* (Niemeyer, p. 217): "We use the axiom, accepted without contradiction among all the pious, that, whenever the sacraments are dealt with, it is customary metonymically to transfer the name of the thing sealed to the seal."

body. The term does not involve a departure from the words of institution; rather, over against the Roman and the Reformed defection from the words, it records our inviolable adherence to the words as they read.

In teaching the *unio sacramentalis* the Lutheran Church is also in full agreement with what St. Paul declares (1 Corinthians 10 and 11) concerning the essence of the Lord's Supper, in his criticism of the celebration of the Sacrament in the Corinthian congregation. We heard above (p. 318) how earnestly the Apostle impresses on the Corinthians, who were observing the Lord's Supper in a trifling and thoughtless manner, that for all who partake of the Lord's Supper the cup of blessing is "the communion [κοινωνία] of the blood of Christ" and the bread broken is "the communion [κοινωνία] of the body of Christ," [78] so that everyone who eats and drinks unworthily becomes guilty of the body and blood of the Lord by "not discerning the Lord's body [μὴ διακρίνων τὸ σῶμα τοῦ Κυρίου]." Also in these Apostolic instructions as to the right spirit in which Christians are to drink "the cup of the Lord [ποτήριον Κυρίου]" and "be partakers of the Lord's table [τράπεζα Κυρίου]," the Lutheran doctrine of the "Real Presence" is so clearly expressed that the rationalist Rueckert is right in saying that only if one rejects the authority of the Apostle Paul can one deny the Real Presence.[79]

---

[78] The first meaning of κοινωνία is of course "communion," *communio*. Whether it can also mean "communication" in the New Testament, as some (Ebeling) affirm and others (Cremer) deny, need not be investigated at this point. Here, at any rate, it is "communion," as Luther translated it. This is demanded by the context. As participation in the sacrificial feasts of the pagans established communion with the demons, so partaking of the cup in the Lord's Supper establishes communion with the blood of Christ. Incorrectly Meyer comments on 1 Cor. 10:16 that Luther did not take κοινωνία to be "communion," but "communication." Where Luther translates, he takes κοινωνία as "communion," as both his translation of the Bible and, e. g., St. L. XX:236 prove. That, in presenting the sense of the passage, he also speaks of a *communication* of the body of Christ results from the fact that whoever maintains the *communio corporis* thereby also teaches the *communicatio corporis*. If the bread is the communion of the body of Christ for all partakers of the Supper of the Lord, the worthy and the unworthy, then naturally the body of Christ is communicated by means of the bread.

[79] *Das Abendmahl, sein Wesen und seine Gesch. in d. alt. K.*, 1856, p. 236, 241 f., 297. Familiar are the words of Luther on 1 Cor. 10:16: "Secondly, besides these four powerful passages we have still another, 1 Cor. 10:16, which reads: 'The cup of blessing which we bless, is it not the communion of the blood of Christ? The bread which we break, is it not the communion of the body of Christ?' That is indeed to my mind a passage, yes, a thunderbolt on the head of Dr. Carlstadt and all his partizans. This passage was the life-giving cordial for my heart in my temptation regarding this Sacrament. Even though we had

Luther, too, confesses, that his flesh tempted him to put a different meaning into the words of institution than they contain because he saw well that thus he "could have given the Papacy a good trouncing." "But," he adds, "I am held captive, cannot escape; the text stands there too powerful and words cannot uproot it from the mind." (St. L. XV: 2050; De Wette, II, 577.) "The Word they still shall let remain," characterizes Luther's stand not only over against Rome, but also over against all Reformed denominations.

Both opponents basically form a united front against Luther and the Lutheran Church in their teaching of the Lord's Supper, in spite of the difference in their conclusions, inasmuch as neither will accept the plain meaning of the statements of Scripture on the Lord's Supper. Lutherans were justified in calling attention to this fact. Krauth (*op. cit.*, p. 626 f.) writes: "It is worth noticing that, widely as Romanism with its Transubstantiation, and Rationalism with its Symbols, differ in their results, they run into their error by the same fallacious principle of interpretation, each applying it with the same arbitrariness, but to different objects. The Romanist wishes to do away with Scripture testimony in regard to the bread and wine; and although they bear their name before the Lord's Supper, during the Lord's Supper, and after the Lord's Supper, he insists that there is

---

no other texts than this one, with it we could sufficiently strengthen all consciences and mightily enough vanquish all opponents." (St. L. XX:235.) On the positive side Luther remarks on 1 Cor. 10:16: "Observe that Paul clearly and lucidly says: 'The same bread that we break is the communion of the body of Christ.' Do you hear it, my dear brother? The bread broken or divided and distributed is the communion of the body of Christ, it is, it is, it is (he says), the communion of the body of Christ. What, however, is the communion of the body of Christ? It cannot be anything else but that those who take the broken bread, everyone his piece, in the same take the body of Christ." (*Ibid.*, 236.) — If one adds what Luther (*loc. cit.*) says regarding the four reports on the institution (232 ff.), and later (240 ff.) goes on to say on Paul's warning that those who eat and drink unworthily become guilty of the body and blood of the Lord because they do not discern the Lord's body, it becomes apparent that this Lutheran confutation of Carlstadt already clearly shows all Reformed interpretations of the words of institution to be impositions. When Meyer opines that Paul's statement about becoming guilty of the body and blood of the Lord (1 Cor. 11:27) proves neither the absence nor the presence of Christ's body and blood in the Supper, and even talks of sophistry ("*Spitzfindigkeit*") on the part of Luther, Meyer forgets that the very words of Paul, according to which those eating and drinking unworthily become guilty of the body and blood of Christ, express the presence of Christ's body and blood. And what the words express one can also prove with them. Meyer would also grant this if he had not decided for himself that the presence of Christ's body and blood in the Eucharist is impossible. But Meyer is going decidedly too far when he expects others to explain St. Paul's words according to Meyer's notions.

neither bread nor wine there, but only their accidents. While our
Lord says: 'This is My body,' the Romanist, in effect, makes it:
This seeming bread is no longer bread, but has become, has been
transubstantiated into, My body. He deserts the letter and reaches
Transubstantiation. The Rationalist wishes to retain the bread and
wine, and therefore holds that what the Scripture calls bread and
wine *is* bread and wine; but he wishes to do away with the Scripture
testimony in regard to the body and blood; and although the Scriptures
say that of that which the Savior tells them to 'Take, eat,' He declares
most explicitly, 'This is My body'; and of that which He tells them
to drink, He says, 'This is My blood' — though it says that the bread
is the communion of His body and the cup the communion of His
blood — though it declares that the guilt of the heedless communicant
is that he does not 'discern the Lord's body,' and that he that eateth
and drinketh unworthily is guilty of the body and blood of Christ;
in the face of all this he insists that there is in the Lord's Supper only
the shadow, image, or sign of the body and blood of Christ, not the
true body and true blood. With what face can a Rationalist meet
a Romanist, or a Romanist meet a Rationalist? No wonder that the
Rationalist, after all, is less violent against Romanism than against
the pure doctrine of our Church.[80] There is the secret affinity of error
between them; and Romanism does not so hate Rationalism, Rationalism does not so hate Romanism, as both hate unswerving fidelity to
the Word of God. That the Romish and rationalizing modes of interpretation are nearer to each other than either is to the Lutheran is
admitted by both Rationalists and Romanists. The rationalizing interpreters make it one of the commonplaces of objection to the Lutheran
view that it has less in a literal interpretation of the Scriptures to
sustain it than the Romish view has: that is, the Romish view is less
decisively opposed than the Lutheran is to rationalistic modes of
literal interpretation."

But how much truth is there in the objection of the Reformed
that the Lutherans themselves do not abide by the literal sense of the
words of institution? Reformed theologians have always raised this
objection. Calvin makes a special effort to expose the Lutherans as

---

[80] Thus Calvin expressly says in his polemic against the Lutheran doctrine:
"I speak not of the Romanists, whose doctrine is more tolerable, or at least more
modest; but some [the Lutherans are meant] are so carried away with the heat
of contention, as to affirm that on account of the union of the two natures in
Christ wherever His Divinity is, His flesh, which cannot be separated from it,
is there also; as if that union had mingled the two natures so as to form some
intermediate kind of being, which is neither God nor man." Allen II, 560.

participes criminis Calvinistici.[81] Hodge, too, says that the literal sense is given up by one part as well as by the other (*Syst. Theol.* III, 662). Generally the following particulars are adduced:

1. That the Lutherans understand by the "cup" not the vessel, but the wine contained in the cup; hence metonymically *contentum pro continente.* Hodge says: "When Christ says, 'This cup is the New Testament,' it is admitted that the cup is used metonymically for the wine in the cup." Yes, but thus we are abiding by the words of institution, for Christ tells us to drink not the cup, but of the cup: "Drink ye all of it [πίετε ἐξ αὐτοῦ πάντες]," Matt. 26:27. And Scripture expressly reports that the disciples complied with the instruction of Christ and drank, not the cup, but of the cup: "And they all drank of it" (Mark 14:23).

2. That the Lutherans use the expressions "in, with, and under the bread" to designate the presence of the body of Christ in the Lord's Supper. Hodge, like his old Reformed predecessors, holds the opinion that this phraseology "makes the language figurative, and the literal interpretations, the main, if not the only, prop of the Lutheran doctrine, is given up" (*ibid.*).[82] But this objection is entirely beside the mark because it evades the real issue. Even the Reformed will admit that stating the sense of the words of Scripture in other and more words does not amount to a changing of the sense of the text and is no relinquishing of the literal interpretation. That is "exegesis" of the right sort. The Reformed themselves do not concede that they are abandoning the literal meaning of a text when they paraphrase the sense of a Scripture statement. Hodge himself (*ibid.*, p. 473) paraphrases the "is" (ὁ ὤν) in the words John 1:18: "Which is in the bosom of the Father" by saying: "He who is, was, and ever shall be in the bosom of the Father, i. e., most intimately united with Him." In this case Hodge will certainly not concede that he is interpreting the passage "figuratively." From Calvin and others he has appropriated the assertion, without testing its correctness, that the Lutherans by their "in, with, and under the bread" are making "figurative language" of the words of institution. Luther himself had to deal with this objection. He writes: "But when this false spirit pronounces us guilty

---

[81] *Inst.* IV, 17, 20. Also in his explanation of the *Consensus Tigurinus;* in Niemeyer, p. 216.

[82] Calvin: "They strenuously insist on the literal meaning of these words, 'This is My body,' yet afterwards depart from their literal precision, and explain them to import that the body of Christ is with the bread, in the bread, and under the bread." *Inst.* IV, 17, 20; Allen II, 544.

of not abiding by the words and the one sense ourselves, because we say that the words, 'This is My body,' must be understood as saying: Under the bread is My body, or: In the bread is My body, etc., I answer: That lying spirit is well aware that he is thereby doing us wrong. . . . I have indeed said in my little book that those who in ordinary conversation say: Under the bread is Christ's body, or: In the bread is Christ's body, are not to be condemned, because with those words they are confessing their faith, that Christ's body truly is in the Sacrament. But thereby we make no different, new text; nor do they desire that these words of theirs should be the text, but they strictly abide by the text. For also St. Paul says: 'Christ is God,' Rom. 9:5, and 'God was in Christ,' 2 Cor. 5:19, and still each passage has its simple and certain meaning, and, in addition, the two do not conflict." (St. L. XX:899 f.) The same understanding of the "in," "with," and "under" is voiced by the dogmaticians.[83]

3. To prove that the Lutherans likewise give up the literal sense, Hodge says furthermore: "If the words of Christ are to be taken literally, they teach the doctrine of transubstantiation." And: "If the bread is literally the body of Christ, it is no longer bread; for no one asserts that the same thing can be bread and flesh [the body of Christ] at the same time." Hodge thinks that by declining transubstantiation the Lutherans are giving up the literal sense of the words of institution. This argument was discussed sufficiently in describing the *locutio exhibitiva* (p. 301ff.). There it was also shown that Hodge himself invalidates his own argument by maintaining, in the doctrine of Christ's Person, that the Son of Mary is literally and without any transubstantiation and simultaneously the Son of God (Luke 1:35). He does not grant the validity of the conclusion: If the words Luke 1:35 are taken literally, they teach the transubstantiation of the Son of Mary into the Son of God, and he rejects the argument: If the Son of Mary literally is the Son of God, then He cannot at the same time be the Son of Mary. Hodge rather is determined to maintain with the Christian Church that one and the same subject can "at the same time" be the Son of Mary and the Son of God.

Reformed theologians make it very hard for themselves to grasp

---

[83] Quenstedt, II, 1201 f.: "It does not follow that an explanation of a text wipes out the text. For thus no translator, no commentator of Scripture, would preserve the text; equipollent terms, grammatical synonyms, oratorical paraphrases, and theological interpretations do not derogate from the text. But he who changes the literal sense into the contrary figurative sense gives up the text; indeed, contradicts the text. Whoever makes of "body" "symbol of body" is changing the text, for body and symbol of the body are two different things.

the meaning of what Lutherans teach on the Lord's Supper. Contending that the Lutherans do not abide by the literal meaning, Hodge observes: "Lutherans themselves cannot avoid saying and admitting that the bread in the Lord's Supper is the body of Christ." In proof he quotes Luther's Small Catechism and Krauth's *Conservative Reformation*. The proof is entirely correct. But he is wrong in assuming that Lutherans are there inadvertently conceding something they do not mean to teach. That the bread in the Lord's Supper is Christ's body is not an unintentional admission of the Lutherans, but is just what they mean to teach and maintain over against the Reformed. The bread in the Lord's Supper is actually Christ's body, of course not by transubstantiation, but because of the sacramental union (*propter unionem sacramentalem*), that is, because Christ's word: "This is My body, which is given for you," has united Christ's body with the bread in the Sacrament of the Altar — just as the Son of Mary is actually the Son of God, not by the transubstantiation of a man into God, but because of the personal union (*propter unionem personalem*). This fact, and nothing more, also Krauth stresses in the words quoted by Hodge. But Hodge does not deal quite fairly with the quotation. He quotes from Krauth: "Just as it would be blasphemy to say, 'Man is God,' and is yet literally true of Christ, 'This man is God,' so would it be blasphemy to say, 'Bread is Christ's body,' and yet it is literally true, 'This bread is Christ's body'" (*op. cit.*, p. 609). What Krauth means to say, and really says, is this: Outside the personal union of God and man in Christ, it would indeed be blasphemous to say, "Man is God," but within the personal union of God and man in Christ it is correct to say, and we must say on the basis of Scripture: "This Man is God." Similarly it would indeed be blasphemous outside the sacramental union of bread and body of Christ in the Lord's Supper to say, "Bread is Christ's body," but within the sacramental union of bread and the body of Christ in the Lord's Supper it is literally true: "This bread is Christ's body." But this bearing of Krauth's words on the personal union in Christ and the sacramental union in the Lord's Supper Hodge effaces by doing two things. First, he omits Krauth's very next words: "*This* man is God personally because of the personal union, and *This* bread is the body of Christ sacramentally because of the sacramental union." Secondly, he omits the italics of Krauth, by which Krauth had sharply marked the bearing of his words on the personal union in Christ and the sacramental union in the Lord's Supper. Krauth had italicized, "*This* man is God," namely, this one certain Man Christ, and, "*This* bread is Christ's body," namely, the bread in the Lord's Supper. These italics Hodge omits. Thus he diminishes the clarity and force of Krauth's presentation and obstructs for himself the correct historical understanding of the Lutheran teaching.

4. Perhaps the objection most widely circulated is the contention that Luther and the Lutheran Church prove the Real Presence not really from the words of institution, but from the doctrine of Christ's Person, especially from the communication of divine omnipresence to the human nature of Christ.[84] Just the opposite is the historical truth, as has already been shown copiously in the doctrine of Christ's Person under the heading "The Communicated Omnipresence and the Lord's Supper" (Vol. II, 190 ff.). Proof was brought both from Luther and from the very emphatic declaration in the Preface to the *Book of Concord*. Moreover, it was established how it happened that in the controversy regarding the Lord's Supper Luther discussed the doctrine of Christ's Person, and particularly the omnipresence of Christ's human nature, so fully and thoroughly. Zwingli and his confreres had asserted that the doctrine of Christ's Person, specifically the article of His ascension and session on the right hand of God, compelled one, upon hearing the words of the Lord's Supper, "Take, eat; this is My body," to think not of the presence, but of the absence of Christ's body, because Christ's human nature could possess no other than the visible, local presence, not exceeding the visible and spatial dimensions of His body. Over against this astonishing Christology Luther and our Lutheran Confession demonstrate that this view reveals a perversion of the Scripture doctrine of the Person of Christ by the Reformed. The Lutherans show that not men, but Holy Scripture ascribe to Christ according to His human nature at least three different modes of presence: (a) the visible or local (*praesentia localis, circumscriptiva*), (b) the invisible, illocal (*praesentia invisibilis, definitiva*), and (c) the illocal, repletive divine mode (*praesentia divina et repletiva*).

It is impertinent for Loofs (R. E., 3d ed., I, 66) here to speak of artifices which exceed the faith of the Christians. Even though many Christians are not familiar with the terms *praesentia localis, praesentia definitiva, praesentia divina sive supernaturalis,* still they know and believe the facts designated by these terms. When they read a Scripture text such as John 4:4: "And He must needs go through Samaria,"

---

[84] Thus also the *Admon. Neostad.*, p. 94 (in Gerhard, *Loci, "De s. coena,"* § 79): "The Lutherans, after they have long sounded forth words, words, words, take refuge in the ubiquity when they are pressed for the reason for their interpretation."

they think of the *praesentia localis*. When, however, they read John
20:19 ff. that Christ came to His disciples, "the doors being closed
[τῶν θυρῶν κεκλεισμένων]," they think of the *praesentia illocalis sive
definitiva*. Lastly, when they read or hear Eph. 4:10: "He . . . ascended
up far above all heavens, that He might fill all things," and Matt. 28:20:
"I am with you alway even unto the end of the world," they think of
the *praesentia divina sive supernaturalis*. The theologians who here
speak of subtleties which Christians find incomprehensible and incredible are attributing to Christians, who in simple faith believe God's
Word, their own deficiency in Christian knowledge.

5

The Variations in the Wording of the Four Records

The variations in the wording of the four accounts of the institution of the Lord's Supper give more than a little trouble to the modern
theologians, even when they declare them to be trifling.[85] They feel
called upon to determine which one of the four holy writers (Matthew,
Mark, Luke, Paul) brings the original words, that is, the exact words
(*ipsissima verba*) used by Christ at the institution and first celebration
of the Sacrament. As to the result of their efforts Cremer declares:
"The *ipsissima verba Iesu Christi* cannot be established" (R. E., 3d ed.,
I, 35). Some report this negative result with a noticeable satisfaction.
To their mind it confirms their assumption that the boundary line
between God's Word and the word of man in Scripture cannot be
exactly ascertained. In other words, these variations in the accounts of
the Lord's Supper, in their opinion, disprove the inspiration of Holy
Scripture.[86]

This problem of the variations does not exist for the old Lutheran
theologians because they cling to the inspiration of Holy Writ. Some
of them ascribe these variations to the intention of the Holy Ghost,
who edited the original words to suit Himself, just as He did in the
case of quotations from the Old Testament.[87] Others believe that all

---

[85] Schnedermann on 1 Cor. 11:24-25.

[86] Thus Kahnis, *Dogm.*, 1st ed., I, 666 ff.; in Baier-Walther, I, 102.

[87] Thus Luther (St. L. XIX:1104) says "that the Holy Ghost purposely so
arranged it that no Evangelist coincides with the other in those words." See my
article in *L. u. W.*, 1886, p. 77 ff.: "The Form of the Old Testament Quotations
in the New Testament."

four versions bring original words. The slight variations in wording they explain by the assumption that Christ did not always use the same words at the first distribution of the elements to His twelve disciples, but varied them somewhat in the course of the distribution. One will have to grant that this explanation is plausible. Also some recent theologians use this explanation. Noesgen, e. g., says: "In repeating the words of the Sacrament on the evening of institution, Jesus is unlikely to have spoken them in a stereotyped form."[88] But Meyer disputes this allegation: "In this moment of sorrowful pathos Christ certainly uttered those few pregnant words but once for all. Such definiteness is what the sadness and sacredness of the occasion calls for."[89] But this is just an opinion, and the opposite might also be deduced from the "sorrowful pathos."

But which are the variations? Comparing the wording of the records, we find that in the words pertaining to the bread all four accounts bring out the essence of the Lord's Supper. They all declare the body of Christ to be the gift of the Sacrament. Matthew and Mark have: τοῦτό ἐστι τὸ σῶμά μου; Luke: τοῦτό ἐστι τὸ σῶμά μου τὸ ὑπὲρ ὑμῶν διδόμενον; Paul: τοῦτο μού ἐστι τὸ σῶμα τὸ ὑπὲρ ὑμῶν κλώμενον.[90]

In regard to the cup the statements in Matthew and Mark also pertain directly to the essence of the Lord's Supper, that is, they directly name the blood of Christ as the gift of the Sacrament. Matt. 26:28 and Mark 14:24: τοῦτό ἐστι τὸ αἷμά μου τὸ τῆς καινῆς διαθήκης.

---

[88] Neutest. Offenb. I, 545. See also Thomasius, Dogm. III, 2, 62. Even disregarding the factor of inspiration, I regard it as very improbable that while Luke in general followed Paul in his report, he substituted for διδόμενον (given) κλώμενον (broken). It is improbable that Luke would have taken this liberty to substitute, especially since Paul says: "I have received of the Lord that which also I delivered unto you." The question whether the shorter or the longer accounts ought to be regarded as the original ones has also been debated. A priori it is improbable that any of the holy writers would have dared to shorten or lengthen the words of institution.

[89] Kommentar zum Matthaeusev., 6th ed., p. 544.

[90] The reading κλώμενον is doubtful. It is missing in ℵ°, ABC°, is found in ℵᶜ, Dᵇ; D° has θρυπτόμενον (broken), others διδόμενον. In the Expositor's Greek Testament Findlay gives as his opinion: "The three participles are various attempts to fill up a seeming ellipsis." Meyer: κλώμενον has "correctly been declared dubious by Griessbach and struck by Lachmann, Rueckart, Tischendorf"; likewise by Westcott and Hort, also Nestle. In case "broken" is the original reading, Calov's interpretation of it, no doubt, is correct: "It shows the gravity of Christ's Passion, because the body felt such torments as though (ac si) it were broken down and crushed." Calov says "ac si" because in the proper sense Christ's body was not broken, John 19:33 ff. [RSV: "which is broken for you." The note is added: "Many ancient authorities omit broken; a few read given."]

In the accounts of Luke and Paul, however, the words regarding the cup state the purpose (*finis*) of the Lord's Supper as means of grace, namely, the new testament, or the remission of sins. 1 Cor. 11:25: τοῦτο τὸ ποτήριον ἡ καινὴ διαθήκη ἐστὶν ἐν τῷ ἐμῷ αἵματι; Luke 22:20: τοῦτο τὸ ποτήριον ἡ καινὴ διαθήκη ἐν τῷ αἵματί μου.

Some have rendered the answer to the question what "the new testament" (ἡ καινὴ διαθήκη) is unnecessarily difficult. The "new covenant," or the "new testament," is the remission of sins. This definition of the new covenant Scripture itself gives. Already in the prophecy of Jeremiah (31:31-34) the new covenant, in distinction from the old covenant, is defined as the remission of sins.[91] This definition of the new covenant is appropriated by Paul (Rom. 11:27) in the words: "For this is My covenant unto them when I shall take away their sins." The same definition of the new covenant is given Heb. 8:8-12 and 10:16-17, where the passage from Jeremiah is quoted more fully: "For this is the covenant that I will make with the house of Israel after these days, saith the Lord. . . . For I will be merciful to their unrighteousness, and their sins and their iniquities will I remember no more." The old covenant, as the covenant of the *Law*, is the imputing to man of his sins; therefore Moses' ministration (2 Cor. 3:9) is called "the ministration of condemnation," ἡ διακονία τῆς κατακρίσεως. The new covenant, or the new testament, as the covenant of the Gospel, is the forgiveness of sins; therefore the ministration of the New Testament (2 Cor. 3:9) is called "the ministration of righteousness," ἡ διακονία τῆς δικαιοσύνης. Because it is placed in contraposition to "condemnation," "righteousness" can here mean nothing else than the *iustitia imputata*, that is, the remission of sins. In short, Luther is right in remarking to the words in Luke and Paul: "This cup is the new testament": "Friend, what else is the 'new testament' than the remission of sins and eternal life, purchased for us by Christ and by Him given to us in the Sacrament?" (St. L. XX:278 f.) The words following, "in My blood" (Paul: ἐν τῷ ἐμῷ αἵματι, Luke: ἐν τῷ αἵματί μου) give the reason or cause why the cup of the Lord's Supper is the new

---

[91] What Philippi states regarding the passage should not have been questioned: "This passage in Jeremiah is no doubt to be considered the Old Testament foundation for the καινὴ διαθήκη [new covenant] to be made with Israel in the future." The "this" (αὕτη) in "This shall be the covenant" points forward, of course, to the words "I will forgive their iniquity, and I will remember their sin no more." Meyer: "This remission of sins, granted by Me, will be My covenant for them." Quenstedt, II, 1285: "Christ Himself calls the cup in the Eucharist the new testament, and Jeremiah affirms this pact as included in the new testament: 'I will forgive their iniquity, and I will remember their sin no more' (Jeremiah 31)."

testament, or the forgiveness of sins. "In My blood" is tantamount to "by means of My blood," "because of My blood." Luther: "For the sake of My blood." Chemnitz: *propter sanguinem meum.* Most of the modern theologians agree. Meyer, too, gives the grammatically correct explanation: "Christ says that the cup is the new covenant by virtue of His blood, which, He says, is in the cup."

This manner of speaking, that the cup is the new covenant, or the remission of sins, is not unusual, but occurs frequently in Holy Writ; for instance, in John 11:25 and John 6:64: Christ is the Resurrection and the Life, and: Christ's words are spirit and are life. The sense is not that Christ merely signifies, or is a sign of, the resurrection and the life, but that through Christ the resurrection is ready and to be had. Again, Christ's words do not merely signify spirit and life, but through Christ's words, or in Christ's words, spirit and life are provided. So, too, the cup in the Sacrament of the Altar does not signify the remission of sins, but in and with the cup the remission of sins is ready and to be had by virtue of, or because of, the blood of Christ, so that everyone who partakes of the cup can also by faith take or appropriate from this cup the remission of sins.[92]

---

[92] The τὸ ὑπὲρ ὑμῶν ἐκχυννόμενον in Luke 22:20, though in the nominative, is best referred to the immediately preceding τῷ αἵματί μου. The irregular case emphasizes the thing stated of the blood of Christ, namely, that this blood is shed for us, more than had the dative been repeated. So Meyer and Philippi hold. That appositional modifiers, when they are given more independence to emphasize them, are given the nominative, regardless of the grammatical construction, is found in the New Testament (James 3:8) as well as in the classical Greek. Cf. Winer, *Gramm.*, 6th ed., p. 471 ff. See in general the entire section in Winer on irregular sentence structure and irregular relation of words in a sentence (*ibid.*, pp. 495—559). In Luke 22:20 Winer prefers to relate ἐκχυννόμενον (shed) to ποτήριον (cup), though he regards it possible that it is connected with ἐν τῷ αἵματι. Luther deals *in extenso* with the question under discussion (St. L. XX:1060 ff.), though he declares it irrelevant as far as the doctrine of the Lord's Supper is concerned.

With Luther it must also be maintained that the phrase "in My blood" belongs to the entire statement, "This cup is the new testament," because it states the reason why the cup is the new testament. It cannot merely be connected with "this cup" because it is separated from "cup" by the words, "is the new testament." Luther: "These words, Luke 22:20, 'This is the cup, the new testament in My blood,' should and cannot be understood as though this word 'in My blood' were intended to belong only to the word 'This is the cup,' as this 'spirit' pretends" (*ibid.*, 278). Again, "in My blood" cannot be connected merely with ἡ καινὴ διαθήκη ("the new testament") because in Paul it is separated from it by ἐστίν. If it was to be grammatically united with ἡ καινὴ διαθήκη, it would have been necessary to repeat the article after ἐστίν, and the text would read: τοῦτο τὸ ποτήριον ἡ καινὴ διαθήκη ἐστὶν ἡ ἐν τῷ ἐμῷ αἵματι. (*Ibid.*, XX, 1059.) That Luther is right in emphasizing the omission of the article against Oecolampadius also Meyer acknowledges. Meyer says: " Ἐστίν decides against the joining

6

The Elements in the Lord's Supper

Because Scripture teaches us to maintain the presence of the bread against the Roman teaching of transubstantiation, and the presence of the body of Christ against the Reformed symbolization, we distinguish a twofold material in the Supper instituted by Christ, which our Church, following Irenaeus, calls the earthly (*terrena*) and the heavenly (*coelestis*) material. Thus we read in the Formula of Concord: "They confess, according to the words of Irenaeus, that in this Sacrament there are two things, a heavenly and an earthly." [93] The earthly element is bread and wine; but, because the Lord's Supper is an act (*actio*), only to the extent that they are dispensed and consumed. The heavenly element is the body and blood of Christ. In every instance where the Lord's Supper is celebrated according to the institution of Christ these are united according to their essence or substance with the bread and wine in a supernatural manner, and are received with the bread and wine. All substitutes for this twofold material are to be rejected.

The Earthly Element in the Lord's Supper. — As water and the application of water are a part of Baptism, so bread and wine and their

---

of ἐν τῷ ἐμῷ αἵματι with ἡ καινὴ διαθήκη, followed by most interpreters (Erasmus, Beza, Calvin, etc.), but correctly rejected by Luther (in his *Grosses Bekenntnis*). Christ says the cup is the new testament in virtue of His blood, which, He says, is in the cup." When on this subject, Philippi (V, 449) bestows upon Meyer a well-merited rebuke. Philippi remarks: "How great, however, the influence of dogmatic bias is becomes apparent when Meyer, in spite of his grammatically correct interpretation, nevertheless can immediately continue: 'For nothing else than His blood, which was quickly to be shed, does the Lord see in the wine of the cup. To this vividly concrete, but symbolical view of this solemn moment the controversy of the churches stands in sharpest contrast.' Meyer therefore decrees *ex scrinio pectoris sui* [from the shrine of his heart] that here there is a symbolical action, as if that were entirely undebatable, and then declares the trope to be in the subject." Meyer, you see, is using the *petitio principii*, very much in vogue among the Reformed, as evident from their universal use of pictures, parables, and allegories in battling the Real Presence. From the very outset they take for granted that the words of institution are to be understood figuratively.

[93] *Trigl.* 977, Sol. Decl., VII, 14. Baier-Walther, III, 497: "*Materia sacrae coenae duplex est, terrena et coelestis.* Thus our men generally, following Irenaeus, who writes lib. IV *Adv. Haeres.*, c. 34: 'What is earthly bread receiving the blessing of God is no more common bread, but a blessing consisting of two things, an earthly and a heavenly.'" On these words of Irenaeus see Loofs, R. E., 3d ed., I, 47 ff.; Kahnis, *Dogm.*, 2d ed., II, 361 ff.; Chemnitz, *Fundamenta*, c. X; Gerhard, *Loci*, "De s. coena," § 103; Baier-Walther, *Comp. theol. historicae*, Loc. XVIII.

reception are the earthly element of the Lord's Supper. As we do not venture to substitute some other fluid for water in Baptism, so neither in the Lord's Supper do we dare to substitute aught for bread and wine.[94] If something else is substituted, doubts must necessarily arise whether our celebration is the Supper instituted by Christ. And as the application of the water is a part of Baptism, so also the giving and receiving of bread and wine are a part of the Lord's Supper. Where the elements are not distributed and consumed, as in the case of the Papistic Mass and the Corpus Christi festival, there is no Lord's Supper and no body of Christ, but solely abomination and fraud. *Nihil habet rationem sacramenti extra usum a Christo institutum* is a perfectly correct axiom.[95]

---

[94] At the institution of His Supper Christ used bread (ἄρτος), Matt. 26:26, etc. In the cup at the first celebration was wine, as we see from τὸ γέννημα τῆς ἀμπέλου, Matt. 26:29, etc. No detailed specifications as to the sort of bread and wine are given. This, therefore, is a matter of free choice. Walther (*Pastorale*, 168 f.), following the older theologians writes: "It is unessential whether the bread is leavened or unleavened, whether it be baked of rye, wheat, corn, barley, or oats, whether it have this or that shape, provided that it is real bread baked of flour and water. It is likewise unessential whether red or white wine be used, or whether the wine be undiluted (*merum*) or mixed with water (as was likely used by Christ, in accordance with the custom of His time), provided that what is used is a potion made from "the fruit of the vine (γέννημα τῆς ἀμπέλου)," Matt. 26:29. The pastor must use every care that nothing but true wine is used in the Sacrament. He should, therefore, not leave the providing of it to the janitor or someone else, but bear in mind that he before all others is responsible for the use of genuine wine. It is false teaching on the part of the Eastern Catholic Church and the Roman Catholic Church when they insist that 'Krama' (οἶνος ὕδατι κεκραμμένος, wine mixed with water) must be used, likewise when Beza and Calvin permit substitution of any element similar to bread and wine, and when the Gnostic Encratites of the second to fourth century forbade the use of wine entirely and used water, a thing imitated by certain temperance fanatics in America." In order not to introduce an element of uncertainty into the Sacrament, one should refrain from using grape juice, since it is doubtful whether it is still "the fruit of the vine" after having undergone the pasteurizing process. R. E., 2d ed., I, 53: "A number of substitutes for wine are found among heretical sects . . . the Encratites used water, others milk, honey, unfermented grape juice. . . . But the Church has not failed to declare all this to be improper and insisted on the use of true wine." Since no doubt can arise if we use genuine wine, the dignity of the Sacrament demands that we refrain from experimenting with all fluids of which it is not certain whether they are, or still are, "fruit of the vine."

[95] Formula of Concord: "For apart from the use, when the bread is laid aside and preserved in the sacramental vessel [the pyx] [reservation of the host], or is carried about in the procession and exhibited [Corpus Christi festival], as is done in popery, they [the Lutherans] do not hold that the body of Christ is present" (*Trigl.* 977, Sol. Decl., VII, 15). If a wafer happens to fall to the floor during the distribution, or some of the wine is spilled, Christ's body does not fall to the ground, nor is Christ's blood spilled, since *extra usum a Christo institutum* no *unio sacramentalis* obtains.

Whether the communicant takes the elements at once with the mouth or first with the hand is immaterial.[96] Lutherans correctly regard also the *breaking* of the bread during the administration of the Supper as adiaphorous or indifferent.[97]

The Heavenly Material in the Lord's Supper. — Likewise with regard to the *materia coelestis* we must abide by the words of institution and reject all man-devised substitutes. It is deplorable that an extensive discussion of this subject is necessary because of substitutes proposed. The following are the principal ones:

1. "The *entire* Christ," "Christ's Person," "Christ's Personality," etc. Reformed theologians assure us that they retain Christ's true body and blood in the Sacrament, inasmuch as that body and blood stand

---

[96] Some Reformed regard it as essential to take the elements with the hand (Chamier, see Quenstedt, II, 1242). But also receiving with the mouth is a true taking, as is evident from John 19:30: "When Jesus therefore had received [ἔλαβεν] the vinegar." Care must be exercised by the pastor that the communicants actually drink (Walther, *Pastorale*, p. 186).

[97] Some of the Reformed (Beza and Zanchi) join Luther and the Lutherans in declaring the breaking of the bread unessential (*adiunctum accidentale*) like other incidental features (nighttime, Upper Room, etc.). Most of the Reformed, however, declare the breaking of the bread to be essential because thereby the manner of Christ's death must be symbolized. They say that, if the breaking of the bread is omitted, the symbolical character of the Lord's Supper is not fully realized. Against this position the valid criticism has been voiced that the thing here supposedly symbolized did not take place at all, for Scripture expressly denies that the body of Christ was broken in a literal sense (John 19:36). Lutherans very correctly say that Christ broke the bread to divide it and to be able to distribute it. They point out that "break" is used consistently in this sense. As the words of institution say: "Jesus took bread, and blessed it, and brake it, and gave it to the disciples," so we also read in the account of the feeding of the five thousand: "And He commanded the multitude to sit down on the grass, and took the five loaves and the two fishes, and looking up to heaven, He blessed and brake and gave the loaves to His disciples" (Matt. 14:19). We read (Mark 8:6) of the feeding of the four thousand: "And He took the seven loaves, and gave thanks, and brake, and gave to His disciples to set before them." V. 19: "When I brake the five loaves among five thousand"; v. 20: "And when [I brake] the seven among four thousand"; Matt. 15:36: "And He took the seven loaves and the fishes, and gave thanks, and brake them, and gave to His disciples"; Luke 24:30: "And it came to pass, as He sat at meat with them, He took bread, and blessed it, and brake, and gave to them"; Is. 58:7: "Is it not to deal ["break"] thy bread to the hungry?" Lam. 4:4: "The young children ask bread, and no man breaketh it unto them." Luther therefore says: "We must not interpret or apply 'break' according to our notions, but according to the usage of Scripture. Now, 'break' in Scripture, especially where it is used of bread or food, plainly means as much as dividing or distributing." (St. L. XX:1066.) [Formula of Concord: "As also St. Paul places before our eyes the entire action of the breaking of bread or of distribution and reception, 1 Cor. 10:16" (*Trigl.* 1001, Sol. Decl., VII, 84)]. Cp. Chemnitz, *Fundamenta s. coenae*, c. 8, p. m. 44 f.; Philippi, V, 426 ff.; Walther, *Pastorale*, p. 169 f.; [*Th. Quarterly* V, 69].

synecdochically for the whole Christ, the entire humanity and entire divinity, the whole Person, etc.[98] The Romanists also are ready to let the "whole Christ" be the *materia coelestis*, to enable them to prove that, in spite of the refusal of the cup to the laity, the lay folk are not being cheated in the Roman Sacrament.[99] Modern theologians, too, including some who call themselves Lutheran, glibly substitute the "whole Christ" for the body and blood of Christ, prompted to some extent by the notion that they are thus enriching Christ's Sacrament.[100]

Per contra we must maintain: The whole Christ is present, of course, as in the universe, so in particular in the Church and in all rites of the Church, hence also in the Lord's Supper. But in His Sacrament Christ gives something to be eaten and drunk with the mouth, and that is not the whole Christ, but Christ's body and blood, as the words of institution read: "Take, eat; this is My body," etc. In the Lord's Supper we therefore receive with our mouth no more and no less than Christ's body and blood, the body with the bread, and the blood with the wine. Therefore the "concomitance," by which Rome endeavors to make the world believe that with the body of Christ one must be receiving also the blood of Christ, since a body is never without blood, must be called a fabrication. Luther properly

---

[98] Quotations in Heppe, *Dogm. d. ref. K.,* p. 466 ff. Trelcatius, *Scholast. et methodica II. Com. s. theol. institutio,* Hannover, 1610, p. 240: "We do not exclude the entire Christ (*Christum ipsum totum*) from the Lord's Supper, since synecdochically the entire human nature, yes, His entire Person is understood by 'body' and 'blood.'" Also Calvin uses "Christ's body" and "Christ" *promiscue:* "The whole Person of Christ is offered to us in the Sacrament." "Only let us hear no more of that calumny that Christ is excluded from the Sacrament unless He be concealed under the bread." (*Inst.* IV, 17, 31; Allen II, 545, 562.) Philippi, V, 295, is right in pointing out Calvin's repeated "arbitrary identification of the body of Christ and the entire Christ."

[99] *Trid., Sess.* XIII, c. 3: "Wherefore it is most true that as much is contained under either species as under both; for Christ whole and entire is under the species of bread, and under any part whatsoever of that species" (Waterworth, p. 78). "If any one denieth that in the venerable Sacrament of the Eucharist the whole Christ is contained under each species, and under every part of each species, when separated (when a separation has been made); let him be anathema" (Waterworth, p. 82 f.).

[100] Nitzsch-Stephan reports: "The conception of the *materia coelestis* has entirely changed. Instead of the substances, namely, Christ's body and blood, the living Personality of Christ and its actions have come to the fore; an *unio sacramentalis* in the old sense between this and the earthly elements, however, is impossible." (*Dogmatik,* p. 667.) Frank (III, 22 ff., 104 ff.) points out that Melanchthon, too, in his later years, when he wavered, uses the terms "body of Christ," "Christ," or "Person of Christ" *promiscue.* He regards it as sufficient to teach, *Christum vere adesse et efficacem esse.* (*Corp. Ref.* III, 514.)

castigates the absurdity of the "concomitance" in his well-known burning words.[101]

Besides, the Reformed teachers do not mean seriously that the "whole Christ" is in the Lord's Supper. They permit "the whole Christ" to be in the Lord's Supper just as little as Christ's body and blood. Calvin not only denies that Christ's promise, "Lo, I am with you," pertains to Christ also according to His humanity, but even declares the Lutheran teaching which so explains the words of Christ to be less tolerable and less temperate than the Roman transubstantiation. See p. 344, footnote 80. It is empty jangling when Reformed theologians, to give the impression that their teaching of the Lord's Supper is particularly rich and full, claim to substitute for the "body" and "blood" of Christ the "whole Christ" or His "whole humanity."

2. The benefits (*beneficia*) of Christ, the virtue (*virtus*) of Christ's body and blood, Christ's merit, the remission of sins, etc. These substitutes Reformed and recent theologians offer.[102]

---

[101] Luther: "The finest piece in the bishop's (of Meissen) proclamation is that the parsons are to teach the laymen that in Communion under one kind there is present the entire Jesus Christ, the Son of God, God and Man, also His body and blood, and is eaten and drunk by the lay communicants. . . . This view is established by concomitance, that is, by inference. Since the body of Christ is not without blood, it follows that His blood is not without His soul; from this it follows that His soul is not without His deity; from this it follows that His deity is not without the Father and the Holy Ghost; from this it follows that in the Sacrament, even when administered in one kind, the soul of Christ is eaten and drunk, and the Holy Trinity with the body and blood of Christ; from this it follows that in every Mass the priest offers up and sells the Holy Trinity; now, since the deity is not without the creatures, it follows from the foregoing premises that heaven and earth are also present in the Sacrament; from this it follows that the devil and hell are also in the Sacrament; from this it follows that any person receiving Communion, also under one kind, devours the bishop of Meissen with his mandate and proclamation; from this it follows that every priest at Meissen in each Mass eats and drinks his bishop twice" (under bread and wine); "from this it follows that the bishop of Meissen must have a larger body than heaven and earth. And who could enumerate all that follows! But lastly this also follows, that all such drawers of inferences are asses, fools, blind, insane, and raving, etc.; this deduction is certain. What devil has enjoined us to imagine such a concomitance? . . . Who has ordered us to include more in the Sacrament than the clear words of Christ state? Who has made you sure that any of these inferences is true? How do you know what God can do? How can you know the measure of His wisdom and power, that He cannot cause the presence of just His body and blood in the Sacrament, in such a manner that His soul and deity are not in the Sacrament, though His soul and deity cannot be outside (extra) His body and blood? Who dare venture to discover and perceive anything beyond what His words state in such miracles of His?" (St. L. XIX:1387 f.)

[102] Heppe, *loc. cit.* Wolleb says: "*Materia interna (coenae Domini) est Christus cum tota satisfactione et merito suo.*" Of Calvin Frank (III, 46 f.) says correctly: "Calvin, who on the one hand asserts that even today the body of Christ

We counter with the simple fact that the "benefits of Christ," etc., are not received with the mouth. This even the Reformed grant. Now, since we are concerned with oral eating in the Lord's Supper, as is evident from the words of institution, "Take, eat; this is My body," the benefits of Christ may not be substituted for Christ's body and blood as *materia coelestis*. Moreover, we must again recall here that in the Sacrament Christ gives us that which is given for us into death and shed for the remission of our sins. But the benefits of Christ, Christ's merit, the forgiveness of sins, are not given and shed for the remission of our sins. Therefore this *alloeosis* of substituting the benefits of Christ, etc., for Christ's body and blood in the Sacrament is manifestly false.

Here, too, the Reformed theologians do not really mean it when they say that "Christ's benefits," "Christ's merit," "Christ's propitiation" are given in the Lord's Supper. According to Calvinistic teaching, the benefits and merit of Christ were not provided for all men and therefore of course cannot be present in the Sacrament for all communicants. So this claim, too, is empty talk.

3. The Holy Ghost and the energy of the Holy Spirit. Calvin, while rejecting the substantial presence of the body of Christ, says that "the exertion of the energy (*virtus*) of His Spirit" is in the Lord's Supper (Allen II, 533). Here Calvin becomes truly eloquent. He says that the Holy Spirit, overcoming all distances, floods the souls of the believers.[103] On the other hand, Calvin's successor, Beza, as we saw (p. 315), considers it absurd to substitute the Holy Spirit and the exertion of His energy for the body and blood of Christ in the Sacrament, because the Holy Ghost and His activity were not given

---

is given, yes, that the Holy Ghost nourishes us with the substance of the flesh and blood of Christ, on the other hand denies the communication of this very substance and substitutes for it the *beneficia, quae in suo corpore Christus nobis praestitit.*" In the *Consensus Tigurinus* (Niemeyer, p. 215) we read of the Lord's Supper: Christ, "remaining in heaven according to His entire body, descends to us with His virtue (*sua virtute*)." Kirn (*Dogm.*, p. 130), too, declines the literal understanding of the words of institution and has Christ "meet" His disciples in the act of the Lord's Supper in such a manner that He "communicates to them the saving virtues of His body and blood given into death." Also Hodge says: "To receive body and blood as offered in the Sacrament . . . is to receive and appropriate the sacrificial virtue or effects of the death of Christ" (*Syst. Theol.* III, 646).

[103] Calvin, *De vera participatione Christi carnis et sanguinis Christi in s. coena* in *Tractatus Theol.*, Geneva, 1576, p. 1167 f.: "One must teach no need of a descent of the essence of the flesh out of heaven to nourish us, but that the energy of the Spirit (*Spiritus virtutem*) suffices to penetrate through all impediments and hurdle all intervals." Also *Inst.* IV, 17, 24, and often.

into death or shed for the remission of sins.[104] Besides, the Reformed
do not seriously mean to put the gift of the Holy Ghost or His exertion
of energy into the Sacrament. For do not Zwingli and Calvin claim
that the Holy Ghost does not use such external means as the Sacraments as His vehicle (*vehiculum, vasculum, plaustrum*)?[105]

4. Spiritual fellowship with Christ and union with His body, the
Church. This is the Reformed and modern theologians' pet substitute
for the *materia coelestis*.[106] To see how impossible this substitution is
we need merely recall how Beza demonstrated the absurdity of substituting the benefits of Christ and the Holy Ghost for the body and
blood of Christ. If we substituted for the *materia coelestis* "spiritual
fellowship with Christ," the words of institution would have to read:
Take, eat; take, drink; this is spiritual fellowship with Christ, given and
shed for you for the remission of sins. And: Take, eat; take, drink;
this is your union with the Christian Church, which was given and
shed for you for the remission of sins. Spiritual fellowship with Christ
as well as membership in the Church Universal indeed belong into
the Lord's Supper. But they belong, as will be shown more fully in
speaking of the purpose of the Lord's Supper, to the fruit and effect
of faith, strengthened through the Sacrament.

5. The glorified body of Christ, the "glorified human nature" of
Christ, the exalted Christ, etc. Calvin has the virtues of the glorified
body of Christ flood the believing soul, and modern theologians speak
of a psychosomatic effect of the Lord's Supper because of a reception
of the glorified body of Christ in this Sacrament. But the words of
institution say nothing of a glorified body, and neither the essence of
the Lord's Supper (the Real Presence) nor its salutary effect (the
remission of sins) is to be based on the glorification of Christ's body.
The fact that the body and blood were not glorified did not prevent
its presence in the first celebration, and the glorification does not contribute to its presence in all succeeding celebrations. The all-sufficient
reason for the Real Presence lies in the words of institution, "This is
My body," and "This is My blood." Only the Reformed objection that

---

[104] *Epist. 5 ad Alemannum*, p. 57, ed. Geneva, in Gerhard, *Loci*, "*De
s. coena*," § 76: "Now then, let us substitute that interpretation for the terms
'body' and 'blood' and say: This is the effect of My death which is given for you,
and this is My Spirit which is shed for you. Can there be anything more absurd
[*ineptius*] than such talk?"

[105] Zwingli, *Fidei Ratio*, Niemeyer, p. 24; Calvin, *Inst.* IV, 14, 17.

[106] Calvin in his *Commentary* on 1 Cor. 10:16; Zwingli in his answer to
Bugenhagen's letter, St. L. XX:517; Kirn, *Dogm.*, p. 129 f.

a human body cannot be at several places at the same time led Luther and his followers to point out that the body of Christ is not merely a true human body, but also the body of the Son of God, which because of the *unio personalis* Scripture expressly endows with divine attributes, also omnipresence.

Walther (*Lectures*, 1874) is entirely right in saying: "The presence of the body and blood of Christ in the Lord's Supper must not be based on the glorification of the body of Christ. The glorification endows the body only with spiritual, not with divine attributes. We believe that Christ's body is present in the Sacrament and received (1) because of the promise of Christ, (2) because Christ's body is the body of the Son of God." And Walther adds the warning: "Men like Sartorius and others, who have otherwise written much excellent material, employ the glorification of Christ's body to support the doctrine of that body's presence in the Sacrament. But this is a false support, and false supports are just as dangerous as open denial. It is a mistake to say: Christ can now give us His body in the Lord's Supper because it is glorified. This unsound argument contains the admission that Christ before His glorification could not give His body, a concession that would cancel the first celebration of the Supper." [107]

---

[107] Against the objection of the Reformed, Kromayer calls attention to the fact that also a glorified body is not omnipresent: "They object on the basis of the Epistle to the Philippians (3:21) that our vile body shall be fashioned like unto His glorious body, while we nevertheless deny omnipresence to glorified bodies. But we answer that one must distinguish between a glorified and a majestic body. Christ will fashion our vile body like unto His glorified body, not His majestic body. What a glorified and spiritual body is we learn from the post-resurrection body of Christ and certain particular actions of His before His resurrection, e. g., when He was made invisible, when He penetrated through closed doors, when He shone like the sun on Mount Tabor. The *corpus maiestaticum* Christ received through the personal union with the Logos and the session at the right hand of God. Whatever is omnipresent pertains to this *corpus maiestaticum. Theol. posit.-pol.* I, 913 f.; in Baier-Walther, III, 501. — Burger (R. E., 2d ed., I, 37): "Against this objection" (that a human body could not at once be at many places) "it was not sufficient to appeal to the state of glorification in which Christ now is. For glorification does not abolish the nature of a body as such, and no one would assert of the children of God that by virtue of their glorification they would now be present simultaneously at all places or at least at many places bodily. But that is not at all what the Lutheran Confessions claim. The power of free disposition over His body, ascribed to Christ in the institution of the Sacred Supper and its continued administration, is His not by virtue of His glorification, but by virtue of the union of the human nature with the divine in His theanthropic Person. From this union of the divine and the human nature in the unity of His Person there results not an amalgamation or blending of the two, but a mutual communication of powers and attributes (*communicatio*

While it is true that communicants today receive the glorified body of Christ, because the identical body once unglorified is now glorified; nevertheless, according to the words of institution, the body comes into consideration not as glorified, but as given into death for our reconciliation (τὸ ὑπὲϱ ὑμῶν διδόμενον), therefore as pledge and medium of the remission of sins.

The Sacramental Union (unio sacramentalis). Since the words of Scripture speak of a twofold material in the Lord's Supper, namely, bread and wine and body and blood of Christ, Scripture thereby teaches also a union (*unio*) of the earthly and the heavenly element. This union has fittingly been called the *unio sacramentalis*. It consists in this, that Christ's body is received with the bread, and Christ's blood with the wine.

All substitutes for the *unio sacramentalis* must be rejected. By distributing, as they claim, only the body of Christ in the Lord's Supper, the Papists supplant the *unio sacramentalis* by transubstantiation.

The Reformed use the term *unio sacramentalis*. But since at the same time they teach that in this union the body of Christ is so far removed from the bread in the Eucharist as heaven is from the earth, they define *their unio sacramentalis* more specifically as a *symbolic union (unio significativa, repraesentativa, symbolica)*. This "symbolic" union is of a very peculiar nature. As there is a connection between a picture of St. Peter and Peter himself in heaven because the picture recalls him to our mind, so the bread in the Lord's Supper on earth

---

idiomatum). They are not joined in such a manner that either can function and operate independently of the other. Rather, wherever Christ is and has promised to be present, there He is entire, unblended, but also undivided, according to both natures. But by virtue of this miraculous, unique, and incomparable assumption of the human nature in Christ unto communion of the divine also all spatial limitation of a body is inapplicable to the body of Christ, and He possesses also according to His body more than one mode of presence wherever He will, not merely the local, according to which He is always within a certain space and cannot at the same time be present at another place, but, as all things are always and everywhere present to Him, so, too, is He present to all things, wherever He has promised His presence, and no spatial barrier hinders Him from exercising His presence in the Holy Supper after He has given His promise to do so. This is the so-called ubiquity of Christ's body, not a spatial extension of His body throughout the universe, a nonsensical thought which would indeed destroy His humanity, but the power that is His, by virtue of the union with the divine nature, of proving Himself bodily present wherever He will, and this miracle He has promised to do in His Holy Supper. The feasibility of this presence, then, rests not on the glorification of Christ, but on the union and mutual communication and penetration of divine and human natures in the unity of His Person."

is united with the body of Christ in heaven by the bread picturing Christ's body to us and thus presenting the body of Christ to our mind. It should therefore be noted that when the Reformed use the term *unio sacramentalis*, they mean exactly the opposite of what Lutherans mean by that term. The Reformed by that term express the absence, the Lutherans the presence, of the substantial body of Christ. And this fact is not altered when many Reformed call the *unio sacramentalis* an *unio vera, realis, substantialis,* etc. Their meaning always remains: As on earth a picture of St. Peter represents to our mind the real Peter in heaven, so the bread in the Lord's Supper symbolizes to us the true, substantial body of Christ in heaven. In spite of their talk of a substantial body of Christ and of a true, substantial union, the Reformed never get beyond a "symbolic union," because they would by all means maintain that Christ's body is as far removed from the Lord's Supper as heaven is from the earth.

The Lutheran Church, in opposition to this view, maintains the Scriptural concept of the *unio sacramentalis*, teaching that the bread and Christ's body are so united in the Lord's Supper that they are received with the mouth in one undivided act (*manducatio oralis*), as the words say: "Take, eat; this is My body."

The discussion of the twofold material and the *unio sacramentalis* gives rise to the question how to define more definitely the manner (*modus*) of the taking of body and blood. We say: (1) Because the twofold material is combined into a sacramental unity, that is, since Christ gives His body with the bread and His blood with the wine, we receive with the mouth (*manducatio oralis*) not merely the bread and wine, but also the body and blood of Christ. (2) Since, however, the union of the *materia coelestis* with the *materia terrena* is not a natural or local, but a supernatural union (no *localis inclusio, impanatio, consubstantiatio*), we receive the body and blood of Christ with the mouth not in a natural, but in a supernatural manner. On the basis of the *unio sacramentalis* the Formula of Concord, on the one hand, adheres to the oral receiving of Christ's body and blood; on the other hand, to the supernatural manner of the reception. It says: "When at the table and during the Supper [*mensae assidens*], He [Christ] offers His disciples natural bread and natural wine, which He calls His true body and true blood, at the same time saying: 'Eat and drink.' For in view of the circumstances this command evidently cannot be understood otherwise than of oral eating and drinking, however, not in a gross, carnal, Capernaitic, but in a supernatural, incomprehensible way." (*Trigl.* 995, Sol. Decl., VII, 64.)

To characterize Luther's doctrine of the Lord's Supper, Adolf Harnack (*Grundriss d. Dogmengesch.*, 4th ed., p. 434) quotes just these few words: "The body of Christ is masticated with the teeth." We cannot help accusing Harnack here of falsifying history. Since Harnack uses quotation marks, he must have looked up the words in Luther. Now, Luther does say: "Whoever eats this bread, he eats Christ's body; whoever crushes this bread with his teeth or tongue, he crushes the body of Christ with his teeth or tongue." But Luther immediately adds: ". . . and nevertheless it remains true in all respects, that no one sees, seizes, eats or masticates Christ's body as one plainly sees and masticates other meat." (St. L. XX:1032.) If Harnack wanted to be true to the historical facts, he should at least have said: Luther teaches both, namely, that Christ's body is masticated with the teeth, and that Christ's body is not masticated with the teeth. If he had then added the references to the passage in Luther, other people could have looked it up and recognized immediately how according to Luther both things are true. Luther, on the one hand, maintains that through Christ's institution a "sacramental union" has come about in the Lord's Supper. He says: "Here two things have become one; I would call that a sacramental union, because Christ's body and the bread are there given us as a Sacrament." Because of this sacramental union the matter comes to this for Luther: "What one does with the bread, is correctly and well said of the body of Christ." On the other hand, Luther maintains that the "sacramental union" is not a local or natural union. He says: "We poor sinners are certainly not so insane as to believe that Christ's body is in the bread in such a coarse, visible manner as bread is in the basket or wine in the cup, a thing the "enthusiasts" would like to pin on us so that they may laugh at our folly." (*Ibid.*, 811.) And in this respect Luther then says: ". . . and nevertheless it remains true in every way that no one sees, seizes, eats, or masticates Christ's body."

Here Frank, too, has become confused. He writes: "The apologetes [of the Formula of Concord] could only urge that Luther says this only because of the sacramental union, and in so much only *secundum quid*, and not *simpliciter*, and expressly adds to it that it nevertheless always remains true that no one sees, seizes, eats, or masticates Christ's body. But this defense does not cover the vulnerable parts. For if it is correct to say because of the sacramental union that Christ's body is masticated, why would it not be correct, because of the same union, to say that Christ's body is digested?" (*Theol.*

d. F. C. III, 141.) Here Frank has lost sight of the fact that the words of institution speak only of an act of eating and drinking and say nothing of any "digestion." According to Christ's institution the bread in the Lord's Supper is not intended to be bodily food, but to be Lord's Supper bread, that is, a means of communicating the body of Christ. Only in this function does the *unio sacramentalis* prevail and does the body of Christ share what is done to the bread. As the bread that happens to fall to the ground during the distribution is not the body of Christ, so also the bread, in so far as it nourishes in a bodily manner as bodily food (*cibus corporalis*) and is digested, is not the body of Christ. Melanchthon, Brenz, and others, very correctly state in an opinion given in 1557 (*Corp. Ref.* IX, 277): So far as the bread in the Lord's Supper is bodily food, the nature of the Sacrament has ceased. "*Cum facta sumptione panis descendit in ventrem et alteratur, estque iam cibus corporalis, desiit ratio sacramenti.*" When the Reformed theologians combat the presence of Christ's body in the Lord's Supper and the *manducatio oralis* with the criticism that then the body of Christ would also be "digested," this objection shows gross ignorance and is an unconscious, at times even conscious, travesty of the Sacrament instituted by Christ. This explains the earnest and sharp words of the Formula of Concord: "Likewise, we consign also to the just judgment of God all presumptuous, frivolous, blasphemous questions (which decency forbids to mention) and (other) expressions, which most blasphemously and with great offense [to the Church] are proposed by the Sacramentarians in a gross, carnal, Capernaitic way concerning the supernatural, heavenly mysteries of this Sacrament. Hence we hereby utterly [reject and] condemn the Capernaitic eating of the body of Christ, as though [we taught that] His flesh were rent with the teeth, and digested like other food, which the Sacramentarians, against the testimony of their conscience, after all our frequent protests, wilfully force upon us, and in this way make our doctrine odious to their hearers; and on the other hand, we maintain and believe, according to the simple words of the testament of Christ, the true, yet supernatural eating of the body of Christ, as also the drinking of His blood (*veram, sed supernaturalem manducationem corporis Christi, quemadmodum etiam vere, supernaturaliter tamen, sanguinem Christi bibi docemus*), which human senses and reason do not comprehend, but as in all other articles of faith our reason is brought into captivity to the obedience of Christ, and this mystery is not apprehended otherwise than by faith alone, and revealed in the Word alone." (*Trigl.* 817, Epit., VII, 41—42.)

7

What Constitutes the Lord's Supper

(Forma coenae sacrae)

The Lord's Supper was not to be celebrated just once or temporarily (cp. p. 290), but Christ wants this Sacrament to be administered in His Church to the Last Day. Therefore we must ask what
makes this sacred rite really the Lord's Supper. We answer: The
Sacrament, instituted by Christ, comes into being not by the state of
the administrant, nor by the faith of the communicants, but by the
institution of Christ, which to the end of time exerts its power wherever
the Lord's Supper is administered according to the institution of Christ.
By way of illustration, the Formula of Concord, appropriating the
words of Chrysostom, says: "And just as the declaration, Gen. 1:28:
'Be fruitful, and multiply, and replenish the earth,' was spoken only
once, but is ever efficacious in nature, so that it is fruitful and multiplies, so also this declaration ["This is My body; this is My blood"]
was spoken once, but even to this day and to His advent it is efficacious, and works so that in the Supper of the Church His true body
and blood are present" (*Trigl.* 999, Sol. Decl., VII, 76).

But at this point, too, the Reformed polemicists from the outset
became untruthful. They sought to attach to the Lutheran doctrine
of the Lord's Supper the offensiveness which Christians properly find
in the Roman teaching of transubstantiation and the magical power
to transubstantiate which is said to be given to the priest by his anointing. They like to represent the matter as if, also according to Lutheran
teaching, the speaking of men and human authority effected the Real
Presence.[108] Luther opposes this misrepresentation and explains ever
so often: Not the speaking of men causes Christ's body and blood to
be present, but solely Christ's word of promise and command. Christ's
word, "This is My body," brought into being the first Lord's Supper,
that is, made the bread the bearer of Christ's body. And because
Christ has given us command to do to the end of days what He did,
therefore also *our* Lord's Supper is what the first Supper was. Christ's
"word of command" (*"Heisselwort"*) makes our word an "effective
word" (*"Taetelwort"*). Luther writes against Zwingli: "Though I spoke
the words, 'This is Christ's body,' over all breads, it would of course
effect nothing. But when, following His institution and command, we
say in the Lord's Supper, 'This is My body,' then it is His body, not

---

108 Thus Carlstadt already in his *Gespraechbuechlein* (St. L. XX: 2356).

because of our speaking or effective word (*"Taetelwort"*), but because of His command, that He has enjoined us so to speak and to do, and bound His command and action to our speaking." (St. L. XX:918.) Also the Formula of Concord discusses this point *in extenso:* "Not the word or work of any man produces [*non efficit*] the true presence of the body and blood of Christ in the Supper, whether it be the merit or recitation of the minister, or the eating and drinking or faith of the communicants; but all this should be ascribed alone to the power of Almighty God and the word, institution, and ordination of our Lord Jesus Christ. For the true and almighty words of Jesus Christ which He spake at the first institution were efficacious not only at the first Supper, but they endure, are valid, operate, and are still efficacious [*adhuc hodie*], so that in all places where the Supper is celebrated according to the institution of Christ, and His words are used, the body and blood of Christ are truly present, distributed, and received, because of the power and efficacy of the words which Christ spake at the first Supper." (*Trigl.* 999, Sol. Decl., VII, 74 f.)

It is imperative therefore that the congregation unmistakably declare at every celebration of the Lord's Supper that its intention is to celebrate the Supper instituted by Christ, or, in other words, that it would repeat the act ordained by Christ. This declaration the congregation makes by consecrating the elements ordained by Christ, namely, bread and wine, for use in the Lord's Supper. Consecration is correctly defined as the act whereby bread and wine are detached from their ordinary use and appointed to the use in the Lord's Supper, that is, are set apart to this end, that with the bread, according to Christ's promise, the body of Christ and with the wine, according to Christ's promise, the blood of Christ be received. We see from 1 Cor. 10:16 that consecration was in use already in the Apostolic congregation: "The cup of blessing, which we bless (τὸ ποτήριον τῆς εὐλογίας ὃ εὐλογοῦμεν), is it not the communion of the blood of Christ?"

Here Calvin goes astray. While correctly rejecting the Roman consecration as a "magical incantation" (*incantatio*), whereby the bread is changed into the body of Christ, he falls into the opposite error, for he adds that the consecration in the Lord's Supper has to do only with persons and not with the sacramental elements. Thereby he plainly contradicts Scripture. According to Paul's words in 1 Cor. 10:16 the object of εὐλογοῦμεν is ὅ, and ὅ refers not to persons, but to the *cup* of blessing, τὸ ποτήριον τῆς εὐλογίας ὃ εὐλογοῦμεν.[109] Hodge, on the

---

[109] *Inst.* IV, 17, 39. How Calvin here mixes the true and the false is evident from the following: "Nothing more preposterous, therefore, can be done with

other hand, says: "When it is said that our Lord gave thanks or blessed the cup and the bread, it is to be understood that He not only thanked God for His mercies, but that He also invoked His blessing, or, in other words, prayed that the bread and wine might be what He intended them to be, the symbols of His body and blood, and the means of spiritual nourishment to His disciples. This is also taught by the Apostle in 1 Cor. 10:16, where he speaks of 'the cup of blessing,' i. e., that cup which has been blessed, or consecrated by prayer, to a sacred use; as is explained by the following words, 'which we bless.'" (*Syst. Theo.* III, 618.) Here everything is right, except that Hodge takes the liberty of inserting into the text "the symbols of His body and blood." According to the text, bread and wine are blessed not to be "symbols," but to be the "communion" of the body and blood of Christ. Also Meyer, in spite of his antipathy for the Scriptural doctrine of the Lord's Supper, admits [in discussing Matt. 26:26] that in 1 Cor. 10:16 we have "a laudatory prayer of consecration [not of persons, but] of bread and wine to a sacred use." In this respect the Lord's Supper differs from Baptism. In the case of Baptism no consecration of the water is mentioned either at the institution by Christ or in its administration in the Apostolic Church. But the consecration of the elements in the Lord's Supper is witnessed to by Scripture both at the institution of the Lord's Supper and in its administration in the Apostolic Church.[110]

---

respect to the Supper than to convert it into a mute action, as we have seen done under the tyranny of the Pope. For they have maintained that all the validity of the consecration depends on the intention of the priests, as if it had nothing to do with the people, to whom the mystery ought principally to be explained. They fall into this error for want of observing that those promises on which the consecration rests are not directed to the elements themselves, but to the persons who receive them. Christ does not address the bread, to command it to become His body; but enjoins His disciples to eat and promises them the communication of His body and blood. Nor does Paul teach any other order than that the promises should be offered to believers, together with the bread and the cup. And this is the truth. We are not to imagine any magical incantation, or think it sufficient to have muttered over the words, as if they were heard by the elements, but we are to understand those words, by which the elements are consecrated, to be a lively preaching, which edifies the hearers, which penetrates their minds, which is deeply impressed upon their heart, which exerts its efficacy in the acomplishment of that which it promises. . . . If the promises are repeated and the mystery declared, that those who are about to receive it may communicate with advantage, we have no reason to doubt that this is the true consecration." (Allen II, 573 f.)

[110] Over against both the Romanist and the Calvinist errors Gerhard (*Loci*, "*De coena s.*," § 151) describes the consecration well in the following words: "This consecration of the Eucharist is (1) not a magical incantation, which by the power of certain words transmutes the bread in its essence into the body and the wine into the blood of Christ, as the Papistic priests pretend that because of

What words are to be used in consecrating? On this point Luther joins issue, on the one hand, with the Papists, who declare it to be a heinous sin if one or the other word is unwittingly omitted in reciting the words of institution. In refutation Luther points to the fact "that the Holy Spirit has purposely shaped things so that no Evangelist uses the identical words with the other" (St. L. XIX:1104). On the other hand, Luther urges that "the order of Christ, appointed in the Supper, be publicly and audibly" sung or spoken, so that in this manner those celebrating Communion confess and become certain that they are observing the Supper instituted by Christ.[111] Similarly the Formula of

---

their tonsure and unction, in virtue of the canon and the intention in the faith of the Church, they brought the Sacrament about *ex opere operato* and changed the essence of the external symbols into Christ's body and blood. (2) It is also not merely a historical repetition of the institution; as the Calvinists make little of the words of institution (thus Bucer on Matthew 26) and assert that it is to be directed at the people and does not at all have the purpose of consecrating the external symbols (Calvin, *Inst.* IV, 17, 39). But (3) it is an efficacious hallowing [*efficax* ἁγιασμός], by which according to the command, ordination, and institution of Christ the consecration [or blessing] in the first Supper, so to say, descends into our Supper and the external elements are destined for this holy use, that with them Christ's body and blood be distributed. We do not, however, ascribe to the recital of the words of institution the power to cause the presence of Christ's body and blood through an occult power inhering in the words (as the sorcerers recite their songs about Jove Elicius, or about drawing down the moon from heaven, in certain set words) much less, that they transmute the nature of the external elements. But we certainly believe and confess that the presence of Christ's body and blood depends solely and entirely on the will and promise of Christ and on the perpetual effectiveness of the first institution; however, we nevertheless add that the repetition of that original institution, done by the servant of the Church in the administration of the Eucharist, is not merely historical and doctrinal, but also consecratory, by which, in agreement with Christ's ordination, the external symbols are truly and effectively designated for the holy use, so that in the distribution itself they are the communion (κοινωνία) of the body and blood of Christ, as the Apostle expressly says 1 Cor. 10:16: 'The bread which we break is the communion (*communicatio*) of the body of Christ; the cup of blessing which we bless is the communion of the blood of Christ.' The Son of God Himself repeats the words, uttered once upon a time, through the mouth of the minister and through them hallows, consecrates, and blesses the bread and wine to be the medium of distributing His body and blood."

[111] Walther (*Pastorale*, p. 173) correctly calls it "a most charming picture" which Luther (St. L. XIX:1279) draws of a truly evangelical celebration of the Lord's Supper: "There our pastor . . . steps before the altar; he sings publicly and plainly the order of Christ instituted in the Lord's Supper . . . and we, especially those who intend to partake of the Sacrament, kneel down beside, behind, and around him . . . all true, holy co-priests, sanctified through the blood of Christ and anointed and consecrated by the Holy Ghost in Baptism. . . . We have our pastor recite the order of Christ not for himself, as only applying to his person, but he is the mouth of all of us, and all speak the words with him from our heart. . . . If he stumbles over the words, or becomes lost and forgets whether he did say the words, then *we* are there, hear him, hold fast the words, and are sure that they were spoken; thus we cannot be deceived."

Concord, likewise referring to 1 Cor. 10:16, says: "Now, in the administration of the Holy Supper the words of institution are to be publicly spoken or sung before the congregation distinctly and clearly, and should in no way be omitted, in order that obedience may be rendered to the command of Christ: 'This do!' and . . . that the elements of bread and wine may be consecrated or blessed for this holy use, in order that the body and blood of Christ may therewith be administered to us to be eaten and to be drunk, as Paul declares (1 Cor. 10:16): 'The cup of blessing, which we bless,' which indeed occurs in no other way than through the repetition and recitation of the words of institution." (*Trigl.* 1001, Sol. Decl., VII, 79 ff.)[112]

With reference to the consecration, queries have been raised that border on *curiosae quaestiones*, e. g., when it is asked whether it would not be a true Lord's Supper if Christians met for its observance and then merely thought in their heart that now they would celebrate the Supper instituted by Christ. Such a question tempts one to answer that sensible people would not think of "consecrating" the elements in such a silent manner. Even the Reformed protest against the omission of the words of institution at the celebration of the Lord's Supper. (*Admon. Neost.*, p. 101; in Frank III, 131.) And if Meyer ever gave his "Eucharistic prayer of consecration of bread and wine for use in the Holy Supper" a practical trial, he must have discovered that one cannot formulate a fitting "Eucharistic prayer of consecration" without the words with which Christ instituted the Holy Supper and gave it to His Church.

Since it is certain that neither the condition of the administrant nor of the communicants, but the institution and ordinance of Christ

---

[112] After saying: "If you would baptize a child with water, but pronounce a Lord's Prayer or another passage from God's Word over the child, that would not be a true Baptism," Luther continues: "Just as in the Supper of the body and blood of Christ — if the command and institution is not observed, it is no Sacrament. For example, if some one read the Ten Commandments, the Creed, or another passage or psalm over the bread and wine, or again, if he substituted something else for bread and wine, such as gold, silver, meat, oil, water, while using the correct words of Christ's institution, that would of course not be Christ's body and blood; and though God's Word is there, and God's creature, still it is no Sacrament. For His ordinance and command is not there in which He named bread and wine and spoke the words: 'Take, eat; this is My body; drink, this is My blood.' In short, you are not to choose or determine for Him either the word or the creature [earthly element] and are to do or omit nothing whatever according to your pleasure, but His command and ordinance should determine for you both word and creature which you are to observe entirely and unchanged." (St. L. X:2068.)

make our celebration the Lord's Supper, it also is certain that both the worthy and the unworthy guests receive Christ's body and blood if they are participating in a celebration which is actually an observance of the ordinance of Christ. Besides, the *manducatio indignorum* is expressly taught when the Apostle says that the unworthy guests become "guilty of the body and blood of the Lord" (1 Cor. 11:27). Luther is not exaggerating therefore when he rates "as one concoction" all who "will not believe that the Lord's bread in the Supper is His true natural body, which the godless or Judas received with the mouth as well as St. Peter and all (other) saints" (F. C., *Trigl.* 983, Sol. Decl., VII, 33). All who deny the *manducatio indignorum* are therewith denying that Christ's institution causes the presence of Christ's body and blood in the Supper. Accordingly the Reformed teach that for the worthy communicants, too, the body and blood of Christ are not in the Sacrament, but in heaven. Thus the *manducatio indignorum* becomes the test question, and Luther was right in insisting upon it that this point be stated clearly in the Wittenberg Concordia of 1536.[113]

From the fact that only the institution of Christ makes an observance His Supper it furthermore follows that the Romanists and the Reformed do not have the Sacrament instituted by Christ, inasmuch as they perform a rite which lacks the institution of Christ. In regard to the Roman Mass the Formula of Concord declares: "When in the papistic Mass the bread is not distributed, but offered up or enclosed, borne about, and exhibited for adoration, it is to be regarded as no sacrament" (*Trigl.* 1003, *ibid.*, 87). Of the Roman Private Mass, in which the priest alone communes, Luther says: "In the Private Mass [*Winkelmesse*] there is not only the abuse and sin that the priest administers and communes unworthily, but though the priest were holy and worthy, *tamen ipsa substantia institutionis Christi sublata est,* that is, they remove the very essence of Christ's ordinance and institution and make an ordinance of their own. . . . For this reason no one can or should believe that Christ's body

---

113 Formula of Concord (*Trigl.* 977, Sol. Decl., VII, 16): "They [the Lutherans] hold that the institution of this Sacrament made by Christ is efficacious in Christendom [the Church], and that it does not depend upon the worthiness or unworthiness of the minister who offers the Sacrament, or of the one who receives it. Therefore, as St. Paul says, that even the unworthy partake of the Sacrament, they hold that also to the unworthy the body and blood of Christ are truly offered, and the unworthy truly receive them, if [where] the institution and command of the Lord Christ are observed. But such persons receive them to condemnation, as St. Paul says; for they misuse the holy Sacrament, because they receive it without true repentance and without faith."

and blood is there present, since His ordinance is not there."
(St. L. XIX:1265.)

In their opinion of the Reformed Lord's Supper the Lutheran
teachers are not entirely of one mind. Fecht, Dannhauer, and others
hold (cf. *Lehre und Wehre*, 1875, 119 ff.) that the Reformed have the
Lord's Supper instituted by Christ, are therefore distributing and receiving Christ's body and blood. They base their opinion on the fact
that the Reformed bodies adhere to the words of institution, though
they give these words another meaning than Christ does. Most of our
old Lutheran teachers hold that the Reformed "Supper" is a rite alien
to the ordinance of Christ and for that reason is not the Lord's Supper.
We feel constrained to agree with this verdict. Because the Reformed
publicly declare that they do not have the intention of celebrating the
Supper with the Real Presence of Christ's body and blood, but pronounce such a Sacrament an abomination, they are in fact not celebrating the Supper Christ gave to His Church. The Reformed doctrine
is an actual disavowal and renunciation of Christ's words of institution.
Hence they have no word of God for their Supper; He did not institute
a Supper in which bread and wine are distributed and received as
symbols of the absent body and blood of Christ.

The situation is analogous to the Unitarian Baptism. As the
Unitarians do not baptize with the Baptism of Christ because they
publicly renounce the Father, the Son, and the Holy Ghost as the one
true God, though they may retain the sound of the words, so, too,
the Reformed do not administer the Supper of Christ because they
publicly renounce the meaning of Christ's words of institution, though
they retain the external sound of these words. Luther writes, and these
words have been embodied into the Formula of Concord: "In the same
manner I also speak and confess concerning the Sacrament of the
Altar that there the body and blood of Christ are in truth orally eaten
and drunk in the bread and wine, even though the priests [ministers]
who administer it [the Lord's Supper], or those who receive it, should
not believe or otherwise misuse it. For it does not depend upon the
faith or unbelief of men, but upon God's Word and ordinance, unless
they first change God's Word and ordinance and interpret it otherwise,[114] as the enemies of the Sacrament do at the present day, who,
of course, have nothing but bread and wine; for they also do not have

---

[114] Frank is right in saying that the phrase "and interpret it otherwise" does
not "independently name another case," but is added epexegetically to the words
"change God's Word and ordinance." III, 66.

the words and appointed ordinance of God, but have perverted and changed them according to their own [false] notion." (*Trigl.* 983, Sol. Decl., VII, 32.) The criticism that we would then have to deny also that the Reformed *Baptism* is Christ's Baptism [115] is not valid, for the Reformed do not renounce the meaning of the words of Baptism, as they do renounce the meaning of the words of the Lord's Supper. The Reformed error in the case of Baptism pertains only to the fruit, not to the essence, of Baptism.[116]

It should be added that the Formula of Concord very definitely rejects the opinion that the consecration by itself, or the mere recitation of the words of institution, makes the Sacrament or brings about the *unio sacramentalis.* Johann Saliger, pastor at Luebeck and Rostock, had tenaciously defended the opinion that the *unio sacramentalis* occurred already *ante usum;* hence before the distribution and reception.[117] But the Formula of Concord says: "However, this blessing, or the recitation of the words of institution of Christ alone, does not make a Sacrament if the entire action of the Supper, as it was instituted by Christ, is not observed (as when the consecrated bread is not distributed, received, and partaken of, but is enclosed, sacrificed, or carried about), but the command of Christ, 'This do' (which embraces the entire action or administration in this Sacrament, that in an assembly of Christians bread and wine are taken, consecrated, distributed, received, eaten, drunk, and the Lord's death is shown forth at the same time) must be observed unseparated and inviolate, as also St. Paul places before our eyes the entire action of the breaking of bread or of distribution and reception, 1 Cor. 10:16." (*Trigl.* 1001,

---

[115] So Fecht and Dannhauer contend; for quotations see *Lehre und Wehre* 1875, 180; cf. also Frank, III, 145 f.

[116] Walther, *Pastorale,* p. 181: "The unworthiness or unbelief or any false intention on the part of the administrant cannot invalidate the Sacrament, otherwise no Christian could have the assurance that he has truly received the Sacrament which Christ instituted. Those false teachers, however, who with the consent of their congregations publicly pervert the words of institution and put a construction upon them according to which the body and blood of the Lord are not truly present in the Lord's Supper, distributed, and received, who therefore retain the sounds of the words, but take away from them the things that make them the word of God, namely, the divine meaning, and thus, as, e. g., the Zwinglians and Calvinists, deny and abolish the essence of the Holy Supper (as the Antitrinitarians deny the essence of Baptism) — such do not administer the Lord's Supper, but distribute merely bread and wine, even though they retain and recite the words of institution." [Fritz, *Pastoral Theology,* p. 146.]

[117] On Saliger see Walther, *Pastorale,* p. 175, note. In vain did a commission seek to convince Saliger; he even carried the controversy into the pulpit. A fuller report on the trouble with Saliger is offered in Frank, III, 146 ff.

ibid., 83 f.) On the contention of Bellarmine that Christ spoke the words, "This is My body," before the act of partaking and that, accordingly, already before its reception the Sacrament must by the consecration be complete (*confectum*), that is, the *unio sacramentalis* must obtain, Quenstedt gives the apposite answer: "Christ does not say absolutely of the consecrated bread that it is His body, but of the bread broken and given to eat. For first He said, 'Take, *eat*'; thereupon He said, 'This is My body.'" (*Syst.* II, 1268.)[118]

8

The Purpose of the Lord's Supper

(Finis cuius coenae sacrae)

The purpose of the Lord's Supper is the remission of sins, as has been shown repeatedly and fully, particularly in the chapters "All Means of Grace Have the Same Purpose and the Same Effect" and "The Relation of the Lord's Supper to the Other Means of Grace" (pp. 108 ff., 293 ff.). This purpose of the Lord's Supper is ascertained not by deduction from extraneous passages of Holy Writ or by theological conclusions, but from the words of institution themselves, where it is clearly stated. See pp. 293, 111. When Christ adds, "which is given for you," to the words: "This is My body," and adds, "which is shed for you for the remission of sins," to the words: "This is My blood," His purpose was to call forth in the mind of His disciples at the first observance and in the minds of all communicants at all succeeding administrations of the Lord's Supper to the Last Day this conviction, that because of the propitiatory death of Christ they have a gracious God, that is, have remission of sins. Other meaning these words absolutely cannot have. We have likewise noted (p. 351) that in the statement about which there has been much dispute, "This cup

---

[118] Walther (*Pastorale,* p. 175) cites Aegidius Hunnius, *Art. s. loc.* "*De sacramentis,*" 1590, p. 712 f.: "As the bread is the communion of the body of Christ only in the act of eating and not before, so, too, the bread is not sacramentally united with the body till this communion and this reception takes place. For if it should happen that after the recital of the words of institution by the minister and after the so-called consecration a fire or tumult broke out before anyone had come to the Lord's Table, and thus the holy rite was prevented by this accident, it would be doubtful whether by virtue of the completed recitation the body of Christ is in some mysterious manner united with the bread, even without the use of the bread, which consists in the eating and was unexpectedly prevented. Here certainly every sensible person would rather negate than affirm the sacramental union."

is the new testament in My blood," the *finis cuius* of the Lord's Supper is directly expressed, since according to Scripture the new testament, or covenant, is nothing else than the remission of sins. Accordingly, we maintain that the Lord's Supper brings forgiveness of sins, the same forgiveness which the Word of the Gospel and Baptism offer.

Peculiar to the Lord's Supper, however, is the wonderful feature that Christ confirms and seals His assurance of the remission of our sins by giving us His body to eat, which was given into death for us, and His blood to drink, which was shed for the remission of our sins. In the Lord's Supper the remission of sins is therefore signed over and sealed to us by giving us the ransom paid for it. Therefore breaking forth in praise of the Lord's Supper, Luther says: "I love it with all my heart, the precious, blessed Supper of my Lord Jesus Christ, in which He gives me His body and blood to eat and to drink also orally, with the mouth of my body, accompanied by the exceedingly sweet, precious words: 'Given for you, shed for you'" (St. L. XIX:1292).

Luther has ever been accused of stressing the substantial presence of Christ's body and blood in the Lord's Supper so much that he lost sight of the "spiritual eating" of Christ's propitiatory death, or faith in the remission of sins. This is one of many misstatements about the *status controversiae* by which Carlstadt, Zwingli, Oecolampadius, and their associates succeeded in deceiving some Christians as to Luther's teaching and thus split the Church of the Reformation. Adolf Harnack and others have reiterated the false accusation.[119] Luther indeed fought tenaciously for the Real Presence because it is taught in Scripture and because a departure from the Word of Scripture at one place would lead to giving up the Scripture principle and making all Scripture uncertain. Still, the Real Presence remained for Luther merely the means unto an end, namely, the means of offering and confirming the forgiveness of sins, and this through the words added by Christ: "Given and shed for you for the remission of sins." After Luther, in his Large Catechism, has proved from Scripture "the first point which relates to the essence of this Sacrament," namely, the Real Presence, he says of the purpose, "on account of which really the Sacrament was instituted," that is, of the imparting of the remission of sins, "which is also its most necessary part, that we may know what we should seek and obtain there" (*Trigl.* 757, 20). Luther by no means puts the Real Presence "in the place of the *sola fides,*" as Harnack (*loc. cit.*) avers, but he lets the Real Presence be the support for the

---

[119] *Dogmengesch., Grundriss,* 4th ed., p. 433.

sola fides, as Christ intended it to be. He sees in the Lord's Supper "a food of *souls*"; "it is given for a daily pasture and sustenance, that faith may refresh and strengthen itself" (*Trigl.* 757, *ibid.,* 23). By this faith, of which Luther here speaks, he means nothing else than faith in the remission of sins. For Luther the Lord's Supper belongs to the *"distributio meriti Christi."* [120] Yes, Luther keeps on inculcating that even the body and blood of Christ in the Supper are not salutary, but only harmful, if faith in the *words,* "Given and shed for you for the remission of sins," is lacking in the heart. And because the Reformed did not cease to shift the *status controversiae,* and spoke of a *carnalis esus* of the Sacrament by the Lutherans [121] and, following Zwingli and Oecolampadius, slandered the Lutherans as cannibals,[122] the Formula of Concord reiterates the teaching of Luther that "without which spiritual participation also the sacramental or oral eating in the Supper is not only not salutary, but even injurious and damning (a cause of condemnation)" (*Trigl.* 995, Sol. Decl., VII, 61). The Formula has Christ state the purpose of the Lord's Supper thus: "Whereby I establish, seal, and confirm with you men this My testament and new covenant, namely, the forgiveness of sins" (*Trigl.* 991, *ibid.,* 53).

To formulate the *finis cuius* of the Lord's Supper as exactly as possible, we shall have to say: Faith in the Real Presence is indeed the indispensable prerequisite for a salutary use of the Lord's Supper. All who disbelieve the Real Presence are not to partake of the Lord's Supper, because they do not discern the Lord's body (1 Cor. 11:29). However, faith in so far as it believes the essential presence of Christ's body and blood in the Sacrament does not necessarily make the use of the Lord's Supper salutary. Only faith in so far as it believes the

---

[120] Luther, St. L. XX:925: "That blind, mad spirit does not know that *meritum Christi* and *distributio meriti* are two distinct things; so he mixes them up. Christ once for all merited and purchased for us remission of sins on the Cross; but He distributes the same, wherever He is, at all hours and all places, as Luke writes, ch. 24:46 f.: 'Thus it is written, and thus it behooved Christ to suffer and to rise from the dead the third day [there you have His *merit*], and that repentance and remission of sins should be preached in His name [there you have His merit's *distribution*].' Therefore we say that in the Lord's Supper is forgiveness of sins, not because of the eating, or that Christ there merits or purchases remission of sins, but because of the word, whereby He distributes this purchased remission among us and says: 'This is My body, which is given for you.' Here you hear that we eat the body as given for us; and while eating it, we hear and believe this; so then forgiveness of sins is there distributed, which was purchased, however, on the Cross."

[121] Calvin, *Inst.* IV, 17, 25.

[122] Beza's κρεωφαγία. Cf. p. 327, footnote 50.

words, "Given and shed for you," that is, believes the remission of sins imparted by the Lord's Supper, makes the use of the Sacrament salutary. We met a similar situation in Christology. The faith that Christ is true God and man is a necessary prerequisite of saving faith in Christ (Matt. 16:13 ff.). But the faith which believes only the true deity and true humanity of Christ is not saving faith. This faith also the devils have (Matt. 8:29). The faith which saves accepts and trusts in the forgiveness of sins which Christ, true God and man, has purchased for the believer and guarantees to him in the Word of the Gospel and in the Sacraments. Similarly, for all who deny the remission of sins as the prime and principal purpose of the Lord's Supper, Christ's Supper loses its practical value, no matter what they believe or do not believe of the essence of the Eucharist.

Into this category we must place the Papists, for they deny that the remission of sins is *finis cuius* of the Sacrament. The *Tridentinum* anathematizes all who declare the remission of sins (*remissio peccatorum*) to be the chief purpose of the Lord's Supper. See p. 338, footnote 69. Carlstadt was of the same opinion, for he says: "That our Christians seek forgiveness of sins in the Sacrament is a common and terrible fault." [123] Zwingli likewise admonishes that one should indeed celebrate the Lord's Supper as a "commemoration" (*commemoratio*) of the death of Christ, but that one should guard against the thought that the remission of sins is dispensed in the Sacrament.[124] The same instruction is given by Calvin. The *Consensus Tigurinus* warns against seeking forgiveness in the Sacrament, "as though the visible sign, while it is being dispensed, in that moment brings with it the grace of God" (Niemeyer, p. 195).

In admonishing their hearers by no means to regard the Lord's Supper as a medium of the remission of sins won by Christ, Zwingli and Calvin were indeed consistent. Since both assert that God's grace in Christ is provided not for all men, but only for the elect,[125] the Lord's Supper cannot be offering a grace that all communicants may appropriate by faith. Moreover, Zwingli and Calvin teach that there is no forgiveness of sins in the Lord's Supper even for the elect, for both teach that the saving manifestation of grace and its operation in

---

[123] *Vom widerchristl. Missbrauch,* etc., St. L. XX:94.

[124] *Opp.* III, 258: "The Lord's Supper, as Paul calls it, is a commemoration of the death of Christ, not the remission of sins." *Fidei Ratio* (Niemeyer, p. 29 f.): "If it works remission of sins, as the one party holds, then the disciples obtained remission of sins in the Supper and Christ therefore died in vain."

[125] Calvin, *Inst.* III, 24, 12, 15; Hodge, *Syst. Theol.* II, 323.

the elect occurs immediately, in a hidden operation of the Holy Ghost, and not through the means of grace.[126] As a means of grace the Lord's Supper, like the Word of the Gospel and Baptism, always presupposes that Christ has purchased grace for all men and that the operation of the Holy Ghost does not proceed without means, or parallel to them, but through the means of grace. Therefore, even if the followers of Zwingli and Calvin left intact the essence of the Lord's Supper, that is, taught with Scripture the real presence of the body of Christ given into death for us and the real presence of the blood of Christ shed for the remission of our sins, their teaching would have no practical value whatever so long as they deny the *gratia universalis* and the operation of the Holy Ghost through the means of grace.

But do not Zwingli and Calvin, in spite of their denial of universal grace in hundreds of places, specifically call the Lord's Supper a seal, sign, pledge (*signum, tessera, pignus*) of the grace and blessings purchased by Christ through His death on the Cross? They do.[127] But they have no right to use such terms so long as they teach the *gratia particularis*. If Christ's body is not given for all, then the sign of Christ's body in the Sacrament cannot point any partaker of the Sacrament to the grace merited by Christ's death on the Cross. If the faith of the individual is to rely on "the sign," then the sign must necessarily be for all. If the sign is not intended for all, it is not a support of faith for the individual, but a source of doubt. True, Zwingli and Calvin point to the "spiritual eating" of the body and blood of Christ as the core of the Reformed doctrine of the Lord's Supper. By their doctrine of the *manducatio oralis* the Lutherans allegedly relegate the spiritual eating, or faith, to the background, even making it impossible. But obviously Zwingli, Calvin, and their followers are the ones that do this very thing by denying that the body of Christ was given for all men without exception.

---

[126] Zwingli, *Fidei Ratio,* in Niemeyer, p. 24 ff. [in Jacobs, *Book of Concord* II, 168]; Calvin, *Inst.* IV, 14, 17; *Consens. Tigur.,* ch. XVII; Hodge, *Syst. Theol.,* II, 684: "Efficacious grace acts immediately."

[127] Calvin, *Inst.* IV, 14, 17; 17, 1, 11. In his *Commentary* on 1 Cor. 11:24: "The Supper is a *speculum* [mirror] which represents Christ crucified to us." In the *Consens. Tigur.* (Niemeyer, p. 193) we read: "This is one among several principal (purposes of the Sacraments), that through them God attests His grace to us, represents and seals it." In his *Expositio* of the *Consens. Tigur.* Calvin even believes it permissible to say: "Away therefore with that rotten calumny that it is theatrical pretense if God does not actually do what He shows by a sign. For we do not say that something is shown which is not really given." (Niemeyer, p. 213.)

This "spiritual eating," which is the same as believing, is prevented by the Reformed teaching of a secret, immediate operation of the Spirit. For one thing, the faith in which spiritual eating consists does not trust in secret operations of the Holy Ghost. Rather, it believes in the gracious disposition in God, brought about by Christ through His reconciling death and offered to men in the Word and the Sacrament. Whoever teaches reliance on secret operations in the heart of man is teaching the Roman *gratia infusa,* not the Christian saving grace, which always is only *gratuitus Dei favor propter Christum.* Secondly, such secret, immediate operations of the Holy Spirit are pure fiction. What is palmed off as operation of the Spirit is man-made. And the faith which trusts in this forgery is likewise an emotion and mood produced by man himself, however much of it is falsely ascribed to the Holy Ghost. It cannot be of the Holy Ghost inasmuch as there is no illumination and operation of the Holy Ghost promised us save that which proceeds through the means of grace.

Furthermore, the followers of Zwingli and Calvin cannot consistently speak of their Supper as a "memorial meal" of Christ's death. Only those can have such a memorial Supper who adhere to the Scripture teaching that Christ died for all mankind. Advocates of the *gratia particularis* do not commemorate Christ's sin-atoning death, but cast doubt upon it. Suppose someone invited a hundred guests to a banquet, but at the same time announced that only twenty elect,[128] known only to him, would actually be admitted to the banquet, would not the invitation become dubious and inacceptable to all? Of the same doubt-harassed frame of mind must all partakers of the Reformed "memorial meal" be as long as they think that Christ's death counts only for the elect and not for all.

Finally, the Reformed have no right to use the term on which they all ultimately agree, namely, that in the Lord's Supper the bread and wine are "symbols" of the body and blood of Christ. The symbol certainly must correspond to the thing symbolized. Now, if the body of Christ was not given into death for all, bread and wine cannot be symbols of that death or of Christ's body and blood for all partakers of the Supper.

Thus Calvin's and Zwingli's doctrine of the Lord's Supper collapses, both when we investigate what they declare to be the essence of the Lord's Supper, to wit, that bread and wine are symbols of the body and blood of Christ, and when we examine what they are minded

---

[128] This is Calvin's estimate, *Inst.* III, 24, 12.

to maintain as to the fruit and effect of the Lord's Supper, that is, that bread and wine are signs, symbols, etc., of the grace of God, a memorial meal of Christ's death, and thus a means of aiding the spiritual eating of the propitiatory death of Christ by faith.

Romanists remove the forgiveness of sins from the Lord's Supper with an anathema, as we have proved above (p. 338) by a quotation from the *Tridentinum*. Why Rome so energetically eliminates the forgiveness of sins from the Lord's Supper is quite understandable. The kingdom of the Pope stands and falls with its doctrine of the uncertainty of the remission of sins. Rome, however, could have saved itself its anathemas, inasmuch as grace necessarily becomes uncertain when the absolution pronounced by the priest is based on contrition, the complete enumeration of all mortal sins with all attendant circumstances, satisfaction by works, and on the intention of the priest to absolve.[129] By laying down these and similar conditions Rome effectively blocks all assurance of the *gratia sacramentalis*.

Just as effectively Arminians and synergistic Lutherans do away with the *finis cuius*, that is, the remission of sins, in the Lord's Supper. If grace cannot be obtained except through co-operation, a lesser guilt, a correct conduct of man, man's own choice, etc., an impassable gulf is set between man and the grace proffered in the Lord's Supper. The Lord's Supper, like the Word of the Gospel and Baptism, will prove to be a means of grace and of benefit to a contrite sinner only when the offer of the remission of sins does not hinge on any human accomplishment, worthiness, lesser guilt, etc. Hence we must maintain against Romanists, Calvinists, Arminian Reformed, and all synergists as to the purpose of the Lord's Supper: The proffer, pledging, and sealing of the free and full remission of sins is the chief and prime purpose of the Lord's Supper. Christ makes us certain of this fact by adding to the words "This is My body" the words "which is given for you," and to the words "This is My blood" the words "which is shed for you." Luther says in his Large Catechism: "Which is also its most necessary part, that we may know what we should seek and obtain there" (*Trigl.* 757, Sacr. of Altar, 20).

All other effects of the Lord's Supper are not co-ordinate, but subordinate to the bestowal of the forgiveness of sins. These other effects have been listed as follows: (a) strengthening of faith, (b) communion with Christ, (c) communion with the spiritual body of Christ,

---

[129] *Trid., Sess.* XIV, *Sacr. of Penance,* c. 3—6, 8, can. 4—10; Waterworth, p. 108 f.

the Church, (d) furtherance in sanctification, (e) kindling of love of God and the neighbor, (f) growth in patience and in hope of eternal life. But all these effects rest not in part only, but entirely on the fact that the Lord's Supper is a means of remitting sins. Christian faith in its very nature is faith in the remission of sins provided by Christ's substitutional satisfaction. For this reason Christian faith can be strengthened only by relating it, through the divinely appointed means of grace, to the object which generates and sustains it, namely, the promise of the remission of sins. Again, there is no other communion with Christ than the one resulting from faith in the forgiveness of sins bought by His blood. To all who, like Rome, Zwingli, and Calvin, substitute for this forgiveness a *gratia infusa* the judgment applies: "Christ is become of no effect unto you, whosoever of you are justified by the Law; ye are fallen from grace" (Gal. 5:4). And there is no other spiritual communion with the body of Christ, the Church, than that which is brought about and sustained by faith in the Gospel of the remission of sins for Christ's sake. All who seek other means of uniting with the Church thereby forfeit both communion with Christ and communion with His spiritual body, the Church. Again, there is no other means to effect Christian sanctification than faith in the mercy of God, according to which God forgives our sins for Christ's sake, as the Apostle writes (Rom. 12:1): "I beseech you, therefore, brethren, by the mercies of God, that ye present your bodies a living sacrifice, holy, acceptable unto God, which is your reasonable service," etc. Again, there is no other means to ignite and set ablaze love for God and the neighbor in the human heart than faith in the divine love which for the sake of Christ's *satisfactio vicaria* forgives the sins of us unworthy sinners. 1 John 4:19: "We love Him because He first loved us." 1 John 4:11: "Beloved, if God so loved us, we ought also to love one another." And so Paul (Rom. 5:1-5) declares the joyous hope of eternal life and patience in tribulations to be solely the fruit of justification, or the remission of sins, by faith. Since, now, in the Lord's Supper the divine forgiveness of our sins is sealed to us with Christ's body and blood, and is thus offered to us in an especially impressive and comforting manner, the spiritual effects mentioned result from the Lord's Supper in peculiar measure. All who, like Rome, Zwingli, Calvin, and modern theologians, will not acknowledge the Lord's Supper to be *primo loco* a means of imparting the forgiveness of sins are actually preventing all the other benefits of the Lord's Supper. They are, when consistent, making of the Lord's Supper a work of man which separates them from the grace of God in Christ.

9

Who Is to Be Admitted to the Lord's Supper

(Finis cui coenae sacrae)

Christian congregations, and their public servants, are only the administrants and not the lords of the Sacrament. The Lord's Supper is not their institution, but Christ's. Therefore they must follow Christ's instructions in administering the Sacrament. On the one hand, they are not permitted to introduce "Open Communion"; on the other hand, they must guard against denying the Sacrament to those Christians for whom Christ has appointed it. Gerhard and Calov are justified in discussing the *finis cui* or the *objectum* of the Lord's Supper also in a dogmatics.[130]

It is common knowledge that "Open Communion" is commended and practiced not only in Reformed churches, but also in church bodies calling themselves Lutheran.[131] A Christian congregation, however, should consider well that the Lord's Supper is not intended for all men, but only for Christians. Here a difference obtains between the preaching of the Gospel and the Lord's Supper. The Gospel is intended for all men, believers and unbelievers alike. The Lord's Table, however, is appointed only for the people who have already come to faith in Christ.

This we learn from the normative example of Christ. Christ preached the Gospel to the Jewish people generally and for that purpose went from place to place (Matt. 9:35 ff.). But the first celebration of His Supper He held in the closed circle of His disciples (Luke 22:11, 14; Matt. 26:18, 20). Neither did the Apostolic Church practice "open" Communion (1 Cor. 11:20; 10:17). Luther says: "Thus Christ did; He delivered His sermons to the multitude for everybody, as the Apostles later did, so that every person heard them, believers and unbelievers; whoever caught it, caught it. We must do the same. But the Sacrament we are not to cast among a crowd. When I preach the Gospel, I do not know upon whom it takes effect; but here I must be convinced that it has taken effect upon those who come to the Sacrament. Here I must not act in doubt, but be [reasonably] sure

---

130 See Gerhard, *Loci,* "De coena s." § 221 f.; Calov, *Syst.,* IX, 195 ff.

131 Regarding American Lutheran circles see A. L. Graebner in *Lehre und Wehre,* 1888, p. 257 ff., 302 ff.: *"Zur Geschichte der vier Punkte."* R. E., 3d ed., I, 68.

that the one to whom I give the Sacrament has laid hold of the Gospel and has true faith." [132]

---

[132] Walther, *Pastorale*, p. 144: "The case of the Lord's Supper is quite different from that of the preaching of the Gospel. The Word is not merely given to sustain the believer in faith, but also initially to awake man from his sleep of sin, to bring him to a knowledge of his sin and to faith; yes, without the Word all this is simply impossible. No one may, therefore, be barred from the preaching of God's Word; for that would mean locking the one door to grace for him. The case is different with the Lord's Supper; by this a man is not to be given the first beginning of repentance and faith, but his existing repentance and faith is to be intensified; by it man is not for the first time to obtain grace and become a Christian, but the grace previously obtained through the Word is thereby to be confirmed to him and he to be preserved, sustained, and furthered in his Christian faith; by this food a man is not for the first time to be quickened unto the life that is of God, but, after having become spiritually alive, to be nourished and refreshed. He, therefore, who would receive the Lord's Supper worthily and for his eternal benefit must previously have come to repentance and faith, must previously have obtained grace and have become a true Christian. Partaking of the Lord's Supper is in and by itself not beneficial; rather the benefit depends on how one partakes. It does not work *ex opere operato*. It is not like a medicine which one need merely swallow to have the benefit. It is rather like a treasure house whose treasures can be taken, grasped, and held only with the hand of faith. He who partakes without faith indeed also receives the genuine and entire Sacrament; for he receives not merely bread and wine, but in, with, and under these elements he with his mouth really and truly receives the body and blood of Jesus Christ as a precious pledge of grace and forgiveness; however, he gets nothing of the blessing contained in it for the salvation of his soul; for what can an ever so precious and costly pledge help a man, and how can it serve to assure him of a fact, if he does not believe that it is so precious and costly a pledge? Moreover, whoever partakes of the Lord's Supper without the right faith, and therefore unworthily, not only loses the grace contained in it, but draws from it wrath instead of grace, death instead of life, curse instead of blessing; he becomes, as St. Paul writes, 'guilty of the body and blood of the Lord; he eats and drinks damnation unto himself, not discerning the Lord's body.' Dreadful therefore is the sin committed by him who partakes unworthily of the Holy Supper; and those who say: 'Still one ought to be glad that the people still come to the Lord's Supper,' thereby reveal how pitiful their knowledge of this holy Sacrament is."

The objection has been advanced that it might occur during the administration of the Sacrament that an unbeliever, hearing the powerful and perfectly clear words of institution ("This is My body, which is given for you; this is My blood, which is shed for you"), would be brought to faith in the essence of the Lord's Supper (the Real Presence) as well as faith in the purpose of the Supper (the remission of sins). This possibility must be granted. The early Christian Church reports how a pagan actor came to faith when in mockery of Christianity he was given Holy Baptism on the stage. But this possibility is none of our concern. What the practice of the Church is to be is established by the divine ordinance. And this reads: "But let a man examine himself, and so let him eat of that bread and drink of that cup. For he that eateth and drinketh unworthily, eateth and drinketh damnation to himself, not discerning the Lord's body." (1 Cor. 11:28-29.) The divine order is that in the Lord's Supper, as Luther expresses it, "we should know with whom it takes effect."

However, not even all Christians are to be admitted to the Lord's Table. To be admitted are:

1. Such as have been baptized. On this order of sequence in the use of the two New Testament Sacraments see p. 292.

2. Such as are able to examine themselves. Scripture expressly declares spiritual self-examination necessary for a salutary use of the Holy Supper: "Let a man examine himself [δοκιμαζέτω δὲ ἄνθρωπος ἑαυτόν], and *so* [οὕτως] let him eat of that bread and drink of that cup" (1 Cor. 11:28). Excluded therefore are children, the sleeping, the unconscious, the dying deprived of the use of their senses, the insane and possessed while not in their right mind, etc.[133]

3. Only such as believe the words of institution, hence believe both that they receive the true body and blood of Christ in the Lord's Supper and that Christ gives them this priceless gift for the remission of their sins. This provision excludes the Christians in Reformed denominations. There certainly are children of God among the Reformed who still preach Christ's *satisfactio vicaria*. Since, however, they lack the right understanding of, and therefore faith in, the words of institution, they are *not in condition* to use the Lord's Supper to their benefit. Paul expressly disqualified all who do not believe the Real Presence, since they do not discern the Lord's body (διακρίνειν τὸ σῶμα τοῦ Κυρίου), 1 Cor. 11:29. With their denial of the Real Presence they also lose the *finis cuius* of the Lord's Supper, namely, that Christ's body and blood is given us in the Sacrament for the remission of our sins. This applies, of course, also to such Lutherans

---

[133] Walther, *Pastorale,* p. 190: "Since according to God's Word everyone who would approach the Lord's Table should first examine himself and discern the Lord's body, it will not do to give the Lord's Supper to children incapable of examining themselves. It was a manifest abuse when this practice, as the examples of even Cyprian and Augustine prove, was quite general from the third to the fifth century, with the sanction also of Innocent I., through a misinterpretation of John 6:53 as referring to sacramental eating and drinking. This misuse was prevalent also among the Bohemian Hussites and is canon law even today in the Eastern Church. Luther writes: 'I cannot side with the Bohemians in distributing the Lord's Supper to children, even though I would not call them heretics on that account.' Furthermore, those who cannot examine themselves and therefore are not to be admitted to the Lord's Supper include also those asleep, or unconscious, those in the throes of death who are already deprived of the use of their senses, deranged people, and the like." Walther, as we saw, points to the fact that the Lord's Supper does not, like bodily medication, work physically, but presupposes consciousness of the essence and faith in the purpose of the Lord's Supper. Further particulars, e. g., the question whether lunatics, raving madmen, yes, also the bodily possessed, may be communed when they have lucid intervals (*"lichte Zwischenzeiten"*) belong to casuistry. See Walther, *ibid.,* p. 192.

as are afflicted with grave doubts as to the Real Presence of Christ's body and blood,[134] or who, though they confess the Real Presence, are not seeking the forgiveness of sins in the Sacrament, but ascribe to it a salutary effect *ex opere operato*.[135]

4. Such as must not first remove a public offense that has been given. The particulars are discussed in Pastoral Theology. The course in Dogmatics must point out that this practice — removing a public offense before partaking of Communion — does not rest on human arbitrariness or legalism, but is demanded by the essence and purpose of the Lord's Supper. Because the Lord's Supper is not intended for believers and unbelievers, but only for Christians, everyone who has made his Christianity doubtful for the congregation must, before he communes again, enable the congregation to become convinced that by God's grace he has risen from his fall. Scripture therefore expressly prohibits us to treat as brothers in the faith those who live in gross, offensive sins, that is, to act toward them as though nothing had occurred. 1 Cor. 5:11: "But now I have written unto you not to keep company if any man that is called a brother be a fornicator, or covetous, or an idolater, or a railer, or a drunkard, or an extortioner; with such an one no not to eat." [136] If the grave offense of a person has become known to the congregation, also his repentance must be made known to the congregation before he again communes with the congregation.

From the essence and purpose of the Lord's Supper it further follows that persons living in the sin of implacability must be suspended from partaking of the Sacrament. For the Lord's Supper is distribution of the forgiveness of sins; only he therefore makes the

---

[134] When some began to doubt the Real Presence because of the preaching of Carlstadt and the "enthusiasts," Luther (XX, 201) gave the advice: "If someone was too weak to take the blow, so that he now has his doubts as to the Sacrament, let him take my advice to do without the Sacrament for the present and to exercise himself without it in God's Word, in faith and love, letting those take the Sacrament who feel safe in their conscience. You are not doomed if you do without the Sacrament." The same thought: XX, 734.

[135] Luther, St. L. XX:748 ff.: "It is not sufficient to know what the Sacrament is, viz., that Christ's body and blood actually is there, but it is necessary also to know *why* it is there and why and for what end it is given us to eat. . . . This, then, we call the right use; not this, that it is simply performed and obedience rendered to the Church. The point is not the performance of a work, but the strengthening of your heart, as the words say, 'Which is given for you, which is shed for you.'"

[136] The συνεσθίειν prohibits any table fellowship. "We are not to have him at our table, nor are we to be found at his table" (Meyer), much less are we to join him at the Lord's Table.

right use of it who there seeks the forgiveness of his sins. But in any
case there can be a true desire for God's forgiveness only in the heart
of him who on his part, too, is ready to forgive the trespasses of his
neighbor, or, if he was in the wrong, to seek reconciliation by asking
the neighbor's forgiveness.[137]

Furthermore, since Christians are forbidden to adhere to teachers
who deviate from the Apostolic doctrine (Rom. 16:17: "Avoid them";
R. V.: "turn away from them"), it is self-evident that members of
heterodox churches must have severed their connection with the
heterodox body and have declared their acceptance of the true doctrine
before they may commune with the congregation. Fellowship in the
Lord's Supper certainly is fellowship in faith or church fellowship
(Fritz: "*Abendmahlsgemeinschaft ist Glaubensgemeinschaft*," altar
fellowship is confessional fellowship, *Pastoral Theology*, p. 154; [Wal-
ther, *Pastorale*, p. 145]). It must also not be overlooked that the Lord's
Supper is private absolution. God's will, however, is that we give
private absolution to him only who, as far as we are able to judge,
sincerely repents. To the unrepentant we are not to say: "Thou shalt
live," but are to give him the ringing warning: "Thou shalt surely die!"
(Ezek. 3:17-18). Therefore Walther (*Pastorale*, p. 146 f.) is right in
holding that by practicing "Open Communion" a pastor becomes "an
unfaithful, careless, and unscrupulous shepherd." Luther, too, warns
against this soul-destroying mingling of Law and Gospel by saying,
as we heard above: "When I preach the Gospel, I do not know with
whom it takes effect; but here I should be convinced that it takes effect
with him who comes to the Sacrament" (St. L. XI:615). He expresses
this thought somewhat more drastically in pointing out what a faithful
pastor must tell an impenitent sinner when he applies God's Word to
him individually: "Repent, and that honestly! If not, you can just as
well go to the devil by yourself, without me and my absolution, as
go doubly to the devil with my absolution and besides by your guilt
drag me along without my guilt. Nay, man; I say: You go to the
devil, I shall stay here; I am not pastor to go to the devil with everybody, but to bring everybody with me to God." (St. L. X:882.)

In vain is love, or charity, appealed to in defense of "Open Communion." The fact is that this practice is contrary both to love of God

---

[137] Cf. Walther, *Pastorale*, p. 194 f. [Fritz, *Pastoral Theology*, p. 151].
Luther: "God will not be gracious and forgive a man's sin unless he also forgives
his neighbor. Besides, a man's faith cannot be sincere unless it bears this fruit,
that he, too, forgives his neighbor and asks his forgiveness; otherwise man may
not appear before God. If this fruit is missing, his faith and his first confession
[his confession "before God"] is also not sincere." (St. L. XI:585.)

and love of the neighbor, for it ignores that the Sacrament of the Altar must be properly used, as prescribed in Scripture, and it leads the neighbor to sin by partaking unworthily of the Sacrament. And what has been said of "Open Communion" applies also to the admission of Reformed to Lutheran altars "as guests." [138]

Accordingly, if a Christian congregation is to prove itself conscientious in the administration of the Lord's Supper, it must have the custom of registration for Communion (announcing one's intention to partake to the pastor). Obviously, only through such registration can the pastor limit Communion attendance to those eligible for the Lord's Supper. Of course, he should explore only those persons with whose faith and life he is unfamiliar. Pertinent is Walther's remark that this exploration before admission to the Lord's Table rests not on a divine command, but solely on the need of the souls. Exploration not only may, but should be omitted in all cases where the pastor is dealing with good Christians well known to him. To explore in such cases would be a needless burdening both of the pastor and of those registering. This is also Luther's opinion. "A person," he says, "may be so well versed in Lutheran doctrine and practice that he need be explored but once in his life or not at all" (St. L. X:2248).[139]

Both pastor and congregation must most carefully guard against denying the Lord's Supper to anyone to whom Christ wants it to be given. In his day Luther had to warn not only against laxity in practice, but also against legalism and unnecessary rigor. He writes to Balth. Thuering in Koburg: "I have written the pastor not to torture the ignorant with long examinations when they announce for Com-

---

138 This "admission as guests" involves a self-contradiction. When Lutheran synods in America indeed wanted to cling to the rule, "Lutheran altars for Lutheran communicants only," but then wanted exceptions to the rule granted, they were again making admission to the Lord's Supper a matter of human caprice and were thus in fact dropping the divine rule.

139 Walther, *Pastorale*, p. 152. It would be contrary to Luther's intention if we applied everything Luther said about the necessary "exploration" before admission to the Lord's Supper without further ado to present-day conditions. We today have congregations to which only those belong "who are earnestly minded to be Christians," a condition Luther strove for, but never attained. Among us, therefore, the pastor usually is personally well acquainted with the spiritual life of his members, and for that reason an exploration is unnecessary. — Also the following reminder is here in place: If the pastor as shepherd must reprove some member of his congregation, he should not wait until the next registration for Communion, lest the day of registration become a general day of judgment in his congregation — a thing that is good neither for the pastor nor the congregation. Walther therefore was wont to give the advice to attend to any case requiring special attention before the day of registration, even though it be the day before.

munion, but also not to refrain entirely from exploring and examining them. To let them partake without any examination is no good. We censure our opponents for being belly servers; but our men are stern and inclined to severity. I pray you therefore, for God's sake, to endeavor most earnestly to teach the Gospel in all humility." (Walch XXI, 1348.) To keep the pastor from denying the Lord's Supper to those weak in Christian knowledge, or frightening timid souls away, Walther gives directions as to what the pastor ought to ascertain and how he ought to explore when people with whose spiritual condition he is unfamiliar desire Communion. The person registering should not be subjected to a "rigorous examination," but be induced by way of a friendly interview to reveal the state of his Christianity and to tell what the Lord's Supper is and why he desires to partake.

But even apart from the cases where the pastor is seeking to discover the spiritual state of practical strangers, there is danger — and the pastor must not lose sight of this fact — that particularly in regard to the use of holy Communion the inherent *opinio legis* is apt to assert itself in the communicants, perhaps also in the pastor himself. It takes this form: Since one receives Christ's body and blood in the Lord's Supper, a salutary use of the Sacrament presupposes a special degree of sanctity and a strong faith. Because of this thought particularly earnest Christians, who feel their infirmity more than others, are prone to postpone receiving the Sacrament until they feel greater fervency of spirit, have waxed strong in faith, and show a progress in sanctification that satisfies them personally. But these are mistaken notions, a result of forgetting that the Lord's Supper is a means of grace. In the Lord's Supper we indeed receive Christ's body and blood. But this wonderful gift is given us for the very purpose of transmitting and pledging to us the free grace of God, based entirely on Christ's *satisfactio vicaria* and demanding no worthiness of our own at all. That Christ receives sinners — this He wants to stress and bring out, as in all means of grace, so particularly by His Supper. Luther says: "The Sacrament is instituted for this very purpose of ministering comfort and strength to us. Therefore let nothing keep you from the Communion. If you feel your weakness, good, for you must feel your unworthiness." (St. L. XI:660.) And earlier: "You must not make of Christ a tyrant, but accept Him for what He in truth is and let Him be unto you nothing but rich, abounding grace. If you feel in your heart that you have not reached this point and do not have such faith, and yet would like to believe, you must, after all, not despair and shun the Communion, but seek your help right there, so that your faith may burst into flame and increase. For though some have been terribly punished for partaking of the Sacrament unworthily and without faith, they are only those whom we described above, namely, the hardened, wicked hearts. You should proceed and think thus: Lord, see, there is Thy Word, and here is my illness and failing. Thou thyself hast said, 'Come unto Me, all ye that labor and are heavy laden, and I will give you rest' (Matt. 11:28). Do you think He said that to those who are already fervid and strong in faith? His kingdom is not established to the end of furthering the righteous (Matt. 9:13), but of helping sinners and making them righteous (1 Tim. 1:15). Hence he who is weak and feels it should go to Communion and let God help him." (*Ibid.*, 653 ff.) Luther also adduces his own example: "It has often happened to me that I hesitated and thus only widened the breach, until I saw that this was no help; so I had to partake. Thus you, too, will find that it is a fraud of Satan, to draw people away from the Sacrament, so that the more they are afraid and want to wait until they feel faith in their hearts, the farther they drift away. And at last, if they continue in this state, all desire and impulse, both toward the Word and the Sacrament, dies out in them, and they never come. Therefore you must thrust aside your thoughts and fears, and partake, and ask God to help you. If you do this often, you will feel how you are gaining more and more desire for it, an increase you would not have gained otherwise. To this end I wish you would follow my example and that the number of those might increase who go to the Sacrament in order that their desire for it might grow and they become stronger and stronger. Otherwise, if you do not partake, you will always remain cold and only grow colder and colder."

To keep a pastor from unjustly refusing Communion, and at the same time to save the pastor unnecessary scruples of conscience, the reminder is in place "that a pastor need not be sure of a living faith in those desiring Communion from him — for who but God could be?—; he must merely be certain that if they are not Christians, this is not manifest or provable. To act according to his moral convictions in admitting or turning away people from the Lord's Table is an inexcusable tyranny over the consciences." (Walther, *Pastorale*, p. 192.) This verdict is not too severe. Suppose a pastor, because of his "moral convictions," turned communicants away from the Lord's Supper, though he cannot prove his conviction to be correct, would he not subject the congregation as well as those desiring to partake of the Sacrament to his caprice?

In certain cases, however, the pastor must suspend from Communion. The pastor's right of suspension has been discussed much in times past and present. However, the discussion has not always been entirely correct (cf. Walther, *Pastorale*, p. 163 f.). The thing that must be maintained is that the pastor is personally and directly responsible not only to the congregation, but also to God, with regard to the persons he admits to the Lord's Supper. Therefore the pastor has both the right and the duty to suspend those whose admission to the Sacrament would be contrary to God's will and ordinance. Walther specifies: "A pastor, though without authority to excommunicate a member of his congregation, must suspend a member from Communion when he has committed or lives in a manifest mortal sin and will not repent; has committed a theft and will not return the stolen goods; has insulted or offended someone or a whole congregation, or has been offended by someone, and in either case will not be reconciled, Matt. 5:23-25; 18:28 ff.; Luke 17:3, etc. In such a situation it becomes necessary to suspend from the Holy Supper, that is to say, the pastor refuses to commune such a member until his offense has been removed, or demands that the member postpone his Communion until he gives evidence of repentance, or of readiness to be reconciled, and the like. A pastor may not and must not become partaker of other men's sins, 1 Tim. 5:22. Certainly he must, then, have the right of suspension from the Lord's Supper in all cases where he by admittance to the Lord's Table would knowingly assist in the commission of a grievous sin and thus become partaker of other men's sin. As emphatically, therefore, as our old orthodox theologians deny the right of pastors to excommunicate without the congregation, so emphatically they defend the pastor's right to suspend from Communion." It must, however, be kept in mind that the pastor by suspending does not excommunicate, as many mistakenly have claimed, but he merely demands postponement of the person's communing until the person in question shows signs of repentance and removes whatever obstacles, according to the Word of God, forbid his going to Communion.

Of course, the suspended person always retains the right of appeal to the congregation from the verdict of the pastor, and this for two reasons: (1) the administration of the Lord's Supper is entrusted originally to the congregation and the pastor has suspended as the servant of the congregation (*minister ecclesiae*); (2) the suspension temporarily affects the relation of the suspended to the congregation. But in the meantime the suspension stands. If it should happen that the pastor justly suspended a person, but the congregation condemned and annulled the suspension, and despite proper instruction and a thorough review of the case, perhaps even by synodical officials, refuses to change its mind, the pastor must nevertheless rather suffer removal from office than give the Lord's Supper to a person to whom, according to God's Word, he must deny it. Under our church polity we have rarely experienced such conflicts. In most cases the pastor succeeded in convincing the congregation of the propriety of the suspension. Now and then the pastor was convinced by his congregation, or by other advisers called in, that the suspension was unjustifiable. At our theological schools a number of typical cases in which suspension ought not to be applied, might well be discussed at length.[140]

The combination of *confession* and the Lord's Supper is a laudable

---

[140] Walther, *Pastorale*, p. 152 ff., 190 ff. [Fritz, *Pastoral Theology*, p. 134] lists these cases: When an "evil rumor" circulates concerning one desiring Communion; when he is directly accused of having committed a grievous sin, but his accuser can bring no witnesses or proof; when the pastor alone knows about his guilt; when a Christian is involved in a lawsuit, etc. The many quotations Walther offers show that even the earlier Lutheran theologians are not entirely dependable guides in this matter because they lived under State-Church conditions and in the exercise of Christian discipline sometimes confused civil and ecclesiastical discipline. It is a correct axiom: *De occultis non iudicat ecclesia.* And this includes that it is not the business of the Church to ferret out secret sins. In quoting the earlier theologians Walther repeatedly refers to his note on page 154 of his *Pastorale*, in which he says: "The confession of particular sins before men is not necessary unless by silence an innocent person is made to suffer. Unless this is the case, or unless the member is unburdening his heart to his pastor, the pastor should not ask whether or not he has committed a certain sin, lest the pastor thus press him to reveal a hidden sin or to tell a lie." Also during private confession interrogation is, according to Walther, to be limited, but a mild *suggestion* may be made to confess a particular sin if the pastor notices that the penitent remains troubled in his conscience in spite of all instruction and consolation (*Pastorale*, p. 290). Walther quotes approvingly from Hartmann's *Pastorale evangelicum*, p. 791: "It is a wrong assumption that a clear and express confession of every single sin, particularly of those sins of which one is accused on the basis of a rumor or a strong suspicion, is necessary, for there is no commandment to that effect in Scripture. It is no less a wrong assumption that he could not be truly sorry for sins committed who does not expressly confess them before the confessor." That express confession is necessary is the well-known horrible doctrine of Rome (*Trid.*, Sess. XIV, can. 4—8), which makes the Church a spy and eavesdropper among men, makes the forgiveness pronounced uncertain, strengthens the priests' shameful tyranny, and exerts a demoralizing influence, particularly on women. When souls in their trials reveal a desire to unburden themselves, the pastor certainly should meet them halfway. But just as earnestly he must guard against ferreting out secret sins. Walther (*Pastorale*, p. 159) says that it is "contrary to a pastor's office curiously to hunt for secret sins," and quotes from the Saxon church regulations: "The servants of the Church are not to ask inquisitively of the penitents what these do not confess of themselves." If a pastor blunders here, he has no cause to be offended if his member tells him: "Pastor, that is not your business," and should not regard such an answer as a sign of impenitence.

church custom, but not a divine ordinance. This statement holds true both of private confession and of the so-called "confessional service," with its confessional address, general confession of sins, and general absolution. Walther (*Pastorale*, p. 168) quotes from the "Instruction for the Visitors" of 1538 (St. L. X:1655): "If the pastor, who daily is occupied with it, desires to go to the Sacrament without a confession or questioning, he may do so. The same thing is true of other well-informed persons who know well how to examine themselves, in order that this confession, which should and must remain a free act, does not again develop into a new papistic coercion and indispensable rite. And I, Dr. Martin, once in a while go to the Lord's Table without having confessed, in order that I may keep from feeling bound in my conscience to observe this custom as necessary; then again I use the confession and would not be without it; above all, because of the absolution, that is, the Word of God." [141]

10

The Necessity of the Lord's Supper

The Lord's Supper is not a matter of choice, an adiaphoron, but a divine ordinance that is to be observed in the Church to the Last Day. See p. 290. It is the gracious will of God that Christians who are able to examine themselves and to discern the Lord's body should partake of the Lord's Supper. The Lord's Supper is of special consolation (pp. 293 ff., 373 ff.) to the Christian with his burden of sin, since the Lord's Supper offers the assurance of grace to the individual and confirms it to the individual by a most singular pledge or seal, namely,

---

[141] See Luther's classic words on confession in his "Sermon on Confession and the Sacrament" (St. L. XI:585—590; see p. 210, footnote 107). Here he distinguishes three kinds of confession, of which the first two (the confession of sin before God and confessing to the offended neighbor) are divinely enjoined, but not so the third. "The third kind is the one commanded by the Pope, which is confessed privately into the ears of the priest. This one is not commanded by God. . . . Still it is advisable and good. . . . For it is deplorable when the conscience is burdened and in fear and knows of no escape or consolation. For that reason, too, it is a noble, fine deed when two come together and the one gives advice, help, and consolation to the other, and things proceed most brotherly and lovely; the one uncovers his ailment, the other heals his wounds for him. On that account I for one would not do without this private confession for all the treasures of the world. Still it should not be taught as commanded, in order not to bind the consciences, as though one had to go to confession before going to the Sacrament." (St. L. XI:590.)

by giving him to eat and to drink the very body of Christ which was given for him, and the very blood of Christ which was shed for him.

Still, there is no absolute necessity of the Lord's Supper, because the remission of sins is not divided among the various means of grace, but each one of them offers the full remission of sins provided by Christ's *satisfactio vicaria* and works, or strengthens, faith. All means of grace have the same purpose and the same effect (p. 108 ff). Hence he who believes the preached or written Word of the Gospel is, through his faith in the Word, in possession of the full remission of sins and salvation, though circumstances keep him from using the Lord's Supper.

Luther is right in rejecting the absolute necessity of either Baptism (p. 280f.) or the Lord's Supper. When Luther heard that Carlstadt's attacks on the Christian doctrine of the Lord's Supper had caused some Christians to doubt the Real Presence, he gave them the advice to suspend themselves from the Lord's Table during this period of doubt, with this reasoning: "You are not lost if you do without the Sacrament"; "train yourselves without this Sacrament in God's Word, in faith, and in love; let those take the Lord's Supper who feel safe in their conscience" (XX:201, 734). Again, decidedly as Luther fought the Reformed teaching of the absence of Christ's body and blood as being a disavowal of the words of Scripture regarding the Sacrament, and positively as he, because of this disavowal of the words of institution, denied that the Reformed had the true Lord's Supper at all, still he was far from denying the salvation of those who from weakness in knowledge did not believe the Real Presence. "After all, we must admit that the 'enthusiasts' have the Scriptures and God's Word in other articles, and whoever of them hears this and believes will be saved, though they [their stiff-necked leaders] are sacrilegious heretics and blasphemers of Christ" (XVII:2212).

This declaration of Luther is reiterated in the Preface to the *Book of Concord.* There it is said, on the one hand, that "the condemnations, censures, and rejections of godless doctrines . . . had to be expressly set forth . . . that all should guard against these condemned doctrines." On the other hand the declaration is made: "We have no doubt whatever that even in those churches which have hitherto not agreed with us in all things many godly and by no means wicked men are found who follow their own simplicity and do not understand aright the matter itself, but in no way approve the blasphemies which are cast forth against the Holy Supper." (*Trigl.* 19.)

John 6:53: "Except ye eat the flesh of the Son of Man and drink

His blood, ye have no life in you," has been adduced to prove an absolute necessity of the Lord's Supper. But recall that this passage does not speak of the Lord's Supper at all. (P. 328 ff.) In short, Luther and Lutheran theologians are right in applying Augustine's dictum, *Contemptus sacramenti damnat, non privatio,* both to Baptism and to the Lord's Supper.

On what occasions and how often the Lord's Supper is to be received Scripture does not specifically state. *Diligent* use of it, however, is not only indicated by the ὁσάκις (often) joined to the imperative preceding: "This do in remembrance of Me," [142] but also follows from the essence and purpose of the Lord's Supper and from the need of Christians. We may well call the more or less frequent use of the Lord's Supper one of the thermometers of the spiritual life of a congregation. On the diligent use of the Sacrament there is hardly a finer and more comprehensive discussion to be found than Luther's in his Large Catechism (*Trigl.* 761, 40–87).

---

[142] Luther, *Large Catechism, Trigl.* 763, V, 45: "These are bidding and commanding words by which all who would be Christians are enjoined to partake of this Sacrament. Therefore whoever would be a disciple of Christ, with whom He here speaks, must also consider and observe this, not from compulsion, as being forced by men, but in obedience to the Lord Jesus Christ, and to please Him. However, if you say: But the words are added, 'As oft as ye do it'; there He compels no one, but leaves it to our free choice, answer: That is true, yet it is not written that we should never do so. Yea, just because He speaks the words, 'As oft as ye do it,' it is nevertheless implied that we should do it often."

The Christian Church

(DE ECCLESIA)

AFTER Christ had reconciled all mankind to God by His vicarious satisfaction and had risen from the dead, He sat down at the right hand of God to gather a Church on earth for Himself until the end of time by the Word of the completed reconciliation (λόγος τῆς καταλλαγῆς), the Gospel.

A. THE CHURCH UNIVERSAL

(DE ECCLESIA UNIVERSALI)

1

Its Nature

The Christian Church consists of all those, and only those, who believe in Christ. Since, however, an anti-Scriptural meaning is today given the words "believe in Christ," we must make our definition more specific and say: The Christian Church is composed of all those, and only those, in whom the Holy Spirit has worked the faith that for the sake of Christ's vicarious satisfaction their sins are forgiven.

Nothing else makes one a member of the Church: neither holding membership in a church body, nor outward use of the means of grace, nor profession of the Christian faith, nor filling an office in the Church, nor zeal for a moral life in imitation of Christ, nor any immediate regeneration or submergence in God of which the "enthusiasts" of all shades talk. Only personal faith in the forgiveness of sins which was purchased by Christ's *satisfactio vicaria* and is proclaimed and dispensed in the Gospel makes one a member of the Christian Church. Acts 5:14 tells us that believers in the Lord were added, προσετίθεντο πιστεύοντες τῷ Κυρίῳ, namely, to the Christian church at Jerusalem. Nothing but that by which man comes to Christ and is justified before God, by which he enters into the communion of God's grace and becomes a child of God, that is, nothing but faith in the redemption (ἀπολύτρωσις) that is in Christ Jesus (Rom. 3:24), makes man a member of the Christian Church. This is a Scriptural axiom: *Sola fides in Christum membra ecclesiae constituit.* Still shorter: *Christiani sunt ecclesia.*

397

Inevitably connected with the personal, Spirit-wrought faith in the remission of sins is, as its fruit and effect, the *unio mystica,* sanctification, "moral conduct," "the recasting of life in its God-pleasing form." Hence we find the members of the Church characterized as, for instance, in Psalm 15; 1 Cor. 6:15-20; 2 Cor. 6:14-18; 1 Pet. 2:5. But this does not depose faith as the constitutive factor. Luther remarks as to the relation of the *sola fide* in justification to the generation and preservation of the Church, that only this article "begets, nourishes, sustains, keeps, and defends the Church; and without it the Church of God could not subsist an hour" (*Opp. v. a.* VII, 512; St. L. XIV:168).

A question that has received much attention is the relation to the Christian Church of the manifestly wicked and hypocrites (*mali et hypocritae*) who are in outward communion with the Church. Scripture teaches: They do not belong to the Church, are not a part of the Church (*non sunt pars ecclesiae*), but have only outward fellowship with the Church (*ecclesiae admixti sunt secundum societatem externam*). None but those in whose hearts the Spirit has wrought faith in Christ are members of the Christian Church, as is evident from all Scripture texts which speak of an inner, spiritual communion of the members of the Church with God, with Christ, with the Holy Ghost. The members of the Church are called the house of God, οἶκος θεοῦ (1 Tim. 3:15); God's building, θεοῦ οἰκοδομή (1 Cor. 3:9); the temple of the living God, ναὸς θεοῦ (2 Cor. 6:16); the temple of the Holy Ghost, ναὸς τοῦ ἐν ὑμῖν ἁγίου πνεύματος (1 Cor. 6:19); Christ's body and the fullness of Him, σῶμα Χριστοῦ, πλήρωμα Χριστοῦ (Eph. 1:23); the children of God, τὰ τέκνα τοῦ θεοῦ (John 11:52). All unbelievers, be they Jews or Greeks, are not God's house, etc., but workshops of the devil, "the spirit that now worketh in the children of disobedience" (Eph. 2: 1-3). To define the Church as the whole number of the elect, a definition for which Luther praises Huss,[1] likewise is Scriptural (1 Pet. 2:9: ὑμεῖς γένος ἐκλεκτόν).

This is the doctrine which with Scripture Luther and the Lutheran Church teach. Clearly pointing out that no outward communion with the Christians and no perfunctory use of the means of grace, but only personal faith in the Gospel makes one a member of the kingdom of heaven on earth, the Christian Church, Luther says: "Otherwise a man would be in the kingdom of heaven just as wood or stone when thrown

---

[1] On Psalm 118, St. L. V:1234 f. Cp. Baier-Walther, III, 614: "Those whom God, according to His eternal decree, has endowed with faith and grace are collectively called the Church." Likewise (*ibid.*) Aeg. Hunnius, *Volum. th. disp.,* Witteb., 1598, p. 329.

among Christians or as the devil is among them." The Apology defines the nature of the Church fully in Articles VII and VIII (*De Ecclesia*) by saying that the true Church consists of "men scattered throughout the whole world who agree concerning the Gospel [*qui de evangelio consentiunt;* German text: *an Christum wahrlich glauben,* truly believe in Christ]," hence believe that their sins are wiped out by the merits of Christ, without works of their own. No less clear is the Apology (*ibid.*) in speaking of the relation of the wicked and hypocrites to the Church. It says that the wicked and hypocrites are not members of the Church; for "it is certain . . . that the wicked are in the power of the devil, and members of the kingdom of the devil, as Paul teaches, Eph. 2:2, when he says that the devil 'now worketh in the children of disobedience'" (*Trigl.* 231, 16). One would, the Apology says, fail to distinguish between the kingdom of Christ and the kingdom of the devil if one regarded the wicked as belonging to the Church. "Although in this life, because the kingdom of Christ has not yet been revealed, they are mingled with the Church [*admixti ecclesiae,* namely, *secundum societatem externorum signorum,* they have the fellowship of outward signs], and hold offices [as teachers and other offices] in the Church," nevertheless the wicked are not "the kingdom of Christ" (*Trigl.* 231, *ibid.,* 17). "And with this clearly agree the parables of Christ, who says, Matt. 13:38, that the good seed are the children of the kingdom, but the tares are the children of the Wicked One. The field, He says, is the world, not the Church." (*Trigl.* 231, *ibid.,* 19.)

In short, according to Lutheran teaching, it is faith in the Gospel which in every case establishes membership in the Christian Church. To him who believes the Gospel, membership in the Christian Church may not be denied. Of him who rejects the Gospel, membership in the Christian Church may not be asserted. Excommunication pronounced against true believers does not deprive them of membership in the Church.[2] Also those who in their ignorance believe false doctrines are members of the Church, whether they belong to an orthodox or heterodox church body, if only they cling sincerely to God's grace in Christ.[3] Also lack of Baptism, if there was no opportunity to receive Baptism, does not deprive believers of membership in the Christian

---

[2] Quenstedt: "The unjustly excommunicated do not cease to be members of the Church Universal, though they have been ejected from some visible and particular church."

[3] Luther, St. L. VI:1629: The sins of the godly "by themselves deserve damnation, but this result does not ensue, because the godly see the impurity of their hearts and trust in Christ."

Church, because Baptism is not absolutely necessary, as was shown in the *locus de Baptismo*.[4]

Since man by nature is inclined to imagine that mere outward affiliation with a church secures his salvation, the great practical importance of ever defining the Church as the communion of believers, or saints, and not as an "institution," an outward polity (*externa politia*), is manifest. A person's membership in the Christian Church depends on his confessing that he deserves damnation before God and at the same time believing that God is gracious to him for the sake of Christ's *satisfactio vicaria*. Cf. Luther's explanation of the Second Article. Of the practical importance of the right definition of the Church the Apology says: "It is necessary to understand what it is that principally makes us members, and that, living members, of the Church. If we will define the Church only as an outward polity of the good and wicked, men will not understand that the kingdom of Christ is righteousness of the heart and the gift of the Holy Ghost [that the kingdom of Christ is spiritual, as nevertheless it is; that therein Christ inwardly rules, strengthens, and comforts hearts, and imparts the Holy Ghost and various spiritual gifts], but they will judge that it is only the outward observance of certain forms of worship and rites. Likewise, what difference will there be between the people of the Law and the Church if the Church is an outward polity? But Paul distinguishes the Church from the people of the Law thus, that the Church is a spiritual people, i. e., that it has been distinguished from the heathen not by civil rites [not in the polity and civil affairs], but that it is the true people of God, regenerated by the Holy Ghost." (*Trigl.* 231, *ibid.*, 13 f.)

We add a few quotations showing that Luther and our Lutheran dogmaticians regarded the Church as consisting only of true believers.

Luther: "Christ is, indeed, Lord of all things, of all the good and the evil, of the angels and the devils, but He is not the Head, except only of the pious, believing Christians, assembled in the spirit. For a head must be united with its body, as I showed above from St. Paul in Eph. 4:15-16, and the members must cleave to the head and receive from it their activity and life. For this reason Christ cannot be the Head of an evil community, although it is subject unto Him as Lord; even as His kingdom, namely, Christendom, is not a physical com-

---

[4] Gerhard, *Loci,* "De eccl.," § 54: "Our men say that catechumens and all others who have faith in the heart are in the Church, even though these have not yet been baptized."

munity or kingdom, yet all things are subject unto Him, be they spiritual or physical, of hell or of heaven." (St. L. XVIII:1025.) Again: "There [at Jerusalem] many wicked fellows, hypocrites, and sinners went in through the gate of the Temple; but here through this gate of the Lord only righteous and saints enter to serve the Lord. For no one is or can be in the congregation of the Christians or be a member of Christendom unless he truly believes, that is, is righteous and holy, as the article of the Creed testifies: 'I believe a holy Christian Church.' But he who does not truly believe, neither is righteous and holy, does not belong into the Christian Church and cannot enter into this gate of the Lord, can also not pray, offer praise, glorify, or serve God, nor does he know God, though it be that he spend his physical life among Christians or even fill an office among the Christians, as rector, preacher, bishop, or outwardly partake of the Sacrament, as also 1 John 3:6 says: 'Whosoever abideth in Him sinneth not; whosoever sinneth hath not seen Him, neither known Him.' And again, v. 8: 'He that committeth sin is of the devil.' And this is the article which that 'laudable' Council of Constance anathematized, together with this verse and the entire Holy Scriptures. For John Huss at that time confessed that there is a holy Christian Church; if the Pope were not pious and holy, he could not be a member, much less the head of the holy Church, even though he held the office in it; for that Huss had to burn as a heretic and be excommunicated. . . . They retort and say: Even if the Pope, the bishops, and all of them sinned grievously, they would still not be of the devil nor of his synagog, but are of Christ and of God, members and heads of holy Christendom. Be sure, they are members of the Church as much as spit, snot, pus, sweat, feces, urine, stench, scab, smallpox, ulcers, syphilis, and all contagious diseases are members of the body; these things, too, are in and on the body; indeed, as blotches and filth that the body must suffer with great danger, pains, and displeasure." (St. L. V:1234.)

Gerhard: "It is called 'catholic Church' primarily and first of all in view of the elect or saints, inasmuch as in its circle it comprehends all who truly believe in Christ, the entire mystical body whose Head Christ is. And this is the genuine and proper signification of this term. In this sense, too, it is used in the Apostles' Creed, when we say, 'I believe one holy catholic Church,' where the term 'believe' plainly shows that the invisible Church is spoken of, which also the added predicate of 'sanctity' shows by itself." (*Op. cit.*, § 151.)

Baier: "Thus it is approved that the Church, properly speaking, is precisely the congregation of the truly believing and sanctified.

For (1) in Eph. 4:16 the Church is described as a spiritual body, which is entirely pendent from Christ according to all joints and bands (out of which compacted, it is set up in the manner of one body), as from the Head, that is, by an influx such as ought to come from the head to the members to this end, that they receive growth befitting the body, and this through love. From this it is correctly gathered that all those, and they alone, are true members of the Church in the proper sense who live a spiritual life through the supernatural grace and influence of Christ, the Head and Soul of this life, and so they are strong not through any kind of faith, but through a supernatural faith, joined with love. To this pertains (2) that the Church is (1 Pet. 2:4-5) described as a spiritual house of living stones, built upon Christ as the lowest Cornerstone, so as to be a holy temple for the Lord, a house of God through the Holy Spirit, which can be the case only through faith in Christ, by which men lean on Christ as the Cause of salvation through the act of faith, joined with love. In the same wise it (3) happens that the Church is compared to an olive tree, the branches of which, in the spiritual sense, are, however, said to be grafted through faith and through the same to remain in it (Rom. 11:16 *sqq.*). And (4) that the Church is the *coetus,* assembly, of the sons of God; sons, however, they become and are through faith in Christ." (*Comp.* III, 617.)

2

False Doctrines Concerning the Church

The doctrine of the Church is of such a nature that if a person erred earlier, all his doctrinal errors will reappear in his teaching concerning the Church. Since membership in the Christian Church is established solely by faith in Christ, the Scriptural doctrine of the Church presupposes a correct understanding of justification by faith: the objective reconciliation of all sinful mankind by Christ's *satisfactio vicaria,* the bestowal of the forgiveness of sins by the means of grace, the appropriation of the remission of sins by faith, created and sustained solely by the Holy Ghost, without any co-operation of man. Without these prerequisites one's concept of the Church cannot be Scriptural. It is necessary and will prove profitable to demonstrate this fact in detail.

1. The Christian concept of the Church presupposes the *satisfactio vicaria Christi.* For all who deny the *satisfactio vicaria* the Christian

Church is not the communion of believers, that is, the whole number of those who through the working of the Holy Ghost believe that God is their gracious God for the sake of Christ's substitutional work. For them the Church is rather a society of people who, inspired by Christ's example, by the "historical Christ," etc., hope to achieve salvation through their own moral life (moral-influence theory). In spite of some differences in their wording and manner of presentation, all Unitarians hold this position, the old Unitarians, such as the Photinians, Socinians, rationalists, as well as the modern Unitarians, such as Horace Bushnell, Ritschl, Harnack of Berlin, Eliot of Harvard. Cf. Vol. II, 356 ff.: Historical Notes on the Doctrine of the Vicarious Satisfaction and Some Theories of the Atonement Examined. It is immaterial whether the factor supposedly making one a member of the Church is then called "faith" or "love" or any other name; ultimately all these presentations, by reason of their denial of the *satisfactio vicaria,* agree with the definition given by the coarse rationalist Roehr (d. 1848): The Church is a "voluntary association of rational beings for accomplishing an earthly and celestial happiness by way of religious enlightenment and virtue." Cf. Hase, *Hutt. red.,* § 124.

But no one is to be advised to join such a "Church" or to remain in it, because Scripture teaches that ever since the Fall men do not get into the Christian Church by way of their own moral life, even if they are incited to do so by Christ's example or the "historical Christ," but remain under the curse (Gal. 3:10), wholly divorced from Christ and His Church (Gal. 5:4; 4:21-31).

Nor ought it to be asserted that men like Ritschl, Wendt, and others have opened a way for a "return" to the original Lutheran concept of the Church because they want the "institutional idea" eliminated from the definition of the Church and prefer to call the Church the "people of God," "true Christendom," etc. Though they give the Church the proper appellation, "the people of God," they deny both the essential deity of Christ and His *satisfactio vicaria.* Hence for them "the people of God," or "true Christendom," is simply a moral-endeavor society.[5] Luther holds that all who deny "the cost,"

---

[5] Ritschl, *Rechtf. u. Versoehn.,* 3d ed., III, 271: "The Kingdom of God are the believers in Christ in so far as they . . . practice love toward one another and thus create that communion of moral attitude and ethical gifts which extends in all possible gradations to the limits of the human family." Modern Unitarians have a special liking for the term "Kingdom of God." For them the Kingdom of God is the realm in which God enforces His autocracy for the moral improvement of mankind.

the substitutional satisfaction of Christ, are in one class with "Turks and Jews" (St. L. XI:1085). Of Horace Bushnell and also of Ritschl it is reported, by the way, that they reverted to faith in the *satisfactio vicaria* at the approach of death. Cf. Vol. II, 255, 370; Vol. III, 79.

The Papacy wants the deity and the merit of Christ to stand. It even anathematizes those who deny the merit of Christ. (*Trid.*, Sess. VI, can. 10a.) But it co-ordinates with the merit of Christ, as necessary for obtaining grace and salvation, the "observance of the commandments of God and of the Church" and the "true merit of the good works of him that is justified" (*Trid.*, Sess. VI, can. 20, 32). Since, however, the conviction that their own works are meritorious excludes men from the grace of God and membership in the Church (Gal. 3:10; 5:4; Rom. 11:6), the Papacy by its official teaching is actually placing itself outside Christendom, *extra ecclesiam*. See Luther, Large Cat., *Trigl.* 693, Art. III, 56. Then the Papacy resolutely takes the next step and excommunicates all who hope to be justified before God solely by faith in the remission of sins for Christ's sake to the exclusion of all their own works, that is, it excommunicates the entire Christian Church (*Trid.*, Sess. VI, can. 11-12). In its struggle *pro domo* the Papacy defines the Church as consisting of those who subject themselves to the supreme authority of the Pope and his dogmas and precepts.[6] There would be no members of the Christian Church under the rule of the Papacy but for the baptized children who believe in Christ, plus a few souls who, in the terrors of conscience and particularly in the agony of death, in spite of the "Church's" interdict and curse, cast aside their own works, together with the merit of the saints, and trust solely in the merit of Christ.[7]

However, not only the avowed Unitarians and "liberal" theolo-

---

[6] The Council of Trent (Sess. VI, *decretum de ref.*, c. 1) calls the Pope *"ipsius Dei in terris vicarius."* No one shall "presume to interpret the said sacred Scripture contrary to that sense which holy mother Church . . . hath held and doth hold" (Waterworth, p. 19). The *Vaticanum* of 1870 expressly adds that the decrees of the Pope on faith and life *"ex sese, non autem ex consensu ecclesiae, irreformabiles esse"* (*Die Canones und Beschluesse des Vatikanischen Konzils,* ed. Schneemann, p. 45 f.). Sess. IV, *decretum de usu s. librorum.* Bellarmine defines the Church as "the congregation of people who are brought together by the profession of one and the same Christian faith and communion in one and the same Sacraments, under the rule of duly appointed pastors and above all of the one vicar of Christ on earth, the Roman Pontiff" (*De eccl. mil.,* c. 2, 9).

[7] Apology, *Trigl.* 225, Art. III, 271: "Even though Popes, or some theologians, and monks in the Church have taught us to seek remission of sins, grace, and righteousness through our own works, and to invent new forms of worship . . . nevertheless the knowledge of Christ has always remained with some godly persons."

gians, such as Bushnell and Ritschl, but also so-called "positive"
theologians, such as Hofmann and Kirn, reject the *satisfactio vicaria*
(Vol. II, 361 ff.). Hofmann is known to have energetically fought the
substitutional satisfaction of Christ (Vol. II, 362 ff.). Kirn demands
that the recasting or reformation of the life of men in its Godlike form
be made a part of the reconciliation with God (Vol. II, 394). This
mingling of sanctification with justification prevents faith in the remission of sins provided by Christ and imparted in the means of grace
and thus keeps men from becoming members of the Christian Church.
All Protestant theologians who reject the *satisfactio vicaria* as too
"juridical" and insist on making the "religico-ethical" reformation of
men a part of the reconciliation with God have gone over to Rome.
For them the Church is not the communion of believers, but an association of men who supplement the merit of Christ by the recasting
or reformation of their own life, that is, by sanctification and good
works. Then it is not faith in Christ's active and passive vicarious
obedience of 1900 years ago which makes one a member of the
Church, but membership depends on the change wrought in men
by Christ's reconciliation, that is, the recasting of their life "in its
Godlike form." Kirn: "God reckons the thing which thus takes
form in the course of history as a part of the complete work of
redemption, and this its effective power is regarded as contributory
to its value before God" (*Ev. Dogmatik*, p. 118). No wonder, then,
that Kirn defines the Church as the "communion of the religico-ethical
life actuated by Christ's Spirit" (*ibid.*, p. 130).

In short, he who does not believe that by His substitutional
satisfaction Christ accomplished the complete reconciliation of all
mankind (the objective reconciliation) has lost the thing a really
justifying and saving faith believes in (its object); for him, accordingly, the Christian Church is no more the congregation of believers,
but an association of supplementers of the merit of Christ. Communion
with God is no more based on *favor Dei propter Christum*, but on an
illusory *gratia infusa*. This *gratia infusa* is an illusion, because true
gratia infusa always is present only as the result and effect of faith
in *favor Dei propter Christum*.

Moreover, all who limit the extent of the *satisfactio vicaria*, that is,
will not let it cover all men, also abandon the Christian concept of
the Church. If some men are not reconciled to God by Christ, then
the means of grace cannot give those who use them full and trust-
worthy assurance that God is gracious to them, can be no *testimonia,
tesserae, signa, sigilla gratiae Dei propter Christum peccata remit-*

tentis. Faith is deprived of the object which calls it forth and sustains it. The Calvinistic restriction of the *satisfactio vicaria* to a part of mankind tends to make the rise of a congregation of believers impossible. Still the Church is found among the Calvinists, for in practice the dire distress of souls struck down by the divine Law leaves the Calvinists no choice but to point these terrified souls to the universal promises of grace for peace and to abandon their self-devised *gratia particularis.*

2. Without the Scriptural teaching of the means of grace the Christian concept of the Church is impossible. Adolf Harnack censures Luther for having fought for the means of grace. Thereby Luther is supposed to have left the Church a "portentous legacy" and, "by declaring certain acts to be 'means of grace,' to have returned to the narrow confines of the Middle Ages he had left." [8] But Luther knew well why the battle for "definite means of grace" had to be fought. We need the means of grace both to get into the Christian Church and to remain in it. All who join Zwingli and Calvin in teaching that the Holy Spirit needs no vehicle (*vehiculum, plaustrum*) for the revelation and operation of His grace and that the operation of saving grace positively takes place without means of grace or alongside them ("Efficacious grace acts immediately. There is here no place for the use of means," Hodge, II, 685), thereby completely give up the Christian Church. Because the assumed immediate working of the Holy Spirit is not real, but illusory, also the Church founded on it is an illusion. That the Christian Church is still found in denominations which officially teach an immediate operation of the Holy Ghost is due solely to the fact (a) that they, contrary to their own official position, do not keep silence, but proclaim Christ's substitutional satisfaction and thus give the Holy Spirit the opportunity to work faith in the Gospel through this Gospel, and (b) that they, again in violation of their official position, incidentally call the Word of the Gospel the foundation of faith and urge men to believe the Word, as Calvin himself did (*Inst.* III, 2, 6).

The experience theologians of our day also surrender the means of grace and with them the Christian concept of the Church. They want to base faith in Christ not solely on the Word of Christ, but in addition on the "historical impression of the Person of Christ," the historical "appearance of Christ," etc. Since it is certain from Scripture

---

[8] *Wesen des Christentums,* 3d ed., 183 f.; *Grundriss d. Dogmengesch.,* 4th ed., 431.

that the "Person of Christ" exerts all "impressions" for the gathering and sustaining of the Church through the Word (John 8:31-32; 17:20; 15:3; 6:63-69; 1 Tim. 6:3-5, etc.), also the Church which experience theologians believe does not exist. Nobody has "experienced" Christ, and nobody will experience Christ to the Last Day, except by faith in the λόγος τῆς καταλλαγῆς, the Word of the reconciliation accomplished by Christ. Experience theologians are walking in the paths of Zwinglian-Calvinistic "enthusiasm," teaching a revelation and operation of the Spirit without and apart from the external Word of the Gospel. If nevertheless their efforts bring men to faith in Christ, it is only because, like Zwingli, Calvin, and their confreres, they are fortunately inconsistent.

3. The Christian concept of the Church as the congregation of believers is given up also by those who follow Rome in teaching an appropriation of grace *ex opere operato* in the Sacraments, that is, without faith on the part of man as the means of appropriation. Thus some Lutherans recently taught a sort of physical action of the Sacraments. Delitzsch takes issue with the view of our older Lutheran teachers, that unbelievers cannot be members of the Church, "which is the body of Christ." [9] But it is a fact that as certainly as the Sacraments are absolutely dependable witnesses of the gracious will of God toward all who use them, so the grace attested and thus proffered can be appropriated only by faith. Where there is no faith, there is, in spite of all use of the Sacraments, no appropriation of grace and, accordingly, no membership in the Christian Church. Thus Article XIII of the Augustana teaches concerning the Sacraments that they are "signs and testimonies of the will of God toward us, instituted to awaken and confirm faith in those who use them. . . . Faith which believes that sins are forgiven is required." (*Trigl.* 49.)[10]

4. The faith which makes man a member of the Christian Church is *in solidum* a work of the Holy Ghost and rests not with "the human powers of the natural free will, neither entirely, nor half, nor in any, even the least or most inconsiderable part" (*Trigl.* 891, Sol. Decl., II, 25). Therefore the Biblical concept of the Church as "the com-

---

[9] See the quotation in Baier-Walther, III, 620; further, the documentation in the second *Proceedings of the Western District.* Books pertaining to this matter are, among others: Franz Delitzsch, *Vier Buecher von der Kirche,* 1847; Loehe, *Kirche und Amt,* 1851; Kliefoth, *Acht Buecher v. d. K.,* 1854; Muenchmeyer, *Die Lehre v. d. sichtb. u. unsichtb. K.,* 1854.

[10] See the proof in *Lehre und Wehre* that this was the doctrine of the old Lutheran teachers, too, 1857, p. 4 ff.; 1856, p. 144 ff.

munion of believers" is forsaken also by those who teach and seek to work a faith which is not *in solidum* a work of the Holy Ghost, but involves also a human accomplishment, such as awakening and confirming faith by an "ethical human deed," "an inner resolve," "self-decision," "self-determination," "correct conduct," "a lesser guilt in comparison with others," etc. Membership in such a "Church" is inadvisable. Against a Church that owes its existence to a human act of the will, man's own choice, self-determination, etc., the gates of hell would very quickly prevail. For that reason Scripture so powerfully emphasizes the divine creation and preservation of the Church (Ps. 100:3; Rom. 11:4 f.). Since only God, without any human co-operation whatsoever, works and sustains faith, it is He alone who plants and keeps the Christian Church.

3

The Attributes of the Christian Church

1. The Church is *invisible* (*ecclesia invisibilis est*) because the constitutive factor of the Church, faith in the heart, is invisible for men and known only to God (1 Kings 8:39; Acts 1:24). Therefore Christ says regarding the visible coming of the Kingdom of God on earth: "The Kingdom of God cometh not with observation [μετὰ παρατηρήσεως, so that it can be seen with the eyes]; neither shall they say, Lo, here! or, Lo, there! for behold, the Kingdom of God is within you" (Luke 17:20-21).[11]

All who declare the Church to be wholly visible (Romanists), or at least semivisible (recent Lutherans), are perverting the nature of the Christian Church. They do not let the Church remain the congregation of believers, but make it, entirely or in part, an outward institute (*externa politia*), in which believers play a varyingly essential or unessential role. Some Lutherans today speak of two sides of the Church, a "visible and an invisible side." The Word and the Sacraments are said to be the visible side of the Church. But such termi-

---

[11] Παρατήρησις (observation) used only here in the New Testament. Wahl: *observatio*, μετὰ παρατηρήσεως, i. e., *ita, ut oculis possit observari*. The verb παρατηρεῖν in the sense "observe" is found repeatedly (Mark 3:2; Luke 6:7; 14:1; 20:20; Acts 9:24). Against the interpretation of ἐντὸς ὑμῶν as *"among you," "in your midst,"* Noesgen on the passage correctly remarks that it conflicts with the context, since whatever is among us or in our midst can also be observable to the senses. For this reason ἐντὸς ὑμῶν is to be interpreted 'within you' (Luther, Calvin, Olshausen, Godet, Keil)."

nology confuses the marks of the Church (*notae ecclesiae*) with the Church proper. The Church is, of course, dependent on the means of grace. The Church is begotten through the means of grace, and so it is sustained only through the means of grace. But the means of grace are not on that account the Church itself or a part of the Church, any more than air and food are man himself, or a part of him, though man cannot live without air and food. However, Word and Sacrament are correctly called *notae ecclesiae*. Just as wheat is to be found only where it has been sown, so the Church can be found only where the Word of God is in use. God's Word is called the seed of the Kingdom of God and has the promise of fruit (Is. 55:10 ff.). The *notae ecclesiae*, however, do not make the Church, the communion of believers, visible, because the constitutive factor, faith, remains invisible.

It is the will of God, on the one hand, that in charity we regard as a Christian everyone who professes faith in the Gospel and does not deny the profession of his lips by a godless life. On the other hand, it would be an encroachment on God's prerogative if we presumed to see what is in the heart of the individual. Scripture definitely warns against this presumption (1 Cor. 4:5). Suppose we could single out every member of the Church, we still would not be seeing the Church, because our mortal eyes can see only the old man in the Christians, while the new man lives deeply hidden in God during this life (Col. 3:3; 2 Cor. 5:4). Not until Judgment Day will the members of the Christian Church differ in their external appearance from the nonmembers (Col. 3:4; 1 John 3:2). The halo with which artists surround the heads of the saints reflects merely our charitable belief.[12]

The Romanists are known to claim that the Church is as visible as the kingdom of France and the republic of Venice.[13] The Papists deride an invisible Christian Church as a Platonic idea, a figment, etc. This jeering we oppose with the truth that according to Scripture this invisible Church of believers is the most powerful reality on the globe,

---

[12] Luther, St. L. IX:702: "For that reason we correctly confess in our holy Christian Creed that we believe a holy Church. For it is invisible, dwells in the spirit at a place into which no man can penetrate; therefore its holiness cannot be seen." Calov, *Systema*, VIII, 264: "The assembly in which the Church is can indeed be seen and distinguished and pointed out with the index finger, namely, the assembly in which the Word is taught and the Sacraments dispensed according to Christ's ordinance; but that assembly which properly is the Church, that is, the communion of believers and saints, is not visible and cannot be pointed out."

[13] Bellarmine, Lib. 3, *"De eccl.,"* c. 2: "The Church is an assembly of men so visible and palpable as the assembly of the people of Rome, or the kingdom of Gaul, or the republic of Venice." The antithesis in Quenstedt, II, 1640.

with this bulwark: "The Lord knoweth [i. e., has elected] them that
are His" (2 Tim. 2:19). It is a reality against which the gates of hell
shall not prevail (Matt. 16:18); in which the Lord's interest centers
to the end of time (Rom. 8:28; Matt. 24:22-24). To the Church the
Kingdom is to be given according to the Father's good pleasure (Luke
12:32). The teaching that the visible Roman Catholic Church is the
Church of Christ is pure fiction. In so far as it is Roman, that is, not
subject to the Word of Christ, but to the word of the Pope, and bases
its hope of grace and salvation not only on the merit of Christ, but
also on human merit, it is outside the Church of Christ both here on
earth (Gal. 5:4; 3:10) and in heaven (Gal. 4:30).[14]

2. The Church is *one* (*una ecclesia,* John 10:16: μία ποίμνη), since
all members of the Church, in spite of all differences in their earthly
circumstances, believe one and the same thing, namely, that God
remits their sins by grace, for Christ's sake, without the deeds of the
Law. Scripture most emphatically declines any variation in the constitutive element of the Church. We are told Rom. 3:23-24: "There is
no difference [διαστολή]; for all [πάντες] have sinned and come short
of the glory of God, being justified freely [δωρεάν] by His grace
through the redemption that is in Christ Jesus." All who lack this
faith, either because they refuse to believe in Christ altogether (1 John
2:23; 5:12), or because they want to supplement Christ's merit by
their works, are not within, but outside the Church (Gal. 5:4; 3:10).
Omnes Christiani de evangelio consentiunt. Accordingly Gal. 3:28:
"There is neither Jew nor Greek, there is neither bond nor free, there
is neither male nor female; for ye are all *one* in Christ Jesus" (πάντες
γὰρ ὑμεῖς εἷς ἐστὲ ἐν Χριστῷ Ἰησοῦ).

3. The Church is *holy* (*sancta ecclesia,* communion of saints),
(a) because by faith in Christ all members possess the perfect righteousness of faith (*iustitia fidei imputata*). Phil. 3:9: "Not having mine
own righteousness, which is of the Law, but that which is through the
faith of Christ, the righteousness which is of God by faith"; (b) because all members have also a true, though imperfect, righteousness
of life (*iustitia vitae*) as fruit of this faith. Rom. 6:14: "Sin shall not
have dominion over you; for ye are not under the Law, but under
grace."

4. The Church is *universal,* or *catholic* (*ecclesia universalis sive
catholica*), because it embraces all believers in Christ, of all eras,
among all nations, and at all places. The Christian faith has never

---

[14] See Luther, St. L. XVIII:1347 ff., against the visible Church of the Pope.

changed its character in the course of the ages. It has always been faith in the remission of sins resulting from Christ's work of redemption. This teaching is not, as is frequently claimed, a dogma devised by Luther and the old Lutheran dogmaticians, but is the doctrine of the Apostles of Christ and of Christ Himself. Peter, Acts 10:43: "To Him [Christ] give all the Prophets witness that through His name whosoever believeth in Him shall receive remission of sins." Christ, John 8:56: "Your father Abraham rejoiced to see My day; and he saw it and was glad." Paul proves justification by faith without works from the Scriptures of the Old Testament (Romans 4; 3:21-31) and calls all who in New Testament times believe the Gospel, without regard to their color, etc., the children of Abraham. Gal. 3:6 ff.: "They which are of faith, the same are the children of Abraham," yes, even calls them "Abraham's seed" (Gal. 3:29). Luther: "That we have forgiveness of sins only for Christ's sake by faith was the faith of the fathers and the Prophets and all saints since the beginning of the world, and later the teaching of Christ and the preaching of the Apostles. They were commanded to bear and spread this forgiveness throughout the world. And even to this day and to the end of time this is the unanimous belief and practice of the whole Christian Church, which always has with one accord and without exception believed, confessed, and fought for this article, that remission of sins is obtained and received solely in the name of this our Lord Christ, and through this faith has been justified before God and saved." (St. L. XII:494 f.)[15]

5. The Church is *Apostolic* (*ecclesia apostolica*) inasmuch as all its members to the Last Day come to faith in Christ through the Word of the Apostles (John 17:20: πιστεύσοντες διὰ λόγου αὐτῶν εἰς ἐμέ) and cling to the Word of the Apostles (Acts 2:42: προσκαρτεροῦντες τῇ διδαχῇ τῶν ἀποστόλων), and this over against all departures from the truth of Scripture. Rom. 16:17: "Avoid them," namely, those who "cause divisions and offenses contrary to the doctrine which ye have learned." The endeavor of the Romanists and the Anglicans to derive the Apostolic character of the Church from the "Apostolic Succession" has correctly been termed childish folly, because Scripture (a) makes no distinction between bishops and teaching elders, or pastors (Acts 20:17, 28; Titus 1:5, 7) and (b) tells us to avoid all teachers who de-

---

[15] Alexander Schweizer, the pupil of Schleiermacher, says (*Ref. Dogm.* II, 114) very correctly: "The universal nature of Christianity cannot be shown more clearly than when it enters in its essentials immediately after the first sin." But Schweizer also misinterprets Gen. 3:15.

part from the Apostolic Gospel, no matter whether they are called bishops, elders, or otherwise (Rom. 16:17; Gal. 1:6-8).[16]

6. The statement that there is no salvation outside the Christian Church (*extra ecclesiam salus nulla*) is true of the Church of Christ, but false when asserted of the Church of the Pope. It is true of the Christian Church, since only those who believe the Gospel enjoy the grace of God and salvation (John 3:16-18, 36). It is not true of the Pope's Church, because this body bases grace and salvation, in part, on the Law (*Trid.*, Sess. VI, can. 20) and thus leaves its members under the curse of the Law (Gal. 3:10).

4

The Dignity and Glory of the Church

The members of the Christian Church as Church owe obedience to no man whatever, but to Christ alone. 1 Cor. 3:23: "Ye are Christ's." Matt. 23:8: "One is your Master [R. V., teacher], even Christ; and all ye are brethren." Christians are firmly admonished to maintain this their sovereignty over against all claims of authority that men might advance. 1 Cor. 7:23: "Ye are bought with a price; be not ye the servants of men."

The Pope, who uses the name of Christ for his pretense that all Christians are subject to him, is *eo ipso* the Antichrist, spoken of in 2 Thessalonians 2. Against his arrogance, hiding behind a Christian mask (lying powers, signs, and wonders), the Christians are specially warned.

Christ indeed equips some members of His Church with special gifts, also the special gift of teaching and ruling other Christians. But this gift does not subject the members of the Church to the rule of men, since all teaching and ruling among Christians extends exactly as far as their one Master's Word reaches (1 Pet. 4:11; Jer. 23:16, 18). Scripture instructs Christians to regard teachers who pretend to know more than Christ's Word contains as bloated ignoramuses (1 Tim. 6:3 ff.). And those who attempt to impose what the Word of Christ leaves free, e. g., forbidding to marry or commanding to fast and abstain from food and drink, are properly regarded by the Christians as arrogant deceivers and disseminators of doctrines of devils (1 Tim.

---

[16] See The Public Ministry, p. 439 ff.

4:1-5; Col. 2:20-23). The Pope may impose a fast on himself, but on no one else in the world.

Christians are not even subject to the persons of the great Apostles. The Smalcald Articles (Power and Primacy of Pope) say: "Let neither the other ministers nor Peter assume for themselves lordship or superiority over the Church" (*Trigl.* 507, 11). As proof they correctly cite 1 Cor. 3:21 ff.: "*All* things are yours, whether Paul, or Apollos, or Cephas, or the world." To be sure, Christians have been given the infallible Word of Christ through the Apostles, and they obey the Word of Christ. But also in the infallible delivery of the Word of Christ the Apostles are merely the servants of the believers. The believers are not there for the Apostles' sake, but the Apostles are there for the believers' sake. On this account Paul explicitly says: "We preach not ourselves, but Christ Jesus the Lord; and ourselves your servants for Jesus' sake" (2 Cor. 4:5). Between Christians and their God neither Mary, nor Peter, nor the Apostles, nor other men stand as mediators, but by faith in Christ all believers have immediate access to God (Eph. 3:12; Heb. 4:16).

To Christians, and to no one else in world or Church, the means of grace are originally given.[17] Christians were not given the means of grace only mediately by receiving them from those persons in the Church (the Pope, the bishops, the ministry) whom Christ supposedly had made their original owners. And because Christians have the means of grace as their own, they, too, hold the keys of the kingdom of heaven (Matt. 16:19; 18:18; John 20:23). To them, and to nobody else, is the authority given to appoint pastors. Their profession of Christ as the Son of the living God, or, in other words, their preaching of the Gospel in the world, is the rock on which Christ builds His Church (Matt. 16:18).[18] Moreover, not only is the world and the

---

[17] 1 Pet. 2:9; Is. 40:9; Matt. 28:18-20; etc. All these points are discussed at greater length, p. 427 ff.

[18] Thus Luther correctly says in his marginal gloss on Matt. 16:18: "All Christians are Peters because they make the profession here made by Peter, which profession is the rock on which Peter and all Peters are built." Referring "rock" to the person of Peter either as an Apostle *primarius* or as representative of the Apostles is utterly precluded by (1) the context, (2) the wording itself. Neither the preceding nor the following context considers Peter as Apostle, but only as believer. Christ asks His disciples what the public (οἱ ἄνθρωποι) thinks of Him. When the disciples report that the people are of divided opinion, but agree on this, that Christ is a mere man, Christ asks His disciples not about their apostolate, but about their faith. When Peter then confesses the faith of the disciples in the words: "Thou art the Christ, the Son of the living God," and this faith is accepted by Christ as the true faith generated by God, Christ utters the words: "Thou art Peter, and upon this rock I will build My Church," and in explanation of His

universe ruled in their interest, but in so far as they by faith possess all that Christ has and do all with Christ that He does (see p. 523), they own the universe, the world, and all things in the world. 1 Cor. 3:21 f.: "All things are yours; whether Paul, or Apollos, or Cephas, or the world, or life, or death, or things present, or things to come,

---

words adds: "I will give unto thee the keys of the kingdom of heaven; and whatsoever thou shalt bind on earth," etc. From the context, then, it is certain that nothing said here pertains to Peter the Apostle, but all pertains to Peter the true believer in Christ and confessor of this faith. — Moreover, that here the person of the *Apostle* Peter is entirely disregarded and only the *believing and confessing* Peter comes into consideration, is certain from the fact that in Matt. 18:18 Christ awards to all believers the keys of the kingdom of heaven, which He (Matthew 16) gave to Peter, and that with the identical words: "Whatsoever ye shall bind on earth," etc. — But also the wording, "Thou art Peter, and upon this rock I will build My Church," forbids referring the term "rock" to Peter. Peter and the rock are two entirely distinct things, as is evident from the fact — as Luther states it popularly but clearly — that Peter is a *"der"* (masculine), the rock a *"die"* (feminine), St. L. XX:282. In the German or English translation this difference does not appear. But in the Greek the rock (ἡ πέτρα) is feminine, while Peter (πέτρος) is masculine. To make the difference appear we would have to translate: "Thou art *Petros,* and upon this *Petra* I will build My Church." Thus as early as 1519 Luther argued against Eck in his *Epistola ad monachos conventus Iutterboccensis et defensio contra malignum Joh. Eccii iudicium, Opp. v. a.* II, 477 ff.; St. L. XVIII:1375 f. After Luther has called attention to the fact that nowhere in Scripture is Peter called "the rock," he continues: "Also in this passage, Matt. 16:18, Christ clearly distinguishes Peter from *petra.* For if He had wanted Peter understood by *petra,* He would have said: 'Thou art Peter, and upon thee will I build My Church'; but by using *petra* in the second instance He indicates clearly that Peter is one thing, *petra* another, which He distinguishes from Peter by the pronoun *hanc* [this, feminine]. In this manner I, from the text before us, easily make it impossible for Eck to prove that Peter is the *petra* (rock)." — Also Meyer, contrary to text and context, refers the *petra* to the person of the Apostle and therefore wants to grant Peter primacy among the Apostles. However, he rejects the Roman deductions, namely, the reference to the Pope, "since Jesus neither had successors to Peter in mind, nor are the Popes such successors." The latter is true, but not the former. Christ indeed had successors of Peter in view, because what He says in ch. 16 of Peter He awards in ch. 18 to all believers. If Meyer wants to attain harmony with the context and the text of Matt. 16:18, he will have to come back to Luther's explanation of the passage, namely, the declaration: "All Christians are Peters because they make the profession here made by Peter, which is the rock on which Peter and all Peters are built." When Meyer expresses the opinion that in the Smalcald Articles Luther's interpretation of the *petra* had been "generalized to the concept *verum ministerium,*" that is an error. The Smalcald Articles expressly declare the *verum ministerium* to be the *ministerium illius professionis, quam Petrus fecerat.* In the English text (*Trigl.* 511, *ibid.,* 25): "However, as to the declaration: 'Upon this rock I will build My Church,' certainly the Church has not been built upon the authority of man, but upon the ministry of the confession which Peter made, in which he proclaims that Jesus is the Christ, the Son of God." — "The Christ, the Son of the living God," is a terse rendition of the entire content of the Gospel, which the Church is to confess and to preach in the world and on which, at the same time, the Church stands with its faith. We have an essential parallel in

all are yours." Meyer's restriction "in the future aeon" is an interpolation. The text does not contain this limitation. In short, the
Christians are the wealthiest and mightiest group in the world.
Heaven's sluices of grace and blessing have opened for them through
their faith in Christ. The believers have everything, the unbelievers
nothing.

5

How the Church Is Founded and Preserved

Because the faith which makes man a member of the Christian
Church is wrought and sustained solely by God's grace and power
(Eph. 1:19-20; 1 Pet. 1:5; John 1:13), Scripture stresses in particular
that the Church is neither entirely nor in part the work of man, but
solely God's work and product. Ps. 100:3: "It is He that hath made us,
and not we ourselves; we are His people and the sheep of His pasture."
1 Pet. 2:9-10: He "hath called you out of darkness into His marvelous
light; which in time past were not a people, but are now the people
of God; which had not obtained mercy, but now have obtained mercy."
Solely by God's grace and power is the Church also preserved from
the gates of hell. The synergistic teaching that faith and perseverance
in faith depend not only on God's grace, but also on man's good
conduct, moves the Church off the foundation which guarantees its
existence.

The means or instrument which God employs to gather and preserve the Church is the Gospel in all its forms (Word and Sacrament),
because only the Gospel creates and sustains saving faith.[19] In so far
as the Reformed teach a creation and preservation of saving faith not
through the means of grace, but through an immediate operation of

---

Eph. 2:20: "Built upon the foundation," etc. The Apostles' word and confession
to Christ and of Christ, however, is no other word and confession than that enjoined
upon all believers. — Luther's understanding of Matt. 16:18 is found not only
among the old theologians (cf. Calov on the passage), but also among recent
theologians (Lange, Ewald, Wieseler). Here, too, the bad habit has crept into
the commentaries of unnecessarily increasing the number of differing interpretations. Thus we usually find adduced as two different interpretations of *petra*:
(1) Christ, (2) the confession of Christ. In fact, we here have to do with only
one exegesis, since faith does not stand on Christ immediately, but always only
mediately, namely, on the Christ whom Peter, the Apostles, and all Christians
confess (*profitentur, praedicant*).

[19] Rom. 10:17; 1 Pet. 1:23-25. See Luther's classic presentation in commenting on Ps. 110:3 (St. L. V:990 ff.) and on Is. 2:2 ff. (VI:31 ff.).

the Holy Spirit, they are divesting the Church of the condition essential to life. Men are organs (*causa instrumentalis*) for the expansion and preservation of the Church only in so far as they proclaim and teach the Gospel (Is. 40:9; Mark 16:15). In this sense Gal. 4:26 calls the Church on earth "the mother" of all who, like Isaac, are the children of promise. See Luther, St. L. IX:573 f. Luther (St. L. IX:575 f.): "Sarah, or Jerusalem, is our free mother, the Church, the bride of Christ, of whom all of us are born. This mother gives birth to children without ceasing, to the end of the world, by exercising the office of the Word, that is, by teaching and spreading the Gospel; for thus she bears children. . . . The Church should do nothing but preach and teach the Gospel properly and purely and thus give birth to children. Thus all of us are one to another fathers and children; for we are begotten one of another. I, having been begotten by others through the Gospel, do now beget others, which in turn shall beget others hereafter, and so this begetting shall continue to the end of the world. . . . The office of the free woman, therefore, is to bear children for God, her Husband, without ceasing; that is to say, such children as know that they are justified by faith and not by the Law."

The question whether the State with its laws and means of coercion is to be employed as a sort of subsidiary means of grace for the building of the Church, has been fully discussed in the section "Means of Grace," p. 178 ff. There we noted that the mingling of State and Church is a characteristic of the Roman and the Reformed Churches, but is rejected upon principle by the Lutheran Church. Likewise we noted that the use of State laws and powers does not advance the building of the Church, because the Church is a congregation of believers and is born and sustained solely by the Gospel. The use of civil powers hinders the growth of the Church if the false principle bears its natural fruits. These fruits are apparent also here in the U. S. A.[20] On the other hand, it must be emphatically pointed out that also the independence of the Church from the State is in itself

---

[20] Though the separation of Church and State is embodied both in the Constitution of the United States and of most of the States, nevertheless Church and State are frequently mingled in practice. One species of this mingling is the appointment of chaplains by the several States and the United States. Now, since in our country most of the citizens are ignorant of what constitutes Christianity, as a rule only such chaplains are appointed as conceive of Christianity, not as the message of Christ Crucified, but as the teaching of civil morality. Others with a better knowledge of what constitutes the Christian religion very often succumb to the danger — in view of the mixed audience — of denying Christ in His substitutional work of redemption.

no means of grace, so entirely does everything in the Church depend on having the pure doctrine of the Gospel. A church body remains a caricature of the Church in spite of its freedom from the State if it cannot be said that in its midst "the Gospel is rightly taught and the Sacraments are rightly administered" (*Trigl.* 47, Augsb. Conf., VII). Of such caricatures the church bodies in the United States furnish examples.[21]

Is it the Church's business to advocate a certain form of civil government? Zwingli wants to introduce democracy; even by revolution if it cannot be done otherwise. See p. 179 ff. and notes 74, 75. Calvin rejects revolution, and as form of government he prefers an oligarchy (*Inst.* IV, 20, 8). Some Anglicans and Lutherans have advocated a monarchy. The Lutheran Church advocates neither democracy nor oligarchy nor monarchy, but simply acknowledges the existing form of government as God's order. Augsburg Confession: "The Gospel teaches an eternal righteousness of the heart. Meanwhile, it does not destroy the State or the family, but very much requires that they be preserved as ordinances of God [*tamquam ordinationes Dei*], and that charity be practiced in such ordinances. Therefore, Christians are necessarily bound to obey their own magistrates and laws, save only when commanded to sin; for then they ought to obey God rather than man, Acts 5:29." (*Trigl.* 51, XVI.) This position is Scriptural. Christ was accused without cause of seeking the crown of the Roman emperor, for He taught: "Render therefore unto Caesar the things which are Caesar's, and unto God the things that are God's" (Matt. 22:21; Luke 23:2). Likewise Peter admonishes the Christians (1 Pet. 2:17, 13): "Fear God. Honor the king." "Submit yourselves to every ordinance of man for the Lord's sake." And Paul does not urge the Christians to start a revolution, but to make supplication "for kings and for all that are in authority," in order that under their rule "we may lead a quiet and peaceable life in all godliness and honesty; for this is good and acceptable in the sight of God, our Savior" (1 Tim. 2:1-3). Cp. Rom. 13:1-7; Jer. 29:7.

Perhaps a few words should be added here on the limits which government officials who are at the same time Christians ought to observe in furthering the Church. Koestlin says of Luther: "Much as

---

[21] In spite of their freedom from the State the Protestant church bodies, including some which appropriate the name "Lutheran," have by and large forsaken the Christian faith. Not the *satisfactio vicaria*, but a moral life inspired by the example of Christ, is preached in most Protestant churches as Christianity. Not only laymen, but also pastors in large numbers are lodge members.

Luther insists that the civil government has no right to force anyone to believe or teach the Christian doctrine, yet he ascribes to the government a vaguely defined power and duty to take steps against public offenses and scandals in doctrine and preaching" (*Luthers Theol.* II, 281). Is the seeming indefiniteness of Luther's statements perhaps merely due to the reader's failure properly to distinguish between the Christian's status as Christian and his status as government official? On the one hand, it must be maintained that the civil authorities as such have neither right nor duty to command or to ordain anything in ecclesiastical matters. On the other hand, public officials, if they are Christians, certainly cannot and should not forget their Christianity. As a Christian should serve the Church with all the gifts that God has given him, so also the prestige and influence that go with a high earthly position should benefit the Church. It is certainly not right if a Christian whom God has elevated to a high position in the world carefully hides his Christianity. Scripture, on the one hand, calls attention to the fact "that not many wise men after the flesh, not many mighty, not many noble, are called" (1 Cor. 1:26). On the other hand, the Holy Ghost did not forget to mention that also prominent people, such as Dionysius the Areopagite, and high officials, such as Erastus, the treasurer of the city of Corinth, belonged to the Christian Church (Acts 17:34; Rom. 16:23). Walther (*Pastorale,* 368) states this point thus: "As the wealthy man with his money, the artist with his art, serves from love, without on that account claiming more authority in the Church than others have, so [according to Luther] the princes with their power should serve, not because they have a greater authority than others, but because love constrains them." But how far should they go? In particular, how far does the "duty of love" go? Rome and all Romanizing Protestants also appeal to the "duty of love" in defense of their twofold demand: (1) that the State must be ruled according to the Word of God, or according to "Christian principles," and (2) that the State must regard itself as the organ of the Church and place also its means of coercion in the service of the Church. Which, then, are the proper bounds? They will be recognized by observing two principles: (1) that the State cannot and should not be ruled with the Word of God, but should be organized and ruled according to natural reason (common sense); and (2) that the Church cannot and should not be built with force and coercion, but only with the Word of God, and that all external coercion in matters of faith blocks the growth of the Church unless God later corrects the errors committed by men.

B. LOCAL CHURCHES

(DE ECCLESIIS PARTICULARIBUS)

1

Nature of the Local Church or Congregation

The preceding discussion was devoted to the one universal Church, scattered over the whole globe, which is expressly called "one fold," μία ποίμνη (John 10:16) and is guaranteed a sure and abiding existence to the end of time by the divine promise (Matt. 16:18; Rom. 11:2-5). In quite a number of texts, however, the Scriptures speak of churches in the plural, of churches which are confined to particular and definite localities on earth. Thus 1 Cor. 16:19: "the churches of Asia," αἱ ἐκκλησίαι τῆς 'Ασίας; 1 Cor. 1:2: "the church of God which is at Corinth," ἡ ἐκκλησία τοῦ θεοῦ ἡ οὖσα ἐν Κορίνθῳ; Acts 8:1: "the church which was at Jerusalem," ἡ ἐκκλησία ἡ ἐν 'Ιεροσολύμοις; Rom. 16:16: "the churches [ἐκκλησίαι, plural] of Christ salute you"; 1 Cor. 11:16: "If any man seem to be contentious, we have no such custom, neither the churches [ἐκκλησίαι] of God." Such churches are called *ecclesiae particulares, local churches,* or *congregations.* They are churches to which one can write and which one can address orally. To local churches, of course, also the following texts refer: Acts 20:28: "Take heed . . . to all the flock, over the which the Holy Ghost hath made you overseers, to feed the church of God"; 1 Tim. 3:5: "If a man know not how to rule his own house, how shall he take care of the church of God?" (τῆς ἐκκλησίας θεοῦ ἐπιμελήσεται); Acts 14:27: "And when they were come and had gathered the church [τὴν ἐκκλησίαν] together"; Acts 14:23: "And when they had ordained them elders in every church" (κατ' ἐκκλησίαν); Matt. 18:17: "Tell it unto the church" (εἰπὲ τῇ ἐκκλησίᾳ); 1 Cor. 14:23: "If therefore the whole church be come together into one place." [22]

What, however, is the relation of the local churches to the Church Universal? The Church Universal and the local churches are not two different churches or two kinds of churches, but the Church Universal consists of all the local churches plus those believers who are prevented by circumstances from joining some local church. When we speak of a Christian congregation, or local church, we always mean only the Christians or believers in the visible communion. The congre-

---

[22] For a complete list see Wahl's *Clavis sub* ἐκκλησία.

gations, too, consist only of believers. As the wicked and hypocrites do not belong to the Church Universal, so they are no part of the congregation either. This is the clear teaching of Scripture. When Paul writes to the congregation at Corinth, he addresses "them that are sanctified in Christ Jesus, called to be saints" (1 Cor. 1:2).

Also all the functions with which the congregations are charged in every case presuppose faith in Christ, e. g., teaching and admonishing one another (Col. 3:16-17); the practice of church discipline (1 Corinthians 5; Matt. 18:17); the supervision of the teaching and the teachers (Rom. 16:17; Col. 4:17); the proclamation of the Gospel (1 Pet. 2:9); Christian conduct (1 Pet. 3:8-17). The hypocrites mingled with the congregation are to be addressed in the same manner as the unbelievers outside: "Repent ye, therefore, and be converted" (Acts 3:19). This, then, is the definition of a congregation: A congregation is the assembly of believers who congregate about Word and Sacrament at a particular place.[23]

<h1 style="text-align:center">2</h1>

The Local Church a Divine Institution

Is the formation of congregations or membership in already existing congregations left to the option of the Christians, or is it God's will and ordinance? This question is of great practical importance because there have at all times been people who, while they claimed to be

---

23 Walther therefore defines also a Lutheran congregation as "a gathering of believing Christians at a definite place among whom the Word of God is preached in its purity according to the Confessions of the Evangelical Lutheran Church and the holy Sacraments are administered according to Christ's institution as recorded in the Gospel" (*Die rechte Gestalt*, p. 1 [*Walther and the Church*, p. 88]). *Precise* in their definition, therefore, are only those older theologians who declare that hypocrites are no part (*pars*) of the congregation either. Thus Dannhauer says: "The hypocrites are by no means members of the invisible Church, neither of the true visible, but only of the collective visible, even as the weeds are not a part of the wheat field as such, but only of the entire field made up of wheat and tares" (*Hodos.*, p. 61). Calov: "Even though hypocrites are in that assembly in which the Church is, still they are not really in the assembly which is the Church. . . . We do not make a twin Church, the one consisting of saints, the other mixed; but we say that this distinction is merely ours, according to which the word 'ecclesia' is used homonymously, in one case for the assembly of the believers, then again for an assembly in which the hypocrites are found mixed with the believers." (Syst. VIII, 253 ff.) Nor does Article VIII of the Augustana say that the false Christians and hypocrites are a part of the Church, but merely that they can be organs of the Church inasmuch as the means of grace remain efficient even if administered by the wicked.

Christians, declared that they were free to join or not to join a congregation, that this was an adiaphoron.[24] We maintain: (1) Because it is the will and order of God that Christians who dwell in one locality should not merely read God's Word privately, but also fellowship with one another, hear God's Word publicly preached, to that end establish the public ministry among themselves, and after its establishment make use of it;[25] and (2) because it is the duty not only of the individual Christian, but also of the congregation to admonish and reprove the sinning brother, the whole congregation is enjoined to exercise Christian discipline;[26] and (3) because in particular the celebration of the Sacrament of the Altar is not merely a church custom, but a divine order for the exercise of brotherly communion (1 Cor. 10:17; 1 Cor. 11:17-21, 33): therefore the formation of Christian congregations, and membership in them, is not a human, but a divine mandate.[27] Accordingly, our Church accepts no "resignation" from membership in a Christian congregation, because neither individuals nor a whole congregation have the authority to grant a dispensation from a divine institution.

On the other hand, the union of congregations into larger church bodies, such as conferences, synods, etc., has not been ordained by God. The command "Tell it unto the church," according to the context, pertains to the local church, or congregation, and it must be restricted to the local church. "Tell it unto the synod," etc., is a human device. Accordingly, Walther (*Pastorale*, p. 393) remarks correctly: "An association of a number of congregations to form a larger church body with governing officers, e. g., by means of a synod with the authority of supervision, a so-called superior board [*Oberkirchenkollegium*], a consistory, a bishop, etc., is not of divine right, but only a human arrangement, and therefore it is not absolutely necessary; of this there can be no doubt because there is no divine command for it." [28]

---

[24] This prompted Walther's brochure of 1880 *Of the Duty of Christians to Join an Orthodox Congregation.*

[25] This point will be discussed more fully in the next section, "The Public Ministry."

[26] Matt. 18:17: "Tell it unto the church; but if he neglect to hear the church, let him be unto thee as an heathen man and a publican"; 1 Cor. 5:13: "Put away from among yourselves that wicked person"; 2 Cor. 2:8: "Wherefore I beseech you that ye would confirm your love toward him."

[27] Walther: "Every Christian is obliged, for the sake of his salvation, to profess allegiance and adhere to orthodox congregations and their orthodox preachers wherever he finds such" (*Kirche und Amt*, p. 144 ff. [*Walther and the Church*, p. 68.])

[28] See, *ibid.*, also the complete evidence that this is *Lutheran* doctrine.

On this fact is based our synodical practice to accept the resignation of congregations from synod if a congregation, in spite of all efforts to dissuade it, remains of the opinion that because of circumstances it would be better for it to sever its connection with synod.

3

Orthodox and Heterodox Churches

Congregations and church bodies must be divided into two classes according to their public doctrine.

It is God's will and command that in His Church His Word be preached and believed in purity and truth, without adulteration. In God's Church nobody should utter his own, but only God's Word (1 Pet. 4:11). Chaff and wheat do not belong together. All "teaching otherwise," ἑτεροδιδασκαλεῖν, is strictly forbidden. 1 Tim. 1:3: "As I besought thee to abide still at Ephesus when I went into Macedonia, that thou mightest charge some that they teach no other doctrine." It is important to point out again and again that in all Scripture there is not a single text permitting a teacher to deviate from the Word of God or granting a child of God license to fraternize with a teacher who deviates from the Word of God. God is against the prophets who proclaim their own dreams (Jer. 23:31 f.). And all Christians without exception are commanded to avoid such (Rom. 16:17; 1 Tim. 6:3 ff.).

The distinction between orthodox and heterodox church bodies and congregations is based on this divine order. A congregation or church body which abides by God's order, in which therefore God's Word is taught in its purity and the Sacraments administered according to the divine institution, is properly called an orthodox church (*ecclesia orthodoxa, pura*). But a congregation or church body which, in spite of the divine order, tolerates false doctrine in its midst is properly called a *heterodox church (ecclesia heterodoxa, impura)*.[29] All children of God should be earnestly concerned to see how real and serious this difference between the church bodies is, because indifference as to the Christian doctrine is rampant today among professed Christians,

---

[29] Orthodox churches in our day are those Lutheran congregations and church bodies which profess and actually teach the doctrines laid down in the Confessions of the Evangelical Lutheran Church, because these doctrines, on examination, are found to be the teaching of God's Word. Impure and heterodox churches are the Roman Catholic Church, the Eastern Catholic Church, the Reformed Church with its many subdivisions, and, moreover, also the church bodies which, though bearing the Lutheran name, do not profess and actually teach the doctrine of the Church of the Reformation.

and the "abrogation of creeds" and substitution for them of a so-called "applied Christianity" is represented as the goal the Church should strive for.[30]

With regard to the orthodox character of a church body note well: (1) A church body is orthodox only if the true doctrine, as we have it in the Augsburg Confession and the other Lutheran Symbols, is actually taught in its pulpits and its publications and not merely "officially" professed as its faith. Not the "official" doctrine, but the actual teaching determines the character of a church body, because Christ enjoins that all things whatsoever He has commanded His disciples should actually be taught and not merely acknowledged in an "official document" as the correct doctrine. It is patent that faith in Christ will be created and preserved through the pure Gospel only when that Gospel is really proclaimed. (2) A church body does not forfeit its orthodox character by reason of the casual intrusion of false doctrine. The thing which the Apostle Paul told the elders of Ephesus: "Also of your own selves shall men arise speaking perverse things to draw away disciples after them" (Acts 20:30), came true not only in the Apostolic Church, but also in the Church of the Reformation and will occur in the Church to the Last Day. A church body loses its orthodoxy only when it no longer applies Rom. 16:17, hence does not combat and eventually remove the false doctrine, but tolerates it without reproof and thus actually grants it equal right with the truth.

We call heterodox church bodies both "churches" and "sects," depending on whether we have in mind the good or the evil in them. Churches they are in so far as they still retain enough of the Gospel of Christ that men can come to faith in Christ and thus can become true children of God. Sects they are in so far as they have combined to further their deviations from the doctrine of Christ and thus cause divisions in the Church and by their errors and separate existence constantly threaten the faith of the children of God.

4

Children of God in Heterodox Churches

Though God desires that all congregations be orthodox, and though all heterodox communions exist only by God's sufferance and contrary to God's gracious will, still it is a fact that also in the heterodox

---

[30] *The Expansion of Religion,* by E. Winchester Donald, Rector of Trinity Church in the City of Boston, 1896, p. 125.

communions there are believing children of God. The term "Christians" covers a wider field than the term "orthodox Christians." Though Christ denies to the Samaritan Church the right of existence as a separate church organization (John 4:22), still He repeatedly acknowledged individual Samaritans as true children of God (Luke 17:16 ff.; 10:33). Luther, too, never thought of making the orthodox Church, the Lutheran Church, coextensive with the *Una Sancta*. Vigorously as he fights against the Papacy and expressly declares it an institution of Satan, he nevertheless does not doubt that God has at all times under the Papacy preserved for Himself a Church, yes, the elite of the Christians.[31] Again, earnestly as Luther fights against Carlstadt, Zwingli, and their collaborators for their deviation from God's Word, he nevertheless grants that there were also true children of God who, ignorant of the evil they were thus supporting, made common cause with these pseudo reformers (St. L. IX:44). Likewise our older Lutheran dogmaticians, "zealots for orthodoxy" though they were, nevertheless decidedly rejected identification of the *Una Sancta Ecclesia* with the orthodox Lutheran Church.[32] The Fathers of the Missouri Synod declare it a calumny when the Lutheran Church is accused of identifying the Church of God with the Lutheran Church.[33] They taught: If a person sincerely clings to the cardinal doctrine of the Christian faith, if he believes that God is gracious to him because of Christ's *satisfactio vicaria,* he is a member of the Christian Church, no matter in which ecclesiastical camp he may be. By denying this truth one would overthrow the cardinal doctrine of the Christian faith, the article of justification. Walther: According to Rom. 3:28 and Acts 4:12 "the unconditional and sole requirement for salvation is fellowship with Christ through faith. The maxim, 'Outside the Church there is no salvation,' 'He who has not the Church on earth for his mother has not God in heaven for his Father,' is true only in this sense, that outside the invisible Church there is no salvation and no state of grace. It has only this meaning that 'there is no salvation outside Christ'; for whoever is not in inward fellowship with the believers and saints is not in fellowship with Christ either. On the other hand, whoever is in fellowship with Christ is in fellowship also with all those in whom

---

[31] St. L. XVII:1019 ff. Also St. L. V:468: "Under the Papacy there have always been some believers, and even today there are some whom we don't know, whom God preserves through His Word and Sacrament, though the devil and the Pope do not relish it."

[32] For substantiation see Baier-Walther, III, 646 ff.

[33] Walther, *Kirche u. Amt,* pp. 95—113 (*Walther and the Church,* p. 65).

Christ dwells, that is, with the invisible Church. Accordingly, he who restricts salvation to fellowship with any visible Church therewith overthrows the article of the justification of a poor sinner in the sight of God by faith alone in Jesus Christ." (*Walther and the Church*, p. 70.)

5

Church Fellowship with Heterodox Churches (Unionism) Is Prohibited by God

It is common knowledge that the presence of children of God in heterodox churches is urged to prove that it is right, even demanded by charity, to fellowship heterodox churches. This is the exact opposite of what Scripture teaches, for Scripture says, "Avoid them." [34]

The argument of unionists is contrary even to *natural reason.* The old Lutheran teachers point to 2 Sam. 15:11 as an illustration. Just as the fact that two hundred citizens of Jerusalem in their ignorance joined Absalom did not give the rest of Israel the right to desert their king and join the rebels, nor even to connive at the rebellion, so the circumstance that some Christians, from ignorance and contrary to God's orders, follow false teachers does not give license to other Christians to do the same thing.

To say that love demands such a practice is a misuse of that word. Love of God and love of the brethren rather requires the opposite practice. He who loves Christ loves Christ's Word, and Christ commands us to avoid all who teach anything that is contrary to His Word. And whoever really loves the brethren refuses to participate in their erring and sinning, seeking rather to deliver them from error and sin.

Moreover, the Scriptures of both the Old and the New Testament state explicitly that God permits false teachers to arise in order that Christians may show their obedience by avoiding them, not in order that Christians may fraternize with them (Deut. 13:3; 8:2; 1 Cor. 11:19). If Christians, against the divine prohibition, fellowship false teachers and tolerate false doctrines, they commit the sin which the Church calls "unionism," "syncretism." [35]

As a matter of fact, this unionism divides the Church and gives rise to heterodox churches in Christendom. Had the Christians always obeyed the divine order to avoid those teaching another doctrine

---

[34] Rom. 16:17; 1 Tim. 6:3 ff.; 2 John 10—11; etc.
[35] Baier-Walther, III, 665 ff.; Apol., *Trigl.* 243, VII, VIII, 48.

(ἑτεροδιδασκαλοῦντες), neither the Papacy nor other sects could have arisen. Where there are no buyers, there is no market. Of course, unionism avers that it aims at the removal of discord among Christians. But because the unity of the Christian Church consists in having one faith and one profession, unionism actually is a caricature, indeed, a mockery of Christian unity.[36] Instead of healing the hurt, it makes it permanent.

In 1 Cor. 1:10 we have an exact definition of Christian unity: "Now, I beseech you, brethren, by the name of our Lord Jesus Christ, that ye all speak the same thing [ἵνα τὸ αὐτὸ λέγητε πάντες] and that there be no divisions among you." This is a demand for uniformity in speech (λέγειν) or in the profession of the Christian doctrine. Then the Apostle continues: "but that ye be perfectly joined together in the same mind and in the same judgment," ἐν τῷ αὐτῷ νοῒ καὶ ἐν αὐτῇ γνώμῃ. Here he clearly says that Christians are to use the same words also in the same sense.[37] Agreement in words with disagreement in meaning is altogether contrary to the unity God calls for, and to seek such a "unity" ("we agree to disagree") is immoral, a trifling with sacred, divine things, which is unseemly for Christians.[38]

The Christian Church can and should have patience with the erring and seek through instruction to remove the error. But never can or should the Church grant error equal right with the truth. If it does, it renounces the truth itself. It is the very nature of truth to antagonize error. Truth which no longer excludes error, but grants it domicile, is *eo ipso* resigning as truth. Pertinently Luther remarks: "Whoever really regards his doctrine, faith, and confession as true, right, and certain cannot remain in the same stall with such as teach or adhere to false doctrine" (St. L. XVII:1180). Unionism in principle abolishes the difference between truth and error, so that only through a "happy inconsistency" can the erring retain their hold on the essential truth. For this reason unionism is a grave threat to the Christian Church. A person is fortunate indeed if, ignoring the words of

36 Cp. Luther on the unity of the Christian Church as a unity of the heart through faith in God's Word (St. L. XIX:344 f.).

37 Meyer on the passage: "Γνώμη nowhere in the New Testament means 'Gesinnung [disposition], rather *sententia, iudicium* [opinion, conviction]."

38 Luther, St. L. XVIII:1996: "Fabius teaches that an ambiguous word must be avoided like a reef; if we undesignedly happen to use such a word, it may be overlooked; but intentionally and purposely to choose such a word is inexcusable and deserving of the most righteous hatred of all. . . . For what else would result if the custom of speaking ambiguously and craftily in religion, in law, and in all important matters were adopted than a thoroughly confused babel, so that finally no one could understand the other?"

Scripture enjoining him to avoid those who teach another Gospel, he yet retains his faith in the words: "The blood of Jesus Christ, His Son, cleanseth us from all sin."

As for the talk current in our day, even among so-called conservative theologians, that "various trends," that is, variations in doctrine and profession, are intended by God, one can merely say that it is shocking that within Christendom the testimony of Scripture should thus be contradicted.

6

Schism (Separatism)

By the term "schism" we mean a division in the Church which God's Word does not enjoin, but which is begun by men for carnal reasons and therefore is sinful, e. g., a separation because of differences in church customs, church terms, order of worship, etc. In practice it is important to distinguish between schismatics acting from spite and schismatics acting from weakness in Christian knowledge and prejudice.[39]

Such, however, as separate from a church body because it tenaciously clings to false doctrine are unjustly called schismatics, separatists, etc. This separation is commanded in Scripture (Rom. 16:17) and is the only means of restoring and maintaining the true unity in the Christian Church.

7

The Representative Church. Church Government

(Ecclesia repraesentativa)

Christ has commissioned neither some one person (Pope, princes, governors, presidents, etc.), nor a college of persons (bishops, pastors, board of directors, consistories, parliaments, conferences, synods,

---

[39] J. Meisner: "Some schismatics are malicious, namely, such as knowingly and willfully, contrary to their conscience, from malice disturb the Church and divide it into two parties disagreeing with each other; others are not malicious, viz., such as do this from weakness, ignorance, and a preconceived opinion which they hold to be very true. The former are not of the Church, because such a malicious schism is a very great sin, extinguishing the faith. . . . The latter are no doubt of the Church, because such disturbance, springing and done from ignorance, does not immediately drive away faith; this happens only when a malicious defense is added to it." *Disput. de eccl. a. 1651 habita*, th. 3, qu. 4; in Baier-Walther, III, 664.

councils, etc.) to decide and ordain ecclesiastical matters for the Church in any way binding the conscience. When the Papacy demands recognition as *iure divino* the supreme binding authority in the whole Christian Church ("the supreme power delivered to the Sovereign Pontiffs in the universal Church," Waterworth, p. 101), it displays one of the marks which identify the Papacy as the Antichrist prophesied in Scripture. When the civil government, whether an autocracy, a monarchy, a democracy, or of whatever form, claims a *ius circa sacra sive in sacra,* we call it Caesaropapism. In general, when the power to make binding decisions and laws in the Church is said to inhere in any body of men, be they ecclesiastics or laymen or a mixed board, this is not a Christian, but a Papistic or Caesaropapistic position, because in the Christian Church God's Word is the only authority and all Christians are and remain responsible directly to God for all they believe and do.

Of course, the Church is free to take care of some things through representatives chosen by it for this purpose. Thus the elders or the church council can represent a congregation, and conferences, synods, councils, etc., can represent other Christians and small or large groups of congregations. But if we ask what authority or power these representatives, these *ecclesiae representativae,* have, the answer is: With respect to the congregation and the individual Christians they always have only advisory power. [The *Handbook* of The Lutheran Church — Missouri Synod, 1949, Art. VII, says of the relation of Synod to the congregations: "In its relation to its members Synod is not an ecclesiastical government exercising legislative or coercive powers, and with respect to the individual congregation's right of self-government it is but an advisory body. Accordingly, no resolution of Synod imposing anything upon the individual congregation is of binding force if it is not in accordance with the Word of God or if it appears to be inexpedient as far as the condition of a congregation is concerned."] The order that obtains in the Christian Church is this: If the question at issue pertains to matters taught and decided in God's Word, the Christian position is that no man and no assembly of men, no matter how learned and renowned they may be, can decide for a Christian what is Scriptural doctrine. This matter every single Christian must decide for himself on the basis of the clear, infallible Word of God.

Let us hear Luther on this subject. He comments on 1 Pet. 3:15 ("Be ready always to give an answer to every man"): "St. Peter spoke these words to all Christians, pastors, laymen, men, women, young, old, and of whatever state they may be; hence every Christian should know the foundation and reason of his faith and be able to give his reason and, when called upon, to answer. Now, so far laymen have been forbidden to read the Bible. That was a cunning move on the part of the devil to draw the people away from the Bible, and his thought was: If I can induce the laymen not to read the Scriptures, I'll lead the parsons away from the Bible *in Aristotelem,* so that they chatter what they please; then the laymen will have to be content with what they preach. Else, if the laymen read the Scriptures, the preachers would have to study so that they would not be reproved and overcome [from Scripture by the laymen]. But take note how St. Peter here says to all of us that we should give answer and show the reason for our faith. When your last hour comes, I won't be with you, neither the Pope; if then you don't know the foundation of your hope and merely say: I believe what the councils, the Pope, and our fathers believed, the devil will answer: Yes, but what if they erred? Then he has won and will drag you into hell. Therefore we must ourselves know what we believe, namely, what God has said and not what the Pope or the councils decree or say. For you dare not trust in men, but must trust in the bare Word of God." (St. L. IX:1235 f.)[40]

Again Luther writes: "Human authorities and teachers have decreed and ordained that the judging of doctrine should be restricted to the bishops and learned and councils; whatever they resolved, all the world should regard as canonical and as articles of faith. . . . Christ takes the opposite stand, denies to bishops, learned, and councils both authority and power to judge the doctrine and instead gives it to each individual Christian and all of them collectively when He says, John 10:4: 'My sheep know My voice,' likewise v. 5: 'A stranger will My sheep not follow, but will flee from him; for they know not the voice of strangers.' Here you certainly see clearly whose is the right to judge of the doctrine. Bishops, Pope, the learned, and everyone has power to teach, but the sheep are to judge whether they teach the voice of Christ or the voice of strangers. . . . Therefore we let the bishops and councils resolve and decree what they will; but where we have God's Word before us, it is for us to decide, and not for them, whether their teaching is right or wrong; and they shall let us rule and shall obey our word." (St. L. X:1540.)

---

[40] Luther is here, as always, insisting on the bare Scriptures, *nuda Scriptura,* in contrast to Scripture interpreted, or commented on, by man, because the "bare" Scriptures are clearer in every case than the exegesis or commentary and because the Christian must in every case judge on the basis of the "bare" Scriptures whether the exegesis or interpretation is correct. This Luther shows *in extenso ad* Psalm 37 (St. L. V:334 ff.).

Nor in things neither commanded nor forbidden in God's Word (*adiaphora*) should Christians take orders from other men, be they few or many, as binding their conscience. To do so would be contrary to Matt. 23:8; and 1 Cor. 7:23; etc. *Adiaphora* are not settled among Christians by compulsion, but through mutual consent (*per mutuum consensum*) according to love.

Attention may here be drawn to the fact that the voting or balloting in the meetings of orthodox congregations has a different significance when it concerns Christian doctrine than when it concerns indifferent matters. The only purpose of voting in matters of doctrine is to see whether all now understand the teaching of the divine Word and agree to it; the purpose of the vote is not to decide the correctness of a doctrine by majority vote or even by unanimous vote. The orthodox Christian Church remains aware of the fact that it cannot by resolution make or give birth to Christian doctrines, but must always merely set forth from Scripture and profess over against the prevailing error the doctrines submitted and settled in Scripture. Axiom: "The decretals of a council neither construct nor give authority to the articles of faith, but if the councils are orthodox, they profess the articles of faith already delivered in Scripture over against the insurgent errors." What holds true of councils applies likewise to all small or large church assemblies. In *adiaphora* a vote is taken to ascertain what the majority regards as the best. The natural order is that in *adiaphora* the minority yields to the majority and acquiesces, not because the majority has the right to rule, but for love's sake. Since, however, love is queen here, it may happen that the majority will yield to the minority. See Walther, *Pastorale*, p. 372 ff. Christians, as Christians, never quarrel about *adiaphora*, since, in so far as they are Christians and walk in the Spirit, "none of them desires to be the ruler of the other, but everyone wants to be the other's servant," as Luther expresses it.[41] A discussion that in an adiaphorous matter becomes vehement and acrimonious indicates that the temper of the meeting is sinking below the Christian level. The discussion of the adiaphoron should then be interrupted and the Christian spirit and frame of mind be restored by instruction and admonition, e. g., on the basis of 1 Pet. 5:5.

Well known are *Luther's theses* (*propositiones*) on the authority of the Church in matters of doctrine and in adiaphorous matters. He says: "The Christian Church has no authority to ordain any article

---

41 "Von welt. Obrigkeit, wie weit man ihr Gehorsam schuldig sei" (St. L. X:406).

of faith, never has ordained and never will ordain one. The Church of God has no power to enact any precept as to good works, never has done it, never will do it. All articles of faith are fully established in Holy Writ, so that there is no need of ordaining even one more. All precepts of good works are fully prescribed in Holy Writ, so that there is no need of appointing even one more. The Church of God has no authority to ratify articles [of faith] or precepts [of good works], or to give sanction to Holy Scripture itself, as though the Church were a higher authority or clothed with judicial powers, never has done it, nor ever will do it. On the contrary, the Church of God is ratified and endorsed by Holy Scripture as its lord and judge. The Church of God approves, that is, it recognizes and acknowledges the articles of faith or Holy Scripture as a subject or a servant does the seal of his lord. For the maxim is sure: He who has no power to promise and grant either the future or present life, cannot ordain articles of faith. The Church of God has authority to appoint rites and customs in regard to festivals, food, fasting, prayers, vigils, etc., but not for others, only for itself; neither has it ever done, nor will it ever do otherwise. A church is a group or assembly of baptized and believers under one shepherd, whether of one city, or of an entire country, or of the whole world. This pastor or prelate has nothing to ordain, because he is not the Church, unless it be that his church empowers him." (*Opp. v. a.* IV, 373 ff.; St. L. XIX:958.)

A part of the Reformed church bodies in America has become infected with the Roman spirit also in this respect, that they ascribe to general assemblies, as synods and councils, the authority to enact laws and ordinances binding on the conscience. True, as a rule, they say that the Church may ordain nothing contrary to the Word of God; thus, e. g., the Episcopalians, the Presbyterians, the Methodists, etc. [Cf. *Pop. Symb.*, pp. 240, 241, 243, 288.] But the same church bodies err egregiously by ordaining things not prescribed in God's Word. In such matters they ascribe to their general church assemblies the authority to enact rules *iure divino*. Thus we read in the *Confession of Faith* of the Presbyterians, chap. XXXI: "It belongeth to synods and councils ministerially to determine controversies of faith and cases of conscience; to set down rules and directions for the better ordering of the public worship of God and government of His Church; to receive complaints in cases of maladministrations, and authoritatively to determine the same: which decrees and determinations, if consonant to the Word of God, are to be received with reverence and submission, not only for their agreement with the Word, but also for the power whereby they are made, as being an ordinance of God, appointed thereunto in His Word." [42]

But this Roman leaven has penetrated also into Lutheran church bodies of America and Germany.[43] They teach a divinely appointed church government that has, besides the office of the Word, the authority to give orders *iure divino,* which the congregation must obey. True, they, too, add the restriction that the church government may not prescribe what is contrary to God's Word. But this limitation is a contradiction in itself, inasmuch as the type of church government they set up is contrary to God's Word.

In defense of their wrong position they invoke the Fourth Commandment, to wit, that parents have authority to order their children to do things that are not commanded in God's Word as long as these things are not in conflict with God's Word. Pastors and other ecclesiastical superiors, it is urged, belong to the spiritual fathers; therefore one owes them obedience by God's order in all things not commanded in God's Word if only they command nothing prohibited in the Word of God. This argument has confused some people, but it is false. Parents may indeed bid their children do things not commanded in God's Word because they have been endowed by God with legislative authority over their children. Col. 3:20: "Children, obey your parents in all things." But God has not invested the Church, or individuals in the Church, with legislative authority; on the contrary, here the rule is: "One is your Master, even Christ; and all ye are brethren" (Matt. 23:8).

He who in the Church seeks to command over and above what Christ has commanded is usurping Christ's authority and infringing on Christ's sovereignty. Christ purchased the Church with His blood for His own, that He might be its only Lord and Master. Whoever now seeks to rule independently of Christ in the Church, no matter to what extent, is thereby encroaching on Christ's position as Savior and Lord. Furthermore, he is infringing on the glory with which Christ has crowned the Christians. With the remission of sins and sonship with God by faith in Christ they have also received the privilege to be subject in spiritual matters solely to Christ and His Word and independent of all commandments of men. This is the glorious liberty of the children of God, purchased for them not with

---

[42] See the quotations in Guenther, *Symbolik,* §§ 154—157. Also, F. Pieper, "Kirche und Kirchenregiment," *Proceedings of Synodical Convention,* 1896, p. 27 ff.

[43] See the quotations in Grosse, *Unterscheidungslehren,* p. 8; *Lehre und Wehre,* 1870, p. 184 f.

gold or silver, but with the precious blood of Christ and presented to them in justification. Now, if men arrogate to themselves the right to impose their will on Christians, they are making God's free children slaves of men and actually expecting them to desert Christ as their only Lord and Master. Therefore Luther says: "Friend, do not regard it as a small matter to forbid what God does not forbid, to destroy the Christian liberty that cost Christ His blood, to load the conscience with sin where there is none. He who does that, and gets away with it, is likely to commit any wrong; yes, he has thereby already renounced all that God is, teaches, and does, including His Christ." (St. L. XX:207.)

Men have derided synods which have only advisory power. They have thought that nothing but "confusion" and "disorder" would have to result if synods were not vested with authority to enact ordinances binding the conscience in matters not regulated by God's Word. This fear is groundless, as can be seen from the history of those Lutheran synods of America which have left consciences entirely unfettered in regard to synodical resolutions. We so-called Missourians have perhaps, as far as peace and order is concerned, experienced the most peaceful time, comparatively speaking, which the Church has ever enjoyed. We can truthfully say that government of the Church solely by God's Word has stood the test of nearly a century among us. Of course, the flesh of the Christians has sought to create disorder also among us. But God's Word has proved its ability to rule and control everything. So firmly has a "free church" government, abstinence from all commanding that exceeded God's Word, united and held us together that outsiders have surmised that we must have a "High Church" government and must be the "High Church" party in the Lutheran Church.

A few *miscellaneous* remarks on the *"ecclesia repraesentativa"*:

1. The convocation of a congregational meeting, or of a conference, synod, etc., naturally rests first of all with those whom the congregation or a group of congregations has commissioned for this purpose. Nevertheless, every Christian has the right to call a meeting of the congregation, synod, council, etc., if he is convinced that conditions demand a meeting and that the officials are lax in doing their duty. (See Luther, St. L. X:278 ff.)

2. The chair in such church meetings is occupied either by a permanent chairman specified in the by-laws and elected by the congregation or by a temporary chairman chosen by the meeting. On the chairmanship of the church council of the congregation,

Walther (*Pastorale*, p. 364) gives this advice: "The pastor of the congregation should open the meetings with a prayer, and since he holds the office of the Word, which is to apply the standard of God's Word to the other offices, it is but proper that he be the chairman. As Luther writes: 'The office of preaching the Gospel is the highest of all, for it is the true Apostolic office, laying the foundation for all the other offices, which all should build on the former' (St. L. X:1592). But even here the pastor must not insist that he be made chairman." Walther (*Pastorale*, p. 372) offers some excellent suggestions on what a chairman must observe in a meeting of the congregation in order that all things may be done decently and in order and the Christian character of the meeting be preserved. They are reproduced by Fritz, *Pastoral Theology*, p. 316 f. Walther's nine points contain also the essentials necessary for conducting larger church meetings (conferences, synods, councils). The handbooks on parliamentary procedure for the most part offer the natural order that should be observed in all deliberative meetings. But the chairman as well as the entire assembly must be careful that the formal application of "parliamentary rules" does not limit free debate and is not employed in a loveless manner against those who are not so well versed in parliamentary procedure.

3. It should be self-evident in the Christian Church that the laymen, too, have voice and vote in synodical meetings. This truth was upheld also by the later Lutheran theologians even under State-Church conditions. Thus Quenstedt says: "Assistants and competent judges are, besides the chairman, not merely the bishop, but also believing Christians, familiar with the Scriptures, both laymen and clerics, sent by the congregations to the council" (*Syst.* II, 1627). The doctrine, which unfortunately intruded also into the Lutheran Church, that in discussions of doctrine the laymen may listen and ask questions, but not judge and vote, is a bald Papistic outrage.[44] Advocates of this doctrine *eo ipso* manifest that they have lost all understanding and judgment in regard to the Christian Church and the prerogatives of the Christians.

Quenstedt's remark, appended to his words quoted above, that all Christian "classes" or "estates," that is, in addition to the public teachers also the civil officers (*politici*) and the laymen, are assistants and competent judges in the councils, requires elucidation. The so-

---

[44] Luther takes a very determined stand against this abomination. He says: "To judge and to decide in matters of doctrine is the prerogative of absolutely all Christians, and so much so that he is accursed who infringes on this right by a hairbreadth."

called "doctrine of the classes" originally had a good intent. It was to emphasize the truth, against the Papacy, that the right to judge in the Church belongs not to certain privileged persons, but to the whole Church, to the Christians of all classes. But the doctrine of the classes can easily be misunderstood as meaning that the secular classes (the working classes and the government, *"Naehrstand und Wehrstand"*) as such are parts of the Church. To be sure, through the Holy Ghost's gracious operation people of all classes (fathers and mothers, employers and employees, lords and servants, sovereigns and citizens, etc.) come to faith and thus enter the Church. But they are in the Church not as a class, but as believers (Gal. 3:28). Also the public ministry (*"Lehrstand"*) is not in the Church as a class or order distinct from the order of the Christians and endowed with special authority, but they are individually, through their call, the servants of the Christians in the public administration of the means of grace, which have all power and efficacy in themselves and do not derive it from the person or order of the administrants.

In speaking of the *ecclesia repraesentativa,* we may well issue the reminder that learned theologians who happen to be present at a synodical convention should present their thoughts in popular form so that all present can understand them. The use of technical language which only specialists can understand ill comports with the purpose of our synodical meetings and is, in fact, somewhat of an affront to the assembly. Here Luther's well-known dictum applies that when theologians are among themselves, they may talk in such scholarly fashion that it astonishes even God in heaven; but when they speak before the people, they owe it to their audience to speak in terms that Hans and Grete can understand.

The Public Ministry

(DE MINISTERIO ECCLESIASTICO)

1

Nature of the Public Ministry

THE term "ministry" is used both in Scripture and by the Church in a general, or wider, and in a special, or narrower, sense. In the wider sense it embraces every form of preaching the Gospel or administering the means of grace, whether by Christians in general, as originally entrusted with the means of grace and commissioned to apply them, or by chosen public servants (*ministri ecclesiae*) in the name and at the command of Christians. In this article we are speaking of the public ministry in the narrower sense, that is, of the office by which the means of grace, given originally to the Christians as their inalienable possession, are administered by order and on behalf of Christians.

The ministry in this sense presupposes Christian congregations. Only a congregation can establish the public ministry. Smalcald Articles (Power and Jurisdiction of Bishops): "Wherever the Church is, there is the authority [command] to administer the Gospel. Therefore it is necessary for the Church [the churches, the congregations] to retain the authority to call, elect, and ordain ministers." (*Trigl.* 523, 67.) This is Scriptural. Only after the mission work on Crete had resulted in congregations did Paul command Titus (Titus 1:5) to ordain elders (πρεσβυτέρους) "in every city," κατὰ πόλιν, in the cities where there were congregations, which elders, or presbyters, he then called bishops (ἐπίσκοποι), v. 7. Furthermore, of the congregations that had come into existence during the first missionary journey of Paul in Asia Minor we are told that Paul and Barnabas on their return "ordained them elders (πρεσβυτέρους) in every church," κατ᾽ ἐκκλησίαν, wherever there were congregations (Acts 14:23).

That the public ministry presupposes congregations is evident also from the fact that Scripture mentions entire congregations and every member of them as coming under the care of this office. 1 Tim. 3:5: "take care of the church of God" (τῆς ἐκκλησίας τοῦ θεοῦ ἐπιμελεῖσθαι); Acts 20:28: "Take heed to *all the flock*" (προσέχειν παντὶ τῷ ποιμνίῳ); v. 28b: "to feed the church of God" (ποιμαίνειν τὴν ἐκκλησίαν τοῦ θεοῦ); v. 31: "to warn everyone" (νουθετεῖν ἕνα ἕκαστον); 1 Pet. 5:3: "being ensamples to the *flock*" (τύποι γινόμενοι τοῦ ποιμνίου).

This office and its functions are called "public," therefore, not because they are always discharged in public, but because they are performed for the good and by the command of the congregation, just as we call civic officeholders "public servants" and their work "public service." Accordingly, the acts of the public ministry are "public" not only when its incumbents proclaim the Word in public to an assembly, but also when they minister privately to a single soul.

Where there are no Christian congregations, as in a pagan country, there can be no public ministry, no service in the name of a congregation. But as soon as the missionary activity has borne fruit and a congregation has come into existence, the public ministry can be established. After showing that a special call is necessary to make one a teacher among Christians, Luther continues: "This is the call to a *public* office among Christians. But if one landed among people who are no Christians, one might do as did the Apostles and not wait for a call; for there [where there are no Christians] the public office of preaching does not exist, and one might say: Here there are no Christians, I will preach and instruct them in Christianity. And if a group formed, chose and called me to be their bishop, I would have a call." (St. L. III:723.)

2

The Relation of the Public Ministry to the Spiritual Priesthood of All Christians

All Christians, that is, all who have come to faith in Christ, are spiritual priests and thus have the call to preach the Gospel. In the words of 1 Pet. 2:9: "Ye are . . . a royal priesthood [βασίλειον ἱεράτευμα] . . . that ye should show forth the praises of Him who hath called you out of darkness into His marvelous light," not elders or bishops, but all Christians are addressed. The public ministry of course presupposes this spiritual priesthood. It is God's will and ordinance that the elders or bishops be chosen not from among the unbelievers, but from among the believers, or spiritual priests, as is evident from the list of attributes which an elder, or bishop, should have. Both the positive attributes (apt to teach, patient, etc.) and the negative attributes (not a brawler, not covetous, etc.) enumerated in 1 Timothy 3 and Titus 1 presuppose personal faith in Christ.

Nevertheless, Scripture distinguishes sharply between the spiritual priesthood and the public ministry. For, besides a general ability to teach, which Scripture ascribes to every Christian,[1] a *special* aptitude to teach is required; and, besides the call which the spiritual priests have to preach the Gospel,[2] a special call is demanded. A congregation would be acting contrary to God's ordinance if it appointed the public ministers by lot, or according to the alphabet, or by any similar method, and in defense of such action claimed that all Christians are spiritual priests, apt to teach, and prompted by the Holy Ghost. No, Scripture on the contrary warns 1 Tim. 5:22: "Lay hands suddenly [R. V., hastily] on no man," [3] and it urges that the choice of elders, or bishops, be made according to the attributes enumerated as requisite for this office (1 Tim. 3:1-7; Titus 1:6-12). Luther: "What qualifications the bishops, or shepherds, to be chosen by the people should have, Paul sufficiently teaches Titus 1:5 ff. and 1 Tim. 3:2 ff." (St. L. X:1598.)

Luther powerfully sets forth the rights, privileges, and duties of the spiritual priesthood and yet sharply distinguishes between the general priesthood of believers and the public ministry. He says with regard to the spiritual priesthood: "When we were made Christians through this Priest and His priesthood [namely, through Christ] and in Baptism were by faith incorporated in Him, we were also given the right and power to preach and profess the Word we received from Him before everybody, everyone according to his station and calling. For, though we are not all in the public office and calling, still every Christian should and may teach, instruct, admonish, comfort, reprove his neighbor with God's Word whenever and wherever he finds someone in need of it; for instance, a father and mother, their children and servants, a brother, neighbor, citizen, or peasant the other. For a Christian certainly can teach the other one who is still ignorant or weak and admonish him with the Ten Commandments, the Creed, Prayer, etc., and he who hears it is in duty bound to receive it from him as God's Word and join in confessing it publicly." (On Ps. 110:4; St. L. V:1038.)

---

1 John 6:45; 7:38-39; 1 Cor. 2:15-16; 1 John 2:27; etc.

2 1 Pet. 2:9; Is. 40:9; Col. 3:16. Moses' wish (Num. 11:29): "Would God that all the Lord's people were prophets and that the Lord would put His Spirit upon them," finds its fulfillment in the New Testament, as Acts 2 reports.

3 Even when the laying on of hands here is taken to mean in general "pronouncing the blessing in various special cases" (Huther), the installation of presbyters is certainly one of those special cases. At any rate, the claim that 1 Tim. 5:22 specifically refers to the laying on of hands at the re-admission of excommunicated persons (de Wette, Wiesinger) is to be regarded as pure conjecture, since such a custom is nowhere mentioned in the New Testament, while the laying on of hands at the induction into the ministry of the congregation is (Acts 6:6).

Luther points out, too, that the means of grace have the same nature, power, and effect, whether administered by common Christians or by ministers in their public office. He writes: "We firmly maintain there is no other Word of God than the one all Christians are told to preach; there is no other Baptism than the one all Christians may administer; there is no other remembrance of the Lord's Supper than the one any Christian may celebrate; also there is no other sin than the one every Christian may bind or loose; again, there is no other sacrifice than the body of every Christian; also, no one can, or may, pray but only a Christian; moreover, no one should judge of the doctrine but the Christian. These, however, certainly are the priestly and kingly functions." (St. L. X:1590.)

On the other hand, Luther sets forth the difference between the priesthood of all Christians and the public ministry. "Though all of us are priests," he says, "we may and should not on that account all preach or teach and govern. However, from the whole congregation some must be selected and chosen to whom this office is to be committed; and whoever holds this office is now, because of it, not a priest (like all the rest), but a servant, or minister, of all the others. And if he can or will no more preach or serve, he steps back into the common crowd, commits his office to someone else, and is now again no more than every common Christian. Behold, thus must the office of preaching, or the ministry, be distinguished from the universal priesthood of all baptized Christians. For this office is nothing more than a public service, which is delegated to one by the whole congregation, though all of them are priests together." (St. L. V:1037.)

Proving further the necessity of a special call for the exercise of the public ministry, Luther says: "Since all things that we have enumerated so far should be common to all Christians, which we have also demonstrated and proved, it would not be seemly for anyone to put himself forward and claim as his sole possession what belongs to us all. Aspire to this privilege and exercise it as long as there is no other who, too, has received this privilege. But because all have the privilege, it becomes necessary that one, or as many as the congregation pleases, be chosen and elected, who in the stead and name of all, who have the same right, administers these offices publicly, in order that no revolting disorder arise among God's people and the Church be turned into a babel, seeing that all things should be done decently and in order in it, as the Apostle has taught in 1 Cor. 14:40. There is a big difference between exercising a common right by order of the congregation and exercising the same right in an emergency. In a congregation, where the privilege is common property, no one should undertake it without vocation and appointment by the whole congregation; but in an emergency anyone may use it." (St. L. X:1589.)

3

The Public Ministry Not a Human, but a Divine Institution

It is not a human, but a divine command that Christians perform the works of their spiritual priesthood; accordingly, preach the Gospel not merely in their homes, but also in their intercourse with their brethren and with the world. Likewise it is not merely a human, but a divine regulation that Christians who live at one place fellowship with one another, form a congregation, and appoint men equipped with the necessary teaching ability to preach God's Word in the name of the congregation both publicly (in the public assembly) and privately (to individual Christians).

As Scripture proof we have not only the example of the Apostles, who "ordained them elders in every church" (Acts 14:23) with the duty to supply the congregations publicly and privately with God's Word, but also the practice of Paul, who, when the congregations in Crete had failed to call elders, or bishops, charged Titus, whom he had left there, to ordain such in every congregation. Titus 1:5: "For this cause left I thee in Crete, that thou shouldest set in order the things that are wanting and ordain elders in every city, as I had appointed thee [R. V., "gave thee charge"]." "Elders" and "bishops" designate pastors in Scripture, for these terms are used *promiscue* (Titus 1:5, 7; Acts 20:17, 28).

These elders, or bishops, Scripture describes exactly both as to their personal qualifications and as to their duties. They must not only be Christians, but exemplary Christians, "ensamples to the flock" (1 Pet. 5:3), also "have a good report of them which are without" (1 Tim. 3:7). The virtues which they are to possess, and the vices which they are not to have, are catalogued in 1 Timothy 3 and Titus 1. As far as knowledge of the Christian doctrine and aptitude to teach are concerned, they must be thoroughly familiar with the "sound," that is, pure, doctrine and be able to handle both thesis and antithesis, that is, be able to teach the congregation the truth and to refute heretics (Titus 1:9-11). In describing further the field of their labor and their work the Apostle tells us: They must not only rule well their own house, but also take care of the church of God (1 Tim. 3:5), "feed the church of God" (Acts 20:28) "feed the flock of God which is among you" (1 Pet. 5:1 ff.), "take heed to all the flock" (Acts 20:28), care for individual souls (Acts 20:31: "I ceased not to warn everyone night and day with tears"), "*watch* for . . . souls, as they that must give account" (Heb. 13:17).

Among others Hoefling of Erlangen questioned the teaching that the public ministry is divinely ordained. He contended that what Paul and Barnabas did, Acts 14:23, and Paul commanded, Titus 1:5 ff., was of only temporary and local significance, was intended for primitive conditions and "newly formed congregations" of the Apostolic Church. But this restriction is not in the text. The text does not urge the ordaining of elders, or bishops, because the congregations were young and inexperienced, or "newly formed congregations," but the congregations are described as congregations in which something is lacking as long as they have no elders or bishops as "stewards of God" (θεοῦ οἰκονόμοι). Besides, newly formed or budding congregations are nevertheless real congregations. A congregation is a congregation because of the presence of Christians, even before the office of the public ministry has been filled. It won't do, therefore, to restrict the command to ordain presbyters, or bishops, to temporary and local conditions of the Apostolic day. The safe course indubitably is to say with our Lutheran Symbols: "Wherever the *Church* is [irrespective of age, size, place, or time], there is the authority [command] to administer the Gospel. Therefore it is necessary for the Church [the churches] to retain the authority to call, elect, and ordain ministers" (*Trigl.* 523, Smalc. Art., *ibid.*, 67). We therefore assert that it is not left to Christians whether or not they would establish and support the public ministry among themselves, but that it is their duty according to God's order. Walther expresses it thus: "The ministry, or the pastoral office [*Pfarramt*], is not a human ordinance, but an office established by God Himself." And: "The ministry of preaching is not an arbitrary office, but its character is such that the Church has been commanded to establish it and is ordinarily bound to it till the end of days." *Kirche u. Amt*, p. 193, 211 (*Walther and the Church*, p. 71, 73). The Apology says: "If ordination be understood as applying to the ministry of the Word, we are not unwilling to call ordination a sacrament. For the ministry of the Word has God's command and glorious promises." (*Trigl.* 311, Art. XIII, 11.)

During the middle of the last century there was considerable dispute in the Lutheran Church, particularly in Germany, regarding the divine institution of the public ministry, but the results were unsatisfactory. Only a few, e. g., Stroebel,[4] took the correct Scriptural position against two aberrations. Hoefling of Erlangen grants that the ministry is divinely ordained, but only in the sense as "everything wise, appropriate, morally necessary" can be said to have "divine sanction," not in the sense that an express divine command for the establishment of the public ministry can be shown. Acts 14:23, where Paul and Barnabas ordain elders in the congregations gathered by them, and Titus 1:5, where Paul charges Titus to ordain elders or bishops in the congregations of Crete, Hoefling gets rid of, as we have seen, by declaring without any good grounds that these passages refer to "newly formed congregations," speak of "primitive conditions," from which, therefore, "no dogmatic deductions for all the future may be made."[5] Hoefling's true reason, however, why he feels that he must reject an institution of the ministry by God, is something else. He holds that if one assumes a divine command for the administration of the means of grace by public servants, one carries over into the New Testament Church an Old Testament feature, a legalistic element, a trace of the Old Testament bondage.

This argument refutes itself as soon as it is applied in earnest. It proves too much. For the use and application of the Word of God

---

[4] *Zeitschrift fuer luth. Theol. u. Kirche*, 1852, 699 f.

[5] Hoefling has set forth his doctrine in "*Grundsaetze ev.-luth. Kirchenverfassung*," Erl., 1850. The entire treatise can also be found in "*Erl. Zeitschr.*," 1850, 317 ff. A third edition appeared 1853. Hoefling's position can perhaps be seen best from his article directed against Muenchmeyer. (*Erl. Zeitschr.* 1852, 102 ff.) There is no material difference between the first and the third edition of Hoefling's book. Also in the third edition he says (pp. 75—76) that the ministry of the Word (*geistliche Amt*) itself is a divine institution, but not the public ministry as established by the congregation; that this must rather be classed with human ecclesiastical and liturgical ordinances, "though it developed from inner necessity." P. 274 he repeats that the Apostles had no divine command to appoint presbyters, or bishops; p. 278 the "appointing of a pastor" ("*Amtsbestellung*") — and this includes the establishment of the public ministry by the church — is put on a level with the observance of Sunday. — The literature pertaining to this controversy is very voluminous: Delitzsch, *Vier Buecher v. d. K.*, 1847; Loehe, *Aphorismen*, 1849; Harless, *K. u. A.*, 1853; Wucherer, *Ausfuehrl. Nachweis*, 1853; Kliefoth, *Acht Buecher v. d. K.*, 1854; Muenchmeyer, "*Das Amt d. N. T.*," *Zeitschr. fuer luth. Th. u. K.*, 1852, 46 ff.; *Das Dogma v. d. sichtb. u. unsichtb. K.*, 1854; Floerke, "*Zur L. v. d. K. u. ihrem Amt*," *Zeitschr. fuer luth. Th. u. K.*, 1852, 1 ff.; Preger, *Die Gesch. d. L. v. geistl. Amt*, 1857 (fine collection of words of Luther, pp. 170—192; criticism of the position of Loehe, p. 192 ff., of Kliefoth, p. 216 ff.); Kraussold, *Amt u. Gem.*, 1858; Dieckhoff, *Luthers L. v. d. kirchl. Gewalt*, 1865; Vilmar, *Erl. Zeitschr.*, Sept., 1859; *Die Lehre v. geistl. Amt*, 1870.

by all Christians as spiritual priests there also is not merely an "inner moral necessity," but besides that an express divine command. All Christians should search the Scriptures, should read the Scriptures, should let the Word of Christ dwell among them, should show forth the praises of God, etc. Here, too, we are dealing with imperatives, therefore with a divine arrangement in the sense of a divine command. If, now, a divine command involved a trace of the Old Testament bondage, we would also have to deny a divine order for the use of the means of grace by all Christians to preserve Christians from drifting into legalism. Also for Baptism and the Lord's Supper there is not merely an "inner moral necessity," but an express divine command. But we would not for that reason think of asserting that a "legalistic trait" attaches to Baptism and the Lord's Supper and, on that account, with modern theologians, deny the divine command or institution of Baptism and the Lord's Supper.[6] Likewise regarding sanctification and good works Scripture teaches not merely an "inner moral necessity," but also a divine will expressed in precept and command.[7] But we do not think of asserting that by such commands Scripture is training Christians to take a legalistic view of sanctification and good works.

In short, Hoefling declares two things to be contradictory which are not in conflict. The divine command, or order, to do a certain thing is not tainted with a "legalistic trait," as Hoefling imagines. In his case, of course, this notion is bound up with the peculiar nature of the Erlangen theology. He expressly refers to the consensus of all his colleagues (*Erl. Zeitschrift*, 1852, 152) and appeals in particular to the Scripture proof which Hofmann is supposed to have furnished for his (Hoefling's) doctrine (*Grundsaetze*, 1850, 50). Hofmann's position is that in presenting the Christian doctrine the theologian must for the first entirely disregard the Bible and permit his "regenerate" ego, or self, to formulate the truth "independently." If one would take the Christian doctrine not from one's own heart, but from an outside source, from Holy Scripture, the doctrine would get the stamp of the Law, and Scripture would become "a collection of faith precepts." (*Schriftbeweis* I, 9 ff.) Only after the "regenerate ego" has

---

[6] Some modern theologians do deny this institution, as we have noted in the doctrines of Baptism and the Lord's Supper. They grant that Baptism and the Lord's Supper were customs in the Apostolic Church, but as the result of free development from Jewish and Gentile analogies rather than because of divine institution.

[7] 1 Thess. 4:3: "the will [θέλημα] of God"; 1 John 3:23: "His commandment [ἐντολή]."

stated its convictions from inner necessity and autonomously, should the product be compared with Scripture and the necessary corrections be made. However, Hofmann did not correct his ego product afterwards. On the contrary, he "corrected" the Scriptures according to the product he had developed with inner necessity out of his own heart, and so much so that he even eliminated the *satisfactio vicaria*.

Hoefling fared similarly. To support his denial of the divine command for the establishment of the ministry, he claims that the Apostolic example and command pertaining to the appointment and installation of elders, or bishops, applied only to the Apostolic age and congregations newly formed. We have seen that Scripture says nothing of such a restriction. He further claims, for the same purpose, that the functions of the office of presbyters, or bishops, in the days of the Apostles are not defined in Scripture. We have shown above that Scripture states very exactly and minutely both what qualifications the elders, or bishops, must have and what they are to do. Hoefling also says that the office of presbyter in the Apostolic age was rather a "governing" (*regiminale*) office. But Scripture declares, as we have seen, that the teaching of God's Word and the refutation of error is the principal work of the presbyters, or bishops.

One is inclined to judge Hoefling less severely because his opponents (Muenchmeyer, Loehe, Kliefoth, etc.) taught a strongly Romanizing doctrine of the ministry, namely, that the office of the public ministry is not conferred by the call of the congregation as the original possessor of all spiritual power, but is a divine institution in the sense that it was transmitted immediately from the Apostles to their pupils, considered as a separate "ministerial order" or caste, and that this order perpetuates itself by means of the ordination. Some also spoke as if the means of grace exerted their full power and efficacy only when they were administered by men of this "order." Against this caricature of the public ministry Hoefling correctly argues that it makes the officiant a "means of grace" alongside Word and Sacrament: "The believers might see themselves with their spiritual needs referred not so much to Word and Sacrament as rather to the organ (the minister) divinely privileged to administer and distribute them. The full efficacy of the means of grace appears dependent on an external legal institution; the Holy Ghost now operates not so much in and through the means of grace as rather through the nomistic organs of their administration."

But Hoefling's polemics do not hold good against the public ministry as taught in our Lutheran Symbols. The circumstance that this office has God's command (*mandatum Dei*) no more makes its public servants "means of grace" or "nomistic organs" than all Christians become means of grace and nomistic organs by the fact that their teaching is likewise done in obedience to God's command and ordinance. Moreover, though the Lutherans teach a *mandatum Dei* for the public ministry, they at the same time maintain and very emphatically stress that the power and efficacy of the means of grace does not at all depend on the persons of the public servants, but that the means of grace have all power in themselves, no matter whether they are administered by believers or godless, laymen or clergymen, duly called pastors or usurpers, the Pope or the emperor, or a youth, etc. It is a false deduction that the teaching of a divine institution of the ministry has the tendency to make "means of grace," in addition to the regular means, of the men filling the office of the ministry. It is just the other way around. When it is maintained, on the one hand, that the means of grace have their power and efficacy from their institution by God, and, on the other hand, that like all Christians also their public servants administer the means of grace by God's order, this very fact of their divine institution will induce all served by the means to disregard entirely the state of the human person administering them and to look solely to the means of grace, as though God in person dealt with them.

In short, Hoefling did not succeed in keeping his balance in opposing a coarse Romanizing error. Thoroughly to refute the immediate divine establishment of the public ministry as Loehe and others taught it, he thought it necessary to deny that the mediate establishment of this office through the congregation is God's ordinance or has divine command. Stroebel [8] gives this summary of the Lutheran doctrine, thereby excluding both Loehe's and Hoefling's doctrine: "Our Church's teaching of the ministerial office is, in short, this: To tell his neighbor the Word of God, to apply the Sacraments to him, to forgive his sins, to lay our hands upon him, these things are every baptized Christian's divine right as a spiritual priest (in case of need, his peremptory duty); however, for the sake of God-pleasing order, he should exercise his right only in case of emergency, normally making use of the service of the pastors regularly called by Christ through the congregation. The Christian congregation should know that it should not abolish the ministerial office ordained by the Lord, nor permit the raving rabble or spiritual or secular tyrants to enslave it, but should ever again fill this office with capable, faithful, pious men until the

---

[8] *Zeitschr. f. luth. Th. u. K.*, 1852, 699.

Lord returns. And the pastors should take this comfort firmly to heart in all trials, that their office received from the congregation is as surely a divine office, to be administered solely in the name of Christ, as if they had been given it directly by Christ. For this is an illogical deduction: He who did not receive the ministerial office directly from the Lord, but from the congregation, has it merely from men and is a servant of men." [9]

4

The Necessity of the Public Ministry

Though the public ministry, which the congregation confers mediately by a call, must be maintained as a divine ordinance, still no absolute necessity dare be ascribed to it. The Holy Ghost is active to generate and sustain faith in the hearts of men also when lay Christians preach the Gospel from inner necessity as well as according to God's command. The preaching of the Word by Christians in their homes, in their intercourse with their brethren and with the world, is not left to their option or caprice, but is God's order. This fact must be stressed unceasingly. In so far as Christians fail to bear witness, they are forgetting their Christian calling and doing the Christian Church untold harm. There have been times — and such times may come again — when unbelief and false doctrine so overran external Christendom that orthodox Christians had to depend on the preaching of the Word in the homes. Of this Luther says: "It may happen that the world will become so utterly epicurean that we shall have no public ministry in all the world and the preaching will be solely epicurean outrage and that the Gospel will be preserved only in the homes by the fathers" (St. L. VI:938).

The Word of God is a means of grace also when merely read. See the full discussion, also over against modern Lutherans, p. 106 ff. Walther points to the words of the Formula of Concord: "The ministry of the Church, the Word preached and heard" (*Trigl.* 1101, Sol. Decl., XII, 30), and: "The Word, whereby we are called, is a ministration of the Spirit" (*Trigl.* 1073, Sol. Decl., XI, 29), and then adds: "This is important in view of those who make a means of grace of the

---

[9] Rejection of the teaching of Hoefling in *Lehre und Wehre*, 1870, 174. Rejection of the position of Loehe, etc., throughout the article "*Antithesen zu d. Thesen v. K. u. A.*," *Lehre und Wehre*, 1870, 161 ff. The first article in Vol. I of *Lehre und Wehre*, 1855, 1 ff., disavows both Loehe's and Hoefling's teaching.

public ministry and co-ordinate it with the Word and the Sacraments and assert that it is absolutely necessary for salvation to every man, so that without the service of an ordained pastor a man can neither come to faith nor obtain absolution for his sins, while our Church asserts this only of the written or outward Word in contrast to an alleged inner word and to every form of 'enthusiasm' " (*Kirche u. Amt,* p. 195).

But the truth that the public ministry is not absolutely necessary dare not be made an excuse for despising this office. The ministry is despised (1) when Christians are remiss in hearing the public preaching of God's Word on the ground that they can read the same Word "at home";[10] (2) when the incumbents of the office are slack in doing their duty and offer the excuse that the flock committed to their care can and should provide its own spiritual food, since Christians are spiritual priests;[11] (3) when Christians are slow to erect and maintain schools for the training of men for public service in the Church.[12]

5

The Call into the Public Ministry

Of the necessity of a call, already mentioned in Chapter Two of this section, Luther says: "It would not be seemly for anyone to put himself forward and appropriate as his alone what belongs to us all." And in the Augsburg Confession we read: "Of Ecclesiastical Order they teach that no one should publicly teach in the Church or administer the Sacraments unless he be regularly called" (*Trigl.* 49, XIV).[13]

---

10 Luther's blunt reproof of this mischief in the Church: "Some smart wise-acres say: But we have books from which we can read it just as well as hear it from the preacher in church. You read down the devil on your head, who is then controlling you. If our Lord God had known that the ministry was superfluous, He certainly would have been so wise and sage not to have had Moses preach to you. . . . He would also in our day surely tell the preachers and pastors to stay at home." (St. L. III:1736).

11 About the want of application on the part of preachers the Church of all ages has had cause to complain. This prompts the admonitions and warnings of Scripture in the Old and New Testaments: Ezek. 3:17 ff.; 33:7 ff.; Is. 56:10 ff.; 2 Tim. 4:2 ff.; 1 Tim. 4:13 ff.; Phil. 2:21. Cp. Luther, St. L. X:5.

12 The best that has been written against this dereliction are Luther's *"A Sermon on Keeping Children in School"* (St. L. X:417) and *"To the Councilmen of All Cities in Germany that They Should Establish and Maintain Christian Schools."* (*Ibid.,* 458 ff.)

13 On the necessity of a call compare the entire section in Walther's *Pastorale,* p. 23 ff. (Fritz, *Pastoral Theology,* p. 32).

The usual distinction between an immediate and a mediate call (*vocatio immediata et mediata*) is Scriptural. Also Luther has it and substantiates it copiously. (St. L. XI:1910 ff.) The Prophets and Apostles, also Paul (Acts 22:21), were called immediately. Paul lays great stress on his immediate call in the headings of his Epistles (Gal. 1:1; Eph. 1:1; Col. 1:1, etc.). The teaching elders or pastors called by the congregation have a mediate call. It is of the greatest importance to bear in mind that the mediate call is no less divine than the immediate. Acts 20:28 says of the mediately called elders, or bishops, of the congregation at Ephesus: "The Holy Ghost hath made you overseers to feed the church of God." This realization is very important for both the public servants and those whom they serve with the Word. See Walther, *Pastorale,* p. 29 f., for details.

Who are the agents through whom God appoints the preachers? This question has aroused great commotion and controversy in and outside the Church. The Pope vociferously claims that only he can make "priests" through the bishops made by him. The Anglicans contend that clerics are made by bishops who have the stamp of the Apostolic Succession upon them. Romanizing Lutherans hold that legitimate servants of the Church can be appointed only by a self-perpetuating "holy order of the ministry." Also political rulers have deemed it their prerogative to appoint preachers without consent of the parishes.

Scripture teaches that neither the Pope, nor the bishops, nor the clergy as an order, nor individual persons within or outside a congregation have the right and authority to confer the public office of the Word, but solely the people to whom is given all spiritual power on earth and to whom Word and Sacrament in particular have been entrusted originally; and these are the believers, or the Christians, and nobody else in the world. The believers possess all things (1 Cor. 3:21); the unbelievers nothing but death and eternal doom. In Matt. 28:18-20 not only the Apostles as such, but the Christians to the Last Day are charged with the administration of Word and Baptism. This is apparent from the closing words: "And, lo, I am with you alway even unto the end of the world." And so in the command pertaining to the Lord's Supper, "This do in remembrance of Me," not only the Apostles as such are addressed, but the Christians to the end of time. This is the interpretation given these words by Paul, who says (1 Cor. 11:26): "As often as ye eat this bread and drink this cup, ye do show the Lord's death till He come." This is the Scripture doctrine so clearly stated in the words of the Smalcald Articles: "For wherever the Church is, there is the authority [command] to administer the Gospel. Therefore it is necessary for the Church ["*die Kirchen*"] to retain the authority to call, elect, and ordain ministers. And this authority is a gift which properly is given to the Church [*proprie* — only to the Church and to no one else], which no human power can wrest from the Church. . . . Here belong the statements of Christ which testify that the keys have been given to the Church [German: "*der ganzen Kirche*" — to every Christian] and not merely to certain persons, Matt. 18:20: 'Where two or three are gathered together in My name,' etc." (*Trigl.* 523, Power and Jurisdiction of Bishops, 67—69.) Individual persons and boards can indeed extend a valid call, but only when they are commissioned to do so by those whose the power originally (*principaliter et immediate*) is, or when these have, at least, given their silent consent. The Smalcald Articles do not, of course, refer to the Church Universal, scattered over the whole world (*ecclesia universalis*), with the phrase "given to the Church," but to the congregation (*ecclesia particularis*), as the passage added indicates: "Where two or three are gathered together in My name, there am I in the midst of them." For the Church possesses all spiritual treasures and privileges, not inasmuch as it is large or small, but inasmuch as it consists of believers.[14]

Against a congregational election of the pastor the following objections have been voiced:

1. The favorite objection is that in Acts 14:23 and Titus 1:5 nothing is said of a calling or choosing by the congregation, but that, on the contrary, these passages only tell what Paul and Barnabas did and what Titus was to do at Paul's command; that no autonomous activity, or even co-operation, of the congregations is indicated. Luther correctly reminds us: "Though Paul charges Titus to ordain pastors, it does not follow from this that Titus appointed them independently, by his own authority, but rather that he ordained them in accord with

---

14 Luther says on Matt. 18:19-20: "Here we hear that also two or three assembled in Christ's name have the same power over everything which St. Peter and all the Apostles have. For the Lord Himself is present, as He says, too, John 14:23: 'If a man love Me, he will keep My words, and My Father will love him, and We will come unto him and make Our abode with him.' . . . We here have present the Lord Himself, the Lord of all angels and creatures; it is He who says that all are to have equal authority, keys, and office, even two common Christians by themselves, when gathered in His name. Of this Lord the Pope and all devils shall not make a fool, liar, or drunkard, but we will trample on the Pope and declare that he is a confirmed liar, blasphemer, and idolatrous devil, who under St. Peter's name has arrogated the keys to himself alone, while Christ has given them equally to all in common." (St. L. XVII:1074.)

the example of the Apostles by the vote of the people; else the words of Paul would conflict with the practice of the Apostles" (St. L. XIX:347).

Moreover, the word used Acts 14:23, χειϱοτονήσαντες, clearly states that in ordaining the elders a vote or election by the congregation took place. Meyer translates χειϱοτονεῖν with "stimmwaehlen." To quote: "Paul and Barnabas chose by vote ["stimmwaehlten"] presbyters for them, that is, they directed their election by vote in the congregations." To explain this translation, Meyer adds: "The analogy of Acts 6:2-6 demands this connotation of the word 'chosen,' a word that, taken from the ancient method of voting by raising of hands, occurs only here and 2 Cor. 8:19 in the New Testament, and this analogy forbids the wider sense constituebant [appointed, placed] (Vulgata, Hammond, Kuinoel, and many), or eligebant [chose for them], (de Wette), so that the appointment took place entirely by Apostolic authority (Loehe). . . . Correctly Erasmus: suffragiis delectos [those on whom it was conferred by suffrage]. . . . Most arbitrarily false the Catholics: it referred to the χειϱοθεσία [laying on of hands] in the ordination of presbyters." History shows, too, that for a long time in the Church of the first centuries public ministers were appointed by congregational vote. The remark of the Smalcald Articles: "Formerly the people elected pastors and bishops" (Trigl. 525, ibid., 70), can be proved to be historically correct.[15]

2. The objection that in Matt. 16:18-19 the keys of the kingdom of heaven were given originally not to the believers, but only to Peter as a special privilege, has been fully refuted above, p. 413, footnote 18. In this passage Peter comes into consideration only in so far as he believes, not in so far as he is an Apostle or a privileged person. Note also that the "keys of the kingdom of heaven" are nothing else, and can be nothing else, than the means of grace, the Gospel. Through the offer of the Gospel, and through nothing else, Christians remit sins and thus open heaven; through withholding the Gospel, they retain sins and thus lock heaven. Now, since the believers are the persons to whom Christ has entrusted the means of grace, they have eo ipso been given the keys of the kingdom of heaven.[16]

---

[15] See Walther, K. u. A., p. 281 ff. Walther (p. 248 ff.) proves that all Lutheran theologians teach that without the election, at least the consent, of the congregation no one can become the pastor of a congregation.

[16] Chemnitz: "Luther taught from the Word of God that Christ delivered and entrusted the keys, that is, the administration of Word and Sacraments, to the whole Church" (Examen, 1667, p. 223). Cp. Walther against Kraussold, Lehre und Wehre, 1870, 179, note.

3. Against the right of the congregation to choose its pastor has been adduced also the statement of the Smalcald Articles "that the office of the ministry proceeds from the general call of the Apostles" (*Trigl.* 507, Power and Primacy of Pope, 10). But this statement does not deny that the ministry is conferred through the call of the congregation: For the same Symbol says: "Therefore it is necessary for the Church [*die Kirchen*] to retain the authority to call, elect, and ordain ministers" (*Trigl.* 523, Power and Jurisdiction of Bishops, 67). The office of the Apostles and the office of the later teachers of the Church is identical in content and power. As the Apostles were commanded not to preach their own word, but God's Word, so the public servants called by the congregation are charged to teach not their own, but God's Word. There is, indeed, this great difference between the Apostles and their "pupils," as Luther calls all post-Apostolic preachers, that the former spoke and wrote the Word of God infallibly, while the latter must take from the Apostles the Word which they preach and are so strictly confined to the Word of the Apostles that Christians are commanded to avoid any teachers who depart from that Word (Rom. 16:17). But in both cases it is the same office, inasmuch as both are concerned only with the public preaching of the Word of God and transmit the same spiritual gifts. Hence that list of Scripture passages in which the Apostles put themselves in one class with the elders, or bishops, e. g., Peter, who says (1 Pet. 5:1 ff.): "The elders which are among you I exhort, who am also an elder [συνπρεσβύτερος]"; and Paul says (1 Cor. 4:1): "Let a man so account of *us*, as of the ministers of Christ and stewards of the mysteries of God." See also 2 John 1; 3 John 1; 1 Cor. 3:5 ff., etc.

6

The Rite of Ordination

Ordination to the ministry by the laying on of hands and prayers is not a divine ordinance, but a church custom or ceremony, for, although it is mentioned in Holy Writ, it is not commanded (1 Tim. 4:14; 5:22; 2 Tim. 1:6; Acts 6:6; 8:17).[17] Hence it belongs to the adiaphorous practices. A candidate for the ministry becomes a pastor

---

17 Walther, *Pastorale*, p. 65: "Scripture indeed mentions ordination, but says nothing of a divine institution of this custom. But in the question Is it a divine institution? the proof *a silentio* is, of course, valid."

not by his ordination, but by his call and its acceptance. Familiar are the words of Luther: "The whole matter depends on whether the congregation and the bishop are in accord, that is, whether the congregation wishes to be taught by the bishop and the bishop is willing to teach the congregation. This willingness settles the matter. The laying on of hands blesses, ratifies, and witnesses this agreement as a notary public and witnesses testify to a secular matter and as a pastor in blessing groom and bride ratifies their marriage and testifies that they have previously taken one another and made this public." (St. L. XVII:114.) The Smalcald Articles expressly declare ordination to be a public ratification of the call: "Formerly the people elected pastors and bishops. Then came a bishop, either of that church or a neighboring one, who confirmed the one elected by the laying on of hands; and ordination was nothing else than such a ratification." (*Trigl.* 525, *ibid.*, 70.) For this reason we do not practice the so-called absolute ordination, that is, ordination of a person before he has received and accepted a call, because it is apt to foster the notion "that by the ordination a man is admitted to the so-called 'order of the ministry' and that only as an ordained priest he is eligible for a charge" (Walther, *Pastorale*, 65 [18] [Fritz, *Pastoral Theology*, 62]). The authority to ordain is, of course, a power delegated by the congregation, as the Smalcald Articles say: "The true Church certainly has the right to elect and ordain ministers since it alone has the priesthood" (*Trigl.* 525, *ibid.*, 69).[19]

Astounding things are taught about ordination within visible Christendom. Rome asserts there is no other way of becoming a "priest" than through ordination received from a bishop created by the Pope. Those called and appointed merely by the Christian congregation are not servants of the Church, but are to be regarded as thieves and robbers (*Trid., de Sacram. ord.,* Sess. 23, c. 4). This zeal for ordination is a zeal *pro domo;* for the things supposedly effected by the ordination are most valuable for the kingdom of the Pope. Not only does ordination *ex opere operato* impart the Holy Ghost and impress a *character indelebilis,* but, above all, it confers the power which neither the angels nor the Virgin Mary have, namely, the power

---

[18] For some quotations cautioning against either overestimating ordination or despising it see Walther, *Pastorale*, p. 65 f.; Baier-Walther, III, 699 f.

[19] Cp. Balduin, Baier-Walther, III, 702; likewise Huelsemann: "The power to ordain does not inhere in some member of the Church, e. g., the bishop, as a permanent condition or character, but as a commission and transitory power, such as a plenipotentiary or envoy with a diplomatic mission receives from his chief." *Praelect. in libr. Conc.,* p. 838.

to celebrate Mass, that is, to produce (*conficere*) the body and blood of Christ as a propitiatory sacrifice for the quick and the dead and thus to secure for the Pope dominion over the consciences of men and access to the treasures of this world. (*Trid., ibid.*, c. 1–4, can. 1–8.) The Episcopalians, needless to say, omit the Pope; none the less they insist upon it that legitimate bishops, priests, and deacons, whose administration of the functions of the ministry is valid, can be made only by bishops of an uninterrupted Apostolic Succession ordaining them.[20] Also Romanizing Lutherans, who refuse to concede that the call extended by a congregation makes a man a minister, but conceive of the ministry as a "distinct Christian order" which perpetuates itself by conferring the office on new members at their initiation, naturally declare ordination to be a divine ordinance.[21]

7

The Ministry No Special Spiritual Order
Superior to That of the Christians

Luther at times follows the custom of his day and calls the public servants of the Church *"geistlicher Stand"* (spiritual order), *"Geist-liche"* (divines), and "priests." (St. L. X:423 f.; XIX:113 f.; etc.) But at other times he calls attention to the fact that these names are not taken from Scripture and are very misleading. Scripture says that all those in whom the Holy Ghost dwells and works through faith in Christ, that is, all Christians, and they alone, are the "spiritual order" or spiritual people (*"Geistliche"*). Not of a smaller circle within the Christian Church, but of all Christians does Scripture assert the "anointing" (τὸ χρίσμα) which "teacheth you of all things" (1 John 2:27). All Christians are "spiritual" (πνευματικοί), Gal. 6:1, and are called "a spiritual house (οἶκος πνευματικός), an holy priesthood (ἱεράτευμα ἅγιον)," 1 Pet. 2:5. It is therefore really an unscriptural usage to call a limited number of people within the Christian Church, namely, the officeholders, the "spiritual order," "divines," "priests." Luther says: "In the New Testament the Holy Spirit scrupulously avoids giving the name *sacerdos*, priest, to any of the Apostles, or any

---

[20] "Form and Manner of Making, Ordaining, and Consecrating Bishops, Priests, and Deacons." Preface. *The Book of Common Prayer*, Philadelphia, 1854, p. 612.

[21] See Grosse, *Unterscheidungslehren*, 1891, pp. 13, 8.

other office, but restricts this name to the baptized or Christians as their birthright and hereditary name from Baptism; for none of us is born in Baptism an Apostle, preacher, teacher, pastor, but solely priests are all of us born; therefore we take some from among these born priests and call and elect them for these offices that they may perform the functions of such office in the name of all of us." (St. L. XIX:1260.)

The incumbents of the public ministry are correctly called the public servants among the Christians (*ministrantes inter Christianos*). The Word and Sacrament, in which they minister, are and remain the immediate property of the congregation, and merely the administration of them in the name of all is delegated to these certain persons by the congregation. In this sense Scripture calls the incumbents of the public ministry not only God's or Christ's ministers (1 Cor. 4:1; Titus 1:7; 2 Tim. 2:24; Luke 12:42), but also ministers, or servants, of the congregation. 2 Cor. 4:5: "And ourselves your servants for Jesus' sake [δοῦλοι ὑμῶν διὰ 'Ιησοῦν]." After saying that the appellation "priest" has been "taken over to the great harm of the Church" from the pagans or the Jews, Luther adds: "But according to the evangelical Scriptures it would be much better to call them ministers, deacons, bishops, stewards. . . . Paul also calls himself *servum*, that is, a servant; he also says more than once: 'Servio in Evangelio,' I serve [minister] in the Gospel. This he does by no means to set up a caste or an order, an authority or a special rank, as our Scholastics assume, but only to praise the office and work and to reserve the privilege and honor of the priesthood for the congregation." (St. L. X:1590 f.) Walther: "The public ministry is not a special order, distinct from and holier than the common order of Christians, as the priesthood of the Levites was, but is an office of service" (*Kirche u. Amt,* p. 221 [*Walther and the Church,* p. 73]). In this sense, too, the Smalcald Articles say that "the Church is above the ministers" (*Trigl.* 507, Power and Primacy of Pope, 11). The Church and its ministers have the same relation to each other as employer and employee or owner and steward.

This relation also is the reason why the congregation has the authority and obligation to supervise the official conduct of its public servants and to dismiss them from office when they no longer possess the required qualifications, become guilty of willful misconduct, or are no longer able to execute the functions of their office (Col. 4:17; John 10:5; Rom. 16:17-18; Matt. 7:15). Contending also against the Roman *character indelebilis,* Luther writes of the power of a congregation to dismiss its minister: "If, then, all of them are servants, their priestly, indelible mark also disappears, and the perpetuity of their priestly dignity, or that one must always remain a priest, is also pure fiction, for a servant may justly be deposed if he cannot be induced to be faithful. Again, he may be left in office as long as he serves well and it pleases the congregation, just as anyone in the secular sphere who administers a public office among his equals; yes, there is far more reason to dismiss a servant in the spiritual sphere than in the secular field; for the former, when he becomes unfaithful, is much more insufferable than an unfaithful worldly servant, who can damage merely the temporal goods of this life, while the spiritual servant ruins and destroys also the eternal goods." (St. L. X:1591.)

It is surprising that even some Lutherans criticize the statement that the public office is committed (*"uebertragen"*) to qualified men by the congregations through the issuance of a call. But the term must be declared adequate if only the teaching of Scripture is maintained that Word and Sacraments have been entrusted by Christ to all Christians for possession and administration. If it is furthermore granted that there is to be among Christians an office of the Word in which one or more persons apt to teach are to serve the congregation, this office can be established only by commission. Even the rationalist Hase declares it to be "the teaching of the Evangelical Church" that "in Christ and in the congregation is the source of all authority in the Church. For this reason every office in the Church is only committed, in case of misuse reverts to the congregation, and in an emergency every spiritual rite can be executed by any member of the congregation." (*Ev. Dogm.*, 3d ed., 494.) Besides, the term "committed" is used frequently by our old Lutheran theologians.[22]

Hase says correctly that "evangelical teaching" makes the congregation the source of all authority in the Church. All that the pastors of a congregation do as pastors is delegated, that is, is done solely at

---

[22] See the quotations in Walther, *K. u. A.*, p. 327 ff. Brenz in his commentary on John 20: "The Church has its ministers, to whom the public administration of the Gospel, that is, the remitting and retaining of sin, is entrusted [*demandata est*]." Polycarp Leyser in his *Evangelienharmonie*, ch. 92, 1748: "This power (to loose and to bind) is in Matt. 18:18 given by Christ to the church, which can in an orderly manner legitimately hand it over [*deferre*] to persons called for this purpose." Huelsemann, *Praelect. in libr. Conc.*, p. 838, says that also the power to ordain inheres in the congregation and other persons have this authority only *per modum commissionis*, by way of commitment. Balduin, *Tractatus de cas. consc.*, p. 1104: "As the keys are given by the lord of the house to his wife, so Christ, too, as the Lord of His house, has given the keys to His betrothed, who then commits [*committit*] them to her servants, who are called the stewards, or administrators, of the mysteries of God."

the command of the congregation. This is true in particular when they pronounce excommunication.[23] The Smalcald Articles say: "It is certain that the common jurisdiction of excommunicating those guilty of manifest crimes belongs to all pastors." But this is not to be done "without due process of law." (*Trigl.* 525, Power and Jurisdiction of Bishops, 74; 521, 60.) This "due process of law" includes, above all things, the hearing of each case by the congregation and the verdict of the congregation. Luther's strong term for an excommunication which has been pronounced without investigation and verdict by the congregation is well known. (St. L. XIX:950 ff.) He says: "The congregation which is to treat him as excommunicated should know and be convinced that he has deserved and fallen under the ban, as this text of Christ (Matt. 18:17-18) states; else it may be deceived and accept a lying ban and thus do the neighbor wrong. . . . Here, where the souls are concerned, the congregation, too, should be judge and mistress." Loescher correctly states as Lutheran doctrine that the congregation passes judgment and pronounces the excommunication, while the pastor as the public servant of the congregation declares, or proclaims, the excommunication.[24]

8

The Authority (Potestas) of the Public Ministry

Since the ministry is the office of teaching God's Word, while man's word is forbidden in the Christian Church, obedience as to God Himself is due the ministry as far as it proclaims the Word of God. Heb. 13:17: "Obey them that have the rule over you, and submit yourselves" (πείθεσθε τοῖς ἡγουμένοις ὑμῶν καὶ ὑπείκετε); Luke 10:16: "He that heareth you heareth Me, and he that despiseth you despiseth Me." To obey pastors beyond God's Word is not commanded, but strictly forbidden to Christians (Matt. 23:8; Rom. 16:17). Also *adiaphora* are not decided by the pastor or the pastors, but settled by the entire congregation of any place by mutual agreement *(per mutuum consensum)*. See p. 427.

Against the appeal of the Romanists to Heb. 13:17; Luke 10:16,

---

[23] Walther, *Pastorale*, pp. 315—354 (Fritz, *Pastoral Theology*, p. 240 ff.), where the whole doctrine of church discipline and excommunication is presented.

[24] *Fortgesetzte Sammlung*, etc., 1724, p. 476; in Walther, *Pastorale*, p. 325. On the rejection of this doctrine by some American Lutherans see the quotations in Grosse, *Unterscheidungslehren*, p. 5 f.

etc., the Apology says: "For it is certain that the expression Luke 10:16: 'He that heareth you heareth Me,' does not speak of traditions, but is chiefly directed against traditions. For it is not a *mandatum cum libera* (a bestowal of unlimited authority), as they call it, but it is a *cautio de rato* (a caution concerning something prescribed), namely, concerning the special command . . . , i. e., the testimony given to the Apostles, that we believe them with respect to the word of another, not their own. . . . 'He that heareth you heareth Me' cannot be understood of traditions. For Christ requires that they teach in such a way that [by their mouth] He Himself be heard, because He says: 'He heareth Me.' Therefore He wishes His own voice, His own Word, to be heard, not human traditions. Thus a saying which is most especially in our favor, and contains the most important consolation and doctrine, these stupid men pervert to the most trifling matters, the distinctions of food, vestments, and the like. They quote also Heb. 13:17: 'Obey them that have the rule over you.' This passage requires obedience to the Gospel, for it does not establish a dominion for the bishops apart from the Gospel. Neither should the bishops frame traditions contrary to the Gospel, or interpret their traditions contrary to the Gospel. And when they do this, obedience is prohibited, according to Gal. 1:9: 'If any man preach any other gospel, let him be accursed.' " (*Trigl.* 449, XXVIII, 18 ff.)

9

The Equality of the Servants of the Church

The fundamental truth that Christ is the one and only Master in the Church regulates also the relation of the servants of the Church to one another. As the servants of the Church are not lords of the congregations, so neither of one another. Superiority or subordination among them is not a divine, but a human arrangement. "Neither is the Pope superior to the bishops," says Luther, "nor the bishop superior to the presbyters by divine right."

The opposite teaching of the Papists,[25] of the Anglicans,[26] and

---

25 *Trid.*, Sess. XXIII, *de sacramento ordinis*, can. 6, 7, 8: "If anyone saith that in the Catholic Church there is not a hierarchy by divine ordination instituted, consisting of bishops, priests, and ministers; let him be anathema. If anyone saith that bishops are not superior to priests . . . let him be anathema. If anyone saith that the bishops who are assumed [for the office] by authority of the Roman Pontiff, are not legitimate and true bishops, but are a human figment; let him be

of other Romanizing Protestants [27] has no foundation whatever in Scripture. As for the alleged specific difference between presbyters and bishops, note that Scripture calls pastors at one place presbyters, at another, bishops (Acts 20:17, 28; Titus 1:5, 7).[28] In short, there is no room in the Church for the rule of man, under whatever name or pretext it may be exercised, because only Christ rules the Church through His Word.

10

The Ministry the Highest Office in the Church

Luther often calls the public ministry the highest office in the Church. In what sense the ministry is the highest office he takes pains to explain. In the Church everything should be done in accord with

---

anathema." Waterworth, p. 174. [See also *Pop. Symb.*, pp. 190, 111, 144, 115, 162.] The *Roman Catechism* (II, 7, qu. 25) enumerates priests, bishops, archbishops, patriarchs, and then places over all of them the Pope as the "visible head and governor of the Church." "He is the archbishop of the entire world, father and patriarch of the earth, sitting in the seat of the prince of the Apostles and possessing the highest degree of dignity and jurisdiction, which he owes to no synod or other human arrangements."

[26] Cp. Guenther, *Symb.*, p. 370, where the prayers at the induction of deacons, priests, and bishops are given.

[27] The Irvingites teach a fourfold office instituted by Christ: Apostles, bishops, priests, deacons (*ibid.*, p. 370 [*Pop. Symb.*, pp. 324, 327, 351]).

[28] Alford remarks on 1 Tim. 3:1: "The ἐπίσκοποι of the New Testament have officially nothing in common with our bishops. The identity of the ἐπίσκοπος and πρεσβύτερος in apostolic times is evident from Titus 1:5-7." In connection with Acts 20:17 he points out what manipulations were practiced very early in the Church and later in England to make the Scripture passages favor Episcopalism. Alford says: "τοὺς πρεσβυτέρους, called v. 28 ἐπισκόπους. This circumstance began very early to contradict the growing views of the apostolic institution and necessity of prelatical episcopacy. Thus Irenaeus III, 14. 2, p. 201: 'To the *episcopis et presbyteris*, who came from Ephesus and the other near-by communities.' Here we see, 1. the two, bishops and presbyters, distinguished as if both were sent forth that the titles might not seem to belong to the same persons, and 2. other neighboring churches also brought in, in order that there might not seem to be ἐπίσκοποι in one church only. That neither of these was the case is clearly shown by the plain words of this verse: He sent to Ephesus and summoned the elders of the church. So early did interested and disingenuous interpretations begin to cloud the light which Scripture might have thrown on ecclesiastical questions. The E. V. [English Version] had hardly dealt fairly in this case with the sacred text in rendering ἐπισκόπους, v. 28, 'overseers,' whereas it ought there, as in all other places, to have been bishops, that the fact of elders and bishops having been originally and apostolically synonymous might be apparent to the ordinary English reader, which now it is not."

the Word of God; in other words, everything should be ruled by God's Word as norm. If, now, the office of the Word in a Christian congregation is committed to a man, his office is to teach how all other offices in the congregation are to be administered. Luther writes: "If the office of the Word is conferred on a man, there are conferred on him all offices which are administered in the Church through the Word, such as the power to baptize, to bless [bread and wine, administer Communion, St. L. X:1576], to bind and to loose, to pray, to examine, or judge. For the office of preaching the Gospel is the highest among them all; for it is the true Apostolic office, laying the foundation of all other offices, on which it is proper to build all the others, namely, the offices of teacher, of prophet, of governors, of those who have the gift of healing." (*Ibid.*, 1592, 1806.) Describing a bishop, who according to 1 Tim. 3:5 is to take care of the church [congregation] of God, Luther observes: "Now, these are the men who should supervise all offices, that the teachers tend to their office, are not negligent, that the deacons distribute the gifts fairly and are not remiss" (St. L. XII:338). Again: "To whom ever the office of preaching is committed, to him the highest office in Christendom is committed: he may then also baptize, celebrate Mass [the Lord's Supper], and perform all the cure of souls [*Seelsorge*]; or, if he prefers not to, he may tend only to the preaching and leave the baptizing and other auxiliary functions to others, as Christ did, and Paul, and all Apostles, Acts 6" (St. L. X:1548).[29]

11

The Antichrist

Scripture uses the term "antichrist" in a wider and in a narrow sense. In the passage 1 John 2:18 all false teachers are called "antichrists" (ἀντίχριστοι πολλοὶ γεγόνασιν). Scripture shows clearly enough why all false teachers are "antichrists." Since Scripture enjoins that in Christ's Church nothing but Christ's Word is to be taught and to rule (Matt. 28:20; John 8:31-32; 17:20; 1 Pet. 4:11; 1 Tim. 6:3 ff.), all who teach another word are *eo ipso* ἀντίχριστοι, opponents of Christ, rebels in His kingdom.

But in 2 Thess. 2:3-12 the "Antichrist" is described as an opponent

---

[29] Cp. Walther on "The Ministry the Highest Office in the Church, from Which All Other Offices in the Church Stem," *K. u. A.*, p. 342 f. [*Walther and the Church*, p. 78 f.]).

of Christ who is altogether unique inasmuch as in him the "many antichrists" meet and the apostasy par excellence (ἡ ἀποστασία κατ' ἐξοχήν) appears. In this special sense ὁ ἀντίχριστος in 1 John 2:18 is singled out from the πολλοὶ ἀντίχριστοι as distinct from them: "As we have heard that Antichrist shall come, even now are there [γεγόνασιν, have become, have arisen] many antichrists." [30] The contrast in which ἔρχεται stands to the perfect γεγόνασιν (have arisen) demands that "cometh" be taken as future. In the many antichrists even now present in all false teachers the same spirit is active which will culminate in the great Antichrist, or to use Paul's phrase: "The mystery of iniquity doth already work," τὸ μυστήριον ἤδη ἐνεργεῖται τῆς ἀνομίας" (2 Thess. 2:7).

The marks of Antichrist as described in detail 2 Thessalonians 2 are these:

1. The position taken by the Antichrist is unqualifiedly called the "falling away" (ἡ ἀποστασία, the apostasy) (v. 3). Obviously this apostasy is not a rebellion against the civil powers, but a defection from the Christian religion, for the entire context speaks not of political or social matters, but of matters in the sphere of religion. What the Antichrist espouses is "all deceivableness of unrighteousness," "a lie," and those who follow him have not received the love of "the truth," that is, of the Christian truth, and shall perish forever (vv. 10-12). Even Luenemann, though he in other respects misinterprets the entire passage, says correctly of the ἀποστασία: "Not disloyalty in the political sense, but solely religious disloyalty, that is, apostasy from God and the true religion, can be meant by the ἀποστασία. We are constrained to agree (1) by what the immediate context says regarding the apostasy of the ἄνθρωπος τῆς ἁμαρτίας, (2) by the characterization of the ἀποστασία (v. 3), as ἀνομία (lawlessness), v. 7, (3) by consistent Biblical usage (cf. Acts 21:21; 1 Tim. 4:1). Accordingly, also the opinion that a mixture of religious and political apostasy is meant must be rejected as inadmissible."

2. The Antichrist has his seat "in the temple of God" (ὁ ναὸς τοῦ θεοῦ), v. 4, that is, in the Christian Church. The notion that the Antichrist will choose the idol temples of the heathen as his seat deserves no serious consideration. Paul never calls the temples of idols "the temple of God," but he does give this name to the Christian Church (1 Cor. 3:16 ff.; 1 Tim. 3:15; 2 Tim. 2:20, etc.). Moreover, if

---

[30] Thus also Huther and Sander correctly render γεγόνασιν.

the Antichrist sat in the temple of an idol, he would be no "mystery of iniquity," but an iniquity at once apparent to the Christians.

3. The conduct of the Antichrist corresponds with his sitting in the temple. He acts as if he were God Himself (v. 4). He "exalteth himself above all that is called God, or that is worshiped" (ἐπὶ πάντα λεγόμενον θεὸν ἢ σέβασμα), claiming to be superior to all authorities in the world, and his insolence is so great that he sits in the temple of God as a god and exhibits himself as God (ἀποδεικνύντα ἑαυτὸν ὅτι ἐστὶ θεός). The words "all that is called God, or that is worshiped," of course, do not include the idols of the pagans, for exalting oneself above these is no iniquity. The words refer to those persons in the world who are indeed not divine in essence, but are called gods in Scripture because of divine functions assigned to them; for instance, the civil authorities and the parents (dei nuncupativi). Also the concept "all that is called God" (λεγόμενοι θεοί) is clearly defined in Scripture.[31]

4. The Antichrist is not Satan himself, as some have thought; however, his "coming [παρουσία] is after the working of Satan" (κατ' ἐνέργειαν τοῦ Σατανᾶ), as his kingdom is built and backed by all manner of lying powers and signs and wonders.[32]

5. The Antichrist will remain until Judgment Day. "Whom the Lord . . . shall destroy with the brightness of His coming" (v. 8). Not till Christ returns visibly for the Judgment will He make an end (καταργήσει) of the Antichrist.

Now, who is this Antichrist? If we take the facts recorded in this text as the constituent features of his portrait, as indeed they are meant to be, then he is neither a political tyrant, such as Nero, Napoleon, Boulanger, etc. (who made no pretense to greatness in the Church), nor a manifest unbeliever and scoffer (who wants nothing to do with the temple of God, as Lehre und Wehre, 1869, 39 ff. makes clear). The features here delineated are those of the Roman Pontiff or of the historical phenomenon of the Papacy.

---

[31] John 10:34-35; 1 Cor. 8:5; Rom. 13:1 ff. Buddeus, Instit. theol. dogm., 1741, p. 1224: "He will sit in the temple of God ὡς θεός, as God, that is, he will appropriate unto himself those things which are solely God's own, even publishing himself fulsomely as a sort of God. To him pertains what Paul at the same place foretells, namely, that he exalts himself ἐπὶ πάντα λεγόμενον θεὸν ἢ σέβασμα, above all that is called or worshiped as God, that is, above all magistrates, kings, and rulers. Thus he ascribes to himself truly divine power, since only God is King of Kings and Lord of Lords."

[32] The "lying" belongs to all three nouns. The powers, signs, and wonders all belong to the sphere of lies, the father of which is the devil (John 8:44).

1. In the Papacy we have the most pronounced and greatest imaginable "falling away" from the Christian religion. Christians know that man is justified and saved only by faith in Christ, without the deeds of the Law. This is the article "which," as Luther states — and all Christians agree — "alone begets, nourishes, edifies, preserves, and defends the Church and without which the Church cannot exist even for one hour" (St. L. XIV:168; *Opp. v. a.* VII, 512). What the air is for the natural life of man, the doctrine of justification by faith without any merit of man is for his spiritual life. But this doctrine is officially anathematized by the Papacy,[33] and the entire machinery of the papal Church is geared to oppose and destroy this doctrine. This truly is the great apostasy, ἡ ἀποστασία, from the Christian religion; and the personal representative of it, the Pope, is truly the worst enemy of Christ and His Church, all the more since he masquerades under Christ's name. Because the Christian Church consists of people whom the Holy Spirit has brought to believe that they have a gracious God without their works, solely for Christ's sake, therefore the Pope, under the cloak of Christ's name, hurls his ban at this Christian Church and is ever intent on destroying it; e. g., by inducing the children who under his rule have become members of the Christian Church by Holy Baptism to forsake Christ and to trust in their own works.

2. The Papacy is found not outside, but inside the Christian Church. For within the domain of the Pope are, besides the many children regenerated in Baptism, a considerable number of adults who, in spite of their seductive environment, through whatever Gospel is still occasionally voiced, trust only in the merit of Christ. (Cf. Luther, St. L. XVII:2191.)

3. The Pope refuses to subordinate himself to anyone; instead, as everyone knows, he insists that he is supreme in Church and world. While he anathematizes and blocks the one way to salvation, he asseverates that only those will be saved who subject themselves to his authority. He alters God's Word and institutions at his pleasure. While he makes himself the judge of all men, he refuses to be judged by anyone. Indeed, he expressly asserts his infallibility. He arrogates to himself rulership over all civil authorities and demands that as secular governments they acknowledge his supremacy and with their powers serve his kingdom.

4. It is likewise common knowledge that the Papacy, past and

---

[33] *Trid.*, Sess. VI, can. 11, 12, 20.

present, employs all manner of lying powers, signs, and wonders to bolster its rule.[34]

5. It cannot be denied that to this day the Papacy has continued to be what it has always been, even though it will never fully recover from the deadly blow dealt it by the Reformation.

Therefore we subscribe to the declaration of the Smalcald Articles: "And the marks [all the vices] of Antichrist plainly agree with the kingdom of the Pope and his adherents" (*Trigl.* 515, Power and Primacy of Pope, 39). Again: "This teaching shows forcefully that the Pope is the very Antichrist" (*Trigl.* 475, Part II, Art. IV, 10).[35]

A number of objections have been raised against this teaching.

1. It has been argued that the Antichrist prophesied in 2 Thessalonians 2 is a single person, one "individual." But the text does not support this view. What the text says rather points to a phenomenon exceeding the span of a human life. The mystery of iniquity is already at work in the days of the Apostle, but there is an obstruction that prevents its full development. This obstruction must first be removed. Then follows the revelation, or unveiling, of the Antichrist and his

---

[34] Luther is right in pointing out that the power exercised by the Papacy can be accounted for only by its diabolical origin. It is contrary not only to God's Word, but also to all reason. Nobody is attached to the Papacy; even its own adherents do not love it; but everybody trembles before it, deceived and held captive by the show of piety and by the signs and wonders of falsehood. (St. L. XVIII:1529; *Opp. v. a.* V, 356.)

[35] Philippi, *Lehre vom Antichrist,* p. 67: "In the Papacy we find the exact counterpart, trait by trait, of the Bible's portrayal of Antichrist. Here is, besides apostasy and false doctrine in general, the man who enthrones himself in the temple of God instead of God (just call to mind his latest dogmas of the *immaculata conceptio* and infallibility); here human authority takes the place of Holy Scripture, human righteousness the place of the righteousness of Jesus Christ; here the commandments of men are placed above God's Law; here passages of Scripture speaking of Christ (e. g., Is. 28;16; Ps. 72:11; Matt. 28:18; Apoc. 5:5) are applied to a man, the Pope; here a man arrogates to himself the highest power not only on earth, but by indulgences, canonization of the departed, transubstantiation, and the like, also in heaven; here a man claims to be *iure divino* the legitimate and sole possessor of all spiritual and secular power on earth, so that from his own infallible sovereign power he presumes not only to ordain the form of divine worship and to decree dogmas, but even to make salvation dependent on faith in his divine authority; here one finds the divine ordinance of matrimony despised (celibacy); here is found a struggle for world domination, collusion with the powers of this world, the exploiting of secular powers for egoistic purposes, the use of unholy means allegedly for a holy purpose; here are found streams of martyr blood shed by him; here one finds lying signs and wonders (just recall Louise Lateau, Lourdes, and Marpingen, the miracle-working images of Mary and of saints, etc.), etc., etc. All these traits are so characteristic of the Papacy that we cannot but say: 'The Pope is the Antichrist.'"

ultimate destruction by the appearance of Christ for the Judgment. Also the many lying powers, signs, and wonders by which the Antichrist builds and sustains his kingdom, the seduction of large numbers to unrighteousness among those who perish (vv. 9-10), suggest a longer period of time. Philippi therefore judges: "There is no contention exegetically more unfounded and arbitrary than that 2 Thess. 2:3-4 could fit only a single concrete person." [36]

2. Against the declaration of our Confessions that the Antichrist prophesied in 2 Thessalonians 2 stands fully grown before us in the Papacy the further objection is raised that this teaching does not rest on Scripture, but on history and that one, accordingly, cannot be divinely assured of having the right answer. However, this objection is an assertion which the objectors themselves are not able or willing to uphold. Whether in Jesus of Nazareth the promised Christ had appeared was also a "historical" question for the Jews of Jesus' day. As the Jews, however, could, on the basis of the prophecies and from the words and works of Christ, know with the assurance of faith that in Jesus of Nazareth "the Christ" had appeared, so by comparing the predictions of Scripture with the words and works of the Papacy we can become divinely sure that in the Papacy "the Antichrist" is standing before us, recognizable by all. [37]

One cannot blame the Papists for denying from their standpoint the *"papam esse ipsum verum antichristum."* But the nearly unanimous denial also on the part of modern Protestant theologians, including

---

[36] *Dogmatik* VI, 181. Buddeus, *Inst. theol. dogm.*, p. 1223: "The things recorded of the Antichrist, 2 Thess. 2:3-4 ff., are of such a nature that they cannot be completed by one man nor in the life span of one man."

[37] Spener says: "But how do we prove that the Pope is the great Antichrist? Answer: In the same manner in which we are accustomed to prove that Jesus of Nazareth is the true Christ, or the Messiah, namely: Jesus is the Christ, or the Messiah, because in Him, and Him only, is fulfilled all that has been foretold of the Messiah in the Prophets. Likewise the Pope must be the Antichrist because everything that Scripture foretells of the Antichrist fits him and cannot be shown to be true of any other. . . . We should diligently note this truth and material, that the Roman Pope is the Antichrist, and not regret the time spent in having listened to this truth. For this is an article which our Church expressly professes in the Smalcald Articles; and we, too, certainly dare not relinquish this truth, and the closer we fear the time to be when the Roman Babylon may be permitted to vent its last fury and persecution upon us, the more need is there that we be fully grounded and confirmed in this knowledge in order that we may learn to guard against it [the Papacy]; for this I regard as a certainty: Whoever does not recognize the kingdom of the Pope as the kingdom of Antichrist is not yet standing so firm that he may not by this or that seduction be converted to it." — *Righteous Indignation Against the Antichristian Papacy*, 1714, p. 39 f. (Baier, III, 681).

Lutherans, that the Pope is the Antichrist (cf. Baier-Walther, III, 683) stems from their opposition to the *sola gratia* (synergism) and their "liberal" attitude toward Scripture (rejection of Verbal Inspiration). Because of this false position they do not see (1) what an outrage the renunciation and anathematizing of the doctrine of justification is, (2) what a heinous offense the Pope is committing by suppressing the authority of the Word of God, and thus of Christ, and supplanting it with his own authority, and that under the cloak of Christ's name and with a great show of sanctity.

3. It has been urged that the Papacy still confesses "fundamental articles" of the Christian faith, such as the article of the Trinity and of the theanthropic Person of Christ. We answer: These "fundamental articles" save no man if at the same time he denies and curses the Christian doctrine of justification. Without the article of justification all other doctrines are empty husks.[38] That the Papacy still confesses some "fundamental articles" is part of the external adornment by which it seeks to cover up its apostasy from the Christian doctrine.

4. Some say that there have been several personally honorable, even "pious" Popes. This objection reveals a lack of Christian judgment. There can be no thought of piety in the case of any Pope, since even "pious" Popes head and direct the machinery that does away with and curses the Christian doctrine of justification, that is, the entire Christian faith.[39] The occasional appearance of an outwardly respectable Pope is a part of the external trappings which hide the inward, spiritual iniquity of the Antichrist. All the marks enumerated in 2 Thessalonians 2 fit all Popes. To the point is the remark of Joh. Adam Osiander: "It should be noted that the essential thing in the case of the Antichrist is not his personal probity or depravity, but the nature of his office. Now, no pontiff, no matter when he reigns or how decent he may be personally, fails to declare himself the ecumenical head of the Church, or to exercise authority in secular and spiritual affairs, or to approve the condemnatory canons of the Council of Trent, though he may, for political reasons, abstain for the time being from slaughter and tyranny." [40] This fact is expressed still more clearly by Luther, who shows that here we are concerned not with the viciousness of the Pope, but of the Papacy, the iniquity not of the person, but of the office. "There is a vast difference," he says, "between the sovereignty which

---

38 See Luther's exposition. (St. L. VIII:629 ff.)

39 Luther XVIII, 1530: "The Papacy is a sovereignty that exterminates faith and the Gospel."

40 *Colleg. theol.* VIII, 162; in Baier-Walther, III, 682.

the Pope has and all other sovereignties in the whole world. To put up with these, be they good or bad, may do no harm, but the Papacy is a sovereignty that exterminates faith and the Gospel. . . . Therefore what we condemn is not the wickedness of the sovereign, but the wickedness of the sovereignty, for it is so constituted that it cannot be administered by a pious, upright sovereign, but only by one who is an enemy of Christ." (St. L. XVIII:1530; *Opp. v. a.* V, 357.)

Does the doctrine that the Pope is the Antichrist belong to the "fundamental articles" of the Christian faith? It certainly does not, for a person is a Christian solely through his knowledge of Christ and not his knowledge of the Antichrist. Before and after the unveiling of the Antichrist there have been many sincere Christians who have not recognized the Pope as the Antichrist. But every teacher in the Christian Church who is familiar with the historical phenomenon called the Papacy and still does not recognize in this Papacy the Antichrist prophesied in 2 Thessalonians 2 is weak in Christian theology.[41]

---

[41] On the Antichrist compare Baier-Walther, III, 672 ff.; *Lehre und Wehre* 7, 267; 13, 297; 16, 312; 5, 311; 15, 39; 15, 198; 16, 339; 17, 47; 26, 94; 50, 489. *Lutheraner* 24, pp. 113, 81, 126, 182; 30, 41; 31, 25. Philippi, *L. v. Antichrist,* 1877.

Eternal Election

(DE ELECTIONE AETERNA SIVE DE PRAEDESTINATIONE)

DOGMATICIANS do not present the doctrine of the eternal predestination, or the election of grace, in the same sequence. Some have dealt with it early, conjointly with the doctrine of God, particularly with the doctrine of the divine decrees (*de decretis divinis*).[1] Others have deemed it appropriate to treat this doctrine under the "grace of God," because eternal election is an election of grace.[2] Still others (e. g., Baier) have discussed it after soteriology, but before the doctrine of the Church, not ineptly, because eternal election stands in a causative relationship to the Church (Rom. 11:1-10; Matt. 24:22). We place the doctrine of election after the doctrine of the Church because Scripture addresses those who by faith have become members of the Christian Church as the elect. (Eph. 1:3 ff.; 2 Thess. 2:13-14, etc.) We prefer this position for the further reason that Scripture assigns to the doctrine of election not a principal, but an auxiliary role. It serves to corroborate the *sola gratia,* a fact which we have noted previously (see Vol. II, 415 ff.), but which we must now amplify. In passing we note that the arrangement of doctrines in dogmatics is immaterial as long as they are taken solely from Holy Writ (Vol. II, 419 ff.).

1

The Nature of Election

Even apart from the doctrine of eternal election, we know that Christians owe their entire state of grace from beginning to end not to any worthiness, any merit, or any effort of theirs, but solely to God, specifically the Holy Ghost, who, prompted by His grace in Christ and operating through the means of grace, calls, converts, justifies, sanctifies, and keeps them in the faith. Of the Scripturalness of this teaching we have previously convinced ourselves. Scripture now adds the revelation that God has from eternity resolved to do for His Christians what He has effected in them in time. This, and nothing else, is the Scriptural doctrine of eternal election. The election of grace may therefore be defined as the eternal act of God by which from eternity out of pure grace for Christ's sake He has decreed to

---

[1] Thus A. L. Graebner, *Doct. Theol.,* § 51.

[2] Thus Quenstedt, Hollaz, etc.

bestow those blessings on the Christians which through His call they now enjoy — conversion, justification, sanctification, and preservation in faith.

This definition follows the procedure of Scripture. For Holy Writ traces the gracious blessings which God bestows on the Christians in time (their call, conversion, justification, sanctification, and preservation in faith) back to their election, an act of God which antedates the Creation, which occurred therefore in eternity. In 2 Tim. 1:9 Paul confesses in the name of all Christians: "God hath saved us and called us with an holy calling," and then proceeds: "not according to our works, but according to His own purpose and grace, which was given us in Christ Jesus before the world began." We read in Acts 13:48 of the Gentiles who came to faith by the Apostle's preaching: "As many as were ordained to eternal life believed." In 2 Thess. 2:10-12 Paul speaks of those who perish by Antichrist's deception, "because they received not the love of the truth," whereas (v. 13 ff.) he thanks God that the Christians at Thessalonica can expect not a wretched, but a blessed end. And this because of their eternal election: "But we are bound to give thanks alway to God for you, brethren, beloved of the Lord, because God hath from the beginning chosen you to salvation through sanctification of the Spirit and belief of the truth; whereunto He called you by our Gospel to the obtaining of the glory of our Lord Jesus Christ." All the wealth of spiritual blessings imparted to the Christians in time the Apostle traces back to their eternal election. Eph. 1:3-6 he writes: "Blessed be the God and Father of our Lord Jesus Christ, who hath blessed us with all spiritual blessings in heavenly places in Christ, according as He hath chosen us in Him before the foundation of the world." Rom. 8:28-30 Paul assures the Christians, inasmuch as they must suffer and endure weakness here in time: "We know that all things work together for good to them that love God, to them who are the called according to His purpose [τοῖς κατὰ πρόθεσιν κλητοῖς οὖσιν]." What is meant by this purpose [πρόθεσις] is not left to our conjecture. The Apostle immediately describes it more definitely as God's foreknowing (προγινώσκειν; Luther: *zuvor versehen*), which includes the predestination (προορίζειν) to glory: "For whom He did foreknow He also did predestinate to be conformed to the image of His Son" (v. 29). But with the predestination to glory are inseparably united the calling, the justification, and the glorification of the elect. For the Apostle proceeds: "Moreover, whom He did predestinate, them He also called; and whom He called, them He also justified; and whom He justified, them He also glorified."

While particulars will be discussed later, two things should be pointed out at once to complete the Scriptural concept of eternal election.

1. Eternal election includes not only a part of the *ordo salutis,* such as the final award of eternal life — "receiving the end of your faith, even the salvation of your souls" — after perseverance in faith unto the end (*electio intuitu fidei finalis*), but it embraces the entire way on which God leads the Christians to salvation, from their calling to their induction into glory. This is the concept of election to which also the Formula of Concord adheres: "The eternal election of God, however, not only foresees and foreknows the salvation of the elect, but is also, from the gracious will and pleasure of God in Christ Jesus, a cause which procures, works, helps, and promotes our salvation and what pertains thereto: and upon this [divine predestination] our salvation is so founded 'that the gates of hell cannot prevail against it,' Matt. 16:18, as is written John 10:28: 'Neither shall any man pluck My sheep out of My hand.' And again, Acts 13:48: 'And as many as were ordained to eternal life, believed.'" *Trigl.* 1065, Sol. Decl., XI, 8.

2. Accordingly in the doctrine of eternal election a person can go astray only if he has previously forsaken the teaching of Scripture regarding the way of salvation. For instance, if one holds that conversion and salvation do not depend solely on God's grace, but also on man's self-conditioning, free choice, correct conduct, lesser guilt in comparison with other men, etc., one will also teach that God from eternity elected individuals to salvation not purely by grace for Christ's sake, but in view of the things mentioned (the *aliquid in homine*).

2

Election in Its Proper Setting

Much and long the doctrine of election has been abused. Luther confesses that for a time the mere thought of eternal election filled him with terror rather than comfort.[3] Many Christians have had the same experience.[4] This effect, both deplorable and contrary to the

---

[3] Luther (St. L. II:180) relates that uncertainty about his election would have killed him if Staupitz had not delivered him from this tribulation.

[4] Luther, *ibid.,* 182: "Under the Papacy, too, there were many pious souls who experienced these spiritual attacks."

true nature of this doctrine and the divine intent, is due to a wrong approach. One must consider eternal election as it actually occurred. Election is, of course, a selecting and appointing in eternity of the persons of Christians to salvation. 2 Thess. 2:13: "God hath from the beginning chosen *you* to salvation." But this choice did not occur "*nude*," in a bare manner. God did not — this bears constant repetition — blindly reach into the mass of mankind with His almighty hand and with His bare omnipotence seize a number of men as His elect; but He seized (αἰρεῖσθαι, "choose") His elect, as is immediately added (*ibid.*), "through sanctification of the Spirit and belief of the truth," ἐν ἁγιασμῷ πνεύματος καὶ πίστει ἀληθείας, so that in this choosing was included the work of the Holy Ghost, approaching the chosen with the Gospel and through the Gospel engendering faith in them. In other words: Like the merit of Christ, so also the sanctification of the Spirit and bestowal of faith are part and parcel of the eternal act of choosing itself and do not merely, as the Calvinists teach, enter into the execution of the decree of election.[5] Hence we have the right conception of our eternal election only if we ever and firmly bear in mind how it actually occurred in eternity, namely, not without regard to the means, or absolutely, but in such a way as to provide for the preaching of the Gospel and the operation of the Holy Spirit through the Gospel for the generation of faith. It was consummated in eternity just as the Formula of Concord describes its execution in time: "For the Father draws . . . by the hearing of His holy, divine Word, as with a net, by which the elect are plucked from the jaws of the devil" (*Trigl.* 1087, Sol. Decl., XI, 76).

With this Scriptural view of the mode of election, we look to Christ and the Gospel to determine whether we are elected, and we are happy to find that all our distress has vanished. We shall enlarge on this subject when we discuss the identification marks of the elect, warning here, however, against all notions leading either to despair or to carnal security. If a person asks: "Am I chosen to salvation?" he should in turn be asked: "Do you sincerely believe in the Gospel?" For the elect have been chosen "through the sanctification of the Spirit and belief of the truth." If the questioner continues: "If I have been chosen from eternity to salvation, I shall inevitably be saved; if I have not been chosen, I shall be lost, no matter whether I now hear the Gospel and believe or not," he should be told that there is no such absolute election to salvation at all, that God does not seize His

---

[5] *Formula Consensus Helvetica* V; in Niemeyer, p. 731 f.

elect by the ears or the neck, but took hold of them in eternity
ἐν ἁγιασμῷ πνεύματος καὶ πίστει ἀληθείας, by means of the sanctification
of the Spirit and belief of the truth, in the same way as He lays hold
of them here in time.

This is the point so emphatically stressed by the Formula of
Concord. Its chief concern is to ensure this correct understanding of
election. First, it establishes that "the eternal election of God's children to eternal salvation" is not identical with "the eternal foreknowledge of God" (*Trigl.* 1063, Sol. Decl., XI, 3—8). Then it sets
forth the truth at length (*Trigl.* 1065, *ibid.*, 9—24), that the election
to eternal life is not "to be considered in God's secret, inscrutable
counsel in such a bare [*nude*] manner as though it comprised nothing
further, or as though nothing more belonged to it, and nothing more
were to be considered in it than that God foresaw [*praeviderit*]
who and how many were to be saved, who and how many were to be
damned, or that He only held a sort of military muster [*militarem
quendam delectum*], thus: 'This one shall be saved, that one shall be
damned; this one shall remain steadfast [in faith to the end], that one
shall not remain steadfast.'" But the correct manner of thinking and
speaking of eternal election, the Confession continues, is "that the
entire doctrine concerning the purpose, counsel, will, and ordination
of God pertaining to our redemption, call, justification, and salvation
should be taken together [*simul mente complectamur*]." The Formula
itself then summarizes the things necessary for a correct conception
in eight points. It says we must consider (1) that God has truly
reconciled the human race unto Himself through Christ;[6] (2) that
God offers and distributes to us the grace purchased by Christ through
the means of grace; (3) that the Holy Ghost works faith through this
offer of grace in the means; (4) that God through this faith justifies
and (5) sanctifies those who are thus justified; (6) that He will not
forsake them in their great weakness and in all manner of temptations;
(7) but will strengthen, increase, and support the good work to the
end; (8) until "finally He will eternally save and glorify in life eternal
those whom He has elected, called, and justified." After the Formula
has thus pointed out this way of salvation for all, it adds that it has

---

6 The Formula of Concord mentions "the human race," or all mankind, not
in order to teach a universal election in conflict with its own declaration (*Trigl.*
1065, *ibid.*, 5), but because we can contemplate "our redemption" only if we
consider that the whole human race is truly redeemed and reconciled with God
through Christ. Our denial of universal redemption would preclude considering
ourselves redeemed.

thereby defined the method, or the mode, by which God in eternity has "in grace considered [*clementer praescivit*, translation of προέγνω, Rom. 8:29] and chosen to salvation each and every person of the elect who are to be saved through Christ, also ordained that in the way just mentioned He will, by His grace, gifts, and efficacy, bring them thereto [make them participants of eternal salvation], aid, promote, strengthen, and preserve them" (*Trigl.* 1069, *ibid.*, 23).

In considering the *terminus vitae* we must proceed in an analogical, or similar, manner. Every man's term of life is determined in God's counsel. Job 14:5: "Seeing his days are determined, the number of his months are with Thee, Thou hast appointed his bounds that he cannot pass." This is likewise a truth we dare not consider in a bare manner (*nude*), that is, irrespective of means, so that we do not pray, nor work, nor eat, nor use assistance in danger or sickness. God has directed us to the means ordained by Him (Acts 9:25; 23:16 ff.; 1 Tim. 5:23, etc.) and has taken the use of these means into account in determining our end. Through the use of these means we therefore arrive at the *terminus* appointed by Him. Similarly, our election is indeed an unalterable fact, as also the Formula of Concord repeatedly emphasizes. (*Trigl.* 1071, *ibid.*, 25; 1079, 45–47; 1081, 54 ff.) However, God did not choose His children absolutely, but ἐν Χριστῷ (Eph. 1:4) and "through sanctification of the Spirit and belief of the truth [ἐν ἁγιασῷ πνεύματος καὶ πίστει ἀληθείας]," 2 Thess. 2:13, that is, motivated by the merit of Christ and providing for the use and effect of the means of grace. By our attitude toward Christ and the means of grace we can therefore tell whether we have been elected from eternity, as the Formula of Concord shows at some length. (1073, *ibid.*, 30 ff.) This is the correct manner of viewing eternal election.

3

The Elect

The *obiectum electionis*, or the elect, are not all men, as Huber (d. 1624) taught,[7] nor the temporary believers as well as those actually saved, as later Tuebingen theologians taught and some modern theo-

---

[7] *Acta Huberiana*, Tueb., 1597, I, 254: "Confession of Dr. Sam. Huber regarding election: I believe and confess from the bottom of my heart that God has in His Son ordained all men and every man to eternal life, passed by no one, but elected all, one as well as the other." In Frank, IV, 281. See *L. u. W.*, 1880, 45 ff.

logians still teach.[8] The elect are only those actually saved, for Scripture teaches that without fail all elect enter life eternal, or, in other words, that none of the elect can be lost.[9] Hence the term "election of grace" is not used in Scripture in a threefold sense, embracing in its widest sense all men, in its wider sense the glorified plus those who believe only for a time, and in its narrow sense only the glorified. "Election," as it is always used in Holy Writ, relates only to those actually saved.

In presenting the doctrine of election, or predestination, the Formula of Concord, like Scripture, from the outset distinguishes between the *praedestinatio ad salutem* and the *praescientia Dei* and shows that the *praescientia* of God pertains to all men, while the *praedestinatio ad salutem* applies only to the children of God. "The eternal election of God, however, *vel praedestinatio* [or predestination], that is, God's ordination to salvation, does not extend at once over the godly and the wicked, but only over the children of God, who were elected and ordained to eternal life, before the foundation of the world was laid, as Paul says, Eph. 1:4-5: 'He hath chosen us in Him,

---

[8] E. g., the Tuebingen theologian J. A. Osiander, d. 1697; *Colleg. Theol. Syst.* VI, 117. See the historical remarks *L. u. W.* 1880, 105; 1881, 100 ff. For a criticism of the Tuebingen position see Fecht, *Compend. univ. theol.*, p. 426 f.; in Baier-Walther, III, 541. Among modern theologians Frank, IV, 177 f., teaches "a twofold order of elect."

[9] Matt. 24:24; Rom. 8:28-30. In the words of Christ (Matt. 24:24): "Insomuch that, if it were possible, they shall deceive the very elect," the "if it were possible" declares that they will not be deceived. This fact is expressly stated in v. 22: "And except these days should be shortened, there should no flesh be saved; but for the elects' sake these days shall be shortened." — Paul shows *ex professo* in Rom. 8:28-30, for the consolation of the Christians, that all elect are assured of eternal glory. The glorification (ἐδόξασεν, aorist) is just as inseparably linked to eternal election as the call (ἐκάλεσεν) and the justification (ἐδικαίωσεν). See Stoeckhardt, *Roemerbrief*, 402. Stoeckhardt quotes Weiss: "To place the glorification on the same level of reliability with the προέγνω, προώρισε, ἐκάλεσε, and ἐδικαίωσε, Paul chose the proleptic (anticipative) aorist." — Those who count the time believers, too, while they have faith, with the called and justified and therefore also with the elect, do so without Scripture warrant, for Scripture limits the eternal election to those actually saved and does not include the time believers. Neither are the time believers included in the texts in which the Church, the communion of saints, or Christendom, is identified with the elect: 1 Cor. 1:2-9; Eph. 1:1 ff.; 1 Thess. 1:5; 2:13; 1 Pet. 1:1-2; 2:9; etc. Accordingly, there is no need of correcting Luther's explanation of the Third Article, in which Luther declares "the whole Christian Church on earth" to consist of those whom the Holy Ghost "calls, gathers, enlightens, sanctifies, and keeps with Jesus Christ in the one true faith." God reckons like the farmer, who does not count the wheat that falls by the wayside during the harvesting and is trod underfoot or eaten by the fowls of the air.

having predestinated us unto the adoption of children by Jesus Christ.'
The foreknowledge of God [*praescientia*] foresees and foreknows also
that which is evil." (*Trigl.* 1065, *ibid.*, 5–7.)

True, there have been Lutheran theologians, especially before the
time of the Formula of Concord, who spoke of a general election
including all men, inaccurately using as synonyms the terms "election
of grace" and universal "will of grace." [10] But the Formula is careful
to distinguish between the two. Though, against the Calvinists, it
testifies very firmly to the universality of God's grace, of Christ's merit,
and of the operation of the Holy Ghost through the Word (*Trigl.* 1071,
ibid., 28 ff.; 837, Epit., 17–19), it never speaks of election as universal.
On the contrary, it says from the beginning that the election embraces
only the children of God who obtain final salvation (*Trigl.* 1065, Sol.
Decl., XI, 5, 8). Some earlier and some more recent theologians
maintain that the Formula of Concord sometimes teaches a universal
or at least a wider election, because it insists that eternal election
must be considered, not as a bare decree (*nude*), but always only in
conjunction with the entire counsel of God "pertaining to our redemption, call, justification, and salvation." However, as we have shown
in the preceding chapter, the purpose of the Formula's insistence is
not to teach a universal election, but to safeguard the Scriptural and
thus the right way of looking at predestination, namely, as including
the operation of the Holy Spirit through the means of grace.

In determining who the elect are one must guard against identifying election with the general rule: "He that perseveres in faith
unto the end shall be saved." This is of course a Scriptural principle
and a divine decree (John 3:18, 36; Matt. 24:13; etc.), but it is not
the election of grace. Scripture teaches that in the election of grace
God chose not a principle, but persons. 2 Thess. 2:13: "God hath . . .
chosen you [ὑμᾶς]"; Eph. 1:4: "He hath chosen us [ἡμᾶς]." It is exactly
as the Formula of Concord states: "And [indeed] in this His counsel,
purpose, and ordination God has prepared salvation not only in
general, but has in grace considered and chosen to salvation each and
every person of the elect who are to be saved through Christ, also
ordained that in the way just mentioned [in the eight points] He will,
by His grace, gifts, and efficacy, bring them thereto [make them participants of eternal salvation], aid, promote, strengthen, and preserve
them" (*Trigl.* 1069, *ibid.*, 23).

When modern theologians assert that election pertains not to

---

[10] Quotations in Frank, IV, 282 f.

individual, definite persons, but to the Church collectively, they are making a self-contradictory statement, since the Church consists of individual, definite persons, namely, of all those individuals who believe in Christ.

4

Being Sure of One's Election

Christians can and should know and be certain of their eternal election. There are Scripture passages which presuppose such assurance, as when the Apostles address the Christians as the elect [11] and comfort them in their trials and temptations with their eternal election.[12] All who assert that Christians cannot be sure of their election prove by this very contention that their teaching of election is not *Scriptural.* Why do many entertain grave doubts about their election?

For one thing, nobody can discern his election from the viewpoint of *divine prescience* or *foresight* (e. g., *intuitu fidei finalis*), because the divine foreknowledge is an inscrutable mystery, hidden from all men. No one is in a position to know what God has foreknown or foreseen concerning him, because "God has revealed nothing to us concerning it in His Word." The theory that God has elected *ex praevisa fide finali* was hatched in the mind of an impractical bookworm and thrives in library dust. No theologian and no Christian has ever been able to put this theory to practical use. We grant that some of the old *intuitu fidei* theologians teach that Christians should and can be certain of their eternal election.[13] However, they reach this conclusion because, forsaking their theory in practice, they direct Christians not to the foreknowledge of God, but to the divine promises pledging preservation in faith.

For this reason the Formula of Concord warns very vigorously against seeking assurance of one's election by prying into the divine foreknowledge. "Thus there is no doubt that God most exactly and certainly foresaw [*praeviderit*] before the time of the world, and still

---

[11] Eph. 1:4 Paul says, including himself with all Christians: "God hath chosen us [ἐξελέξατο ἡμᾶς]"; 2 Thess. 2:13 he tells the Thessalonians: "God hath from the beginning chosen you to salvation" (εἵλατο ὑμᾶς ἀπ' ἀρχῆς εἰς σωτηρίαν); 1 Thess. 1:4: "Knowing . . . your election of God" (εἰδότες τὴν ἐκλογὴν ὑμῶν).

[12] Rom. 8:28-39. V. 33: "Who shall lay anything to the charge of God's elect?"

[13] Brochmand, *Syst.* I, 270 f.; in Baier-Walther, III, 599 ff.; Loeber, *Dogmatik*, p. 495.

knows, which of those that are called will believe or will not believe; also which of the converted will persevere [in faith] and which will not persevere; which will return after a fall [into grievous sins], and which will fall into obduracy [will perish in their sins]. So, too, the number, how many there are of these on either side, is beyond all doubt perfectly known to God. However, since God has reserved this mystery for His wisdom, and has revealed nothing to us concerning it in His Word, much less commanded us to investigate it with our thoughts, but has earnestly discouraged us therefrom, Rom. 11:33 ff., we should not reason in our thoughts, draw conclusions, nor inquire curiously into these matters, but should adhere to His revealed Word, to which He points us." (*Trigl.* 1081, *ibid.*, 54f.)

Furthermore, no one can have any assurance of eternal election so long as he in one way or another limits universal grace (*gratia universalis*). Without faith in universal grace our election is indiscernible, as witnesses the Formula of Concord: "Therefore, if we wish to consider our eternal election to salvation with profit, we must in every way hold sturdily and firmly to this, that, as the preaching of repentance, so also the promise of the Gospel is *universalis,* that is, it pertains to all men, Luke 24:47." (*Trigl.* 1071, *ibid.*, 28.) Man does not see the absolute necessity of *universal* grace so long as the terrors of conscience have not yet seized his heart. But when his conscience is truly terrified (feels the *terrores conscientiae*), he will find nothing consoling but the grace that avails without any limitation for all sinners, which, as Luther expresses it, is meant no less for the malefactor than for St. Peter, no less for the harlot than for the Holy Virgin. Universal grace is denied, however, not only by Calvinists, but in effect also by synergists. Calvinists restrict saving grace, "efficacious grace," to those who are immediately illuminated and regenerated. Synergists predicate the possession of saving grace only of those who by correct conduct, free choice, or lesser guilt qualify for it.

This leads to a third cause of uncertainty. No one can possibly be sure of having been eternally elected if he does not regard predestination an election of grace, but considers it contingent on something or other in man (*aliquid in homine*), no matter whether this "something" is called merit, good works, self-disposition, correct conduct, or lesser guilt. Such a one abandons from the outset the concept of *grace* in favor of some figment of his own mind. Synergists therefore generally and consistently say that nobody can discern his election. If anyone, however, actually believes that God has taken a fancy to him and chosen him to salvation because of some good

he has done or some evil he has left undone, he has in that ᵥ
conceit the mark, not of one of the elect, but of one perishing, becɛ
eternal election is unalterably an "election of grace" (ἐκλογὴ χάριτος),
Rom. 11:5. Hence our Formula of Concord protests against the error
"that not alone the mercy of God and the most holy merit of Christ,
but that also in us [*aliquid in nobis*] there is a cause of God's election"
(*Trigl.* 1093, *ibid.*, 88). The Formula opens its discussion of how we
are to determine our election with a warning against seeking to
establish our identity as elect "according to the *Law*" (*Trigl.* 1071,
ibid., 26).

The assurance of our election, however, we can and should gain
from the Gospel. For the substance of the Gospel is that the grace
of God in Christ is for all sinners without exception, and that this
grace is actually grace, contingent on nothing whatever in man. When
a man hears and believes this blessed truth, he cannot but be assured
that for Christ's sake there dwells in God's heart not wrath, but only
ardent love for him, the sinner. Every poor sinner, therefore, who
keeps his faith focused on the Gospel, without any side glances in
the direction of the Law, is *eo ipso* believing his eternal election.
In short, the recognition of one's election and faith in the Gospel are
identical. Scripture teaches this method of ascertaining one's eternal
election Rom. 8:32-33: "He that spared not His own Son, but delivered
Him up for us all, how shall He not with Him also freely give us all
things? Who shall lay anything to the charge of God's elect?" And
only this fact, that the knowledge of one's election *coincides* with faith
in the Gospel, explains the other fact, that Scripture addresses the
believers in the Gospel as the elect.

However, it is of no use to engage in long arguments about this
matter. It is a fact established by Scripture and confirmed by experience that to contrite hearts seeking grace their election becomes
obvious from the wounds of Christ, as Staupitz taught Luther and
as Luther advises everyone asking about his election. As regards those
who believe only for a time, they are such solely because they do not
believe the Gospel, which specifically promises also preservation in
faith. Commenting on 1 Pet. 1:2, "Elect according to the foreknowledge of God," Luther says: "From this we should learn that predestination does not rest upon our worthiness and merit, as the
sophists hold, for then Satan could every moment make it doubtful
and overthrow it; but it rests in the hand of God and is founded upon
His mercy, which is unwavering and eternal; for that reason it is called
the foreknowledge of God and hence is certain and infallible. There-

fore, when your sins and unworthiness trouble you and the thought comes to you that you might not be elected of God, also that the number of the elect is small and the company of the godless large, and you are terrified by the awful examples of divine wrath and judgment, then do not dispute long why God does this or that so, and not differently, when He could easily do so. Do not presume to explore the depths of divine foreknowledge with your reason, else you will certainly go astray and either sink into gloomy fatalism or turn epicurean. But hold firmly to the promises of the Gospel which teach you that Christ, the Son of God, became incarnate to bless all people on earth, that is, to redeem them from sin and death, justify and save them; and that He did this according to the command and gracious will of God, our heavenly Father, who so loved the world that He gave His only-begotten Son that whosoever believeth on Him should not perish, but have eternal life, John 3:16. If you follow this counsel, namely, first of all acknowledge that you are by nature a child of wrath, worthy of eternal death and damnation, from which no creature, human or angelic, can save you, and then grasp the promise of God and believe that He is the merciful, truthful God, who from pure grace, without our work and merit, faithfully keeps what He has promised, and has sent Christ, His only Son, in order that He make satisfaction for your sins and give you His innocence and righteousness, finally to redeem you from all evil and from death; then do not doubt that you belong to the company of the elect. If we consider election in this manner, even as Paul does, it is comforting beyond measure. If we proceed in a different manner, the thought of election will be terrifying." (St. L. IX:1115.)

From the fact that becoming certain of one's eternal election coincides with faith in the Gospel we learn also what the assurance which Christians have of their eternal election is like. Theologians have inquired whether the certainty is "absolute" or "conditional." Both these terms are equivocal. In speaking of absolute certainty, Calvinists think of an immediate assurance coming through direct revelation and not based on the external means of grace. "Efficacious grace acts immediately." Synergists, in speaking of conditional certainty, think of a certainty contingent on human conduct. The adequate term for a Christian's assurance is "certainty of faith," since it consists in faith in the Gospel and therefore, in harmony with the nature of faith, is not a semicertainty, but full assurance. This normal assurance of faith is described Rom. 8:31-39, a description that closes with the words: "For I am persuaded that neither death nor life, nor angels, nor principalities, nor powers, nor things present, nor things to come, nor height, nor depth, nor any other creature, shall be able to separate us from the love of God, which is in Christ Jesus, our Lord."

The warnings of Scripture against apostasy and its references to those who believe only for a time are most earnestly meant. But they belong to the Law and hence apply to Christians not according to the new man, i. e., in so far as in true contrition for their sins they are concerned about grace, salvation, and election, but according to the old man, in so far as they are indifferent toward grace and salvation and yearn for the things of this world. There is no cause for concern lest time believers be deceived when preservation in the faith is promised them in the Gospel and thus their eternal election is revealed to them. This is a purely hypothetical case. He who confidently believes God's gracious promise to keep him in faith will not fall away finally. This is a truth revealed in Holy Writ. Rom. 10:11 (RV), for instance, says: "Whosoever believeth on Him shall not be put to shame."

5

The Relation of Faith to the Election of Grace

On the relation of faith to election there has been much dissension since the end of the sixteenth century. For this reason we are dealing with it in a special chapter. We must distinguish between the relation of faith to the eternal decree of predestination and the relation which Scripture assigns to faith in the execution of this decree in time.

In eternity faith was neither anterior nor posterior to God's decree of election. At this point both later Lutherans and Calvinists miss the mark. The former regard abiding faith, *fidem finalem,* as logically preceding the eternal election and as its cause, for they teach that God chose those persons of whom He foresaw that they would remain in faith to the end (election *intuitu fidei finalis*). The latter date faith, even in eternity, *after* the election, claiming that faith, like Christ's merit, is solely a part of the execution of the *absolute* predestination.[14] Over against both these positions it must be maintained that in electing the Christians, God resolved to favor them with the gift of faith in the Gospel and thus to single them out of the world. In other words,

---

[14] *Formula Consensus Helv.,* can. 5; in Niemeyer, p. 731 f.

God chose them by deciding to bless them with faith. Accordingly, God did not choose them absolutely, or *nude*, that is, without means, but ἐν ἁγιασμῷ πνεύματος καὶ πίστει ἀληθείας, "through sanctification of the Spirit and belief of the truth" (2 Thess. 2:13). See p. 473 ff.

This is also the teaching of the Formula of Concord. "God in His counsel, before the time of the world [therefore in the eternal election *itself*], decided and ordained that He Himself, by the power of His Holy Ghost, would produce and work in us, through the Word, everything that pertains to our conversion" [that is, to our coming to faith] (*Trigl.* 1077, *ibid.*, 44). And Walther takes the same position: "We teach that God, as He saves us by faith in time, has also in eternity resolved to save the elect by faith; and according to God's Word, our Confessions, and our teaching it is just this fact that constitutes the election of grace. . . . The Calvinists teach an absolute election to salvation and say that after this election God resolved to give faith solely to the elect. We, however, believe, teach, and confess with Scripture and our Confessions that God elected to salvation through faith." [15]

But when we look at the faith of the elect *in time*, it is, like their entire temporal state of grace, a consequence and effect of their election in eternity. 2 Tim. 1:9: "God hath saved us, and called us . . . according to His own purpose and grace, which was given us in Christ Jesus before the world began." Acts 13:48: "And as many as were ordained to eternal life believed." Hence the Formula of Concord teaches: "The eternal election of God . . . is . . . , from the gracious will and pleasure of God in Christ Jesus, a *cause* which procures, works, helps, and promotes our salvation and what pertains thereto; and upon this [divine predestination] our salvation is so founded 'that the gates of hell cannot prevail against it,' Matt. 16:18, as is written John 10:28: 'Neither shall any man pluck My sheep out of My hand.' And again, Acts 13:48: 'And as many as were ordained to eternal life, believed.'" (*Trigl.* 1065, *ibid.*, 8.) Likewise Chemnitz: "God's election does not follow on our faith and righteousness, but precedes all that as one of its causes." [16]

---

[15] *Berichtigung*, etc., p. 147. Luenemann in Meyer's *Commentary:* "'Through sanctification of the Spirit and belief of the truth' belongs neither alone to 'salvation,' nor alone to 'hath chosen,' but to the combined concept 'hath chosen to salvation,' and announces the means through which the election that took place is to be realized." The last part of the statement is inaccurate. The words of the text do not say how "the election that took place is to be realized," but how the eternal election became real, was effected.

[16] *Enchiridion*, Milwaukee, p. 109; in Frank, IV, 336.

Later Lutheran theologians, particularly since Aegidius Hunnius (d. 1603), gave up this doctrine. They had faith, final faith (*fidem finalem*), logically (*notionaliter, in signo rationis*) precede the eternal election. They taught that God chose those from eternity of whom He foresaw that they would remain in faith to the end or at least come to faith before their end (*electio intuitu fidei finalis, ex praevisa fide finali*). They sought to find Scripture proof for this theory by taking the προγινώσκειν, "consider in grace," in Rom. 8:29 in the sense of "to know beforehand," "to foresee" (*nudam scientiam denotans*). But to escape the conclusion that then all men must be elected — since God's mere foreknowledge extends to all men — they needed a restriction of the clause "Whom He did foreknow, did foresee." They obtained it by altering the object of the sentence. They abandoned the object "whom" (οὕς) and substituted for it: "whose constant faith He foresaw or foreknew" (*quorum fidem finalem praescivit sive praevidit*). Among recent Lutheran theologians Philippi, too, adopts this substitution.

To excuse or vindicate this substitution, Philippi says that one of course would have to imagine the "whom" (οὕς) as qualifying for the eternal election, and he regards the "persevering πίστις" (faith) as this indispensable qualification. But Scripture nowhere says that "persevering faith" is the prerequisite of the Christians' eternal election. Scripture says just the opposite. It says that neither *faith* here in time nor perseverance of the Christians even in extreme tribulation antecedes election, but follows it as its result and effect (Acts 13:48; Matt. 24:21-22). So, then, Philippi's *alloeosis*, or substitution of another object for the textual "whom," is not only arbitrary but even unscriptural.

And following mere whim rather than the principles of sound exegesis, others go still farther and substitute for "faith" good works,[17] or love (Weiss, Ebrard); the synergists, taking their cue from the later Melanchthon, insert proper conduct under various names: *facultas se applicandi ad gratiam, voluntas non repugnans, sed assentiens,* self-direction, free self-determination, omission of willful resistance, lesser guilt, etc.

To avoid such arbitrary and unscriptural interpolations and to retain the object "whom" (οὕς) unaltered, we join Luther, the Formula

---

[17] As early as Ambrosius on Rom. 8:29: "He did not predestinate before He foreknew, but to them of whom He foreknew merits (*merita*) He appointed rewards." Baier-Walther, III, 556.

of Concord, and a number of recent theologians in taking "foreknow" (προγινώσκειν) as a synonym of "predestinate," even though conceptually the two terms are not identical. Luther translates: *"Welche er zuvor VERsehen hat."* The Formula of Concord renders προγινώσκειν as "in grace considered," *"clementer praescire," "gnaediglich zuvor wissen" (Trigl.* 1070, *ibid.,* 23). Luthardt describes it as "an appropriating foreknowing." Other recent theologians render it: to make one's own, to ally oneself with.

This definition is fully supported by the *usus loquendi* of Scripture. In Scripture προγινώσκειν, as also the simple γινώσκειν and the Hebrew יָדַע, signifies not merely a knowledge of a thing (thus it is indeed used Acts 26:5 and 2 Pet. 3:17, where men are the subject), but a taking note of someone whereby a mutual relation, an alliance with, or adoption of, a thing or person, is established.[18] Deut. 7:6, for instance, says of God's action toward Israel: "The Lord, thy God, hath chosen (בָּחַר) thee to be a special people unto Himself," and Amos 3:2 expresses the same thought by saying: "You only have I known (יָדַעְתִּי) of all the families of the earth." In this sense γινώσκειν, יָדַע, and προγινώσκειν are used Gal. 4:9; Ps. 1:6; Rom. 11:2. Mere knowledge cannot be meant in these passages. Gal. 4:9 states that in and through their conversion the Gentiles "are known of God" (γνωσθέντες ὑπ' αὐτοῦ). Mere acquaintance with the Gentiles cannot be meant because God had that even before their conversion. Ps. 1:6 says that "the Lord knoweth the way of the righteous," meaning that God befriends the way of the righteous, as is evident from the contrast: "but the way of the ungodly shall perish." Also the words Rom. 11:2: "God has not cast away His people which He foreknew [προέγνω]," would be meaningless if προγινώσκειν expressed mere knowledge, and not appropriation, election.

Now, this established meaning of the term προγινώσκειν (to know fruitfully, to appropriate before, to choose before) in Rom. 8:29 makes unnecessary any change of object and unseemly search for a "fitting" object for προέγνω (faith, conduct, self-determination, love, works). It enables us to keep "whom" (οὕς) as object without any alteration or addition as well as the expressed thought, which not merely fits into, but is demanded by, the context: "Whom God foreknew," that is, appropriated as His own, these He also predestined to participation in the glory of His Son. And this predestination to eternal glory is the

---

[18] Our old theologians defined it as *nosse cum affectu et effectu,* that is, not mere knowledge of a thing, but a knowing combined with a loving appropriation of the object and an effect upon the same.

very comfort the Apostle wishes to give to the Christians groaning under affliction and infirmity here on earth. On the other hand, the whole context rules out mere divine *prescience* as the meaning of προγινώσκειν. Everyone will grant that the intention of the Apostle in this passage is to assure the Christians of their participation in the glory of Christ. If, now, the divine "foreknowledge" is taken as mere divine prescience, the Apostle would place Christian assurance on a totally insecure base, for no Christian knows or can know what God has foreseen in him or of him.

It is a common objection that tautology would result if προγινώσκειν were one of the synonyms of election; for then the objectors hold Paul would be made to say: "Whom He foreordained, them He also foreordained." Philippi, too, makes this assertion, appealing to Hunnius for support. But this objection is one of those traditional untruths that ever find ready and uncritical acceptance. Even if the same word, "foreordain" (προορίζειν), were used in both the relative and the principal clause so that the sentence would read: "Whom He did foreordain, them He also foreordained," there would be no tautology, but real *thought progression,* since the principal clause "them He also foreordained" has attached to it the statement of the *aim:* "to be conformed to the image of His Son." The text would then say that with their foreordination the elect were foreordained to the glory of the Son of God. No one could call this a tautological statement. Besides, προγινώσκειν and προορίζειν, though both serve to describe one and the same divine act, nevertheless differ conceptually. "Whom He did foreknow," οὓς προέγνω, expresses the loving appropriation, or adoption, of the person by God. The conclusion, "them He also foreordained," καὶ προώρισεν, points forward to the aim of the "foreknowing," namely, "to be conformed to the image of His Son" (συμμόρφους [predicate accusative] τῆς εἰκόνος τοῦ υἱοῦ αὐτοῦ).

The teaching of an eternal election *intuitu fidei finalis* finds no support whatever in Scripture. Later Lutheran theologians sought to foist this doctrine on Scripture in place of the doctrine of Luther and the Formula of Concord because, wittingly or unwittingly, they wanted to find an explanation satisfactory to human reason why, with God's grace universal and natural depravity alike in all men, still not all are converted and saved; in other words, why election is not "universal." But the *intuitu fidei finalis* theory fails to solve this mystery as long as one adheres to the divine monergism of Scripture in man's conversion and preservation in faith, or holds that faith *in solidum* is the work of the Holy Ghost. Only with a synergistic basis will

this theory furnish the explanation sought.[19] Of course, if one denies
that faith and constancy in faith are the gracious work of God and
places the decision into the hand of man, making it depend on man's
self-determination, correct conduct, lesser guilt, etc., then one has
indeed arrived at an explanation, but an unscriptural one. It is the
explanation of which Luther said to Erasmus: *Iugulum meum petisti*
(You have seized me by the throat).

6

Purpose of the Doctrine of Election

Scripture explicitly and definitely states the purpose of this doctrine. Its purpose is not to deny or restrict the *gratia universalis*,
as many before and after Calvin have thought,[20] but to confirm and
impress on us the *sola gratia.* Christians, in comparing themselves
with non-Christians, are not to get the idea that God has chosen
them as His people in view of their "different behavior," their better
conduct, or their lesser guilt, etc., but they should always and in all
circumstances remain aware that, compared with the unbelievers,
they, too, behaved wickedly and are themselves just as guilty before
God as are the reprobate. If they took the opposite view, they would
be canceling their membership in the Christian Church, the Kingdom
of *Grace,* and be joining the kingdom of the Pharisees, which lies
under the curse (Luke 18:9 ff.; Gal. 3:10). This is the purpose of
the doctrine of election as revealed in Holy Writ.

This was the purpose also of the Old Testament type of the
election of grace, namely, the election of Israel to be the covenant
people. Reading Deut. 9:4 ff., one gains the impression that Moses
in addressing Israel felt that he could not do enough to cure the people
of the delusion that they received the land of Canaan because they
were better than the heathen. Listen to his words: "Speak not thou

---

[19] This truth also Frank voices (*Theol. d. F. C.* IV, 206): "The theological
expedient, later [namely, among later Lutheran theologians] so popular as a
praevisa fides in connection with the *voluntas Dei antecedens* and *consequens,*
it seems, cannot be made to work, because, on the one hand, faith itself is
supposed to be regarded as effect of grace . . . and, on the other hand, because
the Confession (Formula of Concord) nowhere makes use of this expedient."

[20] See the full historical discussion of this contrast in the sections "Universal
Grace" and "Serious and Efficacious Grace," Vol. II, 21 ff.; also "Terminology
Regarding the Divine Will of Grace," Vol. II, 34—52, where it is shown, too, that
Luther and Calvin agree only in certain expressions, but differ entirely as to
substance.

in thine heart, after that the Lord, thy God, hath cast them out from before thee, saying, For my righteousness the Lord hath brought *me* in to possess this land; but for the wickedness of these nations the Lord doth drive them out from before thee. Not for thy righteousness, or for the uprightness of thine heart, dost thou go to possess their land; but for the wickedness of these nations the Lord, thy God, doth drive them out from before thee, and that He may perform the Word which the Lord sware unto thy fathers, Abraham, Isaac, and Jacob. Understand, therefore, that the Lord, thy God, giveth thee not this good land to possess it for thy righteousness; for thou art a stiff-necked people."

The doctrine of election to salvation serves the same purpose. Here, too, it seems that the Holy Ghost cannot do enough to instill this truth into the Christians, that God's choice of them to salvation is not due to their being better than others, but is attributable solely to the grace of God in Christ. 2 Tim. 1:9: "Not according to our works, but according to His own purpose and grace, which was given us in Christ Jesus before the world began." Eph. 1:5-6: "According to the good pleasure of His will, to the praise of the glory of His grace." Rom. 11:6: "And if by grace, then is it no more of works." Keeping in mind this purpose, the confirmation of the *sola gratia,* we are led to the right understanding of Romans 9—11. These chapters are not directed against universal grace; on the contrary, universal grace is very emphatically taught here too; see 10:21; 11:32. The characteristic feature of these chapters is their polemicizing against the delusion of self-righteousness and superiority to others.[21]

Our Lutheran Confessions, too, declare it to be the purpose of the doctrine of election to confirm the *sola gratia.* Says the Formula of Concord: "It establishes very effectually the article that we are justified and saved without all works and merits of ours, purely out of grace alone, for Christ's sake. For before the time of the world, before we existed, yea, before the foundation of the world was laid, when, of course, we could do nothing good, we were according to God's purpose chosen by grace in Christ to salvation, Rom. 9:11; 2 Tim. 1:9. Moreover, all *opiniones* (opinions) and erroneous doctrines concerning the powers of our natural will are thereby overthrown, because God in His counsel, before the time of the world, decided and ordained that He Himself, by the power of His Holy Ghost,

---

[21] Cp. the résumé (ch. 9:30-33) and the further discussion (ch. 10:1-13), also the Apostle's polemics against the Gentile Christians in so far as they were inclined to regard themselves as better than the Jews. (Ch. 11:18 ff.)

would produce and work in us, through the Word, everything that pertains to our conversion." (*Trigl.* 1077, *ibid.,* 43 ff.) Again: "By this doctrine and explanation of the eternal and saving choice [predestination] of the elect children of God His own glory is entirely and fully given to God, that in Christ He saves us out of pure [and free] mercy, without any merits or good works of ours, according to the purpose of His will, as it is written Eph. 1:5 f.: 'Having predestinated us unto the adoption of children by Jesus Christ to Himself, according to the good pleasure of His will, to the praise of the glory of His grace, wherein He hath made us accepted in the Beloved.' Therefore it is false and wrong [conflicts with the Word of God] when it is taught that not alone the mercy of God and the most holy merit of Christ, but that also in us there is a cause of God's election, on account of which God has chosen us to eternal life. For not only before we had done anything good, but also before we were born, yea, even before the foundations of the world were laid, He elected us in Christ; and 'that the purpose of God according to election might stand, not of works, but of Him that calleth, it was said unto her, The elder shall serve the younger; as it is written concerning this matter, Jacob have I loved, but Esau have I hated, Rom. 9:11 ff.; Gen. 25:23; Mal. 1:2 f." (*Trigl.* 1091, *ibid.,* 87 f.)

Because of its purpose of confirming the *sola gratia* the Scriptural doctrine of eternal election is terrifying to some, consoling to others. For all who think that they are not as other people, who still find in themselves inherent virtue and innate ability, *semina virtutum,* at least a *facultas se applicandi ad gratiam,* a different behavior, a lesser guilt, etc. — for all these the Scriptural election of grace is terrifying because it blasts their whole religion, of which "self-determination, inseparable from human nature," is an important part.[22] On the other hand, all whom the thunderbolt of the Law "has knocked into a heap," who have come to despair of themselves and who see their only salvation in the pure, free grace of God, find the Scripture doctrine of the election of grace very comforting because of its powerful confirmation of the *sola gratia.* "Thus this doctrine," says the Formula of Concord, "affords also the excellent and glorious consolation that God was so greatly concerned about the conversion, righteousness, and salvation of every Christian, and so faithfully purposed it

---

22 Recently again Dr. Schmidt in *Distinctive Doctrines,* 4th ed., p. 230, energetically promotes the idea that man, stirred by grace, still has "an option between obeying the call and yielding to the saving influences of God's Spirit, on the one hand, and refusing to do so, on the other hand."

[provided therefor] that before the foundation of the world was laid, He deliberated concerning it, and in His [secret] purpose ordained how He could bring me thereto [call and lead me to salvation], and preserve me therein. Also, that He wished to secure my salvation so well and certainly that, since through the weakness and wickedness of our flesh it could easily be lost from our hands, or through craft and might of the devil and the world be snatched and taken from us, He ordained it in His eternal purpose, which cannot fail or be overthrown, and placed it for preservation in the almighty hand of our Savior Jesus Christ, from which no one can pluck us, John 10:28. Hence Paul also says, Rom. 8:28-29: Because we have been called according to the purpose of God, who will separate us from the love of God in Christ?" (*Trigl.* 1079, *ibid.*, 45 ff.) Thus the election of grace affords strong consolation to the individual Christians in their weakness and temptations because it confirms the *sola gratia*.

Furthermore, when it seems at times that the end of the Christian Church on earth is at hand, we should regard the election of grace as a guarantee of the survival of the Church under all circumstances. This, too, Scripture teaches as one purpose of eternal election. When Elijah in his pessimism stood before God and lamented: "Lord, I, even I only, am left" (1 Kings 19:10), the Lord informed him that there were still seven thousand left in Israel as fruit of the election. Rom. 11:7: "The election [*abstractum pro concreto:* the elect] hath obtained it." When the distress reaches its climax in the closing days of this world, God will for the elect's sake shorten the days of affliction (Matt. 24:22). Accordingly, the Formula of Concord says: "This article also affords a glorious testimony that the Church of God will exist and abide in opposition to all the gates of hell" (*Trigl.* 1079, *ibid.*, 50). Election is a cause of the continuous existence of the Christian Church.

Those, however, who make some human factor (*aliquid in homine*) the cause or motive of eternal election — whether this is in whole or only in part man's own accomplishment, whether called the "inalienable" option or human free choice or something similar — are all utterly perverting the purpose of the revelation of eternal election into its antithesis. They contort this doctrine, which should confirm and magnify God's grace (Eph. 1:6), into a teaching which actually affirms and magnifies human virtue and good behavior, which removes salvation from the gracious hand of God and places it into the power of man, makes grace and salvation uncertain instead of certain, and is designed to move the Christian Church off its foundation, the *sola gratia.* We dare not forget that as long as a person in his heart and before God holds that there is a cause and reason of election in him personally, he bears the marks of the lost, as Paul reminded the Gentile Christians when they were beginning to forget the truth that "there is no difference between the Jew and the Greek" (Rom. 10:12) and to assume that they were superior to the unbelieving Jews (Rom. 11:18-22).

Another purpose of the doctrine of election is to supply an admonition and warning much needed by all Christians according to their flesh. Since Christians were not elected irrespective of the means of grace (*nude*), but "through the sanctification of the Spirit and belief of the truth," this doctrine powerfully exhorts all Christians by all means to hold to the course in which their election in eternity took place. Thus Christ uses the election for admonition when, after describing the way of salvation, He adds: "Many are called, but few are chosen" (Matt. 20:16; 22:14). Peter, too, uses this doctrine for the same purpose when he urges all Christians to make their calling and election sure (2 Pet. 1:10).[23] The elect on earth are seen in these vestments: they "hear the Gospel, believe in Christ, pray and give thanks, are sanctified in love, have hope, patience, and comfort under the cross, Rom. 8:25; and although all this is very weak in them, yet they hunger and thirst after righteousness, Matt. 5:6." (*Trigl.* 1073, *ibid.*, 30.) The Formula of Concord specifically sets forth the hortatory purpose of the doctrine of eternal election in the words: "From this article also powerful admonitions and warnings are derived, as Luke 7:30: 'They rejected the counsel of God against themselves.' Luke 14:24: 'I say unto you that none of those men which were bidden shall taste of my supper.' Also Matt. 20:16: 'Many be called, but few chosen.'" (*Trigl.* 1079, *ibid.*, 51.)

7

No Election of Wrath or Predestination
to Damnation

The Calvinists categorically teach a predestination unto damnation as the "necessary reverse" or other side of a predestination to salvation. Calvin gives the following heading to the chapter in which he begins his discussion of eternal election: "Eternal Election, or God's

---

[23] See Luther's exegesis of 2 Pet. 1:10 in Vol. II, 544; Luther's disputation on Luke 7:47 in St. L. VII:1461, thesis 57.

Predestination of Some to Salvation, and of Others to Destruction"
(*Inst.* III, 21; Allen, II, 140). And earlier as well as recent Reformed
theologians look down on all who, while teaching an election to salvation, reject a predestination to damnation. Calvin reprimands them
in severe and rude language. He declares the rejection of a predestination to damnation to be exceedingly "puerile and absurd,"
"worse than absurd" (*Inst.* III, 23, 1; Allen, II, 163). Hodge and Shedd
use more polite language, but deny the Lutheran theology the right to
exist because it rejects a predestination to damnation while teaching
an election to salvation. Shedd (*Dogm. Theol.* I, 448) divides all
Christendom on earth into two classes, Calvinists (the deniers of the
universalis gratia) and Arminians (the deniers of the *sola gratia*).
This division leaves no room in the Church for the Lutherans. The
position of the Formula of Concord is called "untenable ground." [24]

But this "necessary reverse" or logical counterpart is purely a
human invention.[25] Scripture strikes this allegedly necessary complement out entirely. Clearly and emphatically Scripture teaches that
Christians owe their whole Christian state in time, specifically also
their faith, to their eternal election; but with the same clarity and
emphasis Scripture also excludes the thought that the unbelief of the
lost can be traced to a predestination to damnation. Compare, for
example, v. 48 of Acts 13 with v. 46. In v. 48 the faith of Gentile
converts is traced back to their eternal election: "As many as were
ordained to eternal life, believed." But the unbelief of the obdurate
Jews is not traced to a predestination to unbelief and to damnation,
but to their opposition to the earnest and efficacious gracious will of
God in the Word: "Seeing ye put it [the Word of God] from you
[ἀπωθεῖσθε] and judge yourselves unworthy of everlasting life, lo, we
turn to the Gentiles." The "necessary reverse" is completely wiped
out also by the passages which testify that the saving grace of God,
the merit of Christ, and the efforts of the Holy Ghost to convert apply
also to the lost. See the discussion of the pertinent Scripture texts
in Vol. II, 21—34. Likewise the Scripture doctrine of obduration

---

[24] Hodge (*Syst. Theol.* II, 325) expresses the same thought.

[25] [This is admitted, practically, in the action recently taken by the Presbyterians. In May, 1938, the daily press reported: "The General Assembly of the
Presbyterian Church in the United States voted 151 to 130 today to omit two
sections of its Confession of Faith, which some speakers said formed the cornerstone of the church code. The sections omitted concerned the predestination of
man by divine election. These sections were criticized by several ministers as an
'overstatement' of the Scriptures which 'keeps our ministers constantly on the
defensive.'"]

proves that the obdurate were in no wise elected to wrath or by-passed with the offer of grace (*praeteritio*). Of course, the hardening of the heart is an act of divine wrath. It does not, however, set in absolutely, that is, without a cause, but rather for "a recompense unto them," εἰς ἀνταπόδομα (Rom. 11:9), in retribution, that is, it results from man's resistance to God's Word and will and to God's gracious visitation. See "Serious and Efficacious Grace," Vol. II, 28 ff.

To substantiate his claim that God "has created" (*creavit*) those ultimately lost, "to a life of shame and a death of destruction," to that end either "depriving them of the opportunity of hearing the Word" or "by the preaching of it increasing their blindness and stupidity," Calvin also appeals to 1 Cor. 4:7: "Who maketh thee to differ from another [τίς σε διακρίνει]? And what hast thou that thou didst not receive?" (*Inst.* III, 24, 12.) We answer: Of course, the Christians recognize their advantage of having the Word of God while others are without it. They also see their advantage of believing the Word, while others do not believe. They acknowledge that they have blessings which others do not possess. But at the same time they realize that they are equally guilty with the rest and still often act reprehensibly toward God's Word; and when comparing themselves with the lost, they find that they are "most similar to them" (*et quam simillimi deprehensi*), and thus they "learn the more diligently to recognize and praise God's pure [immense], unmerited grace in the vessels of mercy," as the Formula of Concord states it (*Trigl.* 1083, *ibid.*, 60).

But this is the surprising thing about the teaching of Scripture regarding the salvation of men that though the vessels of mercy must praise God's unmerited grace, God nevertheless did not pass by the vessels of wrath, the lost, with His grace and salvation, but earnestly sought entrance to their hearts. We saw this clearly in the case of the stubborn Jews, Acts 13:46, who thrust the Word offering them grace and salvation from them and judged themselves unworthy of eternal life, contrary to God's intention. The same fact appears in the words with which Stephen reveals the true situation to the stiff-necked Jews: "Ye do always *resist* [ἀντιπίπτετε] the Holy Ghost; as your fathers did, so do ye" (Acts 7:51). The "resisting" (ἀντιπίπτειν, flinging oneself against Him) presupposes a pressing, aggressive activity of the Holy Spirit. In short, according to the teaching of Scripture, God prefers those ultimately saved in such a manner that He meanwhile does not neglect those ultimately lost, does *not by-pass* them with His effort to convert them. The same truth is taught in Rom. 9:22-23, where the Apostle places in juxtaposition the "vessels of wrath" and the "vessels of mercy." When Paul here says that God endured the vessels of wrath "with much long-suffering" (ἐν πολλῇ μακροθυμίᾳ), he is thereby declaring that God sought to convert and save them too.[26]

A closer study of Rom. 9:22-23 shows clearly that the election to salvation has no predestination to damnation as its corollary. In two respects the vessels of wrath differ radically from the vessels of mercy. 1. While it is said of the vessels of mercy in the active voice that God had afore prepared them unto glory, the passive voice is used of the vessels of wrath: κατηρτισμένα εἰς ἀπώλειαν, ready, ripe for destruction. The passive construction is not to be regarded as accidental, but as intended, since the vessels of wrath and the vessels of mercy are here compared. The more we note how the words "Which He had afore prepared unto glory" (ἃ προητοίμασεν) emphasize God's work in the vessels of mercy, the more it strikes us that in regard to the vessels of wrath, in so far as they are "fitted to destruction" (κατηρτισμένα εἰς ἀπώλειαν), there is no mention whatever of any "doing" by God. Thus the use of the active in regard to the one group and the passive in regard to the other indeed indicates that the preparation for glory and the fitting unto damnation do not have the same author. The fitting unto destruction is not traced back to God.

The Formula of Concord, too, points out this truth: "Hence the Apostle distinguishes with especial care the work of *God*, who alone makes vessels of honor, and the work of the devil and of man, who by the instigation of the devil, and not of God, has made himself a vessel of dishonor. For thus it is written, Rom. 9:22 f.: 'God endured with much long-suffering the vessels of wrath fitted to destruction,

---

[26] Stoeckhardt (*Roemerbrief*) correctly comments: "God endured the vessels of wrath with much long-suffering before venting His wrath on them. This patience does not merely mean, as Hofmann holds, that God postponed wrath and punishment. 'A mere *prolongatio irae*, delaying the judgment, is after all no long-suffering.' Weiss. The μακροθυμία of God always has as its aim the repentance and improvement of the sinner. 'The Lord . . . is long-suffering to usward, μακροθυμεῖ εἰς ἡμᾶς, not willing that any should perish, but that all should come to repentance,' 2 Pet. 3:9. . . . We have shown above that the judgment of obduration, on which the extreme wrath follows, is brought upon men by themselves, always has as its necessary antecedent condition the self-hardening of man. God has previously offered grace to those whom He ultimately hardens and condemns and has earnestly sought to save them, but they would not. And now Paul stresses in our passage that God has been very patient and long-suffering toward the vessels of wrath, that He not merely once, but repeatedly urged and invited them to repent and be converted. And note that God even then endured the vessels of wrath with much long-suffering when they were already fitted to destruction."

that He might make known the riches of His glory on the vessels of mercy, which He had afore prepared unto glory.' Here, then, the Apostle clearly says that God endured with much long-suffering the vessels of wrath, but does not say that He made them vessels of wrath; for if this had been His will, He would not have required any great long-suffering for it. The fault, however, that they are fitted for destruction belongs to the devil and to men themselves, and not to God." (*Trigl.* 1089, 79 f.)

2. While the προ (afore) in προητοίμασεν traces the preparation of the vessels of mercy back to eternity, the προ is missing before κατηρτισμένα εἰς ἀπώλειαν, "fitted to destruction." Here, then, is taught an eternal preparation for glory or for salvation, but no eternal preparation for destruction.[27] In connection with this text, Bengel correctly points to Matt. 25:34, compared with v. 41, and to Acts 13:48, compared with v. 46. In this latter passage the faith of the Gentiles is traced to their eternal election, but the unbelief of the Jews is not represented as a consequence and result of their foreordination to damnation, but as a consequence and result of their resistance to God's gracious will and operation. In Matthew 25 Christ says of the Kingdom of Glory that it was prepared for the blessed of His Father from the foundation of the world, hence from the beginning intended for them. Of the fire of hell, however, Christ says that it is prepared for the devil and his angels. If men go to hell, they go to a place originally not prepared for them. "Hell was originally not built for men."

Against this fact it is urged that in the eternal and immutable God one cannot possibly speak of a first and a second will, an original and a later purpose. True, but the God in whom there is no *prius* and no *posterius* and who is swayed by no cause outside Him is God in His majesty far transcending human comprehension. Nevertheless, since He wants to be known of us, God became man, as in Christ so also in Scripture, as Luther often reminds us. And we must look only to this revelation of God in Christ and in Scripture if we would have a salutary knowledge of God. Christ Himself teaches us in John 3:17-18 that God first of all intends to save all men, and only secondarily intends to condemn those who through not believing on the name of the only-begotten Son leave Him no other choice. It is a mark of folly rather than wisdom to bring in at this point the eternal, immutable God, whom no cause outside Himself determines or in-

---

[27] For a full discussion see Stoeckhardt, *Roemerbrief*, p. 432 ff. [mimeographed translation by Koehlinger, p. 131 ff.].

fluences. Scripture pays tribute to this majestic God, saying, for example, Rom. 11:36: "Of Him, and through Him, and to Him, are all things." But from the context it is plain that this passage states a truth transcending human comprehension ("For who hath known the mind of the Lord? Or who hath been His counselor?") and gives the reason why there are judgments and ways in God which we human beings cannot explain in this life, that is, cannot understand and search out ("How unsearchable are His judgments and His ways past finding out!"). See "Terminology Regarding the Divine Will of Grace" and the discussion of a "change of mind in God," Vol. II, 34 ff.; 367, footnote 69.

Calvinists argue furthermore that there must needs be an election of wrath, a *praeteritio*, or an eternal predestination to damnation in view of the historical fact that so many nations did not have the Gospel and the further fact that of a hundred hearers, who are all alike in total depravity, only about twenty per cent are converted.[28] Recent Calvinists say: "The result is the interpretation of the purposes of God." Here, however, we must maintain that God wants His will toward us determined by His revealed Word, which assures us that His grace is universal, and not by the history of His dispensations upon whole nations or individuals. These ways of God recorded in *history* — that one nation has the Gospel, another not; that, though all who hear the Word are alike guilty, some are converted and the others not — Scripture classes with God's judgments, unsearchable for men, and with His ways that are past finding out (Rom. 11:33-36). Calvin and his followers commit the folly of attempting to extract a doctrine of predestination to damnation from the historical facts which Scripture expressly declares to be incomprehensible and unfathomable for us. They pretend to have a knowledge which they cannot possibly have.

And as for the Formula of Concord, it does not occupy "untenable ground," but takes the doctrinal position of God's revealed Word by saying: "Likewise, when we see that God gives His Word at one place, but not at another; removes it from one place, and allows it to remain at another; also, that one is hardened, blinded, given over to a reprobate mind, while another, who is indeed in the same guilt, is converted again, etc. — in these and similar questions Paul (Rom. 11:22 ff.) fixes a certain limit to us how far we should go, namely, a) that in the one part we should recognize God's judgment. For they are well-deserved

---

[28] Calvin: "The same sermon is addressed to a hundred persons; twenty receive it with the obedience of faith; the others despise, or ridicule, or reject, or condemn it" (*Inst.* III, 24, 12; Allen, II, 191).

penalties of sins when God so punishes a land or nation for despising His Word that the punishment extends also to their posterity, as is to be seen in the Jews. And thereby [by the punishments] God in some lands and persons exhibits His severity to those that are His [in order to indicate] what we all would have well deserved, and would be worthy and worth, since we act wickedly in opposition to God's Word [are ungrateful for the revealed Word, and live unworthily of the Gospel] and often grieve the Holy Ghost sorely, b) in order that we may live in the fear of God, and acknowledge and praise God's goodness, to the exclusion of, and contrary to, our merit in and with us, to whom He gives His Word and with whom He leaves it, and whom He does not harden and reject. . . . c) When we proceed thus far [*eo usque*] in this article, we remain on the right [safe and royal] way, as it is written Hos. 13:9: 'O Israel, thou hast destroyed thyself; but in Me is thine help.' However, as regards those things in this disputation which would soar too high and beyond these limits [*extra hos limites*], we should, with Paul, place the finger upon our lips, and remember and say, Rom. 9:20: 'O man, who art thou that repliest against God?' " (*Trigl.* 1081, *ibid.*, 57—63.)

Also the words (Rom. 9:18): "Therefore hath He mercy on whom He will have mercy, and whom He will He hardeneth," are incorrectly adduced as proof for a predestination to damnation. They do not mean that in God's heart there is no mercy for a part of mankind, namely, for those who are finally lost. The Apostle expressly says the very opposite (ch. 11:32): "God hath concluded them all in unbelief that He might have mercy upon all." And this mercy the Apostle does not conceive as a "will of complacency," that is, a will without any intention of securing its fulfillment, for in ch. 10:21 he quotes God as saying: "All day long I have stretched forth My hands unto a disobedient and gainsaying people." Why not take note of the scope of the text? The words, Rom. 9:18, "Therefore hath He mercy on whom He will have mercy, and whom He will He hardeneth," are not directed against the universal grace of God, but against work-righteousness, that is, against the delusion of man that by works he can merit something before God, and against the conceit that he can by works make God his Debtor. This scope of the passage is evident from the entire preceding and subsequent context, particularly also from the words: "I will have mercy on whom I will have mercy, and I will have compassion on whom I will have compassion. So, then, it is not of him that willeth, nor of him that runneth, but of God that showeth mercy."

It may be well to add a remark with reference to Rom. 9:18, since this text has suffered much at the hands of exegetes. Quite generally they are ready to let this statement stand: "Whoever is saved, is saved only by grace; whoever is lost, is lost by his own fault." Now, the words that God has mercy and hardens according to His will do not in their meaning go one inch beyond the sentence that the critics are ready to accept. The clear teachings of Scripture must, of course, be upheld, that those ultimately lost are not lost because of a lack of grace, but solely through their own fault, because of their wicked conduct toward God's Word and gracious operation, as we have shown; and that furthermore such as are saved are equally guilty with the others and no better in their conduct. In these two truths we have the substance of Paul's words: "Therefore hath He mercy on whom He will have mercy, and whom He will He hardeneth." The Formula of Concord states the meaning thus: "For no injustice is done those who are punished and receive the wages of their sins; but in the rest, to whom God gives and preserves His Word, by which men are enlightened, converted, and preserved, God commends His pure [immense] grace and mercy, without their merit" (*Trigl.* 1083, *ibid.*, 61). There is but one deduction of which we must beware, which the Calvinists as well as the synergists take the liberty to make contrary to Scripture, to wit, the inference that the affirmation of the *sola gratia* has as its "necessary reverse" the denial of the *gratia universalis et seria*.

8

The Cause of Error in the Doctrine of Election

The cause of aberrations from the Scripture doctrine of election is the attempt to unravel a mystery in this life the solution of which we can expect only in eternal life. This topic has been discussed under Universal Grace and Universal Redemption, as also under Conversion and Preservation in Faith (Vol. II, 21 ff.; 379 ff.; 486 ff.; Vol. III, p. 98). Therefore a brief summary here will suffice. Why, with the same divine grace for all and the same total depravity in all men, not all mankind, but only a part, is saved is beyond our limited ken in this life.

The attempt to solve this mystery has given birth, on the one hand, to Calvinism (denying the *universalis gratia*), and on the other, to *synergism* (denying the *sola gratia*). Correctly Thomasius says: "The Reformed teaching solves the problem facing us by amputating the one side (universal grace)" (*Dogmatik*, 2d ed., III, 464). With the same end in view, synergism amputates the other side, the *sola gratia.*

The fact that the synergists are intent on solving the mystery indicated becomes apparent from their whole Melanchthonian argumentation. The heart and core of all their multiform arguments is always: It is necessary (*necesse est*, Melanchthon) to assume a difference among men with regard to their conduct and their guilt before God. If there were no difference among men before God, but an equal guilt and an equally contrary behavior, we would not be in a position to explain why not all men believe and are saved or, in other words, why some believe and are saved and others not.

This statement of course is true. We cannot explain this mystery. In the light of the facts clearly revealed in Scripture, that the grace of God is universal, and that all men are alike totally depraved, we cannot answer the question: *Cur non omnes? Cur alii, alii non? Cur alii prae aliis?* But Scripture directs us to hold our tongue. The question should remain unanswered. Scripture (Rom. 11:33), speaks of God's "unsearchable judgments and ways past finding out" in His guidance of individuals and nations; and the Scriptural reason for the incomprehensibility and inscrutability of these judgments and ways is the fact that no one has first given something to God, for which God should recompense him.

Luther teaches that in this matter there is an inexplicable mystery, the solution of which we can expect only in eternal life. Cf. Vol. II, 49, note 93. The Formula of Concord teaches the same mystery by maintaining equal guilt and equally wicked behavior on the part of those who are saved, and by instructing us not to attempt in this life to go beyond this boundary of human knowledge: Whoever is saved, is saved by God's grace alone; whoever is lost, is lost solely by his own fault.[29] This mystery is taught also by the Lutheran dogmaticians of the 16th century before the *intuitu fidei* theory appeared. Cf. Vol. II, 487, note 64. This mystery the Missouri Synod as well as the entire Synodical Conference taught in the controversy on the doctrines of conversion and election, and thus, on the one hand, it upheld the *universalis gratia* over against Calvinism, and, on the other hand, it resisted the denial of the *sola gratia* inherent in the opposite contention that conversion and salvation, and therefore also eternal election, depend not only on God's grace, but are contingent on the different conduct and the lesser guilt of man. Cf. Vol. II, 490, footnote 69.

---

[29] *Trigl.* 1083, *ibid.*, 61, 62. Frank is mistaken, therefore, when he (*Theol. d. F. C.*, I, 124) opines that the Formula "withholds judgment as to whether a scientific harmonization is possible or not."

It has therefore been well said that in the doctrine of election a theologian takes his final examination. This Scripture doctrine sweeps the last remnants of Pelagianism and rationalism out of one's theology. The *sola gratia* many praise *bona fide* as the very heart of the Christian doctrine. But the moment they come face to face with the question whether those who are saved are, compared with those who are lost, equally guilty before God and equally contrary, they feel constrained to predicate a better conduct and a lesser guilt on the part of those who are saved and thus to deny the *sola gratia*. Again, many *bona fide* praise Scripture as the only source and norm of Christian doctrine. But as soon as you expect them to cling to both the *universalis gratia* and the *sola gratia* without any rationalistic compromise, simply because Scripture teaches both, then also some professed Lutherans abandon the Scripture principle and reason themselves, with the later Melanchthon, into the synergistic camp. Goeschel remarks on Article XI of the Formula of Concord: "This article certainly makes it clearer and clearer how the Formula of Concord, without regard of persons, forcefully assails all rationalism, also the subtlest, the rationalism of believers. That is the very reason why it draws the criticism of so many to this day; it is opposed to rationalism of all sorts, and for that reason rationalism of every kind has an antipathy to this Confession, also that rationalism which does not regard itself as rationalism." [30]

---

[30] *Die Konkordienformel*, etc., p. 144 f.; cp. Pieper, *Grunddifferenz*, p. 12 ff., espec. p. 28, note 3; F. Pieper, *Zur Einigung*, 2d ed., p. 29 ff.

Eschatology, or the Last Things

(DE ESCHATOLOGIA)

THIS section presents: (1) Temporal Death, (2) the State of the Souls Between Temporal Death and the Resurrection, (3) the Second Advent of Christ, (4) the Resurrection of the Dead, (5) the Final Judgment, (6) the End of the World, (7) Eternal Damnation, (8) Eternal Life.

1

Temporal Death

(De morte temporali)

Its Nature. — Scripture teaches that physical death [1] is not annihilation, but the separation of the soul from the body.[2] The death of the rich man whose ground had brought forth plentifully is described in this way: "This night thy soul shall be required of thee [τὴν ψυχήν σου ἀπαιτοῦσιν ἀπὸ σοῦ]," Luke 12:20. Likewise of the dying Christ's suffering a real death, it is stated: ἀφῆκεν τὸ πνεῦμα (Matt. 27:50) and παρέδωκεν τὸ πνεῦμα (John 19:30). Quenstedt: "The nature of death is the loosening, and local [τοπική *seu localis*] separation, of the soul from the body" (*Syst.* II, 1701).[3]

Its Cause. — Death is not due, as both heathen [4] and some professed Christians [5] asserted, to the constitution of human nature. The Scriptures of the Old and New Testaments know of no cause of death but sin. When God warns (Gen. 2:17): "In the day that thou eatest thereof thou shalt surely die," and after the Fall pronounces

---

[1] For a discussion of spiritual, temporal, and eternal death, see Vol. I, 535 f.

[2] Gerhard, *Loci, "De morte,"* § 54: "Neither the soul nor the body of man is annihilated in death. Not the soul, because it subsists immortally (Matt. 10:28) when separated from the body. Not the body, because, when dormant in the sleep of death, it rests in the dust of the earth, expecting its resuscitation on the Last Day (John 5:28)."

[3] *Localis* Quenstedt explains by adding: "Since the soul really parts from the body and no longer stays in it, it leaves the latter both as to its presence and as to its instruction."

[4] Seneca: "That you die is the nature of man, not punishment." In Gerhard, *loc. cit.,* § 27. The extensive antithesis, § 38.

[5] The Pelagians, Hoenecke, *Dogm.,* II, 461. The old and the modern Unitarians, *Catech. Racov.,* s. 2, c. 1, qu. 2—6. Modern theologians: Nitzsch-Stephan, *Ev. Dogm.,* p. 358; Kirn, *Ev. Dogm.,* p. 92. Cf. the full antithesis in Gerhard, *op. cit.,* § 39.

the verdict (Gen. 3:17 ff.): "Because thou hast hearkened unto the voice of thy wife . . . unto dust shalt thou return," He plainly declares that death does not inhere in the nature of man as originally constituted, but came into the world only as a consequence of the transgression of the divine commandment. In the same way the New Testament speaks of the cause of death. Rom. 5:12: "Death by sin," διὰ τῆς ἁμαρτίας ὁ θάνατος, and Rom. 6:23: "The wages of sin is death," τὰ ὀψώνια τῆς ἁμαρτίας θάνατος. The idea that death prevailed even prior to sin, but after the Fall was connected with sin as its judgment (and thus was given a special meaning),[6] has no Biblical warrant. Scripture knows of no death except the one that is the divine judgment on sin.

All other causes of death mentioned in Scripture are such only because and in consequence of sin. God Himself is the cause of death inasmuch as He, as the righteous Judge, according to His retributive justice (*iustitia vindicativa*), inflicts death on the sinner as a punitive evil (*malum poenae*). Ps. 90:7—8: "We are consumed by Thine anger. . . . Thou hast set our iniquities before Thee." The devil is a cause of death — he is called a "murderer" of men, ἀνθρωποκτόνος (John 8:44) — inasmuch as he seduced man to sin. Also Adam, the first man, is expressly called the cause of death (Rom. 5:15): "Through the offense of one many be dead," τῷ τοῦ ἑνὸς παραπτώματι οἱ πολλοὶ ἀπέθανον. But "the many" died through Adam's sin because his sin was imputed to the many and thus transmitted to posterity. Disease, old age, fire, water, war, etc., come into consideration only as intermediate causes of death. Behind these, as the ultimate and proper cause, lies the fact that sin has come into the world and all men have become sinners. Scripture expressly ascribes to sin the fact that men die after seventy or eighty years, are killed in accidents, in war, etc. From Psalm 90 we see that it is not the number of years that cause death, for not only the deaths we call untimely, but also those at seventy or eighty are attributed to the anger of God provoked by the sin of man. And speaking of the death of the eighteen on whom the tower of Siloam fell and of the Galilaeans whose blood Pilate had mingled with their sacrifices, Christ exclaims: "Except ye repent, ye shall all likewise perish" (Luke 13:1-5), thereby declaring the accidental death of some men the consequence of the wrath of God at the sins of all men.

To bolster their notion that death would have been man's lot

---

[6] Thus Kirn, *Dogm.*, p. 92 f.; Nitzsch-Stephan, *Dogm.*, p. 357 f.

even without sin, men resort chiefly to the argument that the human body, being matter, must disintegrate, or that such heterogeneous elements as the immaterial soul and the material body cannot possibly live endlessly in harmonious union. This argument dates back to heathen philosophers.[7] But even in Nitzsch-Stephan we read: "Composed of the same elements as the rest of nature, the body can hardly defy the general law of dissolution" (*Ev. Dogm.*, p. 358). Does such reasoning make sense? Whoever grants an almighty God must also admit that Almighty God can easily preserve what He has created. And when rationalists boast: "According to the incontestable results of physiological science the body of the first man, even without sin, would finally have disintegrated," they are mouthing unscientific bombast. They can furnish no evidence of such "incontestable results of physiological science."

Of all who attribute death to the very nature of man instead of to the guilt of sin one can only say that they have not begun to understand that ever-present, all-important fact — the death of man as the punishment for sin, and are therefore, according to Scripture, minus a knowledge all men need.[8] Secondly, such people do not grasp the meaning of the death of Christ, which likewise is a momentous fact because Christ's death is the propitiation for the sins of mankind, reconciling men unto God, and thus is our life. And their prejudice, witting or unwitting, against the *satisfactio Christi vicaria* is the underlying cause of their denial of the guilt of sin as the one cause of death.[9]

The Subjects of Death. — All men are subject to death because sin, the cause of death, is found in all. Rom. 5:12: "Death passed upon all men [διῆλθεν, spread] for that all have sinned." [10] The claim,

---

[7] Further details in Gerhard, *loc. cit.*, § 38.

[8] Ps. 90:12: "So teach us to number our days, that we may apply our hearts unto wisdom." Awareness not of the mere fact that we die, but that we die in consequence of our sin is meant; cf. vv. 7-11: "Thou hast set our iniquities before Thee," etc.

[9] An eminently personal interest prompted the old rationalists energetically to espouse the theory that death is not the punishment of sin, but a "natural, original order of the Creator." (Bretschneider, *Dogm.*, I, 845 ff.) They did not want the fact of death to disturb their delight in their own righteousness and to oblige them to seek consolation against death in the reconciling death of Christ. Therefore they taught men "to develop and to use their powers and aptitudes of both body and soul according to the laws of truth, goodness, and beauty and thus to become worthy and capable of a higher and more blessed existence."

[10] Death is personified. This mighty warrior, "so to say, accompanies all the generations and branches of the human race" (Stoeckhardt). Death clings to the heel of all men because they have become sinners.

voiced from time to time, that a preventive of death has been discovered is a deception and delusion, disproved also by experience (Ps. 89:48; Job 14:1-2). He who would deliver men from death must strike at the root of the evil. He must free men from the cause of death, the guilt of sin and the wrath of God at sin. Christ has achieved this feat by His vicarious satisfaction, and for this cause He is the only Deliverer from death. "He hath abolished death" (2 Tim. 1:10).

But here the question arises why Christians, though they have remission of sins, still must die. This fact has ever been used to prove that death cannot be the result of sin. Scripture teaches two things regarding the death of Christians: (1) Christians, except those living when Judgment Day arrives, must pass through death as a judgment upon the sin dwelling in them. Rom. 8:10: "The body is dead because of sin," τὸ σῶμα νεκρὸν δι' ἁμαρτίαν; (2) The dying of Christians is no longer death in the full sense because they are delivered from the thing that makes death terrible — the *sensus irae divinae*, as the Apology states.[11] Through their faith in Christ this sense of divine wrath has been supplanted by the assurance of divine grace, so that in dying they commend their soul into the Lord's hand.[12] Moreover, the essence of death is really the fact that if nothing intervenes, it is followed by "the second death" (ὁ θάνατος ὁ δεύτερος, Rev. 20:14), eternal torment. This consequence has been replaced in the case of Christians by its direct opposite. Through death they pass into life. Christ says of every believer (John 5:24) that he "hath [ἔχει] everlasting life and shall not come into condemnation, but is passed [μεταβέβηκεν] from death unto life."[13] (To what extent this truth

[11] *Trigl.* 299, XXIV, 56: "That sting and sense of wrath of which Paul speaks 1 Cor. 15:56: 'The sting of death is sin; and the strength of sin is the Law.' This strength of sin, this sense of wrath, is truly a punishment as long as it is present; without this sense of wrath, death is not properly a punishment."

[12] Examples: Acts 7:59; Luke 2:29. Luther, St. L. I:1512: "Natural death, consisting merely in the separation of body and soul, is a simple death. But where the feeling of death, that is, the fright and terror of death, grips one, there is the real and genuine death. Where there is no terror, death is no death, but a sleep, as Christ says, John 8:51, 'If a man keep My saying, he shall never see death.' For when the terror is taken away, the death of the soul is gone, too."

[13] The perfect used (μεταβέβηκεν) is proleptic. The passage from death to life is an accomplished, certain fact for faith. The same perfect is used (1 John 3:14) in the confident assertion of faith: "We know that we have passed from death unto life." Luther, St. L. I:1514: "If you listen to the Law, it will tell you, as we sing in the old Christian hymn, 'In the midst of life we are encompassed by death.' But that is a hymn of the Law. The Gospel, however, and faith invert this hymn and sing: 'In the midst of death we are in life.' We laud Thee, God, our Lord, that Thou art our Redeemer, hast raised us from death, and given us eternal life."

applies to the state of the soul between death and resurrection we shall discuss in the next chapter.) Accordingly, we find Scripture replete with *epitheta ornantia* (embellishing epithets, or euphemisms) regarding the death of the believers, which the early teachers of the Church as well as Luther and our dogmaticians have compiled.[14] Every Christian, and especially every teacher in the Church, ought to know them well and use them.[15]

2

The State of Souls Between Death and Resurrection

Holy Writ reveals but little of the state of the souls between death and the resurrection. In speaking of the last things, it directs our gaze primarily to Judgment Day and the events clustering around it. With their coming to faith, the blessedness of the Corinthians was complete except for the bliss awaiting them at "the coming of our Lord Jesus Christ" on Judgment Day (1 Cor. 1:7). And with Paul the Philippians and all Christians confess: "We look for the Savior, the Lord Jesus Christ, who shall change our vile body" (Phil. 3:20-21). See also Col. 3:4; 1 Thess. 4:13 ff.; 2 Tim. 4:7-9; Titus 2:13. Great significance the Day of Judgment and its sequels have also for unbelievers. They "shall be punished with everlasting destruction from the presence of the Lord and from the glory of His power when He shall come" (2 Thess. 1:9-10). But what meanwhile becomes of the soul? What is the state of the souls between death and the resurrection?

Of the souls of the unbelievers (ἀπειθήσαντες) Scripture declares that they are kept ἐν φυλακῇ, "in prison," a place of punishment

---

14 [Such *mortis dulcia nomina* are: being gathered to one's own people, Gen. 25:8, 17; departure in peace, Luke 2:29; departure and being with Christ, Phil. 1:23; a turning away from the evil to come, Is. 57:1; sleep, Matt. 9:24; John 11:11; 1 Thess. 4:13; Dan. 12:2; rest, Rev. 14:13; Heb. 4:11; passing from death unto life, John 5:24; deliverance from all evil, 2 Tim. 4:18; gain, Phil. 1:21.]

15 Luther says: "Scripture has a lovely manner of speaking of death and the deceased," and then proceeds to set forth this "lovely manner," St. L. XIII:1328 f.: "Scripture does not call it death, but a sleep," etc.; VIII:1230: "We must henceforth learn a new speech and language in speaking of death and the grave. . . . That is not a human, earthly language, but a divine, celestial language. For the like you find in none of the books of all learned and wise on earth. . . . But among Christians this should be a familiar, common, and current speech." "We must learn to scrape our tongue." Quenstedt on *mortis dulcia nomina*, II, 1699. Even more copiously Gerhard, *loc. cit.*, § 17 ff.

(1 Pet. 3:19-20).[16] Of the souls of the believers we are told not merely in general that they are in God's hand (Acts 7:59; Luke 23:46), but also in particular that they dwell with Christ and in Paradise, Phil. 1:23; "I have a desire to depart and to be with Christ; which is far better." (Luke 23:43.)[17] The "being with Christ" or "in Paradise" of the departed believing souls must certainly be an augmentation of the communion with Christ which Christians enjoy here on earth, because Paul adds: "which is far better," πολλῷ μᾶλλον κρεῖσσον, better than his communion with Christ here on earth. Moreover, the life "in Paradise," which Christ promised the soul of the believing male-factor, certainly bespeaks a blissful state of the soul after death.[18] These texts surely make it evident that the departed souls of the believers are in a state of blessed enjoyment of God, even though we know nothing further as to the manner of their blessed communion with God. Deductions from the nature of the soul, e. g., that it cannot be inactive,[19] are uncertain and therefore not to be urged in theology.

A soul sleep which excludes a blessed enjoyment of God [psychopannychism] [20] must be definitely rejected on the basis of Phil. 1:23 and Luke 23:43. A sleep of the soul which includes enjoyment of God (says Luther) cannot be called a false doctrine.[21]

The Roman purgatory (*purgatorium*), to which Rome consigns the souls of the believers for the purpose of suffering temporal punishments still due, is pure invention, for by their faith in Christ the believers, as Scripture teaches, possess not purgatory, but eternal life

---

[16] Ideas of the heathen on the state of departed souls, Gerhard, *ibid.*, § 163.

[17] Luther on this passage, St. L. I:1763.

[18] Erroneous ideas of Church Fathers regarding the Paradise of believing souls as *paradisus terrestris*, Gerhard, *loc. cit.*, § 163 f. Luther on Luke 23:43: "Here heaven and Paradise are one."

[19] Thus, e. g., Baier teaches (II, 232, note b).

[20] On this error of many Church Fathers see Quenstedt, II, 1745 ff. Bizarre is Hofmann's notion, *Schriftbeweis*, 2d ed., II, 480: "The soul of him who dies in faith is in a state corresponding to the state of death of the distintegrating body that awaits the resurrection."

[21] Luther, St. L. I:1758 ff.; II:215 ff. A complete history of this doctrine in Gerhard, *loc. cit.*, "De morte," § 293 ff. Luther speaks more guardedly of the state of the soul between death and resurrection than do Gerhard and the later theologians, who transfer some things to the state between death and resurrection which can be said with certainty only of the state after the resurrection. Luther: "It is divine truth that Abraham [after death] lives with God, serves Him, and also rules with Him. But what sort of life that is, whether he be asleep or awake, that is another question. How the soul rests, we are not to know; it is certain, however, that it lives." (II:216.)

(John 5:24; 3:18, 36).[22] And this holds true not merely of the souls of Paul (Phil. 1:23) and Stephen (Acts 7:59), but also of the soul of the believing malefactor (Luke 23:43).[23]

Recent Protestant theologians likewise teach a sort of purgatory for the departed believing souls. Kahnis (*Dogm.*, 2d ed., II, 498), for example, opines: "The idea of purgatory, no doubt, contains some truth, viz., that many Christians still stand in need of a purgation. There are many Christians of whom one cannot say that Christ is their Life. Still they feel themselves drawn to Him, and of what they do know of Him they bear witness with a sincerity, self-effacement, and devotion which cannot but shame many Christians who are stronger in words than in deeds. Is there to be no hope for such? There are, finally, the numerous Christians who, as far as men are able to judge, have true faith, but whose faith is still permeated with the dross of the old man, so that one is inclined to judge that, as they now are, they cannot enter Paradise, if Paradise is to remain Paradise. Do not tell me that with the body also much of the old man will fall away. . . . The peculiar traits of a person cannot be wiped out by one magic stroke. How should a Christian who was lacking in love suddenly by death be equipped with a flow of love? Hence we can hardly do otherwise than assume that there is room in yonder world for refining and development." These words of Kahnis show that he is contending for a purgatory on the basis of the Roman position of salvation by works. He has lost the central truth of Christianity, that through His *satisfactio vicaria* Christ has purchased for all men full remission of sins and complete salvation and that man possesses (ἔχει, John 3:36; 5:24) this remission of sins and salvation the very moment he comes to faith in Christ as his Savior through the working of the Holy Spirit. Accordingly, Kahnis has lost sight of the power of Christian faith as far as both justification and sanctification are concerned. He describes Christians as they are not. For Christ is the Life of all Christians, even the weakest. All confess Christ, too, and walk in a new life according to the new man, or in so far as they believe in Christ. Their life is, of course, still greatly impaired by the dross of the old man. But Christians believe that this imperfection

---

[22] Luther, St. L. I:1762: "Especially what is said of a purgatory is nothing but lies; for it is based on nothing but wicked life and unbelief. Since they deny the doctrine that faith saves, they substitute penance for sin as the cause of salvation."

[23] Luther on the Papistic purgatory, St. L. II:2067 f.; Smalc. Art., *Trigl.* 465, Part II, Art. II, 12—15; 485, Part III, Art. III, 26—27. Gerhard discusses purgatory in more than one hundred paragraphs (*loc. cit.*, §§ 181—292).

is richly and daily forgiven them so long as they continue in faith (1 John 2:2). If because of this dross they were to be consigned to a purgatory after this life, none of them would escape this fate, not even the Apostle Paul. For he avers, on the one hand, "The life which I now live in the flesh I live by the faith of the Son of God, who loved me, and gave Himself for me" (Gal. 2:20); on the other hand, he deplores the dross of the old man still inherent in him, saying: "O wretched man that I am! Who shall deliver me from the body of this death?" (Rom. 7:23-24.)

With regard to Kahnis' remark that the faults of a person cannot be wiped out as "by a magic stroke," note: (1) In the very moment in which the Holy Spirit succeeds in creating faith in him, man is regenerated and delivered from the dominion of sin (Rom. 6:2, 14). Faith is not the product of human deliberation, self-decision, or concurrence, etc., but as much a creative work of God as the calling forth of light out of darkness at Creation (2 Cor. 4:6). (2) Luther and the old Lutheran teachers certainly are right when they teach that in death the soul of the believer is purified of all the remaining dross of original depravity, as the phrase "in Paradise" (Luke 23:43) proves.[24] Paradise is the dwelling place of sinless man. Inasmuch as after its separation from the body the believing soul dwells in Paradise, it must have become sinless. Also, "being with Christ" (Phil. 1:23) is such an enhancement of the communion with Christ that the soul is completely free of sin. Luther therefore calls death the last *purgatorium* of the soul.

Men have also dreamt of an intermediate body for departed souls. Kahnis reports: "Theologians (Schleiermacher) and philosophers (Fichte, Weisse, Goeschel) have come to the conviction that without a material foundation the survival of the soul is inconceivable" (*Dogm.*, 2d ed., II, 522). This idea appeals to Kahnis himself. Likewise to Macpherson, who reasons: "It may fairly be assumed that during the period that elapses between the death of an individual and the coming of Christ, which brings with it the general resurrection, he wears a body suitable to his condition during that period, which in the resurrection to judgment is changed for that spiritual body which he will wear throughout eternity" (*Christ. Dogm.*, 1898, p. 453). He adds: "Schleiermacher, in particular, has dwelt upon the impossibility of our conceiving or imagining a human spirit unassociated with a body." But this idea of an intermediate body is foreign to Scripture.

---

[24] Luther X:2119 ff.; Gerhard, *loc. cit.*, § 55; Philippi, VI, 7.

Schleiermacher's inability to conceive of a human spirit unassociated with a body does not warrant the adoption of this notion. Schleiermacher would not have had to worry about a bodiless soul had he borne in mind that there is a personal and omnipotent Spirit, fully able to keep a soul in existence without its body.[25]

Before leaving the subject of the souls of the departed, we record the following facts: 1. Departed souls do not return to this world. This is a standing rule and divine arrangement (Luke 16:27-31). Moses and Elias, who appeared on the Mount of Transfiguration and spoke with Christ (Matt. 17:3), are to be counted with the risen.[26a] 2. There is no Scripture warrant for attributing to the souls of the departed a direct knowledge of particular things and happenings on earth (Is. 63:16: "though Abraham be ignorant of us, and Israel acknowledge us not"). To invoke the departed saints for their intercession and help, as Rome enjoins,[26b] is not only idolatry, but also folly.[27] 3. Scripture offers no hope for the conversion of departed souls. Such wishful thinking rests entirely on human speculation. In 1 Pet. 3:18-19 a preaching of judgment, and not a preaching of the Gospel, is meant. See Vol. II, 315 f., for details.

3

The Second Advent of Christ

Scripture teaches that, in divine majesty and surrounded by the hosts of His angels,[28] Christ will return visibly,[29] in the sight of all

---

25 Thomasius, while declining the intermediate body (*Dogm.* III, 2, 445), assumes that the soul is clothed with the glorified body of Christ during the interval of death. Neither for this is there any basis in Scripture. This fancy is a consequence of the delusion of a physical action of the Sacraments.

26a He who assumes that in 1 Samuel 28 God Himself made an exception to His rule and actually had the soul of Samuel appear must at the same time teach that this exception does not abolish the clear rule enunciated by Christ that the spirits of the dead do not return to this world and that therefore Spiritism is devil worship and a fraud, for which God punished the Canaanites with extermination (Deut. 18:11-12).

26b *Trid.*, Sess. XXV: "that it is good and useful suppliantly to invoke them." Smets, p. 65 f.; Waterworth, p. 234.

27 Cf. Apology, *Trigl.* 343, XXI, on the adoration of saints.

28 Matt. 25:31: "The Son of Man shall come in His glory and all the holy angels with Him." Also Matt. 16:27. Baier (*Comp.*, ed. Walther, II, 260) says: "It will be the office of the angels not merely to accompany Christ and by resounding trumpeting to manifest His advent (1 Thess. 4:16), but also to gather

men,[30] for the purpose of the final Judgment of the world [31] and the induction of His Church into eternal glory.[32] Luther: "He will then not be bedded in the manger, nor ride on an ass, as He did in His first advent, but burst forth from the clouds in great power and glory." [33]

This return of Christ is to be maintained as a positive fact against both the direct denial of it by the scoffers who say: "Where is the promise of His coming?" [34] and the forgetfulness of the Christians, who according to their flesh are very apt to fail to remember the return of Christ.[35]

However, certain as Christ's visible return is, the exact time and hour of its occurrence is hidden, as Christ says: "But of that day and hour knoweth no man, no, not the angels of heaven, but My Father only" (Matt. 24:36).[36] In vain, therefore, do men try to compute the time of His arrival.[37] They should, however, carefully take note of the

---

all men from all parts of the earth, not only the risen dead, but also the surprised living (Matt. 24:31); then to segregate the believers from the unbelievers (Matt. 13:49); thereupon to drive the damned into hell (Matt. 13:42)."

[29] As Christ was taken up "while they beheld," so "this same Jesus, which is taken up from you into heaven, shall so come in like manner as ye have seen Him go into heaven" (Acts 1:9, 11).

[30] That Christ will not appear successively to nation after nation, but to all at once is not only stated in Matt. 24:27, 30 and Luke 17:24 ("As the lightning, that lighteneth out of the one part under heaven, shineth unto the other part under heaven; so shall also the Son of Man be in His day"), but is also implied in His appearance to all living on earth "as a thief in the night" (1 Thess. 5:2), "in such an hour as ye think not" (Matt. 24:44), so that, for example, Europe will not be able to flash word of His coming to America.

[31] Matt. 25:32: "And before Him shall be gathered all nations; and He shall separate them one from another."

[32] Heb. 9:26, 28: "In the end of the world [the time of the New Testament] hath He appeared to put away sin by the sacrifice of Himself. . . . And unto them that look for Him shall He appear the second time [ἐκ δευτέρου] without sin unto salvation [εἰς σωτηρίαν]."

[33] St. L. IX:951. The texts that speak of the spiritual coming of Christ in the means of grace (John 14:21-23) cannot be confounded with those that speak of the visible return of Christ for Judgment. Cf. Thomasius, *Dogm.*, III, 2, 462, note.

[34] 2 Pet. 3:3-4. This talk of the scoffers also proves that the future return of Christ was general Christian teaching.

[35] Particularly Matthew 24 and 25 and their parallel in Luke 21 pertain to this forgetfulness. The fact that these references to the return of Christ are intended as warnings also for Christians is evident from their content, but is also expressly stated Mark 13:37: "What I say unto you I say unto all, Watch."

[36] On the added "neither the Son" (Mark 13:32) see Vol. II, 163 ff.

[37] In spite of Christ's express declaration that the day and hour of His return should remain hidden, even theologians like Bengel (who expected Christ in 1836) could not refrain from attempting to fix the date. This fact shows how

numerous signs of Christ's return (τὰ σημεῖα τῆς παρουσίας) which Scripture reveals.[38]

The Signs Revealed in Scripture. — "All parts of Creation . . . shall herald that day." (Luther, St. L. XI:59; I:255 f.) These signs are abnormal conditions or disturbances (a) in the social world (general hostility among nations, wars, pestilence, famine, persecution of the Christian Church, etc.); (b) in the realm of nature (earthquakes, floods, disturbances among the stellar bodies, etc.); (c) particularly in the Church (false teachers, the falling away from the Gospel, the rise of the Antichrist κατ' ἐξοχήν, who comports himself in the Church as though he were God and, using Christ's name, seduces many to apostasy from Christ by his lying powers, signs, and wonders). Just as the irregularities and ailments in man, the microcosm, are heralds of his approaching death, so these abnormal occurrences and disorders in the realm of nature, the macrocosm, and in the Church are the harbingers of the approaching great Judgment and the end of the world. Luther: "Heaven and earth creak and crack like an old house ready to crash and collapse and act in every way as though they divined that the world is soon to come to an end and that The Day is close at hand." (St. L. VII:1480 f.)

Man's failure to recognize these abnormalities as precursors and signs of the approaching advent of Christ, and the tendency even of Christians to overlook them, is caused by the "astounding stupor" (*mirabilis stupor*) dulling our eyes, mind, and heart since the Fall. (Luther, St. L. I:256; *Opp. Exeg.*, I, 266). "We are living in a more than Egyptian darkness" (I:255, 265). Things actually abnormal and unnatural we regard as normal and natural. But, as Luther reminds us, the fact that in all these things we are face to face with most unnatural conflicts surely ought to "strike our eye." Since men were created for mutual love and service, it is a horrible abnormality that their interests clash and a *bellum omnium contra omnes* is going on and that entire nations and coalitions of nations wage devastating and bloody wars. Abnormal, furthermore, are epidemics and famines, for man is to

---

deeply forbidden curiosity is rooted in the flesh of Christians. In Luther's day Michael Stiefel set Judgment Day for October 19, 1533, about the eighth hour. Stiefel regarded himself as the seventh angel, who with his revelation would precede Judgment Day (St. L. XXII:1334), and he became very angry because Luther would not believe him. Luther reports: "No opponent, as long as I live, ever scolded me so vehemently as did he." Semisch (R. E., 2d ed., III, 201 f.) reports other calculations as to the hour of Judgment Day. "Disappointment [miscalculations] served to stimulate to all the bolder attempts."

[38] Particularly in Matthew 24; Luke 21; 2 Thessalonians 2.

replenish the earth, and the earth is to nourish and support man. It is a monstrous phenomenon, moreover, that the world hates the Christian Church, which proclaims to the world for its salvation the perfect reconciliation achieved by the blood of God's incarnate Son. Instead of accepting this Word and welcoming the preachers of it as benefactors, decorating the streets in their honor and giving them medals, the children of the world fulfill the words of Christ: "Then shall they deliver you up to be afflicted and shall kill you; and ye shall be hated of all nations for My name's sake" (Matt. 24:9).[39] And when the earth quakes and demolishes the works of men's hands and buries man himself under the wreckage; when floods swallow man and his goods, these surely are no normal phenomena. Christ wants us to regard them as signs of the imminent collapse of the world.[40]

Christ specifically declares the rise of false teachers in the Church to be a sign of the end. Why they are signs is not difficult to see. The Gospel has been purchased by Christ at great price through His *satisfactio vicaria;* at His command it is being proclaimed in the world; and "it is the power of God unto salvation to everyone that believeth." Should not therefore all who profess to be Christian teachers be most diligently intent on delivering this message to men pure and unadulterated, without detracting from it or adding to it? But what happens is what Christ foretold: "Many shall come in My name, saying, I am Christ; and shall deceive many" (Matt. 24:5). The denial of Christ's vicarious satisfaction itself has become general among professed Christians. This is a state of things so abnormal, so contrary to the purpose for which the Church exists, for which the world continues to exist, that false teachers stand out among the signs of the Judgment and the end of the world.

From among the catastrophes indicative of the nearness of Christ's

---

[39] John 16:2; Matt. 10:17; Rom. 8:36; etc. Examples: Acts 14:5-6, 19; 16:22 ff.; etc.

[40] Luke 21:25-26. Luther: "Christ would say that the whole creation shall be shaken and shall herald that day; sun and moon with darkening, the stars with falling, the nations with wars, men with hearts failing from fear, the earth with convulsions, the waters with storms and roaring, the air with infection and pestilence, and the heavens with their collisions" (St. L. XI:59). — To the objection that the things mentioned, particularly the phenomena in sun, moon, and stars, could also be explained as natural and therefore could not be signs of the end of the world, Luther answers: "The courses of the celestial bodies have been so arranged from eternity that they must produce these signs before the Last Day. . . . The blind leader Aristotle wrote a book about the phenomena in the sky and attributed all of them to nature and made them out to be no signs. Him our learned men follow, and thus one fool fills the world with fools." (St. L. XI:51.)

appearance Scripture singles out the Flood, the destruction of Sodom and Gomorrah, and the destruction of Jerusalem as particularly significant. These striking divine punishments are preludes to the general Judgment of the world.[41] Notice also that Christ connects the preaching of the Gospel in the whole world with the end of the world when He says: "And this Gospel of the Kingdom shall be preached in all the world for a witness unto all nations; and then shall the end come" (Matt. 24:14).

To what extent have these signs been fulfilled? Like Luther, we must, on the one hand, speak guardedly on this point; on the other hand, however, we shall have to say with him "that the greater part of these signs have already occurred and not many others are to be expected." [42] These signs, it should be added, are purposely so designed as to make computing the exact time of Christ's return impossible,[43] with a view to keeping Christians constantly alert. The Lord warns (Matt. 24:42): "Watch, therefore, for ye know not what hour your Lord doth come." Here Meyer becomes indignant. He says (*Komm. zum Matthaeusev.*, 6th ed., p. 504) against Olshausen: "If the Lord had intended, as Olshausen imagines, that His coming be considered possible at all times, yes, even probable, and if for that reason He spoke as Matthew reports Him to have spoken, He used deceitful

---

41 For this reason the destruction of Jerusalem and the final Judgment are woven together Matt. 24:2-14, 15-21, 22-51. Also Matt. 16:27-28. Stoeckhardt: "The destruction of Jerusalem appears, on the one hand, as a sign of Judgment Day; on the other hand as the beginning of the final Judgment" (*Bibl. Gesch. d. N. T.*, p. 256). Meyer censures Luther for assuming "a medley of type and antitype" in Matthew 24. Thomasius (*Dogm.* III, 2, 460), however, says: "As to the prophecy of Christ in Matthew 24 (cf. Luke 21) I regard as faulty exegesis the attempt to separate what pertains in it to the judgment on Jerusalem from what pertains to the end of the world. Both flow in a mingled stream; the former forms a prefigurative foreground, the latter the background, which is the true theme of the entire prophecy. In the type of end that Jerusalem will have the Lord sees and shows the end of all things in such a manner that the features of what occurs at the end of the world are related to and connected with the fate of the city and at every point shine forth through it."

42 Luther, St. L. XI:50 f.: "Here again I do not want to blaspheme, but will give my opinion. Some think that the sun is to be darkened so as never to shine again. But this cannot be the meaning, for day and night must continue to the end, as God has promised, Gen. 8:22: 'While the earth remaineth, seedtime and harvest, and cold and heat, and summer and winter, and day and night shall not cease.' This sign must therefore not interfere with day and night, and still must be fulfilled before Judgment Day, for it is a sign of its coming. It cannot, therefore, be more than an ordinary eclipse of the sun."

43 Even in the days of the Apostles it could be said with good reason that the preaching of the Gospel had penetrated into all the world (Rom. 1:8; 10:18; 1 Thess. 1:8; Acts 19:10; 1 Tim. 3:16).

means for a moral end." Meyer should have recalled the analogy
between the life span of man and the time allotted to the world before
the second advent of Christ. With regard to man's span of life, too,
God has arranged matters so that every man can and should expect
the end of his life at any time. Still God has a very "moral end" in
view, namely, that man be ready for a blessed end at all times.

Fictitious Signs of Judgment Day. — First among these is a mil-
lenarian kingdom, still lying in the future, in which Christ, together
with His Christians, particularly the risen martyrs, is to rule visibly
here on earth. The idea of such a kingdom of Christ on earth took
root very early in the Christian Church and was given the name
chiliasm. There are many varieties of chiliasm, and there may be cases
that do not fit perfectly into one of the usual three divisions: *chiliasmus
crassissimus, crassus,* and *subtilis.*[44] The grossest (*crassissimus*)
chiliasm anticipates a full measure of not only spiritual, but also
carnal delights and pleasures in a future millennial kingdom on earth.
Gross (*crassus*) chiliasm teaches a future golden age and era of peace
for the Church on earth, in which the Church, after a universal conversion of the Jews and the fall of Antichrist, will reign over the world
for a thousand years and control also all secular affairs. This chiliasm
teaches two future visible returns of Christ and a twofold resurrection
of the dead, with or without the "establishment of the kingdom of
Christ on earth" in Jerusalem and the Holy Land. Subtle (*subtilis*)
chiliasm omits a twofold return of Christ and two resurrections of the
dead and confines itself to a "hope of better times" ("*Hoffnung besserer
Zeiten,*" Spener) for the Church, to set in before the end of the
world. But individual teachers of chiliasm manifest various differences
even in the fundamental ideas.

Chiliasm has no basis in Scripture, for Scripture itself explains the
passages to which chiliasm appeals as speaking of the spiritual glory
of the New Testament Church, which dawned with the coming of
Christ into the flesh and the preaching of the Gospel in the world.
The passages involved are Is. 2:2-4; 11:6-9; Zech. 9:9-10; Joel 2:23 ff.;
3:18 ff.; Micah 4:1-4, and especially Revelation 20.

Is. 2:2-3 indeed clearly teaches that all nations will come to Mount
Zion: "All nations shall flow unto it, and many people shall go and say,
Come ye, and let us go up to the mountain of the Lord, to the house
of the God of Jacob; and He will teach us His ways." This prophecy
of the congregating of the nations on Mount Zion, at Jerusalem, etc.,

---

[44] Pfeiffer's division in his *Antichiliasmus,* p. 111 f.; in Baier-Walther, II, 252.

runs through the entire Old Testament. Scripture, however, does not place the *fulfillment* of this prophecy in a future millennial kingdom, but says of all believers who, without leaving home, have come to faith in the Gospel during the New Testament era (Heb. 12:22): "But ye are come [προσεληλύθατε] unto Mount Sion and unto the city of the living God."

Again, Is. 2:4 definitely prophesies that on Mount Zion abundance of peace will reign: "They shall beat their swords into plowshares and their spears into pruninghooks; nation shall not lift up sword against nation, neither shall they learn war any more." The same promise of a state of rejoicing and peace among the nations we have, though in somewhat different words, in the other Old Testament passages mentioned. Is. 9:5 (R. V.): "All the armor of the armed man in the tumult shall even be for burning, for fuel of fire." Is. 11:6-9: "The wolf also shall dwell with the lamb," etc. "They shall not hurt nor destroy in all My holy mountain" Zech. 9:10: "And I will cut off the chariot from Ephraim, and the horse from Jerusalem, and the battle bow shall be cut off." Micah 4:1-4 repeats Is. 2:2 word for word. The chiliasts admonish us to accept these statements as to the great peace ruling on Zion in their "full, actual value." And we take this admonition to heart.

But we also do not forget that the *Gloria in excelsis* of the angels sounds forth its glad message, "Peace on earth," not in some future millennial kingdom, but at the birth of Christ and the preaching of the Gospel at that event, and that Christ says not of the citizens of a future millennial kingdom, but of all who believe the Gospel: "Peace I leave with you, My peace I give unto you" (John 14:27), and: "These things I have spoken unto you that in Me ye might have peace. In the world ye shall have tribulation." (John 16:33.) The Apostle Paul takes the same view of the matter. He calls the Gospel "the Gospel of peace" (Eph. 6:15) and attributes to all who believe the Gospel "the peace of God, which passeth all understanding" (Phil. 4:7). In other words, what these Old Testament texts prophesy of a future peace in the world is realized in its "full, actual value" not in a still future millennium, but in the appearance of the Son of God in the flesh, in the reconciliation of the world to God, in the proclamation of this news in the world, and in the sending of the Holy Spirit, who through this message works faith in people's hearts, thus creating children of peace in the whole world and among all nations. By faith in the Gospel the Christian Church on earth possesses a peerless state of peace.

Scripture expressly forbids us to refer these Old Testament passages to a worldly or external peace. Matt. 10:34: "Think not that
I am come to send peace on earth; I came not to send peace,
but a sword." Thus the New Testament interprets these texts. But
even the Old Testament texts themselves connect the peace they
predict with the coming of Christ in the flesh and with the New
Testament preaching of the Gospel; they represent it as an immediate
consequence and effect of these events. The declaration of peace in
Is. 9:2-5 has as its cause: "For unto us a Child is born; unto us a Son
is given," etc. The state of peace described Is. 11:6-9 ("The wolf also
shall dwell with the lamb," etc.) is immediately preceded by its
causa efficiens: "And there shall come forth a Rod out of the stem of
Jesse, and a Branch shall grow out of his roots." Similarly, the Old
Testament itself as well as the New clearly states that the coming
of the nations to Mount Zion is not local or physical, but comes to pass
when Zion goes into all the world with the Gospel, for through faith
in the Gospel the Gentiles and "the remnant" of Israel come to Zion
without leaving home. Hos. 1:10: "And it shall come to pass that in
the place where it was said unto them, Ye are not My people, there
it shall be said unto them, Ye are the sons of the living God."

Again, what the Old Testament passages prophesy of the abundance of spiritual knowledge in Zion (e. g., Is. 11:9: "The earth shall
be full of the knowledge of the Lord, as the waters cover the sea";
particularly Joel 2:28 ff.: "Your sons and your daughters shall prophesy," etc.) finds its fulfillment in the outpouring of the Holy Spirit at
the first Pentecost in the New Testament, as Peter expressly declares
in his sermon. (Acts 2:16 ff.) What is said of the raising up of the
tabernacle of David and of the fruitfulness of the land of Canaan —
so that seedtime and harvest occur simultaneously, the mountains drop
sweet wine, and all the hills flow with milk (Amos 9:11 ff.; Joel 3:
18 ff.) — James at the council of the Apostles at Jerusalem (Acts
15:13 ff.) declared to be fulfilled by the entry of the Gentiles into the
Christian Church.

All interpretations of these texts as pertaining to a still future
millennium instead of to the Christian Church of the New Testament
and its consummation in eternity set aside the explicit exegesis of
Scripture itself. Gerhard aptly says that the Old Testament passages adduced by the chiliasts "speak of New Testament matters in
Old Testament terms" (*Loci,* "*De consumma. seculi,*" § 90). Besides,
as Philippi (*Glaubenslehre* VI, 223) points out, the chiliasts refute
themselves by themselves giving a figurative interpretation of certain

expressions in the Old Testament passages, e. g., Mount Zion becoming the top of the mountains, exalted above the hills (Is. 2:2), the mountains dripping with wine and the hills flowing with milk (Joel 3:18).

Turning to Revelation 20, we find that this passage, aside from all other points, cannot be used to prove a millennial reign of Christ on earth because the "reigning with Christ a thousand years" (vv. 4, 6) takes place in heaven. Also Franz Delitzsch grants the validity of this argument. On the one hand he goes so far as to assert that "today there is hardly a pious Christian who does not share the chiliastic view of the last times"; on the other hand he concedes: "Apoc. 20:4 by no means furnishes a sufficient Scripture basis for the *regnum millenarium*." [45] It should not strike us as strange that Rev. 20:4 reports that the souls of believers rule with Christ in heaven. Just as surely as Christ, sitting on the right hand of God, rules the universe, the souls of the believers in heaven and on earth rule with Him, since the believers concur in all that Christ does. See p. 414. Christ has made them not only "priests" but also "kings" (Rev. 1:6; 1 Pet. 2:9). What the Second Psalm says only of Christ, Christ Himself in Rev. 2: 26-27 ascribes to all that are His: "He that overcometh and keepeth My works unto the end, to him will I give power over the nations; and he shall rule them with a rod of iron; as the vessels of a potter shall they be broken to shivers; even as I received of My Father." It is true, of course, that the reign of the believers over the world will become manifest only on Judgment Day. But even now, before Judgment Day, this reigning of believers is a fact, though to all appearances they are the oppressed, the dying, the slain. In short, according to the explanation which Scripture itself offers, the promises in Holy Writ to which chiliasm appeals are consummated in all that the Church of the New Testament already has by faith in the Gospel and looks forward to in heaven.

On the true meaning of the "binding of Satan for a thousand years" (Rev. 20:2) Scripture gives all needed information. It teaches that all mankind is in the power of Satan because of its burden of guilt. But Christ by His propitiatory death has put an end to this lordship of Satan. As He enters upon His Passion, Christ Himself interprets its significance, saying: "Now shall the prince of this world be cast out [ἐκβληθήσεται ἔξω]" (John 12:31; 16:11). For the individual the reign of the devil ends, and the devil accordingly is bound, the very moment that man is converted through faith in the Gospel, that is, through

---

[45] *Die bibl.-proph. Theol.*, 1845, p. 6, 136; in Baier-Walther, II, 256.

believing that Christ fully expiated man's sin. Again Scripture itself declares this to be the case. Paul's mandate as Apostle reads: "Unto whom [the Gentiles] now I send thee to open their eyes and to turn them from darkness to light and from the power [ἐξουσία] of Satan unto God." (Acts 26:17 f.) To the Colossians Paul writes that all who believe the redemption through Christ's blood, even the forgiveness of sins, are delivered from the power [ἐξουσία] of darkness and translated into the kingdom of God's dear Son (Col. 1:13-14). There are no other means of freeing men from the power of the devil than the preaching of the Gospel and faith in the Gospel. Such factors as science and education, recognition and world-wide influence of the Church since the days of Constantine, are in themselves no means of binding Satan. On the contrary, it was the harassed and persecuted Church which through its faith in the Gospel overcame Satan and the world.

Now, since it is certain that Satan is chained for believers only through faith in the Gospel, we shall with Luther (St. L. XIV:137) have to say that the thousand years began when the Gospel began to be preached to mankind to convert it from darkness to light and from the power of Satan to God. Accordingly, we are of the opinion that the "thousand years" plus the "little season" (μικρὸς χρόνος), Revelation 20, constitute the entire New Testament era, because the "little season," joined to the thousand years (v. 3), is immediately followed by the general judgment of the world (vv. 9-10).

When the "little season," during which Satan is loosed again, begins, or has begun, cannot be computed exactly, any more than Doomsday. But this season is characterized as a period of general assault on "the camp of the saints and the beloved city," that is, the Christian Church. This is no reference to secular wars. In the recent World War, for instance, neither the Central Powers nor the Allies were the camp of the saints and the beloved city, but on both sides the unbelievers were the vast majority. The general assault on the Christian Church occurs through universal opposition to the Christian doctrine of the gracious forgiveness of sins for the sake of Christ's vicarious satisfaction. This doctrine is the foundation on which the Christian Church stands by faith. Since the opposition to this foundation of the Christian Church is general in our day, our conviction is that we are now in the "little season." We are not thinking primarily of the Social Democrats.[46] As to their majority, they are, of course,

---

[46] Against Philippi, *Glaubenslehre*, VI, 220.

a division, but after all only one division of the army, "the number of whom is as the sand of the sea" (Rev. 20:8), which is assaulting Christendom in the four quarters of the earth. This host is also not made up merely of Rome, though it is using the Pope's decretals and doctrine of works with increased zeal to destroy the Christian Church. But a part of this Gog and Magog is also the multitude of Protestants who refuse to accept Scripture as the Word of God and deny the *satisfactio vicaria Christi* and thus undermine the Christian Church's foundation of faith. Also the secret orders (lodges), prevalent the world over and particularly powerful in our country, are a part of this throng, for they are built on the rejection of Christ as the only Mediator between God and man. Even certain mission societies belong to this hostile multitude. Though they declare it their aim to Christianize the world in a generation, they set a mundane goal for their work by not seeking to save men out of the world and from eternal damnation unto heaven, but by endeavoring to raise the moral standard of men, to imbue them with "Christian principles," and particularly to "popularize democracy." In the measure in which they actually put this rationalism into practice,[47] such mission societies belong to the "Gog and Magog" that assault the camp of the saints and the beloved city.[48]

Here are the marks by which chiliasm is recognized as anti-Scriptural:

1. Chiliasm teaches a future twofold visible return of Christ, a visible advent to establish the millennium and a visible coming to judge the world. In Heb. 9:28 Scripture enumerates the visible advents of Christ and, contrary to chiliasm, expressly says that after Christ's coming into the flesh for the purpose of bearing the sins of men only His second coming to conduct His own into eternal life is to be expected. Heb. 9:28: "So Christ was once offered to bear the sins of many; and unto them that look for Him shall He appear the second time [ἐκ δευτέρου] without sin unto salvation."

---

[47] Fortunately this is not always the case; occasionally, just as in the Roman Church, the *satisfactio vicaria* also raises its voice so that the Holy Spirit can make some members of the Christian Church.

[48] The attempts to identify Gog and Magog as certain nations are folly. The predicate makes it clear who is meant by Gog and Magog, for it speaks of a battle against the Christian Church fought from all over the globe: "And they went up on [R. V.: over] the breadth of the earth and compassed the camp of the saints about" (Rev. 20:9). Gog and Magog, therefore, are all powers in the whole world which war against the Christian faith that the incarnate Son of God by His substitutional satisfaction has reconciled God and men and that men are saved from hell for heaven solely by faith in the accomplished reconciliation.

2. Chiliasm teaches two resurrections of the dead, a resurrection of the martyrs and specially pious Christians to join in Christ's millennial reign on earth, and a resurrection of the general run of Christians and of all men for the Judgment. Christ, however, refers all who believe in Him only to the resurrection on the Last Day. John 6:40: "Everyone which seeth the Son, and believeth on Him, may [R. V., should] have everlasting life; and I will raise him up at the Last Day [τῇ ἐσχάτῃ ἡμέρᾳ]."

3. Chiliasm perverts the teaching of Scripture on Christian hope. By its assumption of a still future millennium on earth which includes world peace and the rulership of the Christians over the unbelieving world, it centers the hope of the Christians first of all in a this-worldly felicity, the millennium of peace in this world and the Christians' reign of a thousand years over the unbelieving world. The Scriptures, on the contrary, describe the way ordained for all Christians from the days of the Apostles to Judgment Day as a *via crucis*. Acts 14:22: "We must [δεῖ ἡμᾶς] through much tribulation enter into the Kingdom of God." Rest and reward are to follow only in heaven. Thus Christ presents it in the Beatitudes (Matt. 5:3 ff.: "Blessed are the poor in spirit, for theirs is the kingdom of heaven [ἡ βασιλεία τῶν οὐρανῶν])." V. 12: "Rejoice, and be exceeding glad, for great is your reward in heaven [ἐν τοῖς οὐρανοῖς]." And when Paul (Phil. 3:20-21) describes the hope common to himself and all Christians, he, too, refers to no millennium of peace and rulership on earth, but says: "Our conversation [R. V. citizenship, πολίτευμα] is in heaven; from whence also we look for the Savior, the Lord Jesus Christ, who shall change our vile body."

And what is the effect of chiliasm on the spiritual life of Christians? Chiliasm's misdirection of the Christian hope is extremely harmful and dangerous. Where chiliasm is taken seriously, that is, where it controls the heart, it turns heart and mind away from the invisible spiritual glory of the Christian life, which consists in the assurance of the remission of sins and of the future heavenly heritage, and supplants it with the expectation of an outward and mundane greatness. It depreciates such mighty and glorious words as these: "Peace I leave with you, My peace I give unto you; not as the world giveth, give I unto you" (John 14:27), and: "These things I have spoken unto you that in Me ye might have peace. In the world ye shall have tribulation; but be of good cheer; I have overcome the world" (John 16:33). Chiliasm is not content with the "Behold, the Kingdom of God is within you" (Luke 17:21), but would have the

Kingdom of God come with outward display so that one might say: "Lo, there it is!" In short, Scripture does not teach chiliasm, but warns against it.[49]

The General Conversion of the Jews. — Chiliasm usually includes the tenet of a future general conversion of the Jews. Luthardt says in his *Dogmatik,* p. 406 f.: "When, in accord with the prophecy of Christ, the Church will have branched out over all nations, the hour for the conversion of Israel will also strike, according to Romans 11." At the same time Luthardt charges that Luther and "the majority of Lutheran exegetes and dogmaticians "by a novel interpretation seek to evade" the "all" in Rom. 11:26: "And so all Israel shall be saved [πᾶς 'Ισραὴλ σωθήσεται]." The advocates of a general conversion of the Jews usually credit themselves with greater exegetical keenness and charge their opponents with "violent exegetical measures." Philippi, too, at first made this charge in his *Commentary on Romans,* p. 537, but in the third edition (p. 552 ff.) he retracted in an appended note. Some Lutheran theologians in America have also raised this accusation. Voigt, for example, says in his *Bibl. Dogmatics,* p. 231: "It is a violent exegesis which would transfer these promises, the constant theme of the prophets, to a spiritual Israel. Nor can St. Paul's distinct prediction of the conversion of Israel (Rom. 11:11-29) be turned from God's ancient people to a spiritual Israel, that is [?], 'Christians generally.'" But, as noted, Philippi recanted and then conceded that both wording and context of Rom. 11:25 f. speak not for, but against, a future general conversion of the Jews. Even more thoroughly Walther discusses this subject in *L. u. W.,* 1859, 307 ff.

The supporters of a general conversion of the Jews, for one thing, do not accept the term "all Israel" without limitation. But taking "all Israel" to mean Israel according to the flesh (all Jews), they may not, like Luthardt, interpret: "Not every single one, but Israel as a whole." Nor may they interpret: Israel "for the most part," "very many" of Israel; or, like Voigt (*loc. cit.*), even limit "all Israel" to "enough of them to represent the race." There are, it is true, Scripture texts in which "all" is used in the sense of "for the most part," "very many," etc.

---

[49] Bibliography on Chiliasm: Walther, *L. u. W.* 1872, 97 ff.: "*Lehren die Kirchenvaeter wirklich einen sogenannten biblischen Chiliasmus?*" Theo. Brohm, *Lutheraner,* 1847, p. 11: "*Ist der moderne Chiliasmus mit dem 17. Art. d. Augsb. Konf. vereinbar?*" (A brief but very careful examination of this question.) *L. u. W.,* 1860, 208 ff.: "*Das sogenannte tausendjaehrige Reich.*" For further literature see the theological encyclopedias, e. g., the article by Semisch, R. E., 2d ed., III, 194 ff., which, revised by Bratke, is found also in R. E., 3d ed., III, 805 ff.

(Luke 3:21). But in Romans 11 this construction of "all" is excluded because it stands in contrast to "in part." And this restriction of "all" is all the more inadmissible in the case of the advocates of a general conversion of the Jews. They assume two periods for Jewry: the one running parallel with the time of the Gentiles, during which only a part of Israel is blinded and always some of Israel are being saved; the second period, following the first, during which "all Israel" is saved. Hence they even sharpen the contrast of "all" with "in part." This very contrast, however, makes it utterly impossible, as also Philippi points out in his recantation, again to restrict "all Israel" in the second period of Jewry to a part, to "representatives" of Israel, etc. All who understand "all Israel" in Rom. 11:26 to mean Israel after the flesh may not restrict this term in any way, but must understand it to embrace all "individual Israelites," not one excluded. Yes, they must go even farther. "All Israel after the flesh" includes not only all Israelites living when the world ends, but also all previously deceased Jews. Consistency therefore demands that these exegetes, with Petersen (d. 1727), in the supposed second period of Jewry, include a resurrection and conversion also of all Jews who died in unbelief.[50] Then only do they really have all Israel after the flesh. Whoever is not ready to include these has no right to appeal to Rom. 11:26 in support of his opinion.

It is evident, then, that only they give "all Israel" its full value who, with Luther and the majority of Lutheran exegetes, understand it really to mean all Israel, namely, all spiritual Israel, the whole number of elect among the Jews. In several ways the wording of the text demands this view of "all Israel" as the spiritual, or elect, Israel.

1. "All Israel" ($\pi\tilde{\alpha}\varsigma$ 'Ισραήλ) parallels "the fullness of the Gentiles" ($\tau\grave{o}$ πλήρωμα τῶν ἐθνῶν). Now, as the "fullness of the Gentiles" does not denote all Gentiles after the flesh, but the whole number of elect among the Gentiles, so also "all Israel" denotes the whole number of elect among the Jews. In other words, all Israel will be saved in the same sense and to the same extent as the fullness of the Gentiles. As we cannot say that all Gentiles according to the flesh will be saved, that no Gentile whatever will be lost, so we cannot say that

---

[50] A complete list of the writings of Joh. Wilh. Petersen and the numerous rebuttals is offered in Walch, *Bibl. Theol.*, II, 803 ff. On Petersen's life and doctrine see Walch, *Gesch. d. Religionsstreitigkeiten d. luth. K.*, II, 586 ff. On Spener's relations to Petersen see H. Schmid, *Gesch. d. Pietismus*, p. 258 f.; Wagenmann, R. E., 2d ed., XI, 499 f.

"all Israel" according to the flesh will be saved, or that "all Israel" means all Jews.[51]

2. "The spiritual Israel" must be meant here because the Apostle expressly states how all Israel is saved. The Apostle's argument in this entire section from v. 11 on is directed against Gentile Christians who presumptuously imagined that the acceptance of the Gentiles implied the hardening and rejection of the whole Jewish nation. Against this misconception Paul clearly sets forth the fact that not all the nation is hardened, but that "blindness *in part* happens to Israel," and this situation is to last "until the fullness of the Gentiles be come in," "and so," καὶ οὕτως, in this manner, by the hardening of Israel in part, but not in its entirety, "all Israel shall be saved," that is, the entire Israel that is not obdurate, but believes. Thus also Philippi explains the words in his retraction: "In part Israel is hardened until the fullness of the Gentiles has come in, and in this manner, viz., by a continual gathering in to the end of time of a great number of believers from this people hardened only in part — in this manner 'all Israel' as really meant by the Old Testament Word of God, as the texts immediately adduced from the Prophets prove, is saved." [52] The advocates of a general, still future conversion of the Jews can evade the force of this argument only by taking the liberty of substituting for the adverb of manner "and so" (καὶ οὕτως) an adverb of time, "and then" (καὶ τότε).[53a]

---

51 True, Meyer and others assume also a conversion of all Gentiles before the end of the world, a teaching that necessarily, as Philippi shows (*op. cit.,* p. 555), must degenerate into Origen's and Petersen's restitution of all things (*apokatastasis*). Also Thomasius (III, 2, 465) visualizes a conversion of all Gentiles, but then modifies his thought by adding: "in which connection, however, one need not necessarily think either of a conversion of all individuals or of a genuine conversion of all." Accordingly there would be an entry of the Gentiles into the Christian Church without "genuine conversion"!

52 The Old Testament texts quoted by the Apostle (Is. 59:20 and Jer. 31: 33 f.) do not treat of the time immediately before the end of the world, but of the entire time of the New Testament, beginning with the incarnation of Christ. The texts furthermore do not speak of a saving of all Jews, but of those in Israel who turn to Christ. Even rationalists like Rueckert and Meyer grant this limitation, though they think that the Apostle here, as on other occasions, erred in his proof from the Old Testament. First they mistakenly ascribe to the Apostle the doctrine of a general conversion of the Jews just before the end of the world, and then they accuse him of adducing faulty evidence from the Old Testament, or of trying to prove the conversion of all Jews with texts which speak only of the spiritual Israel. Cf. Walther, *L. u. W.,* 1859, 227; Quenstedt, II, 1817.

53a On this interchange of terms compare Stoeckhardt, *Roemerbrief,* p. 542 f. Philippi against Meyer: "The οὕτω does not simply sum up what has been said, in the sense of 'and then,' not even in the passages from the classical writers adduced by Meyer (Thuc. 3, 96, 2; Xen., *Anab.* 3, 5, 6; cf. in addition Xen., *Cyrop.*

The objection that "until [ἄχρις οὗ]the fullness of the Gentiles be come in" refers not only to the event mentioned, but implies an event still to follow, is arbitrary. Philippi is undeniably right in saying that ἄχρις οὗ in itself indicates only the time up to which an action or occurrence is to last. Walther, too, says: "The particle ἄχρις οὗ, *until,* keeps its natural meaning of denoting the time when a fact ceases." "Until" states no more and no less than the fact that the hardening of only a part, and not the whole of Israel, and therefore the conversion of a part of Israel, will continue until the fullness of the Gentiles is come in. Walther: "Jews are to be converted as long as Gentiles are converted." Now, Christ states very definitely that the time of the Gentiles lasts to the end of the world: "And this Gospel of the Kingdom shall be preached in all the world for a witness unto all nations; and then shall the end come" (Matt. 24:14). Also in Luke 21:24 ("Jerusalem shall be trodden down of the Gentiles until [ἄχρις οὗ] the times of the Gentiles be fulfilled") a succeeding time of the Jews is an arbitrary interpolation; for the immediately following words (v. 25 ff.) speak of the signs heralding the end of the world without any mention of a time of the Jews. In the passage we are discussing (Rom. 11:25-26) the thought of a time of the Jews still to follow is expressly excluded by the fact that the statement "all Israel shall be saved" is attached to the preceding words not with καὶ τότε, but with καὶ οὕτως. We must say that since καὶ οὕτως certainly means "and so," "in this manner," the conversion of all Israel is definitely described as an event running parallel with the hardening of a part of Israel and with the coming in of the fullness of the Gentiles. Walther is right in saying: "There is no choice, therefore, but to seek in the immediately preceding words the definition of the manner in which the thing stated by Paul in the words 'all Israel shall be saved' occurs. With the little word 'so' the Apostle cuts short all man-made thoughts regarding a saving of all Israel and refers the reader to his own preceding words."

The further objection that the Apostle would not have used the term "mystery" if he had merely wished to say that during the entire time of the Gentiles all believing Israel would be saved is disposed of by a reference to Eph. 3:3 ff., where Paul calls the fact that "the Gentiles should be fellow heirs and of the same body and partakers

---

2, 1, 1; *Hellen.* 2, 3, 6), but it always emphatically stresses the previously stated mode in which the succeeding event happens or did, will, or shall happen. This is the case also in the New Testament texts: Acts 7:8; 17:33; 20:11; 27:44; 28:14; Rom. 5:12; 1 Cor. 7:36; 11:28; 14:25; 1 Thess. 4:17; Heb. 6:15."

of His promise in Christ by the Gospel" a mystery made known unto him by revelation (κατὰ ἀποκάλυψιν ἐγνωρίσθη μοὶ τὸ μυστήριον), in spite of the ample testimony regarding this great fact in the Old Testament. Walther makes this pertinent remark in regard to Paul's use of the term "mystery": "It is true, to us who look back on eighteen centuries of history of the Christian Church, who still have the Jewish nation before our eyes, who know of the conversion of Jews in all ages and countries, who observe how God even today faithfully keeps His covenant with Israel — to us this no longer appears as a great mystery, as little as the wickedness of Antichrist revealed to us by the Reformation. However, if we imagine ourselves in the position of the Roman Gentile Christians to whom Paul wrote, it will soon become clear to us that for them the Apostle's prophecy of Israel's survival and admittance to the Kingdom of Christ to the Last Day was bound to be an unexpected, great, marvelous mystery. . . . This is the mystery that the Jewish nation would never fall prey to obduracy entirely, that its hardening would always remain a hardening in part only, so that as long as Gentiles were converted, Jews also would be converted, so that as long as the time of grace for the Gentiles lasted, the time of grace for the Jews would also last, and therefore a time when only Gentiles would enter into the kingdom of Christ would never come. . . . In this grand, admirable, and adorable manner all Israel 'which He foreknew' (v. 2), without a single exception, shall, through God's inexplicable good faith, veracity, compassion, patience, and long-suffering, be saved. In view of this situation, do you Gentile Christians still want to boast?"

3. Finally, the interpretation that "all Israel" means Israel after the flesh conflicts also with the remoter context, with the whole exposition of the Apostle from ch. 9 on. In ch. 9:1-5 we have the Apostle's pathetic lamentation over Israel's unbelief and doom. He even says that he could wish to be banned from Christ for his kinsmen after the flesh. But immediately he also states that the unbelief and doom of the majority of Israel does not prove that God's promise to Israel had come to naught. For "they are not all Israel which are of Israel," "the children of the flesh, these are not the children of God; but the children of the promise are counted for the seed" of Abraham. Just as clearly the Apostle states (ch. 9:27 ff.) that of the great number of the children according to the flesh (of Israel "as the sand of the sea") only "a remnant [κατάλειμμα] shall be saved." From ch. 9:30 ff. through ch. 10, he demonstrates that everything depends on faith and that Israel, in spite of God's efforts to win over that disobedient nation,

refused to believe. And then he again raises the question (ch. 11:1) whether God has actually cast away His people. He answers in the negative, again asserting that, as in the days of Elias, so "at this present time also there is a remnant according to the election of grace" which does believe and is saved: "The election hath obtained it, and the rest were blinded" (v. 7).

Then, beginning with v. 11, Paul, whose office it was to be the Apostle of the Gentiles, becomes the champion of Israel because the Gentile Christians in their self-conceit imagined (vv. 17-24) that their call into the Kingdom of God excluded Israel from salvation. Paul refutes this error by showing in the entire section up to v. 32 that the time of grace for the Gentiles is also the time of grace for Israel. The Apostle very definitely declares at the very outset (v. 11): The purpose of sending salvation to the Gentiles is not to exclude Israel from salvation, but, on the contrary, to incite Israel to emulation by the example of the believing Gentiles and thus to save them also. Therefore it was the practice of the Apostle in executing his ministry among the Gentiles always to keep the Jews in mind and to provoke them to emulation with a view to saving some of them (τινὰς ἐξ αὐτῶν). Summing up his case against all particularistic thoughts of the Gentiles, against their tendency to exclude Israel from salvation, the Apostle states (v. 32): "God hath concluded them all (πάντας) in unbelief that He might have mercy upon all." In view of this situation there can be no doubt that like "the fullness of the Gentiles," that is, all the elect among the Gentiles, so also "all Israel," that is, all the elect among Israel, will be saved.[53b]

[53b] Bibliography on a general future conversion of the Jews: Walther, *Lutheraner*, 13, 85 ff.: *"Von der Hoff. einer noch bevorsteh. allg. Bekehrung."* Walther, *L. u. W.* 1859, 307 ff., 331 ff.: *"Wird Roem. 11:25-27 eine noch zu erwartende solenne Judenbekehrung gelehrt?"* Both articles reveal careful preparation and belong to the most thorough discussions of this question. In the article in the *Lutheraner*, Walther first shows historically what Lutheran teachers have held as to a general conversion of the Jews. He divides the Lutheran teachers into three classes: (1) such as at first were convinced of a future universal conversion of the Jews, but later retracted; (2) such as never entertained this hope; (3) such as taught a general conversion of the Jews either as probable or as certain. Then Walther discusses the chief passages of Scripture that have been adduced for chiliasm in general, or for a general conversion of the Jews in particular, and shows that this teaching is not contained in these texts. The article in *L. u. W.* expounds Rom. 11:25 ff. and takes issue with the opinions of modern theologians regarding this passage. The old Lutheran theologian Calov copiously and thoroughly discusses a general conversion of the Jews in his *Biblia Illustrata* in connection with Rom. 11:25. Calov at the same time furnishes a history of the exegesis given by the Church Fathers, the Romanists, the Reformed, and the Lutherans. Philippi in his recantation adopts the conclusions of Calov's exegesis.

The lesson of Romans 11 present-day Christians likewise have every reason to take to heart. Only too easily we come to think that God's grace has been withdrawn from that nation whose ancestors crucified the Savior of the world. And particularly the protagonists of a future general conversion of the Jews, as appears from rather dubious utterances of theirs, are inclined to this error. Luthardt (to Romans 11 in the *Zoeckler Commentary*) speaks of a "special judgment ban" at present resting on Israel. He says: "The present state of Israel is that of πώρωσις (hardening of the heart)." That is a mistake. It is the express declaration of the Apostle that the present state of Israel is not one of hardening of the heart, but there is a hardening only of a part of Israel, and Paul's words (Rom. 11:32): "God hath concluded them all in unbelief that He might have mercy upon all," apply to the Jews till the end of the world. Walther says well: "True though it be that the Jews have crucified and rejected their own Messiah, still, according to the mystery unfolded by the Apostle, Jews shall be converted as long as Gentiles are converted. Not only will the door of grace remain open till the end, but there shall always be a number of both who actually enter the Kingdom of God." It may be correct to say that since the first Pentecost proportionately as many Jews as Gentiles have been converted to Christ if we compare the relatively small number of Jews in the world with the great number of Gentiles.

But whatever this ratio may be, we are assured by Scripture that the door of grace stands open no less for the Jews than for the Gentiles and that God has dispersed the Jews among the Gentiles not to exclude them from salvation, but by the testimony and example of the believing Christians to incite them to believe that in Jesus of Nazareth the Messiah of the Jews and the Savior of the world has come. Only if this knowledge lives in us will we take the right attitude toward Israel, whereas the unscriptural opinion that the present state of Israel is one of hardening of heart and that the "judgment ban" will not be lifted until later will prove harmful to Christians and Jews alike. On the one hand, it will prevent the Christians from confidently preaching the Gospel to the Jews; on the other hand, it will divert

---

Among the elder theologians who treated this subject are also Gerhard, *Loci*, "*De extremo iud.*," § 111; Quenstedt, II, 1812 ff.; Hollaz, *Examen*, "*De iud. extr.*," qu. 16. All essential material furnished by modern theologians who contend for a general conversion of the Jews one will find assembled under Rom. 11:25 in Tholuck, Meyer, Luthardt, Hodge, Alford, and Philippi (before his recantation). For references see also Walther's documentary proof against Dr. Seiss that Papias, Justin, Irenaeus, etc., taught crass chiliasm. (*L. u. W.*, 1872, 97 ff.)

the attention of the Jews from the Gospel which in their dispersion they now hear and are to believe to a future age.

This pernicious effect is intensified if this dream of a future "time of the Jews" is made attractive to them by promises of Jewish nationalism, a return to, and possession of, the land of their forefathers, and a rebuilding of the Temple in Jerusalem, with re-establishment of its elaborate worship. One of the many deplorable consequences of the World War is the promise of the Allies to give Palestine to the Jews as their national home. Instead of repenting of their sins and believing in the Messiah who has come, the Orthodox Jews dream of a return to Palestine and the rebuilding of the Temple with its worship (Zionism), and the Reform Jews envision a spiritual domination of the world by Jewish intellectual superiority and erudition, to be achieved by means of a Jewish university on the Mount of Olives.[54]

4

The Resurrection of the Dead

(De resurrectione mortuorum)

Human reason not only doubts the resurrection of the dead (1 Cor. 15:35), but even ridicules it (Acts 17:32). Such an attitude involves a denial of what man knows by nature. Because rational man knows that there is an omnipotent God, this fact being evident to him from the mighty works of Creation (Rom. 1:19-20), he ought at least to acknowledge the possibility of a resurrection of the dead. Therefore Paul says of the deniers (1 Cor. 15:34): "Some have not the knowledge of God," and Christ says (Matt. 22:29), Ye know not "the power of God."

Turning to Holy Scripture, we find that it clearly teaches the resurrection of the dead throughout the New Testament (John 5:28-29; 6:39-40; Mark 12:18-27; 1 Thess. 4:16; 1 Corinthians 15; 2 Cor. 5:10; etc.), and also clearly affirms the resurrection of the body in the

---

[54] Cf. Dr. Weizmann's remarks at the cornerstone laying of the Hebrew University on the Mount of Olives (*L. u. W.*, 1920, p. 93). The Jews might build the Temple because they have the wealth and an exact description of the Temple in the Old Testament (1 Kings 6 and 2 Chronicles 3). But the restitution of the Old Testament worship is impossible because for it they need priests from the house of Aaron and the tribe of Levi (Esra 6:62; Neh. 7:64), and the genealogies are lost. (Cf. Baumgarten, *Glaubenslehre*, II, 160 f.; Winer, *Realwoerterb.*, 3d ed., II, 516; Eusebius, Kirchengesch., I, 6.)

Old Testament. Christ charges the Sadducees, who had nothing but the Old Testament, with ignorance of the Scriptures ("not knowing the Scriptures," Matt. 22:29), because of their denial of the resurrection of the dead. At the same time He points to a large group of Old Testament texts which teach the resurrection of the dead: "But as touching the resurrection of the dead, have ye not read that which was spoken unto you by God, saying, I am the God of Abraham and the God of Isaac and the God of Jacob? God is not the God of the dead, but of the living." [55a] Accordingly, wherever in the Old Testament we find the divine promise of grace: "I will be thy God" (at the institution of circumcision, etc.: Gen. 17:7; 26:24; 28:13; Ezek. 37:27, etc.), the resurrection of the dead is taught. The same holds true of Gen. 3:15, where together with the crushing of the head of the serpent by the Seed of the woman, that is, the destruction of the rule and works of the devil, is promised also the abolition of death, inasmuch as death is solely the consequence of sin, which was introduced into the world by the devil's seduction of man. Luther's comment on Gen. 3:15 is fully warranted: "This passage at once includes deliverance from the Law, sin, and death and reveals a clear and sure hope of the resurrection and restoration in the hereafter. For if the serpent's head is to be crushed, certainly death, too, must be done away with and destroyed." [55b] The Christian faith is as ancient as the first promise of Christ, Gen. 3:15, and includes deliverance from death along with deliverance from the guilt of sin.

Today a very gradual development of a resurrection faith among the Old Testament believers is generally assumed. Also Luthardt opines: "In the Old Testament the teaching of a resurrection becomes evident only very gradually" (*Dogm.*, 11th ed., p. 412). For the Old Testament teaching on the resurrection such theologians point to a few texts in the later books, particularly to Dan. 12:2, sometimes also to Ps. 17:15, and to "prefigurative" passages, such as Hos. 13:14; Is. 26:19; Ezekiel 37; possibly also to Job 19:25-27. Voigt, for instance, says: "The doctrine of resurrection is found only in the later books of the Old Testament" (*Bibl. Dogm.*, p. 239). But this opinion reveals a poor understanding of the Old Testament Scriptures and directly contradicts

---

[55a] Matt. 22:31-32. These words do not merely teach the survival of the souls after death, but also, as Christ expressly says, treat "of the resurrection of the dead [περὶ τῆς ἀναστάσεως τῶν νεκρῶν]."

[55b] St. L. I:240. Also III:84 f.; especially detailed in a sermon on Gen. 3:15 preached 1526 (III:650f.)

Christ Himself, who definitely states that in the words of Ex. 3:6, "I am the God of Abraham," etc., the resurrection of the dead is taught.[56]

Hofmann, however, in spite of Luthardt's contradiction (*Dogm.*, p. 412), asserts: "Nothing can be more erroneous than the opinion that the resurrection is a later idea, the product of human reflection, the first trace of which, if it did not indeed first come from the Parsees to the Jews, we are supposed to have in Isaiah and Ezekiel, perhaps, it is conceded, even in the Psalms of David. . . . No age can be found when one could conceive of faith without this hope, and there is no period after the first promise when it might first have arisen. . . . Hengstenberg says on one occasion that when men regarded death as the punishment of sin, faith in an eternal life necessarily had to spring up as soon as the hope of a deliverance had taken root. The hope of deliverance, however, took root when that solemn word of God after our first parents' fall told of the victory of mankind [ought to read: of the victory of the Seed of the woman] over their seducer. In this victory also death is swallowed up. But would not faith appropriate to the individual what is promised to mankind? If men knew that their sins were remitted to them, how could they do otherwise than comfort themselves with the hope that they would not remain in death?" (*Schriftbeweis*, 2d ed., II, 2, 490; quoted approvingly by Philippi, *Glaubenslehre*, VI, 80, note.)

Scripture clearly states that the doctrine of the resurrection of the dead belongs to the fundamental doctrines (see Vol. I, 84 f.), rejection of which makes Christian faith impossible. It says of Hymenaeus and his confederates, who contended that the resurrection had already taken place, hence denied the bodily resurrection on Judgment Day, that they "concerning the truth have erred [περὶ τὴν ἀλήθειαν ἠστόχησαν]" and "concerning faith have made shipwreck [περὶ τὴν πίστιν ἐναυάγησαν]" (2 Tim. 2:18-19; 1 Tim. 1:19-20).

Raising the dead is never a work of man, but always a work of divine omnipotence. 2 Cor. 1:9: "God, which raiseth the dead"; Rom. 4:17: "God, who quickeneth the dead and calleth those things which be not as though they were." Since, however, divine omnipotence is common to the three Persons of the holy Trinity without division or

---

[56] The author of the article *Resurrection* in the *Calwer Bibellexikon* deems himself qualified to accuse Christ of false exegesis: "What Jesus deduces from the name 'God of Abraham, Isaac, and Jacob,' namely, that the communion of the believer with God extends beyond the grave (Matt. 22:32), was in general hidden from these men themselves and from the believers of the Old Covenant generally." According to this assertion, Christ groundlessly reproached the Sadducees for not knowing the Scriptures.

multiplication (see Vol. I, 415 ff.), we find that the Son of God, too, ascribes this single act (*eandem numero actionem*) of the raising of the dead to Himself (John 5:21: "As the Father raiseth up the dead and quickeneth them, even so the Son quickeneth whom He will"), just as He attributes the single act of world preservation to Himself (John 5:17-20). At the same time Scripture teaches with great emphasis that the divine act of raising the dead and judging the world is performed by the incarnate Son of God, that is, in and through the human nature of Christ. John 5:22: "The Father judgeth no man, but hath committed all judgment unto the Son," and this "because He is the Son of Man" (v. 27). Cf. Vol. II, 160. Therefore no man need marvel (v. 28) that the hour is coming in the which all that are in the graves shall hear His (the Son of Man's) voice. In the divine economy the Redeemer of the world is also the Reviver of the dead and the Judge of mankind. As the Son of God became the Bearer of the sins of the world not ἄσαρκος, but ἔνσαρκος, that is, in His assumed human nature, and thus destroyed the works of the devil, so He judges the world in His assumed human nature, and the preceding raising of the dead is performed "by that Man whom He hath ordained" (Acts 17:31). The notion that the actions (*actiones*) of the deity of Christ cannot be communicated to His human nature is indeed to be found in Reformed writings, but not in Holy Writ (cf. Vol. II, 243 ff.).

Who rises (*subiectum quod resurrectionis*)? Scripture answers: "All men, not only the believers, but also the unbelievers." John 5:28: "All that are in the graves." Before Felix (Acts 24:15) Paul speaks of "a resurrection of the dead, both of the just and unjust." That the unbelievers will rise is denied by many.[57] But here the bodily resurrection differs from the spiritual. Christ's call to arise spiritually (John 5:25), that is, to believe the Gospel (Matt. 11:28: "Come unto Me, all ye that labor and are heavy laden, and I will give you rest"), is resistible (Matt. 23:37, "Ye would not"), because during the time of grace Christ works through means. On Judgment Day (John 5:28) Christ's call to the body to arise works irresistibly, because then "the Son of Man shall come in His glory," in uncovered majesty, and therefore works *efficacia irresistibili* (Matt. 25:31-32).

As to what rises (*subiectum quo resurrectionis*), Scripture instructs us: Whatever of man is "in the graves," hence the bodies of men.

---

[57] Cf. the antithesis in Gerhard, *Loci*, "*De resurr.*," § 100—102; in Guenther, *Symb.*, 4th ed., p. 422 f. (Socinians, Adventists, Russellites, Christadelphians). [See *Pop. Symb.*, pp. 132, 357, 419, 416.] Strong, *Syst. Theol.*, p. 1016, against Stevens, *Pauline Theol.*, p. 357.

The identity of these bodies with those which men had here on earth is implicit in the very term "resurrection." What had died, decayed, rises and becomes alive. "The word ἀνάστασις denotes the raising again of what previously stood and had fallen." He who denies the numerical identity of the deceased and the risen bodies is *eo ipso* denying the resurrection of the dead. Neither the instantaneous transformation (ἀλλαγησόμεθα) of those living at the break of Judgment Day (1 Cor. 15:51-52) nor the resurrection of the dead erases the identity of the bodies. Objections such as that the elements of the body turned to dust have been assimilated by other bodies, etc., are brushed aside by the word of Christ: "Ye know not the power of God" (Matt. 22:29).

The risen bodies of the faithful, however, will then be spiritual (σώματα πνευματικά). 1 Cor. 15:44: "It is sown a natural body; it is raised a spiritual body." What is meant by a spiritual body we may, of course, not determine by speculation, but can learn only from Scripture, which describes the resurrection bodies, in contrast to their character in this life, as incorruptible, glorious, vigorous. 1 Cor. 15: 42-43: "Raised in incorruption — in glory — in power." The term "glorious" is further explained Phil. 3:21: "Fashioned like [σύμμορφον] unto His glorious body," and Matt. 13:43: "The righteous shall shine forth as the sun."

The term "equal unto the angels" (ἰσάγγελοι, Luke 20:36; ὡς ἄγγελοι, "as the angels," Matt. 22:30) is interpreted by the words added: "They neither marry nor are given in marriage." The similarity with the angels is therefore not to be widened to include incorporeity or loss of sex. In regard to asexuality Baier correctly says: "They receive the sex and all the parts or members that they had in this life, of course not for the restoration of the former use, but for the integrity of the organic body."[58] Since seedtime and harvest, food and raiment, etc., cease with this world, the spiritual body — as Luther expresses it (St. L. IX:1243) — will "no more be an eating, sleeping, digesting body, but will be spiritually fed and sustained by God and be indestructible life."[59]

[58] *Comp.*, ed. Walther, II, 248. Luther: "The constitution of the body remains the same, but not the use of the body," (St. L. IX:122).

[59] Cf., *ibid.*, Luther's also philologically classic explanation of σῶμα ψυχικόν, natural body: "The term *animale corpus*, which we translated 'a natural body,' comes from the Hebrew *nephesh* (*anima*) and means not merely a part of man, as we Germans speak of the soul, but means the entire man as he lives in his five senses and must sustain himself by eating, drinking, house and home, wife and child." This fact also Meyer sets forth in commenting on this text.

The opinion that everyone will rise in the stature he had at his death is the most probable.[60] In the saints all bodily defects (*deformitas*), also the marks of old age, will of course be removed, since all physical defects and aging are wholly the consequence of sin. Because sin becomes inveterate in persistent unbelievers, the consequences of sin (the *deformitas*) will also become more pronounced in their bodies in yonder life.[61]

5

The Final Judgment

(De iudicio extremo)

The judgment of the world is joined closely to the visible return of Christ and the resurrection of the dead. The description of the glorious visible appearance of Christ (Matt. 25:31) is immediately followed by the words: "Then [τότε] shall He sit upon the throne [θρόνος] of His glory, and before Him shall be gathered all nations [πάντα τὰ ἔθνη]; and He shall separate [ἀφοριεῖ] them one from another, as a shepherd divideth his sheep from the goats; and He shall set the sheep on His right hand, but the goats on the left." In the divine economy Christ in His human nature, radiating divine glory, will be the Judge of the world, as has been set forth in the preceding chapter.

As subjects of the Judgment, Scripture mentions all men, pious and wicked,[62] dead and living,[63] and besides mankind also the evil angels.[64]

---

60 Rev. 20:12: "I saw the dead, small and great [τοὺς μεγάλους καὶ τοὺς μικρούς], stand before God." On this entire chapter see the comprehensive historical and exegetical discussion in Gerhard, *loc. cit.*, under the heading "*De materia resurr.*," §§ 67—90.

61 Gerhard gives this description of it, *loc. cit.*, § 52: "But if the malefactors and criminals in this life bear testimony by their scowling face of the hidden impiety of their hearts, 'murder and theft glare from their eyes,' how much more will the indelible marks of their sins appear in the bodies and faces of the damned!"

62 2 Cor. 5:10: "For we must all appear before the judgment seat of Christ, that everyone may receive [κομίσηται, take along] the things done in his body, according to that he hath done, whether it be good or bad." Rom 14:10: "For we shall all stand before the judgment seat of Christ."

63 Acts 10:42: "He [Jesus of Nazareth] was ordained [ὡρισμένος] of God to be the Judge of quick and dead."

64 2 Pet. 2:4: "For if God spared not the angels that sinned, but cast them down to hell, and delivered them into chains of darkness, to be reserved unto judgment [παρέδωκεν εἰς κρίσιν τετηρημένους]." There has been debate as to whether 1 Cor. 6:3: "Know ye not that we shall judge angels?" refers to evil or

The norm of the judgment (*norma iudicii*), Scripture says, are the works of men. 2 Cor. 5:10: "According to that he [everyone] hath done, whether it be good or bad." [65] But the righteous are judged only according to their good works because these works are the proof of their faith in Christ; the evil works of the believers are not even on Judgment Day brought to light again because through the believer's justification they have been cast into the depths of the sea (Micah 7:19), that is, have been forgiven. This is expressed also in Matt. 25: 34-40 by the fact that in the judgment of those on the right hand only good works and no evil works whatever are mentioned.

The opinion voiced also by some Lutheran theologians (even though they add all manner of restrictions) that also the evil works of the believers will be brought to light again in the last Judgment is certainly a strange opinion. To reject this curious, unscriptural view, we harmonize in a Scriptural manner two groups of passages that seem to contradict each other. Holy Writ states two things most definitely: (1) All men, including the believers, will be judged;[66] (2) The believers are not judged.[67] Holtzmann abandons the attempt to harmonize these Scripture statements. He assumes that here, as in justification and sanctification, there are in Paul two "disharmonious"

---

good angels. Cf. Calov and Meyer on the passage. Meyer here assumes good angels and claims to be observing a more faithful exegesis because the term "angels" without a specific modifier always is used of the good angels. However, Meyer forgets the universally accepted exegetical rule that the predicate defines both the subject and the object more closely. The predicate "judge" defines the object "angels" more specifically as angels encumbered with sins, as evil angels. Meyer himself searches further for a definitive qualifier in favor of his "good angels" and imagines he has found it in Heb. 1:14, which states that the good angels have to serve the Christians, a service for which they must be held "responsible." However, the general concept "responsible" will not suffice to save Meyer's argument. He must transform the general concept of responsibility into the specific concept that the good angels sin in connection with their service of man. Thus, to obtain a fitting object for the predicate "judge," he himself again arrives at the interpretation which he rejects in "most" commentators as unexegetical. In vain does Meyer appeal to Gal. 1:8, where "in an assumed case" the anathema would strike the good angels, for in 1 Cor. 6:3 we are not dealing with an assumed case, but with reality: "We shall judge angels." The Christians "judge" inasmuch as they do with Christ everything that He does.

[65] Specific mention of good and evil works Matt. 25:35-40, 42-45; 12:36: "Every idle word."

[66] The texts cited above; Rom. 14:10: "We [the Apostle is speaking in the name of all Christians] shall all stand before the judgment seat of Christ," etc.

[67] John 3:18: "He that believeth on Him [the Son of God] is not condemned [judged]." John 5:24: "He . . . shall not come into condemnation [εἰς κρίσιν οὐκ ἔρχεται]."

trends of thought and speaks of a "yawning contradiction." (*Neutest. Theol.* II, 223.) Meyer in his comments on 1 Cor. 6:2 harmonizes by first judging the believers and then making them associate justices of Christ. But Scripture knows nothing of this "first" and "then." The Scriptural manner of harmonizing these statements is this: Since in the judgment of the righteous only their good works, and not their evil works, come into consideration, as we clearly see from Matt. 25: 35-40, this procedure amounts to the declaration of Christ that "he that believeth on Him is not condemned [judged]" (John 3:18; cf. 5:24). A procedure in which evil works are disregarded and only good works performed are praised has lost the character of a judgment. In other words, these two series of Scripture passages are harmonized by the proper distinction of Law and Gospel. Gerhard remarks: "*Nomistic* statements must be distinguished from those that are properly evangelical. This is Law: 'Every idle word that men shall speak, they shall give account thereof in the Day of Judgment,' Matt. 12:36; this is Gospel: 'He that . . . believeth . . . shall not come into condemnation,' John 5:24. This is Law: 'Thou treasurest up unto thyself wrath against the day of wrath and revelation of the righteous judgment of God,' Rom. 2:5; this is Gospel: 'Look up, and lift up your heads; for your redemption draweth nigh,' Luke 21:28." (*Loci*, "*De extremo iudicio*," § 65.) Because the believers have forgiveness, their *norma iudicii* is not the Law, but the Gospel, which means that they are not judged at all.

But why, then, are statements that are Law, *e. g.*, "We must all appear before the judgment seat of Christ," addressed to the believers in this life? The proper reply is: As in general the preaching of the Law is necessary and salutary for the believers because of the flesh still clinging to them, so in particular the words of the Law pertaining to the Judgment on the Last Day. These nomistic statements should warn them against carnal security and keep alive the knowledge of their sin. When this purpose is attained, that is, when they in daily repentance realize their sinfulness and in faith flee to Christ as their Redeemer from all sin, they are dealt with according to the word: "Christ is the end of the Law," hence also of the judgment. "He that believeth on Him is not condemned" (Rom. 10:4; John 3:18). Luther: "The judgment is abolished; it concerns the believer as little as it does the angels. . . . All believers pass from this life into heaven without any judgment, and will even be the judge of others." (St. L. VII:1974, 1975.)

Finally, the observation is correct that we should not conceive of the Judgment of the Last Day as a long-drawn-out trial (*iudicium discussionis*) eventually leading to the separation of the righteous from the wicked. According to Matt. 25:32, the parting of the righteous from the wicked precedes all discussion or explanation.

6

The End of the World

(De consummatione mundi)

Scripture says expressly that "the heaven and the earth," that is, the universe created by God "in the beginning" (Gen. 1:1) will pass away or perish. Luke 21:33: "Heaven and earth shall pass away [ὁ οὐρανὸς καὶ ἡ γῆ παρελεύσονται]." Heb. 1:10-12 quotes Ps. 102: 26-28: "Thou, Lord, in the beginning hast laid the foundation of the earth, and the heavens are the works of Thine hands: they shall perish [ἀπολοῦνται] . . . and they all shall wax old as doth a garment; and as a vesture shalt Thou fold them up, and they shall be changed [ἀλλαγήσονται]." But while heaven and earth pass away and are changed, God will continue forever (σὺ δὲ διαμένεις, v. 11), and so will the words of Christ (οἱ δὲ λόγοι μου οὐ μὴ παρελεύσονται, Luke 21:33).

Our old Lutheran theologians are not agreed on whether this passing away is to be defined more specifically as a total annihilation (*interitus mundi secundum substantiam*, κατ' οὐσίαν) or only as a transformation or conversion (*interitus mundi secundum accidentia*, κατὰ ποιότητα). Luther, Brenz, Althammer, Ph. Nicolai, and others teach a transformation, principally on the basis of Rom. 8:21: "The creation itself also shall be freed from the bondage of corruption into the glorious liberty of the children of God." [68] Most of the earlier Lutheran

---

[68] Luther: "It is quite comforting to hear Paul draw in the whole creation and make of it a person one with us in the desire to leave this life for another. He wants us to become sure that our present life is not yet our destiny, but that we are to expect another life, which is to be our true life. Just as the sun is waiting for a new attire to be given it, and the earth and all other creatures; a cleansing from the misuse by the devil and the world. This, he says, will come to pass when the children of God are made manifest. Even now, here on earth, they are truly God's children, but they are not yet in their glory. Just as the sun is not yet in its true glory because it is subject to vanity; but it is awaiting the end appointed, when its servitude shall have an end. For this it is waiting together with all creatures and all saints, with much sighing. Meanwhile it remains subject to vanity, that is, to the devil and the wicked world, solely because God has subjected it; however, in hope that this is not to continue forever." (St. L. XII:729;

theologians join Gerhard, Quenstedt, and Calov in assuming that the world will perish *quoad substantiam.* Gerhard (*Loci,* "De consummatione seculi," §§ 37—63) treats the subject extensively. He quotes the arguments pro and con and then gives his reasons why he regards a destruction according to the substance as corresponding more fully to the statements of Scripture.[69]

Nevertheless Gerhard says (*ibid.,* § 38): "We do not defend our opinion of the destruction of the world according to its substance as an article of faith, but we assert that this opinion is more in conformity with the emphatic statements of Scripture concerning the end of the world. Hence we do not rashly accuse those of heresy who are of the opposite opinion and describe the destruction of the world as a transformation. Many therefore would rather reserve judgment in this question [ἐπέχειν] and leave this matter to future experience than take a definite stand now."[70] All who assume a transformation of the creation must teach a change whereby the world in its entire present outward form really passes away on Judgment Day or comes to an end (τέλος). 1 Cor. 7:31: "The fashion (σχῆμα, form) of this world passeth away." Luther: "In short, whatever belongs to the nature of these temporal goods, whatever constitutes this transitory life and activity, shall all cease" (St. L. VIII:1222).

Erl., 2d ed., 9, pp. 117, 108 f.) Brenz (Homil. 53, *in Lucam*): "Will heaven and earth pass away in such a manner that nothing whatever of them remains? By no means. They will not pass away entirely, but will be changed. They will cast aside the vestment of corruption and put on the new vestment of incorruption. It will be a change of heaven and earth, but not a total abolition of them." More quotations in Gerhard, *loc. cit.,* § 38. With the words of Luther quoted above, however, compare passages such as St. L. VIII:1187 ff.

69 The chief mistake of those who seek to prove a mere transformation of the Creation from Romans 8 is, according to Gerhard, that they do not heed properly the term "bondage" (δουλεία) in the statement: "The creature itself also shall be delivered from the bondage of corruption into the glorious liberty of the children of God." They interpret as if the Apostle said that the creatures were to be delivered from corruption, while the Apostle merely speaks of a deliverance from servitude (*servitus*) to corruption. "We add," says Gerhard, "that the Apostle nowhere says that the Creation shall be delivered from corruption, a phrase that could seem to be opposed to a destruction of substance, but delivered from the servitude of corruption, a phrase that does not conflict with the destruction of substance." It is the bondage of corruption from which the personified Creation longs to be delivered. But this deliverance from bondage could take place, according to Gerhard, not only by a renewal (*renovatio*), but just as well by a cessation of existence. In illustration of this type of deliverance Gerhard points to the words of Seneca to Marcia that death brings man freedom from all evils, although Seneca at the same time maintains that in death man ceases to exist. Calov agrees with Gerhard.

70 Gerhard mentions as Lutherans who would not assert anything definite: Heerbrand, Mylius, Hutter, Balth. Meisner, and others.

7

Eternal Damnation

(De damnatione aeterna)

In a measure the conscience of natural man still convinces him that damnation awaits men after this life because of their sins. This knowledge belongs to the sphere of the Law, and the Law is still active in natural man not only as norm, but also as condemning judge. Rom. 2:15: "Which show the work of the Law written in their hearts, their conscience also bearing witness and their thoughts the meanwhile accusing or else excusing one another." Accordingly, belief in a Hades with its punishments after this life prevails among the heathen.[71]

Holy Scripture teaches the truth of an eternal damnation so clearly and emphatically that one cannot deny it without at the same time rejecting the authority of Scripture. Scripture parallels the eternal salvation of the believers and the eternal damnation of the unbelievers. Whoever therefore denies the one must, to be consistent, deny the other. Matt. 25:46: "These shall go away into everlasting punishment [εἰς κόλασιν αἰώνιον], but the righteous into life eternal [εἰς ζωὴν αἰώνιον]." We find the same juxtaposition and antithesis in other passages of Scripture, e. g., John 3:36, etc. This parallelism proves that the term "eternity" in the sense of limited duration, as sometimes used in Holy Writ (Ex. 12:14, 24; 21:6; etc.), is inapplicable here. We must take the predicate "eternal" in its proper, or strict, sense, in the sense of *sine fine*, in all Scripture texts which use it to describe the duration of the penalties of the wicked in yonder life (2 Thess. 1:9: "everlasting destruction"; Matt. 18:8: "everlasting fire"; Mark 3:29: "eternal damnation"). The Apology, too, so defines it: "Christ shall appear, and shall raise up all the dead, and shall give to the godly eternal life and eternal joys, but shall condemn the ungodly to be punished with the devil without end (*sine fine*)" (*Trigl.* 335, XVII, 66).

---

[71] In connection with Rom. 1:32 Philippi quotes from Aeschylus' *Eumenides*, lines 259—265:

> You will see whoever else of the mortals has sinned,
> Committed a crime against the deity, against the guest,
> Against the dear parents.
> Everyone has there his due reward;
> For Hades is the great judge of mortals
> Below the earth,
> He sees and records everything in his heart.

Similarly, the Augustana: "They condemn the Anabaptists, who think that there will be an end [*finem*] to the punishments of condemned men and devils" (*Trigl.* 51, XVII, 4).

The objections raised in all ages to the endlessness of the infernal punishment are understandable; for the thought of a never-ending agony of rational beings, fully realizing their distressing plight, is so appalling that it exceeds comprehension. "*Mein ganz erschrocknes Herz erbebt, dass mir die Zung' am Gaumen klebt*" (*Gesangb.* 434, 1). But all objections are based on the false principle that it is proper and reasonable to make our human sentiments and judgments the measure of God's essence and activity. This is the case in particular with those who contend that an everlasting punishment of a part of mankind does not agree with the unity of God's world plan ("dualism"), or that it is compatible neither with divine love nor with divine justice, who accordingly want to substitute for eternal damnation eventual salvation by gradual improvement in the next life or an immediate or later annihilation of the wicked.[72] Against such views we must maintain the general principle that God's essence, attributes, and actions exceed our comprehension,[73] that we can therefore not know *a priori*, but only from God's revelation in His Word, what agrees, or conflicts, with God's essence and attributes.

The *nature* (*forma*) of eternal damnation consists in eternal banishment from the sight of God, or, in other words, in being forever excluded from communion with God. To the doomed Christ says, Matt. 25:41: "Depart from Me [πορεύεσθε ἀπ' ἐμοῦ]"; and Matt. 8:12 we read: "They shall be cast out [ἐκβληθήσονται] into outer darkness."

---

[72] Quotations in Guenther, *Symb.*, 4th ed., pp. 420—423. On "conditional damnation" Bretschneider (*Syst. Entwicklung*, 3d ed., p. 847 f.) says: "By eternity of the punishments of hell our old theologians understood an uninterrupted continuation of punishments in intensity as well as duration and an everlasting confinement of the damned in the eternally unchangeable place of torment. . . . The numerous criticisms of this ecclesiastical conception, however, induced more recent theologians to assume the possibility and probability of an improvement of the damned and with it an improvement of their state. They drop the absolute eternity of infernal punishments and either assume a conditional eternity, that is, if the damned would never reform, hence declare the punishments eternal only in the case of such as will never let the punishments improve them; or they regard them as only relatively eternal, that is, in this respect eternal, that the damned forever lag behind the perfection and blessedness of the pious, even though they reform and become happier, so that, because of their irremovable retardation in virtue and bliss, they always feel the eternity of their punishment."

[73] 1 Tim. 6:16: "dwelling in the light which no man can approach unto"; Rom. 11:33-34: "How unsearchable are His judgments, and His ways past finding out! . . . Who hath been His counselor?"

Man is made for God, that is, for communion with God. Now, as living in communion with God is supreme joy and delight for man (Matt. 17:4, the prelude: "It is good for us to be here"), so banishment from God's face involves the most unbearable suffering of body and soul. In describing the state of damnation, Scripture uses a variety of terms, but all of them express intense agony of body and soul: "tribulation and anguish" (Rom. 2:9), "being in torments" (Luke 16:23), "tormented in this flame" (Luke 16:24), "the fire that never shall be quenched; where their worm dieth not" (Mark 9:43-44), "there shall be weeping and gnashing of teeth." (Matt. 8:12; 13:50; etc.) To illustrate the terrible agony setting in with this banishment from the sight of God, the dogmaticians point to the agony of a fish removed from its element. But there is this difference: the fish which is removed from its element soon dies, whereas the man who is banished from communion with God must by God's judgment live on, "is guilty of eternal judgment [ἔνοχός ἐστιν αἰωνίου κρίσεως]," Mark 3:29.

A number of questions still need to be discussed. To begin with, Is hell-fire physical or hyperphysical fire? Gerhard (Loci, "De inferno," § 69) recommends deferring judgment (ἐπέχειν, restraint), though personally he favors (magis propendemus) the immaterial interpretation. Quenstedt (Syst. I, 820 ff.) sides more definitely with the hyperphysical conception, giving as his reason: "Scripture usually speaks of the things of the future world in terms belonging to this life, as it, e. g., describes the joys of the celestial life as a wedding and a banquet, Matt. 8:11; Luke 22:30." Therefore Quenstedt interprets the fire of hell as figurative for extreme agony. "This opinion is confirmed by Is. 66:24: 'Their worm shall not die, neither shall their fire be quenched.' Now, as the nature of the worm, so is also the nature of the fire. 'Fire' is metaphorical designation of excruciating pain." (Ibid., 823.) As a rule our old theologians conclude their presentation with the remark: "It is wiser to be concerned about escaping this eternal fire by true repentance than to engage in an unprofitable argument as to the nature of this fire." (Gerhard, loc. cit.) One thing is sure, hell contains no atheists, because the damned actually experience God as the righteous Judge. There is no more room in hell for the lie that there is no God.

Can ceaseless sinning be predicated of the damned? Since the damned remain morally responsible beings, subject to God's Law, and yet are wicked, there is unending sinning on their part. The claim that the punishments of hell are intended to be remedial or restorative (hypothetical damnation) is just as unscriptural as the claim that these punishments are a means of annihilation. — But to the question whether God will suffer the damned continually to blaspheme Him by outward acts some of our old Lutheran theologians do not risk an affirmative answer. The words Rev. 16:11: "They blasphemed the God of heaven because of their pains and their sores," are correctly referred by these teachers to the conduct of the wicked while on earth. In describing the state of the damned in body and soul, it is a good rule for us not to draw on our imagination, but to employ the language of Scripture.

Degrees of torment, determined by the nature of the sins to be punished, are plainly taught in the Bible. Matt. 11:22: "It shall be more tolerable [ἀνεκτότερον] for Tyre and Sidon at the Day of Judgment than for you." The severest punishment follows on the rejection of the Gospel by those to whom it had been preached in rich measure, as Christ testifies in regard to Chorazin, Bethsaida, and Capernaum (Matt. 11:16-24).

As to the *location* of hell, it is best to refrain from trying to define it geographically or otherwise. For this reason our theologians simply speak of hell as a "somewhere," πoῦ *inferni sive damnatorum*. They decline to conceive of this πoῦ as a definite physical locality because there is no Scripture proof for such a locality. Quenstedt (I, 810) says: "Where this πoῦ is, is uncertain. Some say it is within the universe, yes, definitely at the center of the earth, as do the Papists; others say that it is outside the universe, and this seems probable." Positively we can only say that hell is where God pours out His endless righteous wrath on the condemned by banishing them forever from His face.[74] Here, too, our theologians, following the lead of some Church Fathers, give the discussion a practical turn by saying that we should concern ourselves not so much with determining the place of hell as rather with escaping it. Quenstedt: "Chrysostom states correctly: 'We search not where it is, but how we may flee it.'"

---

[74] Hutter (*Libri Conc. Explic.*, p. 945 ff.), after declining futile efforts to determine its place, says: "Purer and truly orthodox is the opinion that hell is by no means to be defined as some physical or bodily place or some other part of this universe, but is a certain spiritual, illocal, and entirely incorporeal division or "somewhere" (πoῦ) outside this universe, in which the tortures of perpetual divine wrath rave and rage now in the bodies, now in the souls of men. Just as, vice versa, heaven, or the place of the blessed, is not some bodily or physical place, nor any part of the sky, but a certain spiritual and illocal πoῦ or "somewhere" in which the elect are showered with everlasting happiness and ineffable joys. However, where this division "hell" is to be, yes, where it is already, we cannot definitely state, especially since Scripture itself says nothing certain on this matter."

The Cause of Eternal Damnation. — Holy Writ expressly declares that since Christ by His vicarious satisfaction is the Propitiation for the sins of the whole world, only faith can save and only unbelief can actually condemn sinners. John 3:36: "He that believeth on the Son hath everlasting life; and he that believeth not the Son [ὁ ἀπειθῶν τῷ υἱῷ] shall not see life, but the wrath of God abideth on him"; Mark 16:16: "He that believeth not [ὁ ἀπιστήσας] shall be damned." Of course, all sins, original sin and actual sins, are indeed damnable in themselves (*natura sua, ut sic, meritoria*), and this truth must be urged against all who minimize sin; but in fact (*actu*) only unbelief results in damnation. This truth must be brought home to all who minimize the work of Christ, the complete reconciliation He brought about through His vicarious satisfaction. Quenstedt (I, 807): "Although all sins as such are *causa meritoria* of damnation, nevertheless the express, proper, immediate, and adequate cause of damnation is *finalis* ἀπιστία, or unbelief, which not only deserves, but in fact brings on eternal death and damnation, by virtue of the words Mark 16:16; John 3:18, 36." But where unbelief reigns, all other sins again assume their condemnatory character. This is what Scripture teaches when it names as causes of damnation, besides unbelief, also the other sins, e. g., Eph. 5:6: "Because of these things [adultery, filthiness, covetousness] cometh the wrath of God upon the children of disobedience [marg., unbelief]." Cf. also Gal. 5:19-21; 1 Cor. 6:9-10; Rev. 22:15.

The purpose of this shocking doctrine of eternal damnation is to warn against unbelief and carnal security and thus to save from eternal damnation. When John the Baptist preaches: "His fan is in His hand, and He will thoroughly purge His floor and gather His wheat into the garner; but He will burn up the chaff with unquenchable fire [πυρὶ ἀσβέστῳ]," this preaching of damnation is to serve his main message: "Repent ye, for the kingdom of heaven is at hand" (Matt. 3:12, 2). When Christ points to the fact: "Many shall come from the east and west and shall sit down with Abraham and Isaac and Jacob in the kingdom of heaven, but the children of the Kingdom shall be cast out into outer darkness; there shall be weeping and gnashing of teeth" (Matt. 8:11-12), He is thereby warning "the children of the Kingdom" against proceeding farther on the wrong way of the Law. When Christ admonishes that it would be better for a person to cut off his offending hand or foot than be cast into hell, into the fire that never shall be quenched (Mark 9:43 ff.), He impressively reminds also believers of the necessity of merciless crucifixion of the flesh in order to escape eternal destruction. The same purpose the statement concerning Judas is to serve: "It had been good for that man if he had not been born" (Matt. 26:24); likewise the statement about the "wicked servant" upon whom the Lord comes unawares with His judgment: "He shall cut him asunder and appoint him his portion with the hypocrites; there shall be weeping and gnashing of teeth" (Matt. 24:48-51). And when Paul writes: "But after thy hardness and impenitent heart treasurest up unto thyself wrath against the day of wrath" (Rom. 2:5), this statement is, according to text and context, an admonition to repentance, and the aim of the Apostle is to save his readers from the wrath of the Last Day.

This purpose is thwarted by all theologians who treat the Scripture doctrine of eternal damnation as if it were debatable and subject to the expert opinion of theologians and consequently either deny eternal damnation outright or substitute for it doctrines that are "more worthy of God" and more in accord with "human consciousness," or "Christian consciousness." The annihilation of the wicked, "conditional damnation," the possibility of a probation after death, etc., are such substitutes. But a Christian theologian must insist that the doctrine of eternal damnation is not something submitted in Holy Scripture for human criticism, but eternal punishment is taught as an incontestable fact which the Christian Church should preach to the world as well as to Christians without reservation or apology. The "mercy theologians" (*misericordes theologi*), as Quenstedt (*Syst.* I, 828) calls the deniers and critics of this Scripture doctrine, actually are most merciless. Instead of sounding the alarm against the menace of hell, they actually, as far as they are concerned, plunge men into eternal perdition.

Also the Calvinistic doctrine that God's will is twofold from the outset, that is, God from eternity willed to exhibit the glory of His grace in the case of some people and the glory of His punitive justice in the case of all the rest, thwarts the end God would attain through the Scriptural doctrine of eternal damnation. For the anti-Scriptural nature and the pernicious effects of this Calvinistic teaching, see Vol. II, 24ff.; 50; 508; Vol. III, 118ff. Of course, eternal damnation ultimately serves to demonstrate also the punitive justice of God. But such retribution overtakes only those who decline to avail themselves of the first and original will of grace that God for Christ's sake has toward all men. If it is objected that this distinction would impose the relation of time on the eternal God, we answer that our human conceptions are bound by time and space. See Vol. II, 36 ff.

8

Eternal Life

(De beatitudine aeterna)

The Fact of Eternal Life. — We know that there is an eternal life and that believers will come to behold God as He is and to enjoy unspeakable bliss in soul and body, but we have this knowledge only through God's revelation in His Word, that is, the Gospel of Christ. Natural theology knows nothing either of the incarnation of the Son of God or of the eternal salvation which He won for men through His *satisfactio vicaria* and which is the portion of those who believe in Christ.

The pagan teaching of the immortality of the soul must not be mistaken for the Christian doctrine of eternal life.[75] Paul declares of all Gentiles, also of Gentile scholars who, like Plato and others, have made a special study of the immortality of the soul,[76] that "they have no hope [ἐλπίδα μὴ ἔχοντες]," Eph. 2:12. The hope of eternal life springs from faith in the Gospel of Christ as its only source, for, to cite only one text, "God so loved the world that He gave His only-begotten Son, that whosoever believeth in Him should not perish, but have everlasting life" (John 3:16).

The Nature of Eternal Life (forma beatitudinis aeternae). — Since eternal life consists in seeing God, only this beholding of God beatifies man. While the believers in this life know God only through His Word, hence in an image (*cognitio Dei abstractiva*), God reveals Himself to the blessed without image or veil, face to face, immediately (*cognitio Dei intuitiva*). Scripture distinctly teaches that this beholding of God is the cause of heavenly bliss, since such seeing will transfigure the believers both in soul and in body, the glory of God being reflected in them. 1 John 3:2: "Beloved, now [νῦν] are we the sons of God, and it doth not yet appear [ἐφανερώθη] what we shall be; but we know that when He shall appear, we shall be like Him [ὅμοιοι]; for we shall see Him as He is."

---

[75] Rationalists showed a special interest in the proofs for the immortality of the soul. Cf. Bretschneider, *Handb. d. Dogm.*, 4th ed., II, 357 ff. But the rationalist Hase (*Hutt. rediv.*, § 139) tells them: "Because of the possible counter-arguments to which each one of these proofs is subject, faith in an eternal life should be based on Christ and not on philosophical demonstrations or doubtful stories. For that reason you will find a more vigorous faith in eternal life in the hut of the poor peasant than in the lecture halls of great philosophers."

[76] On the belief of the Gentiles, especially the Greeks and Romans, in the immortality of the soul see the first book of Cicero's *Tuscul. Disputt.*

In 1 Cor. 13:8-12 the Christians' knowledge of God through God's Word in this life is compared with the knowledge of God which Christians will have in yonder life by seeing God, and compared with their present knowledge, their future knowledge is declared to be perfect. V. 12: "For now we see through a glass darkly [δι' ἐσόπρου ἐν αἰνίγματι], but then face to face; now I know in part [ἐκ μέρους, piecemeal], but then shall I know even as also I am known." Our old theologians, in discussing eternal life, speak justly of a *visio Dei beatifica*. And they are right, too, in adding that the *visio beatifica* excludes every possibility of defection from God. Aside from the fact that in heaven there no longer is any deception, the deceivers having forever been thrown into the lake of fire (Rev. 20:10), the blessed by their beholding of God will enjoy God so perfectly that *eo ipso* every yearning after any other good is absolutely excluded.[77]

The question has been raised whether we shall behold God with our bodily eyes (*visio corporalis*) or only with our spiritual eyes (*visio mentalis*). The Scripture terms "face to face" and "they [αὐτοί] shall behold God," etc., point to a *visio corporalis*, that is, a seeing with our bodily eyes. How this is possible can hardly be a problem for a Christian.[78]

Besides seeing God as He is, the blessed will also know one another, even though they did not meet in this life (Matt. 17:3-4).[79] The question whether the blessed will also recognize the damned in hell is best left unanswered.[80] If the blessed do know the damned, such recognition will self-evidently not dim their bliss, since their will is in perfect accord with the will of God.[81]

Some Particulars. — Scripture describes both the negative and the

---

[77] This is the *confirmatio voluntatis in bono* (Baier-Walther, II, 1, 7—9). Gerhard, *Loci*, "De vita aet.," § 75: "Because the blessed know God, the highest Good, intuitively and perfectly, they also adhere inseparably to this highest Good, perfectly known, through the holy action of their will, and for that reason there will be expelled from their mind every mist of ignorance and from their will every proclivity toward evil. . . . Just as the angels, because they always behold the face of the Father which is in heaven (Matt. 18:10), are confirmed in the good and freed from the danger of sinning, so the blessed will be perfectly holy and confirmed in the good through and because of the beatific vision of God."

[78] A detailed discussion also of the historical side of this question in Gerhard (*ibid.*, §§ 143—144).

[79] At the transfiguration of Christ the disciples knew Moses and Elias, whom they had never seen before.

[80] The conversation between Abraham and the rich man in hell (Luke 16:23 ff.), like all accessory details in parables, may not be stressed.

[81] Thus Gerhard (*ibid.*, § 148) says: "The will of the blessed will perfectly conform to the divine will."

positive side of eternal blessedness. Negatively it will consist in perfect freedom of the blessed from every evil (2 Tim. 4:18; Rev. 7:16-17; 21:4); positively, in their being filled with unutterable bliss (1 Pet. 1:8; Ps. 16:11; John 17:24). The very description of the heavenly life as "hid with Christ in God" here on earth (Col. 3:3) intimates that the bliss of heaven surpasses all earthly comprehension. In order to give us some conception of the glory of our inheritance, the Bible pictures it to us in terms of this life; e. g., as a wedding (Matt. 25:10; Rev. 19:9), as a feast (Matt. 8:11; Luke 13:29), as a sitting upon thrones (Luke 22:30). Scripture expressly states that these are merely images symbolizing the spiritual bliss of life in heaven in contrast to mundane glory.[82]

Participation of the bodies of Christians, which shared their tribulation and labor on earth, in the bliss of heaven, is evidenced by the fact that the body is an essential part of man, by the very concept of resurrection, and by the description of the nature of the resurrected body. The body will be a spiritual body, σῶμα πνευματικόν (1 Cor. 15:44), similar to the glorified body of Christ, σύμμορφον τῷ σώματι τῆς δόξης αὐτοῦ (Phil. 3:21). It will "shine forth as the sun," οἱ δίκαιοι ἐκλάμψουσιν ὡς ὁ ἥλιος (Matt. 13:43). Perfect immortality, strength, and beauty will adorn it, because sin, the sole cause of decay, weakness, and ugliness, is completely done away with. 1 Cor. 15:42-43: "It is sown in corruption, it is raised in incorruption; it is sown in dishonor, it is raised in glory; it is sown in weakness, it is raised in power." The language of heaven will be a celestial tongue, once heard by the Apostle Paul in Paradise, the like of which earth does not know (2 Cor. 12:4).

There are no *degrees* of bliss, because all the blessed are perfectly happy, that is, every one of them will find full contentment for himself in beholding God. However, Scripture does teach that there are degrees of glory (δόξα, *gloria*) corresponding to differences of work and fidelity here on earth. This teaching has been summarized in the Latin verse: *"Omnibus una salus sanctis, sed gloria dispar,"* and it is proved by Scripture texts such as 2 Cor. 9:6 f. and Dan. 12:3.[83]

---

[82] Luke 22:24-30 in contrast to earthly dominion; Matt. 22:30 in contrast to marriage on earth; Matt. 8:12 in contrast to weeping and gnashing of teeth in hell.

[83] 2 Cor. 9:6-7: "He which soweth sparingly shall reap also sparingly; and he which soweth bountifully shall reap also bountifully [ἐπ᾽ εὐλογίαις]." Meyer: "with blessings, that is, according to the context, richly." Meyer is none too clear, but he does point to Calov, who says of the promise and reward mentioned here: "It is to be referred not to eternal life as such, but to the rewards in eternal life,

Luther: "It is true, there will be a difference in yonder life, according as they have labored and lived here. For example, St. Paul was an Apostle, Samuel or Isaiah a Prophet, etc. One will have greater brightness than the other because he worked or suffered more in his office. . . . Thus everyone will have his distinction and glory according to his office, and still one God and Lord will be in all, and one and the same joy and bliss. In his person none shall be more or have more than the other, St. Peter no more than you and I. None the less there must be a difference because of the works. For God did not do through Paul what He did through Isaiah, and vice versa. For that reason everyone will bring along his works, through which he will shine and praise God so that people will say: St. Peter has done more than I or another. This man or this woman has led such a fine life and done such great things. In short, all are to be alike before God in faith and grace and celestial bliss, but they are to differ in their works and their honor." (St. L. VIII:1223 f.) Self-evidently degrees of glory in heaven will not call forth envy, but only praise of God, because sin has been completely eliminated.

The Location of Heaven. — This can no more be fixed than the location of hell. Every attempt therefore to locate heaven geographically is folly. As the ποῦ *damnatorum* is wherever God manifests His eternal wrath, so the ποῦ *beatorum* is wherever God reveals Himself in His uncovered glory, "face to face." During their service on earth the angels are in heaven, too, because they "do always [διὰ παντός] behold the face of My Father which is in heaven." [84]

The Subjects of Eternal Life. — Only those who believe in Christ

---

not to the essence of blessing and glory, but to the degrees of glory." In Dan. 12:3 those who have led many to a knowledge of salvation and to righteousness are specially mentioned among the risen saints. Cf. Keil on the passage. On the point of comparison in 1 Cor. 15:35 ff. see *L. u. W.*, 1884, 408 ff.

[84] Matt. 18:10. Also Luke 1:19: "I am Gabriel, that stand in the presence of God." Cf. the quotation from Hutter, p. 547. Strong disagrees. He answers the question: "Is heaven a place?" by saying (*Syst. Theol.*, p. 1032): "We answer that this is probable, for the reason that the presence of Christ's human body is essential to heaven, and that this body must be confined to place. . . . As the new bodies of the saints are confined to place, so, it would seem, must be the body of their Lord." Thus Reformed Christology plays havoc even with eternal life. But Strong did not consider that his assumption creates a difficulty to which, for example, Gerhard points: "The blessed who have their mansion at one end of heaven will rarely and slowly come over to the others living at the other extremity because of the very great distance between; and what is worse, when Christ stays at one extremity of heaven, He will be withdrawing His most lovely sight and conversation from the rest of the blessed living in the opposite part; and more such ideas come to a person in reflecting on this puerile opinion of the heaven of the blessed." (*Loc. cit.*, § 170.)

in this life will enter eternal life. The love of God in Christ indeed embraces the whole world, for "God so loved the world that He gave His only-begotten Son" (John 3:16), but to these words the purpose clause "that whosoever believeth in Him should not perish, but have everlasting life" is added. And that this clause refers to faith in this life is clear from v. 18: "He that believeth not is condemned already." This is the way to salvation which Scripture reveals, and a Christian teacher should not venture to arouse hopes of a possible conversion after this life or — even worse — to declare honorable heathen saved on the basis of their civic righteousness, *iustitia naturalis et civilis.*[85] The *necessitas fidei in hac vita ad salutem in futura vita consequendam* is also the basis of Christ's command to His Church to "preach repentance and remission of sins among all nations" (Luke 24:47) and thus "to open their eyes and to turn them from darkness to light and from the power of Satan unto God, that they may receive forgiveness of sins and inheritance among them which are sanctified by faith that is in Me [πίστει τῇ εἰς ἐμέ]," Acts 26:18.[86] Furthermore, the necessity of faith in this life is the basis (1) of the admonition, addressed to all servants of the Word, diligently and faithfully to perform their office lest by indolence and unfaithfulness they become contributory causes of the eternal perdition of souls committed to their care;[87] (2) of the admonition, directed to all Christians, to instruct, admonish, and reprove a sinning brother, who is in danger of being lost (Matt. 18:15-17); (3) of the admonition, also addressed to all Christians, to lead a blameless life before the world lest they become implicated in the eternal perdition of the world by giving offense. Matt. 18:7:

---

[85] This is done by the Unitarians, past and present (Guenther, *Symb.*, 4th ed., p. 115), Zwingli in his *Expositio Fidei* (Niemeyer, p. 61), also recent theologians such as Hofmann, who (*Schriftbeweis*, 2d ed., I, 568 f.) ascribes to the Gentiles, on the basis of God's testimony regarding Himself in their conscience, "a conduct toward God which on the Day of Judgment . . . He will reward with eternal life." Against this figment compare *Trigl.* 127, Apol. IV, 22 ff.; Luther against Zwingli's translation of Hercules, Theseus, Socrates, etc., into heaven (St. L. XX:1766 f.) The difficulties arising here for the human mind (harmony of history and the Word of God) were pointed out in Vol. II, 26 ff. Cp. the remarks on 1 Pet. 3:18 ff. in Vol. II, 314 ff.

[86] Meyer correctly remarks on the passage that πίστει τῇ εἰς ἐμέ belongs to λαβεῖν and is in emphatic position.

[87] Ezek. 3:18-19: "When I say unto the wicked, Thou shalt surely die; and thou givest him not warning, nor speakest to warn the wicked from his wicked way, to save his life; the same wicked man shall die in his iniquity; but his blood will I require at thine hand. Yet if thou warn the wicked, and he turn not from his wickedness, nor from his wicked way, he shall die in his iniquity; but thou hast delivered thy soul." New Testament passages: 2 Tim. 4:1-2; 2:23-26; 1 Tim. 4:15-16.

"Woe unto the world because of offenses! For it must needs be that offenses come, but woe to that man by whom the offense cometh!"

The Purpose of This Doctrine. — Just as the doctrine of eternal damnation is to be a deterrent against unbelief and carnal security lest men perish, so the doctrine of eternal life is to be an incentive to men to believe in the Gospel and persevere in faith that they may obtain eternal life. A Christian life uncharted and unmotivated by the sure hope of eternal life is inconceivable.[88] We must remember that here on earth Christians, like Christ Himself, are woefully underrated.[89] To keep up their courage and Christian morale, they follow the directions of Christ and fix their gaze on the eternal blessedness awaiting them in heaven. Matt. 5:12: "Rejoice, and be exceeding glad; for great is your reward in heaven." In particular the teachers of the Gospel in church and school are a despised lot here on earth. The Gospel of the crucified Christ has never been popular with the world, has always been, and will continue to be to the end of time,[90] "a stumbling block to the Jews and foolishness to the Greeks" (1 Cor. 1:23). However, Christians do not grow faint, but rise above all these tribulations (Rom. 8:37: "In all these things we are more than conquerors [ὑπερνικῶμεν] through Him that loved us"), if they do not take their eyes off the heavenly inheritance (παραθήκη, sacred trust), but follow the example of the Apostle, who says (2 Tim. 1:12): "I am not ashamed, for I know whom I have believed and am persuaded that He is able to keep that which I have committed unto Him against that day." Luther: "We have the promise and hope of heaven, and the recompense and reward of our present misery will be so great that we shall rebuke ourselves severely for ever having dropped one tear or sigh on account of this contempt and ingratitude of the world. Why, we shall say, did we not suffer even worse things? I never would have believed that there could be such surpassing glory in eternal life; else I should not have so dreaded to suffer even much worse things." (St. L. II:1237; Erl., *Exeg. Opp. Lat.* 9, 235.) From this practical viewpoint the Christian dogmatician should teach the whole Christian faith and particularly eschatology.

SOLI DEO GLORIA

---

[88] See Luther's sermon on Titus 2:13. (St. L. IX:930 ff.) This important truth was discussed on p. 84 f.

[89] 1 John 3:2: "Now are we the sons of God."

[90] 2 Tim. 4:1-8, a description of the time up to the appearance of Christ for Judgment. V. 4: "And they shall turn away their ears from the truth and shall be turned unto fables."